The American Biblical Repository
by Bela Bates Edwards

THE

AMERICAN

BIBLICAL REPOSITORY.

DEVOTED TO

𝕭iblical and 𝕲eneral 𝕷iterature, 𝕿heological 𝕯iscussion, the 𝕳istory
of 𝕿heological 𝕺pinions, etc.

CONDUCTED

BY ABSALOM PETERS, D. D.

SECOND SERIES.
VOL. FIRST.—NOS. I, II.—WHOLE NOS. XXXIII, XXXIV.

NEW YORK:
GOULD, NEWMAN AND SAXTON, PUBLISHERS.
BOSTON :
PERKINS & MARVIN, AND CROCKER & BREWSTER.
LONDON : JAMES S. HODSON.
1839.

CONTENTS OF VOL. I.

NO. I.

NO. II.

CONTENTS.

THE

AMERICAN

BIBLICAL REPOSITORY.

JANUARY, 1839.

SECOND SERIES, NO. I.—WHOLE NO. XXXIII.

ARTICLE I.

INTRODUCTORY OBSERVATIONS.

By the Editor.

IT has been the fate of most periodical publications in our country, whether political, literary or theological, to be of short continuance. They have been commenced, each in its turn, to meet an exigency. As the exigency has ceased, the periodical has passed out of existence or assumed a character supposed to be better adapted to the changed position of things.

Such a result was to be expected in a condition of society so rapidly advancing as that of the North American States. A few years only, in most sections of this country, produce such changes in the number of the population, their wealth, and the state of education, as demand new facilities of supply and improvement. Institutions of learning have thus been multiplied, each of which has been anxious to avail itself of the influence of a separate periodical to subserve its own interests, as well as to promote the general cause of education. Other sectional or party interests have often been found to conflict with each other. These too have demanded, for a time, the support of rival publications which have ceased with the occasions that produced them;—and the conductors of the periodical press, like other men, are not suffered to continue by reason of death. Their works fall into the hands of new proprietors and editors, whose talents and relations fit them for other spheres of real or supposed usefulness, and thus the identity of their publications, though continued with no change of name or of declared object, is frequently lost in the progress of events.

There are, however, certain departments of knowledge, which the periodical press is adapted to promote and which are of universal and perpetual interest to mankind. Religion, sacred philology, morals, politics, the natural sciences, etc. are of this sort. For the support of instruction adapted to these and similar subjects, the *exigency*, in an advancing state of society, never ceases. The demand is perpetually growing, and to meet it in the best manner, periodical publications are essential. Whatever changes may be produced in the external form of these publications, and in their modes of discussion, by the causes already noticed, in some form, and in a manner adapted to their end, they must be sustained, or society will retrograde.

Yet, even in regard to topics of universal interest and necessity, it may not be wise to continue a periodical for many years in an unbroken series. However ably conducted, and however valuable may be its contents, when it is extended beyond ten or twenty volumes, the work becomes heavy. Many, who do not possess the means to purchase the whole, would gladly own a portion of it. But so long as it is continued unbroken, it is the same work, whatever changes it may undergo. The purchaser knows not where to break the series, and whatever portion of it he may procure, he will possess but a fragment of the whole. To obviate this inconvenience, and at the same time to preserve the value of the entire work for such as are able to own it, experience has taught the conductors of the press that it is wise, as often as the termination of every ten or twelve years, to interrupt the series of their periodicals and commence them anew. This is convenient for purchasers and subscribers. It also furnishes a proper occasion for any change in the name or character of a work, which circumstances may render expedient, the better to accomplish the object of its continuance.

The editor, who is also now a proprietor of the Repository, has been induced, by the foregoing considerations, to commence a *new series* with the present Number. It will not, however, be a new work. The new series is a continuation of the old, with only such changes in the plan of the publication, (not affecting its leading characteristics, and objects,) as have been suggested by considerations of support and usefulness. The principal object of this measure is to accommodate new subscribers who may not feel able to purchase the former volumes of the work.

The BIBLICAL REPOSITORY was commenced in 1830. Its object was to collect and embody matters of permanent value relating to the literature of the Scriptures and to questions growing out of that literature. Articles to some extent were also inserted pertaining to sacred rhetoric, historical theology and other subjects adapted to promote the advancement of sound biblical and theological learning. The work was conducted four years under the charge of Professor Robinson, then of Andover, its founder and original editor, whose learned labors received the high approbation of eminent christian scholars and divines in this and in foreign lands.

In January, 1835, the Repository passed into the hands of Mr. B. B. Edwards, as editor, who continued to conduct it with distinguished ability until January 1838. Since that time it has been under the charge of the present editor, and has reached its twelfth volume.

In the hands of Professor Edwards both the plan and the size of the Repository were enlarged by uniting with it the "*American Quarterly Observer,*" and by embracing the principal topics to which that work had been devoted. These were the discussion of those principles of literature, politics, morals and religion, which are of general interest and are recognized as such by the mass of Christians. With this enlargement of plan the work received a considerable increase of subscribers, which have continued, with but little variation in number, to the present time. It has, however, never been well supported, though highly valued by the learned and intelligent generally.

The object of its founder was to produce a work distinctively and mainly *biblical*. The christian public having failed to sustain that original design with sufficient liberality, the object of all subsequent arrangements has been, without changing materially its *biblical* character, to give such enlargement and variety to the work as to make it more acceptable and useful to the mass of the intelligent and the educated, and thus to secure that increase of pecuniary patronage which is essential to its ample support.

It has been the aim of the present editor, as well as of his immediate predecessor, by concentrating the largest possible amount of talent and patronage in one publication, to augment the power and usefulness of the periodical press. In one respect this object has been attained to the full extent of their reasonable expectations. A work has been produced which holds a high rank in the estimation of learned and christian scholars both in this country and in Europe. It has already become so interwoven with the American Biblical and General Literature, and, to some extent, with the important theological discussions of the times, that no biblical scholar or clergyman can well do without it. It is extensively quoted in Lexicons and other learned works, and is not only a valuable, but almost an indispensable appendage to a good theological or biblical library. In this respect there is no lack of material or of talent to continue the work with the same elevated character, and greatly to increase its permanent value. The editor is assured of the coöperation of a sufficient number of the best writers in this country, and of some in foreign lands. His principal solicitude is to obtain such an increased circulation of the work as shall enable him to afford a suitable compensation to writers, and in other respects to sustain it on a liberal scale.

To secure a still greater union of talent, as well as support, to the Repository, the present proprietors have purchased the subscription list of the " Quarterly Christian Spectator," heretofore published in New Haven, and have induced the proprietor of that work to discontinue its publication from and after the commencement of the current year. As many of the learned and talented writers, whose contributions have hitherto sustained the high character of that publication, will be expected hereafter to enrich the pages of our work, it is hoped that most of the readers of the Spectator, who are not already subscribers to the Repository, will transfer to the latter the patronage which they have heretofore given to the former.

In thus entering upon a field which has heretofore been occupied by another publication, the editor is aware that he has assumed new responsibilities of great delicacy and importance. He has, however, in making this arrangement, carefully avoided coming under any obligations in regard to positions heretofore maintained, or opposed, in the Spectator. His responsibilities will extend only to such articles as shall be offered for publication in his own work, of the propriety of whose introduction he will be the sole judge. In this way it is hoped that a profitable direction will be given to some existing controversies, while new discussions may be commenced with great promise of usefulness and harmony. Writers will be relieved from the embarrassments of any personal conflicts or misunderstandings, into which they may have fallen in the support of former positions, and will be encouraged to commence anew the discussion of such topics as shall be judged important to the illustration of the christian system. The editor, in the mean time, (if he may be permitted, informally, to assume that office,) will serve his brethren, as Moderator, to decide all points of order among the contributors to the work. He will not, however, be responsible for the correctness of every sentiment which may be advanced by writers. As a general rule, each article will be published with the name of its author, who will be held responsible for the defence of his own positions, while the editor will guard against the introduction of articles of hurtful tendency, or which contain sentiments unworthy of a candid discussion in a work of this character. He thus proposes to allow as much freedom of inquiry and discussion as can be reasonably desired, and at the same time to preserve that courtesy and personal respect between writers of differing views, which is as essential to the highest usefulness of their productions, as it is to the preservation of harmony and brotherly love among the writers themselves.

By the expressions of approbation which have been received from all to whom the foregoing suggestions have been submitted, the editor is encouraged to expect the happiest results from their accomplishment. After much deliberation, therefore, and a consultation with his brethren, as extensive as has been in his power, he has determined on the following enlargement of the plan of the Repository. It will hereafter be denominated, as in the present No., THE AMERICAN BIBLICAL REPOSITORY. *Devoted to Biblical and General Literature, Theological Discussion, the History of Theological Opinions,* etc.

In thus extending the title of the work the editor designs to express more fully, in the first of the explanatory clauses, what the Repository has been almost from its commencement. It has never been wholly *biblical,* but has embraced general literature and other matters of permanent value. These characteristics it is proposed still to retain, and to make the first of them, as it ever has been, a prominent and leading characteristic of the work, to whatever variety of topics it may be extended. Its theology, as well as its literature, is designed to be distinctively biblical.

"Theological Discussion and the History of Theological Opinions" are now added to meet the arrangement already referred to, and an exigency which is believed to exist in our country at the present time.

For a number of years past there has been an extraordinary agitation of the public mind on the subject of theological doctrines. The signal blessing of God upon the churches, in numerous and extended revivals of religion, has been attended with instances of extravagance and enthusiasm. These have been regarded by some with simple regret, by others with alarm and distrust. Opinions have also been broached by bold and zealous preachers, which have been assailed by others as erroneous in principle and of dangerous tendency. Animated discussion has ensued, in which distinguished clergymen and the Professors in several of our Theological Seminaries have taken part. Religious periodicals have assumed these debates, and have thus served to sustain, for a time, the several parties or sectional interests which produced them. In many instances also *newspapers* have taken up the disputes which have arisen. The combatants have thus exposed themselves to numerous points of attack ;—and, being pressed on every side, have been driven, as it were, by a sort of self-supporting impulse, to the unprofitable work of personal defence and crimination. Thus, to a lamentable extent, not only in the weekly sheet, but also in the monthly and quarterly periodical, many writers have seemed almost to lose sight of the principles in question, and have indulged their own excited feelings and amused a portion of the public, (to little profit,) in discussing the *men*, and not the principles, which at first provoked them to controversy.

Differences of opinion and of practice in regard to ecclesiastical order and discipline, and the forms of benevolent action, have been added to the existing diversities of theological views to separate brethren of the same essential faith and increase the acrimony of their disputes. Distrust and suspicion have thus been promoted and extended, until large portions of the church and of its ministers, who might otherwise walk together in delightful harmony, are divided asunder.

The causes which have produced this state of things are worthy of serious consideration and a candid review. How much of it may be justly attributed to the influence of periodicals and papers, each having a limited circulation and being read only by its own partizans, it is not easy to judge. It cannot be doubted, however, that many of the calamities referred to have come upon us from these sources. The vehicles of public instruction and discussion, which ought to be bonds of union and peace, have, in too many instances, been the occasions, however unintentionally, of disunion and alienation. This has become not only a real, but an acknowledged evil. The wisest and best men of every school, whose prayer to God for Israel is that they may be saved, and made the light of the world, are looking with intense interest for its correction. *It can be corrected ;*—and to many the state of the public mind appears to present a high degree of encouragement to the effort for this purpose at the present time. A large majority of intelligent Christians, of different denominations, it is believed, have become tired of the existing personal warfare. They sigh for the calm and candid discussion of the points of religious truth which have been brought into controversy. They are partizans, not from choice, but by a sort of necessity. And what is that necessity ? It is that the conductors of the periodical press have so generally introduced a partizan theology, a partizan benevolence, and a partizan literature. If a reader of one publication of this character drops it, and gives his patronage to another, he gains little or nothing, in this respect, by the exchange, so long as both are alike partizan and exclusive. And this will not cease to be the case, so long as each party in the church shall continue to issue and sustain its own separate periodical. Their readers must submit to be partizans, or by taking them all, at an expense which few can afford, be thrown into confusion, and distrust of all, by the conflicts which they often raise on the simplest principles of Christianity.

The most effectual relief from these embarrassments which can be proposed, it is believed, will be to concentrate in one periodical, as far as shall be found to be practicable, the talent and patronage which have heretofore been devoted to the support of different publications. In this way a work may be produced which shall be truly *American,* as well as biblical and orthodox, an honor to our country no less than to the cause of literature and religion. Thus associated in the organ of their communications to the public, writers would conduct their discussions with the knowledge of each other's positions, and with a common, and not with a rival interest in the success and usefulness of the work. They would almost of necessity become more guarded and courteous, and, their productions being examined,

not by different editors, without concert, but by a single judge
of their fitness, who is equally indebted to all and equally devoted to the interests of all, the temptation and the exposure to
wrangling disputes will be vastly diminished. The readers too
of such a publication would soon learn that, with all the diversities of views which it might exhibit on the minor and debata-
ble points of theology, there is a unity of essential faith among
all who love our Lord Jesus Christ. They would be conscious
of the freedom of their own opinions, and of the influence of
calm and dignified biblical discussion and exposition to elicit
truth and impress it on the mind. A work thus conducted, it
might be hoped, next to the influence of associated action to
promote the conversion of the world, would tend to make the
mass of Christians ONE, in the true sense of the sublime inter-
cessory prayer of our Saviour.

Whether the Repository shall be made the organ of such a
concentration of talent and of salutary influences as are here
suggested and invited, they who, under God, have the power
to exert or to withhold such influences will determine. The
editor, however, is by no means so sanguine as to hope for the
immediate coöperation of all parties in the church. Such a
result, at once, is rather to be desired than expected. Yet an
approximation to it may be practicable without delay. A large
majority of our christian scholars and able divines, it is believed,
are prepared to associate in the diligent study of the Scriptures,
apart from the influence of what may be peculiar in their several creeds and confessions. They are, in fact, thus associated
already; and nothing is wanting but a common organ of communication to make it manifest to all. The progress which has
already been made in sacred philology and exegesis has brought
the mass of the educated upon common ground. They have
learned to interpret the Bible according to the common laws of
language, and that it is orthodox fearlessly to abide the issue of
such an interpretation. Original investigation, therefore, and
free and fair biblical exposition and argument must go on and
prevail. The strength of the church is in this;——and whatever
else in Christianity is excellent and glorious, it is by the diligent and prayerful study of the Bible by each generation of
scholars and divines, for themselves, that intellectual vigor and
pure and undefiled religion can be maintained on the earth.
But they who thus study the Bible are not divided. They derive their learning from the same original source, and use sub-

stantially the same helps.   They are ready, unless prevented
by party influences derived from other associations, to unite in
a common effort to inculcate a knowledge of the Bible and of
its doctrines upon others.   They have one end in view, and why
should they not be associated in their endeavors to accomplish it ?

In soliciting the free discussion of all biblical subjects and
theological doctrines, it may be proper to remark, to prevent a
suspicion of the contrary, that the editor regards the great fundamental doctrines of the christian system as settled.   On these
he supposes the writers who will unite to sustain the Repository are substantially agreed.   They may be viewed, however,
in numerous and widely different aspects and bearings, and may
be profitably discussed, elucidated and defended.   There are,
also, numerous secondary and explanatory doctrines, which are
matters of opinion, and not essential to the true faith.   Yet, in
their tendencies, they may affect, more or less, the power of
fundamental truths, and thus become the subjects of intensely
interesting and important discussion.

The principal fundamental doctrines, on which it is supposed
all Christians are substantially agreed, and which are proposed
as subjects of investigation and defence in this work, we shall
state with some accuracy, to assure our readers, that in the freedom of discussion which we invite, the foundations of religious
truth shall not be endangered.   To secure a favorable hearing,
especially from the great body of the Presbyterian and Congregational churches, as they are at present diversified with
shades of differences in theological opinions, our statement of
doctrines has been copied from the correspondence between Dr.
Woods and Dr. Beecher in 1832, as published in the "Spirit
of the Pilgrims," Vol. V. p. 496 seq.   In this statement the
two distinguished and enlightened divines above named express
their cordial agreement.   They also express it as their united
opinion " that, with few exceptions, the ministers of the orthodox Congregational church in New England, together with
most, if not all of the Presbyterian ministers, throughout the
United States, will give their full assent to this statement."
They also regarded it as " a solid basis of ministerial fellowship
and coöperation."   It is as follows :

1. *Being and Attributes of God.*

God is a Being of infinite perfections, both natural and moral, and, in consistency with his unity, exists in three persons, Father, Son, and Holy Ghost.

2. *Decrees and Providence of God.*

The design of God in all his works is the manifestation of his glory in the holiness and happiness of a moral kingdom. His plan for the execution of this design comprehends the creation of a universe of free, rational, accountable, and immortal beings, under the government of perfect laws perfectly administered.

The purposes of God are, like his nature, eternal, wise, just, good, immutable, and universal, extending to, and implying the certainty of, whatsoever comes to pass ; and yet, by his providential administration, events are so ordered, that they " fall out according to the nature of second causes, either necessarily, freely, or contingently ;" and so that " thereby God is not the author of sin, nor is violence done to the will of the creature, nor is the liberty or contingency of second causes taken away, but rather established." The providence of God extendeth itself to the " sins of angels and men, and that not by a bare permission, but such as hath joined with it a most wise and powerful bounding, and otherwise ordering and governing of them, in a manifold dispensation, to his own holy ends ; yet so as the sinfulness thereof proceedeth only from the creature, and not from God, who being most holy and righteous, neither is nor can be the author or approver of sin."*

3. *Original Rectitude and Fall of Man.*

Our first parents were in the beginning holy, after the image of God, to the exclusion of all sin ; but by transgression they lost all rectitude, and became as depraved, as they had been holy.

4. *Consequences of the Fall upon the Posterity of Adam.*

In consequence of the sin of Adam, all his posterity, from the commencement of their moral existence, are destitute of holiness and prone to evil ; so that the atoning death of Christ, and the special, renovating influence of the Spirit are indispensable to the salvation of any human being.

* **Confession of Faith.**

5. *Obligation, Free-agency, and Accountability of Man.*

The obligation of intelligent beings to obey God is founded on his rights as Creator ; on his perfect character, worthy of all love ; on the holiness, justice, and goodness of his law ; and on the intellectual and moral faculties which he has given his subjects, commensurate with his requirements.

" God hath endued the will of man with that natural liberty, that it is neither forced, nor by any absolute necessity of nature determined to good or evil."*

Man having been corrupted by the fall, sins voluntarily, not with reluctance or constraint ; with the strongest propensity of disposition, not with violent coërcion ; with the bias of his own passions, not with external compulsion.†

" By the fall, however, man does not cease to be man, endowed with intellect and will ; neither hath sin, which has pervaded the whole human race, taken away the nature of the human species, but it hath depraved and spiritually stained it."‡

" The moral law doth forever bind all, as well justified persons as others, to the obedience thereof.——Neither doth Christ in the Gospel any way dissolve, but much strengthen this obligation."§

6. *Atonement.*

An atonement for sin was indispensable to reconcile the exercise of mercy with the maintenance of law ; and such an atonement was made by Christ's dying for us.   " This death of the Son of God is a single and most perfect sacrifice and satisfaction for sins ; of infinite value and price ; and abundantly sufficient to expiate the sins of the whole world."   On the ground of this all-sufficient atonement, the universal offer of salvation is authorized and made, and the command to accept it given ; and " the promise of the Gospel, that whosoever believeth in Christ crucified, shall not perish, but have everlasting life,—ought to be announced and proposed promiscuously and indiscriminately, to all nations and men, to whom God in his good pleasure hath sent the gospel, with the command to repent and believe."   " But as many who are called by the Gos-

---

* Confession of Faith, Chap. ix. Sec. 1.   † Calvin.
‡ Synod of Dort, Chap. iii. and iv. Sec. 16.
§ Confession of Faith, Chap. xix. Sec. 5.

pel do not repent and believe in Christ, but perish in unbelief, this doth not arise from defect or insufficiency of the sacrifice offered by Christ, but from their own fault."*

7. *Regeneration.*

Regeneration is not to be regarded as the creation of any new natural faculty or capacity of the soul, without which obedience is a natural impossibility ; but as a special act of the Spirit of God, whereby he " maketh the reading, but especially the preaching of the word, an effectual means of convincing and converting sinners ;"† or that " work of God's Spirit, whereby, convincing us of our sin and misery, enlightening our minds in the knowledge of Christ, and renewing our will, he doth persuade and enable us to embrace Jesus Christ, freely offered to us in the Gospel."‡ But this persuasion of the Holy Spirit in effectual calling is not that moral suasion of man's exerting, or sufficient grace of God's giving, whose efficacy turns on the will of the sinner, and not on the energetic and transforming influence of the Holy Spirit,—" as the Pelagians do vainly talk ;" nor is it of a kind, which, when exerted, the sinner by his free will ever does resist ; " but it is manifestly an operation supernatural, at the same time most powerful and most sweet, wonderful, secret, and ineffable in its power, according to the Scripture not less than, or inferior to, creation, or the resurrection of the dead : so that all those, in whose hearts God works in this admirable manner, are certainly, infallibly, and efficaciously regenerated, and in fact believe. And thus their will, being now renewed, is not only influenced and moved by God, but being acted on by God, itself acts and moves. Wherefore the man himself, through this grace received, is rightly said to believe and repent."§

" This divine grace in regeneration does not act upon men like stocks and trees, nor take away the properties of their will, or violently compel it while unwilling ; but it spiritually quickens, heals, corrects, and sweetly, and at the same time powerfully inclines it : so that whereas before it was wholly governed by the rebellion and resistance of the flesh, now prompt and sincere obedience of the spirit may begin to reign ; in which

---

* Synod of Dort, Chap. ii. Sect. 3, 5, 6.
† Assembly's Shorter Catechism, Ans. 89.   ‡ Ibid. Ans. 31.
§ Articles of the Synod of Dort, Chap. iii. and iv. Sec. 12.

the renewal of our spiritual will and our liberty truly consist. And unless the admirable Author of all good should thus work in us, there could be no hope to man of rising from the fall by that *free will*, by which, when standing, he fell into ruin." " But in the same manner as the omnipotent operation of God, whereby he produces and supports our natural life, doth not exclude, but require the use of means, by which God, in his infinite wisdom and goodness, sees fit to exercise this his power; so this fore-mentioned supernatural power of God, by which he regenerates us, in no wise excludes, or sets aside the use of the Gospel, which the most wise God hath ordained as the seed of regeneration and the food of the soul. For grace is conferred through admonitions; and the more promptly we do our duty, the more illustrious the benefit of God who worketh in us, is wont to be, and the most rightly doth his work proceed. To whom alone, all the glory, both of the means, and their beneficial fruits and efficacy, is due for everlasting. Amen."*

The dependence of man, as a sinner, on the Holy Spirit, is so real, universal and absolute, that no human being ever was, or ever will be saved without special grace. The natural ability which avails to create obligation, and to bring on the disobedient a just condemnation, never avails, either alone, or by any power of truth, or help of man, to recover a sinner from alienation to evangelical obedience,—*because of the inflexible bias of his will to evil.* The necessity of the regenerating influence of the Spirit lies wholly in the sinfulness of man's heart, or the obstinate obliquity of his will, which overrules and perverts his free-agency only to purposes of evil. " We are oppressed with a yoke," says Calvin, " but no other than that of voluntary servitude. Therefore our servitude renders us miserable, and our will renders us inexcusable." It is the same impotency of the will to good, and slavery to evil, of which Luther speaks, and all who follow him. An obstinate will demands as really and certainly the interposition of special divine influence, as if the inability were natural, though the difference in respect to obligation and guilt and deserved punishment is infinite.

8. *Election.*

All the subjects of God's special renewing grace were chosen in Christ before the foundation of the world, that they should

---

* Synod of Dort, Chap. iii. and iv. Sec. 16, 17.

be holy and without blame before him in love, to the praise of the glory of his grace ; not on principles of law as meriting this favor, and not on the ground of repentance, faith, or good works foreseen ; and yet not without a wise reference to the effect of this discriminating grace to corroborate the law, to deter from sin, and promote evangelical obedience.

9. *Perseverance.*

' All who have been renewed by the Holy Spirit, and have truly accepted of Jesus Christ, as he is offered in the Gospel, will persevere in holiness to the end and be saved ; not because the falling away of a saint, if left to himself, would be impossible ; but because the unchangeable love, and purpose, and promise of God, the power and faithfulness of Christ, and the agency of the Spirit, all make it certain that he who believeth shall be saved.'*

10. *Justification.*

Justification includes the forgiveness of sin, and the restoration of the offender to the protection and privileges of an obedient subject. The meritorious ground of justification is the atoning death and righteousness of Christ. And this, by God's appointment, is set to our account, and becomes available to our salvation, when it is received and relied upon by faith.

11. *Good Works.*

Good works can never be the meritorious cause of our justification, like the obedience and death of Christ ; nor the instrumental cause, like faith ; and yet they are a part of that obedience which is due to God, the unfailing effect of faith, and indispensable as the fruit and evidence of repentance, and as the means of adorning the profession of the Gospel, glorifying God, and stopping the mouths of gainsayers.

"Works done by unregenerate men, although for the matter of them they may be things which God commands, and of good use both to themselves and others ; yet because they proceed not from a heart purified by faith, nor are done in a right manner, according to the word, nor to a right end, the glory of God ; they are therefore sinful, and cannot please God, or make

---

* See Synod of Dort.

a man meet to receive grace from God;"* nor can they be lawfully proposed as a substitute for immediate repentance, or as a sort of minor obedience as good as the sinner can render, and as having a promise of special grace to help out their deficiency.

12. *Future State.*

" God hath appointed a day, wherein he will judge the world in righteousness by Jesus Christ, to whom all power and judgment is given of the Father ; in which day, not only the apostate angels shall be judged, but likewise all persons, that have lived upon earth, shall appear before the tribunal of Christ, to give an account of their thoughts, words, and deeds ; and to receive according to what they have done in the body, whether good or evil."†

On the basis of the preceding doctrines it is believed that biblical scholars generally, and the ministers of the different evangelical churches in our country, may agree to coöperate in the illustration and defence of the christian system. Such a coöperation, the editor is assured, is earnestly desired by many. To encourage an endeavor so worthy, and of so high promise of usefulness, a portion of the Repository will hereafter be devoted to discussions pertaining to these subjects.

Intimately connected with theological discussion, as interesting to the same classes of readers, is the consideration of the various forms of associated action for the spread of the gospel and the promotion of christian morals. The present is not only an age of light and knowledge, but of benevolent action. It is now generally conceded by Christians that all who are partakers of the gospel are bound to extend its blessings to others. The Scriptures are understood to impose upon the church, by which we mean the whole body of professing Christians, the solemn duty of communicating the means of salvation to the whole world. And each individual Christian is bound to sustain his share of the common responsibility. It becomes therefore an intensely interesting question, for each individual to decide for himself, in what manner he may best exert his agen-

---

* Confession of Faith, Chap. xvi. Sec. 7.
† Ibid. Chap. xxxiii. Sec. 1.

cy to promote, with the blessing of God, the coming of his kingdom, the conversion of the world.

In the primitive age of the christian church, and especially at the commencement of the christian dispensation, this question does not seem to have occasioned much perplexity. The church was then a feeble body of converted men in possession of the truth, for the benefit of the world. Their association was voluntary and cordial, and their discipline simple. They needed no extended Societies, such as those with which we now associate the idea of missions, because they were not then divided into sects, as Christians are at the present day. They were all united and the acknowledged business of the members of the church, both individually and collectively, was to promote the spread of the gospel by sustaining the apostles in their labors, and others whom they had enlisted in the same service. They pursued their work with a common sympathy, and in the most free and unrestrained manner. They seem to have felt at full liberty to avail themselves of every expedient, whether by individual or associated action, to do the best they could. The simple principle of individual dedication to God, which is so directly inculcated in the language of the New Testament, and so strikingly exhibited in the example of the primitive Christians, relieved them from all embarrassment on this subject. The same principle, were it universally cherished by Christians now, might prove equally efficacious. Let a man imbibe this principle, and it seems to us, that the Bible would say to him,—"follow it out—act upon it—try what you can do—do it faithfully, and in the best way you can, that by all means you may save some."

This position, it is believed, lays a foundation for the right of voluntary Societies for useful purposes, in all ages. Each individual not only possesses the right, but is under a solemn obligation to judge for himself in what manner he ought to exert his agency to promote the salvation of his fellow men. Yet he may not act alone. He occupies a condition of important social relations and influences. He is therefore under social, as well as individual responsibilities; and if, by associating with others in extended measures for the benefit of the whole race of men, he may hope to accomplish more than by the separate exertion of his individual agency, he is bound thus to associate. But the simple act of association with others, for such purposes, is not his only duty. There are various existing and possible forms of association, which are submitted to his free choice. From among these he is bound to select and adopt that which he judges to be best adapted to promote the great end of his high endeavors as a Christian. If he judges that, in the present condition of the church and of the world, it is the duty of each denomination of professing Christians to act by themselves in all things, without conference or coöperation with other denominations, and to conduct their missions under the exclusive control of their own ecclesiastical courts, he has, doubtless, a right so to judge, and to act accordingly. His choosing, however, to be thus associated is voluntary, and he is individually responsible for the results of his choice, in this respect as well as in all others. If, on the other hand, his opinion be that sectarian organizations, thus controlled and directed, are adverse to the best and most effective exercise of the true spirit of missions,—if he conscientiously believe that the great work of the world's conversion requires the united and concentrated action of all who desire and pray for its accomplishment, he has as clear a right so to judge and to promote such a union among Christians by associating with others, like-minded, of all denominations, irrespective of their denominational preferences in regard to church order and discipline. No authority which forbids the exercise of this right can be legitimately derived from the Scriptures. No such authority has been constituted by the great Head of the church. On the contrary, the divine command is on record, and is of universal obligation, "Let there be no divisions among you." And the Saviour's prayer for his disciples, in all ages, is, " That they all may be one, as thou, Father, art in me, and I in thee, that they also may be one in us, *that the world may believe that thou hast sent me.*"

In these divine instructions we find our warrant for voluntary Societies to counteract the influences of all existing anti-scriptural divisions of the church, and the better to accomplish the great work of the church, as the light of the world. It is apparent also to the eye of every observer, that more unity of principle, as well as of action, is needed in the work of missions, and that whatever benefits may have arisen, in other respects, from the divisions of the church, under different names, and with conflicting opinions, it surely ought to occur to us, more frequently than it does, that, in the beginning, it was not so, and that it will not be so in the end.

The Repository, therefore, will continue to be the advocate

of the right of voluntary associations, and will freely discuss the principles involved in this right.　At the same time it will cherish and maintain a charitable and catholic spirit and bearing towards the friends and supporters of other organizations, however objectionable in form, for benevolent purposes.

Natural history, geology, astronomy, etc., are acknowledged to be of more or less importance in illustrating the facts and the truths of revelation.　They are therefore interesting to the christian scholar.　" The works of the Lord are great," says the Psalmist, " sought out of all them that have pleasure therein."　Many of the facts, also, of natural science have been forced away from their due connections and relations and made to subserve the cause of infidelity.　They have been mingled, in distorted shapes, with the learning of more than one profession, and, through the medium of popular authors and lecturers, have been made to exert a perverting influence not only upon the mass of the community, but upon the minds of many of the intelligent and the educated.　On these accounts, therefore, as well as on account of their essential importance, the facts and principles of the natural sciences require to be understood. They should be thoroughly investigated by all such as would defend with ability the truths of revelation against the cavils of skepticism.　Articles on the leading topics of natural science will accordingly be invited from such as are especially engaged in these studies.

Mental science will also find a place in the Repository.　It cannot be doubted that well digested and discriminating views of the powers of the human mind, clearly stated, would do much towards settling many of the points now in controversy between theologians of different schools.　There are fixed principles in the science of mind on which, considered by themselves, all intelligent men agree, and certain mental phenomena, the existence of which is supported by the testimony of universal experience.　These constitute the foundation of the science ; and existing, as they do, in nature, and being admitted by all, whence has it occurred that so many conflicting theories have been formed by different authors ?

It is admitted by all writers on this subject that most of the confusion which exists has arisen from indefiniteness in the use of language.　Each succeeding author, therefore, feels himself bound to define with accuracy the terms which he is pleased to use, that he may, at least, be consistent with himself.　His definitions, however, differ in some slight degree from those of others of equal authority. Disputes are thus originated, in which each contends for the definition which is adapted to sustain his own theory, and the common sense of mankind and the true nature of the subject is not perfectly reached by any of the contending parties. To us it appears plainly that the true remedy for these evils is not only *accuracy* of definitions, but *agreement* in definitions. In the most important fixed principles of the science all are agreed. Why should they not agree in their definitions ? If a system of mental philosophy is ever to be formed which shall be worthy of all acceptation, there must be this agreement. But in order to produce it, writers must cultivate the habit of placing themselves in each other's positions, and of thus approaching the several topics embraced in the science at the various points of access in which they present themselves to other minds. The periodical press furnishes the happiest facilities for the comparison of views which is here suggested, and it is hoped that the contributors to the Repository will not be slow to avail themselves of these facilities.

Our work will also be open to the free discussion of all questions of morals. Moral and religious sentiments have a natural sympathy with each other. Christianity recognizes this sympathy, and blends them in her precepts of love to God and love to man. Moral science, therefore, rightly understood, is but another name for Christianity in its application to the affairs of men. It is a part of the religion of every Christian to understand and perform his duty to all with whom he is associated in life, however remotely. The subject of christian morals, therefore, is one of universal interest to mankind. And it is not only every man's highest interest, but his duty to seek proper instruction in regard to his moral obligations.

It has been justly remarked that "the law of duty, in the abstract, is simple, and not liable to be mistaken ; but its applications are often complex and delicate, requiring the exercise of a strong and cultivated reason." The *idea* of duty, in every case, must be fully comprehended, or the *authority* of duty cannot be strongly felt. When it is considered, therefore, that our moral obligations are infinitely various, that they comprehend the whole range of our duties to God, to ourselves and to our fellow men, it will be manifest to every reflecting mind that they open a field for the deepest research and the most interesting and profitable discussion. The mutual duties which result from the social relations, the duties of individuals to society, those of society to individuals, and those of different societies or communities to each other, must all be considered. Much is probably yet to be learned in regard to each of these departments of duty. And free institutions, as they greatly increase the sphere of efficiency, proportionably enlarge not only the sphere, but the variety of duties, both of individuals to society and of society to its members. The duties of societies, states and nations to each other demand also the special consideration of moralists.

Political economy, therefore, in all its departments, should be discussed as a branch of christian ethics. The politician, the magistrate and the statesman, no less than the private citizen, owe allegiance to the moral law. Though their individual duties are various according to the relations which they severally sustain to society, the same general principles pervade the whole, and are designed to govern the intercourse of nations, as well as of individuals. That " *social selfishness*," which, in every country, is cheered and flattered by the name of patriotism, which has led the mass of every nation to merge their individual in their social responsibilities, and thus to justify acts and feelings from which, as individuals, they would shrink with abhorrence, finds no sanction in the system of morals which we propose to advocate and defend. Nations, as well as individuals, are bound to honor one another, and, in all their intercourse, to observe the law of love.

Each nation, however, is bound to sustain its own institutions and to guard its own interests against the encroachments of hurtful influences, both from within and from without. As Americans, therefore, we shall not fail to defend and support, according to the measure of our ability, American institutions, so far as they accord with the code of morals inculcated in the Bible. Education, both common and professional, the Sabbath and its ordinances, the right of free discussion and inquiry on all subjects of interest to the nation and to mankind, the various societies of our country for benevolent purposes, etc. will each find an advocate in the Repository, as occasion may require.

The criticism of books is a department of labor in which the editor hopes to make the Repository highly useful to the general reader. It is not his purpose to devote a large portion of the work to *Reviews*, properly so called. Productions of this sort will be occasionally inserted on subjects and authors of special interest and importance. Our remarks upon books will be generally classed under the head of "*Critical Notices*," the object of which will be to furnish the reader, in as few words as possible, a clew to the leading topics of the most important publications which shall issue from the press both in this country and in Europe, with such opinions of their merits or defects as we may judge it suitable and useful to express.

This department of the Repository will be hereafter somewhat more extended than it has been in the former series of the work. It is proposed to furnish in each No. a Quarterly list of the most important new publications. This we shall make as complete as shall be practicable, and publishers will greatly oblige us by furnishing for our use the titles of their books, or the books themselves, as soon as they are issued. In this way we shall endeavor to keep our readers apprised of the productions of the press from time to time, and to aid them in forming a correct judgment of the merits of such works as shall invite their attention.

To the notices of new publications will be added in each No., such literary and miscellaneous intelligence, as shall appear to be of special interest and of permanent value to the christian scholar. We shall thus aim to make our work an interesting miscellany, a *repository* of useful knowledge and of articles adapted to promote the advancement of sound biblical and theological learning, as well as to elevate the standard of general and professional education in all our institutions. We shall hope also to contribute something to advance the cause of morals and religion in our country generally, and to promote the purity and peace of the American churches, as well as their christian efficiency in the several works of benevolence and philanthropy which now invite their exertions and animate their hopes.

ARTICLE II.

On some of the Causes of the Corruption of Pulpit Eloquence.*

By Rev. Leonard Bacon, Pastor of the First Church, New Haven, Conn.

THERE is always some touch of melancholy in the feelings, however pleasant, with which we revisit scenes once familiar, but grown strange by long absence. The changes that take place around us, and in our own persons, come on successively, and, for the most part, gradually; and if there is now and then some sudden and violent shock which agitates us for the time, we soon recover ourselves, and the mind in all its habits becomes adjusted to its new circumstances, and ceases to realize how great is the difference between what is, and what was. Thus we pass along from one period of life to another; everything is changing around us; we ourselves are changing continually; and yet we are ordinarily little conscious of the rapidity of our progress. But when, in mid life, we come back to the scenes of youth, the changes of half an age crowd at once upon the consciousness; and the pleasure of reviving the past is tinged with melancholy.

Fifteen years ago, I parted here with my theological classmates. I find myself standing where I stood when as a class we bade farewell to these hallowed scenes. The same walls are around me. The same windows look out upon the same broad landscape. The same sort of an assembly is before me, the old, the young, the learned, the venerable, the lovely;— and in the assembly, how many of the same forms and faces, looking to me, almost as they looked that day. But all are not

---

* [This Article is the substance of an Anniversary Discourse, pronounced by Mr. Bacon, in the chapel of the Theological Seminary, Andover, Mass., Sept. 4, 1838, before the *Porter Rhetorical Society*. This will account for several remarks which it contains and the form of address which it preserves throughout. We have thought it proper also to retain the touching introductory remarks of the author. Though local and personal, and especially adapted to the occasion that produced them, they are too rich and various in their allusions to be objected to, even by readers who are strangers to the scenes to which they refer.—ED.]

here. One tall, spare figure*——one wrinkled, speaking countenance——is here no more ; nor shall we ever catch again one
whisper of that impressive utterance. And where are they,
the hearts of youthful manliness that were then around me,
beating with grateful affection, and with common impulses?
The same affections and hopes, the same high impulses, are
here to-day, but the hearts in which they were then beating,
can never meet again. Where are they ? As I run over the
catalogue, and think, Whose names are these ?——I find the names
of men who are beginning to grow gray in the ministry. One,†
in this Commonwealth, has seen a great seat of learning rise
under his labors and those of his successive associates, from the
germ. One, worthy to bear a sainted name,‡ has served out
his weary years of imprisonment in a Southern penitentiary, a
noble martyr to liberty and truth, and is still pursuing his missionary work among the grateful barbarians whose language his
translating pen has helped to enrich with the living oracles of
God. Others, more in all than one out of every five, are in
their graves. The first,§ sleeps in the old church-yard, where
the shadow of the sanctuary in which he was baptized, falls on
the green turf that covers him. Another——to me the most intimate of all my early friends‖——rests among the sepulchres of
the people who, during his brief ministry, honored him as an
angel of God. The third is buried under the palm-trees of India.¶ The fourth,** whose soul was made of fire, lies at the
base of hoary Argeus on the utmost bounds of Cappadocia,
where stranger hands have written on his tomb in a strange
tongue,

> "A bright star of the new world arose from the west,
> And with wonderful swiftness, went down in the east."

And the fifth,†† having gathered wisdom in various regions and
climates, and having just shown, as a writer, and as a pastor,

---

* The Rev. Dr. Porter, deceased, Professor of Sacred Rhetoric and
the first President of the Institution.

† Prof. Fiske, of Amherst College.   ‡ Rev. S. A. Worcester.

§ Joseph Hyde, of Green's Farms, Fairfield, Conn.

‖ Rev. Chester Isham, of Taunton, Mass.

¶ Rev. Edmund Frost, Missionary at Bombay.

** Rev. Elnathan Gridley, Missionary in Asia Minor.

†† Rev. William Shedd, of Abington, Mass.

what might be expected from his gifts and graces, found his grave where those whom he taught, are to rise with their pastor in the last great day. Such are the departed; when I think of them, and think to what purpose some of the survivors have outlived them, it seems a sentiment as just as it is natural, "The good die first."

Returning then to myself, and looking around on these familiar scenes, I realize that I am no longer young. Life is fast passing away;—and O, to how little effect! How little have I accomplished in the fifteen years since I began to be a preacher! And why so little? I can see that I might have done much more, had I been more faithful, more industrious, more fearless, more single-minded, and more abundant in prayer to Him who giveth the increase; but, at the same time, I can see, just as every other minister can see, in reviewing the past, that I might have done more, had I been more skilful, had I been furnished with larger stores of knowledge, had the powers which God has given me been disciplined by a more complete education, and had my honest efforts to do good been guided by a sounder wisdom.

The great question with a minister of the gospel—the great question too with a student for the ministry—is, How shall my ministry be made most effective for the glory of God in the spiritual well being of my fellow men? The end of the ministry is the effect which is to be produced upon men by this instrumentality. All that preparatory study, all that various disciplining and furnishing of the mind, by which a man is educated for the ministry, has its value only in its relation to this end. If you study the Scriptures in their original languages, and in the principles and methods by which they are to be interpreted, it is that you may preach effectively. If you study the great scheme of christian doctrine, seeking to refer every part to its principle, and to see every principle in its harmonious relations to the vast system, it is that you may preach effectively. If you study any other branch of knowledge, sacred or secular, history, politics, jurisprudence, the philosophy of mind, the wonders of physical science, as a part of your preparation for the ministry, it is that your ministry may be effective. And most of all, or rather most immediately and obviously, in that department of study and discipline which is the special object of this Association; when you give your thoughts and efforts to the act itself of preaching; when you inquire after the best modes of exhibiting the gospel ; when you train all those faculties of body and mind, which are employed in the just exposition and in the vivid, winning, and majestic utterance of the truth ; it is that you may be efficient ministers of the word of God. And, permit me to say, that as the years of your life of labor roll away, however God may bless you with success, the saddest thought, in the review of the past and in the prospect of the ever lessening future, will be the thought that your efforts are accomplishing so little in a work so magnificent. You will have occasion, doubtless, great occasion to ascribe the deficiency to your unfaithfulness ; but you will have equal occasion to ascribe it to your unskilfulness. The longer you labor in the ministry, if you are not too wise in your own conceit to learn anything, the more you will see, not only of your own moral imperfection, but of your actual inability to do justice to the work. The more experienced you become in the ministry, the higher will be your estimate of the value of a complete equipment for the ministry. The longer you go on improving in this work, the keener will be your sense of the mischievousness of every influence upon your habits of mind or heart, of thought or style, that has impaired the efficiency of your efforts as a preacher.

In selecting a subject with which to occupy the hour assigned to this exercise, it would be unseemly to depart from the range of topics indicated by the name and object of your Association. I must speak of something relating to eloquence, and particularly to the eloquence of the pulpit. Let me attempt then to point out some of the causes which may operate, in our day, to produce a vitiated and inefficient style of preaching.

1. There are dangers arising from a misunderstanding of the end at which the preaching of the gospel ought to aim. I do not allude here to those who, rejecting such truths as are declared to be the wisdom of God and the power of God to salvation, consider the end of preaching to be nothing else than the cultivation of men's natural affections, and the promotion of social and domestic enjoyment, by lectures on ethics. It would be easy to show how such views of the end of preaching affect the eloquence of the pulpit—how naturally that preaching, the character of which is determined by such views, loses all vital warmth, and though perhaps magnificent with the creations of a poetic philosophy, or brilliant with the light of genius, becomes, to those sensibilities of man's nature which the gospel is designed to quicken, cold as a grotto of icicles glittering in the

wintry moonlight.   But it will be more pertinent to speak of
such misapprehensions as may exist, among those who intend
to hold fast the great principles of what we call the evangelical
system ; and particularly of such misapprehensions as are naturally engendered, in opposite quarters, by the theological discussions which divide evangelical divines at the present day.

On one side, in these discussions, it is maintained that conversion, the turning of the soul to God, is, and in the nature of
the case must be, voluntary, a decision by the will of an intelligent mind ; that the Spirit of God, in producing that change,
operates by the instrumentality of motives addressed, not indeed
to the passions of the natural heart, but to the constitutional susceptibilities of the human soul ; that the end of preaching being
the conversion of the hearer to God, the aim of the preacher
should be to bring men to the act of renouncing selfish and
worldly enjoyment as their highest good, and of choosing it as
their chief end " to glorify God and to enjoy him forever."   I
state this view, not to call it in question as heresy, nor yet to
contend for it as orthodoxy, or as common sense, for here we
have nothing to do with questions of heresy or orthodoxy.   I
make the statement, only for the sake of showing what unpro-
pitious effects, on the method and style of sermonizing, may be
produced by a too zealous partizanship for the view referred to.

Suppose then a preacher who is so intent upon the idea that
conversion is a voluntary act, as to forget or overlook every
other aspect and relation of the subject.   Suppose him to forget that the act in question, however voluntary, is an act that
goes to the very basis of all specific voluntary action, being
nothing less than the choice of what shall thenceforward be pursued by the soul as its supreme good.   Suppose him to forget,
or not to remember, that however voluntary this act may be,
intelligence is as essential to it as volition.   Suppose him to forget what is *the* truth by which men are converted or renewed ;
suppose that in the eagerness with which he contends for the
doctrine of the soul's voluntary activity in turning from rebellion
to obedience, from stubbornness to repentance, from unbelief to
faith, he insensibly comes to regard this as the great doctrine,
the essential thing in preaching, the very truth by which the
soul is renewed to holiness.   Suppose that in the strenuousness
with which he maintains that conversion is an act of choice, and
resists whatever he imagines to be contrary to that view, he
forgets what it is which is chosen in the act of conversion, and

under what motives the choice is determined. How will his preaching be affected?

Is it not obvious, that he will be very likely to insist, disproportionately, upon a few common-place propositions and arguments nearly connected with his favorite doctrine? The constitutional or physical ability of man, as a moral agent, to repent of sin committed, and to determine his own moral character—the nature of moral agency, and how it differs from mechanical or physical passivity—the certainty that man is able to do what God requires him to do, and that God cannot without injustice require him to do what he is really unable to do—these and some other points of the same kind, are the topics immediately connected with the doctrine in controversy. Who will tell us that the preacher who becomes enthusiastically engaged in maintaining the doctrine of the voluntariness of men in conversion, against all supposed opposition, will not be in danger of insisting frequently, largely, and even continually, upon these topics? And who will tell us that such preaching does not, after a little while, however exciting to those who never heard such views before, become dull, tedious, and as ineffectual to move man's higher and moral sensibilities, as the preaching of mathematical theorems.

This, however, is an effect which is always more or less apparent, when the preacher has become engrossingly engaged in asserting some particular point of controversial divinity. To use a familiar but significant expression, he has mounted his hobby; and though the zeal with which he rides it may be extremely interesting for a while, it presently becomes, first to the people, and afterwards to himself, a trite and sleepy affair. Whatever his hobby may be, be it the millennium, or the doctrine of election, or anti-slavery, or temperance, or the unlawfulness of voluntary associations for doing good, or the divine right of congregational churches, or, as in the instance before us, the doctrine of man's voluntariness in conversion, the same sort of result is likely to be manifested. The temporary interest in the subject which enthusiasm naturally produces, will as naturally be succeeded by weariness in the hearer, and wearisomeness in the preacher. But in the instance now in question, there is another effect upon the preacher. The hobby which he rides not only carries him round one narrow circle, but carries him off from the preaching of the gospel itself, to the preaching of some particular points touching the reception of the gos-

pel.   Men are renewed and made holy, by the objective truths
of Christianity, brought home to the mind by the power of God
himself, and received there, by a living faith, as springs of emotion and of action.   The doctrine of Christ crucified and its cor-
relate doctrines—those awful and subduing revelations of the
character and government of God, and of the nature, character
and moral relations of man, which form the orb of light around
the cross—are the wisdom of God and the power of God to
salvation ; and these doctrines, the objects of christian faith, the
motives to christian holiness, the sources of christian joy, it is
the first great duty of the preacher to inculcate.   The preaching of these doctrines, not by rote, or as received by mere tradition, but from a mind that perceives their evidence, their
meaning, their grandeur, and from a heart that feels their power, will be full of life and various and unfailing interest.   But
that preaching which, habitually omitting the objective grounds
of religious affection, has to do only or chiefly with the analysis
and description of certain subjective processes of mind, cannot
be—however perfect in its kind—cannot be of the highest order of eloquence.   If eloquence would make the hearer weep
with pity, is it to be done by metaphysical disquisitions on the
subjective feeling of compassion, or by a clear exhibition of the
object of compassion ?   If you would waken in a hearer the
highest feeling of sublimity, will you read lectures to him on
the nature of the emotion and set him upon the inspection of
his own mental exercises ?   Or will you, by the power of description, place him under the roaring of Niagara, and make him
see that rushing world of waters, and show him the rainbow
which, from century to century, still sits upon the boiling surges,
"like hope upon a death-bed."
    There is another view to be taken here.   The preeminent
glory of pulpit eloquence, is its dignity, simplicity, and direct-
ness.   Preaching, when it is what it should be, is nothing else
than truth, naked truth, truth from eternity, grappling with the
intellect, the conscience, the affections, and bringing them into
captivity to Christ.   How does such eloquence disdain all artifice and trick—all the devices of the stage and of the stump.
How is it degraded, and God himself dishonored, when it is
forced into so mean an alliance.   But if the preacher is continually insisting upon the voluntariness of conversion ; if that, in
one shape and another, comes to be the beginning and end of
all his sermons and addresses ; if he falls into the habit of telling

his hearers, how easy a thing it is to be converted—"nothing but an act of choice"—"nothing but changing your mind"— "as easy as to move from your seat, or to turn your hand over;" if he feels that all he has to do is simply to make them choose, to bring them to some determination, to get them to commit themselves in favor of religion; how naturally may his preaching degenerate into a mere appeal to the nerves by hideous descriptions and hideous noises and grimaces, or into a reckless endeavor to get the hearers upon what he calls with appropriate barbarism the "anxious-seat." How naturally may preaching, under this influence, become a painful mixture of serious and eternal themes with coarse anecdotes and low caricature, and pantomime, and artifices to get people to commit themselves before they know it. From such debasement of the pulpit and the sanctuary, may the God of our fathers save his churches!

5. Thus far of the danger arising from a too enthusiastic asserting of the doctrine of man's voluntariness in conversion. Let us now see if everything is safe in the opposite quarter. On the other side, in these theological discussions, it is maintained that men are converted from their sins, and renewed to holiness, by the power of God; that the sinner is dependent on God for a divine influence, by which a new moral disposition is to be created within him; and that till the grace of God thus interposes, all arguments and motives addressed to the sinner will be in vain. It would be aside from my present purpose to inquire whether there is really any contradiction between this view and the other; or whether any of those who maintain the other are willing to be considered as rejecting this. I state this view, as I stated the other, only for the sake of showing what danger may arise to the pulpit from a too zealous partizanship.

Suppose then a preacher to become so zealous for the doctrine of the dependence of the sinner on the grace of God, that he forgets, or overlooks, the fact of the sinner's voluntary and responsible nature. Suppose him to dwell in his preaching upon the doctrine of man's passivity in regeneration, till he no longer remembers that regeneration is a change wrought by the instrumentality of truth in an intelligent and active mind, or that motives, arguments, appeals to the soul's nature as sensitive and active, have anything to do with the result. Suppose him to become so alarmed at the progress of inquiry and speculation, and the mixture of philosophy with religion, that he begins to be shocked at hearing men called upon in the language of Scripture, " Make you a new heart," and still more at hearing it argued that the sinner's plea of inability is false. Suppose him to fall into the habit of feeling that the great thing to be preached in these days of Arminian and Pelagian error,—the beginning and end of the gospel, or at least of the gospel as suited to these degenerate days, is the absolute inability of men to repent, or to believe, or to lay hold on the hope set before them, and their absolute incapacity to be moved to anything but sin by the appeals and arguments of the word of God. What will be the effect on his preaching considered as pulpit eloquence ?

Need I say of this preacher, that he too has mounted his hobby, and is as likely as the other to tread perpetually a narrow round of dry and barren topics? Need I say that as he performs that circuit from year to year, his intellect, and his heart too, will shrivel into littleness? Need I say that he, as really as the mere partizan on the other side, is diverted from the preaching of the gospel itself, in the infinite variety and grandeur of its disclosures, to the preaching of propositions and disputes respecting the nature of the mind and its agency in receiving the gospel? Need I say that the great and central doctrine of true Christianity, the doctrine of Christ crucified, the doctrine of pardon and reconciliation by the blood of the Lamb, is as likely to be omitted or thrown into the shade in his preaching, as in the preaching of the other? Nay, if by any strange concurrence, there should come into his congregation some breath of religious excitement, ruffling the surface of the dead and heavy waters, and if he should sympathize with the movement, still forgetting the dependence of regeneration, as an end, or truth, as the means, what but his party associations and prejudices, is to hinder him from resorting to all sorts of empirical expedients and measures and extravagances, as readily and madly as the other ?*

But the most obvious tendency of that misapprehension of the end of preaching which we are supposing,—and some ap-

---

* Is it not a fact, that " anxious-seats," and camp meetings, and similar expedients are as common at the South and West, among those who abhor the so-called new divinity, as they are in some other regions among those who regard the old divinity with like abhorrence ? Were not the new measure men of 1740, strenuous assertors of passivity in regeneration ?

proximation to which is certainly more than a mere hypothesis, —is peculiar to itself.   According to this view, when pushed to this extent, the only end of preaching is to make manifest its own inefficiency, that God may have the glory,—first, of having appointed and employed, in order to the conversion of men, an instrumentality which has no tendency or adaptedness to the end ; and, then, of interposing to perform, independently of all means, that to which in the nature of the case, no instrumentality whatever can contribute anything.   Now where a man has wrought himself into this view, or into any view that comes pretty near to this, the most natural inference, and certainly the most practical, is, that the poorer the preaching, and the more signal and unquestionable its unadaptedness to move men and to bring their thoughts and wills into captivity to Christ, the more perfectly will the only legitimate end of preaching be accomplished ; and, if any body is converted, the more impossible will it be to suspect that the preaching had anything to do with the conversion.   Tell us, then, what sort of eloquence will be likely to proceed from under that man's old sounding-board ? What drowsiness comes over us at the thought of one of his afternoon sermons !   What physical appliances of fennel and dried orange-peel—not to speak of anything more pungent—are necessary to keep his congregation decently awake through the performance.

Can there be anything more deadening to effort—anything that strikes through the heart with a more complete paralysis of its energies—than the conviction that what you are doing has no tendency to any desirable result ?   Could you discourse eloquently in your mother tongue, to a congregation of Chinese or Persians, not one of whom understands one word of your utterance ?   If you could do it once, by the force of imagination, could you continue to do it, twice every Sabbath, and still be eloquent ?   Could you preach, like the saint in the monkish legend, to a congregation of fishes, and preach eloquently, persuasively,—thoughts, words, all burning from a burning heart ? If not, why not ?   If the truths of the gospel have no intrinsic adaptation, as motives, to man's constitutional susceptibilities, and if I am perfectly convinced of it, why can I not argue out of the gospel with a shark, as earnestly and pointedly as with a lawyer,—or with a shoal of mackerel, as eloquently and fervently as with the most enlightened congregation of unconverted men that ever crowded a New England sanctuary ?   Sup-

pose it were your appointed duty, every Sabbath day, summer
and winter, storm or calm, to take your station by the sea shore,
and when, at the fit hour, the scaly troops and families have
gathered in due order before you, to preach to that assembly.
How terrible would be that bondage!   How tiresome and tedious the labor of preparing and delivering those sermons! How
somnolent the flow of your discourse!   Old ocean, methinks,
soothed by the sound, composes all his waves to slumber, and
his perpetual murmur subsides into a snore.

II. Another, and a very different source of danger to the pulpit, is found in a common misapprehension of the nature of elo
quence, and, consequently, of the manner in which it is to be
cultivated.

True eloquence is nothing else than wisdom fitly uttered.
Proposing to itself some worthy end, it brings out that which is
pertinent to the end.   Eloquence does not consist in words,
but in the meaning of words, and in the fitness of the meaning
as conveyed by the words, to move and control the minds of
the hearers.   The elements of such eloquence, or to speak
more correctly, the qualifications necessary to the production of
such eloquence, are everything which gives intellectual dignity
or moral worth to man.   The achievements of eloquence, are
the highest achievements of cultivated mind.   The action of
mind on dead unconscious matter, taking advantage of the laws
of matter to mold or wield the most terrific agencies of nature
for the use of man, is majestic.   Majestic is the action of mind
on the vast arena of investigation and scientific discovery, penetrating the obscure, analyzing the complex, measuring the infinite, bringing up bright truth from the profoundest deep, and
resolving all the appearances of things into their principles and
causes.   But more majestic is the action of mind upon other
minds ; intellect concentrating light, as reflected from a burning
mirror, upon other intellects ; feeling sending its electric impulses through other hearts ; the soul rising to dominion over other
wills, and swaying them with an imperial power.

The first element or condition of eloquence, is knowledge of
the subject to be discoursed upon.   Read any of the speeches
of Burke, as for example the famous speech on conciliation with
America, or that on the debts of the Nabob of Arcot ;——read
any of the best speeches of our own illustrious orators, as for
example any one of those great speeches on constitutional questions that have made the name of Webster so proud a name for

all our country ;—and the first and strongest impression on your mind is that of the mastery of the speaker over the subject of his discourse. You are reminded of that maxim of Cicero, which might well be the motto of such an Association as this, " Ex rerum cognitione, efflorescat, et redundet, oportet oratio." This " cognitio rerum" is what weighs in a deliberative assembly ; this is what weighs with a jury, when addressed by advocate or judge ; this is what weighs everywhere, except with fools. Whoever has occasion to speak where the " knowledge of things" is of secondary importance, may be assured that his speaking will be to little purpose, and may as well be omitted. Whoever undertakes to speak without the " knowledge of things,"—is himself a fool.

What then is, and must be, the first thing in the eloquence of the pulpit ? Knowledge of the subject with which the eloquence of the pulpit is expected to be conversant ; knowledge of the Bible, and of all that it contains ; knowledge of the doctrines which the Bible teaches ; knowledge of all the bearings of those doctrines, of all the perversions to which they are liable, and of all the arguments by which they are defended ; perfect knowledge, familiar knowledge, knowledge at command ; knowledge consisting not of confused and contradictory notions, but of clear and definite views of whatsoever is " profitable for doctrine, for reproof, for correction, or for instruction in righteousness." Thus only it is that " the man of God may be perfect, thoroughly furnished to every good work."

Another constituent of the power of eloquence, is the knowledge of men, of the state of men's minds in respect to the subject of discourse, and how they are to be reached and controlled by the speaker. " Nisi qui naturas hominum, vimque omnem humanitatis, causasque eas, quibus mentes aut incitantur aut reflectuntur, penitus perspexerit, dicendo, quod volet, perficere non poterit." He who is to speak with cogency on any subject, or to any auditory, must understand not only human nature generally, but the particular errors, prejudices, and infirmities, of those whom he is to move. Otherwise, though he understand his subject well, he is like an artist who, with excellent instruments, works in the dark, and does only ruin the materials that he works upon. His speaking will not be pertinent to his end, will not be wisdom, and therefore will not be eloquence. The speaker who, not knowing how to make a way into the minds of his hearers, begins by getting them into a passion, by needlessly irritating their prejudices against himself, or against that of which he wishes to convince them, by something as unsuited to the actual state of their sentiments as " vinegar upon nitre," or " songs to a heavy heart,"—will not be likely to carry his point.   This is as true of the preacher, as of any other speaker.   His knowledge of the Bible will be very inadequate ; his knowledge of objective religion will be of little avail, unless he knows also what kind of creatures his hearers are, and how they are to be instructed, convinced, and persuaded.   This is what we call *tact ;* and who does not know that *tact* is as important in the church as it is in the senate-house.

A third ingredient in that constitution and equipment of mind which makes the orator, is some degree of sympathy with those who are to be spoken to.   Indeed that knowledge of human nature, of which I have been speaking, cannot exist in the mind that has not a living ready sympathy *with* human nature.   What is called *tact*, is not so much art, as instinct—a quick inward perception, guiding the speaker, perhaps without his being aware of it.   Conscious that his mind and feelings are the same with other men's, he knows that this statement, that argument or illustration, that objection or reply, that appeal to sensibility,— will strike other minds as it does his.   Speaking from the human intellect and reason of his own soul, and from the human imagination and sensibilities within him, every word wakens a living echo.   There must be such congeniality between the speaker and hearers ; or eloquence is not.

Is it not on this principle that God employs the agency of men, of converted sinners, in calling sinners to repentance ? Who does not believe that the gospel itself, passing through a human mind as the medium of its conveyance to other minds, spoken with the persuasive tones of human utterance, breathed out with the sweet modulation of human affections and sensibilities, and with the deep earnestness of human experience, is far more eloquent to men, far better adapted to the end for which the preaching of the gospel is appointed, than if it were sung on earth with angel harps and voices, or sounded out from the trumpets of the seraphim ?

Nay, in those inimitable discourses of the Son of God, what is more striking than their strong sympathy with human nature. Every word is of one who took not on him the nature of angels, but was formed in fashion as a man.   Every word is from a heart that can be touched with the feeling of our infirmity.   It is humanity, stainless indeed, refined, exalted, refulgent with the incarnate Divinity,—but still humanity, with its smiles and tears ; our nature, with its quick strong impulses of affection, of sorrow, and of joy.

Would you be eloquent, as a preacher ? Be a man—not a monk, but a man—not an ascetic, or a cynic, or a pedant, or an owl ; but a man, with all the thoughts, associations, interests, relations, affections, sympathies, of perfect manhood. Be able to say, and every body will feel that you are able to say with the poet,

" Homo sum, et nihil humani à me alienum puto."

In addition to these elements of power, the eloquent man must have the power of illustration, which is nothing else than the ready perception of analogies, with an abundant store of various and familiar information ; in other words, the ready perception of analogies and the possession of analogies to be perceived. How often will a man thus furnished accomplish more with one well chosen word, that goes like a live arrow to its mark, than another man will accomplish with hours of flowing and flowery declamation.

What more is necessary to eloquence ? Words, you will tell me,—the command of language. True, without words there can be no eloquence ; for eloquence is not wisdom laid up in the mind, but wisdom in the act of utterance ; it is power, not in repose, but in action. But how are words to be had. Not surely by committing a dictionary to memory. Not by being conversant with wordy people, whose flow of language without thought, is a disease, instead of an accomplishment. But by having thoughts. The living thought will seize for itself the winged word. " Thoughts that breathe" will find, or will create " words that burn."

If now, this is the true idea of eloquence, and of the way in which the power of eloquence is to be cultivated, there is danger in our day of a vitiated and inefficient sort of pulpit eloquence. It seems to be supposed in some quarters that eloquence, for which the highest honors are claimed of course, is concerned only with words, and figures, and style, and gesticulation ; and that the matter of a discourse has very little to do with its merits considered as eloquence. Such a man is said to be eloquent. Why ? Why, what a beautiful speaker he is !—

how graceful !—what a sweet voice !—what elegant figures !—
what a command of language !—how beautifully he brought out
that quotation from Lord Byron !

There is more favor shown toward that sort of inane and puerile rhetoric in the pulpit, than anywhere else.   The advocate
at the bar, who should indulge himself in such an exhibition,
would see the jury looking vacant and puzzled ; he would see
the judges scowling at him from the bench ; and he would catch
some glimpses of the faces of his brethren of the bar grinning
with contemptuous merriment.   Every advocate knows that if
he is to get fees, it must be not by rhetoric and poetry, but by
a knowledge of whatever a lawyer ought to know, and by the
thorough study and perfect comprehension of his cases.   So in
the senate, a man may sometimes rise for the purpose of making
a rhetorical display ; but he talks to the galleries, and mean-
while the conscript fathers are sleeping, or filing their papers
and putting their desks in order, or writing letters to their constituents.   But in the pulpit how often are such rhetorical exhibitions considered as eloquence.   And how often do we see
the effect of such an idea upon the studies of young men preparing for the ministry.   Such an expectant of the great office
of interpreting the recorded teachings of the Holy Spirit, and
of justifying the ways of God to men, omits, or passes over
slightly, the hard and heavy learning of Hebrew and Greek ;
for what connection is there between the Greek grammar, or
the Hebrew lexicon, and eloquence ?   He has no taste for metaphysics and systems, or the distinctions and questions of Didactic Theology ; for he can find in these subtleties and dry chips
of logic no savor of eloquence.   The history of doctrines and
opinions, of persecutions and martyrdoms, of controversies, corruptions, and reformations, is to him an arid waste ; for he sees
there no flowers of eloquence.   To him all these departments
of study are barren ; and if he does not absolutely turn away
from them, he only aims to give them so much attention as will
enable him to pass through some Seminary, and get an introduction to the pulpit.   His favorite study is fine writing ; and you
will find him great in belles lettres, well read in Bulwer and
Cooper, profoundly familiar with Childe Harold and Lalla
Rookh, and always among the first to try the merits of the last
new novel.   He is for eloquence ; and when he pronounces his
orations, let Baxter and Edwards, Dwight and Hall, hide their
diminished heads ; for here is a preacher—pardon me—a pul-

pit orator, whose eloquence has been formed by means and processes which they never dreamed of.

No ; the eloquence of the pulpit is not a parade eloquence, but a business eloquence.   It is not at all kindred to the rhapsodies of the stage, which have no other end than to delight the imagination, or to excite the passive emotions.   It aims not to amuse, nor merely to excite, but to instruct, to persuade and to control.   The eloquence of the senate, when the grandest interests of an empire are in debate,—the eloquence of the bar, when the whole living, the character, the liberty, or the life of a client, is depending on a certain conviction to be produced in the minds of the hearers,—the eloquence of the popular assembly, when prejudice is to be made docile, when passion is to be subdued, when the reluctant will of the multitude is to be swayed and determined by argument,—is not more a business eloquence than the eloquence of the pulpit ought ever to be.   But this lisping poetry, this mincing elegance of diction, this trumpery and moonshine of superficial rhetoric, this would-be eloquence, which is uttered only to be admired—how impious the impertinence !

III. Another danger to the eloquence of the pulpit is the danger of cutting off sympathy and mutual confidence between the pulpit and the people.   I can describe this danger in no way so well as by referring to some two or three sorts of preachers, who more or less effectually isolate themselves from the people at large, and live and think and move in some peculiar and narrow world of their own.

The first specimen then of those preachers who lack sympathy with the common mind, may be the preacher who is smitten with the love of factitious and fashionable life.   He sighs for elegant society ; he is shocked with the coarseness and clownishness of plain people who wear homespun, and whose hands are hard with labor, and their faces bronzed with exposure to the sun.   To be the pastor of a country parish, to be doomed to perpetual association with men and women who are always at least a year behind the fashion, and who go neither to Washington in the winter nor to Saratoga in the summer,— would be putting his light under a bushel, he might as well go to the heathen, as to spend his life among such christianized barbarians.   He must be settled in a city, where he can have a genteel congregation, that shall appreciate his polish and refinement.   Can this man be the master of a living and persuasive eloquence? This *man!*—let me rather say, this compound of buckram and broadcloth,—can he preach effectively? No. Wherever he may undertake to preach, there is no sympathy between him and the people. His sympathies are not with man as God made him, but with man as the tailor made him. He judges of people, not by their human minds and hearts, but by their clothes and their cards. And therefore if he attains the very place of his poor ambition, and preaches from a mahogany pulpit to a city congregation, his preaching will be good for nothing; for the human nature of the city is after all the same with the human nature of the country, and, if touched to any salutary purpose, must be touched by the same appeals and arguments. He who does not respect the people, even in the rude rough mass, cannot be respected, or trusted, by the people, anywhere.

Next, we have the scholastic preacher, who knows nothing but what he finds in books, set down under the forms of science, and who therefore knows nothing in common with the people in their most familiar ideas and associations. The man whose propositions, and arguments, and language, all savor of the technicalities of the schools, cannot have the full confidence of the people at large; for though he may mean something very true, and very simple, they know not what he would be at. Nor can the people have his confidence; for after he has tried them a while, he cannot but esteem them too ignorant to be taught, and too dull to be moved by anything which he has to say to them. He whose talk is of major and minor propositions, of subjects and predicates, of entities and quiddities, of substratum and accidents, and who cannot translate into the language of common life, that philosophy of the human mind which he has learned from books and professors, will find, or at least will show, that there is no conducting medium between his mind and the minds of the people at large. And if all the preachers in the land were of such a sort, the perfect inefficiency of the pulpit would soon expose it to universal and unbounded contempt.

I confess, however, that I see no particular occasion, just now, to fear the growth of scholasticism in the pulpit, except among those who are led to affect the doctrines and the language of a mystical or transcendental philosophy. There is something in that philosophy, especially as recommended by the poetic genius of Coleridge, and by the enthusiasm and learning of some who in this country have undertaken to be his expounders; there is something in its air of profundity, in its appeals to the imagination, in its very obscurity and incomprehensibleness; there is something too in its lofty contempt of Edwards, and Locke, and the great morning star of modern science,—which strangely and strongly fascinates the minds of young men of a scholastic turn, and of an inactive imaginative temperament. But nothing is more fatal to an effective eloquence in the pulpit, than the fascination of such a philosophy; for nothing more effectually cuts off the communion of sympathy and of mutual confidence between the preacher and the people. The preacher exalted above common sense by transcendentalism, will be likely to shoot above the heads, not only of ignorant men, but of all men, and even to project his arrows into some infinite vacancy, "the reign of chaos and old night." He may write well, in his way; he may write (some of the class do write) much better than Coleridge; he may write as well as Plato himself; and if he could afford to say,

"Fit audience let me find, though few,"—

if he could have a congregation of mystical philosophers, perhaps he might be eloquent. But a congregation of mystics is not to be found this side of the moon; and therefore he who has been engrossed with the things of the inner and higher consciousness, till he has pretty much forgotten the things of that outer and lower consciousness which belongs to other men,—cannot preach with anything like effective eloquence. Between the man transcendent in the pulpit, and the men transcended in the pews, there is "a great gulf," over which there can be no communication of sympathy, or of conviction and persuasion. Vain are the preacher's sonorous periods, vain his vast obscurities:

"The hungry sheep look up, and are not fed."

Beside these, there is the conservative preacher, equally cut off from healthful sympathy with the people. I call him conservative, not because he has any particular right to be so called, but because he chooses that name as a name of honor. Need I describe him to you? He is the man who has found out that whatever looks like progress, in these days, is, on the whole, only a progress from bad to worse. He sees only the dark side of everything that is, and the bright side of everything that was. He refers all things to the standard of the good old times, before the beginning of this disastrous nineteenth century. He is panic-struck with the innovations that he sees, and still more with those of which he has no information but by common fame. Tell him of the religious awakenings and revivals with which God visits the churches ; and he groans over the " machinery," and the " animal excitement" and the " new measures," all which are, as he thinks, peculiar to these times. Speak to him of the movements and enterprises of associated benevolence, which are filling our country with the institutions of Christianity, and sending out the gospel to the ends of the earth ; and you touch upon another of his fears,—not that he would express any disapprobation of efforts for the propagation of Christianity, if they are only properly conducted ; but he fears what these organizations will grow to ; he fears that they are constructed on a wrong principle, and that they tend to promote the designs of innovators. He does not like to hear this perpetual talking about responsibility. His soul thirsts for those old quiet days, when there were no societies for the conversion of the world, no theological seminaries, no sabbath school libraries, no religious newspapers, and no religious news ; and when every man was allowed to smoke his pipe in peace, and mind his own business. All the agitations of the age alarm him, as if the earth were moved out of its place. The improvements in science, in commerce, in the arts, which are so fast revolutionizing the world and bringing all nations into mutual contact and dependence, help to alarm him. To him, the glorious experiment of popular governments, in this country, and of a federal union, seems to have failed entirely. He despairs of the republic, and is much inclined to the opinion, that it will never be well with us, till we introduce something of those hereditary distinctions which give such stability to the institutions of the old world. He looks upon this age, as one of the darkest in the history of man. His office is to prophesy in sackcloth, and he expects daily the slaying of the witnesses. In a word, he is so frightened with the hissing of steam, the noise of many running to and fro, the general excitement attendant on the increase of knowledge, and the commotions and jarrings incidental to the rapid progress of society, that he feels as if it were the chief end of man to stand still and hold back.

This is our conservative. You have heard him. How did he preach ? Powerfully, do you say ? But have you heard him for weeks and months, so as to know the effect of his preaching, as a whole, on the people ? Perhaps there is power in a single discourse of his, if you give yourself up to the illusion which he throws around himself, and which has become a part of his identity. Nothing is more thrilling than the talk, sometimes, of a hypochondriac, or monomaniac, especially if you fall in, for the moment, with his hallucination. But as soon as you remember what the fact is; as soon as you go out of his close and darkened apartment, and begin to perceive the reality of things, and breathe the free air, and look upon the face of blooming and rejoicing nature,—the spell of such eloquence is broken. So whoever hears our conservative preacher, harping upon his one idea of the progressive degeneracy of this iron age, may be impressed, so long as he forgets the facts, or while he happens to be in a melancholy mood of feeling. But when he goes out into the real world, and sees things as they are; when he sees every interest of society actually advancing—science continually making new discoveries, and art instantly turning each discovery to account for the use of man—knowledge diffused more copiously in all directions, and among all classes—the means of human comfort endlessly multiplied—great reformations of morals, brought to pass by the voluntary efforts of good and patriotic men arguing with their fellow-citizens—the press free, the pulpit free, the churches free from all subjection to the state—the school and the sanctuary, rising in every new settlement that intrudes upon the wilderness—an educated and devoted ministry, coming forward by thousands, to build up the waste places—missionaries going out in companies to preach the doctrine of Christ crucified in every quarter of the world—presses and schools set up on the darkest and remotest shores, and barbarous tongues learning the name and praise of Jesus—it is impossible for him to believe that the night of the dark ages is again closing in upon the world. He who is continually crying out that an age like this, an age of freedom, peace, and universal progress, is, of all ages, most disastrous to the Church, ought to know that the people can retain their confidence in the divinity of the Christian religion, only by losing their confidence in him.

Let it not be so with you. Beware how you fall into this morose and green-eyed humor of ultra-conservativism. Never be afraid of improvement. Show that you have in you the spirit of reform and progress. Be co-workers with him who is making all things new. Remember that, in this age, above all others, if ministers of the gospel stand as the guardians of old errors or abuses, if they look upon improvements with a jealous eye, if they always exalt the days of fifty years ago as better than these days, their hold upon the popular mind is gone; their sympathy with the popular heart is gone; and the power of the pulpit is no more.

My young brethren, you are to preach the gospel,—truth into which angels desire to look; truth from God, and worthy to be revealed by the ministry of angels, and by the incarnate brightness of the Father's glory; truth adapted to man's nature, and appealing to every capacity of this spiritual and immortal being; truth, the power of which, if you are not deceivers, you have experienced upon your own hearts. Preach that truth, then. Preach it with all your souls. Preach it, conscious of the grandeur of your commission. Preach it as it is, in all its variety of awfulness, sweetness, and power. Let it not be mutilated or dishonored in your exhibition of it.

You are to preach to men—created in God's image, but ruined by their own apostasy; to men with the affections and sensibilities of your own nature, the nature which Christ assumed, and in which he taught and suffered; to men who are to be saved from sin, or forever abandoned, according as they receive or reject that gospel which you are commissioned to preach to them. Preach, then, as men to men, pleading with them, in God's behalf, for their salvation.

You are to preach to freemen; — not to slaves trodden into the earth, whom the gospel can only teach to suffer meekly, and to perform their servile toil with cheerfulness, as to the Lord; not to the subjects of a spiritual despotism, who have never learned to use their own intelligent faculties, and never dare to think, save at the bidding, and according to the will, of those who rule them; but to freemen, accustomed to manly inquiry and argument, to manly sentiment, and manly action. He who preaches to such hearers, ought to preach well. Dull, prozy dogmatism, supercilious authority, merely traditionary answers to traditionary questions, will not serve his turn, who has to deal with freemen, accustomed to free thought. He must commend himself to their consciences by the MANIFESTA-TION of the truth. And how is the truth to be manifested, but by clear statement, vivid illustration, and cogent argument, all accompanied with the demonstration of the Spirit? See, then, that you preach well; so that the gospel, in your ministration, may triumph over the hearts of freemen, and enlist their manly affections and energies in the service of the reigning Saviour, who still leads his elect to war upon the darkness of this world.

You are to preach in an age of revolution, an age alive with the excitement and progress of changes greater and more rapid than ever before agitated the world. In such an age, he who speaks timidly, feebly, and as not quite knowing what he would say, must expect to find himself unheeded, and his voice drowned in the rushing and clamors of this vast theatre. In such an age, to which all ages past have been tending, and which is itself the crisis of all ages to come, how great the privilege, how great the charge, to be entrusted with the ministry of that truth which is the most powerful of all the instrumentalities that affect the destinies of men.

With what earnestness, then, with what self-denying industry, with what carefulness to redeem the time, with what prayer to that Almighty Spirit who can enrich with all knowledge and utterance, ought you to pursue your preparation for so great a ministry. The desire to preach well is indispensable; but, in reference to the end of the ministry, the power to preach well is no less so. A fervent piety, a heart kindling with holy love, a confidence in God which cannot be shaken, a constant sense of the grandeur of those interests which are to be affected by the preaching of the gospel,—all this is to be sought by watchfulness and prayer, and by the constant discipline of the heart, under the means of grace; but, in reference to the end of the ministry, something more than this is equally necessary. The power to wield the sword of the Spirit, which is of God, the skill rightly to divide the word of truth, the faculty of illustration and expression which commands attention, and carries truth into the minds of the hearers, in all its fair proportions,— without these, though a man were as fearless as a martyr, as indefatigable as the winds, and blazing like a flame of fire with zeal, what is he worth as a preacher? Cultivate, then, the power to preach well. As you would save the souls of them that hear you,—as you would give account to God, of the good thing committed to your trust, and of opportunities of usefulness beyond all value, *study* to preach well; yes, STUDY TO SHOW YOURSELVES APPROVED, WORKMEN THAT NEED NOT BE ASHAMED.

ARTICLE III.

CHRISTIAN PERFECTION.

By Enoch Pond, D. D. Bangor Theol. Seminary

THE pretenders to Christian Perfection may be divided into *three classes*, as they rest their claims on three different grounds.

1. There are the advocates of *imputed* perfection. These are perfect, not in their own righteousness, but in the *imputed righteousness of Christ*. By an act of faith, they devolve all their sins upon Christ, and take all his righteousness upon themselves ; so that they are as perfect, as righteous, as the Saviour.

Of this theory it must be said, not only that it is unscriptural and anti-scriptural, it is altogether of an antinomian character. The individual who fancies himself in possession of all Christ's righteousness holds usually, not only that he does not, but that he *cannot* sin. What would be sin in others, is no sin in him. Let him do what he may, he sins not. Of course, all moral restraint is taken off from him, and he becomes as unprincipled as an atheist. Besides ; this theory of imputed perfection involves an *absolute impossibility*. This supposed transfer of moral character, one way and the other—this putting over of our sins to Christ, and taking his righteousness upon ourselves, is, in the nature of things, impossible. It is what never was, and never can be, done. Moral character is not transferable property. It adheres to its possessor, and to him alone, and can never become the character of any other being.

2. The second class of perfectionists are those who claim what they call an *evangelical* perfection. They do not profess to obey perfectly the divine law, or think that this is at all necessary. The *moral* law has been superseded by the law of *faith*. It has been annulled, in whole or in part, and the milder and less rigorous requisitions of the gospel have taken its place. It is these milder requisitions that the *evangelical* perfectionist (as he chooses to term himself) professes to fulfil, and not the strict demands of the law.

To this theory it is sufficient to reply, that the moral law has *not* been superseded or annulled, but is in *full force now throughout the universe*. Our Saviour came to vindicate and honor the law, not to annul it. The dispensation of mercy is based upon it, but does not supersede or abate one iota of its claims. No person can become interested in the grace of the gospel, till he consents to the entire law that it is good, and condemns himself for all his transgressions of it. We may frame for ourselves a standard of character, if we will, and live up to it, and call this *perfection ;* but the Bible knows nought of such perfection. It is of no value in the sight of God.

3. The third class of perfectionists are those who profess to *fulfil perfectly the law of God.* They admit that the moral law—the great law of love—stands in unabated force ; that it is binding on themselves ; and insist that they can and *do* fulfil it. They love the Lord their God with all their heart, and soul, and mind, and strength. They love their neighbor as themselves. From day to day, and in many instances from year to year, they come short of the requisitions of the divine law in nothing. They are as free from sin, as was the man Christ Jesus. They are *perfect*, even as their Father who is in heaven is perfect.

This latter scheme of perfection is that which has been most recently promulged, and most plausibly advocated.* It contains more of truth than either of the former theories, and on that account is more likely to prevail. It is to this latter theory—the claim of *fulfilling the whole divine law*—to which attention will be given at the present time.

The advocates of this theory hold it in connexion with much important truth. They agree, in several points, with other evangelical Christians ; and it may be important, in the commencement of this discussion, to notice some of these points of agreement.

We agree, then, in insisting that the moral law, the great law of love, has never been *repealed* or *abated.*† It is the only standard of character which God has ever fixed, or ever will. It is in full and binding force now, in heaven, on earth, and throughout the intelligent universe.

We agree in insisting, that this law requires a *constant, unwavering obedience.* It makes no allowance to human infirmi-

---

* Particularly by Rev. Charles G. Finney, in his Sermons to Christians.

† At least, we agree in *words*. It may be questioned whether this class of perfectionists do not, in their *conceptions* of things, very considerably diminish the high demands of the law.

ty ; — no compromise with our delinquencies. Every thing which comes short of it, or passes over it—all want of conformity to it, or transgression of it, it denounces and punishes as sin.

We agree with the third class of perfectionists, that men have all the requisite *natural faculties* to keep the divine law. The reason why the law is not obeyed perfectly is, not that men are destitute of the requisite *faculties*—not that they lack a proper *natural ability*—but solely because they lack the right *feelings* or *dispositions* of heart. The law is obeyed perfectly by saints in heaven ; and if saints on earth had the same *feelings of heart*, the same *moral affections*, which they will have when they arrive at heaven, the law would be perfectly obeyed here. The difficulty with us, I repeat, is, not that we lack the requisite faculties, but that we are wanting in right *affections*, or holy *desires*.

We agree further with the class of perfectionists of whom I speak, that the law of God is to be *approved* and *loved*. It is the great standard which we are to keep ever before us, and towards which we are constantly and earnestly to aspire. We are to believe and feel, that the divine law requires nothing which is not altogether reasonable—that it is not at all too strict —and that we are *to blame* for all our transgressions of it. Like Paul, we are to say, " The law is *holy, just, and good*, but we are carnal, sold under sin." Like him, we are to forget the things which are behind and reach on to those which are before. We are to aim continually at a sinless perfection, and to be satisfied with nothing that comes short of it.

On all these points, and perhaps others, we agree with the class of perfectionists of whom I now speak. And these are very important points. Christians cannot have them too deeply imprinted on their memories, and engraven on their hearts. We are not to feel that we are under a natural, invincible *necessity* to be imperfect, and therefore may rest satisfied with our imperfections. There is nothing in the way of our moral perfection—our perfection in holiness, but the corrupt desires and propensities of our hearts ; and for these we should ever feel that we are to blame. With these, we should never allow ourselves to be satisfied, till the last remains of them are overcome, and we are made meet for the inheritance of the saints in light.

But if we agree with the class of perfectionists to whom reference has been made, in so many points ; wherein, it may be asked, do we differ ? In what does the difference consist ?

To this I reply, that the question between us is simply one of *fact*. The perfectionist asserts, not only that Christians *ought* to be perfect in the present life, but that they often *are* so ; — not only that perfection is metaphysically attainable, but that, in frequent instances, it is *actually attained*. Christians come *to be perfect*, in the present life. They are free from sin. They keep the whole law. They may be said to have entered into their rest.

This position of the perfectionist he endeavors to sustain by various arguments, the more important of which it will be necessary to consider.

1. The *testimony of the perfect* is sometimes alleged in proof of their own perfection. Certain individuals *think* they are perfect. They *say* they are perfect. And their testimony in the case is to be admitted.—But do not persons often think of themselves more highly than they ought to think ? Do they not often think themselves better than they are ? And are we under obligations to *believe* all that individuals take it upon them to say, in regard to their own attainments in holiness ? The young man in the gospel thought that he had kept all the commandments from his youth ; whereas, in their proper spiritual import, he had not kept any of them.

2. But to the testimony of the perfect respecting themselves is added, in some instances, the testimony of *others*. Others around them, express the opinion that they are perfect. — But *their* testimony is not conclusive for this reason, among others, that they have no means of looking into the heart. " Man looketh on the outward appearance, but God looketh on the heart." Persons sometimes appear much better externally, than they are internally. They draw nigh to God with the mouth, and honor him with the lips, while their heart is far from him. Partial friends may see no palpable imperfections in one another, while God may see great imperfections in them all.

3. The *command of God* is sometimes urged in proof of perfection in this life. We are *commanded* to be perfect, even as our Father who is in heaven is perfect. — But does it follow, because Christians are commanded to be perfect, that they actually are so ? Do men in this life actually *perform* all that God has commanded them ? He has commanded us to remember the Sabbath day, and keep it holy ; and yet by multitudes the Sabbath is dreadfully profaned. He has commanded all

men to love him with their whole heart ; and yet millions upon millions do not love him at all.

4. It is urged again, in proof of perfection in the present life, that it is our duty to *pray that we may be perfect.* In the Lord's prayer, we are directed to pray that we may be *delivered from all evil.* Paul prays for the Thessalonians, that the God of peace would sanctify them *wholly,* and preserve their *whole spirit, soul, and body, blameless,* unto the coming of the Lord Jesus, 1 Thess. 5: 23. But admitting that it is the duty of Christians to pray for perfection in the present life, is it certain, from this circumstance, that any of them actually arrive at it ? Do Christians receive here all that they pray for, and all that they may with propriety pray for ? Were the Thessalonian Christians sanctified *wholly,* and were their whole spirit, soul, and body, preserved blameless, unto the coming of the Lord Jesus, in answer to the prayer of Paul ? Paul's heart's desire and most fervent prayer for the Israelites was, that they might be saved ; and yet the great mass of them were not saved. He prayed also for the removal of the thorn in his flesh ; but the thorn was not taken away. No more is it certain that Christians arrive at perfection in the present life, because they may with propriety pray for it.

5. Various passages of Scripture have been urged, in proof of perfection in the present life. Thus it is said that " Noah was a just man, and *perfect* in his generations." Job, too, was " *perfect* and upright, one that feared God, and eschewed evil." In addressing the Philippians, Paul says, " Let us, therefore, as many as be *perfect,* be thus minded." But the perfection here spoken of, can only be a *comparative* perfection, not a sinless one. This we know, from the subsequent history of Noah and Job, and from the connection of the passage quoted from Paul. It was long after Noah was spoken of as perfect, that he was found drunken in his tent, Gen. 6: 9. 9: 21. It was subsequent to the alleged perfection of Job, that we hear him abhorring himself, and repenting in dust and ashes for his sins, Job 42: 6. And in the verses *immediately preceding that,* in which Paul speaks of himself and others as perfect, he represents himself as not having yet attained, neither as being *already perfect,* Phil. 3: 12—15. Noah, and Job, and Paul, were just and devout men. In comparison with men generally among whom they lived, they may be said to have been *perfect* men ; yet we know from their history, and from what they said of themselves

in other connections, that they were not sinless in the sight of God.

In proof of perfection in the present life, there are often quoted some of the *promises* of God to the Israelites. Thus it is said in the Psalms, " He shall redeem Israel from *all his iniquities,*" Ps. 130: 8. There is a promise, also, to the Jews, when returned from their captivity, that they should be cleansed from *all their idols,* and *their filthiness,* and saved from *all their uncleanness,* Ezek. 36: 25. In regard to the first of these promises, there is nothing connected with it to limit its application to the present life. God will redeem his people from all their iniquities ; but will he do it before they arrive at heaven ? In regard to the latter promise, we know that the restored Jews, although for a time a reformed people, were not a strictly *perfect* people. The promise was fulfilled to them in its intended *comparative* sense, but not in an *absolute, unqualified* sense.

Certain expressions are used in the first Epistle of John, from which it has been inferred that some Christians are perfect in the present life. " Whosoever is born of God *doth not commit sin ;* for his seed remaineth in him, and he *cannot sin,* because he is born of God," 1 John 3: 9. That this passage is not to be understood absolutely, and without qualification, is certain from two considerations. In the first place, if we thus understand it, it proves too much. It proves, not that some few Christians only, of eminent attainments, are free from sin, but that this is true of *all regenerated persons* : " *Whosoever is born of God* doth not commit sin." Yea, more than this, such an one " *cannot sin,* because he is born of God." But this is saying more than the advocates of perfection would be willing to admit. It is saying that not one of those ancient worthies, of whose imperfections we read in the Scriptures—indeed, that no one, who does sin, or *can* sin, is a regenerated person.—But there is another objection to an unqualified interpretation of this passage. Such an interpretation would make it contradictory to other plain declarations of the apostle John, in the same Epistle. " If we say that *we have no sin,* we deceive ourselves, and the truth is not in us." Again, " if we say that *we have not sinned,* we make him a liar, and his word is not in us," 1 John 1: 8, 10. Now we are not at liberty so to interpret one passage of Scripture, as to make it contradictory to another, and to the general current of Scripture testimony on the same subject. The passage under consideration, like many of the sweeping generalities of the Bible, needs qualifying; and the qualification which it needs is very obvious. ' He that is born of God doth not sin as he *once* did;—with his *whole heart*—with the same eagerness and pleasure.' He cannot *so* sin, because the seed of divine truth and grace abideth in him, and he is born of God. Or, as Dr. Watts expresses it,

> " Immortal *principles* forbid
> The sons of God to sin."

This is the plain and full import of the passage; and thus understood, it goes not a step towards establishing the doctrine of sinless perfection.

We have thus considered the principal arguments by which the doctrine of perfection has been attempted to be supported, and have shown that they are all defective. They fail to establish the point for which they are advanced.

Let us now look at the other side of the question, and consider what arguments may be adduced to prove, that Christians, in the present life, are *not perfect.* They ought to be perfect; they are metaphysically capable of becoming so; they are to blame for all their imperfections or sins. Still, it may be laid down as a general truth, that *none ever do attain to this state of perfection, in the present life.*—In proof of this I urge,

1. Several plain declarations of Scripture. "There is no man," saith Solomon, "that sinneth not," 1 Kings 8: 46. Again, "there is not a *just man* upon earth, that doeth good, and sinneth not," Ecc. 7: 20. "In many things," says the apostle James, "we offend all," or (as is the sense of the original) we *all offend,* Jas. 3: 2. The apostle John, in a passage before quoted, says, "If we say *we have no sin,* we deceive ourselves, and the truth is not in us," 1 John 1: 8. Such is the plain and general testimony of Scripture on this subject; proving, I think, beyond a doubt, that, however much perfection is to be desired and aspired after, it is never attained, so long as we live in this world.

2. In proof of the same point, I urge the *example* of some of the holiest men whose names are recorded in the Bible. To the fall of Noah, after his wonderful preservation through the deluge, I have already adverted. The imperfections of such men as Abraham, and Lot, and Isaac, and Jacob, and Moses, and Aaron, and David, and Solomon, and Peter, and Barnabas, are all faithfully recorded by the pen of inspiration. Such men as

Isaiah, and Jeremiah, and Job, and Daniel, and Paul, and John, and James, we hear confessing, and often bewailing and lamenting their sins.   In short, we read of no sinlessly perfect man in the Bible, with the single exception of the man Christ Jesus. But if patriarchs, and prophets, and apostles—those holy men of old, who spake as they were moved by the Holy Ghost, were not perfect ; where are we to look for perfection on this side the grave?   Who will have the arrogance to pretend that he is more perfect than they ?

3. In proof of the same point, I may refer to the example of some of the holiest men, who have lived between the days of the apostles and the present time.—Of the ancient christian church, the celebrated Augustine of Hippo may justly be regarded as the great luminary.   And he was distinguished, beyond all his contemporaries, by the deep and humbling sense which he habitually entertained of his own sinfulness.   Of this, his published Confessions will stand as a monument, to the end of time.*

John Bunyan, a man distinguished for piety and deep christian experience, wrote a memoir of himself, entitled "Grace abounding to the *chief of sinners.*"   This was the light in which Bunyan, like Paul, was constrained to view himself, the *chief of sinners.*

When we look into the lives of such men as Brainerd, and Cowper, and John Newton, and Fuller, and Martyn, and Payson, and Porter, and Mills, we find that they were not more distinguished for their piety, and zeal, and usefulness in the church of God, than they were for their deep, and often painful, and ever abiding convictions of sin.

The immortal Edwards, whose spiritual attainments have not, probably, been exceeded upon earth, since the days of the apostle Paul, thus expresses the views which he entertained of himself, years after his conversion.   "My wickedness, as I am in myself, has long appeared to me perfectly ineffable, and swallowing up all thought and imagination, like an infinite deluge, or mountains over my head.   I know not how to express better what my sins appear to me to be, than by heaping infinite upon infinite, and multiplying infinite by infinite."

The experience of the church upon this subject has been remarkably uniform.   Wherever we find an eminently holy

---

* The Confessions of Augustine are in thirteen books, the first ten of which relate chiefly to his religious experience.   They may be found in the first Tome of his Works, Benedictine Edition.

person, we are sure to find one who is—not doting or dreaming of his perfection—but humbly abasing himself before God, and confessing and lamenting his great sinfulness.

4. That Christians do not attain to perfection here, is evident, since this life is to them a state of *warfare.* So it is represented in the Scriptures. " The flesh lusteth against the Spirit, and the Spirit against the flesh." "The good that I would I do not, but the evil that I would not, that I do." This account of the christian life, drawn by the unerring hand of inspiration, has been verified in the experience of all the children of God. They have all been *conscious* of this war in the members—of this struggle, this conflict between the flesh and the Spirit. They have all felt the necessity of girding on the gospel armor, and of contending against the enemies of their peace. But the very existence of this warfare—a warfare which terminates only with the Christian's life — is conclusive against the idea of perfection here below. If Christians were delivered from all sin, they would, of course, have no sin to contend with, and no warfare to maintain.

5. If we compare *the claims of the divine law* with *the measure of Christian attainment* in the present life, we shall perceive, at once, that there is no perfection here.—What, then, are the claims of the divine law? " Thou shalt love the Lord thy God, with all thy heart, and with all thy soul, and with all thy strength, and with all thy mind ; and thy neighbor as thyself." " Whether ye eat, or drink, or whatsoever ye do, do all to the glory of God." " Whatsoever ye would that men should do to you, do ye even so to them." Such, in substance, is the divine law — a law which the Psalmist has well represented as " *exceeding broad.*"

What now would be the state and character of an individual, internal and external, who should perfectly obey this holy law ?

In the first place, his *understanding,* in all its departments, would be completely rectified. I do not mean that it would be infallible, but it would be delivered from everything calculated to mislead or pervert it. His thoughts, his conceptions, his imaginations, his recollections, his judgments—all would be under the most happy influence, and would be regulated in the most perfect manner.

Next, the whole range of the *sensibilities* would be reduced to exact order, and be held under the most wise control. The evil propensities would all be extirpated. The baser passions of the soul would be thoroughly subdued ; while the nobler sensibilities, such as the feeling of gratitude, the sense of moral obligation, the power of conscience, would be raised to their proper standard, and would exert a sovereign control.

Then *the love of God* would fill the whole heart, and soul, and mind. It would be exercised continually, and with the utmost strength. Our fellow creature, too, would be loved, as we love ourselves, and we should feel the same regard for his interest, as for our own. This love to God and our neighbor, dwelling, reigning constantly in the heart, would of course displace every evil affection. We should feel no longer the motions of pride, or envy, or discontent, or of selfishness in any form. We should no more be slothful, or indolent, or remiss, or neglectful, in the performance of that which God required. Our heart would be ever warm, and our hand ever engaged, in appropriate duty. Our duties to *ourselves*, whether relating to body or soul, to time or eternity, would be promptly and perfectly performed. Our duties to our *neighbor*, whether public or private, relative or social, moral or religious, would be performed in the same manner. And so also would be our duties to *God*. We should walk in all the commandments and ordinances of the Lord blameless, neither rising above, nor sinking below—passing over, nor falling short of, the full measure of the divine requirements.

In short, if we obeyed the divine law perfectly, we should be just such persons (according to our measure of knowledge) as was the Lord Jesus Christ. We should perfectly copy his example. We should be just such persons (in proportion to our knowledge) as we shall be when we arrive at heaven.

Now it is certainly desirable—in itself *most desirable*—that we should all be such persons as I have here described. This state of perfection should be earnestly aspired after, and prayed for. Every Christian, like Paul, should press towards this mark for the prize—this measure of the stature of a perfect man in Christ Jesus. But do any *attain* to it, in the present life ? This is the question. Paul tells us expressly, that he had not already attained, neither was he already perfect. John also tells us, in extreme old age, that he had not yet attained. David, and Daniel, and Isaiah, and Jeremiah, and all the prophets, and all the apostles, who say anything on the subject, tell us the same story. Who then has attained ? Where is the already *perfect* Christian, who perfectly obeys the whole divine law? Really, when I hear Christians occasionally speaking of their perfection (and it is but occasionally that we hear such things) their testimony, so far from establishing the validity of their claims, serves rather to convince me of one of three or four things;—either that the persons in question have no adequate conception of what the *law of God* is—or that they know not what *sin* is—or that they know not what their own *heart* is—or (which is more probable) that they are sadly, grievously blinded and ignorant in regard to all these important matters;—so that in place of their alleged perfection, they have need to go back to the very alphabet of religious knowledge, and learn again what be the *first principles* of the oracles of God.

6. In disproving the claim to sinless perfection, I urge but another consideration, which is, that the *nearer* Christians arrive to perfection in the present world, *the further they seem to themselves to be from it.* This may appear paradoxical to some, but both Scripture, and observation, and reason confirm its truth.——It was when Job was favored with the clearest manifestations of the divine presence and glory, and his heart was warmed with unwonted measures of divine love, that he began to abhor himself and repent in dust and ashes. He had justified himself before, and protested his innocence; but now he lays his hand upon his mouth, and says, 'Behold I am vile.' It was when Isaiah had that wonderful vision of Jehovah, sitting upon a throne high and lifted up, with his train filling the temple, that he cried out, 'Woe is me, for I am undone; because I am a man of unclean lips.' And from the days of Isaiah to the present, it has been universally true, that those Christians who have had the clearest views of divine things, and have made the greatest progress in holiness, have uniformly had the deepest sense of their own unworthiness and vileness. The strong language of President Edwards on this subject, I have already quoted. Now President Edwards was led to use this language in regard to himself, not because he was more wicked than others; for he was a pattern, so far as the eye of man could follow him, of all the christian graces and virtues. But the reason of his using such language was, that he was *holier* than other men. His standard was higher; his affections purer; his attainments in divine knowledge and holiness greater. He saw further into his evil heart than most men, and the evils which he saw there appeared more odious to him. He could not endure the sight of them, but turned away from them with detestation and abhorrence.

In this respect, it is in religion as in other things. In the different branches of *learning*, to use the language of another, " he who knows nothing, or knows but little, is confident and eager ; while he who seriously enters on the pursuit, soon loses his presumption. He acquires, by degrees, a new standard of judging. New views present themselves. The circuit continually widens around him. The point of perfection moves further off. And after years of patient study, he still sees that he has acquired but very little, in comparison with the unbounded field which stretches itself before him.''

And thus it is in the pursuit of personal *holiness*. The worldly man knows nothing of the subject, and of course if he speaks of it, he will betray his ignorance. The young Christian knows but little, and must therefore be an incompetent judge. But the *experienced* Christian, who has been long in the school of Christ, and has been growing there, uniformly finds his confidence in himself to diminish, in proportion as his spiritual attainments increase. He sees more of the extent and purity of God's law. He feels more deeply the defilement and guilt of sin. He sees more clearly the beauty and excellency of holiness. His spiritual senses become more acute. He daily finds new sources of evil discovering themselves, and new points of duty calling for attention. And thus, while he is improving in all goodness, he seems to himself often to be deteriorating. He seems to remain at a vast and increasing distance from that point of perfection to which his heart aspires. The beautiful language of Pope, on another subject, is so illustrative of this, that I shall be excused for quoting it :

" So pleased, at first, the tow'ring Alps we try,
Mount o'er the vales, and seem to tread the sky ;
The eternal snows appear already past,
And the first clouds and mountains seem the last.
But these attain'd, we tremble to survey
The growing labors of the lengthen'd way ;
The increasing prospect tires our wand'ring eyes ;
Hills mount on hills, and Alps o'er Alps arise.''

The fact here illustrated, viz. that the greater the advances which Christians make in holiness, in this life, and the nearer they approach to the point of sinless perfection, the further they seem to themselves to be from it, is to my own mind indubitable. And if it be so, it stamps as utter *delusion* all those pre-

tences to perfection which are sometimes made.   " I've seen an
end of what they call perfection here below." There is no
such perfection here.

Nor are these pretences to perfection a harmless delusion.
Their influence on the heart and character is uniformly hurtful.

The man who thinks himself already perfect will, almost of
necessity, be led to lower down the standard of duty. He may
not intend to do it, but *he will.** The law of God will not appear to him, as it did to David, to Paul, and to President Edwards.   It will receive such modifications in his hands, that he
can easily bring himself up to what he conceives to be the measure of its requisitions.

He will also be a *self-confident, self-righteous* man.   He
will be strong in his own strength, and will look down with
pity, perhaps with scorn, on those whose attainments he deems
inferior to his own.   He will be disposed to find fault with other
Christians ; to judge of them censoriously ; and to withhold
from them the hand of christian fellowship.

A connection has commonly been observed between a fancied
perfection, and *wild enthusiastic notions.*   After Mr. Wesley
began to preach the doctrine of perfection, and a considerable
number of his followers in London had attained to that state,
he complains that, in spite of him, " enthusiasm broke in. Two
or three began to take their own imaginations for impressions
from God, and thence to suppose that they should never die.
The same persons, with a few more, ran into other extravagancies, fancying that they could not be tempted—that they should
feel no more pain—that they had the gift of prophecy, and of
discerning of spirits.   At my return among· them," adds Mr.
Wesley, " some stood reproved ; but others *had got above instruction.*"†

Persons who fall under the delusion of which we speak are
usually led to undervalue *christian ordinances,* and *religious
means.*   The Sabbath, the house of God, sacraments, and set
times of prayer, may be needful for those who are struggling
under the bonds of sin ; but what necessity have the perfect

---

* Mr. Wesley did not intend, perhaps, to depress the standard of
duty ; but he held to the repeal of " the Adamic law," and thought it
very consistent with perfection that persons should fall into great *errors* and *faults.*   See his Plain Account, pp. 93, 54.

† Plain Account, p. 76.

for any of those things? Every day is to them a Sabbath, and every place a temple, and every breath as the incense of heaven. For persons in this state, ordinances are low and carnal things.

In short, I have no hesitation in saying, that those who think themselves perfect in the present life, are the subjects of a miserable, hurtful delusion. Instead of perfection, they too often manifest to all around them, in their *tempers* and their *lives,* that they are exceedingly imperfect — far gone in error and in sin*—and have need to have their eyes opened, and their hearts humbled, and to come back, in penitence and sorrow, upon the ground of *salvation,* as offered in the gospel.

I must not be understood, in anything I have here written, as *excusing* or *palliating* the imperfections of Christians. For their imperfections admit of no good excuse. They *feel* this; they are *sensible* of it; and this is that which humbles them in the sight of God.

Nor must I be understood as discouraging the *desires,* and *prayers,* and *endeavors* of Christians to get forward in the divine life, and press toward the mark of sinless perfection. For such desires, and prayers, and efforts, are an essential *element* of the christian character. No person, who is not conscious of them, can have any real evidence that he is a child of God.

---

* In illustration of what is here said, I cannot forbear quoting a few sentences from Mr. Wesley's "Plain Account" of some of his *perfect* followers in London. "Some," says he, "are wanting in *gentleness.* They *resist evil,* instead of turning the other cheek. If they are reproved or contradicted, though mildly, they do not take it well. They behave with more distance and reserve than they did before. If they are reproved or contradicted harshly, they answer it with harshness; with a loud voice, or with an angry tone, or in a sharp or surly manner. They speak sharply or roughly, when they reprove others, and behave roughly to their inferiors.

"Some are wanting in *goodness.* They are not kind, mild, sweet, amiable, soft, and loving at all times, in their spirit, in their words, in their looks and air, in the whole tenor of their behavior. They do not study to make all about them happy. They can see them uneasy—perhaps *make* them so; and then wipe their mouths and say, It is their own fault.

"Some are wanting in *fidelity,* or a nice regard to truth, simplicity, and godly sincerity." "Some are wanting in *meekness,* composure, evenness of temper." "Some are wanting in *temperance,*" etc. pp. 113, 114.

But I would discourage Christians from vainly pretending that they have arrived at the point of sinless perfection, when this is not the case. I would discourage them from thinking of themselves more highly than they ought to think; — from flattering themselves that they are rich, and increased in goods, and in need of nothing, when they are wretched, and miserable, and poor, and blind, and naked.

If Christians would be safe in this respect, let them study faithfully and prayerfully *the law of God.* They must carry it always with them. They must keep it ever before them, in all its extent, its spirituality, its strictness, its purity. Let them keep up the standard high, where God has set it; and labor to bring themselves up to the standard, instead of laboring to bring the standard down to them. In this way, while they are ever active, and growing, and fervent; they will be ever humble, penitent, and contrite. While they are gaining new conquests over the world and sin, and advancing nearer and nearer to the standard, the standard may seem to recede faster than they approach, and they may think themselves further from it than ever. In the measureless distance which lies before them, they will think little of the way over which they have already travelled. In their zeal to get forward, they will forget the things which are behind. And thus will they go on, from strength to strength, and from attainment to attainment, to the end of their mortal conflict — till they lay down their bodies in the dust of death; and then will the last remains of sin be overcome, and their triumphing souls will be 'set at liberty. Then will they lay aside their armor, and cease from all their toils and sufferings, and enter into glorious rest.

ARTICLE IV.

The Writings of John Foster.

By Rev. Daniel Butler, Dorchester, Ms.

Among the theological writings of the present age, few have obtained a wider circulation, or gained for their author a more lasting fame, than the volumes of John Foster. I grant, indeed, that if we estimate this writer merely by the number and size of his works, he will be lightly esteemed in comparison with many of his contemporaries. While their huge octavos, in shining array, occupy the lower shelves of every respectable library, his three or four small duodecimos are thrust away on the upper shelf, content to stand beside Annuals, Almanacs, and books simplified, or made extremely simple, for children. But if, on the other hand, we regard the truth he has given us, the just views he has taken of many important subjects, the valuable ideas he has suggested, the new fields of thought he has opened to view, and the tone of piety which pervades all his writings, we are bound to assign him a high eminence among those whose productions have blessed the world.

One of Foster's most prominent characteristics is his *originality.* This is displayed even in the selection of his topics for discussion. Several of them are new altogether, and of a nature which would seem, at first sight, to repay but poorly the labor of investigation.

But the originality of the selection is not more conspicuous than that displayed in the treatment of his subjects. He follows no leader. He does not content himself with dressing up anew shapes borrowed from preceding writers. As the subjects are his, so the treatment is eminently all his own. He seems a spark struck out from the seventeenth century, that antiquated period, when men were content to think their own thoughts.

It is another excellence of this writer, that he displays a *mastery of his subject.* If he has chosen themes seldom considered, he has not done so without a full understanding of their nature. His mind is deeply imbued with them, and displays its fulness in every line. Successive views are taken, and the great question appears to be, not what shall be said, but what omitted. Like the successful adventurer to distant lands, who, on his return, unable to bring all his wealth, casts his eye doubtfully along the glittering heaps, uncertain which to leave ; so he, from his rich stores of thought, seems laboring to select, where all is too valuable for omission.

As a consequence of this fulness, he is all the time making progress in his subject. He does not grasp, in conscious poverty, every idea presented to his mind, and hold it up again and again, under different aspects. Like the sun in its progress round the world, no sooner has he poured light upon one part, than he hurries forward to illuminate regions yet in darkness. You feel, as you pass from sentence to sentence, that you are really advancing—gaining views of what is already past, and discovering what has hitherto been hid in the distance. Like the aspiring conqueror, instead of sitting down to enjoy the fair fields already won, each point gained becomes the signal for new conquests. And when the theme is dropped, an impression of completeness is left upon the mind, as though it had obtained a full and symmetrical view of the subject discussed.

The correctness of many of this author's conclusions, is easily admitted, from the fact that they are founded upon operations of the mind of which all are conscious. This remark is especially applicable to his *Essay on Decision of Character.* No one can read this, without the conviction that the writer possessed an intimate knowledge of the workings of the human mind; and yet in so happy a manner does he introduce his metaphysics, that they lose their offensive features, and become interesting to all classes of readers, who are but willing to *think.* In the masterly description which he gives of Indecision of Character, one cannot but feel that he is speaking from his own experience; and it is probably from this circumstance the report has arisen that the author is distinguished for this very Indecision. Certain it is, that he has described it far better than the opposite quality.

Another characteristic of our author's writings is, that they are eminently suggestive. Many writers possess the power of amusing and instructing us by what they actually say, and that is all; they leave nothing to be done by the reader. A person perusing their productions, like the traveller on the banks of the Nile, sees much that is beautiful immediately around him; but his heart sickens as he beholds, at a little distance on either hand, the prospect bounded by a hopeless desert. With the writer before us, the case is far different. If he says much, he suggests more. He excites the mind to vigorous action by the glimpses of truth, no less than by what he actually reveals. He conducts us along a high road, where many attractive objects present themselves, while ever and anon our path is intersected by others, which, stretching far away over hill and dale, disclose to our hasty glance views dim yet beautiful, and each inviting the labor of a separate journey. He gives us the materials of thought, no less than the thoughts themselves. He surrounds us with the fairest fruit, but the toil of collecting it is our own. With admirable skill he points out the position of the ore, but leaves to us the labor of removing it from its bed and preparing it for use. Hence, it is no easy thing to *read* this author. If you go with him, you must *work your passage*. He does not take you up in his arms and carry you gently along over a level surface, pointing out the flowers that bloom here and there by the way-side. He leads you through regions hitherto untrodden ; and when, from some high eminence, you survey the magnificent prospect, the pleasure experienced results, in no small degree, from the reflection that it has been procured, in part at least, by your own agency. Thus the mind becomes emulous of the toil so abundantly rewarded. The power of rousing others to vigorous exertion, is one of the greatest proofs of a vigorous mind. None but a Hannibal or a Buonaparte could conduct an army over the horrid precipices and the eternal snows of the Alps ; none could go with them without imbibing something of their vigor and decision.

The materials out of which many compositions used in the arts are made, have, by modern discoveries, been concentrated, by the removal of substances naturally existing with them. They are kept in this state for convenience, and prepared for use by admixture and dilution. The author before us seems to have understood the art of concentrating thought, and many writers have availed, and many more will yet avail themselves of his skill. His writings afford an abundant supply for almost any number of religious publications of a certain order. In the empty brain of most modern book-makers they may be expanded indefinitely, like a drop of ether in an exhausted receiver. Out of this lumbering baggage-wagon loaded with gold, as Robert Hall significantly calls these writings, multitudes obtain the material for trinkets and small wares, which they manufacture for the religious world, and which, like the jewels given on one occasion to Aaron, are far more likely to make Calves than Men.

The crowning excellence of this writer is the high tone of moral feeling displayed in his productions. His philosophy is imbued with the principles of the Bible, and in all his plans for improvement he keeps prominent the fact of our dependence upon God. With deserved severity he rebukes those who hope by any *merely* human means to reform the world, and shows that not only infidels, but Christians even, are too little sensible of their impotence when unaided from above.

The style of the author has been justly censured as harsh, and sometimes obscure, and some of his positions are doubtless stated with less qualification than truth will warrant. His sentences are occasionally too long, yet it may fairly be questioned whether, as a general thing, it is possible to express the author's meaning more clearly or in fewer words than he has done. One of the most distinguished living writers remarks, that these faults are justly chargeable, not to the author, but to the language, which is unable better to express his vast conceptions. Allowing him to be guilty of all the faults ascribed to him, it is certain they bear a small proportion to his excellence ; and no one can attentively read his works without becoming a better thinker, a better reasoner, and a better man.   While the metaphysician admires his luminous depths, and the philosopher is delighted at the soundness of his reasoning, " the Christian," in the words of another, " indulges a benevolent triumph at the accession of powers to the cause of evangelical piety which its most distinguished opposers would be proud to possess."

ARTICLE V.

Genuineness of several Texts in the Gospels.

By M. Stuart, Prof. of Sac. Lit. Theol. Sem. Andover.

As I have already intimated, in my review of Mr. Norton's work contained in the preceding numbers of this Miscellany, there are several other passages of the Gospels, besides Matt. i. ii., which this writer affirms to be of a suspicious character, or more probably spurious.   The length to which my remarks on Mr. Norton have already been extended, will not permit me to examine these in minute detail.   A brief notice of each, with some general remarks on the whole, is all that seems to be requisite and proper at the present time.

In passing to the examination of Matt. 27: 3—10, which Mr. Norton supposes to be an interpolation, he remarks, that " we have but a single authority, the Greek translation, the representative perhaps of but one copy, probably not of many, for determining the text of Matthew."   This, he thinks, " is evidence of no great weight against a strong presumption of the spuriousness of a passage." p. lxiii.

It is unnecessary for me to repeat here the considerations, which may well induce us to decide against the probability that our present canonical Matthew is a *translation*. It bears no marks of such a character; and the conduct of the ancient churches in regard to this whole matter, is decided evidence that it was never practically treated by them as such, whatever a few individuals may have said or conjectured in respect to this subject.

Even if it were a *translation*, how can any one now tell how many copies of the Hebrew Gospel were compared when it was made, in order to ascertain the best text ? Why should we presume that a work so well done as this translation surely is, (if indeed it be one), was so negligently performed as to consult only one or a very few copies of the text ? If we do so, we must venture, not upon one, but upon several *presumptions*, in order to proceed with Mr. Norton in the work of excision.

The passage in question, which is suspected by Mr. Norton, respects the repentance and suicide of Judas, and the manner in which the thirty pieces of silver he had received for his treachery, were disposed of by the chief priests. Mr. Norton tells us, that " at first view this account of Judas has the aspect of an interpolation." The whole story, if true, he asserts to be " out of place." According to him, it refers to " a subsequent period of time." The narration states, that Judas repented, when he saw that *Jesus was condemned ;* and early in the morning " no condemnation had yet been passed upon Jesus by the Roman governor ; and Judas could have no new convictions that the Sanhedrim would use all their efforts to procure the death of Jesus." The suspected passage further " represents Judas as having had an interview with the chief priests and elders (i. e. the Sanhedrim) *in the temple ;* which is irreconcilable with the course of events as represented by Matthew in the context of the passage, as well as by the other Evangelists." ' Matthew could not have represented the council as held in the house of Caiaphas, and at the same time as conferring with Judas in the temple.'

To this last remark one may well reply, that Matthew does not so represent it. He does not say where the council was actually held. He merely tells us, that the *chief priests and the elders* met in council, *early in the morning, πρωΐᾳ ;* and Mark also says, (which amounts to the same thing), that the *whole Sanhedrim* (ὅλον τὸ συνέδριον) were assembled. *Where ?*

No one says, as Mr. Norton assumes, *at the house of Caiaphas*, on this occasion.   Nor is this at all probable.   I do not understand, from any thing which we know respecting this subject, that the hall of the high-priest's house was the place for the meeting of the Sanhedrim.

Judas, then, who, no doubt, had passed a night of dreadful horror, appeared before the Council thus assembled, and cast the money down in their presence.   Then he went forthwith and hanged himself.   That money they dared not put into the sacred treasury.   What should be done with it?   They decided to purchase with it the Potter's Field, as a burial place for strangers.   It is not necessary to suppose that all the particular transactions of actual purchase were gone through with on this very morning.   Enough that they directed the money to be so appropriated; and inasmuch as this was done, the Evangelist, naturally enough, mentions the purchase with other particulars of the story in the same connection.

Thus far then there is nothing in any degree improbable. but Mr. Norton tells us that *Jesus was not yet condemned*, and that 'there was no new ground of conviction, in the morning, that the Sanhedrim would pursue their bloody persecution.'

Yet the circumstances of this occasion appear to my mind very differently from what he represents them to be.   After the apprehension of Jesus, the evening before the crucifixion, he was brought immediately to the house of Caiaphas.   On this occasion, no intimation is given by the Evangelists that the whole Sanhedrim were assembled.   Plainly they were not.   It was the *next morning*, that ὅλον τὸ συνέδριον was assembled, and doubtless at the temple, where they usually met, and not at the house of the high-priest.   In this council, after the examination of Jesus, which was very short and summary, the high-priest asked his colleagues in council: "What think ye?   And they answered and said: ᾿Ένοχος θανάτου ἐστί," Matt. 26: 66. Mark makes use here of the very expression employed in Matt. 27: 3, which is regarded as a part of the interpolation by Mr. Norton.   He says: Οἱ δὲ πάντες κατέκριναν αὐτὸν εἶναι ἔνοχον θανάτου, Mark 14: 64.

Now all this could have been done, and probably was done, very early in the morning, even before the sun had risen.   The mock-trial did not require one half-hour.   Judas, beyond all doubt, was present.   His conscience urged him too much to allow of absence.   The *condemnation* of Jesus, moreover, is plainly stated in this account of the doings of the Council ; and this is enough to gainsay what Mr. Norton alleges, when he avers that ' there was no new ground of conviction in the morning, that the Sanhedrim would use all their efforts to procure the death of Jesus.'   Surely there was new evidence, and that of the highest and most authentic kind, viz., the unanimous sentence of the whole Sanhedrim that *he was guilty of death.*

What is there then in all this paragraph, which has ' the aspect of an interpolation ?'   Luke, moreover, tells the story of Judas's suicide, Acts 1: 18, 19 ; and also of the purchase of the Field of Blood.   Is his account an *interpolation?*

To say, as Mr. Norton does, that the paragraph in question *interrupts* the narration of Matthew, is at most only a *rhetorical* objection, if it be well founded.   How many passages of such a nature can be found, in the Old Testament and in the New, every critical reader must well know.

But at all events, if the narration of *Luke* respecting **Judas** be admitted, Mr. Norton thinks the narration of Matthew now in question must be rejected.   In his apprehension they are inconsistent with each other.

In Acts 1: 18 Peter is represented by Luke as stating, (1) That " Judas *purchased* a field with the reward of iniquity." At first view this would seem to mean, that Judas himself made the purchase ; but the true meaning of the speaker I apprehend to be, that Judas, instead of keeping in possession and enjoying the price of his treachery, by expending it for his own gratification, was obliged to relinquish it ; after which, it was bestowed on the purchase of a burying-place for strangers.   (2) Luke also says of Judas : " Falling headlong, he burst asunder, and all his bowels gushed out."   " This," he adds, " was known to all the inhabitants of Jerusalem."   The question now before us is, whether this account is inconsistent, as is alleged, with that in Matthew.

A difficulty on this subject is indeed a matter of long standing.   I must limit myself, however, on the present occasion, to a few remarks upon it.

In the first place, is it certain that the words in Luke's account, or rather in Peter's address, are to be *literally* understood? It seems to me more like a figurative description than a literal one.   I am inclined to understand Peter as affirming, by the manner in which he speaks of Judas, that he came to a sudden, violent, and dreadful death, such as takes place in the case of criminals, who are precipitated from some high tower or rock, (the *Tarpeian rock* will be readily called to mind as an example by the reader), and are dashed in pieces. But if any one should feel, that this is taking too much liberty with the language of Peter, (although cases enough of the like nature, in both the Old Testament and the New, might easily be produced), I will not dispute the point with him. There is no absolute inconsistency between the facts as stated by Luke and as stated by Matthew, if we interpret both of the statements literally. If Judas, when he hanged himself, swung himself off from a height, and was cut down, or fell in consequence of the breaking of the cord by which he was suspended, either of which events is far enough from being impossible or even improbable, then did he "fall headlong, and his bowels gush out." Certainly the latter circumstance is perfectly natural, on the supposition that he fell on pointed rocks below the precipice, or on any hard or sharp substance which might be beneath him. Peter chooses one of the circumstances to describe the manner of his end; Matthew another. That such apparent discrepancies are frequent in all parts of the three first Gospels, every one knows who has made a diligent comparison of them.

But we are met, by Mr. Norton, with another objection against the passage in Matthew, which is, that the Evangelist has, in quoting the passage from the Old Testament respecting *the thirty pieces of silver*, ascribed the words to *Jeremiah*, and not, as they should be, to Zechariah (11: 12, 13).

So it stands in our text, indeed; and the reading (*Jeremiah*) is approved by Griesbach, and many other critics. Yet all the sources of authority, in this case, are not agreed. An excellent Codex (No. 22 in Griesbach) and the Philoxenian Syriac Version here read Ζαχαρίου; two Codices of good note, (Nos. 33, 157), with the Peshito or old Syriac, wholly omit the proper name, and read ῥηθὲν διὰ προφήτου. The majority of Mss. however, and the present weight of authority, seem to be in favor of the reading Ἰερεμίου.

Griesbach thinks the quotation before us to be a plain case of lapse of memory in Matthew. Kuinoel, on the other hand, supposes Matthew to have quoted from an *apocryphal* Jeremiah then extant, (which Jerome testifies he had seen), both because of the name of the prophet mentioned at the beginning of the quotation, and because the sense given to the passage by the Evangelist, is very different from the sense of Zech. 11: 12, 13.

Many other conjectures have been made, which it would be little to our purpose to mention.

In a case like this, which as to one particular is *unique*, (there being no other which will in all respects compare with it in the New Testament), it does not become any critic to be very confident. I have but two suggestions to make, and they are brief. (1) The ancient and well known order of the prophets among the Hebrews was, that *Jeremiah* should stand *first* or at the *head* of all the rest. The reasons assigned for this I need not now mention. The fact is notorious, and will not be denied. If now, as was often the practice when a general reference only was to be made to the place of a text of Scripture, we may suppose that *Jeremiah was quoted as the title of the prophetic volume*, (and this because he stood at the head of it), then there is, after all, no serious difficulty in the case, and (I may of course add) no serious improbability. If the reading 'Ιερεμίου be genuine, I should incline to this solution. It does not seem to me likely that Matthew, or whoever was the author of Matt. 27: 3—10, was ignorant of the particular place where such a peculiar text of Scripture was found as that before us.

But the old Syriac, it seems, was not made from a Ms. which presented the difficulty in question. If the solution above be not admitted, I should incline to believe that the original Ms. did not contain the name of the prophet. Matthew, indeed, has frequently appealed to the prophets, particularly to Isaiah, by name; but in all cases, besides the present one, without any error. I cannot proffer positive proof that he did not commit an error, and write 'Ιερεμίου here; but in the present state of disagreeing testimony, and of other circumstances, I do not feel at liberty to conclude that he has committed a mistake, certainly not such an one as Mr. Norton supposes to exist.

But passing all the difficulties about the name of the prophet quoted, Mr. Norton thinks " the words of the Old Testament perverted," as to the sense given to them. That Zechariah makes a use of the words in question in some respects different from that made by the Evangelist, I readily admit. But so it is in respect to a multitude of quotations from the Old Testament by the writers of the New. Yet the admission of this does not settle all the questions that occur in relation to this subject. One question I have to ask is, whether the action of Zechariah, described in the passage quoted from him, was *symbolical?*

That it was, is certain.   Nearly the whole chapter from which it is taken is *parabolic* in a high degree, and is designed for instruction by similitudes.   Another question is, whether the treatment which the prophet represents himself as receiving from the hands of the Jews, is similar to that which the Saviour received from Judas and the unbelieving Jews.   And here the similitude is very striking.   The services of the prophet were valued at thirty pieces of silver; the Saviour was prized at the same.   The silver in the first case was given to the *potter*, — probably the one whose business it was to make vessels for the house of the Lord ; in the second, it was appropriated in the like way, in order to purchase a burying-ground, for the poor, of a potter probably holding the same relation to the temple. I ask now : Are there not many cases of *ἵνα πληρωθῇ* in the New Testament, where the resemblances are even less striking than here ? And why then should Mr. Norton speak of " a perversion" of the ancient Scriptures in this case, like that of which the Rabbies are guilty ?

But Mr. Norton appeals to his friend Mr. Noyes for proof, that the word usually rendered *potter* here should be rendered *treasury*.   Yet, after all, this matter is not quite so plain as it seems to be to the minds of Mr. Noyes and Mr. Norton.   The Hebrew word in question, which is employed in Zech. 11: 13, is יוֹצֵר.   Now that this may mean *figulus* (*potter*), there is and can be no doubt ; for the verb יָצַר, which means generally *to form, to fashion*, means also in particular *to form* or *fashion as a potter does his vessel*.   Hence when God himself is called יוֹצֵר, *creator*, it is in reference to his *plastic* power.   No instance except the controverted one in question can be produced, where יוֹצֵר is supposed to mean *treasury*.   There is nothing either in the verb itself which is the root, or in the nature of any particular case, that would lead us to such a signification. It is only by asserting that יוֹצֵר is equivalent to אוֹצָר, that Gesenius in his Lexicon gets at the meaning of *treasury*—a meaning, moreover, which only one of all the ancient Versions (the Syriac) has given.   The whole matter, then, stands upon mere *conjecture*, and the meaning thus given has no actual authority in its favor.

Which now are we to trust, in the present case ?   The Hebrew usage of יוֹצֵר universal in other cases, all the ancient Versions but one, and most of the modern ones, not to mention the weight of authority given by the rendering itself in Matthew ?

Or shall we trust to the *guess* of Gesenius, and after him of Mr. Noyes following in his track, and then of Mr. Norton, rather than to all the sources just named above?

When Mr. Norton says, that 'the words of Zechariah are applied here in so strange a way, that there is nothing else resembling it in the whole book of Matthew,'—he says what I do not think will bear the test of close examination. There are other passages whose πλήρωσις is decidedly more obscure than that of the present.

I merely add here, that when Mr. Noyes translates thus: " I took the thirty pieces of silver, and cast them *into the house of Jehovah into the treasury*," he certainly takes a somewhat large liberty with the Hebrew text. Zechariah says: וָאַשְׁלִיךְ אֹתוֹ בֵּית יְהוָה אֶל־הַיּוֹצֵר, *and I cast it* [the silver], *at* (or *in*) *the house of Jehovah, to the potter*, i. e., as I understand the passage, to the potter who was at or in the house of Jehovah, and whose business it was to make vessels for its use. Mr. Noyes has rendered בֵּית יְהוָה, INTO *the house of Jehovah*; whereas the *into* is wanting in the Hebrew, and the person to whom the money was given, or (if you insist on it) the place into which it was thrown, is designated by אֶל־הַיּוֹצֵר. *Two* places of depositing the money we cannot well suppose to be designated. Surely, then, the simple Accusative (בֵּית יְהוָה), after the verb אַשְׁלִיךְ, cannot be translated with propriety as Mr. Noyes has translated it. The בֵּית יְהוָה, no doubt, designates the *place where* the transaction mentioned by the prophet occurred, but not the place *into* which (as Mr. Noyes has it) the money was thrown.

If what I have said is well founded, then it would seem that Mr. Norton's objections against Matt. 27: 3—10, when deliberately examined, do not amount to any thing like the sum of difficulty which he has so strongly alleged.

It is not even pretended by him, in the present case, that there is, the world over, a Ms. or a Version, ancient or modern, which *omits* the passage under examination. In a question of *lower* criticism then, are we, from mere conjecture, or at most from mere theological or exegetical difficulties, to disregard all authorities from the first century down to the present day? In *theologizing*, some may make this a question; in *criticising* respecting the genuineness of a particular text or passage, I do not see how such a question can be raised.

Another passage which Mr. Norton rejects, is found in Matthew 27: 52, 53.   It respects the resurrection of the saints at the time when Jesus expired on the cross, and who are said to have ' gone, *after his resurrection*, into the holy city, and to have appeared to many.'

Here Mr. Norton finds a multitude of difficulties ; they are all, however, of a like nature with those in the preceding case. He does not even pretend that any Ms. or Version favors the position, that here is an interpolation.   All his objections amount to the allegation, that *the thing is incredible.* 'Who are the saints ?   How long had they been dead ?   For what purpose were they brought to life ?   What converts to Christianity were made by such a miracle ?   Did they die a second time ?   How could the writer forbear to tell us the consequences of a miracle more astounding than any other on sacred record ?   How could the other Evangelists omit the mention of such a thing ?'   Such are his grounds for believing that here is an interpolation.

I need not dwell on most of the allegations implied by raising questions of this nature.   If one should undertake to raise questions of the like kind about the miracle of the water turned into wine, the barren fig-tree that was cursed, the swine that rushed into the lake, and other like things, he could easily outstrip Mr. Norton himself.   And why, I might ask in the like spirit of suggesting difficulties, did no other Evangelist but John tell us of the resurrection of Lazarus, or of the cure of the infirm man at the pool of Bethesda, or of the man born blind whose sight was restored ?   These were astonishing miracles ; and why then did not all the Evangelists record them ?   And why has even John forborne to tell us of the " consequences" of all these things, excepting merely that the multitudes were rendered the more eager to hear and see Jesus—a thing that we should of course expect and believe, without any particular information.

As to any speculations about the *subsequent* state or experience of those who were raised from the dead, according to the passage in Matthew, I have none to proffer, except such as seem to lie upon the face of the narration.   I understand the writer as meaning plainly to impress the idea upon the reader, that this resurrection was but temporary, perhaps merely apparent, the apparitions being as it were the *umbrae* of the dead.   I know indeed that σώματα is employed in the description. But this is perfectly natural, as the σῶμα was all which could be deposited in the tomb. But when the writer says, that ἐνεφανίσθησαν πολλοῖς, ' *they made their appearance, or shewed themselves*, to many persons,' it would be strange indeed if the reader did not receive from this the impression, that their appearance was short and incidental. As the account in Matthew now runs, it would seem that they were raised from the dead at the time when the tombs were opened by the groans of the expiring Saviour, but that they did not actually *appear* in Jerusalem until after the resurrection of Jesus, μετὰ τὴν ἔγερ- σιν αὐτοῦ. This intervening time was, however, only one day and a small part of two more. Some twenty-six or twenty-eight hours are all the time which it is necessary to make out, between the death and the resurrection of the Saviour. More may be supposed or conceded ; but more is unnecessary.

Now as to the facts themselves, I do not see how we can shew the impossibility, or even the improbability of them, any more than of the rending the veil of the temple, darkening the sun, cleaving the rocks, etc. That there may be difficulty in freeing the passage from all the objections which might be rais- ed *theologically*, or *physiologically*, I would not gainsay ; but that there is any stable ground for *critical* objections to the gen- uineness of the passage, I see no good reason to believe.

Mark 14: 8—20, i. e. the concluding paragraph of Mark's Gospel, is also regarded by Mr. Norton as an *interpolation*. And here it cannot be said that he is entirely destitute of any critical support ; for the Codex Vaticanus, a Ms. of great age and of high authority, omits the paragraph in question. In a number of other Mss., (Mr. Norton states them to be more than forty), there are remarks of the following purport in connection with these verses, viz., " Wanting in some copies, but found in the ancient ones ;" " in many copies ;" " considered spurious, and wanting in most copies ;" " not in the more accurate cop- ies ;" " generally in accurate copies," etc.

That some of the ancient fathers had doubts concerning the genuineness of this passage, is clear from what Eusebius says, in his Quaestiones ad Marinum, pp. 61, 62. Gregory of Nys- sa avers, that the passage is not found in the more accurate

Greek Mss. ; and Jerome, that it is wanting in many of them. Greg. Opp. III. 411. Jerome, Opp. IV. P. I. col. 172.

After all, however, only one Ms. (Cod. Vat.) is known which omits the paragraph under examination. It is in all the Versions, unless some Codices of the Armenian should be excepted, which is doubtful. No recent critic has ventured to thrust it out from the corrected text of the New Testament. No one, I apprehend, can do so, and justify himself on grounds that are purely critical, while the state of the evidence continues to be as it now is.

As in the preceding cases, Mr. Norton here resorts to *internal* difficulties, and depends principally upon them. He notices the apparent discrepancy between Mark 16: 9, ἀναστὰς δὲ, πρωῒ πρώτῃ σαββάτου ἐφάνη πρῶτον Μαρίᾳ τῇ Μαγδαληνῇ, and Matt. 28: 1, ὀψὲ δὲ σαββάτων, τῇ ἐπιφωσκούσῃ εἰς μίαν σαββάτων, ἦλθε Μαρία ἡ Μαγδαληνή. He admits, however, that the difficulty here is nothing more than in *appearance.* Mark asserts, (if his text be rightly pointed), that *Jesus, when risen, appeared early in the morning on the first day of the week* (first, as the Jews counted days, for their Sabbath was the *last* day of their week), *to Mary Magdalene.* He does not say *when* Jesus rose from the dead. Matthew asserts, that sometime on the evening of the Sabbath, (which here means the evening that *followed* the Jewish Sabbath, if we so translate the passage), or (as we may translate) *on the evening of the week which dawned toward the first day of the week, came Mary Magdalene,* etc. Nothing more need be said than simply to explain the two passages, in order to shew that there is no contradiction between them. Both unite in the sentiment, that Jesus shewed himself to Mary Magdalene, early on *the first morning which followed the Jewish Sabbath.*

Mr. Norton here ingenuously declares, that " there is no ground for believing that transcribers are to be charged with *omitting* passages in one Evangelist, because they found, or fancied, them to be irreconcilable with those in another ; " p. lxxiv. yet, on p. lxix. he represents some copyist of Matthew's Gospel as having thrown in the clause in Matt. 27: 53, μετὰ τὴν ἔγερσιν αὐτοῦ, in order to avoid contradicting another passage of Scripture, which states that *Christ was the First-Born from the dead.* What an inconsistent part, then, does Mr. Norton make these copyists to act ! Did they not know that the penalty was the same for *adding* to the Scriptures, that it is for *taking away* from it ?

Mr. Norton appeals to the language of Mark 16: 9 seq. as differing from that of the rest of his Gospel. 'Here,' says he, 'Mark uses πρώτῃ σαββάτου, while he uses μία σαββάτων in 16: 2; as do the other Evangelists.' But what does this amount to? *Μία σαββάτων* is a Hebraism, and πρώτῃ σαββάτων is conformed to the usual Greek idiom. Had not a Hebraistic writer his choice, who wished to avoid repeating the same phrase too often?

'But *Ἐκείνῃ* in v. 10, and *Κἀκεῖνοι* in v. 11, are not used demonstratively, nor emphatically; which occurs no where else in Mark's Gospel.'—Yet it lies on the face of the narration here, that Mary Magdalene is spoken of emphatically, or at any rate demonstratively, in order to render plain the distinction between her and the other Marys. As to κἀκεῖνοι, whoever attentively reads the preceding verse may see, that the word is here altogether in its place.

Several ἅπαξ λεγόμενα Mr. Norton has also selected from the passage, p. lxxv. But I can attribute no weight of importance to this argument. We may select passages from Matthew's account of the Sermon on the Mount, from almost any of Paul's epistles, or from the book of Acts, and disprove the genuineness of each passage on the same ground. When are we to become sufficiently aware, that the same writer is not confined to one and the same mode of expression, on all subjects and at all times?

But Mr. Norton's main reliance is on the internal improbability of the things asserted in the paragraph under examination. 'The enumeration of miracles' he says 'is strange.' Some of these were to be such as neither Jesus nor his disciples were accustomed to perform. *They were liable to be confounded with the tricks of pretended magicians.* Some of the powers promised could be of no use to others. The promise appears to be to Christians in general; while we know that all private Christians never possessed miraculous powers.' pp. lxxvi. seq.

The passage I have marked in Italics (which Mr. Norton does not) seems to me somewhat strange. We open our New Testament at Luke 10: 19, and find the Saviour declaring to the Seventy disciples whom he sent forth on a special mission: "Behold I give you power over serpents and scorpions, and over all the power of the enemy, and nothing shall by any means hurt you." Acts 28: 5 tells us that 'Paul shook off a viper from his hand, which did him no harm.' Did the Saviour not know that magicians had played tricks with tamed serpents and scorpions, and that the Seventy would be in danger of being taken for magicians?

Casting out devils is another miraculous power mentioned in the passage before us. Yet the Seventy Disciples before mentioned were commissioned with such a power: "Lord," say they, in the account there given of their missions, "even the devils are subject to us through thy name;" Luke 10: 17. Let the reader turn to Acts 5: 16. 8: 7. 16: 28. 19: 12, and he will see whether the apostles are represented as being possessed of the power in question.

They shall speak with new tongues, is another part of the commission in Mark. And here we need only to ask the reader to peruse Acts ii. and 1 Cor. xiv. I am aware of what Herder, Eichhorn, Bleek, and others, have said against the usual interpretation of these passages; but I am not in any measure satisfied with their views, and verily believe them to be philologically inadmissible.

They shall lay hands on the sick, and they shall recover. If the reader wishes any explanation of this, the book of Acts, the First of Corinthians, and the Epistle of James, chapter v., may be appealed to, without any room for doubt as to what was promised and what was bestowed.

What remains, then, of this list of *extraordinary* and *improbable* miraculous powers? No one thing—except what is designated by the following phrase: *If they shall drink any deadly thing, it shall not hurt them.* But is not this virtually contained in the commission to the Seventy Disciples, Luke 19: 19, when the Saviour says that they shall be *over all the power of the enemy, and nothing shall by any means hurt them?* There is, however, no need of further defence. It is enough to say, that when *serpents* and *poison* are mentioned (as in Mark), two obvious and usually irremediable causes of death are particularized, merely as a symbol or specimen of all dangers. The passage, then, contains a promise of protection from all dangers, even the worst, until their work should be finished. What can be more common in the Scriptures, than such a mode of speech as this, where a part is particularized, and stands as representative of the whole genus?

As to miraculous powers being granted to *Christians in general,* I do not see how Mr. Norton gets at such an interpretation of the passage before us. Whom does the Saviour address?

His *eleven apostles;* (Judas was dead).   Does all which he promises to *them,* belong also to every individual Christian in the world ?

But enough.   Mr. Norton says, at the close, that 'there is a conciseness and brevity of statement here, [i. e. in the paragraph before us], which is unusual for Mark, who commonly details facts with more particularity than any of the other Evangelists.' And yet, this very characteristic detail of Mark seems to be conspicuous in the passage before us.   Matthew represents the Saviour as simply saying : *Lo ! I am with you always, even to the end of the world.*   Luke, in Acts 1: 5, represents the Saviour as saying : *Ye shall be baptized with the Holy Ghost, not many days hence.*

What these two writers have thus so briefly expressed, Mark has designated in his usual way, i. e. by detailing particulars. This lies on the very face of his record.   And when the other Evangelists have said so much as has just been recited and referred to, what objection can lie against the narration in Mark, with respect to the miraculous powers which it promises should be bestowed on the apostles ?

One more remark, and I have done with the discussion of this topic.   I must request the reader to open his Greek Testament at Mark 16: 8, i. e. at the verse which immediately precedes the paragraph that Mr. Norton thinks to be an interpolation.   What kind of *ending* the Gospel of this Evangelist would have, if vs. 9—20 should be rejected, may be seen at once, viz. the following: καὶ οὐδενὶ οὐδὲν εἶπον · ἐφοβοῦντο γάρ. Now as this would be truly a ἅπαξ λεγόμενον, if I may so speak, in the whole world of books, and as it is, moreover, too improbable for rational belief, so Mr. Norton suggests, that probably sudden death or accident interrupted Mark in the midst of his work ; and then, that 'some individual who was taking copies of his work, with good intention but not with the best judgment, added the paragraph under consideration, in order to complete the work !'   Mr. Norton here forgets what he has so well said, in the body of his volume, on the impossibility that even a single sentence should be added by an interpolator, without its being detected, so difficult is it to imitate the style of the Gospels, and so marked is this style.   He seems also to have forgotten the powerful argument which he urges against the probability of the corruption of the Gospels, from the fact that any one copy, or even a considerable number of copies, if interpolated, could produce no influence on the remainder. How strange, now, that Mr. Norton should contend at the same time, that both Matthew and Mark received *large* additions in the way of interpolation, even in the primitive age — yea, while some of the apostles themselves and evangelists were living! For if these books were interpolated, it must have been thus early. A later period renders it impossible, as Mr. Norton himself has even demonstrated, for interpolations to change the great body of Mss. in circulation among Christians.

The Evangelist Luke has almost escaped the *abrading* criticism of Mr. Norton. Only a very short paragraph in chap. xxii. 43, 44, respecting the agony and bloody sweat of the Saviour, and the interposition of an angel on the occasion, can, as he thinks, with good reason be doubted ; p. lxxix.

Here, indeed, with respect to the verses specified, Mr. Norton may claim more *critical* support than in most of the other cases. The Cod. Alex. and Cod. Vaticanus omit the passage ; as does the Sahidic Version. In ten Mss. it is marked as doubtful. Hilary says, that many Greek and Latin Mss. omit it. Jerome merely states, that *some* copies contained the passage.

On the other hand, Justin Martyr quotes it ; Irenaeus appeals to it in order to confute those heretics who denied the real body of Christ; and so does Epiphanius also. It is contained in all the Mss. and versions except those mentioned above. There is no doubt of its being universal in the Codices of the New Testament, or at any rate nearly so, after the fourth century.

How Mr. Norton reconciles what he says here in one place, with some of his previous declarations, I am unable to see. Epiphanius says, that " the passage is found in Luke's Gospel, *in those copies which have not been subjected to a revision.*" His meaning plainly is : In those copies which have not been purposely altered so as to conform to certain opinions. But Mr. Norton in commenting on this declaration of the good father, makes it tantamount to saying : " It is found in copies not inspected after the transcriber had done his work, by some person responsible for the correctness of the text ; " to which he subjoins the following clause : "*A care which was undoubtedly taken of all copies pretending to accuracy ;* " p. lxxx. I have underscored these remarkable words of Mr. Norton here; for remarkable they truly are, when we find them in a writer who has told us repeatedly of whole chapters and long paragraphs being added by copyists to Matthew and Mark, without any embarrassment at all, as it would seem, from "persons responsible for the correctness of the text." Mr. Norton does not thus commit himself, when he is pleading in behalf of a cause that is well grounded.

But the *internal* difficulties, again, are in his view the principal objections to the passage. 'The agony of the Saviour takes place *after* the angel has interposed. The bloody sweat is such an occurrence as physiology would decline undertaking to explain. The firmness and fortitude of the Saviour's character are rendered doubtful by such an event. No one was present to witness the events here related. If Jesus told the story to his disciples, how could Matthew omit the mention of it? The story interrupts the connection of the discourse.'

A brief reply to these objections, is all that seems to be needed. When the angel *strengthened* the Saviour, it was that he might bear the agony which awaited him, not to deliver him wholly from it. The cup must be drunk; it could not pass from the Saviour. Mr. Norton indeed, in his subsequent remarks, seems to imply a distrust in the interposition of angels on any occasion; but this is a point I need not stop to argue with him here.

As to the *bloody sweat* being a physiological impossibility, I have only to remark, that the Evangelist makes no statement liable to physiological objection; at least, as I understand him. His words are: ὁ ἱδρὼς αὐτοῦ ὡσεὶ θρόμβοι αἵματος καταβαίνοντες ἐπὶ τὴν γῆν, i. e. 'his sweat was like drops of blood falling to the ground.' I understand by this, that the agony of Jesus was such as to force from his body a copious and viscous perspiration, which fell down in conglomerated drops, like blood, to the earth; an occurrence perfectly within the pale of common physiology. Even if this sweat was discoloured, and of a reddish hue, there is nothing very strange in the occurrence. But the words of the Evangelist do not at all oblige us to suppose this. Mr. Norton himself has presented us here with that which Paulus calls a *philological wonder*.

But the firmness and fortitude of Jesus, it seems, are in danger of being compromitted on such an occasion. Then three of the Evangelists have compromitted them; for so many relate his agony in the garden, and that which he endured on the cross, and also his complaints while thus suffering. On the other hand, my view of this case is very different. That Jesus persevered in his resolution, peacefully and unresistingly to suffer death, in the midst of such agonies, shews his firmness and fortitude in a most conspicuous light. Had he been merely stupid or insensible; had he exhibited only stoical apathy, or haughtily put at defiance (like the heathen of our western wilds) all torments however exquisite; how different would he have been from that tender-hearted " man of sorrows acquainted with grief," which the Evangelists have shown him to be! Now, all is well. ' Having been tried himself, he knows how to succour those who are tried.'

Nor can I forbear here to add one thought more; which is, that the peculiar sorrows and agonies of Jesus, who was perfectly free from sin, must ever remain inexplicable to those, who will not admit that " he bore our griefs and carried our sorrows," or that " he bore our sins, in his own body, on the tree."

As to the allegation that ' Jesus was alone, and therefore his disciples or others could know nothing of the agony in the garden;' if it be of any avail, one must by implication make out from it, that Jesus did not communicate this to his disciples, during his forty days' converse with them after his resurrection, or that the Holy Spirit did not instruct the mind of the Evangelist in respect to it. How either of these views is to be established, we have not yet seen.

That Matthew must have necessarily mentioned the circumstance of sweating as it were drops of blood, in case he knew of it, no more follows, than that he must have mentioned the raising of Lazarus from the dead, or the cure of the man born blind, because he knew of these.

Here again, also, Mr. Norton tells us at the close, how the " mistake of transcribers took [the passage before us] into the text of Matthew." In the preceding page he has told us, as we have already seen, what effectual care was taken to prevent such mistakes.

The story of the impotent man at the pool of Bethesda we might expect to find doubted by Mr. Norton, who seems to be anxiously desirous to dispense with all *angelic* interposition. But this passage has been so often discussed, and information respecting it is so accessible, that it is unnecessary for me to go into detail. It is well known, that a great variety of readings are to be found in the Mss. here, and some of great authority omit John 5: 4, which contains the special account of angelic interposition. Knapp marks the latter clause of *v.* 3 and the whole of *v.* 4 as suspicious ; but he does not venture to reject it.

I shall make but few remarks on the subject. My first observation is, that scarcely any two Mss. which differ from the Textus Receptus here, agree with each other in their readings. The adverse testimony is remarkably discordant ; and cross-examination would very much embarrass the witnesses.

My second remark is, that on the ground which Mr. Norton and others take, viz. of rejecting the story respecting the angel and the moving of the waters, no satisfactory account can be given of what the impotent man says, when addressed by the Saviour, and which all Mss. and versions agree in representing as genuine : " Sir, I have no one, *when the water is troubled,* who can put me into the pool ; for whenever I come, another goes down into it before me." Now several things are necessarily involved in this answer, (1) That the waters were agitated only occasionally, or at certain times with intervals between. (2) That unless a person was put into the waters at the critical moment of agitation, no healing virtue was to be expected. (3) It would seem that only one person at a time was healed. (4) Not the least doubt appears to be entertained by the impotent man and others, that the healing virtue of the pool, when agitated, was a matter of fact.

All these things are plainly involved in the answer of the impotent man, i. e. that he and others firmly believed them all. Now if the preceding account of the agitation of the pool, of the interposition of the angel, and of the peculiar healing virtue of the pool when agitated, should be all *omitted,* (and this Mr. Norton contends for), then this answer of the impotent man must appear to be so abruptly and mysteriously introduced by John, that it would be one of the most unaccountable things that I can even imagine. According to the best edition of the *amended* text the matter would stand thus : " There was a pool called Bethesda, having five porches. In these lay a multitude of impotent, blind, maimed, withered. . . . Now there was a certain man there, etc." For what purpose then did all these valetudinarians resort there ? Not surely for common bathing, which could be had every where. Yet the Evangelist, as his emendators would have it, has not told us a word of the specific object of the visitors at this place ; and yet in the sequel he introduces an impotent man, whom he represents as saying things that must in this way appear to the readers more mysterious than the riddle which so long perplexed Oedipus.

I cannot read this whole account without a deep conviction that the Received Text is in the right here, if the succeeding part of the story is to be retained ; and of this we have no authority to doubt. It must be admitted, at least I cannot but admit, that the weight of authority is on the whole upon the side of the usual reading. If now, in addition to this it be a matter of fact, that the internal state of the composition renders necessary this reading, (and that this is so I appeal to the simple unprejudiced reader), then may we be contented with the text as it is.

As to Mr. Norton's objections on the score of *angelic interposition*, and the extraordinary nature of the case, I can allow them only when, with the Naturalists, I may come to disbelieve all which is miraculous. At present, I am a great way from such a position.

Mr. Norton thinks that the pool was " an intermitting medical spring." Did he ever hear of such a spring, that would heal *but one*, and that only when it was agitated ? The words of the impotent man shew at least, that the popular belief was very different from this view of Mr. Norton. As to the *fact* itself, I shall have a word to say in the sequel.

Mr. Norton says, that ' the story of the angel is founded on the superstition of the Jews, who, in common with the heathen, were accustomed to ascribe any remarkable natural phenomenon to supernatural agency.' This is not a very honorary account of the Jews ; and what is of rather serious import is, that it involves along with them, their patriarchs and prophets and apostles. The Scriptures are full of accounts which present us with such views. But how are we to *disprove* angelic agency ? How are we to show that it is improbable even in any small degree, that there are intermediate beings between us and our Creator, who are " ministering spirits ?"

As to the matter of fact in respect to the virtues of this Spring or Pool, much need not be said. The *impossibility* of such virtues by such means, no man can prove ; the *improba-*

bility can be shown merely by trusting to physiological reasoning. But on the same ground, Hume has objected to all miracles; and so might others do. Yet this cannot prove, that he who made the world may not and does not interpose—and this in a variety of ways—in order to accomplish special ends which the usual laws of nature will not accomplish.

But let us view the subject, for a moment, in another light. Suppose a writer should now appear on the stage, who, in describing the occurrences of the last generation in Boston, should state the existence there of such a pool as that of Bethesda. What should we say of him, in case matters were as we now know them to have been? We should say: ' This author is either a fool or a madman.' And what would become of his book? Of course it would be regarded with universal contempt.

Now John, in telling the story of the impotent man, has made an appeal to all Jews, and to all the world who knew any thing of Jerusalem, as to the facts which he has stated. Even omitting the disputed part of the account, the words of the impotent man still imply, for substance, all which that contains. John, then, has either represented this man as being a madman, or else John himself was mad, when he published such a story, if it be not founded in fact. There was not a place of any note, in all the eastern world, which did not contain Jews who had been up to Jerusalem to the feast. They must all have known whether the story about such a pool as John's Gospel mentions, was well or ill founded; and in the latter case, the credit of his Gospel must have been ruined at once. Was John so destitute of common sense, as to throw out upon the world such an idle fabrication, at the risk of all credit and all respect? So I cannot think; and therefore I admit the fact as stated in the *Textus Receptus*.

But it will be said, that in this statement I assume the fact that John did publish the paragraph now disputed. I have done so; but I am willing to assume the ground that the paragraph marked in Knapp as suspicious, is to be omitted. How do matters then stand? They stand thus, viz. that the representation of the impotent man renders it necessary to suppose, that his own views of the healing virtues of the pool were the common and popular views; else why the porches, and the numerous valetudinarian visiters there? Otherwise, moreover, John has introduced a man as telling a story, which has not, and never had, the least foundation in point of fact, or even of supposed fact; a story which every inhabitant of Jerusalem, not to say of Palestine, could of his own personal knowledge contradict.   In fact we cannot for a moment imagine, that the views of the multitude were not such as the answer of the impotent man implies that they were. Surely John has not represented this man as gravely saying what every body knew to be false or ridiculous.   What then could have occasioned such a popular belief as this?

But after all, it will be said, there is this advantage in leaving out the disputed clause, viz. John is not then made responsible for the truth of what is said concerning the virtues of the pool of Bethesda ; he merely states what the popular belief was, through the medium of what is said by the impotent man.

To this I should reply, that the aspect of the whole story is such, even on the ground of omitting the disputed passage in it, as seems to my mind plainly to imply, that John did not deem the account given by the impotent man as inconsistent with truth, or as varying from it.   No qualifying word of John's gives us even a hint, that he supposes the man to be merely speaking out his own superstitious and groundless views.   I do not, therefore, think any substantial difficulty is avoided by rejecting the disputed passage ; and the rest of the account is such as, in my view, to render the admission of it apparently necessary.

Even if John did not himself write the disputed part of the paragraph before us, whoever did insert it, he must have done so at a very *early* period ; certainly before the close of the second century, or rather, before the middle of it ; for the Peshito contains it in full.   The interpolator, then, must have been a very strange man, if he could suppose that a fact like this would not be generally known among the readers of John's Gospel, to be either true or false.   If false, how could his interpolation escape being detected?

In a word ; the difficulties are not by any means confined to the Textus Receptus.   The omission of the disputed passage seems to me to throw more difficulty in our way, than the reception of it.   At any rate I am far enough from thinking, as Mr. Norton says he does, that ' John did not adopt the common error of his countrymen respecting the agency of an angel in the case in question, because he appears to have been free from a more general error, viz. the belief that diseases were occasioned by demoniacal possession ; ' p. lxxxvi.

The narrative of the woman taken in adultery and accused before the Saviour, related in John 8: 3—11, Mr. Norton believes to be true, but says : " We may conclude with confidence that it was not written by St. John ; " p. lxxxvi.

There is, indeed, a strange discrepancy of Mss. as to this account.   Not to mention others of less importance, the Codices B. L. omit it, while D. G. H. K. M. N. insert it.   The Versions and the Fathers are also divided.   But still, the majority of testimony seems plainly to be in its favour.   In this state of things, and when there is nothing in manner or matter which affords any serious hindrance to the reception of this paragraph, I do not see how we can ' *confidently* conclude that John did not write it.'

The two last verses of John's Gospel are also suspected by Mr. Norton.   But here, for a cogent reason, he does not appeal to critical authorities.   His objections therefore are, that in v. 24 the writer says οἴδαμεν (first person *plural*), while in v. 25 he says οἴμαι (first person *singular*) ; that he says, ' *the world could not contain the books,* if the life of Jesus had been fully written,' which is " extravagant hyperbole ; " and that the passage wears the appearance of an appended editorial note.

As to the first objection, one need only read a little way in Paul's epistles, in order to find the change of person from *we* to *I*, and he will see that it is a matter of very frequent occurrence ; as indeed it is elsewhere.   The second objection may easily be met by asking, whether, when Jesus says : " It is easier for a camel to pass through the eye of a needle, than for a rich man to enter into the kingdom of God," this is *extravagant hyperbole ?*   Who can well suppose the meaning of John to be any thing else, than that in his opinion the state of the world was such, in regard to the publication of books, that a biography so copious as to include every thing which Jesus said and did, would not be acceptable, or would not be tolerated ?

In one sense I can admit what is said by Mr. Norton about an " editorial note."   But then I must suppose *John* to be the *editor* of his own Gospel.   That others should be vouchers for him, as Mr. Norton supposes, would be a strange occurrence in the New Testament books.   I omit any remarks on the peculiar sense which Mr. Norton says is given to several words in this passage, because they do not seem to me to be of sufficient importance to establish his position.

Thus have I summarily gone through with the examination of Mr. Norton's reasons for rejecting from the text various passages in the Gospels as they now lie before us. I do not say, that there is no ground of doubt in any of these cases; but it is my apprehension, that according to the state of the evidence now before us, there is not sufficient reason to reject any of these passages; and in respect to some of them there is evidence, which at present is incontrovertible, that they ought to be received as genuine parts of the text.

I have now, at the close of these discussions, some brief reflections to make, on the general method chosen by Mr. Norton of discussing or managing this very important topic, viz. the genuineness of particular passages in the Gospels. Having bestowed so much attention upon his views, and canvassed to so great an extent his objections, I am unwilling to take my leave of the subject, without suggesting a few things which appear to me of great importance, in relation to such an affair as adding to or taking from the word of God.

I cherish no superstitious feelings in relation to this subject, which would induce me, in any way, to impede or restrain the most free and full investigation. It must be perfectly plain to every thinking mind, which has any acquaintance with subjects of this nature, that the first *printed* editions of the New Testament have no peculiar claim to accuracy above other and subsequent editions with which far greater pains have been taken. The first printed edition was of course copied from Mss. Some of these appear to have been since lost; and with respect to the others, there is no ground to suppose that they had any unusual claims to accuracy. It is quite probable, that other and better Mss. have since been brought to light.

The simple question in respect to any or all New Testament Mss. is: Which, in all probability, comes nearest to the original autographs of the authors? Any evidence, internal or external, which will enable us to judge soundly in regard to this subject, should be attended to with eagerness and received with thankfulness.

I fully coincide with the sentiment that has sometimes been expressed, viz. that there is as much reason to be on our guard against *adding* to the word of God as there is against *taking from* it. The penalty is the same in both cases: and on the ground of justice and propriety *it ought to be the same.*

In all investigations of this nature, then, a judgment strictly impartial should, if possible, be made out. But in order to do this, one must conform the whole process of his efforts to find what the true text is, to the simple and impartial rules of criticism. These have been established, so far as they may be considered as settled, on grounds independent of any particular theological bias or opinion. They are rules which apply to the investigation of all books alike, whether sacred or profane.

One remark more I may add, before I make the application of these principles to the case before us. This is, that questions of *lower* criticism, i. e. questions which simply respect the state of the text, have, and can have, with few exceptions indeed, little or nothing to do with the opinions or sentiments which may be expressed in any particular passage, or even book. The real critical question in every such case, is not whether the author's opinions are true or false ; it is simply, *whether he wrote what is seemingly attributed to him.*

I do not say this, however, as I have intimated above, without some limitations. There may be cases, where a passage has been foisted into a writing, which passage is so entirely irreconcilable with the tenor of the author, either as to sentiment, or manner, or as to both, that no external evidence can wholly overcome the probability of its spuriousness. Such are the passages exhibited by Mr. Norton in pp. xcv. seq. of his work. The bare reading of them seals at once their condemnation.

It is easy, moreover, to imagine many cases, where the same thing might be truly said. But then it is not common to meet with such passages in any works of importance, which are popular and well known, and have had an extensive circulation. The difficulty must have always been very great, when Mss. (and not *books*) were in use, of making any interpolation of this nature which would be generally adopted.

Setting aside then such flagrant cases, which occur rarely indeed, let us confine our views to the more practical parts of the subject before us. Is it true, in the cases produced by Mr. Norton which he believes to be *interpolations,* that there is such marked differences of style and manner, as would rank them with cases such as I have just mentioned ? I venture to say, that it is not. My belief is, that a reader, who never had heard any thing of the various readings of the New Testament, and knew nothing of the contests about the genuineness of particular passages, and whom we will suppose to be well acquainted with the subject of criticism in relation to classic authors, would never think of objecting to the passages selected by Mr. Norton, any more than to a multitude of others which present difficulties at least equally great. That there are many others of this character, it would be easy to shew. I deem the work superfluous, however, for every intelligent and well-informed reader of the Gospels must have observed them in the course of his own studies.

I must object, therefore, on general grounds, to the aspect at large of Mr. Norton's criticisms on these particular topics. It wears the air of theological prejudice—of *a priori* reasoning. I may say of it, I think truly, *non sinit ratio nec loci nec temporis.* In mere questions of lower criticism, difficulties of theology, or of rhetoric, or of concinnity, should all hold quite an inferior place. I would not say, that they should be entirely kept out of sight ; but I would aver, that they are by no means to constitute a *prominent* part of all that we have to say on such an occasion.

Are they not, however, prominently exhibited in the remarks of Mr. Norton ? For example ; what *critical* authority does he adduce, in order to establish the spuriousness of Matt. i. ii. ? Not even one. And yet he is quite in earnest, that we should reject these chapters. Why ? Because they contain narrations exhibiting, in his view, various incongruities and improbabilities. But did not the Ebionites reject them on the like ground ? Did not Faustus the Manichaean, whom Augustine so severely reproves, prune away these chapters because of his particular views respecting the nature of evil as necessarily attached to all which is material ? Did not Marcion prune away some parts of Luke, for the reason that he could not reconcile them with his philosophy or theosophy ? Did not even Luther reject the epistle of James, because he thought that it took sides against him, in his dispute with the Romanists respecting justification ? And did he not at first reject the Apocalypse, because he could not understand it, and afterwards incline to admit it because he learned that it might be turned to good advantage against " the scarlet beast at Rome ?" Where shall we begin and end with such processes as these ?

If Mr. Norton, in reply to this, should say, that the cases of interpolation produced by him, are of so flagrant a nature, that he rests his objections against them on this ground ; then I must appeal to what has been said in the preceding pages, in order to disprove such an assertion.

In a word ; it is to me a matter of deep regret, that what Mr. Norton has built up so ably with one hand, he should pull down with the other. His book contains much that has, in my view, more than ordinary excellence. With the maxims of lower criticism which he seems to hold on almost all occasions, I should fully accord. With his application of them, or rather (I should say) with his failure to apply them, in the supposed cases of interpolation, I cannot be satisfied. I cannot think that he has been consistent with himself.

At all events, if the liberty he has taken with the Gospels is a matter of common right, (and why should it not be ?) then we may expect to find almost every sect in Christendom applying the shears of criticism to the New Testament, and cutting out such parts as become troublesome to them whenever they are urged against their particular opinions by a skilful antagonist. Should they follow the example of Mr. Norton, they would not need the support of Mss. and Versions, in order to justify themselves in such a process. It is enough, if they are persuaded that some parts of the Gospels which they approve seem to be embarrassed by other parts which they would willingly spare. *Actum est*, in regard to the latter. Scripture cannot contradict reason, i. e. their reason ; and so that cannot be Scripture which seems to contradict their reason. Where can we stop, now, in such a process as this ?

Highly, then, as I think of Mr. Norton's book in many respects, and cheerfully as I concede to him the well earned praise of great diligence, much learning, and cultivated style ; much as I truly wish him success in the further prosecution of his interesting and important labours ; I must, so far as is proper for me to do, enter my most solemn protest against some of the *practical* developments of his criticism, and against their results in respect to those portions of the Gospels, the integrity of which he has called in question. I do not assert in a categorical manner, or with a dogmatical air, that these portions are genuine ; for of what use could such an assertion be ? But it is my most sincere and hearty belief, that, as critics, we are not entitled by the present state of evidence to pronounce against them. I go one step further. I cannot even admit, with the evidence before me which as yet has been proffered, that a great portion of them are even of a doubtful character. I must on the whole, therefore, continue to regard them and to appeal to them as genuine, until new and different light shall be poured in upon them. It is on every ground safer to do so, than it is to substitute subjective feelings and difficulties for external evidence, theological opinions for critical reasons, and to launch forth on the boundless ocean of conjecture without rudder or compass.

ARTICLE VI.

Some Remarks on Hebrews 12: 25.

By T. D. Woolsey, Professor of Greek Literature in Yale College, New Haven.

THERE are one or two points connected with this verse, which may profitably be made the subject of more extended remark, than is usually found in a general commentary. It has been doubted not a little who is meant by τὸν ἀπ᾽ οὐρανῶν, and the opinions of critics have not been entirely united with regard to τὸν ἐπὶ γῆς. The construction also of χρηματίζοντα is somewhat questionable. I beg leave to offer some observations on these points and on the verse generally, although, on account of having given little study of late years to New Testament Greek, not very well qualified for the task.

In the first place let me ask, who is meant by τὸν ἐπὶ γῆς χρηματίζοντα? As ἐκεῖνοι indisputably carries the mind back to those Jews of v. 19, who were witnesses of the scenes on Mt. Sinai, τὸν ἐπὶ γῆς can only point either to God or Moses. It appears that so excellent a scholar as Grotius, after the Greek commentators Theophylact and Oecumenius, has referred these words to God. But in this way, God is contrasted either with himself or with Christ. In either case, the reasoning from the less to the greater,—so evident in the passage,—is destroyed or very much weakened. Again, the form of the sentence,—τόν contrasted with τόν,—seems necessarily to point at *two* different objects. And, as if utterly to demolish this interpretation, in the very passage of Exodus (20: 22) where the first transactions on the sacred mountain are recorded, to which these commentators suppose an allusion, God is represented as speaking from *heaven*; ὑμεῖς ἑωράκατε ὅτι ἐκ τοῦ οὐρανοῦ λελάληκα πρὸς ὑμᾶς. The author of the epistle must then have been strangely forgetful, to have conceived of God as speaking on earth. But a far more important question is, who is intended by τὸν ἀπ' οὐρανῶν, God, or Christ? Of modern commentators, whom I have consulted, Mr. Stuart decides, with some hesitation, in favor of Christ; Heinrich, in a trifling note, has no doubt that God is meant—"id quod sequentia necessario flagitant." Kuinoel thinks that Christ is undoubtedly spoken of. The general opinion is in favor of Christ, speaking through his apostles, or his gospel.

That Christ, and no other, can have been in the writer's mind, may be made evident, I think, by several considerations. *In the first place,* Moses and Christ are before compared in similar passages of the epistle (3: 1—6. 10: 28, 29); what, then, so natural, as here to argue from the danger of rejecting Moses to that of rejecting Christ? *Secondly,* not only are Moses and God no where else contrasted, but it would be inapposite and unsuited to the state of the Jewish mind to contrast them here; for God was the author of the old economy as well as of the new, so that he would be equally rejected in both cases; and a Hebrew would not suppose that he rejected God, but only Christ, when he gave up the gospel, and clung to the law which God had confessedly given. *Further,* it deserves to be mentioned, though it may be a weaker argument, that by interpreting the latter clause of God, we take χρηματίζοντα in two different shades of meaning. For, when used of Moses, it points to him as making divine communications,—as introducing the Jewish system; but if spoken of God, it must be understood of him as promulgating the christian system from heaven in a figurative sense. As referring to Christ, it compares him, the head of the christian system, with the head of the Jewish; and then the same *nuance* of thought is preserved. But *finally,* the preceding context leads us irresistibly to regard Christ as intended. For τὸν λαλοῦντα of v. 24 is plainly the same as τὸν ἀπ' οὐρανῶν of v. 25. But the person there is defined by what goes immediately before —"Jesus the mediator of the new covenant, and the blood of sprinkling which speaketh—." What that blood speaks, is plainly spoken by Christ.

A third point, to which some attention is due, is the construction of the participle χρηματίζοντα in relation to τὸν ἐπὶ γῆς, τὸν ἀπ' οὐρανῶν. In connexion with this, the meaning of the parts of the verse, its relations to the context, and some points touching the language, may occupy us with advantage.

I formerly thought that our translators were wrong in taking τόν with χρηματίζοντα, and that τὸν ἐπὶ γῆς, τὸν ἀπ᾽ οὐρανῶν were to be separated from the participle; τόν being the subject of ἐπὶ γῆς ὄντα, ἀπ᾽ οὐρανῶν ὄντα, and the participle indicating the action in which the two persons were engaged when they were or might be rejected. The prepositions and genitives would then denote the origin of the persons, ἐπὶ γῆς being equivalent to ἐπίγειον terrestrial, of earthly origin. The sense would be, "if they escaped not when they rejected the earthly one, when he spake, much more (shall not) we escape who turn away from him that is from heaven, when he speaketh." The reasons for this change in the translation seemed to be, 1. and especially, that the participle of the *Aorist* was needed, if τόν and χρηματίζοντα were taken together in the first clause. A matter of history, the rejection of Moses by the Jews, is the subject of thought; the rejectors are spoken of in the historical tense, παραιτησάμενοι, ἔφυγον; and there seemed to be no assignable reason why the imperfect participle should be used of the person rejected; as the mere fact was insisted upon. 2. Moses and Christ are before contrasted in regard to their origin or official dignity. (See c. 3, c. 10 u. s.) 3. There seemed to be something frigid, and rhetorical, in comparing them as to the place from which their communications to man were given forth, especially as those of Christ were equally made on earth. 4. The separation of χρηματίζοντα, by παραιτησάμενος, from its clause, seemed to add some little weight to these reasons. But the other construction produced a sense so natural for the writer, so true and elegant, as to commend itself, without much weight of argument. On looking into Kuinoel, I find the same view adopted by him, and ascribed to Cramer, Storr, and Böhm. He calls the explanation that arises from taking τον ε. γ. χρημ. together, 'frigidam paene ab reliquâ oratione ornatâ et vividâ alienam;' he has no hesitation in explaining ἐπὶ γῆς (ὄντα) to be the same as ἐπίγειον, but does not seem to feel the argument derived from the tense of the participle.

But, notwithstanding this sanction of a critic respectable for his knowledge both of classical and Hellenistic Greek, the opinion must, I think, be abandoned as untenable. For first: common as are phrases consisting of the article ἐπί and a genitive with ὤν understood (e. g. ὁ ἐπὶ τοῦ κοιτῶνος, Acts 12: 20. ὁ ἐπὶ πάντων, Ephes. 4: 6.) I know of no example like the present, in which ἐπί and a genitive may be resolved into an adjective consisting of the same elements, and yet such that the *proper sense* of the preposition *out of composition* is departed from.   In other words, granting that ὄντα is understood, the phrase must still mean *who was on earth*, and not *who was of earth.   Secondly*, where Christ's heavenly origin is spoken of, he is said to come, not ἀπ', but ἐξ οὐρανῶν.   This I believe is altogether true, though the argument itself is rather calculated to throw suspicion on an explanation otherwise doubtful, than to produce any independent conviction.   *Thirdly*, the participle with τόν in such a case as this, can be used substantively with the exclusion of the idea of time, so that the sense here is, ' the maker of divine communications.'   I believe Winer, in his grammar, explains it thus.   But the whole context seems necessarily to require us to regard it as expressing time, i. e. as not laying aside its participial power.   Or the participle may have an imperfect force, and denote a person not 'speaking' historically considered, but engaged in a series of acts of this kind. And there was this additional reason for using it, that the present participle being understood after οὐρανῶν, must have been in the writer's mind.   It is perhaps separated from its company by an intervening word, in order to throw emphasis upon ἐπί γῆς. But, *fourthly*, the preceding context requires us to think of Christ as addressing his communications from heaven.   And this leads to the consideration of the manner in which this context is related to the verse before us.

In the former parts of the epistle, the writer recurs more frequently perhaps to the ascension of Christ to heaven, than to anything else.   (See 1: 3. 7: 26. 8: 1. 10: 12.)   But especially does he speak of Christ in heaven, when he compares him with the Jewish high priest.   " If he were on earth, he could not be a high priest" (8: 4) ; but he has " passed through the heavens" (4: 14), which are the more noble tabernacle (9: 11), not made by hands but fashioned by God himself, and bearing his offering of blood with him, (διὰ τοῦ ἰδίου αἵματος), has entered the most holy place above the heavens (7: 26), now to appear in the presence of God for us.   And in the present chapter, he is thought of as in heaven.   In v. 18—24 we have the earthly dispensation of terror compared in a sublime strain with the spiritual one of hope and joy.   Ye have come, says the writer, not to earthly scenes, but to amazing heavenly realities ; and among the rest, to Jesus the mediator of the new covenant, and to the blood sprinkled in heaven that higher most holy place, which blood by opening the way there to believers (10: 19), speaks better things than were spoken by Abel, that is, by Abel's blood. The scene here is wholly laid in heaven, and the writer now makes use of these sublime strains to inculcate the danger of rejecting Christ.   It is not a Saviour ascended to heaven only that the Hebrews were liable to turn away from, but one, whose blood spoke to them ; one who by his blood made divine communications to them, as being by it the founder of Christianity. Nor is there any thing frigid, as Kuinoel thinks, in the contrast of earth and heaven here as the places whence the words of Moses and Christ came.   For with the idea of speaking on earth, is connected, in the writer's mind, that of an earthly system and its earthly founder ; and with that of speaking from heaven, the idea of Christ's exalted dignity at the right hand of God.   Thus it seems to be shown that the interpretation advocated in these remarks arises most happily out of the context.

A word ought to be added in regard to the ensuing context. If Christ is clearly meant at the close of the 25th verse, he must unquestionably be the subject of the next verse also.   Now here in τότε we have an obvious reference to v. 19.   Hence this verse contains one of the most illustrious testimonies in the New Testament in favor of the exalted nature of Christ ; for both the transactions on Mt. Sinai and those prophesied of by Haggai are ascribed to him.   And hence it appears to be taught by the author of this epistle, not only that God " made the worlds" by his Son, but also that all divine manifestations under the Jewish system were made by him.

A remark or two upon particular words and phrases shall close what we have to say concerning this verse.

Oὐx ἔφυγον.   Here we have οὐ and not μή after the conditional, a usage which is so common in the New Testament that some one has remarked that εἰ μή is seldom found except in the sense of *nisi*.   Winer lays it down (§ 59. 5.) that εἰ οὐ are used where the emphasis is on the negative.   A special reason here perhaps is, that the condition is only a rhetorical one ; a matter of fact being put into that form.   They did not escape ; much less then shall we escape.

Ἔφυγον, come off unpunished.   Some commentators, as Prof. Stuart, supply δίκην after this word.   It is obviously more true to say, that nothing is understood.   The context limits the meaning, and the verb is used without an object.

Ἐπὶ γῆς.   This is the best reading.   Respecting the use and omission of the article with this word in the sense of *the earth*, and with οὐρανός, where the insertion of the article is not necessary to avoid ambiguity, no general rules can be laid down. On the whole, I suspect that the Nominative, and Accusative, as the object, incline to take the article in prose, and that the cases, at least of γῆ after a preposition incline to omit it. Thus we have φαίθων—τὰ ἐπὶ γῆς ξυνέκαυσε, (Plat. Timaeus, 22. c.) and a little below, τῶν ἐπὶ γῆς φθορά. And yet on the next page we have τῶν ὑπὸ τὸν οὐρανόν. With us the article is never needed when *heaven* in its monadic sense is spoken of, but is freely added or left out in prose with *earth*: yet in such expressions as ' who on earth, no one on earth,' it is perhaps better suppressed. And yet we must always say *the world*, *the sun*, when those words are used in their monadic sense, except in exclamations. There are, perhaps, reasons for all this that may be ascertained ; but such instances show the necessity of considering each of such words by itself, and the folly of reasoning from one language respecting the article to another.

Χρηματίζοντα. Perhaps the translation of this word in our version is unfortunate, as it is far from meaning *speaking* in general, and as that is remote from its original sense. It denotes more exactly making communications. In the Septuagint it occurs several times almost solely in Jeremiah, and answers to דִּבֶּר in every instance, I believe, except one. It is used of God both in the Septuagint and New Testament, except in one passage of Jeremiah, which I cannot at this moment find. Its common meaning in profane Greek, *to do business* (especially of a public nature, as an ambassador, president of an assembly, etc.), may be illustrated by the word *negotior*, which, in Latin, is limited, I believe, to the act of *trading*, but the derivative of which, *negotiate*, is almost technically applied to certain actions of ambassadors.

ARTICLE VII.

CAMPBELLISM.

By Rev. R. W. Landis, Jeffersonville, Pa.

"Our country is full of pretended reformers, who never read the Bible, and who, animated by a blind impulse, vainly imagine they are turning the world upside down; while in fact, they are only turning upside down in the world."—CLOUGH's DISCOURSES.

By *Campbellism* I mean the system of theology promulgated by Mr. Alexander Campbell, of Bethany, Brooke County, Virginia.   But inasmuch as the followers of this gentleman reject this designation as offensive, we disclaim all intention of employing it as a term of reproach.   It is used simply to avoid circumlocution, in discriminating this sect of religionists from other professors of Christianity.   It is as foreign from our wishes to offend the Campbellites by this appellation, as it is from theirs to offend others by using the terms Lutheran, Calvinist, Arminian, and Papist, for a similar purpose.

Mr. Campbell was born, and educated with a view to the Presbyterian ministry, in Ireland.   He subsequently, with his father, (who was a preacher in the same denomination) being in straitened circumstances, emigrated to America; and arriving in the western part of Pennsylvania, it was found necessary to attempt something for their relief.   Contributions were made by a number of Presbyterian churches for this purpose.   We mean this as no reflection upon Mr. Campbell, but we desire to obviate the influence of some of his statements upon the minds of his followers.   He has often asserted that in emigrating to America, he voluntarily relinquished many advantages not to be here enjoyed, and turned his back upon brighter and more attracting prospects than this country afforded.   The proof of disinterested benevolence in this case is by no means so clear as to be satisfactory.

Soon after arriving in this country, Mr. Campbell forsook the communion of the Presbyterian church, and united himself with that of the anti-paedo–Baptists.   He still professes to be a Baptist, but (as will appear hereafter) it would be doing the greatest injustice to that intelligent and evangelical community to identify it with Mr. Campbell and his followers.   They have long ago, in the general, repudiated both him and his system.*

The leaders of this sect boast that it is very numerous.   Mr. Campbell himself, in 1830, affirmed that he had 150,000 followers ; another of their popular writers, in 1833, estimates the number at 200,000.   Their number cannot now be ascertained with precision, but they are numerous in the Southern and Western States.

The questions are not unfrequently asked, What are the distinguishing doctrines of this sect ?—and, On what do they rely in support of their views ?   It is the intention of the present article to give a distinct answer to these questions ; and to examine, with some thoroughness, the system itself ; together with their adopted translation of the New Testament.

It is a trite remark, that there is no new error in theology ; and that what in the present day is regarded as such, is nothing more than the resuscitation of error which existed, and was exploded, in a former age.   Were we disposed to illustrate the truth of this remark, we should look in vain for a better or a more confirmatory instance than the one now under consideration.   Though it may be true that the whole system was never before advocated by any single errorist, it is still a fact that there is scarcely a weatherboard or a tile which Mr. Campbell has fastened on his singularly heterogeneous structure, that cannot be shown to belong, appropriately, to the demolished fabric of some other opposer of the gospel in former days.   We had, at the first, some thoughts of making this apparent ; but have abandoned the design, believing that such is not the kind of investigation demanded by the present age.   Nor could it accomplish any good end, that may not be better answered by conducting the investigation in the method which we have resolved upon.

---

* By the Appomattox (Va.) Association, in 1831, then comprising 24 churches, 14 ministers, 4 licentiates, and 4000 communicants, of whom 962 had been added by baptism during the preceding year, the following resolution was adopted.

"*Resolved*, that in view of the distracting ravages of Campbellism in the bounds of the Meherrin Association, this Association will cease to correspond with that Association, until the old leaven be purged out ; and that this Association will not knowingly correspond with any other, holding in fellowship Campbellite churches, or Campbellite preachers." *Ab uno disce omnes.*

Errorists, where the Bible is acknowledged, when they set out to establish a favorite theory in religion, invariably claim to be supported by the word of God, and manifest an anxious desire that this claim should be acknowledged by others: — or, at least, that their opinions, however wild and extravagant, should be admitted to be the result of honest conviction on their part. Public sentiment, to an extent that is truly remarkable, sanctions this claim, and regards it as uncourteous and uncivil to doubt whether such an individual honestly believes that his views are sanctioned by inspiration. No matter how hallucinary, or preposterous, or abhorrent to the dictates of Scripture and common sense, the sentiment in question may be, we can express no doubt of the intelligent sincerity of the convictions in the mind of the errorist, without subjecting ourselves at once to the imputation of bigotry or uncharitableness. The same fate, also, pretty generally awaits us, when we venture to pronounce such sentiments repugnant to Scripture and to common sense. To such an extent did the late erratic, though transcendently gifted Irving urge this claim, that he considered himself harshly treated and persecuted by his opponents, because they affirmed that his views could not be supported by their Confession of Faith,— a measure which he even seriously attempted. The Mormon prophets of our own country, and the Christyans, and Campbellites, furnish other and not less remarkable instances.

It is not our intention to speculate upon this topic. But this abuse of public confidence appears to us, to annihilate the distinction between truth and error, at least as respects everything that pertains to its discovery and profession. It makes it equally meritorious for an individual to profess and suffer for error, as for truth. It assumes that man is not culpable for error, and loses sight of the fact that Paul has placed "*heresies*" along with other "*works of the flesh,*" with "lasciviousness, idolatry, hatred, envyings, drunkenness," etc. ; and involves the absurd supposition that the Atheist's honesty ought not to have been doubted when he affirmed that he could " prove everything by the Bible, except that there is no God."

It is clearly a doctrine of the Bible, that error in religion is, to say the least, much more the result of depravity of heart, than of honest and conscientious mistake. And though we cannot here pause to ascertain it, yet, there certainly must be some principle which will justify an individual in speaking decidedly, in terms of reprehension, of that which is clearly contrary to the word of God, without being justly the subject of censure. Surely if there are errorists, and if mankind are furnished with the means of ascertaining truth ; if Christians are called upon to contend earnestly for the truth originally revealed ; there must be some principle that justifies them in peremptorily refusing all such demands upon their christian fellowship and charity as are thus made by every one who chooses to represent himself as inspired of Heaven.

But errorists themselves practically concede the existence of such a rule or principle as the one referred to.   The Mormons, the Christyans, and the Perfectionists, perpetually admonish all the churches in the land, hitherto regarded as Christian, that they are in dangerous error, that they are not Christian, but are corrupt, anti-apostolic, and have nothing to look for at the hand of God but his uncovenanted mercies.   The Campbellites assume precisely the same position, as we shall see hereafter. Nor is this all ; for, if we except the fact that the Campbellites and Christyans have, within a few years past, professed an agreement on all the essential points of their systems, they, with the utmost bitterness, denounce each other.   Of this denunciatory spirit, we shall present here one brief example, from the writings of Mr. Campbell.   He is speaking of the Mormons, (whom, we doubt not, it will be admitted, before we are through with this discussion, have quite as valid claims to be regarded as Christians, as Mr. Campbell himself and his followers,) and thus remarks : *   " I would say nothing to the disparagement of this deluded people.   But 'tis a disgrace to the christian character, to the name, to any man who has ever read a Bible, to believe that absurd book, called ' the book of Mormon.'   It is a matter of astonishment and grief, to think of a man in the exercise of reason, for one moment, to give credit to this wretched bundle of lies.   It must have been written by an ATHEIST, who did not believe that God would ever call him to judgment for lying in his name.   A Yankee trick to make money.   The author must have studied barrenness of sentiment and expression, a poverty of style, without an equal in the English language for the purpose of deception," etc.

Mr. Campbell, therefore, admits the existence of the rule, or principle in question.   We also admit it.   And without further

---

* See Mr. Campbell's *Millennial Harbinger* for April, 1834, Vol. V. p. 148.

preliminary, proceed to remark distinctly that the Campbellite system of theology, in all its essential features, possesses no just claim to be regarded as the religion of the cross. It is essentially " another Gospel." We also venture to affirm that the course which Mr. Campbell has pursued in relation to his pretended translation of the New Testament, has been such as cannot fail to fill every one with the deepest horror, who will favor our remarks with a perusal.

The conduct of that gentleman has been such, at least in the particular last mentioned, as calls loudly upon all who have been deluded by his speculations, and by his dreadfully corrupt version of the New Testament, to consider seriously the consequences that may result from following him any further. We are well aware of the consequences which cannot fail to ensue to ourselves, residing as we do in an enlightened christian community, should these observations prove to be either unfounded or but equivocally supported ; and are willing to meet all these consequences if we fail to sustain them by an abundance of stubborn and unambiguous facts. The importance of the subject at the present time, especially in those parts of the country where Campbellism prevails, demands this investigation, and all we ask of the reader is a patient and candid attention to the proofs which follow.

§ I. *The fundamental principles of Campbellism pointed out and examined.*

It is to be lamented that the propagators of erroneous sentiments in religion, are in general so very reserved in their communications, that not unfrequently a considerable length of time is suffered to elapse before their most constant auditors become fully acquainted with the distinctive fundamental principles of their system. While it is a fact that such persons uniformly agree to misrepresent and vilify other denominations, it is rarely indeed that they venture immediately and unreservedly to make known their own sentiments, or even to give a tangible statement of the points whereon they differ from those whom they decry. They are satisfied with making the general statement that other denominations are corrupt, anti-apostolic and the like ; leaving it to be inferred that of course *they* are the very reverse. In those, however, who declare themselves conscious of advocating truth, such conduct can admit of no justification. It is the very opposite of that of our blessed Lord, of Paul, of Peter, and of his other apostles.

We are led to these remarks by having observed the silence, respecting their distinguishing tenets, which is observed by the advocates of Campbellism. This silence is indeed surprising, if we consider the numerous declarations made by them to the effect that " the gospel as promulgated by Mr. Campbell is the same as was propagated by Christ and his apostles ;"*—that " all other protestant churches are daughters of the mother of harlots ;"—and that " altogether they constitute the Babylon of Revelation, out of which all true Christians are commanded to flee." Such declarations as these are teeming in their writings and discourses. Yet they keep their own sentiments concealed, either by not declaring them openly, or by the employment of a phraseology so ambiguous that few can be found, aside from their own denomination, who can give a rational account of even a few of the distinctive features of the system. Hence the frequent inquiry, " What are the sentiments of this people ?" Distinctive indeed must be their sentiments, if they alone entertain in its purity the true gospel of Christ, while all other denominations lie exposed to the wrath of God.

Of later years, however, Mr. Campbell himself has become somewhat more emboldened in the advancement of his views. Backed as he is by a numerous host of followers, he no longer feels that restraint which formerly held him in check, and prevented his coming fearlessly before the public with his system in a tangible form. Though it is still true that his doctrines are, to a great extent crude and undigested, and wrapped in a tedious verbosity, yet any one who has the requisite patience to wade through his tomes may reasonably entertain the prospect of ultimately detecting his sentiments.

That we may avoid misrepresenting this denomination, (a conduct of which they constantly complain, and often without the shadow of a reason) we shall, as far as possible, employ their own language in the expression of their views.

1. On Faith.

In Mr. Campbell's narrative of the debate between himself

* " I do most unhesitatingly avow my conviction that not one single truth or fact of the gospel, as taught by him (Mr. Campbell) can be disproved." See *Mill. Harbinger*, Vol. V. p. 174.

and the late Dr. Obadiah Jennings of Nashville, he asserts that " *Faith* ranked amongst the fruits of the Spirit, is *fidelity*, associated with temperance and meekness." *Mill. Har. extra*, No. 1.

His fundamental position in relation to the faith which the gospel requires, or that belief which is to the saving of the soul, is, that it is " *in its nature purely historical*, consisting in the belief of a few simple facts, and not doctrines ; that there neither was, nor could there possibly be any difference between that belief of the gospel which is requisite to the salvation of the soul, and that credence, which we usually with readiness yield to any other well authenticated history." Vide *Debate*, p. 32, 33, etc. ut supra.

He also furnishes the following illustration of his views, which cannot be misunderstood. When he was a young man he read, " three histories"——one of Asia, one of Africa, and one of the United States. He believed them all. His faith, he tells us, in the History of the United States, was fully equal to that faith which the gospel requires, and which is connected with salvation ; for he was thereby led to leave his own country and come to this. " And what better, or higher faith," he asks, " could the gospel require than this, which exerted such a powerful influence upon the mind ?" It is not probable, however, that the reader will be very forcibly impressed with the parallel between this case and that of the patriarch Abraham.

The following passage will present the view in a yet stronger light, especially as regards the *object* of saving faith. In his *Christian Baptist*, Vol. III. No. 7, he replies to an " anxious inquirer" who desires to know what he must do to be saved. In this reply, after attempting to prove that *the religious experience of every Christian corresponds with the religious education he has received*, Mr. Campbell thus remarks : " If by your *own efforts* you can believe that Jesus is the Messiah, the Son of God, by your own efforts you can believe on him to the saving of the soul. *That is saving faith* (for there is but one faith) which purifies the heart and works by love." It is not possible to misunderstand this. Mr. Campbell asserts, that to believe that Jesus is the Messiah, the Son of God, is to believe on him to the saving of the soul.

Another of the popular writers of this sect, in a work entitled " A Mirror of Ismatic Religions," p. 11, 12, which Mr. Campbell has pronounced an *able* work, speaks on the same subject as follows : " The catholic church of Christ (not of Rome) is held and compacted together by the belief of this truth, that *Jesus is the Messiah, the Son of God, the living one, and that God raised him from the dead on the third day*—their belief, if I may so term it, comprehends, in the words of Paul to the Ephesians, ' the one Lord, one faith, and one immersion,'—hence they are all of *one mind, one judgment, one spirit,*—and not being required by their master to be of one opinion, every one concedes to his brother his own particular views."

In his Preface to his New Testament Mr. Campbell repeats this view : " When one question of fact is answered in the affirmative, the way of happiness is laid open, and all doubts on the nature of true piety and humanity are dissipated. The fact is a historic one, and this question is of the same nature. It is this—*Was Jesus the Nazarene, the son and apostle of God?* This question is capable of being converted into various forms, such as—Are the subsequent narratives true? Did Jesus actually and literally rise from the dead after being crucified and interred? Did he ascend into heaven in the presence of his disciples? Is he constituted the Judge of the living and the dead? Or, was he an impostor and a deceiver of men? It may be proposed in many a form ; but it is still a unit, and amounts to this—*Is Jesus the Nazarene, the Son of God, the Apostle of the Father, the Saviour of men? When this question is answered in the affirmative, our duty, our salvation, and our happiness are ascertained and determined.*" *Mill. Har.* Vol. VI. p. 82.

As this topic is closely connected with the succeeding one, we shall omit any further remarks upon it until we shall have pointed out

2. *The Doctrines of Campbellism on Regeneration.*

The following statements and extracts from the works of the leaders of this sect will exhibit fully their views on this topic.

(1) *They with one consent declare that regeneration, or being born again, is essential to salvation.*

To prove this they constantly quote John 3: 5, and Tit. 3: 5, and several other passages of similar import. As their agreement on this point is perfectly unanimous, it is quite unnecessary to tax the patience of the reader with more than the following passages. In *Mill. Har. Extra*, No. 1. p. 12. Mr. Campbell himself thus remarks: "Whatever this *act of faith* may be, it necessarily becomes the line of discrimination between the two states before described. On this side and on that, mankind are in quite different states. On the one side, they are pardoned, justified, reconciled, adopted and saved: on the other, they are in a state of condemnation. *This act* [*of faith*] *is sometimes called immersion, regeneration, conversion;* and that this may appear obvious to all we shall be at some pains to confirm and illustrate it." The meaning of this passage it is impossible to misunderstand.

The following passages show this to be the settled opinion of the sect. "He who loves his God, loves and consults his word; nor does a lover of God's word find *non-essentials* upon its pages. Yet our teachers have found *non-essentials* among the Master's commands in God's word!!" *Mill. Har.* Vol. V. p. 146. Again: "*No man of learning and candor can, in the face of this generation, say, that immersion is not commanded.*" *Ib.* p. 177. "Our Paedobaptist friends say that we make too much of the *water.* Be that as it may, I can assure them that I have felt more peace and comfort in six months since, than in ten years before I was immersed, as I am now able to rejoice in all things, giving glory to God for opening my eyes and enabling me to do his will," etc. *Ib.* p. 188. And in Vol. VI. (for 1835) p. 59, 60, it is remarked again, "To say that any institution that Messiah has imposed upon us is a mere non-essential, is directly and emphatically offering violence to the whole system of morals laid down by him." Again: in *Extra* No. 1. p. 30, "One thing we know, that it is not a difficult matter for believers *to be born of water,* [which he explains to mean being immersed into it, and raised up out of it,] and if any of them wilfully neglect or disdain it, we cannot hope for their eternal salvation." And in *Extra* No. VI. p. 355: "All that is now promised in the gospel, can only be enjoyed by those who are born again, and placed in the kingdom of heaven under all its influences."

From these passages it is clear that, in the Campbellite view, regeneration, or being born again, is essential to salvation.

2. *Mr. Campbell and his friends declare, that immersion in water is essential to regeneration.*

They employ the terms "regeneration, conversion, and immersion," as synonymes. See *Extra*, No. 1. "The apostle Peter, when first publishing the gospel to the Jews, taught them that they were not forgiven their sins *by faith*, but by *an act of faith;* by a believing immersion into the Lord Jesus.——Christian immersion, frequently called *conversion*, as that act *is inseparably connected with the remission of sins*," p. 16. "No man can, scripturally, be said to be converted to God, until he is immersed." "*Conversion, regeneration,* and *immersion,* are terms all descriptive of the same thing." "Remission of sins cannot be enjoyed by *any person* before immersion," p. 34. "All the saints are said to be saved by immersion," p. 55. "The act of immersion is the act of conversion," p. 27. "Whatever this act of faith may be,——it is sometimes called immersion, regeneration, conversion," p. 12. "From the day of Pentecost, to the final *Amen* in the revelation of Jesus Christ, no person was said to be converted, or to turn to God, until he was buried in, and raised up out of the water," p. 35. "Immersion *alone* was that act of turning to God," p. 35. "That such was the import of the apostolic term [conversion] we have no doubt. No person was said to be converted, until he was immersed; *and all persons, who were immersed, were said to be converted,*" p. 16. "All who, believing, are immersed for the remission of their sins, have the remission of their sins in and through immersion," p. 55. "Down into the water you were led.——In its womb you were concealed.——There your consciences were released; for there your old sins were purged away," p. 55. "Peter taught all the saints in Pontus, etc. that the water of baptism saved them, as the water of the deluge saved Noah in the ark; and that in immersion a person was purged from all his former sins," p. 55. "Born of God he cannot be, until born of water," p. 30.

In Mr. Campbell's *Christian Baptist,* (published previously to the *Millennial Harbinger,*) Vol. VII. p. 164, he advances the same views. "Have you, my dear brother, ever adverted to the import of the participle in the commission, Matt. xxviii, 'Disciple the nations, *immersing* them?' I need not tell you that this is an exact translation. Let me ask you, then——Does not the *active* participle *always,* when connected with the imperative mood, express the manner in which the thing commanded is to be performed? cleanse the room, *washing* it; clean the floor, *sweeping* it; cultivate the field, *ploughing* it; sustain the hungry, *feeding* them; furnish the soldiers, *arming* them; convert the nations, *baptizing* them; are exactly the same forms of speech. No person, I presume, will controvert

this. *If so, then no man could be called a disciple, or convert,
— no man could be said to be discipled, or converted, until he
was immersed.*"

In his *Extra*, No. VI, p. 355, he thus speaks: " The subject
of this great change (regeneration) before the new birth existed
in one state ; but after it, he existed in another.   He stands in
a *new relation* to God, angels, and men.   He is now born of
God, and has the privilege of being a son of God, and is consequently pardoned, justified, sanctified, adopted, saved.   The state
which he left was a state of condemnation, called by some ' the
state of nature.'   The state into which he enters is a state of
favor, in which he enjoys all the heavenly blessings through
Christ ; therefore it is called ' the kingdom of heaven.'   *All
this is signified in his death, burial, and resurrection with Christ;
or in his being born of water.   Hence the necessity of being
buried with Christ in water ; that he may be born of water ;
that he may enjoy the renewal of the Holy Spirit, and be placed
under the reign of favor.*"

On p. 354, 355, " Our great Prophet, the Messiah — when
speaking of being born again — when explaining to Nicodemus
the *new birth*, says, ' except a man *be born of water*, and of the
Spirit, he cannot enter the kingdom of God.'   May not we,
supported by such authorities, call *that water of which a person
is born again*, the water or bath of regeneration ? "

These sentiments are in exact agreement with those of all the
leading men of this sect.   Mr. Ballantine, by far the most learned
among them, thus remarks : "All that you say of your modern
regeneration, except thereby you mean immersion, is mere chaff
before the wind.——Here is the head and front of our offending :
we make baptism regeneration.   *So does Jesus, so does Peter,
and so does Paul.*"   *Strictures*, p. 29, 30.

The author of the *Mirror*, before referred to, says, (p. 11,)
" *The institution of immersion* reminds us of the death, burial,
and resurrection of Christ ; it shows us the necessity of our
dying to this world, being *buried* with him in *immersion*, and
rising again to newness of life ; it shows us how we may become acceptable in the sight of God ; it shows us how we may
obtain access to his blood, shed for the remission of sins ; it
teaches us to look with an eye of faith, through the water, at the
great anti-typical sacrifice for sin ; it teaches us to leave the
kingdom of Mammon on one side of the water, and to enter the
kingdom of Christ on the other," etc.

Mr. Joseph Marsh says (*Gospel Luminary*, Vol. III. p. 270 —273, 1830), "I have said, and now contend, that repentance and baptism are inseparably connected." Remarking on Mark 16: 16. Acts 2: 38. 22: 16, he says, "These and other passages positively place baptism before salvation or forgiveness of sins." "The Samaritans, and the Eunuch, were not filled with joy until they were baptized." "Paul's sins were not forgiven, or washed away, until he was baptized."

It is justice, however, to remark, that Mr. Campbell and his friends do not say, (as has been charged upon them,) that immersion will itself save, without a belief of the "facts" of the Bible ; but simply that *no one can possibly be saved, who is not immersed.* See *ut supra*, in connection with *Mill. Har.* Vol. VI. p. 83, 84.

(3) *Mr. Campbell and his friends teach, that immersion in water is absolutely essential to forgiveness of sin.*

This is apparent from some of the preceding extracts. But, that the system may be perfectly understood, we will give this position a more particular consideration.

In *Mill. Har. Ex.* No. 1. p. 31, Mr. Campbell says, "Those who are *thus* begotten and born of God, [i. e. by immersion] are children of God. It would be a monstrous supposition, that such persons are not freed from their sins. *To be born of God, and born in sin, is inconceivable.* Remission of sins is as certainly granted to the *born of God*, as life eternal and deliverance from corruption will be granted to *the children of the resurrection,* when born from the grave."

Again, p. 41 : "Some ask, how can water, which penetrates not the skin, reach the conscience ? But little do they think, that in so talking, they laugh at and mock the whole divine economy, under the Old and New Testament institutions."

Again : "Under the government of the Lord Jesus, there is an institution for the forgiveness of sins, like which there was no institution since the world began. The meaning of this institution has been buried under the rubbish of human traditions for hundreds of years. It was lost in the dark ages, and has never been, till now, disinterred," p. 2.

"Under the former economy, blood was necessary to forgiveness ; and under the new economy, water is necessary." *Christian Baptist*, Vol. VII. p. 163.

"He (God) appointed baptism to be, to every one that believed the record he has given of his Son, a formal pledge on his part, of that believer's personal acquittal or pardon; so significant and so expressive, that when the baptized believer rises out of the water, *is born of water*, enters the world a second time, he enters it as innocent, as clean, as unspotted as an angel." *Debate with Mr. M'Calla, as reported by A. Campbell*, p. 137.

The following illustration will make it manifest that these extracts do not misrepresent the views of this sect on the subject before us.

"In religion a man may change his views of Jesus, and his heart may also be changed towards him, but unless a change of state ensues, he is still unpardoned, unjustified, unsanctified, unreconciled, unadopted, and lost to all christian life and enjoyment." "Begotten of God he may be, but born of God he cannot be, until born of water."—"Lavinia was the servant of Palemon, and once thought him a hard master. She changed her views of him, and her feelings were also changed towards him; still, however, she continued in the state of a handmaid. Palemon offered her first his heart, and then his hand, and she accepted them. He vowed, and she vowed before witnesses, and she became his wife. Then, and not till then, was her state changed. She is no longer a *servant*,—she is now a *wife*. No change of views and feelings led to this change of state; for Maria, who was another handmaid of Palemon, changed her views of him, and her feelings towards him, as much — nay, more — than did Lavinia; yet Maria lived and died the servant maid of Palemon and Lavinia." *Extra*, No. 1.

We might greatly extend these extracts, but think it best to permit the foregoing pathetic "analogy" to conclude them, that the impression may remain in full force upon the reader's mind. There is one other topic, however, in connection with this subject, that we must here introduce, to place the system fully before the reader's mind.

(4) *The Campbellites declare that immersion in water, and regeneration, are two names for the same thing.*

However inconsistent this may be with the foregoing statements, we, of course, are not answerable. The inconsistency will be seen upon perusing the subjoined extracts, if the preceding passages have not already made it apparent.

In *Mill. Har. Ex.* No. 6. p. 360, *Note*, Mr. Campbell thus speaks: "We contend that being born again, and being immersed, are, in the apostle's style, *two names for the same thing*." and "When we speak in the *exact style* of the living oracles on this subject, we must represent *being born again* (John 3: 5), and *regeneration* (Tit. 3: 5), *as relating to the act of immersion alone.*"

He says, however, at the same time, that he does not, by regeneration, mean *all* that evangelical Christians mean by it.[*] But it is sufficient for us to know, that he professes to mean by *immersion*, or the act of immersion, *all that the New Testament means by regeneration, or being born again.*

In *Extra*, No. 1. p. 27, 28 : "Being born again, and being immersed, are the same thing." " Regeneration and immersion are, therefore, two names for the same thing." " Immersion and regeneration are two Bible names for the same act."

In showing the amazing power which immersion in water exerts upon the soul, and illustrating the *velocity* which it thereby acquires, Mr. Campbell remarks : " Like a strong impulse given to a ball, which puts it into motion, immersion for the forgiveness of sins carries the mind forward, far beyond all the experiences formerly demanded as preparatory to immersion. A change of state so great, so sensible, so complete, so sudden, operates more like the ancient cures, than the cold, dark, and tedious *mental* regenerations of the philosophising theologues." And then we have the " analogy," or illustration, which is as follows : " He that passes from Virginia into Pennsylvania, passes over a mere imaginary geographical line, without scarcely perceiving the transition ; but he that passes from Virginia into the state of Ohio, *by swimming the river*, the natural and sensible boundary, immediately realizes the change."

These quotations are surely more than sufficient to give the reader an idea of this ridiculous travesty of the gospel. We would, however, before leaving this topic, remind Mr. Campbell that his claim to originality in this discovery of a method to cleanse the soul from sin, is not so clear as to be indisputable. For we recollect that shortly after " the dark ages," there was a certain old gentleman at the head of a denomination, who made the same discovery, and affirmed that, " If any one shall say that baptism is indifferent, that is, not necessary to salvation, let him be accursed." [†] He affirmed many other things in re-

---

[*] His words are : "Our opponents deceive themselves and their hearers, by representing us as ascribing to the word *immersion*, and to the act of immersion, all that they call regeneration." Ut supra, p. 369.

[†] Si quis dixerit, Baptismum liberum esse, hoc est non necessarium ad salutem ; anathema sit. *Conc. Trid.* Les. VII. die Mart. iii. 1547. Can. 5. de Baptismo.

lation to it, which have been summed up by the Roman Catholic bishop Hays, in his *Abridgement of the Christian Doctrine*, approved by archbishop Maucal ; and some of them are as follows : " Baptism brings to the soul sanctifying grace—washes away the guilt of original and actual sin—gives a new and spiritual birth—makes us Christians—entitles us to actual grace—preserves the sanctity gotten at baptism,—and gives a right to eternal happiness."

We are not sure but Mr. Campbell must also yield to another claimant. One of our missionaries some time ago meeting an old Brahmin, aged eighty, asked him : " Do you know how your sins are to be pardoned, and what will be your state after death ?" He replied : *" My hope is in the Ganges."* And when further pressed, he confessed that *" If the Ganges could not take away his sins, he knew not what could."* See *Miss. Her.* Vol. XXIX. p. 97. It would be amusing to speculate upon the manner in which a Campbellite would have treated the subject with the aged priest.

We should be sorry to take away from Mr. Campbell all merit of originality in relation to his illustrious discovery ; but as he has so boldly ventured his claim, it may be proper to introduce to his acquaintance one other old gentleman, who, previous to Mr. Campbell's having advanced his pretensions to originality, published the same discovery in a work entitled " *A Refutation of Calvinism.*" The reader can compare the following extracts, and then decide for himself, to whom belongs the palm. " Those who are baptized are immediately translated from the curse of Adam to the grace of Christ. They become reconciled to God—heirs of eternal happiness,—acquire a new name, a new hope, a new faith, a new rule of life. This great and wonderful change in the condition of man is as it were a new nature, a new state of existence ; and the holy rite by which these invaluable blessings are communicated is by St. Paul figuratively called regeneration, or new birth. The word regeneration, therefore, is in Scripture solely and exclusively applied to the one *immediate effect* of baptism once administered," etc.

These, then, are the great fundamental, or distinctive doctrines of Campbellism. If we have been prolix in our citations, it was to avoid misrepresentation, and because we wished to hold up the system in every point of view, in which it is presented by its advocates.

As the remaining sentiments of this sect, which it is our intention hereafter to notice, are not so strictly distinctive as the foregoing, we shall treat *them* in a historical, and not a controversial manner. We propose, however, first, to subject the foregoing principles, and especially those relating to regeneration, to a somewhat thorough examination. The views entertained of this last subject, especially, constitute the difference between this sect and other sects of Unitarians, as we shall show hereafter. Mr. Campbell himself admits that these views of faith, forgiveness, and regeneration, are essential to the very existence of his system. Hence, if *they* are proved to be erroneous, or destitute of support, this whole theological fabric, confessedly, falls to the ground.

The foregoing Views Examined.

We observe, 1. That the *faith* which the Campbellites contend for, has, confessedly, no connection whatever, with regeneration. They are truly separate. A man may exercise this faith truly, and properly, and yet be entirely unregenerated ; as much a child of hell as the vilest infidel. The proposition, therefore, that " we are justified by faith" is to this sect intrinsically absurd.

2. They teach that faith has no real connection with the pardon of sin. For a man may exercise it in the fullest manner, and yet be unpardoned.

3. From the preceding extracts it further appears that, agreeably to Campbellism, a sinner believes to the saving of the soul, without the agency of the Spirit of God ; by his own unaided efforts alone. In fact Mr. Campbell repeatedly ridicules the idea of the agency of the third person of the Trinity either in the exercise of saving faith or in regeneration.

How very opposite all this is to the whole tenor of the gospel will be seen by a mere allusion to such passages as the following. " He that believeth hath everlasting life," John 5: 24. 3: 16, 36. " *With the heart* man believeth unto justification," Rom. 10: 10. " By grace *ye are saved, through faith*," Eph. 2: 8. " Sirs, What must I do to be saved ? And they said, Believe on the Lord Jesus Christ, and thou shalt be saved, and thy house," Acts 16: 30, 31. " Being justified by faith we have peace with God, through our Lord Jesus Christ : by whom also we have access by faith into this grace wherein we stand, and rejoice in hope of the glory of God," Rom. 5: 1, 2. "Know ye therefore that they which are of faith, the same are the children of Abraham?" Gal. 3: 7. "The blood of Jesus Christ his Son cleanseth us from all sin," 1 John 1: 8. With multitudes of kindred passages which will immediately occur to the memory of all who are familiar with the word of God.

The folly of the Campbellite view of this subject might be further exhibited, by entering into a discussion of the nature of faith. But this is not here called for. And we pass on, for the present, to consider the leading or distinctive principle of the sect—*regeneration by immersion into water.*

From the foregoing extracts we learn, 1. That Mr. Campbell and his sect believe that no person can be saved unless regenerated or born again.

2. That immersion in water is essential to regeneration.— That no person can possibly be regenerated without being immersed.

3. That immersion in water is the medium through which sins are remitted.

4. And, however inconsistent with the foregoing, that immersion is regeneration itself. "Being born again, and being immersed, are, in the apostles' style two names for the same thing."

Hence nothing can be clearer, than that, according to the Campbellites, *immersion in water is indispensably necessary to salvation.* It follows syllogistically, thus :

1. Regeneration is essential to salvation. But immersion in water is essential to regeneration, inasmuch as no one can be regenerated without being immersed : therefore immersion in water is essential to salvation. Or thus :

2. "Immersion and regeneration are, in the apostles' style, two names for the same thing :" so that being immersed, is itself being regenerated. But no one can be saved without being regenerated. Therefore no person can be saved without being immersed.

COROLLARY. Infants who die in infancy, are either lost, or if saved, they are saved without being regenerated. Even the infants of the Campbellites ; for they do not baptize their children.

3. The same conclusion follows in another way. Immersion is essential to remission of sins. But no one can be saved without remission of sins. Therefore, no one can be saved without being immersed.

COROLLARY. All mankind, therefore, according to the Campbellites, who are not immersed, perish forever.

This, then, is the ground occupied by the foregoing views. And our object here, is merely to give a plain and compendious summary of them, for the convenience of reference ; and not to prove them false by their consequences. Mr. Campbell and his friends appeal to the Bible to sustain their views ; and if that fairly sustains them, it is in vain to talk of *consequences.* Our next step will therefore be, to take up and consider the passages on which they profess to rely.

Argument founded on John 3: 5.

This passage has ever been regarded by Mr. Campbell and his friends as containing a complete, and unanswerable argument in favor of their position, that *baptism is essential to regeneration, and consequently to salvation:* "Jesus answered, Verily, verily, I say unto thee, except a man *be born of water,* and of the Spirit, *he cannot enter into the kingdom of God.*" On this verse, with Tit. 3: 5, there has been more controversy with this sect, than on any other texts of Scripture.

To avoid the force of Mr. Campbell's argument, it has been observed, that the phrase "kingdom of God" does not refer to *heaven,* but to the *invisible* church on earth. Others have supposed that it referred to the *visible* church. Both positions, however, have been swept away simply by the Campbellites asking, ' Whether the objector did not believe that many were members of the *invisible* church who had never been baptized with water ?' and ' whether there were not members of the *visible* church, who, though they had been baptized with water, had not been baptized with the Spirit ?' As both are admitted by all evangelical Christians, the objectors could not, in consistency with their own sentiments, maintain such a view of the subject. And thus their false exposition has been refuted, and Campbellism has triumphed.

It is in vain that some have maintained that baptism is not here enjoined as essential, but merely as obligatory *when it can be attended to.* The Campbellites have triumphantly answered, that ' Being *born of water* is placed by our Saviour upon an equal footing with being *born of the Spirit.* If, therefore, the one may, under any circumstances, be dispensed with, the other may be likewise under the same, or similar circumstances.'

But as no Christian could admit such an inference, the position sustaining it must be abandoned.

Thus the Campbellites, from this passage conclude, that to be born of water is equally essential to salvation as to be born of the Spirit ; for the text says, " Except a man be *born of water* AND *Spirit.*" But all Christians admit that to be born of the Spirit is essential ; and therefore agreeably to this admission, baptism is essential to salvation. This is the argument of Mr. Campbell and his friends ; and the above is their method of wielding it.

Now to attempt to answer an argument of this kind by sneering at it, as has been already too often the case in this controversy, only betrays the utter imbecility of him who makes the attempt. However ridiculous an argument may appear, it is puerile to undertake its refutation by a witticism, when we know that our opponents rely upon it in support of opinions which they profess to believe to be as worthy of veneration and regard as we consider any of our own to be. If solid reasons cannot be given for dissenting from its conclusions, the argument will be deemed unanswerable, and its conclusions true, no matter whither they may lead.

Mr. Campbell and his friends have frequently avowed their conviction that this argument is unanswerable. We do not agree with them, however ; for

1. *They take for granted the very point in dispute.* Without offering one particle of proof, they assume that ὕδωρ, *water,* is here to be understood of the *element* water. But this is by no means so clear as might be thought. The same word is constantly employed in the New Testament in a sense quite the reverse. E. g. see John 4: 10. Eph. 5: 27. Rev. 22: 1, 17, and John 7: 38, 39. " He that believeth on me, out of his belly shall flow rivers of living water. *But this he spake of the Spirit.*" The argument is therefore of no value, unless it be shown that ὕδωρ refers to the element water.

Of course Mr. Campbell will not plead in support of his argument that many divines have understood *water* here to refer to baptism ; for in matters of this kind he professes to place no reliance on human authority.

But though Augustine and some other eminent men have understood the word in this manner, there are very great authorities, (and it is not improper here to refer to them,) on the other side. *Basil* understands it very differently. See his book on the Holy Spirit, cap. 15.   *Bullinger*, understands it not of *external* baptism of water, but of internal and spiritual regeneration.   *Brentius* understands it metaphorically.   See also *Bellarmine*, De Bap. lib. 1. c. 4.   *Lombardy*, lib. 4. dist. 4. cap. D. E.   *Grotius*, and *Pareus* also *in loc.*

Now since the Campbellites claim to deduce such sweeping conclusions from this passage, why should this point be granted without their offering a particle of proof?

But further: Let it be observed that ὕδωρ here, even allowing it to refer to the *element*, cannot without manifest absurdity be understood of the water of *Christian* baptism.   For the simple reason, that the Jewish dispensation was not abrogated at the time these words were spoken; and of course christian baptism was not instituted.   That the ceremonial law was still in full force, is clear from the fact that when Christ had healed a leper on a certain occasion (Matt. 8: 4) he commanded him to go show himself " to the priest and offer the gift that Moses commanded for a testimony unto them."   And the institution of christian baptism was immediately antecedent to the ascension.   How then can Christ be understood here to refer to that ordinance, (at least so as to be understood by Nicodemus,) when that ordinance was not yet instituted?   But,

2. *The Campbellite exposition of this passage is directly contrary to fact.*

To say nothing on the subject of the emphasis being laid by our Saviour upon *Spirit* and not *water*, as appears from the fact that he directly, in the explanation of his meaning, entirely drops the mention of water and speaks of being born of the Spirit alone :—there is another consideration which we might largely insist upon ; to wit, that if regeneration and immersion in water are one and the same thing, the illustration adopted by our Redeemer is necessarily inappropriate : " The *wind* bloweth where it listeth, and thou hearest the sound thereof, but canst not tell whence it cometh, and whither it goeth, *so is every one that is born of the Spirit ;*" which certainly was intended to teach us that although the reality of the new birth could no more be doubted, than the existence of the wind ; yet that there was something in its nature, and in the manner whereby it was effected, wholly inexplicable by man; and that there most assuredly is nothing in the act, and in the circumstances attendant on, immersion, that cannot be fully comprehended by any person.   But, to say nothing on these topics, I would remark that the Campbellite exposition is directly contrary to the conduct of our Saviour and to the word of God.

The reader will bear in mind that this exposition is, that " no one can be regenerated, or saved without being immersed." But I answer that unambiguous *facts* prove this to be a false exposition of the language of our Saviour : for *after* this conversation with Nicodemus he repeatedly remitted sins without baptism.   Take for example the case of the palsy-stricken, Mark 2: 1—12, with Matt. 9: 1—9: "Son, be of good cheer, thy sins be forgiven thee."   Or the case of Mary, Luke 7: 36—50 : "Her sins which are many are forgiven for [not *she has been immersed*, but] she loved much.—And he said unto the woman, thy *faith hath saved thee ; go in peace."   But lest the advocates of the system under consideration rather than admit the only obvious and proper inference, should maintain that these instances did not occur *after*, but *previous* to the conversation with Nicodemus ; or, that if they did occur afterward, they prove nothing, for the persons may not have been regenerated if even their sins were forgiven, we shall produce one more instance.   It is that of the dying malefactor.   He came to execution a hardened impenitent sinner, Matt. 27: 44, and Mark 15: 32.   While hanging on the cross he repented, and was forgiven, Luke 23: 40—43.   Now the foregoing objections cannot here apply.   For 1. No one will maintain that this occurred before the conversation with Nicodemus ; and 2. No person will maintain that the malefactor was not regenerated ; he was saved, and no one can be saved unless regenerated..   He therefore came to the cross impenitent ; on the cross he repented ; on the cross Jesus pardoned his sins ; and from the cross received his soul to mansions of endless bliss. Here then, was a soul pardoned, regenerated, sanctified, and saved, without the application of water.   Of course then, water is not essential to regeneration, nor baptism absolutely essential to salvation.   And consequently the foregoing exposition of John 3: 5, is false.

But their exposition is equally contradictory to facts of another description.   Mr. Campbell and his followers admit that the phrase " born of water and of the Spirit," is only another form of expression for "being regenerated," or " born again." In other words, that the term regeneration signifies everything that Christ intended by the phrase " born of water and of the Spirit."   This is undoubtedly correct ; for we have the fullest confirmation of it in **v. 3** and **8** of the same chapter. The question then arises, How are persons regenerated, agreeably to the Scriptures? And this question we shall answer in the phraseology of the Bible. *God regenerates mankind through the truth.* 1 Pet. 1: 23, "*Being born again*, not of corruptible seed, but of incorruptible, *by the word of God*," διὰ λόγου Θεοῦ. John 8: 32, "The truth shall make you free." John 17: 17, "Sanctify them through thy truth, thy word is truth." Jas. 1: 1, "Of his own will *begat he us* with the word of truth." Mr. Campbell makes a distinction between "being born of God" and "being begotten of" him, but this distinction is unavailing. For the above cited passages declare that persons are both born of God, and begotten of God, "by the word of truth." Other passages in great abundance, declaring the same, can be easily adduced. If therefore men are regenerated, or born again, by *the truth*, and if the phrase "born of water and of the Spirit," signifies nothing more than being regenerated, which the Campbellites admit, it follows that Mr. Campbell's exposition of this passage, so far at least as regards his inferences from it, is false.

This passage being regarded as the great pillar of the system under consideration, it may reasonably be demanded, that, having exposed the falseness of the foregoing exposition, I should at least attempt to make known the true import of the phrase ἐξ ὕδατος καὶ πνεύματος, *of water and of the Spirit.* I shall proceed to do so with brevity.

We shall first consider the *occasion* of Christ's introducing this phraseology, and then its *import.*

It is an excellent observation, which lord Bacon somewhere makes, that "being unlike man, who knows man's thoughts only by his words, Christ, knowing man's thoughts immediately, *never* answered their words, but their thoughts:"——that is, he always answered their *thoughts*, whether their words really expressed them or not. Le Clerc, profiting by this suggestion, has remarked upon the passage before us, (see his *Harm.* fol. p. 520,) that the answer of Jesus does not seem direct, but that Nicodemus, having premised what is contained in ver. 2, was about to ask Jesus what he ought to do in order to be admitted into the kingdom of heaven, which was at hand; and that it is this unuttered part of his address that the remarks of Jesus are a reply to." Hence nothing can be more to the point than our Lord's reply; though, without this clew, (or, at least, granting the supposition that the whole of the conversation is not recorded,) it

has somewhat the appearance of abruptness : " Verily, verily,
I say unto you, unless a man be born again, he cannot see the
kingdom of God." Nicodemus, not comprehending the import
of this declaration, Jesus proceeds to explain it ; in which explanation he uses the phrase immediately under consideration.

By referring to the original, we find a clew to the meaning
of the passage, which will at once divest it of the apparent obscurity of our Saviour's allusion to water ; in which, in fact, the
chief obscurity exists. We refer to the appellation given to
Nicodemus, ὁ Διδάσκαλος, not "*a* master of Israel," (as our
translation renders it,) but "*the* teacher ;" and critics have labored
very much from finding the definite article in this connection.
But it is only necessary to suppose that Nicodemus, a member
of the Sanhedrim, had been, in his regular turn, *officer of the day*,
who presided over the dispensation of baptismal water, in the
constant, and almost innumerous Jewish purifications ; and all is
plain. The reason then is at once apparent, why he is denominated "*the* master of Israel," and also why our Saviour makes
the allusion to water.

But what is the meaning of the phrase ἐξ ὕδατος καὶ πνεύματος?
Ans. Our Saviour, instructing a Jew to whom the prophetic
writings were known, uses these two words in the order in
which they are recorded, that the latter might interpret the former, meaning by the phrase, *spiritual water :* i. e. "You have,
sir, been baptizing with water, but let me tell you, that outward
baptism will not qualify you for being an inhabitant of the kingdom you speak of. Unless you are baptized internally, or with
spiritual water, you cannot," etc. That such is the meaning
of these two words, and that thus Nicodemus understood them,
we see not how it can be disputed by any who will attend to
the phraseology of the Scriptures. See e. g. Matt. **3**: 11,
πνεύματι καὶ πυρί, *with spiritual fire.* Matt. **4**: 16, ἐν χώρα
καὶ σκιᾷ θανάτου, *in the region of the shade of death.* 1 Cor.
2: 4, ἐν ἀποδείξει πνεύματος καὶ δυνάμεως, *in the demonstration
of the powerful Spirit.* Coll. **2**: 8, διὰ τῆς φιλοσοφίας καὶ
κενῆς ἀπάτης, *by the vain deceits of philosophy.* So also Acts
17: 25, πᾶσι ζωὴν καὶ πνοήν, *to all the breath of life ;* an expression equivalent to πνοὴν ζωῆς (of the LXX) in Gen. **2**: 7.
So also 2 Macc. **7**: 23, τὸ πνεῦμα καὶ τὴν ζωὴν ὑμῖν, *he shall
restore to you the breath of life.* Gen. **3**: 16, τὰς λύπας σου
καὶ τὸν στεναγμόν σου, *thy sorrow from,* or *by, thy conception.*
See also 1 Peter **3**: 18. Exodus **34**: 9. Ephesians **2** : **2**. Heb.

2: 14.   See this very happily illustrated by Grotius, *in loco*, to whom, to save space and the reader's patience, I beg leave to refer.

But Mr. Campbell strenuously objects against interpreting one part of the passage figuratively, and the other literally, as he says is done when we take the word *Spirit* literally, and *water* figuratively.   He contends that the whole verse "*must* be either literal or figurative throughout."   But in this assertion there is betrayed a great want of consideration ; for there are innumerable passages of Scripture which demonstrate its falseness.   Not to insist on Matt. 3: 11, take John 7: 38, " He that believeth on me, out of his belly shall flow rivers of living water."   The phrase " He that believeth on me," every one will admit, is to be understood literally ; and yet the concluding phrase is figurative, as John himself tells us in the next verse, " *But this spake he of the Spirit.*" See also Is. 44: 3. John 4: 13, 14, etc.

The Campbellites also object very strenuously, (and with apparent reason,) against making the two words *water* and *Spirit* refer to Spirit alone.   They maintain that " such a construction must make nonsense of the whole passage."   We have known them to be exceedingly witty while sermonizing on the subject, affirming that it made the Saviour say, " Except a man be born of Spirit *and of the Spirit*,—which is unintelligible."   And then the exegetical ability of their opponents would fairly smoke again beneath the scorchings of their ridicule.   But before they should have ventured to ridicule the exposition which we give of this passage, it would have been wise in them to have enquired whether their witticisms could not be successfully retorted. For in the present instance they have been peculiarly unfortunate.   In their exposition of the phrase, they do the very same thing for which they have undertaken, in so contemptuous a manner, to sneer at others.   They assert that " regeneration and immersion in water, are *two names for the same thing.*" Of course, then, if (as they assert) ὕδωρ, *water*, in the text refers to immersion in water, it of course refers to regeneration, for " they are two names for the same thing."   But they also declare that the whole phrase " water *and* the Spirit," refers only to regeneration ; and therefore πνεῦμα, *Spirit*, must likewise refer to immersion.   And thus water refers to immersion, and Spirit refers to it likewise.   So that the Campbellites' sneers might be returned with interest.

We proceed to consider their

Argument from Titus 3: 5.

In the present controversy, this passage is the one next in importance to the preceding. " Not by works of righteousness which we have done, but according to his mercy he saved us, *by the washing of regeneration, and the renewing of the Holy Ghost.*" This is supposed to be a full proof of the doctrine that baptism is equally essential to salvation as " the renewing of the Holy Ghost." By the phrase " washing of regeneration," the Campbellites understand *immersion in water;* and they take for granted that it can mean nothing else. See *Mill. Har. Ex.* Nos. 1. and 6. and Vol. II. No. 3. This argument may be thus stated : If the " renewing of the Holy Ghost" relates to being born again, which our opponents admit ; and if the phrase " washing of regeneration" refers to baptism, which it would be absurd to deny ; and if God saves us " by the washing of regeneration, (i. e. baptism,) AND the renewing of the Holy Ghost," it follows that water baptism is, on their own principles, no less essential to salvation than is the renewing of the Holy Ghost. This is their argument, and at first sight it seems plausible ; for the received text reads διὰ λουτροῦ παλιγγενεσίας, καὶ ἀνακαινώσεως πνεύματος ἁγίου.

But how perfectly preposterous does this reasoning appear when viewed in connection with the principles under discussion. The advocates of those principles sagely inform us that regeneration and immersion are the same thing ; " in the apostle's style, *two names for the same thing ;*" and yet they aver that immersion is here said to be equally essential as regeneration ; that is, immersion is equally essential as immersion ; which it is presumed that few would deny.

I make these remarks, not to evade the apparent difficulty before stated ; (the argument is one that has been, in substance, long employed by the papists, and we therefore deem it important to consider it carefully ;) but it is an argument which Mr. Campbell and his followers cannot employ seriously without surrendering into the hands of their opponents more than they gain by it. This will be fully seen presently.

The preceding argument is plain, unambiguous, and admits of no exceptions. Let us then pause and ask, Whether the conclusion does not directly contradict the scripture facts already adverted to under our examination of John 3: 5 ? And if it does, whether that conclusion is not necessarily false ?

But further, the Campbellites must admit, that if baptism is the "laver of regeneration," if it is the "scripture method of being born again," it must be so in every case, at least when administered by an apostle. But can any one seriously believe that all whom the apostles baptized were regenerated in the scripture sense of the term? That Simon Magus was scripturally "born again, converted, regenerated," at the precise moment that he had "no part nor lot in the matter," and was "in the gall of bitterness and bonds of iniquity?" and so of Ananias, Sapphira and others. Can it be possible for a rational man to give assent to such a proposition? But until it is assented to, this passage cannot be pressed into the service of supporting their scheme.

Now, however plausible an argument founded on the foregoing translation of this passage may appear to be, yet when critically investigated it fades away as the murky vapor before the rising sun. For λουτροῦ παλιγγενεσίας and ἀνακαινώσεως πνεύματος ἁγίου, manifestly refer to the same thing; the latter clause being exegetical of the former.

Any one conversant with scripture criticism will readily admit that it is no uncommon thing for the latter clause of a passage to be explanatory of the former. "When he shall have delivered up the kingdom to God *even* (καὶ) the Father," 1 Cor. 15: 24. See also 1 Thess. 1: 3, 17, (in Campbell's translation) Titus 2: 13. And in the Old Testament see Gen. 6: 17. 7: 21—24. 37: 24. 40: 23. 42: 2. 49: 25. Judges 5: 3. Ezek. 34: 11. Judges 3: 10. But to cite all the passages would be to quote a large part of the Bible.

Mr. Campbell knows perfectly well that the only correct rendering of καὶ in numberless instances in the New Testament is "*even;*" and he knows too that in a great number of instances in his version of the New Testament he has thus translated it; see e. g. Acts 7: 5. 1 Cor. 15: 24. 1 Thess. 1: 3. 2 Thess. 2: 16. And the reader can judge for himself, whether Mr. Campbell would not have given it the same rendering in the instance before us, could he have subserved the interests of his sect as well by doing so, as by the translation which he has given.

There is also a manifest and strong reason for adopting this rendering. Baptism, when properly performed is "*a work of righteousness which we have done;*" but Paul declares that it is "*not* by works of righteousness which we have done, *but* according to his mercy he saved us *by the washing of regeneration*," etc. ; of course then, *baptism* must be something different from this washing, because by *it* we *are* saved. Hence " washing of regeneration" can be referred only to " the renewing of the Holy Ghost."

The Latin Vulgate (*Basil*, anno 1578,) renders the passage thus : *per lavacrum regenerationis Spiritus Sancti*, " By the laver of regeneration of the Holy Spirit." Whatever this " laver " therefore may be, it is here referred exclusively to the agency of the Holy Spirit. But it would be preposterous to suppose that the Holy Spirit operates upon the soul by water.

Here, then, we have in favor of this rendering the approved version of the whole Romish church ; which will certainly be considered as of great weight when it is remembered that this church makes water baptism essential to salvation.* It would therefore have been to their interest (as like the Campbellites, they are very much pressed for proof-texts,) to have given this passage a rendering similar to that contended for by Mr. Campbell. Yet with a knowledge of all the advantages that their cause would thereby have gained, we find them without hesitation repudiating such a rendering. To be sure, they have in the margin added the phrase " et renovationis," *and renewal*, as a marginal gloss or reading ; but this only proves that it was not left out of the text by mistake. They must therefore have had solid reasons for thus omitting it, when its insertion would have been of so much advantage to their cause. And as the passage now reads, the " regeneration " spoken of, is referred entirely to the operation of the Holy Ghost. The Rhenish translators of the Vulgate, it is true, have added to the text, the clause " et renovationis," but it is not difficult to determine their motives for doing so. Such an act tends to display their faithfulness as translators in its true colors.

The reader will not understand me as attempting to insinuate that the phrase καὶ ἀνακαινώσεως, is a spurious rendering. The proper inference to be deduced from the fact, that the copyists and correctors of Jerome omitted the words *et renovationis* would be, not that they regarded the phrase referred to as spu-

---

* " The law of baptism as established by our Lord, *extends to all*, insomuch that, *unless* they are *regenerated by baptism*, be their parents Christians or infidels, they are born to eternal misery." *Douay Catechism*, p. 171.

rious, but that they considered *per lavacrum regenerationis Spiritus Sancti*, a full and complete translation of the whole passage. No one ever thinks it necessary, in order to give a faithful translation of a language, to render it word for word. If the idea can be expressed perfectly in fewer words than are employed for that purpose in the language from which the translation is made, no one would think of objecting to the translation on that ground.* So the author of this translation, believing that the phrases " washing of regeneration," and " renewal of the Holy Ghost," referred to the same thing, viz., spiritual regeneration, saw no impropriety whatever in expressing the idea in fewer words, thus: " The washing of regeneration of the Holy Spirit;" that is, as we have above rendered it, " the washing of regeneration, *even* the renewing of the Holy Ghost."

Since writing the foregoing criticism, I perceive that the learned Dr. Williams of England in his answer to Bishop Tomline, and also Dr. Cleland of our country give the passage the same rendering.

Argument from Acts 22: 16.

This passage is adduced in support of the position that baptism is essential to remission of sins. " And now why tarriest thou? *Arise and be baptized, and wash away thy sins*, calling upon the name of the Lord." The Campbellites produce these words with an air of triumph; and pretend that it is only necessary for them to quote the passage, in order to demonstrate that their doctrine of remitting sins by baptism is true. They are perpetually asserting that " Here is an instance in which sins were actually washed away by water baptism. Of course, therefore, the truth of the doctrine that they are washed away in this manner, cannot be questioned." One of their writers says, " Paul's sins were not forgiven till he was baptized." Another says, " Until a man is baptized, invoking the name of the Lord, he is in his sins." Of course then, agreeably to this doctrine, Paul was not a pardoned sinner until he was baptized! It would be difficult to account for the utter recklessness of such an assertion, on any other supposition than that partiality to a

---

* The reader will call to mind the precept of Horace:
" Nec verbum verbo curabis reddere fidus
Interpres."—*De Arte Poetica*, 133.

favorite theory has blinded the minds of these men. How otherwise could they have failed to discern the overwhelming evidence of the fact, that Paul was regenerated and converted, (and, of course, his sins were pardoned,) before Ananias called upon him? One would have thought that the bare perusal of Acts ix. must have satisfied the mind of any one, however prejudiced, of the truth of this. But as the fact is thus disputed, and even denied, we shall briefly exhibit a few of the proofs which support it, after which we shall explain the passage.

1. In Acts 9: 11, he is directly represented as converted: " *Behold he prayeth.*" Paul, as a Pharisee, had undoubtedly constantly prayed before this. What then is the import of this declaration? Why, that he now prayed *aright.* And praying aright is of course an evidence of conversion. This too is the evidence that the Lord gave to satisfy Ananias that Paul was no longer a persecutor ; and it did satisfy him to that degree that he from that moment regarded him as a christian brother.

2. The *object* for which he was sent is sufficient to convince any one that Paul must have been at that time a sincere believer ; and of course a pardoned sinner. " Go—*that he may receive his sight, for* (γὰρ) behold he prayeth." If the words " behold he prayeth" do not in their connection denote an essential change of character, what words can?

3. Let any one review the actions and words of Ananias towards Paul, and he will find that the same fact is established. The cause for which he was blinded, was now removed. Ananias gives him the strongest evidence of this, by restoring his sight. The same kind of evidence that the sick of the palsy had when Jesus said, " Thy sins be forgiven thee." Moreover Ananias salutes him by the distinguishing christian appellation of " *brother ;*" a term that Paul constantly opposes to *unbeliever.* See 1 Cor. 7: 12, 13. 5: 11. 6: 8. 8: 11, etc.

4. It is quite unnecessary to enlarge here. But I would just remark, that the same fact is established by the following declaration of the Lord to Ananias: " He *is* a chosen vessel to bear my name before the Gentiles, to suffer for me," etc. See v. 15, 16.

Now the only reason for maintaining that Saul was not converted until he was baptized, is, it is said, " Arise and be baptized, and *wash away thy sins ;*" and it is argued that, If he were a Christian before his baptism, his sins were of course washed away before his baptism : But his sins were not washed away until he was baptized ; and therefore he was not converted, regenerated, or pardoned until then.

But even admitting that there is an *immediate* connection between baptism and remission in this passage, (a fact that is by no means clear, as we shall show,) surely it would not require any great stretch of credulity to suppose that Ananias meant by these words no more than, " Receive the external sign of having obtained the remission of sins."

By a little attention to the original the Campbellites might have seen the blunder which they have committed in their argument. For ἁμαρτίας σου, translated " thy sins," is not, as they pretend, here used to designate the sins of his whole life— *all his sins ;* but simply the reproach, or stains that rested on his character as a persecutor of the church. And these stains could be washed away, only in the manner prescribed by Ananias, viz., *by calling upon the name of the Lord.* For that the connection is (as the passage reads) between *washing away sin,* and *calling upon the name of the Lord,* and not between *baptism* and *washing away sin,* is clear from the fact that these sins could be removed by calling upon the name of the Lord, much more effectually than by baptism administered privately, as his was. Now the distinguishing appellation of Christians, at this time, was *" those that call upon the name of the Lord."* See Acts 9: 11, 14, 21. 1 Cor. 1: 1, 2. Acts 2: 21. Rom. 10: 13, etc. Hence the idea is, " Wash away thy sins—remove them, by calling upon the name of the Lord." As if Ananias had said : " Go, call publicly upon that Lord, whose disciples you have persecuted even unto death ; associate with them, and those stains which you have contracted as their persecutor will be washed away—will be forgotten." See 2 Cor. 7: 1. Is. 1: 16, 17. Jer. 4: 14.

In support of this rendering, we will produce *one* authority which must be admitted to be in this controversy completely decisive. We refer to Mr. Campbell himself. In Vol. VII. p. 164 of his *Christian Baptist,* he thus speaks : " Have you, my dear brother, ever adverted to the import of the participle in the commission, Matt. xxviii. : Disciple, or convert the nations, *immersing* them. I need not tell you that this is the exact translation. Let me ask you, then, *does not the active participle always, when connected with the imperative mood, express the manner in which the thing commanded is to be per-*

formed? Cleanse the room, *washing* it ; clean the floor, *sweeping* it ; cultivate the field, *ploughing* it ; sustain the hungry, *feeding* them ; furnish the soldiers, *arming* them ; convert the nations, *baptizing* them ; are exactly the same forms of speech. No person I presume will controvert this." Very good, indeed. Now let us try the clause under consideration by this *famous* and *incontrovertible* rule ; and in order to do Mr. Campbell perfect justice, we shall take his own translation of the passage : " *Wash away thy sins, invoking his name.*" Here then is " the active participle" (*invoking*) connected with the " imperative mood" (wash away). Of course then, as " the active participle when connected with the imperative mood, *always* expresses the manner in which the thing commanded is to be performed," Paul was to wash away his sins by *invoking* the name of the Lord, and not by baptism. How then can this text be adduced to prove that sins are washed away by baptism.

But suppose we allow that " *sins*" here refers to *all* the sins of Paul's whole life ; the important query arises, *How did he wash away his sins?* He was *commanded* to wash them away (ἀπόλουσαι τὰς ἁμαρτίας σου) ; and we are told he obeyed the command. Now how did he obey it ? Campbellites say that " it was done by the waters of baptism." But how did he wash away his sins by the waters of baptism ?" This phrase is utterly unintelligible. Did he baptize himself ? This surely will never be pretended : and yet, if his sins were washed away by baptism, this is the only way in which it could with propriety be said that " he washed away his sins." But this is so preposterous that Campbellites will not admit it ; for it would be establishing a precedent with them of rather a singular character, and of disastrous effect ; and it is also said in Acts 9: 18, that " he *was* baptized," in the passive voice. How then did Paul wash away his sins by baptism, if he did not baptize himself ? There can be no way whatever. And this further proves that the connection is not between *baptize* and *wash away*, as Campbellites pretend, without the shadow of reason ; but between *wash away* and *invoking.* For thus it is perfectly plain how Paul obeyed the injunction ; and did actually " wash away his sins."

If it were of any use we could pursue this subject still further, and show that the most ridiculous consequences follow to the Campbellite scheme from their own exposition of this passage ; but we prefer to pass on to their

Argument from Mark 16: 16.

" He that believeth *and is baptized* shall be saved ; but he that believeth not shall be damned." From this it is argued that the Saviour has put water baptism upon an equal footing with believing ; and as believing is confessedly essential to salvation, baptism must of course be. But a very few remarks will show that this argument is very far from being conclusive.

As no person can dispense with any *acknowledged* command of Christ, and be in a salvable state, I conceive water baptism to be essential to the salvation of all who admit the ordinance to be enjoined by Christ ; provided it be in their power to obey the command. It was not however essential to the salvation of the dying malefactor ; nor is it, to the person who may truly repent on his death-bed, or in any circumstances in which it is impossible to render obedience to the command. A Quaker may likewise be saved without it ; for he believes that the injunction of the Redeemer on this subject has reference only to spiritual baptism. There is a wide difference between simply mistaking the import of a command, and wilfully neglecting it. The former is compatible with a sincere desire to obey it, but the latter is not.

But to proceed. The passage before us says, " He that believeth and is baptized shall be saved." Now this is perfectly plain. It contains a proposition that no Christian can dispute. We are assured by it, that such as believe and are baptized " shall be saved." It does not, however, assert that such *only* shall be saved ; but merely, *that such will be saved, whatever becomes of others.* The same as when Paul and Silas said to the jailor (Acts 16: 31), " Believe on the Lord Jesus Christ, and thou shalt be saved, and thy house," they did not intend to convey the idea that the jailer and his house were the only persons that should be saved ; but that *they* should be saved, on the terms then specified, whatever might become of others. If the Campbellites can here discover any proof in favor of their theory, they certainly possess the faculty of acute discrimination, in a degree to which few others can pretend to lay claim, without very great presumption.

But it may be asked, " Does not this declaration *imply* that those who are not baptized, will as certainly not be saved, as those who do not believe ?" I answer, that such an inference would be indeed plausible if this declaration contained *all* that our Saviour has said on the subject.   But it does not ; for he immediately adds what renders it altogether nugatory to *infer* anything from the foregoing clause : " He that believeth not shall be damned."

If, then, the Campbellites will resort to inference, we have no objection ; as, of course, we have the same privilege.   They are welcome to infer from the *former* clause, that such *only* as are baptized shall be saved ; and that all others must be lost, if even they do believe.   We, on the contrary, have of course the same right to infer from the *latter* clause, that those *only* who do not believe shall be damned, and that all others shall be saved, whether they have been baptized or not.   And how much Campbellism can gain by such a procedure, every one will judge for himself.

The last that we deem it necessary to examine is their

Argument founded on Acts 2: 38.

This passage thus reads : " Repent and be baptized, every one of you, for the remission of sins : " and from it the Campbellites argue that baptism is as intimately connected with remission as repentance is : and that remission cannot be obtained without baptism, any more than without repentance.   But repentance is essential to salvation, and therefore so is baptism.

It will not be disputed that the idea contained in this passage may, with propriety and correctness, be rendered " Repent and be baptized, every one of you, in the name of Jesus Christ, that your sins may be remitted :" εἰς ἄφεσιν ἁμαρτιῶν.   In our translation, *for* seems to convey a meaning not supported by the original.   The word is not γάρ but εἰς ; " be baptized *unto* the remission of sins."   It steers clear of the idea of *desert* being attached to baptism ; and this in fact is Mr. Campbell's own rendering : " Reform, and be each of you immersed in the name of Jesus Christ, in order to the remission of sins."

The confidence with which Mr. Campbell relies on this passage, in support of his system, may be seen by the following quotation from his *Extra*, No. 1. p. 14. " They were informed that though they now believed and repented, *they were not pardoned ;* and must reform, and be immersed, for the remission of sins." — " This testimony, when the speaker, the occasion, and the congregation, are all taken into view, is itself alone sufficient to establish the point."

But what is it, I ask, to be baptized εἰς ἄφεσιν ἁμαρτιῶν ?
The clause can easily be understood by a reference to a few of
similar construction.   "John preached the baptism of repentance (εἰς) *into the remission of sins*"—the same phrase. See
Mark 1: 4.   So Rom. 6: 3, " Know ye not that as many of us
as were baptized (εἰς) *into* Jesus Christ," etc.   1 Cor. 10:
2, "And were all baptized (εἰς) *into* Moses."   Matt. 3: 11, " I
indeed baptize you with water (εἰς) *into* repentance."   These
references are sufficient.   The construction is precisely parallel
to the one under consideration.   And now we ask,—What did
John the Baptist mean by " I baptize you unto repentance ?"
Did he mean that *repentance was brought about by baptism ?*
If not, how can it be imagined, that when Peter used the expression, " Be baptized into the remission of sins," he meant
that baptism was to bring about remission of sins ?   A similar
question may be asked in relation to the other passages referred to.
   But let us take another brief view of it.   With what is εἰς
ἄφεσιν ἁμαρτιῶν (remission of sins) here connected ?   With repentance, or baptism, or both ?   Peter himself, who uses the
expression, shall also answer the question : " *Repent ye therefore, and be converted, that your sins may be blotted out*," etc.
Acts 3: 19.   If then water baptism is in every case as inseparably connected with forgiveness as repentance is, Peter has here
committed an unpardonable omission.   If he has made no omission, then the vital connection in the text under review is not
between baptism and remission, but between repentance and remission.
   But further :   The peculiar circumstances of the case mentioned in Acts 2: 38, prove it to be a *particular instance* in the
strictest sense of the term : and it is illogical and utterly out of
the question to deduce *general* conclusions from it, and apply
them to the present circumstances of mankind at large.   I have
no objections to allow that in the case of the persons here spoken of, baptism may have been essential to remission ; and yet
this case would afford no ground for concluding that baptism is
essential to remission *in every case*.   But unless this can be
shown, the passage confessedly affords no support whatever to
the system.   A few remarks will show how peculiar were their
circumstances.
   1. The persons here spoken of, must either have obeyed the
command, and have been baptized, or have remained open and
avowed enemies to the cause of Christ.

2. It was the best possible, and in fact the only satisfactory evidence that they could then give, of their sincerity in renouncing Judaism and embracing Christianity. The step involved the loss of all things.

3. *They*, circumstanced as they were, could not even *innocently* mistake, or misunderstand the command. The apostles were present, and if any difficulty occurred it could be promptly obviated. Hence it was not even possible for them to be in error respecting their duty on the subject.

4. They had ample time and opportunity to obey the command.

Now to disobey under such circumstances, must argue an impenitent, unhumbled heart. And to the possessor of such a heart remission could not be granted. And hence baptism was essential to the remission of their sins.

In the same sense that baptism was essential to the remission of sins in this case, it is also essential to remission at the present time; e. g. when it is admitted that baptism is positively enjoined on all his followers by Christ; and when there is time and opportunity to obey the command. Under these circumstances I do contend that no one can be in a salvable state while he lives in the open violation of this command. We have no more right, under these circumstances, to dispense with this, than with any other acknowledged command of the Saviour.

But then it does not follow that if baptism be essential to the salvation of persons thus situated, it therefore is essential in the case of persons not similarly circumstanced; e. g. of sick persons, or of others, in whose cases it would be impossible to administer the ordinance. Yet unless it does follow that baptism is absolutely essential to remission *in every instance,* the passage confessedly affords no support to the theory that baptism is essential to the forgiveness of sin. If but *one instance* can be produced (and I have produced a number already), wherein it is admitted that remission of sins either was, or may be granted without baptism, the argument attempted to be deduced from this passage is false.

But on this subject we want no better authority than that of Mr. Campbell himself. Let us therefore hear him. On p. 165, Vol. VII. of his *Christian Baptist,* he says: "*I doubt not* but such Paedobaptists as simply *mistake* the meaning and design of the christian institution, who nevertheless are, as far as they know, obedient disciples of Jesus, *will be admitted into* *the kingdom of glory.*"*   Now Mr. Campbell maintains that Paedobaptists are not baptized.   Of course then, he himself being judge, the passage under consideration does not prove that baptism is equally essential to salvation as repentance. For while he admits that no sinner can be saved without repentance, he also "*doubts not*" that the unbaptized Paedobaptist may be saved.   It follows therefore, that according to Mr. Campbell's own testimony, the Campbellite exposition of Acts 2: 38 is false.

It is also worthy of remark that although in this instance we find " repentance, baptism, and remission of sins," in connection ; yet in other passages we find " repentance and remission of sins" without any reference to baptism.   A fact wholly inexplicable on the theory that sins are remitted by baptism.   An instance of this has been given above ; and the following are a few others.   Acts 5: 31, " Him hath God exalted with his own right hand, to be a Prince and a Saviour, to give repentance unto Israel and remission of sins."   Luke 24: 47, " That repentance and remission of sins should be preached in his name among all nations."   See also Acts 9 : 18.   2 Cor. 7 : 10. Hence Paul also tells us, (1 Cor. 1: 17,) that " Christ sent him not to baptize but to preach the Gospel ;" and he thanks God that he baptized "*none*" of the Corinthians, save a very few.

There are a few other passages which the Campbellites adduce (though the foregoing are the chief ones,) such as Acts 26: 17, 18, " I send thee (Paul) to open their eyes, and to turn them from darkness to light, and from the power of Satan unto God ; that they may receive forgiveness of sins, and inheritance among them which are sanctified by faith."   On which Mr. Campbell remarks, here is " first faith, or illumination ; then conversion ; (i. e. baptism,) then, remission of sins ; then, the inheritance."   That is, Paul was sent to *baptize* the Gentiles !   A direct contradiction to the Apostle himself.   It is quite unnecessary however to investigate any more of their

---

* But alas ! it is hard to know whether we can even take comfort from this *charitable* concession ; for in *Extra* No. 1. p. 30, he says, " But whether they may enter into the kingdom of eternal glory after the resurrection, is a question much like that question long discussed in the Schools, viz. : Can infants who have been quickened, but die before they are born, be saved ?   We may hope the best, but cannot speak with the certainty of knowledge."

" *Scripture* arguments." Our brief examination of the chief passages on which they depend for the support of their system, has evinced, it is believed, that not the shadow of a reason can be adduced in its favor from the word of God.

[NOTE.—We regret that our limits will not allow us to conclude this article in the present No. of the Repository. In the remaining sections, the author presents a brief synopsis of direct arguments against Campbellism, considers, at some length, the Unitarianism of the system, and reviews with much point, and in a very satisfactory manner, the *Translation of the New Testament,* adopted by the Campbellites, showing it to be a gross deception practised upon the public. His arguments are characteristically biblical, and the article, as a whole, appears to us highly valuable and appropriate at the present time, as an able and learned refutation of the scheme of a pretender, whose popularity in some parts of our country has given him the power of destroying much good. The reader will also perceive that the strong language of disapprobation used by Mr. Landis, is fully justified by the facts in the case. The conclusion will appear in the Repository for April next.—EDITOR.]

ARTICLE VIII.

ADVANTAGES AND DEFECTS OF THE SOCIAL CONDITION IN THE UNITED STATES OF AMERICA.

By Calvin E. Stowe, D. D. Prof. of Biblical Literature, Lane Seminary, Cincinnati.

"He hath not dealt so with any nation."—*Psalm* 147: 20.

" What could have been done more to my vineyard, that I have not done in it? Wherefore, when I looked that it should bring forth grapes, brought it forth wild grapes?"—*Isaiah* 5: 4.

IT is obvious that the people of the United States are placed in a different position from any which has ever before been occupied by a nation. Our providential advantages are such as ought to work out a state of society far superior to any which has ever existed before, in the universality of its intelligence, virtue and happiness; while our abuse of these advantages has been such as in some respects to throw us backwards from the point whence we started.   A brief notice of these advantages and defects is the subject of this article.

I. Our Advantages.

1. In our very origin we started from the highest point of civilization which the human race had then reached.

If we trace the progress of man from the commencement of history in the great Egyptian and Oriental monarchies, through the republics of Greece and Rome, down to the ripened age of modern Europe, we find that the advancement of civilization has been uniform ; that it has gradually but steadily enlarged its sphere, and proceeded from the few towards the many ; and that each successive development of man has been more extensive and more free than the last.   It is also true that each point of transition has been marked by bloody revolution, by the violent disruption of the old forms of society, and modelling them all anew.

In Egypt and Old Assyria the history of human cultivation commences, and in many respects these ancient nations had advanced quite as far as any of their successors.   The stupendous remains of their architectural efforts which still exist, excite the astonishment and exceed the skill of the most ingenious of modern architects.   The ablest engineers of the French Army, when they surveyed the ruins of Memphis and Thebes, acknowledged that they were acquainted with no mechanical contrivances by which such immense masses of heavy material could be moved and arranged in the admirable order in which they found them.   Nor was it in the massive and heavy only that they excelled.   In the lighter arts they were equally successful.   Colors which, though laid on four thousand years ago, are found as fresh and bright as if mingled but yesterday, attest the progress of the old world in the lighter ornamental arts.

Civilization, the arts, and sciences, were carried to a very high degree of perfection ; but what proportion of the people partook in this progress ? how extensively was the human race benefitted ?   Probably not one man in a hundred thousand of that ancient era enjoyed the benefit of its advancement, or participated in its civilization.   A very few were hereditary lords, the many, the vast majority, were hereditary, hopeless slaves.   No luxury, no self-indulgence was too great for the noble ; no oppression, no deprivation too much for the plebeian ; till at length when human nature could endure no longer, and the vengeance of God could no longer sleep, those old systems were dissolved in blood.

To these monarchies succeeded the republics of Greece and Rome. Civilization was carried forward, the refinements of life were increased, the arts were practised in a style of greater finish and better taste ; and the benefits of this progress became far more widely diffused. Where there was one in Assyria or Egypt who enjoyed all the privileges of a man, there were ten in Greece and Rome. But in Greece and Rome two thirds of the people were slaves, or in circumstances which shut them out from all participation in the progress of society. Corruption debased the high, and oppression brutalized the low ; till they all together fell a prey to the hardy courage of the barbarians of the north ; who, after gorging themselves with the blood and treasure of their victims, were the instruments of Providence for working out a new state of society in modern Europe, as much superior to the Greek and Roman, as that was in advance of the Egyptian and Assyrian. The civilization of modern Europe is a much greater advance on that of Greece and Rome, than this itself was on that of the ancient oriental world, both in respect to its quality and also in regard to the extent of the diffusion of its benefits among the mass of society.

But of all the kingdoms of modern Europe, England had, two centuries ago, made the farthest advances in everything calculated to elevate the intellect and the morals of the whole people, and give them the dignity and self-respect of freemen. It was from the best portion of this most advanced of the nations of the earth, from that very class of the population which had made her what she was, and given her her distinction, that our nation took its origin. We began therefore in advance of all the nations of the earth, and ought always to have kept in advance of them in all that is civilizing, ennobling and excellent. Nay it is our destiny and our duty here in this western world, to work out a fourth development of man as much superior to that of modern Europe, as modern Europe herself is superior, not to Greece and Rome merely, but to Egypt and old Assyria. And sooner or later this will be done——it is the decree of Heaven ——the whole analogy of Providence shows it——and it cannot be reversed.

2. We sprang from an enlightened and conscientious ancestry.

The history of nations has generally commenced in rude barbarianism, in savage and plundering wars, in ambition and selfishness and violence. But in the history of this country, particularly the north-eastern section of it, we have the singular spectacle of religious men, animated with the purest zeal and directed by an enlightened conscience, leaving their homes of ease, respectability and affluence, and penetrating a forested wilderness, to lay the foundations of a new empire, for the purpose of themselves enjoying and transmitting unmolested to their posterity, certain great moral principles, which they held dearer than all the blandishments of life, or even than life itself. They were truly men of principle ; they not only held to the principle distinctly and decidedly in theory, but uniformly acted on principle, and reckoned no sacrifice too costly, when called upon to make it for the sustaining of principle. This characteristic feature of their own moral development, they took unwearied pains to transfer to their descendants ; and at the earliest period of their history, and at an expense which they could not sustain without denying themselves all the luxuries and many of the physical comforts of life, they laid the foundations of those institutions, which, if they have not given to the children all the exalted virtues of the fathers, have at least endued them with a strength and energy of character which has sent their influence to every quarter of the globe, and conferred on them an almost resistless power in every circle where they move.

3. The equality and freedom of development which exist among us is another advantage which distinguishes ours from all preceding conditions of society.

One of the first peculiarities which attracts the notice of the intelligent traveller on coming among us, is the perfect equality of rank which obtains in our free States, so different from the artificial forms of society which prevail in the old world. For this the human race has been struggling from the very commencement of its history ; to this it has at length arrived by slow degrees and through a series of revolutions which have deluged the earth with blood. The few have all along obstinately resisted the efforts of the many ; the ground has been contested inch by inch ; but here at last the victory of the many over the few has been completely achieved, and here there is no rank but what each man makes for himself by his own efforts. The field is entirely open, and the same incentives to exertion are held out to every member of the community.

Accordingly, whatever advances any one may make, they are speedily within the reach of all, and whatever elevates any one class contributes directly to elevate the whole mass of society.   No one family, no one order, can appropriate to its exclusive benefit a single improvement produced by the progress of society, any more than it can monopolize the light of the sun or the rains of heaven.

Very different from this is the condition of the old world. There the lower orders have but little direct participation in the improvements of the higher.   The nobility, the clergy, the military, may each avail themselves to any extent, of the progress of civilization, while the mass of the people, the *vulgar herd*, are still shut up to the inferior condition in which they were born, and receive only a remote and a very inferior kind of benefit.   This is strikingly true at the present time throughout modern Europe, and still more painfully was it true of all the states of society which preceded this.   The American traveller in Europe sees that everything there is arranged for the convenience and luxury of the *few*, while in regard to the great *many*, the problem seems to be to crowd together the greatest number possible, into the least possible space.   Hence the spacious, splendid castle of the nobleman surrounded for miles with unproductive pleasure grounds, and the little, crowded, narrow, dirty, treeless villages of the poor, where thousands herd together without ground enough for a cabbage garden, and expecting nothing more from their griping landlord than a bare shelter from the heat and the storm.   The independent, healthful mode of each farmer's building his own house on his own farm, and thus dotting the whole surface of the country with comfortable dwellings is there unknown.   There, the princely mansion, the open field, and the crowded village, are the only objects that diversify the scene.

4. Religion in this country is disconnected with politics ; and is therefore comparatively pure, moral and free.

Where religion is interwoven with the state it becomes almost entirely a political matter ; and the character of the minister sinks to that of a simple governmental officer.   The sacredness of his character is gone, and an irreligious or vicious clergyman excites no more remark, and is regarded as in no way more peculiarly unfit for his office, than an irreligious or vicious magistrate.   In countries where there is a state religion, the amount of moral worth that would make a justice of the peace respectable is all that is required to make a respectable clergyman. It is easy to see how essentially the moral efficacy of religious institutions is broken by such a public sentiment. The clergyman is simply an officer appointed by government to perform certain duties, and if he is regularly commissioned, whatever his private character may be, the value of his public performances is not affected by it.

As a striking illustration of this, I will mention what occurred more than once in Mr. Wesley's chapel in London, as related to me by an old member of the society, who was admitted to it by Mr. Wesley himself. In his will Mr. Wesley directed that the ordinances in that chapel should be administered by a regularly ordained clergyman of the Church of England. In early times it was often difficult to find such a clergyman who was willing to perform these duties in the chapel. And more than once the trustees have gone to Newgate prison and found among the convicts some regularly ordained clergyman of the Church of England, who has been brought to the chapel guarded by two constables, under the inspection of this guard has administered the sacrament of the Lord's supper to the church members, and returned again to the prison with a constable on each arm. His Episcopal ordination gave him full authority to administer the ordinances, and the value of an ordinance is not affected by the personal unworthiness of the minister.

In this country, where religion has no connection with the state, the character of the minister is in no danger of being confounded with that of the magistrate. Every minister must stand on his own individual moral worth, every minister must ostensibly, and in profession at least, be a good man. No denomination, no society can tolerate an openly vicious and irreligious minister. The vast amount of moral influence by this means exerted on society, and the strong attraction thus put forth to keep religion pure, are seldom estimated by us at their true value. One must visit some country of the old world to see this thing in its true light.

5. We enjoy in this country entire freedom of action.

If one is disposed to do good there is no law and no governmental authority to prevent him. Whatever obstacles may be interposed by public prejudice or popular violence, they are but transient, and can have no permanent influence to injure the cause against which they are used. Our government has so little power

to interfere with the movements of individuals, that in all our benevolent operations, it scarcely occurs to us that we are under
any government at all.

In most other countries, (Great Britain is an exception) benevolent efforts are obstructed in a thousand ways by the watchful jealousy of the governments. In France, though now governed by a king who is a man of strong mind and benevolent
feelings, and under the direction of a prime minister (Guizot)*
who is a decided protestant and most enlightened man, the efforts of protestants are constantly impeded and often counterac-
ted by the timidity of the government. In Prussia, though
governed by a religious king, whose long reign of nearly half a
century has exhibited an almost unbroken series of efforts for
the intellectual and moral good of his people, no religious society dare employ an agent to present their cause to the
churches, and their meetings for prayer must always be held
in private houses, because the king dislikes itinerating agents
and chooses that all should be done by settled pastors, and because he thinks it best that the churches should not be opened
except for the regular services of the Lord's day and on such
other occasions as he himself may appoint. If the best governed kingdoms in the world be thus restricted, what must the
state of things be where selfishness, bigotry, and ignorance occupy the throne ?

6. We have means in abundance for the accomplishment of
any good we may desire.

Industry and economy in this country everywhere may secure a competency and something more. Almost any man, if
he chooses to make the effort, can become wealthy, and no
Christian who has health, need debar himself the luxury of
giving support to benevolent objects. We have no idea of the
hopeless poverty to which great masses of people in other
countries are condemned. We know not what it is to toil
early and late, to be scantily fed and poorly clothed, to be
obliged habitually and as one of the conditions of existence, to
suffer from hunger and from cold, because the utmost effort of
industry and parsimony cannot secure a sufficiency of food and
fuel. Millions of industrious and virtuous families in Europe
can afford in the severest weather to keep a fire only an hour
or two in the morning, and all the rest of the day they must

---

* This article was written while Guizot was minister.

shield themselves from the cold as they best can. A poor boy in northern Prussia being asked once in a school examination, what he thought of the happiness of heaven, replied very seriously, that he supposed it *to be a place where good people would keep warm the whole day.* Coarse black bread and water alone constitute the usual food of the laboring people, and happy do they consider themselves if they can get enough of this. Early in the morning, the whole family, men, women and children leave their comfortless cottages and toil till night in the field. The women bring the produce from the fields and take it to the markets in large baskets fastened to their shoulders ; and in none of the slave States which I have visited, have I ever seen negro women drudging in such toilsome, out-of-door labor, as falls to the lot of the laboring women of Germany and France. And all this they do for less than the bare necessaries of life. In one of the most fertile and wealthy provinces of gay, polite, sunny France, I have seen blooming girls of from twelve to eighteen lugging manure into the vineyards in baskets. How different the state of society here. The extent, variety, and fertility of our territory, the enterprise and activity of our people, the great demand and ready reward for every kind of useful labor, makes poverty wholly unknown or entirely inexcusable.

7. We have had all the advantage of starting anew and for ourselves.

Societies have generally originated fortuitously. Institutions have grown up as it were by accident, and have been the product of circumstances over which the people had no direct control, or they have had very little regard to the laws of reason, or the general good, and have been continued generally for the exclusive advantage of the few who happened to have the preponderance at the time of their origin. Habits extremely detrimental to the progress of society have thus become fixed and interwoven with all the relations of life ; and as society must advance, the tearing away of these prepossessions, when the time comes that they must be broken up, is the occasion of violence, bloodshed, and retrogradation.

How different was the inception of our institutions ! Men of enlightened views and correct principles, with the advantage of all the experience that had preceded them, applied themselves, of set purpose, to the work of framing a body politic expressly designed to secure the greatest happiness of the greatest number. Prescription and prejudice were laid aside, and actual utility was the guiding principle. Our country has afforded the first instance since the creation of the world, of a great nation, meeting by representatives or delegates of their own choice, to form and adopt a frame of government for themselves.

The peopling of our country from various European nations has fallen in with and helped forward this great advantage. Local prejudice has in this way been disarmed, narrow views enlarged, and opportunity given for selecting the best from a great variety of examples. The superiority of modern Europe was caused, in great part, by a similar fact in its early history ; but there the mingling of the people took place in a much lower grade of civilization and under circumstances far less propitious. Here the combination takes place under the attractions of peace and mutual advantage ; there it was attended with conflict, war and deadly hate. If the English character was so essentially benefitted by the forced coalition of the Briton, the Saxon and the Norman, what advantage may we not expect from the peaceful combination of the various elements which compose our society ?

Hence originates in a great measure our characteristic readiness to receive improvements, and our habitual expectation that everything is susceptible of improvement and will improve.

8. Our welfare depends entirely on ourselves, and all our evils are susceptible of a speedy remedy.

By the form of our government our destinies are put into our own hands, and it is made the interest of every member of the community to labor for the intellectual and moral advancement of every other member. If we are plunged in difficulty and disgrace by the folly and wickedness of our rulers, the folly and wickedness are our own, for the rulers are but the creatures of the people ; and mortifying as the reflection may sometimes be, without doubt our legislative and executive officers are usually a fair representation of the majority of those whom they govern.

If we are exposed to suffering from the giddy and unprincipled movements of an ignorant and vicious populace, it is an ignorance and a viciousness for which we are in great part directly responsible ; for nothing hinders our exerting ourselves to educate and reform every portion of our population ; and suitable efforts on the part of those who are themselves sufficiently educated to undertake the enterprise would soon accomplish the object. No tyrants can oppress us but our own indulged vices ;

no ignorance or wickedness can annoy us, but that which we ourselves permit to grow ; for it admits not of doubt that there are enlightened and virtuous men enough in the country, if every such man would exert himself to the extent of his power, there are enough, I say, to banish ignorance from the land, and compel wickedness to hide its head. God has put it in our power to do this, and if we neglect to do it, the evil consequences on our own heads will be dreadful.

Talk not to me of the swarms of papal emigrants who are to destroy our free institutions. I affirm, that for the very purpose of sparing us the expense and hazard of a foreign mission to popish countries, God has brought to our very doors that class of the papal population whom there can be most hope of benefitting, placed them in the midst of us, where there can be no penal enactments to obstruct our efforts for their conversion, where we can labor for them without interfering with any other objects, and be foreign missionaries without leaving our own homes or putting the church to one cent of expense ; where such efforts may be attended with the greatest mental, physical and moral advantages, and where they become necessary as a means of self-defence as well as a christian duty.

Finally, the present aspect of the world in reference to permanent and universal peace is another circumstance highly auspicious to the welfare and superior growth of our nation.

In the savage state, where there is no law, each man seizes whatever his strength may enable him to grasp, and defends his own possessions against the aggressions of others as he best can. The only law is violence, the only authority force. As man emerges from the savage state he allows himself to be governed by law, and instead of relying on the strength of his own arm to repel aggression, he appeals to the magistrate and sustains his claims by the moral power of the government.

Hitherto this civilization has extended only to individuals and to small communities united under one government, while nations in their intercourse with each other have still acted as savages and known only savage law. There has always been between nations, even of the christian profession and the farthest advanced in civilization, the same readiness to resort to violence, the same thirst for revenge, the same quick sensitiveness, falsely termed honor, the same love of mutual annoyance, murder, blood, and destruction, as exists between individuals and tribes in savage life. When nations as such become civili-

zed, then their intercourse with each other will be regulated by
such laws, and their differences settled by such tribunals as
regulate the intercourse and settle the differences of individuals
in well ordered communities.

Several circumstances show that the progress of civilization
in this respect, though slow, is still certain ; and our country
possesses the singular advantage of passing its youthful and
forming period under the influence of these circumstances.

1. The acknowledged grounds of war have been very greatly diminished, and are still diminishing. In ancient times, a
desire of conquest, a love of what was called glory, or the mere
want of something else to do, were considered sufficient reasons
for a nation's attacking and butchering its unoffending neighbors ; and much of the glory celebrated by the poets of antiquity is the glory of being robbers and murderers without provoca-
tion.   Christianity very early exerted influence enough on national character to abolish this system of national pillage ; and
the people who would now go to war avowedly for such purposes would justly be regarded and treated as pirates by the
whole civilized world.   Even after the spread of Christianity
in Europe, the propagation of religion or the extinction of idolatry or heresy was considered a just ground of war ; and many
of the most bloody scenes were enacted in these so-called religious wars.   But the thirty years' war which was terminated
by the peace of Westphalia in the year 1648, after a seven
years' negotiation, was the last war of this kind ; and public
sentiment is now so firmly settled on this point, that the pope
himself would no longer dare proclaim a crusade against heretic
or infidel.

Again ; the preservation of the balance of power, as it is
called, was long considered a sufficient ground of national hostility, and it was in wars of this kind that Marlborough acquired
so much glory by making so much misery.   But no cabinet in
Europe would now dare to make war on this pretext only.   Indeed the grounds of war acknowledged at present are reduced
to two, the preservation of national honor, and the repelling of
aggression; and in regard to these, the first will soon be confessed a mere illusion, and the second will be obsolete.

2. The increasing facilities of communication between the
most distant parts of the earth, and the intimate financial connections between different nations are a strong security against
war.   Constant habits of personal intercourse and the mutual

dependencies of mercantile transactions are quite inconsistent with the device of mutual destruction ; and governments who now devise to make war, must ask council of the merchant as well as the soldier.

3. The aristocratic influence over governments is continually diminishing, and that of the industrious classes as constantly increasing.

One great reason of the continuance and popularity of wars has been, that human butchery has been regarded as the only employment worthy of a nobleman. It would disgrace the son of a noble to do anything beneficial to society ; a place in the army or navy is all that is fit for him, and to have a sufficient number of places in the army and navy, there must be something for the army and navy to do. All the honors and profits of war belong to the few who hold its high places, while its unmitigated miseries and horrors fall upon the great many, the industrious classes, who have been so long the dupes and slaves of the higher orders, but who will be so no longer. They already feel their strength and assert their rights, and so decided already has their influence become, that even noblemen now begin to make themselves useful as farmers and merchants, and kings and emperors are emulating the honors of the schoolmaster.

When the industrious and productive portions of the community fully understand their interests and their rights, then wars will be impossible. Hear what an ingenious living writer appropriately calls, ' The purport and upshot of war :' "What, speaking in quite unofficial language, is the net purport and upshot of war ? To my own knowledge, for example, there dwell and toil, in the British village of Drumdrudge, usually some five hundred souls. From these, by certain 'natural enemies' of the French, there are successively selected, during the French war, say thirty able bodied men. Drumdrudge at her own expense, has suckled and nursed them : She has, not without difficulty and sorrow, fed them up to manhood, and even trained them to crafts, so that one can weave, another build, another hammer, and the weakest can stand under thirty stone avoirdupois. Nevertheless, amid much weeping and swearing, they are selected ; all dressed in red, and shipped away at public charges, some two thousand miles, or say only to the south of Spain ; and fed there till wanted. And now to that same spot in the south of Spain, are thirty similar French artisans, from a French Drumdrudge, in like manner wending ; till at length, after infinite effort, the two parties come into actual juxta-position ; and thirty stand fronting thirty, each with a gun in his hand. Straightway the word ' Fire !' is given ; and they blow the souls out of one another ; and in place of sixty brisk, useful craftsmen, the world has sixty dead carcasses, which it must bury and anew shed tears for. Had these men any quarrels ? Busy as the devil is, not the smallest ! They lived far enough apart ; were the entirest strangers ; nay, in so wide a universe, there was even, unconsciously, by commerce, some mutual helpfulness between them. How then ? Simpleton ! their governors had fallen out ; and instead of shooting one another, had the cunning to make these poor blockheads shoot."* Can such things be when men become sufficiently enlightened to understand their interests and their rights ?

4. In our own country we have a farther security against war in the very curious balancings of the various interests of the different portions of the nation. No one interest is sufficiently strong to hold out against all the others, and the connections of the different interests are so complicated, that it is impossible to form extensive hostile classes.

In the rapid increase of commercial intercourse, it will not be long before the whole world will be linked together by similar ties ; and the associations for Atlantic steam navigation are among the most efficient of Peace Societies.

II. Our Defects.

Having thus spoken of the advantages of our condition, I must now, with the same plainness and simplicity, proceed to notice our defects.

1. We have in the United States a vast amount of vulgar and obtrusive vice, in addition to our full share of the more decent and secret modes of wickedness, which always attend a high degree of worldly prosperity.

No man or woman can travel in our stage coaches, on our canals, or in our steamboats, without being often offended with outbreakings of profaneness and filthiness against which there is no remedy but uncomplaining silence ; for any manifestation of displeasure or any attempt at reproof, unless contrived and exe-

---

* Sartor Resartus.

cuted with very unusual skill, will increase tenfold the obnoxious torrent. There is no country on earth where the traveller is so much exposed to this species of annoyance; and as our great lines of public conveyance are the scenes which first present themselves to the notice of strangers, is it any wonder that foreigners should sometimes become prejudiced against us and our institutions? There is nothing like it in Europe; and the nearest approach to it is found in the low, uneducated, and vicious part of the populace of France. While in that country I was at no loss to conjecture where the instruments were found to perpetrate the horrid excesses of the French revolution; and I trembled when I traced the too visible features of resemblance to a large and, I fear, an increasing part of our own population.

The source of this evil in the United States is easily pointed out. What must be the inevitable result of permitting large masses of active, ardent mind to grow up without culture, and continue from year to year engrossed in the business and pleasures of sense, without any of the modifying influences which arise from cultivating the imagination and taste or the religious sentiments? The class of population to which I refer enter on the business of their lives, with little or no training from schools, and once engaged in their occupations they have no Sabbath to break the current of worldly thought and feeling, and no objects of veneration to soften or to awe the rougher propensities of their nature. No, they have no Sabbath. Griping avarice, contemptible demagogueism, and a supercilious disregard of authority, which practically denies to God himself the right to rule except so far as the *democracy of numbers* shall please to permit, has swept away from our great lines of conveyance that palladium of our safety, that great source of modifying influences over minds let loose from governmental restraints—and our country offers no substitute in the shape of venerated usages, traditional customs, or artificial and imposing forms of society.

Those political men, (for statesmen they are not,) who have dared hazard the consequences of desecrating the Sabbath from the example of Europe, have shown themselves extremely short-sighted; for in Europe, where the day is not strictly appropriated to religious duties, a part of it is devoted to elevating and civilizing amusements, to visiting the ornamental public walks, the works of art, the statues and paintings, the venerated castles and cathedrals, the cherished antiquities which continually impress the mind with the hallowed recollections of ancient times, and thus soften and refine it—and with all this the constant presence of an armed police accustoms every man to suppress the outward expression of his rougher feelings.

But with us there are no such customs, no such linkings with antiquity, no such restraining influences on our manners. Take away the religious character of the sabbath, and everything civilizing and humanizing in the day is gone, and there is nothing left but one continued stream of worldly pursuit, interrupted only by bursts of drunkenness and brutalizing debauchery. With us the desecration of the sabbath brings with it its natural and most appropriate punishment, in the degrading and brutifying of that part of our population who have little opportunity of intellectual or moral culture, except what the hallowed rest of this day is designed to afford. And yet this institution of God, so essential to the civilization and moral culture of the mass of our people, so necessary to our political safety, this most important institution must be set at nought, lest a business letter should be delayed a few hours on the road, or a package of merchandize not quite so rapidly change owners, or an imbecile demagogue lack a hobby to ride into office with!

"Shall I not visit you for these things? saith the Lord; and shall not my soul be avenged on such a nation as this?" Jer. 5: 9.

"Thou hast despised my holy things, and hast profaned my sabbaths. Behold, therefore, I have smitten my hand at thy dishonest gain which thou hast made.—Can thy heart endure, or can thy hands be strong, in the days that I will deal with thee? I the Lord have spoken it and will do it." Ezek. 22: 8, 13, 14.

Surely without speedy repentance and reformation the visitation will come; and, as God's visitations usually are, it will be the natural result of the transgression. Already has the appropriate retribution been commenced, and every year the rod is felt with increasing severity. Whence result those terrible steamboat explosions, but from the recklessness of men, made wanton by entire political freedom, without the checks of intellectual and religious instruction? Every year, the destruction of life from this source increases at a fearful rate. In 1836, 400 were destroyed in this way; in 1837, 600; and during the first half of 1838, more than 1000.

Are we so blind that we cannot see the hand of God, so deaf that we cannot hear his voice, in these fearful catastrophies?

Are we so unreflecting that we cannot here see the natural result of leaving freemen entirely beyond the influence of educational and religious institutions?

Restore to us the sabbath as a means of popular improvement, or give us the iron hand of a Prussian despotism, which though it may hold us with a tight rein, will at least cultivate our minds and our morals, and protect our lives and property.

2. A vast number of children among us grow up in ignorance, disorder and wickedness, without the restraints of religious institutions, schools, or family government.

This is true to an extent exceedingly alarming to one who looks at the facts as they really exist, and does not allow himself to be dazzled by the habits of self-applause to which we are so much addicted. As to the first point mentioned, it is making liberal allowance to admit that one third of the inhabitants of the United States are regular attendants on any species of public worship, or come at all under the direct influence of our religious institutions. The population of the United States must be now nearly 16,000,000. From statistics furnished by the American Almanac for 1838, (p. 172,) I estimate the whole number of communicants belonging to all the different religious denominations at 2,045,129. Reckoning the communicants to comprise only one third of all the different religious societies, there will be 6,135,387 persons connected with the different religious societies. This number subtracted from 16,000,000 leaves 9,864,613 not connected with any religious society whatever. With every allowance, therefore, the regular attendants on public worship, of every description, cannot exceed one third of the whole population.

In regard to schools, though schools generally are much more popular than churches, the state of things is but little better. On this subject I am satisfied there have been many flattering estimates, which a minute and impartial examination would prove to be entirely groundless. The estimates for the State of New York, for example, would show a very thorough extension of the benefits of the common school system. But the extent to which these estimates may be relied upon as an accurate representation of the facts, may be seen by the following paragraph from the First Annual Report of the superintendent of common schools for the State of Ohio, (p. 13.) "The returns from the counties in New York would, if taken in the aggregate, show a general attendance thus: there are 538,396 children in the State, and 532,167 are reported as in the schools. The schools are taught seven months, on an average, in the year. The whole amount expended for tuition, was $738,937,67, or a fraction less than $1,40 per scholar. Of course it will pay for teaching the whole number less than three months in the year; but some have attended nine months, and the average is seven months, so that either they all had less than three months' schooling, or something less than half attended seven months, and the others did not attend at all. To prove still further that this review is fair, one county has 10,799 children, and the same tables show 11,931, or 1,132 more than the whole number, have attended school in the same year, an average of seven months, for $14,257,21, or for $1,20 per scholar. The true average for the whole number is about three months, if they all attended; and that the school was an average of seven months for that number proves that all did not attend steadily. Their statistics do not pretend to furnish the time that each scholar attended; all are numbered that attend, however short the period. Add to this the fact that of those reported as at school, a large number are either over or under the ages included in the reported whole number; and a greater deficiency will be found than appears at first view."

Of the system generally, Judge Duer, of New York city, says, " It is, in fact, so imperfect and scanty, as hardly to deserve the name of elementary. It is unconnected with anything resembling moral discipline, or the formation of character, the teachers inexperienced and transitory, snatched up for the occasion; are paid by salaries which hardly exceed the wages of a menial servant; and as a necessary consequence, ignorant and disqualified, they are perhaps over-paid by the pittance they receive." (Same Report, p. 13.)

I believe it will be admitted that Ohio is as intelligent and as well provided with educational institutions as any other State south and west of New York; and that taking the whole United States into the account, where there is one in a better condition, in this respect, than Ohio, there are at least three in a worse. What then is the result of the laborious investigations of our single-hearted and truth-telling superintendent? From an examination of the large statistical table, and the synopsis given on page 49 of his First Annual Report, I obtain the following results.

Whole number of persons between the ages of four and twenty-one,

	Males,	254,530
	Females,	238,309
	Total,	492,839

Number reported as in a public or private school more than two and less than four months,

	Males,	45,311
	Females,	38,985

Number reported as in School more than four months,

	Males,	31,664
	Females,	30,480
	Total,	146,440
Supposed to be in school not reported,	. .	81,365
	Total,	227,805
Not in schools at all,	. . . . .	265,032

Making every requisite allowance, and comparing the above numbers with the results of my own observations, so far as I have had opportunity to observe, I am persuaded that scarcely one half of the children of Ohio between six and eighteen years of age were, in 1837, in attendance on any school whatever, either public or private, for even the short period of two months.

From this, making what I consider a fair estimate for the whole United States, I am persuaded that not more than one third of the whole number of children of proper school age attend school at all, either public or private ; and I will be entirely silent as to the real value of about one half of the schools that actually exist. Certainly *keeping school* is a more common employment among us than *teaching children.*

Let it not be supposed that two thirds of our population are provided for, one third by religious institutions, and another third by schools ; for it is a notorious fact, that those who neglect religious institutions usually neglect schools also, and that it is the same families who attend our churches, that attend our schools.

But is not the deficiency in church and school made up by family government and family instruction ? In some few instances it may be ; but as a general fact, alas ! alas ! for family discipline and family teaching ! If this be the only substitute, it is much like another substitute not unfrequently met with in the western country, namely, wading through the mud with a rail on one's back as a substitute for riding in the stage-coach.

Let me not be misapprehended. I am neither *croaking* nor *lugubriating* ; but simply stating plain facts in the plainest language.

The crowds of idle, profane and vicious boys which infest our large cities and swarm on our great thoroughfares, afford painful proof of the sad deficiency in school and parental instruction. The following paragraph, which has appeared in our newspapers during the present month, (July, 1838), is a vivid illustration of the same point. "*Irresponsible Boys.*—Several lads of from seventeen to twenty years, have been taken up in Baltimore on suspicion of being concerned in the late house-burnings. There is a class of youth growing up in our large towns, free from the restraints of a proper guardianship, of whom society has much to fear. Hundreds come in from the country in pursuit of trades and employment, who are thrown into promiscuous association in boarding-houses, over whom there is no sort of supervision whatever, except during the working hours of the day. Thus left to themselves without instruction, or the attractions of domestic society, they naturally seek excitement in the streets, or elsewhere. Something, we are persuaded, might be done by masters and parents to remedy this defect in our apprenticeship system. And until something is done, we must expect to be cursed with intemperance, street brawls, and incendiarism of every sort."*

If it be the indispensable condition of a republic, that a majority of its citizens be intelligent and virtuous, our prospects for the future, without greatly increased exertions, are none of the brightest.

In England, the education of the *lower orders*, as they are called, has always been grossly neglected ; and what is the consequence ? Every nook of the kingdom swarms with mischievous boys and boyish men ; every work of art, every beautiful object, every pleasure ground, every garden, every cluster of flowers, every fruit tree, must be fenced in and guarded, to preserve it from wanton injury. The same propensity to wanton destruction and mutilation of everything that is unguarded is notorious among ourselves, and it is owing to the same cause, neglect of early education ; shall I not rather say, want of civilization ? Who, in any of our large cities, that has a choice flower garden, a gallery of paintings, a saloon of statues, would ven-

---

* **Newark Sentinel.**

ture to throw them open, unguarded, to the promiscuous concourse of the public ? It would be nearly as unsafe here as in England itself. Flowers would be plucked and trampled upon, pictures soiled with handling, statues would be mutilated, and in a few years the whole collection would be rendered almost worthless. It has fallen to my lot to act as librarian to three different public institutions in parts of the United States remote from each other. Each of these institutions had collections of rare books and expensive plates, which were open to the inspection of visitors who were respectably introduced, and to them only ; and yet I must testify with shame and indignation that in every institution, notwithstanding the utmost vigilance on my part, plates have been torn and soiled by careless handling, and rare copies of valuable works have been dog's-eared and pencil-marked.

Where children are properly educated, this species of Vandalism does not exist. In Bavaria, in Saxony, in Wurtemburg, in Prussia, the public walks and private gardens, the collections of statues, paintings and other works of art, the great libraries, are freely open to all observers, and thronged, particularly on holidays, with men, women, and children, from every class in society ; but not a flower is broken, no picture is soiled, no statue bruised, no book mishandled, unless it be by some Vandal foreigner.

By order of government the roads in Prussia are lined on each side with fruit trees. Riding once early in September from Berlin to Halle, I noticed that some of the trees had a wisp of straw attached to them. I inquired of the coachman what it meant. He replied, that those trees bore choice fruit, and the straw was a notice to the public not to take fruit from those trees without special permission. " I fear," said I, " that such a notice in my country, would be but an invitation to roguish boys to attack these very trees." " *Haben sie keine Schules ?*" (Have you no schools ?) was his significant rejoinder.

It is a fact that the children of the convicts in the Prussian prison have, through the assiduous care of their government, better advantages of early education, than many of our wealthy citizens are willing to afford to their own sons. It is true, and I thank God for it, that the spirit of the people is now to some extent aroused, and much is done ; but by how few, how very few, in comparison with the whole number who ought to be at work, is it all done !

But juvenile lawlessness is not the only proof of defective early education which exists among us. What a sad want of knowledge and of conscience in regard to moral principle is manifested even by many who are communicants in christian churches! Whose conscience reproaches him for making what is called a good bargain? that is, taking more for a thing than it is worth, or buying a piece of property at half its known value? On whose word can you rely to keep a contract, when breaking it will bring more money? A man who uniformly keeps his word, is a prodigy and a wonder.

Again; how much knowledge of the true principles of free government is manifested by a goodly number of our voters? What sort of argument is it that has the greatest influence in procuring their suffrages? What intelligent freemen they must be, who bawl for liberty with their throats, and with ther hands tear down their neighbor's house for holding and publishing opinions which offend them! Men whose feelings are raised to the highest point of indignation, that any one should be restrained in his liberty to sell rum and destroy the bodies and souls of his fellow-citizens; but who at the same time will shoot a man for publishing a newspaper which asserts that negroes should not be slaves! And as to a knowledge of international law and the true principles of foreign policy, the recent proceedings in regard to Canada and Texas, afford pregnant illustrations.

I cheerfully admit and rejoice in, the good sense of the great mass of *the people;* but all these things exist, and they are mortifying in the extreme; and must be remedied!

3. We are prone to self-estimation, self-applause, and an all prevalent *egoism.*

German philosophy makes a distinction between *egotism* and *egoism,* the latter indicating that one esteems himself of great importance and makes himself the centre of his own efforts. It is one of the greatest curses of despotism, that it robs the great mass of the people of self-respect, and one of the greatest blessings of free institutions, that they make each individual feel that he is an important member of the community, and lay upon him the responsibilities of a man. But self-respect, unregulated and unchecked, may degenerate into habits of self-applause and self-idolization; and that this has been the case to some extent in our country, no impartial observer can doubt. Hence the disgusting airs and intolerable assumptions of the ignorant and noisy though successful aspirants, for wealth or popular favor. Hence also the great intolerance, the want of reverence, the coarseness of thought and language, which have infected to some extent even our religion, and produced addresses to the Deity which would be disrespectful even to a fellow creature.   On this topic let us hear the testimony of a very intelligent foreigner, who has written a sensible book respecting us and our institutions.

" The ruling power in the United States (says M. De Tocqueville) must not be jested with ; the smallest reproach irritates its sensibility ; the slightest joke, which has any foundation in truth, renders it indignant ; everything must be made the subject of encomium, from the very structure of their language to their more solid virtues.   No writer, whatever be his eminence, can escape from this tribute of adulation to his fellow citizens.   The majority lives in the perpetual practice of self-applause, and it is only from strangers or from actual experience, that the Americans have any chance of learning some truths.   If no great writers have as yet appeared in America, the reason is clear.   Literary genius cannot exist without freedom of opinion, and freedom of opinion does not exist in America."[*]

If there is some exaggeration in the above, there is also much of plain, honest truth.

To the same principle of egoism and self-worship are to be attributed the interminable, irrelevant, loose harangues, (so different from the plain, short, straight forward talks in the British Parliament,) which consume the time of our Congress.   These harangues are made, not for the sake of convincing any one, not for the purpose of elucidating the subject under debate, for the haranguer knows very well that nobody listens to him, and by the hour together he makes no allusion to the subject before the house, but he wishes only to hear himself talk, and does not even pretend to be speaking to his colleague representatives, but says he is addressing his constituents a thousand miles off; and this imaginary audience is the only one he ever fancies to be listening to him.

An amusing instance of this verbal flux recently occurred in the U. S. Senate.   The Senate were ready to pass a certain measure by *unanimous vote*, but one honorable member was dying to deliver himself of a speech in *favor* of the measure—and in compassion to him the Senate adjourned and spent the whole of the next day in waiting for the end of his speech in *favor* of

---

* Democracy in America, Vol. II. p. 162.

the measure, which they had all declared the day before they were *ready to adopt* without further debate !

4. We are characterized by great violence and illiberality of party spirit, both ecclesiastical and political.

Here *public sentiment* (as it is called), is the great arbiter and sovereign, and public measures are carried, not by the authority of an elevated few, but by the combined energies of a great mass. Hence every party strives to gain as many adherents as possible, whatever may be their moral worth ; and these adherents must all be committed and identified with the party, that numbers may give them weight, and unbroken union enable them to control public sentiment. This is the great object of party, *to control public sentiment ;* and the public sentiment of the party, is too often put in the place of God. This leads to a rigorous and uncompromising party discipline—a discipline which tolerates no individuality of character or opinion, and has no patience with the scruples of a too tender conscience or of a too tardy and hesitating reason. Many men are urged to courses which both their judgment and feelings disapprove, because they have not courage to breast the torrent of the public sentiment of the party. If one should so far resist as to refuse himself to take an active part in that which he regards as wrong ; this sacrifice at least he is expected to make to the spirit of party, to content himself with a silent non-coöperation, and avoid all public expression of disapprobation. This would be to weaken the influence of the party—to detract so much from its power to control public sentiment ; and this must not by any means be permitted. Thus party spirit prevails over conscience, and the enlightened dare not resist the illiberal. Men acknowledge in general that it is their duty to bear an open testimony against all sin ; but in regard to the sins of their own party, they act as though a private testimony or even no testimony were sufficient. On what principle of christian morality is such conduct to be justified ? Whence does a man derive his authority to conceal or palliate the sins of his associates and declaim openly against those of his opponents only ?

"But our party is engaged in a good cause—its principles and its aims are right—and therefore its influence ought not to be broken." Admit that its principles and its aims are right—do its vices therefore become virtues, or does the end sanctify the means ? Does not any one see that such a position is a constant snare to one's conscience, a continued and powerful temptation to wrong doing?

Equally disastrous, in a moral point of view, is such a position in regard to one's opponents. A man from conscientious conviction resists the course of a party. He therefore stands in its way and breaks its power of controlling public sentiment. The party are willing to persuade him by argument, if they can, to fall into their ranks, or at least to stand out of their way and offer no obstacle to their progress. But if argument fails to persuade, still he is in their way, and must be put out of their way—and if his influence is exerted against them, that influence must be destroyed. Something must be found against him; and if nothing can be found, something must be made. The process usually is to trace some resemblance between something which he has thought or done, and something which has been thought or done by some odious party—to insist upon it that he belongs to that party—and then take the worst acts of the worst men of the party, and hold them up with their features all distorted as a fair representation of his character.

A man opposes the establishment of an abolition newspaper in a certain town, because he thinks it will do harm instead of good. A mob with different motives and widely differing means also opposes its establishment, and straightway the man is set down as an encourager of mobs, and is told that he is just as bad as the worst of the mob, for he and they think and feel just alike. Another declares his conviction that to hold and treat men as merchandize is a sin against God, and a violation of all the laws of humanity; and in certain circles he is immediately decried as a fanatic, an incendiary, an *abolitionist.* A man comes in possession of slave property which he does not immediately abandon—and it is not enough to call him a slaveholder—he is a thief, a man-stealer, a murderer, a cannibal; and it is all proven against him by a new and most exquisite system of logic.

Even if one be a bad man, it is grossly immoral to accuse him of things of which he is not guilty, in order to help forward the impression produced by his real guilt. We have no right to call the duellist a thief as well as a murderer, in order to increase the odium against him. We are in every way as strongly bound to strict, conscientious truth in our treatment of a bad man as of a good one. Lying never promotes truth, and *the wrath of man worketh not the righteousness of God.*

There is great injustice in classing a man with a party which he disclaims, because some of his opinions accord with a tenet or two of the party. It is also equally unjust to hold a good man responsible for the evil use which bad men may make of his right actions and opinions. Our Saviour set himself against the formal hypocrisy of the Pharisees. So did the Sadducees and the Herodians. Did our Saviour therefore belong to the Sadducean or Herodian party? or did he lend his influence to build up those licentious sects? In Jewish writings we find this very course of argument pursued to prove that Jesus was an impostor and a bad man; and the argument is worth as much in reference to him, as it is in reference to many others in regard to whom it is now used. It is by no means certain that a cause is right because bad men oppose it, or that good men who oppose it also, are lending their influence to help the bad. At the time of the reformation many bad men opposed popery, and from very bad motives too; and it was often objected to the Reformers that they were in league with all the lawless and the infidels of the time. Were the Reformers therefore in the wrong? and ought they to have abandoned their cause till all bad men had ceased to hate the papal tyranny?

A state of public feeling which tolerates such excesses cannot be healthful; and when such methods are called to the aid of religious enterprises, it shows a sad departure from the precepts and the example of the New Testament. In a nation where such is the character of the *godly*, what must the ungodly be!

It has been said by the philosophic traveller quoted above, that there is less freedom of opinion in America than in any of the European despotisms. His words are these:

"I am not acquainted with any country in which there is so little true independence of mind, and so little freedom of discussion, as in America. The authority of a king is purely physical; it controls the actions of the subject without subduing his private will; but the majority in America is invested with a power that is physical and moral at the same time; it acts upon the will as well as upon the actions of men."—

"In America the majority draws a formidable circle round the exercise of thought. Within its limits an author is at liberty to write what he pleases—but wo to him that dares to pass them! Not that he is threatened with an 'auto de fe,' but he is exposed to annoyances of every sort. His political career is forever closed if once he offends the only power which can open it to him. Every kind of compensation is refused him, even that of celebrity. Before he published his opinions he imagined he had partizans—but no sooner has he declared them openly than he is loudly censured by his opponents, while those who think with him, without having equal courage to give expression to their thoughts, hold their peace and abandon him. He yields at length, oppressed by the daily efforts he has been making, and subsides into silence, as if he were tormented with remorse for having spoken the truth."*

5. The existence of negro slavery, and the conduct of our people in reference to it, is a sad blight on our social condition and prospects.

Slavery was first introduced into the American colonies against the will of the colonists generally, and in spite of their active resistance. When the revolution separated them from the parent country, it was universally acknowledged as an evil and a wrong, and there was a general understanding that it should be gradually extinguished. This was done in more than half the States, and was fast advancing in the rest, when a new generation inherited the possessions of their fathers. The making of money now became the ruling passion ; and the gains of slave-labor were esteemed of more importance than the inalienable rights of thousands of our fellow men. Political men also were too intent on their own advancement to obstruct their progress by listening to the cry of the oppressed ; and by degrees the whole nation was becoming tolerant towards slavery—*and behold the tears of the oppressed, and they had no comforter ; and on the side of their oppressors there was power, and they had no comforter.*

At length the efforts of the Colonization Society began to awaken the sympathies of the nation in behalf of the slave ; and now a man loudly proclaims himself the advocate of the oppressed and by a singular concurrence of influences, becomes very conspicuous. But what is his character, and what qualifications does he bring to the work ? Smarting under injury, and swollen with a spirit of self-adulation that seems almost like insanity, and incapable of appreciating the proprieties and decencies of civil society, he exhausts the stores of the English language for a vocabulary of abuse to reform the nation with. Others who engage in the same work become infected with something of the

---

* Democracy in America, Vol. II. p. 160, 161.

same spirit ; and one of the best of causes is rendered intolerably odious by the abusiveness, and self-complacency, and disregard of the established order of society, manifested by some of its more prominent advocates. Their abuse is returned with equal violence, (for it is always true *that they who take the sword must perish by the sword ;*) men become enraged by false accusations and unmerited insults—moral violence gives occasion to physical—and Lynch-courts and mob champions come in to defend that which is utterly indefensible.

As the result of the contest we have now the mortifying spectacle of men professing to be saints, the disciples of Jesus Christ, on the one hand excusing and palliating and even defending American slavery, and on the other attacking it with a spirit and language more appropriate to a brawler in the streets than to a defender of great moral principles and an advocate of human rights. It is all wrong, and shows a state of public conscience that must be anything but pleasing to a God of purity and love.

I would not pass indiscriminate censure. Many abolitionists are men of great purity of motive, temperate in their language, calm, and disinterested as well as indefatigable in the pursuit of their object, and every way worthy the entire respect of all good men ; and the same is true of many of the opponents of their measures. I only speak of the general aspect of the controversy as it has appeared to me. I am happy to believe that a better spirit on both sides is now fast gaining the preponderance ; and that ere long all good men will unite to *do justly and love mercy*, and *to walk humbly*, in respect to this exciting subject.

Finally, Our government has not guarded with sufficient care the sacred honor of the nation, in the fulfilment of its treaties, particularly in respect to the aborigines of the country.

The violation of public faith is properly regarded as the last step in national degeneracy. Governments notoriously profligate in their morals generally, guard this point with peculiar care, because they know that if the honor of the nation cannot be trusted, there is an end of all confidence, and other nations can deal with them only as they deal with pirates and outlaws. But the most solemn treaties have been violated by the United States. The poor Indians have been torn from lands guarantied to them by treaty after treaty, and allured or driven to a distant wilderness, under a promise that if they would go there, they should be no more molested. But what are such promises worth ? Scarcely has the Indian had time to construct his wigwam in the desert of his exile, before the State government is clamoring for his removal, and the general government has the same right and may have the same inducement to violate the public faith for Arkansas, that it had to do so for Georgia.

I mention the evils here specified, not as universal, for happily there are numerous exceptions to all of them, and many ameliorating features of each, (and indeed except the Lord of hosts had left unto us a very small remnant, we should already have been as Sodom, we should have been like unto Gomorrah ;) but I allude to most of these evils as being very general, and to a considerable extent characteristic of our social condition. Now when we compare such a moral atmosphere as this with the opportunities which God has given us for the highest advancement in all that is good, who but must feel the applicability to us of the affecting passage in holy writ : *What could have been done more to my vineyard that I have not done in it ? wherefore when I looked that it should bring forth grapes, brought it forth wild grapes ?* And it is not the mere existence of these evils, nor even their general existence that is so alarming—but the alarming fact is the very great apathy, the want of conscience, the want of shame which the whole nation exhibit under them.

III. What then must be done in the present crisis ? How can our condition be bettered ?

1. Men of principle and piety must interest themselves in the political affairs of the country.

If God has given to a religious man political influence, he is just as much responsible for it as he is for wealth or talent or any other gift. If he has given us the privilege of choosing our own rulers, it is our duty to see that our public offices are filled with capable and honest men. If we neglect our duty, and in consequence of our neglect bad men bear rule, we are responsible for the mischief done ; and if we suffer through misgovernment, we do but suffer the natural effect of our own sins. Why has God permitted such a form of government to be established, and established too in the first instance by religious men, if not for the very purpose of giving men of principle an entire and unobstructed field for the exertion of their influence ? And why should they refuse to exert an influence,—why withdraw entirely from this wide open field, as if a republican government were the devil's own legitimate possession with which no worshipper of God had any right to interfere ? How seldom do we hear even a prayer for our rulers, though the Bible expressly enjoins it on ministers of the gospel always to pray for *all that are in authority!* (1 Tim. 2: 2). In monarchical governments it is not so. In England you can enter neither church nor dissenting chapel without hearing the sovereign prayed for by name, and the same is true on the continent generally ; but in this country alone, in the only country where the people can exert a direct influence on their rulers—the apostolic injunction is almost totally neglected! It is a sin against God, and treason to our country, and treachery to the great interest of free institutions throughout the world, thus to disregard the rulers of our own choice, and who are directly responsible to ourselves. Already have we felt the rod of Heaven's indignation for our culpable neglect, and unless we repent we shall feel it more and more. Providence has showered down his bounties on us with an unsparing hand, but in spite of this bounty we have contrived to bring ourselves to the extremity of pecuniary distress and the very verge of universal bankruptcy. No calamities are so intolerable as those which God permits an infatuated people to inflict on themselves, as the whole Jewish history witnesses.

2. All men of influence must unite to help forward the cause of universal education.

Here is our only hope. If the Democracy is to rule, as it surely must in this country, then the democracy must be enlightened and well principled, or it will speedily run into reckless anarchy, and end in military despotism, as it did in France. To effect this purpose in such a country as ours, so extensive, so free, so rapidly filling up from its native population, swarming with emigrants from the old world, and withal so excitable, adventurous and headstrong, all men of influence must unite. Much is already done, but by how few is it done, in comparison with the whole number who ought to be at work! and how little is accomplished in comparison with the actual wants of the country! If all would work, the whole might be done ; but while scarcely one in ten does anything, none are safe. Who will excuse himself from taking a part in this work ? The man who does so, does it at his own peril. If such an one were on the wide ocean in a leaking ship, would he refuse to work at the pump, because he was a passenger forsooth, and not a sailor ?

3. The whole nation must repent and forsake its wrong doings.

In the wrong doings of this nation, all the citizens either by actual participation or passive acquiescence, have been more or less implicated, and every one has work for repentance. Repentance secures the favoring smile of heaven, reformation, the necessary result of true repentance, removes our evils and our dangers. If each one will reform one, the whole work will be completed ; but while each waits for another, nothing is done. Every citizen is bound to feel a share of responsibility in what is done by the mass, and no man who enjoys the privileges of this country can withdraw himself from an interest in its public affairs, and be innocent or safe. In answering the question, *Who must repent and forsake wrong doing*? let every citizen of the United States be told, THOU ART THE MAN.

CONCLUSION.[*]

I have thus endeavored, honestly though feebly, to give expression to my views respecting the destinies of our country, our defects, and the duties of her citizens at the present crisis. Never have I had such glowing and burning impressions of the immense importance in the world's history of the position which we hold, of our capabilities for working out the most glorious results that human eyes have ever witnessed, such irrepressible desires to exert every power which God has given me, to help forward this great work—as while abroad examining the institutions of the old world[†] and comparing them with our own. Our national character is now in its forming state, and our destiny, the temporal and eternal destiny of millions yet unborn, the emancipation of a world, the decision of the great question of coercion or self-government, of physical force, or moral power, for ages yet to come, depends on its being formed aright.

And it is here at the West, especially, that this character must

---

[*] The substance of this Article was originally written as an address to the students in the Colleges of Marietta and Hudson, Ohio. The concluding part, with but little alteration, is retained as an appeal to the young men of the whole country.

[†] [Our readers are aware that Professor Stowe was commissioned by the Legislature of Ohio to examine the various systems of education adopted in Europe, and to collect such information as he might deem useful to the State in regard to this general subject. He did so, and made an able and interesting report to the Legislature in Dec. 1837, which we have noticed. See Repos. Vol. XI. p. 517. April, 1838.—ED.]

be formed; it is here that that which is appropriately and distinctively American is most rapidly developing itself — our society and institutions are now peculiarly democratic and less affected by influences of the old world than those in the States peopled before our political severance from Europe — and here there is more a feeling of citizenship, more of jealous pride in being American, more of the distinctive features of nationality, than in any other part of the Union.　On us then, more particularly, on the young men of the Western Colleges, and others who shall emigrate hither, does this responsibility rest.　You, young men, who have the flower and the prime and the strength of life before you, and have this central, teeming, glowing West for the scene of your labors, you, I say, hold in your hands the destinies of a world for ages yet to come, of a world beyond comparison greater than past ages have ever witnessed, and destined to a glory or a wretchedness, which will throw all past history in the shade, according as you lay the forming hand on the fused and gushing tide of human nature which is billowing around you.　Men to whom such responsibilities are entrusted, should be men of thoughtful, upright, thoroughly furnished minds, men at the farthest possible remove from rashness, selfishness, and superficial views—they should have the steadiness, the religiousness, the far-reaching forecast of the pilgrim fathers of New England, united with the buoyancy, the enterprise, the sprightly, adventurous fearlessness of the pioneers of the West.

Religion and the laws—God and your country—let these be the rule of your conduct, the object of your labors—hold on upon the great principles of eternal right—never consent that they be set aside for a moment for the sake of more speedily accomplishing any object, however immediately desirable, a fault too prevalent among our impatient and impetuous countrymen—let all party rivalries, and mean jealousies, and local prejudices which prevent united effort, be repelled as utterly unworthy of men in your position—labor with all your might and disinterestedly with this grand object in view, *the entire accomplishment of the providential destinies of this new world in the West*—and by the blessing of God this glorious work will be completed, and the object secured before you die.

But should you neglect your great duty, and live, as many have done before you, only for mean and selfish ends—still the ends of providence will not be frustrated—God's word will not return to him void.　The great development of man will be wrought out here at last—but it must be far in the distant ages of futurity, and only through long years of agony and oceans of blood—and you, taking no part in the conflict, can share in none of the glories of the triumph.

ARTICLE IX.

THE MORALS OF SOCRATES.[*]

Translated from Schweighauser's Opuscula Academica, by F. M. Hubbard, Teacher of a Classical School, Boston.

In the following inquiry into the moral principles which governed the life of Socrates, we have thought it best to examine first, the evidences which are left to us of his piety towards God ; secondly, of his singular earnestness in promoting the happiness of men, which in him was united with a generous disregard of his own personal advantage ; and lastly, of his fortitude and constancy of mind.

CHAPTER I.

THE REVERENCE EVER MANIFESTED BY SOCRATES TOWARDS GOD.

§ 1. *Is shown the Piety of Socrates.*

Whoever would form a just estimate of the piety of Socrates, ought most carefully to study and most thoroughly to apprehend the religious opinions and moral sentiments of the age in which he lived ; lest, while he would judge the character of an Athenian citizen, he may incautiously carry back his own opinions and feelings to those times, and measure by a wrong standard. Only a strict adherence to this rule can lead us to a fair and true judgment. Though in the minds of the Greeks, as of other ancient nations, the notion of many deities was deeply seated and inveterate, and though, with them, an acceptable worship and their whole religion consisted of only an outward observance

[*] [For an account of the Theology of Socrates, by the same author, see Bibl. Repos. First Series, Vol. XII. p. 47.—ED.]

of prescribed forms ; we are by no means to imagine that the mind of Socrates also was subject to these erroneous and diseased opinions. For while he in a spirit of true obedience honored the institutions of his country,[*] and mingled with his fellow citizens in the observance of those rites which his country had appointed, we can have no doubt, if we consider his habits of thought and the method of his life, that, his own convictions were far removed from the then universal belief. As in a whole people the character of their religious notions must give a form, to the outward service, and the reason and spirit of those notions, must be the actuating spirit of that service ; so in an individual, the style and spirit of his inward worship must be derived from his idea of God, and must vary with the distinctness and truth of that idea. Now when we learn that Socrates formed to himself an apprehension of the Deity which surpassed in pureness and grandeur those of all philosophers who had gone before him, viz., that God is mind separate from all matter, the creator of the universe, almighty, good, wise, forecasting, everywhere present, knowing all things, invisible, one and single in the peculiarity of his own being ;[†] we must believe that ideas of God so true and exalted could not coëxist with only that narrow system of worship which is satisfied with a mere sensuous expression of reverence and devotion, with offerings which the hands can handle, and the eyes look on and measure. Nay, if we regard Socrates in his very prayers and sacrifices,[‡] there is sufficient and abundant reason to believe, that he held firmly the conviction, that under whatever form he is worshipped, God looks not so much at the outward, the manner, as at the inward state and habit of the soul. In what he conceived the most worthy worship of the Supreme Being to consist, can be gathered from what has been said, and likewise and perhaps more surely from the whole plan of his life. For he judged not, that our whole duty to God is comprised in those rites, to the performance of which human laws bind every member of the State, but that undoubtedly the entire course and method of our life ought to breathe only reverence and adoration of the Most High.[§] And so he judged that every purpose of our soul, every act of our life, should be grounded on some

---

[*] Xen. Mem. Socr. I. 3. 1. IV. 3. 16. (cf. Cic. de Leg. II. 16.)

[†] See Bibl. Repos. Vol. XII. p. 66.   [‡] Mem. Socr. I. 3, 2. 3.

[§] Mem. Socr. I. 1, 18. 19. 20. I. 3, 4.

intimation of the will of God ; that wrong should be avoided as odious to the divine nature, that the beautiful, the good, the honorable and true are to be sought after and followed as harmonizing with the divine nature ; and in fine, that men, who may, if they will, perfect step by step their own nature, ought in all their actions to imitate God, who has manifestly impressed on all his works through the whole universe of created things, tokens of a plan devised and directed to the common advantage of all sentient natures, and has willed that nothing should exist purposeless and useless in this theatre, as it were, of his perfections.* Led by a like desire of the common advantage of all, Socrates would fain express his own piety, not only in the blamelessness of a life free from every stain of vice, but, aiming at a diviner attainment, by freely pouring forth whatever of truth and virtue he had for the benefit of every man.† Nowhere, not amid the snares of envy and calumnies, do we see him swerving from that scheme of life and those principles, which he held. Full of faith in Him, whose cause he always cherished, he chose rather to die. This is it, which most strongly attests the eminent devoutness of Socrates, and which betokens the unvarying inclination of his will to that which seemed pleasing and acceptable to God. Himself affirmed, with cheerful countenance, when his death was near, that it was the will of God that he now should die.‡ One can hardly question, with these evidences before him, that resignation to the divine will, was a permanent feature in the character of Socrates, and one which gave a color and strength to the rest.

§ 2. *An answer to those who censure Socrates, for his observance of the religious institutions of his country.*

Yet there are those who charge Socrates with superstition or a base hypocrisy, because, following in all things the traditional and appointed service of the gods, he offered incense on the altars of Neptune, of Jupiter, of Vulcan, and that he used auspices and other rites pertaining to divination, and advised his friends to do the same.§ But such should consider, that our philosopher, if he had dared to supersede, and suddenly to withdraw

---

* Mem. Socr. IV. 3, 17.
† Mem. Socr. I. 6, 14. IV. 4, 1. add chap. II. infra.
‡ Mem. Socr. IV. 8, 5.   § Mem. Socr. I. 1, 2. 9.

his countrymen from those usages, which they had been taught
to regard with reverence from their infancy, would soon have
incurred universal hatred, and surely would have fallen under
the suspicion of atheism ; and thus', having made shipwreck of
all good reputation among his fellow citizens, if even he escaped the loss of life or years of exile, all the fruit and advantage
of his doctrine would have perished.   But I do not see that he
is worthy of a severe censure, who, that he may gain the name
of an upright and obedient citizen, follows in anything the ordinances of his country, provided it be not repugnant to propriety
and honor, and involve no tendency to a corruption of morals.
So when we behold Socrates not hastily and untimely rejecting
those rites which belonged to the religion of his country, so far
is he from deserving censure on that account, that rather we
should approve the calmness and moderation of his temper, under the control of which like a worthy subject he observed himself the appointments of the State, and exhorted others to do
the same.   Not less here ought we to commend the rare prudence which this same purpose displayed, and by which he most
clearly saw that the feelings of men are to be cultivated and
their opinions rectified, and themselves brought to a perception
of the folly of mistaken religious usages, not so much by the
importance given to external ceremonies, as by promulgating
more adequate apprehensions of the divine mind.   By the invitation therefore of his own example he called men to the observance of the established customs of devotion and worship ;
yet more earnestly did he labor to impart to his fellow citizens
a better and more salutary knowledge of God, by the natural
efficacy of which they would gradually and of themselves come
to understand what was superstitious and vain in the popular religion.*

---

* Some have been disposed to charge Socrates with superstition, because, as Plato near the end of his Phaedo relates, he is reported to have
said with almost his last breath, that " he owed a cock to Æsculapius."   Which no one will suppose him to have uttered in earnest,
who regards his well known habit of irony, but will rather agree
with many, both ancients and moderns, that in this saying we are to
understand Socrates, who had often said that the soul so long as it is
in the body is in a state of disease, to have meant by Æsculapius,
health, and to have intimated by this form of expression, that he had
now recovered from this long disease.

CHAPTER II.

THE REMARKABLE ZEAL OF SOCRATES IN PROMOTING THE HAPPINESS OF MEN.

§ 3. *Hence is explained his strong disposition to a free inter-course with men, and his peculiar method of moral instruction.*

We now proceed more closely to inquire into, what we have as yet only touched upon, the ardor with which Socrates labored to advance the happiness of men, and more fully to unfold the power which he has exerted on the course of human life. So great do we conceive to have been the ardor of that desire, that postponing all considerations of personal advantage, he aimed only at this, applied to this all the energies of his great genius, and directed the plan and action of his whole life to this one purpose of rendering his fellow men wiser, better, happier, in matters of the highest moment to them, and of disseminating the principles of true safety and the most stable and honorable happiness for the behoof not more of those among whom he lived, than of all future ages.* This noble impulse of his spirit, seems to me the more worthy of all reverence, when I consider it as the source of all the illustrious actions which he performed and of that busy life of practical goodness which he led. Hence came his perpetual custom of free intercourse and conversation with all men, to which he was so much inclined, that his whole life was public, open and in the sight of all men, and in hearty fellowship with all. In the morning he was wont to visit the public walks,† the gymnasia, the forum, and so in the rest of the day he used to fre-

---

* Mem. Socr. I. 2, 60. 61. I. 3, 1. I. 6, 14. 15. III. 10. IV. 1, 1. And on every occasion Xenophon intimates that in all things and in every manner, he rendered himself useful to his fellow citizens and friends, and this in reference to their true advantage, so that nothing could be more profitable to any than an intimacy with Socrates, since not less in his sportive than his serious conversation he studied the best good of those with whom he associated.

† Unless indeed what Xenophon here calls περιπάτους are to be understood rather public schools, and the assemblies of studious men, than public walks, respecting which meaning of the word, I have given an opinion in the notes to Cebetis Tabula, cap. 13. p. 307 seq. (Lipsiae 1798), and in Animadv. ad Athenaei Lib. III. p. 103. d.

quent those places where he would meet the most numerous assemblages of men.* He thought it by no means necessary for a public teacher to hide himself in the seclusion of a school, which shaded life, the moral philosophers who succeeded him affected ; but, that of all men, he who would devote all his powers to reforming and purifying the moral habits of his fellows, should pass his life in the utmost publicity, and in open intercourse with all orders in the State. Wherefore he would not invite his disciples to his own house, or open a public school at an appointed place and at fixed hours ; but chose himself to go out to meet men, to enter their shops and working places, to be present at public meetings and places of general resort, and find his pupils engaged in the active business of their life. In this plan, among many other conveniencies he found especially these ; that those who committed themselves to his instruction, were stimulated to the imitation of their teacher's example thus rendered conspicuous and open to the observation of all ; but chiefly under it men were not forced to learn his peculiar doctrine wrapped up in the forms of a system, but in the living act, were they instructed the method of a right judgment on whatever subject at the moment occupied them ; if in anything they had erred, they were led to a wiser course for the future ; if they had been guilty of any delinquency, they might be admonished ; was there need of action, they might have an adviser to action the most honorable and strenuous ; were they in perplexity and doubt, they might avail themselves of the prudent guidance, not of an arrogant master, but of an intelligent friend, who would kindly and courteously adapt himself to the understanding of every questioner, and suit his advice to every variety of circumstance. This scheme of instruction in morals, which found its appropriate place amid the bustling life and the busiest activity of men, Socrates, the father of that philosophy which has been rightly named the *philosophy of human life,* eminently perceived to be the most excellent and the most efficacious. Another advantage, by no means to be passed unmentioned, in his plan, was this ; that while he sought by all means to profit all, he also found means to know, and select from the youth who flocked to hear him, and become more intimate with those, from the training of whom to virtue, wisdom, and judicious counsels, the commonwealth might derive the greatest advantage.

---

* Mem. Socr. I. 1, 10.

§ 4. *Hence his disregard of all sciences that are rather difficult than useful.*

To the same noble desire of human happiness do I ascribe it, that both he himself made no account of the labor which the philosophers of his age were accustomed to waste in discussing questions respecting the origin of the universe, the causes which produce and determine all things and everything, and other kindred topics, and constantly dissuaded others from inquiries at once difficult and trivial.* Indeed our truly named philosopher, who was ever animated with a divine zeal to examine those subjects only which might bring some advantage to the life of men, to the utter neglect of all others, as he at once perceived how little true utility could arise from such a style of investigation, as then prevailed, and of such subjects, and how barren and unsuited to the actual condition and wants of humanity; turned away from them all his thoughts and efforts, and was the adviser of every man, that he should not wear away his life in the vain pursuit of sciences beyond the reach of the human intellect, and which, if thoroughly understood even, could have no relation to the melioration of our life.† From this statement it ought not to be inferred, as some have falsely done, that Socrates was a despiser altogether of those sciences whose object is the study of nature and her laws, to which sciences he was by no means a stranger.‡ He wished this only, which every wise philosopher must wish, that men should not entangle themselves in vain subtleties, and fruitless and useless investigations; but, so far as each of those sciences, for which the sophists in those days made great pretensions, contained anything which might become a source of knowledge profitable for daily life, so far they should study it, and so much they should gather from it. Nor was he satisfied with giving such directions to his disciples, summarily and in general terms; but he was accustomed often and with much care to take up the various kinds of science one by one, and instruct them what was the limit and measure of each, and of what use each might be to the right ordering of domestic or civil affairs, and on the contrary what classes of sciences were so removed from practical

---

* Mem. Socr. I. 1, 11. 12. 15.

† IV. 7, 6. 7. cf. Diog. Laert. in Vita Socratis, Lib. II. § 21.

‡ Mem. Socr. IV. 7, 5.

utility, that it were an abuse of leisure to pursue them, and by such exercises he trained them to a just judgment, and a skilful selection.* If there were any subjects of which he had too little knowledge to be a teacher of them, and which he yet perceived to be practically useful, he recommended to his friends those teachers whom he knew to be well skilled in them; totally unlike in this those falsely styled philosophers, who, while they regarded more their own gain and reputation, than the profit of their disciples, professed to know and teach all things.

§ 5. *Hence his perpetual commendation of inquiries which have relation to the duties of life.*

Accordingly, when Socrates perceived that other sciences and arts have in themselves alone no power sufficient to render human life better and happier, he devoted his whole study to that science which contains the grounds of true acting and of duty, and the institutions of the whole life of man, and by consequence the principles and means of human perfection and of human happiness. Hence his high estimate of those studies which involve a practical benefit and use, which he judged most appropriate for man and of the greatest concern to him. Hence his continual questionings of what is right, what wrong; what just, what unjust; what honorable, what base; what harmonizes with wisdom and prudence, and what is contrary to them; the definitions and estimates of which he had ever on his lips.† Of his habit in this particular, the words of Cicero may justly be reckoned a description, when Socrates is said, "first to have called down philosophy from the heavens," (that is from the study of celestial things, for an accurate knowledge of which he conceived them to have no sufficient means,) "to have given her a dwelling in our cities, to have even introduced her to our homes, and to have forced her to inquiries concerning life and manners, and things good and evil." How liberal was his notion of general utility, Socrates showed in this, that he did not stop with commending a regard to single virtues only, such as temperance, frugality, benevolence, and the like duties, but embraced also in his teachings, every department of domestic and civil life, and the whole range of duties to the com-

---

* IV. 7, the whole.

† Mem. Socr. I. 1, 16. IV. 2, 22. 23. IV. 4, 6. IV. 6. 1. cf. Cic. Tusc. Quaest. I. 4.

monwealth : and while he used no arts to obtain, by favor of his fellow citizens, his own advancement to places of trust and honor in the State, he yet exhorted others, whom he thought competent, to seek a part in the management of public affairs, and either aided them to a wise and successful administration, by most salutary counsels, in their preparation, or, by his suggestions, guided them in the pressure of official perplexities and cares, and, in fine, whatever might be the position of any one in the State, he would clearly set forth to him the duties which belonged to that position.*

§ 6. *His generous disregard of personal advantage.*

With this wonderful zeal for promoting the universal happiness of men, Socrates joined a noble contempt of his own private emolument, which led him constantly to decline and refuse all those rewards and gains, which from the value of his instructions, might have made him rich.† No one will deny that a man may be a sincere lover of truth, and yet act rightly and suitably to that character, if he derives a profit and reward to himself from that doctrine which he communicates to others. For how is the cause of truth injured, if the tokens of gratitude from their disciples are received by those who teach it ? But when Socrates observed that the Sophists, with whom Athens at that time abounded, never contented with the tribute of an honorable regard, which their instructions might have won for them, and contending only for an immoderate gain, sold and prostituted for the vilest consideration, their boasted wisdom ;‡ animated by an ingenuous and most righteous indignation, he determined to pursue an opposite course, lest men should confound his most noble scheme of discipline with their trivial though specious shows, and his loftiest reward, in the forming and culture of the minds of men, should be lost and perish. And so declaring that to him it was a wonder that any man, professing to be a teacher of virtue, should claim a price for his labor, he set to himself this law,§ that to any one who truly desired to attain the knowledge and practice of virtue, with no regard to his condition, and with no exception, whether he were a citi-

---

* Mem. Socr. III. 1, 3. 5. 6. sc.
† Mem. Socr. I. 6, 5. cf. Diog. Laert. II. 24. 27.
‡ I. 2, 6 and 6. 5 and 13.   § I. 2, 7.

zen or foreigner, rich or in the deepest poverty, he would impart, without fee or reward, whatever he might have of useful
knowledge and salutary counsel ;* accounting himself to have
an ample reward, if he should make those who came to him for
instruction wiser and better, and truer friends to himself and to
all good men.†

CHAPTER III.

THE FORTITUDE AND CONSTANCY OF SOCRATES.

§ 7. *The strong-mindedness of Socrates shown in his contempt of effeminate pleasures.*

No one who has studied the principles and course of the life of
Socrates, can have failed to perceive everywhere in his character the brightness of that steadfast mind and constancy, which,
in all the changes of mortal life, proclaims the great man.   Of
this strong and constant mind we have proof in the vehement
disdain of effeminacy, which everywhere and in all circumstances appears in him.‡   The spirit of effeminate indulgence had,
in his day, breathed over Athens as from a pestilential comet ;
the manliness of all in body and mind had been broken and destroyed ; the empire of depraved desire was uncontrolled.   Socrates, who had learned to employ the supremacy of the mind,
and the ministerial service of the body, was aloof from the con-
tagion ; but foreseeing the peril which sprung from it, he sought
to meet the evil insidiously stealing among the people, and stifle
as it were the envenomed plant in its earliest growth.   How
can a man, who has the consciousness of his humanity, and is
swayed by a love of ingenuous freedom, submit his neck to the
yoke of lusts ?   Will he, who has, to keep his freedom, spurned
the allurements of gain, throw away that freedom for the service
of enticing pleasures ?   What else does voluptuousness (*molli-
ties*) propose to itself, but to furnish those conveniences and delights, which indulge the body and wear away the vigor of the
soul ?   The freedom then of that man is an empty name, over
whom passion and lust have obtained dominion.   With so anx-

---

* Mem. Socr. I. 2, 60.   † I. 6, 9. and 14. I. 2, 8. and 61.
‡ Mem. Socr. I. 2, 1—3. cf. Sympos. Xenoph. A. ed. Leunclav
p. 691.

ious care did Socrates, under a persuasion of their essential baseness and dishonor, avoid every vice by which the energy of the
body may be impaired, that he may be set forth a fit exemplar,
not to his own age only, but to the whole human race.   As
touching frugality in respect of dress and personal convenience,
and temperance in food and drink, which he declared to be the
basis of all other virtues,* no one more highly regarded it, or
more faithfully practised it than Socrates. " So frugal was he,"
says Xenophon, " that I know not if there be any one who
might not by easy labor provide for himself that portion, which
he thought necessary for him.   For whether he remained at
home, or accepted an invitation to sup with a friend, he made
it his uniform practice, which likewise he commended to others,
never to eat unless he was hungry, or drink unless thirsty.†
This too he affirmed to be the most excellent remedy for a
qualmishness and loathing of food, to limit the amount of our
food by the demands of the natural appetite.‡ Not less in other
matters in which an effeminate habit inclines most men to yield,
did Socrates study and exemplify a strict temperance,§ as we
may infer from the reasons which induced him to cultivate frugality and other virtues.   For he deemed it an evidence of a
weak mind, to allow oneself to be overcome by lust, or sleep,
or impatience of labor, and other such things.   But temperance
follows that method which, while it supplies the necessary
means of sustaining life, and things needful for the body, leaves
the mind master of itself, and refuses that superfluity which
may minister to depraved desires.   Hence Socrates used to say,‖
that " those who are given to excess are in a most wretched
slavery, are forced away from the pursuit of wisdom, often are
reduced to the necessity of embracing an evil for a good, and
can never know the true pleasure which may be derived from
food and drink, from love and sleep, from the knowledge of
good and evil, and from the pursuit of things that are necessary
to an upright and honorable life ; that they are alien from all vir-

---

*Αρητῆς χρηπίδα, Mem. Socr. I. 5, 4.

† Mem. Socr. I. 3, 5. 6. cf. Diog. II. 25. Xen. Cyrop. I. 3. 10. where
he introduces Cyrus discoursing of his father : διψῶν παύσται.

‡ Mem. Socr. III. 13, 2.

§ Mem. Socr. II. cc. and Diog. II. 25. cf. Gell. N. A. II. 1. Ælian,
Var. Hist. XIII. 27.

‖ Mem. Socr. IV. 5, 2—12.

tue, and live after the manner of the brute beasts.   On the contrary, the temperate, as they follow after a real good and abstain from evil, day by day become better and happier, and are better fitted for all noble and honorable action." The truth and salutariness of this teaching, himself the most continent of all men, evermore proclaimed in his own example.*

§ 8. *Socrates, while he thought the body ought not to be pampered, thought also it is not to be despised, but made a higher account of the mind.*

But some may say, what remarkable thing is it to abstain from the pleasures of love, of wine, and the like multitude of depraved desires?   Does not every prudent man, and every one even who has a regard to his own health, shun everything which may harm him, and pursue that only which may profit his body and keep it in a sound state?   We cannot deny, that so high praise is not merited by a temperance which springs from a peculiar love and inordinate care for the body, and the object of which is to provide merely, in indolent ease and luxurious security, the conditions of personal convenience and advantage.   But so far from rightfully imputing such a temperance, (rather a voluptuous epicurism,) to Socrates, we find him austere and morose even in the culture of the body, and to some he might seem almost neglectful of it.   We have the express testimony of Xenophon,† as well as evidence from other sources, that he did not himself disregard a sound physical culture, nor approved such disregard in others.   In his conversation with the youthful Epigenes,‡ he earnestly recommends an honorable care of the body, such care, to wit, as should render it a suitable dwelling, or a strong instrument for the soul, and fit for every duty to it.   We infer the same when we read that Socrates loved and practised the art of dancing, and advised his friends to learn it, to make the limbs supple and firm.§   And we are pleased to read his adroit and witty replies to the Sophist Antipho, who unfairly censured the frugal fare and cheap raiment of Socrates.|| Still higher was the estimate which, he

---

* Mem. Socr. I. 2, 1.   † I. 2, 4.   ‡ III. 12.

§ Diog. Laert. II. 32.   Xen. in Sympos. p. 693.   Lucian, de Saltatione, cáp. 25.

¶ Mem. Socr. I. 6 5—7.   "Do you think my food vile," says he,

affirmed, a man ought to have of the culture of the mind, for the pleasures of the body indeed fill the sense with a present and exquisite delight, but a sedulous and ingenuous culture of the soul brings with it not only sublimer and nobler delights, and a more honorable enjoyment, but assures us of an eternal and imperishable satisfaction.*

§ 9. *An answer to those who have charged Socrates with an indulgence in impure pleasures.*

To me, therefore, meditating on the character of Socrates, nothing has seemed more lamentable than that many have falsely accused that man, who died a martyr to virtue, of intercourse with the vilest women, and even to have been addicted to the foul crime of pæderasty. As touching the former part of this charge, I notice that they who accuse Socrates of this crime, commonly adduce as evidence of it, the conversation he had with the courtesan Theodota, recorded in the Memorabilia of Xenophon.† 1 confess my ignorance how the charge could have been derived from that conversation. Nay, 1 am firmly persuaded that any one who shall come to the perusal of it, with no preconceptions of its purport, and give it a careful study, must perceive, from the whole plan and structure of the dialogue, that Socrates by no means intended seriously to instruct that woman in the arts of a harlot, but that his whole discourse was

---

" because you suppose me to eat food less healthful than yours, and imparting less strength ? Or because what I eat is more difficult to be procured than what you eat ? Or that your food is more to your taste than mine is to me ? Are you not aware that as one eats with a better appetite, he less needs nice condiments, and when he drinks with a stronger thirst, he feels less need of a draught that is difficult to be procured ? Now when men change their garments they do it on account of the heat or cold, and they wear sandals, that they may not be prevented from travelling, by things that might hurt their feet. And did you ever know me to stay at home on account of the cold, or quarrel with any one for a shady place on account of the heat, or not go where I wished on account of sore feet ? Do you not know that men of most infirm frame, have enabled themselves by exercise to excel those the most robust even, who have not exercised themselves in the same things ? And can you not suppose that I, by continual experience and practice, can bear anything more easily than you, who have had no practice ?"

* Mem. Socr. I. 6, 8. 9. III. 9, 1 seq.   † III. 11.

manifestly ironical; especially will this appear from the close of
the conversation, when disregarding all her requests and entreaties that he would visit her at her house, he promised to receive
her at his own, if he is not engaged with more valued friends.
If any are disposed to infer this charge from the fact that Socrates in company with his associates went to the house of a courtesan, let them remember that he lived in a city and an age, in
which it was the custom for the young men, when a beautiful
stranger arrived, to go and see her.   We ought, then, rather to
commend the watchful and provident care of Socrates, who
would not suffer his youthful friends, alone and unguarded to
approach one whose beauty and skill in deluding the unwary
had become notorious, and preferred to accompany to the place
of danger, those who could not be persuaded to stay away from
it—a place too where he might fill her with shame by his judicious reproof, and dissuade her companions from pernicious crimes,
and lead by wise instructions all who might be there, to a purer
and better way.

The crime of pæderasty, which with less reason even is
charged upon Socrates, any one who has found him guiltless of
the other, will readily concede to be unsustained and false.
But those who believe him guilty, call in Xenophon as a witness, and claim him as an express assertor of it.   What indeed?
That Xenophon who has declared in the most precise terms
that of all men Socrates was most continent in the pleasures of
love?[*]   Who affirms that he more easily abstained from the
most beautiful than others from the most deformed?[†]   Who on
every occasion introduces Socrates's most severely censuring
those who were in the habit of that crime, and with the most
earnest solicitude exhorting his intimates to shun with the utmost care, not only the act of crime, but everything that might
excite or furnish materials for lust?[‡]   These most weighty
charges are forsooth derived from another book of Xenophon,
which is entitled Convivium; in which book, among many other
things uttered wittily and in jest, yet not without grave and serious purpose, Charmides is introduced affirming sportively, that
he had seen Socrates, at the house of a certain schoolmaster,
while he was turning over the same volume with young Crito-
bulus, and reading something in it, applying his head to the
head, and his naked shoulder to the naked shoulder of Critobu-

---

* Mem. Socr. I. 2, 1.   † I. 3, 14.   ‡ I. 2, 29. I. 3, 8 seq.

lus.* Since this statement occurs in a passage in which that vile practice, then too common in Athens, was made the subject of conversation, it has seemed to some to have a meaning more serious than the natural import of the words, and that in the answer which he is said to have given to Charmides, we have the confession of Socrates himself, that he had been guilty of the foul deed.   But such persons, if they would read without prejudice the whole book in which the conversation occurs, might see that the plan and object of the whole discussion, which Xenophon has thus recorded, are discrepant and utterly at variance with the interpretation.   Nay, if they would consider only the reply of Socrates to the declaration of Charmides, or a very few words which immediately precede the passage, they would find enough to convince them how foreign from the truth is the charge which they have unadvisedly endeavored to sustain by this testimony.   Surely if elsewhere, most clearly in the whole discussion which forms the subject of this book, has Xenophon presented to us Socrates, in deep earnest, with an open profession of his purpose, and most studiously representing to his companions the unworthiness and meanness of the crime of which they were discoursing, and dissuasively warning them of the first spark of lust, that he might invite them to the enjoyment of pleasures nobler and worthier of men, and pleasures too which yet are to be derived from an intimacy with men and even young men ; to wit, from the chaste union and intermarriage of souls, from the delights of friendship, than which nothing can be more grateful to an ingenuous spirit, and from the forming, encouraging, and exciting youth, on whom nature has freely bestowed her gifts, to every honorable and glorious action, thus binding these youthful disciples, by the perpetual bond of a thankful remembrance, to all the offices of gratitude, and securing to themselves a return of kindness from all good men and from the commonwealth.   These golden precepts and warnings, this wise man, conspicuous not less for prudence and courtesy of manners, than for integrity and chastity, proposed to his hearers, with no stern countenance, or sad and supercilious moroseness, which Socrates never put on, and which would have been most unfitting the time and place of this discourse ; and he most plainly saw, withal, that men may be offended by such a course, and alienated from true virtue with a certain disgust and dread, but are

---

* Xenoph. Conv. p. 698. ed. Leunclav.

not used thus to be reclaimed from their vices and recalled to the love and practice of it.   And as in his other conversations we have found, as Cicero says,* " Socrates to have been pleasant and witty, of mirthful speech, and in his whole discourse a feigner, of that class which the Greeks term ironical," so especially do we apprehend this convivial discourse, that it might gain a readier hearing from his fellow banqueters, to be sprinkled over with well meant hilarity, and exquisite irony.†

§ 10. *The strength of character of Socrates is displayed in the wonderful constancy, with which, overcoming the greatest obstacles, he pursued the plan he had adopted, both of life and doctrine.*

This careful avoidance of voluptuous indulgences, which we have shown to have been so conspicuous in Socrates, proves beyond question or doubt his eminent strength and greatness of mind. Yet, we think his possession of this energy and greatness more amply displayed in his steadfast adherence through the whole course of his life, to his peculiar scheme of doctrine and of life. We are all of us inclined to select good and generous plans of action, but when the hour of their execution comes, if any serious hindrance stands in our way, our energy becomes weakened by indecision and our activity rendered useless by reluctance.   Nothing seems to us more easy than the consummation of the scheme we have chosen, and the more splendid we persuade ourselves are more easy ; we are deceived by their specious and plausible magnificence ; we impose upon ourselves by a false anticipation of the renown which their achievement will bestow ; our eyes are dazzled by their splendor ; we behold them already accomplished, and hear already the voices of men celebrating our praises ; when from this ecstasy of vision and of hope, we betake ourselves to the laborious working out of our plans, we are suddenly overwhelmed with impediments, our mind is vexed, our resoluteness begins to waver, we omit, neglect, lay aside what we had conceived with such cheerful ease, and entered on with so glad promise, and abandon forever and forget our purpose. How

---

* De Officiis, I. 30.

† We may refer, among other instances occurring in the same conversation, especially to the boast of Socrates, p. 695, " that he had great confidence in the skill of a pander, which art," he says, " if he were willing to exercise it, would bring him much money."

alien and remote from those who are destined to do great deeds, the inconstant, and faltering will should be, the nature of the thing itself declares to us. For will any one call that glorious, which can be attained in the ordinary sluggishness of human action, without severe toil and intense activity of all our energies? Nay, but that we justly deem most glorious, which we have brought to a happy issue, having overcome great difficulties, resisted the mightiest force of trouble and of obstacles, and despised the insinuated claims of great advantage. But that a great scheme may be well carried, and brought to a successful accomplishment, what steadfastness and strength of mind are needed! This very steadfastness and strength, this stable and changeless perseverance gave its dignity and priceless worth to the character of Socrates. From the moment in which he had persuaded himself that the highest happiness of men lay in the knowledge and practice of virtue, he yielded up his noble powers to the sublime and inspiring purpose of diffusing among his fellow men that virtue and that happiness, with an effort never to be suspended, and a laborious devotion that should know no weariness. That the reader may now readily perceive how great was the constancy of Socrates we will show in a brief sketch, how many and how great were the obstacles he encountered by reason of the times in which he lived.

The doctrine which Socrates proclaimed to the dwellers in Athens was new, and a strange one to every ear. Not even the Philosophers, before him, though they had been used to dispute among themselves about a universe of subjects far above the reach of human intellect, had ever directed their investigations to the condition of man and the wants of his nature, and as the result of such an investigation, taught as they should have done, what man should aim at, and what shun, and by what means he might become the sure partaker of a sure blessedness. Socrates therefore was the first who unfolded in the assemblies and daily intercourse of men this divine philosophy, the purpose of which is the regulation of morals, and so the inward perfection of the soul. Superstition ingrafted into their minds in the freshness and tenderness of infancy strengthened and confirmed by the evil arts of the sophists, and invested by the authority of ages, with a certain august and reverend majesty, had struck deep its roots among the people; and when we remember how tenaciously those opinions are defended, which we have as it were drawn in with our mother's milk, and have been accustomed to cherish and sustain in mature years, we can conceive how hardly this unheard of doctrine of Socrates might gain a welcome among the inhabitants of Athens. A notable perverseness of opinion respecting all that pertained to the worship of the gods was to be rooted from their minds, before the good seed which he would sow there could blossom and bring its fruits to ripeness; and the experience of all ages shows how slowly and with what resistance, this sublime philosophy of reformation finds access to the minds of men through the thick darkness of superstitious opinions.

Another kind of obstacle was found in the universal levity and corruption of morals of the age. In the licentious mode of living which then prevailed, if a teacher of morals, wise, ingenious and sagacious, should dare to insist on a purer way, what expectation could he entertain, that himself should derive any profit from his instructions? Whom more would abandoned and voluptuous men, given to every lust, shrink from and dread, than him who directed them to put a restraint upon their passions, and exhorted them to make wisdom their counsellor and return to a healthful course and sounder principle of life? Socrates therefore could not expect from such men, who like brute beasts were prone to every lust, rather than disposed to follow the precepts of a well regulated life, that they would readily listen to his severer discipline. Rather was it probable that they would do and devise every thing to seduce those who might seem willing to become his disciples, from any tendency to virtue. No slight obstacle is overcome, when the might of such a torrent is resisted and stayed.

Finally, the pernicious arts of the sophists with which they sought to entangle the people and especially the young, to bring upon Socrates by every species of calumny, the suspicion, contempt, and hatred of his fellow citizens, are by no means to be omitted in recounting the obstacles which obstructed the career of this most noble philosopher. Which yet had not the power, accumulated and mighty as they were, to turn him aside, for a moment, from the steadiness of his purpose.

§ 11. *The greatness of Socrates shines out most brightly in his noble endurance of an unjust death.*

This wonderful steadiness of purpose shone with the brightest light, in the closing period of his life. That he was compelled to suffer death unjustly many of his contemporaries among the Athenians acknowledged, and posterity have unanimously affirmed. But no one was more firmly convinced than Socrates himself, of the cruel wrong of the fate that awaited him.[*] Yet, although he might, by entreaties or a tearful defence, have gained the favor of his judges, or by aid of his friends, have found means of escape and safety in flight,[†] scorning such evasions, he preferred to endure cheerfully whatever the magistrate should decree, and submit to his will without resistance or reluctance, be that will what it might. With a quiet composure therefore and joy, he suffered the sad sentence, and in that act, gave ample testimony to his fellow citizens and to posterity, of a steadfast and great soul.

The more I contemplate the constancy with which our Philosopher chose to abide by his principles in his life and in his death, the more I feel myself filled with admiration of the excellence and eminence of the man. Nor do I see that I can more fitly close these pages, than in the words, with which Xenophon has concluded his Memorabilia of Socrates. " To me indeed, since Socrates was such a man as I have related, (to wit, so religious that he would do nothing without the asking counsel of the gods, so just that he would harm no man in the slightest thing, but render every assistance to all who sought it of him, so temperate that he never preferred pleasure to goodness, so sagacious that he seldom erred in discriminating the better and the worse, and needed no man's assistance in making this judgment ; in fine who excelled all in the art of aptly and acutely expressing his own thoughts, of exploring the sentiments of others, of convincing the erring, and inspiring men with virtue and honor ;) he has seemed the best and happiest of men. If any think otherwise, let them contrast his morals with those of others, and thus judge."

---

[*] Mem. Socr. IV. 8, 9.

[†] Mem. Socr. IV. 4, 4. cf. Diog. II. 24. Cic. Tusc. Quaest. I. 29.

ARTICLE X.

A Secular View of the Social Influences of Christianity.*

By Hon. Caleb Cushing, Member of Congress, Newburyport, Mass.

If the social condition of the family of nations to which the United States belong, be compared with that of other political communities, past or present, having pretensions to be ranked as civilized, ours will be found distinguished by some all-important peculiarities. That of ancient Egypt, of Greece, of Rome, —with its extraordinary advancement in the fine arts, and in liberal knowledge whether of abstract philosophy or of government,—an advancement scarcely yet surpassed in modern times, —wanted the elementary ingredient of Christianity, which, it would seem, has done and is doing so much more than any other single agent for the refinement and cultivation of the human race. It was deficient, also, in another great instrument of civilization, the peculiar boast of the nations of modern Christendom, namely, the social influence and authority, and the singular dignity of character, of the female sex. For though polygamy, the great source of degradation in Asiatic countries, did not obtain among the Greeks and Romans, yet cultivated, intellectual, and accomplished woman played but a casual, and that no honorable, part, in polished Attica or Ionia; nor, in the economy of Roman society, though more considered than at Athens, did women of ingenuous rank and pursuits occupy the position assigned to them by the loyalty and attachment of the stronger sex in modern Europe and America. And these, the two most distinctive features of modern society, are intimately associated one with the other.

Indeed, wherever the religion of the Gospel has gone, it appears to have carried with it more or less of the blessings of cultivated life ; among the barbarian conquerors of the Roman Empire, in America, in Asia and Africa of our own day, in the

---

* This Article is the substance of a Discourse delivered by the author at Providence, R. I. Sept. 1838, before the Phi Beta Kappa Society of Brown University.

Australian and Pacific Islands.   And in so many rich and fertile regions of Asia and Africa, once replete with a refined population and studded with splendid cities, barbarism and social debasement have spread like a pestilence over the land, in proportion as the institutions of Christianity have given place to the forced establishment of a hostile faith.   Such and such things, at any rate, are found coëxisting together.   Are they to be regarded as cause and effect respectively, or as the joint effects of other causes?—Let us commence with a more careful inspection of the facts, and proceed afterwards to the deduction of conclusions and principles.

Our religion, our learning, our liberal knowledge, the essence of whatever is purely intellectual in our social condition, as distinguished from government and manners, springs from that auspicious region of the Mediterranean Sea, so long the seat of empire and of art.   How much is there in the round of that glorious water, how much even in the wrecks of what has been, for the traveller to visit and contemplate and study, if he would enter into the true spirit of our own institutions!   First, he might pause upon that Arabic race, which occupies the northern belt of Africa, and its continuous range along the shore of Asia. Here he should consider the remains of the Phœnician power, whether in Syria or Africa, from Sidon of the one hand to Carthage of the other, the wings as it were, or outposts, of that antique civilization, whereof the Nile was the abode.   In the narrow valley of the Nile, shut in by the sands of the desert or its eternal walls of sienite, he will inspect the mysterious pyramids, the colossal statues and sphinxes and temples, the innumerable depositories of the living dead, the half deciphered hieroglyphics upon a world of monuments, which bear witness to him of the departed glories of ancient Egypt.   Among the hills of Palestine, he makes his pilgrimage to the cradle of Christianity, and to

> ————" Silou's brook that flowed
> Fast by the oracle of God."

Turning thence, he will arrive at the shores of Greece, her isle-spangled seas, her vallies of the vine and the olive, her ruined temples and her thousand remembrances of liberty and of learning, that land of the memory, not long, perhaps, to be desecrated by the presence of Tartar invaders.   Proceeding along, he will come to Italy resting upon Germany and France, with so many relics of the old civilization mingled and combined with the marks of the new, and inhabited by races the result of the union of the northern barbarians with the people of the Roman Empire.   There, if he see much to remind him of the power and refinement of old Rome, as the language spoken, the monuments of art, and even the very municipal laws of the Republic now in full force on every side, he will perceive, also, that the tribes of the North, in their commingling with the conquered inhabitants of Italy and Gaul, brought with them, and infused into the blended mass, their own great peculiar sentiment, that restless love of personal freedom, which has changed the face of Europe.   Thence he may repair to the Spanish Peninsula, to see like monuments of the past, similar general characteristics in the forms of religion or government and the social habits of the people, modified, however, by the effects of Moorish domination and the near proximity of Africa.   Planted on the very Pillars of Hercules he will find the foot-print of the Island-Queen,—their everlasting rock marvellously quarried by her into a fortress bristling with cannon,—and learn of the refinements of civilization extended, at length, to the Ultima Thule; whence, reaching forth upon the broad Atlantic, he may descry ' the star of empire' bending its course westward to these remote regions of the New World.

Let us dwell a moment on a single one of this bright succession of splendid objects.   Follow me to imperial Rome,—to so much of her, at least, as pestilence, and war, and domestic rapacity, and the elements, and civil rage, have spared to modern times.   Pause amid the chaos of ruins, which two thousand years have heaped together on the site of the mistress of Italy, the queen of Europe, the conqueress of the world.—The ' lone mother of dead empires,'

> "The Niobe of nations !   There she stands,
> Childless and crownless in her voiceless woe !"

Time has been, that her senators were princes of the earth ; that pleading nations came to receive dispensation of justice at the hand of her magistrates ; that her consuls placed their feet on the necks of great monarchs ; that, like a spendthrift's patrimony turned into jewels and lavished upon a wanton, the riches of the world were poured into her lap ; that the industry and art of the whole universe were taxed to pamper her profusion, to adorn her palaces, to amuse her populace ; that earth, and sea, and sky, the elements, and all created things, seemed to be chained as tributaries to the triumphal car of Rome.

Would you apprehend the perfection of art lavished in her decoration? Look, then, at the scattered remains of her magnificence, the fragments of her basilica and arches, the mutilated statues and columns, or here and there a solitary tomb or temple left standing unharmed by time, and in its matchless beauty and glory. Would you appreciate, in a glance, the splendor and wealth of the old imperial city? Enter the Coliseum; and,—as the moon-light bathes in radiance its deep masses towering before you like some stupendous cyclopean* fabric of the extinct race of giants, or of the genii of oriental fable,—summon up to the mind's view that vast amphitheatre in the days of its pride, filled with near a hundred thousand spectators, with the blood of thousands of victims flooding its arena at a single festival, and captive warriors fighting, not in mimic battle, for the entertainment of the degenerate subjects of the Cæsars.

Those the ages of her greatness and her crime have passed away; and the structure of power, which generation after generation had bled and toiled and suffered to rear, has, like the marble monuments of its presence, crumbled into the dust. But not with the downfall of the empire of its arms did Rome cease to be potent; for religion gave to her a dominion over the minds of men only secondary in force to the allegiance she once claimed of their persons; and when the deluge of barbaric invasion had swept across the land, as its waters subsided, Christianity, like the missionary dove of the ark, flew forth over the waste a blessed harbinger of hope, recalling science and art once again to the genial shores of their own Italy.

Suppose, then, that we stand near by the bank of the famed Tiber, in the precincts of the seven-hilled city, and on the brow of the Vatican, where papal magnificence has built up an assemblage of palaces and churches, in themselves alone equal in extent to the capital of a great kingdom. It is the site of Nero's amphitheatre. You emerge from a labyrinth of narrow avenues, to enter upon a noble square, with its beautiful fountains throwing up their sparkling jets to the sun-beam, and its antique Egyptian obelisk, covered with mysterious inscriptions,

* ——"Vos et cyclopea saxa
Experti."—*Aen.* i, 201.

if unexplained, yet eloquent to the eye, to the memory, to the imagination, like a spirit from the Nile, rising up from the slumber of ages, to address you in the sacred tongue of the Pharaohs.   But lift your eye to that colossal basilic of St. Peter's, its enormous front,—the elliptic colonnades, the galleries, arcades, pilasters, statues, lavished upon its exterior in stintless prodigality,—and above all its cupola soaring over the subject city, the crowning ornament, the diadem, the pontifical tiara as it were, appropriate for the capital of Christendom.

Ascend the marble steps, pass the vestibule and its equestrian statues, enter this richest and proudest of the temples of religion, reared to the humble fisherman of Galilee.   Is it not grand, magnificent, overpowering, sublime ?—Your footstep is unconsciously arrested, the heart almost ceases to beat, as you gaze upward and onward, in mute admiration of the splendor and immensity of the long-drawn aisles, the gorgeous altars and chapels, the colossal statues, the columns of marble and bronze, the beautiful pictures, the gilded vault, and above all that inimitable dome, the miracle and masterpiece of human art, the classic Pantheon hoisted up and poised in mid-air by the genius of Buonarroti.   As you continue to gaze around, the sense of awe, of stupor, of self-debasing littleness, which first fills the soul, yields to a loftier sentiment of stupendous grandeur, of vastness that dilates rather than humbles the beholder, of elevation of spirit suited to the majesty and power of the scene. In a word, while you admire this monument of papal pride, you realize the lofty aims and outreaching spirit of those fathers of the Roman Church, who, by thus appealing to the imagination and the senses, led captivity captive, and conquered the rude conquerors of Europe.

If the place and the spectacle have not yet had their full effect on the mind, view them in the midst of the imposing ceremonies of Holy Week.   Join yourself to the crowds of the peasantry or populace of Rome, and of strangers of all civilized nations ; rove in weary wonder through the thousand halls and chambers of the Vatican palace, with its libraries, its galleries of painting and sculpture, its rich collections in every various form of human genius ; go to the Sistine Chapel, with the sublime figures of Michel-Angiolo's Last Judgment looking down upon you in the gathering gloom of twilight, and listen to the invisible choir, chanting in darkness the sad and solemn strains of the Miserere ; and then repair once more to St. Peter's, no longer bright with the beams of an Italian sun flashing upon its polished marbles or gilded ceilings, but imperfectly lighted with an illuminated cross, image of the blazing sign of Constantine, suspended from the dome in front of the high altar, and pouring its rays upon the head of the Roman Church prostrate in the act of worship, while arch and column project their shadowy masses upon the immense aisles, thronged, but not filled, with the multitude gathered to witness the scene from every quarter of Christendom.

Such is modern Rome; such the great Catholic Church, out of which, as it grew corrupt, all the sects and denominations of western Christendom took their departure; such is social refinement, in its grandest efforts, associated with religion.

But, you will say, this was a degenerate church; its forms overlaid with superstition, its doctrines wide of the pure standard of the gospel. True. Its ministers, its followers, were men, full of the infirmities, which still cling to poor humanity, raise it as you may by teachings or by discipline. It was a domineering, a persecuting church. True, again. It is the attribute of power, wherever it exists, to whatever it attaches itself, in religion as in politics, to be prone to exact conformity with its opinions, and obedience to its commands. And we have to do with the actual, not the ideal,—the world as it is, not as we would have it to be. Even the Puritan fathers of New-England, the very zealots of liberty, who abandoned their native land, with all that is dear in the name of country and of home,—dared the perils of unknown seas, and planted themselves on these inhospitable shores of the New World, amid untamed savages, or in the solitudes of the primeval wilderness,—that here they might found an asylum for unrestricted freedom of conscience,—even they, upright and highminded as they were,—did they escape the infirmities of our common nature? Fleeing from religious persecutors, did they learn to eschew religious persecution? Let the history of their times,—let the sufferings of the men and the women of other persuasions with whom they fell into conflict,—let this free-spirited plantation of Providence, founded on the broad platform of pure toleration, by Roger Williams cast out from Massachusetts for religious dissent,—answer the question. What then? Shall we, because of the corruptions of this society, or the intolerance of that, condemn Christianity in the general, and with Gibbon and his disciples infer that its social influences are only evil continually?

Here is a great problem.   To the statesman, and to society in general, this becomes a curious and most instructive inquiry, namely, to ascertain precisely what Christianity has done for the advancement and cultivation of social life in Europe and America.   To reach the solution of this problem, it needs that we take note of the condition and vicissitudes of Christianity at certain proscribed epochs of modern history.

In the prosecution of which, I desire to be understood as examining the point under a laical, not a clerical, aspect ; that is, I shall avoid, the most I may, any observations affecting controverted matters of religious opinion or belief; and shall presume to touch the tenets of Christianity, only so far as they bear upon the social and intellectual state of mankind in the diverse countries of Christendom.

Just as the minister of religion has frequent occasion to consider the social relations of mankind, so the layman would but imperfectly discharge his duty, if he did not sometimes reflect on the social uses of religion.   Each may thus aid the deliberations of the other; and by comparison of thought strike out the holy spark of truth, the common pursuit of both.   Individuals deeply and conscientiously pledged to any set of opinions, especially where those opinions belong to the social position of such individuals, are prone to fall into professional trains of thought ; whereby it not seldom happens that a man profoundly versed in some precise branch of knowledge, errs for that very cause in his estimate of the mutual relations of things.   His facts and reasonings are grouped around his own point of view ; what he sees, he sees clearly ; what he knows, he knows accurately and thoroughly ; but only with reference to the range of his own line of observation.   Another person, although quite superficially informed upon such questions, will sometimes arrive at sound conclusions respecting them relatively, by reason of the very fact of his less exclusive engagedness in any one of them ; according as, in war, a spectator, curiously overlooking the field, has a better idea of the general ordering of the battle, than the brave soldier, who is contending for victory and life at his appointed post in the very thick of the combat.

These explanations I interpose, not at all in proof or justification of what is to follow, but simply to forestall any misconstruction of what is intended only as a secular view of the social influence of Christianity.

Begin at the reign of Constantine, and look back and around

on what Christianity had been, and what it then was, in the proud days of the greatest extent of the Roman Empire. In the very infancy of our religion, the early Christians appear to have assembled as voluntary associates, without fixed or uniform ecclesiastical discipline. They were apostles and inferior teachers on the one hand, and converts or disciples on the other, alike engaged in the mutual enjoyment of the same religious emotions and convictions, and in the propagation of the new faith over the Greek and Roman world ; but they had not yet become an organized social institution. At the period in question, there was no established hierachy in the Church, independant of the whole body of believers ; no government, except of their own choice or assent ; no laws or discipline acting upon them by the unappealable will of human superiors. And this, it is believed, is the characteristic of the Church in the primitive years of Christianity.*

Fortunately, or it should rather be said providentially, things had undergone a material change at the epoch immediately preceding the dissolution of the Roman Empire. There had grown up a body of clergy having a distinct being as such ; a clerical society administering the services and teaching the doctrines of religion to the lay society of the time ; the Church as a public institution. The assistant or elder had become a priest ; the inspector, a bishop.—Christianity, having triumphed over paganism, was now the recognized religion of the Roman Empire. Its ministers and teachers were objects of distinction and observance. In fact, they were the only class of men, who, at this time, possessed a marked personal authority, founded on public respect and confidence, apart from the holding of military force ; they were the only men, having moral strength of character ; and these peculiarities in their condition led to a new and singular change in their social position, which was, their being invested with large secular power in the internal administration of the Empire.

Was this the result of spiritual pride on the part of the clergy ? Was it an act of clerical usurpation or ambition ?—Not at all. Power devolved upon them, because they alone were able and willing to undertake its responsibility. At the period of the invasion of the Empire by the barbarians, the municipalities were all that survived, in a political form, to attest the grandeur and

---

* Guizot, Civ. de l'Europe.

wisdom of the Romans, that proud race, whose national art it was

> Regere imperio populos,—
> Parcere subjectis et debellare superbos.

The dissolving world broke up into cities; it had not yet assumed the form of separate nations.   But the *curiales*, the ordinary municipal magistrates, shrank from the labor and responsibility of administration.   Amid the vexations of despotism, the decay of industry, and the universal crash and confusion of the social elements, which foretokened the downfall of the Empire, common men grew weary even of governing their fellows : —it sufficed them to live,—if indeed they could make sure of that poor boon.   Hereupon, impelled by the necessities of the times, one emperor after another *imposed* municipal duties on the bishops and priests, as appears by various examples in the civil code.*   Ravaged, depopulated, miserable as the cities then were, they retained a share of their ancient dignity and importance ; and they did so, chiefly by the reason of the activity and self devotion of the clergy, who preserved public affairs from falling into utter chaos, and stood as a sort of connecting link between the Roman population and the conquering barbarians.

It is demonstrable, therefore, that whatever of civilization survived the destruction of the Empire, is mainly due to the influence of the Christian Church.   Its ministers were the life and soul of the civic organization of that period.   Armed only with the holy weapon of the cross, they opposed the moral power of conviction, reasoning, example, religious profession, to the brute power of mere physical force.   They extended the ægis of a divine religion over the prostrate body of the ancient civilization.   They strove to redeem the earth from the empire of sheer violence.   See Alaric and his Goths, pausing amid the fury of the sack of Rome, to respect the churches of the apostles, and to conduct the emblems of religion, and the fugitive multitudes who accompany them, into the sanctuary of the Vatican.†   Hearken to St. Ambrose, arresting the great Theodosius at the entrance of the catheral church of Milan, because of the emperor's unatoned massacre of the people of Thessa-

---

* Cod. Just. L. i, tit. 4, s. 26 and 30.—Ibid. tit. 65, s. 8.
† Aug. de Civ. Dei, l. i.

lonica, and sending this mighty monarch away to penance and repentance as if he were the humblest man of the people. "Sir, you seem not to perceive," said Ambrose, "the guilt of the murder you have committed ; or perhaps the greatness of your power prevents your acknowledging your offence. But it is not fit you should suffer the splendor of the imperial purple to deceive you. With what eyes will you look on the house of our common master ? With what feet will you tread his holy pavement ? Will you stretch forth those hands, still dropping with the blood of that unjust murder, and take therein the holy body of the Lord ?"* Noble rebuke ! Objectors may say what they will of the idle though bloody controversies, the spiritual pride, and the world-seeking ambition, of the clergy of those times :——it is obvious to reply that the clergy alone served to rescue from extinction the expiring flame of civilization, and pass it down to modern Europe.

Would you realize all which the Church,—that is, I mean, the clergy and the visible institutions of Christianity in the general,—did for religion and for society in the fifth and sixth centuries ? Make present to the imagination the unspeakable disorders, the chaotic confusion, the misery, desperation, and abandonment, of a rich and cultivated nation deluged by one overwhelming flood of barbarians following on the track of another, each successive horde wasting, burning, slaying, as if sent on a mission of divine vengeance for the curse and ruin of the universe. Conceive the exanimate frame of the Roman Empire struggling in vain against all these lawless bands of Lombard, Goth, Vandal, Hun, Frank, and whatever else of horrid name the frozen North vomited forth upon the sunny fields of Gaul and Italy. What men might do to stay and withstand the torrent of destruction, the Romans did ; but the fatal hour of the Empire was come. In that dread season of Night and Erebus returning to brood once again over the earth, the clergy sustained the drooping strength of the municipalities ; they endeavored to save the power of the Empire and the supremacy of their religious opinions from a common overthrow ; and failing in this, they betook themselves, in the true spirit of saints and missionary martyrs, to the sacred task of converting their barbarian conquerors to the faith of Christ. Victorious in vain over the paganism of the Empire, the Christian Church saw itself compelled to renew its exertions and zeal to gain to the cross these new masters of

* Ward's L. of Nations, ii, 25.

Europe. It appealed to the reason and conscience of the barbarians ; it addressed itself to their imagination by the imposing splendor of its rites and ceremonies, then chiefly invented, or at least extended, for this purpose ; it labored to overcome their brutality, their recklessness, their violence, their indiscriminate love of pillage and bloodshed ; it spared no pains to wean them from their idolatry of Woden and Thor to the worship and obedience of the true God.

At the same time, to preserve itself from being swallowed up and utterly destroyed by the barbarians, the Church introduced into Europe a new principle and a new institution. The new principle was, in the language of the day, the separation of spiritual from temporal things ; that is, the rendering whatever appertained to religion independent of the secular authority, so that the Church should have not only a distinct legislation of its own, but the undisturbed control of the property belonging to its various members and denominations. This, the fundamental doctrine of religious freedom, therefore, originated with the Church itself, in defence of its own weakness. The new institution was the adoption, or rather the development and extension, of monachism. Monasteries became the chief asylum of religion and learning,—the strong holds of spiritual and intellectual cultivation,—the repositories of books, whether of sacred or profane literature,—the places of education ;—and of course, how much soever abused in the sequel, and howsoever unfitted to the advanced refinement of the present day, they were at that time among the effective instruments of the diffusion and safety of the Christian civilization of Europe.

Bearing in mind the general facts in the history of Christianity as an institution down to the period of the twelfth century, let us consider more distinctly the details of its influence in the countries of Western Europe subsequently to the conversion of the barbarians, and to the reign of Charlemagne, who contracted a close alliance with the Church, receiving at the hands of Pope Leo III. title and coronation as emperor and successor of the Cæsars, and repaying this boon with such concession of authority and domain, as raised the Roman See to the general supremacy of Western Christendom, and gave it the means to rear up that fabric of ecclesiastical power, that dominant monastic church, which, in association with the feudal system, controlled the affairs of Europe in the middle age.*

---

* Sismondi's Ital. Rep. p. 36.

At the close of this period, the Church presents itself in the attitude of a powerful body, valuable as a friend, dangerous for a foe. Within itself, there was cultivation, development, intellectual progress. All the knowledge of the time sought refuge in the cloister and the chapter-house. Whatever the sense of intellectual and moral responsibility, good knowledge, the study and inculcation of virtue, and the pursuit of religious truth, may do for the characters of men, it did for the clergy of that day, to such a degree at least as the circumstances of the age would permit. Consequently, they alone were competent to the due management of civil affairs; and they of necessity were the statesmen and jurists of the time. Laymen had one great argument for all occasions,—force,—and the use of this was the chief thing they understood: to the clergy remained the realms of the soul, and superiority of reason as their main reliance in conflict with a corrupt and disorganized world.

Not only was moral and intellectual culture the separate domain almost of the clergy, but the interior institutions of the Church were in many respects radically democratic, and so admitted and induced the exercise of much political discussion, and the collision of mind with mind, among its members. It was the chief road whereby simple intellect, unaided by force or other adventitious means, ascended to eminence and power. It recruited itself in all ranks, high or low, indiscriminately; out of it, birth and privilege were everything; in it, nothing. Its ecclesiastical functions, from a parochial cure up to the papacy, were open to all men alike, whether prince or peasant. And its high dignities were for the most part obtained by free election, as in a pure republic.

Whatever might have been the faults of the clergy, therefore, they were so much superior in cultivation, so much more civilized in their habits of thought and action, than all other possessors of authority, that the oppressed people continually appealed to their mediation or their authoritative intervention, for protection against the intolerable misrule and violence of the age. Seeing as they must their own intellectual preëminence, we cannot wonder, though we lament, that they should have aspired to govern the rude iron-handed and iron-headed chieftains of the Goths and Franks. But it is not true, as often rashly and superficially stated, not merely in books of religious controversy, but in others of more impartial pretension, as for instance in the words of a deservedly popular author of the present day, that, in the middle age 'the great mass of the priesthood assumed the sacred habit for the mere purpose of indulging more effectually in the worst and most licentious passions and appetites, and surpassed all the rest of the community in the irregularity and scandal of their lives.' It is not true. I know, and any body else may know who chooses to inquire, that such an assertion could only come from gross ignorance of the facts, or a culpable indifference to common veracity. It might as well be averred of this or any other age. It is a libel on the Christian Church, it is a libel on the principles and social influence of Christianity; whose general tendency, its better spirit, appears incontrovertibly on the inspection of its ordinary social influence among the people at large, in all things independent of the question of heresy.

Nothing, of the history of the middle age, is more familiarly known, to those who desire to know it, than the efforts of the Church to soften the hardships of every day life, and by example and precept to better the general condition of mankind. Thus, it never ceased to labor for the abolition of personal servitude, which prevailed so generally in those times. Most of the forms of manumission alleged a religious motive for the act; as love of God, the safety of the soul, the religious equality of all men, and their common hope of salvation through the mediation of Christ.* The clergy labored equally to humanize the penal laws of the barbarians. They proposed rational punishments in place of the rude and cruel ones of the feudal lords. They protested against the ridiculous modes of proof in vogue at that time, such as ordeals, judicial combats, and the oath of compurgators. If the Church was rich, it was not rich for itself alone; since the condition of its tenants was proverbially good and happy, and it freely dispensed its wealth in the succor of the needy and the sick. It was never weary of struggling against the universal spirit of rapine and warfare, which converted the whole of Europe into one great battle-field, sprinkled all over with walled towns and military posts, and with every dwelling-house a fortified castle. Who has not heard, for example, of that merciful expedient, namely, the well-meant, but ineffective, truce of God,† as it was called, by which the clergy sought to rescue one short day of the week from the horrors of private war, waged by men on all hands as if they

---

* Roberts. Cb. V, int. n. 20.   † Ib. Cb. V, int. n. 21.

were incarnate fiends inspired with infernal hate ? Christianity did more than any other cause to introduce notions of justice and humanity into the intercourse of European monarchs, to make itself the arbiter of public controversies, and thus to lay the foundation of the modern law of nations, that is, to substitute a rule of right instead of the rule of force, in the mutual dealings of the sovereign states of Christendom.

How contradictory and inconsistent with itself is the human mind ! We perceive the blessings which Peace brings with it, leaving all the energies of man to be exerted in the development of the natural resources of the country, and his affections to flow in a deep stream, of prosperity unbroken by violence, of beauty undefiled by blood. In the smiling presence of Peace, life seems to be lighted up with gladness, reflected from fair eyes, which speak only of joy and of hope. No dread alarms disturb the night, no anxious perils harass the day. Boon Nature yields to us ungrudgingly the wealth of land and sea, which is to be expended in the cultivation and adornment of the earth, not in its devastation. Monuments of religion, of education, of the fine arts, and of humanizing commerce, rise around us, instead of the ramparts and citadels, whose frowning masses bear witness only to rapine, treachery, cruelty, and bloodshed. How blissful might be the condition of a nation, which, possessing within itself all the elements of greatness and power, a broad and rich territory opened to internal commerce by numerous natural avenues of communication, a soil teeming with agricultural and mineral wealth, a congenial climate, free institutions of government, and a high-spirited, intellectual, civilized and christianized people,—how happy might be the condition of that people, if, under the blessing of God, its own disposition, or the conduct of others, would suffer it to dedicate itself forever to the lovely arts of peace !

Yet how few and brief are the intervals of time, in which, throughout all the civilized world, the gates of the temple of Janus have been shut, the sword sheathed, the panoply of war laid aside, and man has reposed awhile from the destruction of man ! Ambition, interest, revenge, rouses the ever-watchful passions within us ; the trumpet sounds to arms, and its notes thrill through the kindling frame ; all the surpassing pomp of martial array glitters before us, to dazzle the senses, and to madden the soul ; ' the rapture of the strife' burns in our bosoms, and the emulous love of glory hurries us forward into the field, where Death gathers his great harvest, and Havoc lords it over the smoke and the clash of battle. We resemble the bull in the Spanish arena, phrenzied by the scarlet shawl that is fluttered before him, and rushing blindly on the knife of the *matador*. We resemble the race-horse in others of the countries of Europe, where he is placed on the course unincumbered by bridle or rider, but with streaming ribbons on his head, and little bells with jagged points suspended over his back. He might, if he would, stand still at the starting post ; for there is nothing to force him from it ; but the bugles ring ; the gazing multitudes shout ; he is animated or startled by the sights and sounds about him ; he begins to move ; his movement shakes the bells, which jingle in his ears and prick his flanks ; and he dashes forward in the race for life or death, self-impelled and self-spurred to the goal. Is not this a true picture of our own lives ? Are not we also, in the sanguinary wars which from time to time convulse the world, the self-immolated victims of our own headlong passions and unreasoning animal instincts ? Oh, when will civilized communities learn that war, even upon those rare occasions when it is hallowed by a just and high cause, is after all but a necessary crime and the scourge of our kind ! When will they conspire, not in overreaching and encroaching upon one the other, but in bringing their choicest oblations, the flowers and fruits with which the bounteous hand of Heaven begems the unspoiled earth, and the aspirations of a fraternal concord, to lay them lovingly together on the altar of Peace ?

Remote as that auspicious day may seem to be, certain it is, that in nothing is the progress of refinement more visibly manifest, than in the gradual melioration of the belligerent usages of the European race ; and equally certain it is, that, though Religion has been the incentive or pretext of many wars, yet that the general influence of Christianity has been signally promotive of this melioration. Alexander III spoke the true voice of the Gospel, when he interposed as mediator between Henry of England and Louis of France. 'Among other good things,'—said he, 'which renders men lovely to their fellows and pleasing to God, that good we deem to be specially acceptable, which infuses charity into their hearts and binds together their souls. This is PEACE ; which dispels hatred, casts aside rancor, drives away envy, and shakes off rage ; which pacifies the mind, conciliates the heart, tranquillizes the breast, aud harmonizes the will. It is this we seek to plant, to propagate and to nourish in the soil of the

Church; this we would bring to fruit among princes, kings, and great men.' Such is the not ineloquent language of this pastoral letter; language worthy to be addressed to monarchs by the consecrated ministers of Christianity.*

Without dwelling any further on the influence which Christianity exerts over the progress of society in these relations, I pass to another branch of the subject. Hitherto, I have discussed it in reference to the world at large, its institutions of government, its general well-being, its condition of peace or war, its outward aspect, and the monuments of its civilization;—that is, in reference to man, the chief actor in those events which occupy the page of history. But whilst the well-being of general society has been so beneficially affected by the doctrines and establishments of Christianity, there is one portion of the human race, which, as I intimated in the outset, is more peculiarly indebted to its influence; and that is Woman. Let us test this, by example and by analysis.

Suppose that you reside in Paris at the opening of the French Revolution. You are in the very centre of the civilization and social refinement of Europe. Abuses exist in the government of the country; social evils in the condition of the people of a most malignant type; but yet learning, religion, the useful and liberal arts, polished manners, law, everything which marks and embellishes society or man as a member of society,—all these are abundantly possessed by the French. Place yourself, then, for the scene that is to come, on the field of the Place de la Révolution. In the midst is the perpetual guillotine. Power, hurled down from her ancient place in the palace of kings,— Power sits enthroned here, a drunken harlot upon the gallows, and calls herself Liberty. The soil beneath is forever soaked with human gore. The victim of to-day comes, undistinguished by pomp or state from those who have gone before, but still no common personage. On the same spot, you may, perhaps, have seen Louis of Bourbon executed, at the fiat of a voice mightier than of kings, that of an oppressed people goaded into madness by the combination of civil discord and foreign invasion. Led up the slippery steps of the scaffold by a file of armed men, appears one, equally illustrious in descent, equally unfortunate in destiny, with the dead Louis; the daughter, wife, and sister of kings, but queen herself no longer, the_dethroned, uncrowned, condemned Marie Antoinette.

---

* Ward's L. of Nations.

Do ten thousand blades leap from their scabbards, not merely to avenge a look that threatens her with insult, but to rescue
her from an impending ignominious death ?   No, she perishes,
like the meanest of her fellow-victims ; a single roll of the drum
drowns her death-cry ; her mangled remains are pushed aside ;
and the idle crowd, glutted with blood, or palled with sights of
woe, when the emotion of the moment is passed, waits listless-
ly for the next in turn among the doomed of the Reign of Terror.   She, the purple-born,—πορφυρογεννητη,—nursed in the
lap of imperial greatness, for a life-time the idolized object of
the adulation of courts, has just emerged from the subterranean
cell of a common prison-house, to be drawn amid the coarse
cries of a frantic rabble to the scaffold.   Is the age, then, of
chivalry gone ?   And is the glory of Europe extinguished forever ?   No.   You witness, to be sure, acts damning to their
doers, perpetrated in the delirium of national fury ; but only in
christian Europe or America would they be peculiarly memorable as public crimes.

A woman has been tried, condemned, and executed according to the law of the land.   And why not ?   Why not, I say ?
What is there of remarkable in it ?   Why is it, that we feel
shocked, revolted, horror-struck, by the spectacle of such an
execution ?   Simply, because in Christendom, and Christendom
only, there is an admiration, an affection, a gallantry, a religious
sentiment, that like the heaven-descended cloud which the
goddess of Love caused to gather about her favorite Paris at the
siege of Troy, invests woman with a sort of halo of immunity
and of respect.   In other countries and times, and under other
religious dispensations, it would seldom, if ever happen, that a
woman could possess sufficient consequence to be thought deserving of the solemn death of Marie Antoinette ; or to cause
that death to send a shock of grief and of horror through surrounding nations.   In Turkey, the everlasting oblivion of a
loaded sack, and a moon-light plunge into the Lethean waters
of the Bosphorus, would quietly follow the guilt, real or imputed, of a woman.   In the remote East, it would be happiness
enough for her, were she the pride of her sex, to be offered up
as a burnt sacrifice on the funeral pyre of her husband.   In more
barbarous communities, her fate might have combined the cruelty of the latter case, with the obscurity of the former.

We have present before us, in various parts of the United
States, a complete example of human life in its rudest and

lowest condition, that of the savage, of a race, not only without Christianity, but with scarce the least tincture of civilization.

The Indians of North America are for the chief part at the earliest stage of existence, the hunter-state, subsisting by the chase or its products, averse to agriculture, wedded to the life of the woods, possessing only the most imperfect rudiments of social institutions, devoted to predatory war, and in the brief intervals of battle or the chase given up to habits of sloth, and of brutality, which the very beasts of the wilderness would scorn to imitate. We reproach ourselves as a people for the wrongs the Indians have sustained at our hands, banished or wasted as they are from the river-banks and the woodlands they once occupied, and perishing away by the diseases and vices they have caught from us. We have ample cause of self-reproach. But, are we wholly or chiefly blamable in this? The Indians take from us the vices of civilized life,— and they die. Is that our fault? Why do they not copy our virtues? Are not our virtues open to their imitation as well as our vices? Are we responsible, if they perseveringly choose the latter, and perseveringly reject the former? Have we not strenuously endeavored to educate them, to christianize them, to wean them from their obstinate vagabondage of life, and to bring them to habits of industry and respectability? It is our misfortune quite as much as theirs, that, thus far, we have poorly succeeded in these benevolent purposes; that the millions upon millions, expended by the government or the citizens of the United States in the attempt to civilize them, have been as waters spilled on the ground; that, in general, they have not, and can neither be persuaded nor driven to adopt, any of those institutions of society, which alone are competent to protect one people against the violence or the fraud of another.

The Indian no longer dwells by the pleasant valley of his fathers, by the islands they loved to frequent, by the waters where they were used to launch the light canoe; and the forests, whose deep solitudes were to them a congenial home, have disappeared before the axe of the European. True. And did the all-wise Providence who created this beautiful land, who over-canopied the earth with this bright sky above us, who caused the heavens to send down refreshing showers upon it, and the sun to shed over it his kindling and fecundating rays, did that Providence design this beautiful land to be the desert lair of wild beasts, or of a handful of men wild as they?

Shall we lament that the hut of the savage has given place to the populous city; that smiling harvest-fields have sprung up in the bosom of the wilderness; and that these temples of religion consecrated to the service of the true God, have superseded the barbarous rites of the heathen? To them also the Word was preached, to them civilization was offered; they refused it, and they died in their unbelief; their own licentious propensities being the means appointed by Providence for their punishment. It would be to impeach His wisdom and goodness, to regret that we the millions of christian men have been raised up by His hand to succeed the bands of naked savages, who once wandered over, rather than occupied, the fairest regions of the New World.

These, I say, the aboriginal inhabitants of our country, present a ready example of men at the lowest stage of human condition. There is among them not only the absence of Christianity, but of all that cultivation which usually accompanies it in the countries of Europe. For it is the delusion of idle dreamers to imagine there is anything of great or good or wise in the customs or character of the Indians, to be put in competition with the civilization of Europe and America, unless it be that stoic impassionness of theirs under pain or death, which is the result of physical rather than moral causes, and among which causes the destitution, misery, coarseness, and stupor of their ordinary life are not the least prominent. Excepting this, there is nothing in them, which, when regarded in its simple truth, and freed from the optic illusions of the fancy, is comparable to the blessings of civilized life :——what they have peculiar, consists chiefly in the absence of those blessings. Doubtless, there may be pointed sayings and striking acts culled from their history; but the very rarity of which chiefly renders these remarkable. And the peculiar barbarism of the red men has its climax in their treatment and estimation of the female sex. Do we admire the patriot hero rendered glorious by his high deeds in the field of battle? I go to the woods to observe 'the feather-cinctured chief' on the war-path, and I detect a vulgar savage, half clad in a rude blanket, his person bedaubed with red earth, skulking around the solitary hamlet, that he may spring upon it in the dark night, to tomahawk its unwarned and defenceless inmates amid the flames of their dwellings ;——or I perceive him returning proudly to his brethren, and laden, not with the arms of a brave foeman won in honorable encounter, but with the scalps of murdered women and babes, and exhibiting in triumph these disgraceful trophies of his treachery and his cowardice;—for it is upon woman and her helpless offspring that the North American Indian, and he alone of all mankind, makes systematic war.—Do we bless the great lawgiver, who lays deep the foundations of the happiness of states, and bequeaths wise institutions to posterity? Where is the lawgiver of the Indian? Ages upon ages had rolled along with him, and he had not yet bethought him of that which is the very beginning of a state, the separate cultivation of the earth; nor was it until our own day, after three hundred years of association with Europeans, that a Cherokee began to apply alphabetic letters to the language of his race.—Do we cherish and honor the man, the husband, the father, who worthily discharges the duties of life in the sphere which God may have assigned to him? Go to the wigwam of the Indian, and you find him weltering in stolid baseness,—whilst his wife is a wretched drudge, who tills his cornfield, and carries his burdens, —his servant, his slave,—the handmaiden, not as in oriental countries of his luxury and his pleasure, but of his sottishness and his sloth. For woman is with him at once the means of his debasement, and the cause of its continuance. To him, idleness is a principle, not an accident. To her, life is but another name for toil. He will not work, because Nature, which endowed him with superior strength, which gave fierceness to him, and gentleness to her, has enabled him to impose work on her; and to participate in it would, in his estimation, sink him to the level of that sex, which in his mind is the impersonation of lowness and of labor. And you cannot, in my opinion, elevate the Indian above his present degradation, until you teach him, until you compel him, if he will not be taught, to love, to cherish, and to respect woman, alike in peace and in war.

Such is a true picture of the condition of woman among the unchristianized races of North America. You may object to this, perhaps, that it is an unfair example; that the degradation of the female sex among them arises from their peculiar barbarism of manners, not from the absence of Christianity; and that in a highly civilized, though unchristianized, community, it might be otherwise. The objection is a proper one; and must be met. In doing this, I shall not select the case of a civilized people in which polygamy prevails; though I well might, because Christianity has done so much to eradicate the practise of polygamy; but I take for an example the most refined and cultivated of all the pagan nations known to authentic history,—I mean the Athenians.

In proportion as men are elevated by the habits of civilization, the traits which distinguish them in their social relations are more delicately marked, and therefore, to be duly understood, require a more careful and accurate observation. This truth is material to be remembered in the present case; for in the Attica of the days of Pericles, the highest point perhaps of the greatness of the Republic, it is obvious to be seen, by many signs, that woman was neither the toy of the harem as in some pagan countries, nor the thrall of the field as in others. Men had learned to prize in the gentler sex the grace of manners, and the refinement of mind, which above aught else heighten the zest of her personal charms. Pericles himself was the constant and devoted admirer of Aspasia; there was a Lais, the pride of Corinth, and a Phryne, in whose house stood a golden statue in the temple of Delphic Apollo.—But these were not the matrons of Greece, the mothers and the wives of her sages and her statesmen. The Attic usages required of ingenuous women to live a life of domestic seclusion; to depart from it was to lose their social estimation; they of course could not form the centres and the arbiters of refinement and of social intercourse as with us: and hence that intellectual converse of the other sex, which, with the Ionians and Athenians, as with us, had become a necessity of existence, devolved upon the Leænas and the Sapphos, who, in the cultivation of the intellect, had laid aside the purity of the heart.

While such is the testimony of history and biography, the facts are singularly illustrated by the poetry of the Athenians, especially their drama, which is itself a mirrored image of life, and the personation of its passions. In the dramatic poetry of modern Europe, as in our prose fiction, it is the passion of Love, which plays the prominent part. Of the thirty-three plays ascribed to Shakspeare, there are but Macbeth, Coriolanus, Timon, Julius Cæsar, Lear, and perhaps here and there one of the English historical plays, in which Love is not more or less the active operator of the plot. It is the master-passion of the modern drama. But, in Greek tragedy, Destiny, irrevocable Destiny secretly working out the happiness or misery of men and of nations, is the chosen agent of dramatic interest. It is

Prometheus, bound by the gods to a wild sea-rock because he had snatched fire from heaven for the good of mankind, listening to the chant of the oceanic nymphs, as with stern composure he awaits until, after innumerable ages have passed away, his predestined vindication and deliverance shall come.   It is Œdipus, the fore-doomed murderer of his father, and the husband of his mother, the greatest of criminals by no crime of his own, in his guilt and in his expiation the helpless instrument of Fate.   It is Orestes predestined to avenge the murder of his father by himself becoming the murderer of his mother.   It is the lovely Antigone, the appointed victim of filial duty and of sisterly affection.   It is Iphigenia predestined to be slain by Agamemnon at Aulis, the unconscious object of her father's vow for the salvation of Greece.   It is the Ion of Talfourd,—who in that exquisite composition has caught the true inspiration of the Greek muse,—it is the pure and noble Ion, preordained to expiate in his person the sins of the royal race of Adrastus so that the offended gods may redeem his country's desolation.   Such was the comparative absence of the passion of Love from the dramatic poetry of the Athenians; such its eminent conspicuousness in that of christian Europe.   Which remarkable difference between the ancient and the modern drama, it seems to me, is imputable, in no small part, to the new social position acquired by Woman in the countries of Christendom.

We have witnessed her condition in Attic Athens.   Change the scene.   Select any spot you choose in christian Europe or America,—I care not where, so that a single ray of the illumination of religion and civil culture has reached it,—and observe the wider influence, the higher respect, which Woman has attained.   When Philip of Spain's armada threatened England, queen Elizabeth repaired to the camp at Tilbury, clad in a steel corslet, with a general's truncheon in her hand, and rode on horse-back bare-headed through the ranks of the armed host. "I know I have the body but of a weak and feeble woman," said she, "but I have the heart and stomach of a king, and of a king of England too; and I take foul scorn that Parma or any prince of Europe should dare to invade the borders of my realm. Wherefore I am come to you at this time, being resolved, in the midst and heat of the battle, to live and die amongst you all; to lay down for my God, and for my kingdom, and for my people, mine honor and my blood even in the dust."   Earth and sky reëchoed the enthusiastic hurrahs of twenty thousand brave

English hearts as she rode along their glittering files ; and the men, who saw that sight, and heard that speech, would have battled to the death in her behalf against the armies of all Europe. Again. When Maria Theresa of Austria saw her generals defeated, her armies dispersed, her cause almost desperate, she threw herself upon the generosity of her martial Hungarians. She appeared in their assembly with her infant son in her arms ; unfolded to them her wrongs ; besought their succor. Excited to enthusiasm by the spectacle of her beauty, her desolation, her trust in their loyalty, the gallant nobles rose spontaneously to their feet, their hands clanged instinctively upon their sword-hilts, every blade flashed forth upon the eye, and the hall rang with their shout of acclamation,—"Moriamur pro rege nostro Maria Theresa!" These and a hundred other like scenes, which lie scattered up and down in the history of modern times, have no parallel out of the limits of christian Europe.

For it is in Christendom alone, that woman is the coëqual companion of man ; the joint heir with him of the common heritage of immortality ; the chosen partaker of his joys and sorrows on earth, and of his hopes of heaven ; the object of his chivalrous adoration in youth, and of his respect and affection in age ; placed on thrones, to be obeyed with a loyalty born of love, and devotion that is half a worship, or if she fall on evil times, and become the victim of civic strife, then to see the world shake at the story of her wrongs ; and though excluded from ordinary political life, yet thus only when exclusion is shelter not dishonor, as the most precious jewels are guarded from the soil and contamination of vulgar use. Well might the holy women of the Evangelists cling to the cause of Christ ; well might the early female martyrs of the church persevere unto death ; well might Helena seek to infuse her faith into the heart of Constantine, and make it the religion of the Empire ; well might Clotilda strive to gain over to it her Clovis and his Franks ; well might the female sex in past and present times be distinguished for their devotion to Christianity. It has raised them to the rank that is their due, and redeemed them from a bondage of the soul worse than captivity of person. In our Europe and America, she is no longer shut up in household retirement, as in some countries, to be loved without respect, or issuing forth as in others, to be caressed without respect or love. Education, taste, knowledge, virtue, religious culture, intellectual embellishment, the grace and beauty of soul, are now conjoined in woman with her native loveliness of form and feature. We open the writings, which do honor to the literary cultivation of the age, and we find them strown with roses from the tasteful hand of woman ; for to her also is the inspiration of genius imparted. We go abroad into the world, and we find the influence of her tender and benevolent spirit pervading life. We enter the gay saloon, and she is there, radiant in beauty, animating society, cheering, exalting, spiritualizing it, and beaming, like some bright particular star, the cynosure of all eyes. And we retreat into the domestic circle, there still to find her the dispenser of happiness,—and there to bestow the homage of our hearts at an altar such as the old idolatry never knelt before,—to bow down to the incarnation of beauty enshrined in that sanctuary of home, where the vestal flame of true love is purified and hallowed by the divine precepts of Christianity.

Upon the whole matter, then, we may receive this for proved :—The Church exercised a large influence over the moral and intellectual condition of modern Europe, its ideas, sentiments and manners. It gave impulse to intellectual cultivation ; it stamped itself upon legislation, literature, science, and moral debate. And its influence upon all these points was in the main salutary ; though in affairs of government, its doctrines were not congenial with freedom ; for it always aimed to control the opinions of men, and their conduct also, in the article of their ethical relations, and ultimately aspired to the general dominion of society.

But in the very moment of the greatest power of the Church, appeared its incapacity of running successfully the race of empire ; for, long before the world was ready for the Protestant Reformation, it was presaged by the schisms and dissensions of the churchmen themselves, and by the universal development of society in Italy, France, Britain, and elsewhere, consequent on the crusades. For, in the fourteenth century, the epoch of the revival of letters, intellectual cultivation, so long peculiar to the clergy, began to diffuse itself abroad ; and in proportion as it augmented the intelligence of the laity, tended to throw back the clergy into their appropriate place, of the moral and theological guides of men, instead of their temporal and intellectual sovereigns. The Protestant Reformation naturally followed. It was the insurrection of European mind against the usurped dominion of thought and opinion asserted by the See of Rome. Whatever other considerations, of ecclesiastical reform in the purgation of abuses, of political contention, or of personal inducement as in the conduct of Henry Tudor and his advisers, may have mixed themselves up in the affairs of Europe, that,—namely the emancipation of intellect and of conscience from the fetters of ecclesiastical servitude,—was the true motive spring of the Reformation.

In reflecting on the religious wars,—the sanguinary local persecutions,—the reciprocal confiscations of property, massacres and burnings,—of the Catholic and Protestant divisions of the Christian Church at the period of the Reformation, we shall do injustice to Christianity as an institution, if we do not remember that throughout the progress of this long and desperate struggle of the mind to be free to have its own conscientious convictions, it was the learning and practice of discussion acquired within the Church, by the clergy themselves,—by the Martin Luthers, the Cranmers, the Calvins,—which successfully guided the less informed thinkers of lay Europe to the end of the religious revolution of modern Christendom. That stupendous mass of power, which the See of Rome had for so many ages been rolling together, was shaken and rent asunder, like the terrestrial globe in the agony of earthquake, not by assault from without, but by the irrepressible fires of freedom, which burnt within its own breast.

Thenceforth, Christianity ceased, except in particular countries, to act upon men so potentially as an institution, and is to be viewed, in respect of its connection with the progress of social refinement, rather as a faith. In the matter of its rites and tenets, it visibly pervades all the relations of life, and gives a coloring and a character to all the social institutions of Europe and America. Our thoughts, our language, our writings, our conduct, our laws, all the elements and the monuments of our civilization, bespeak its influence. And our peculiar moral condition, it is safe to say, is what it is, because of Christianity ; for no man of whatever creed or profession, who listens to reason, and makes comparison of our own civilization with that of the ancients or of existing nations out of the pale of Christendom, can fail to perceive and avow the salutary influence of the tenets of Christianity upon the general organization of society ; the spiritualizing and of course elevating effect of its continual reference to the immortality of the soul, and the aid derived by government and law from the soundness of its unequalled ethical code. In addition to which, consider how deeply our literature, our general intellectual cultivation, is imbued with the doctrines and associations of Christianity ; and how much of the sculpture, painting, and architecture, of our world is religious or ecclesiastical in its uses and origin, as exhibited in the edifices and other monuments of religion, with which all the countries of Christendom abound.

In the United States, a pervading universality of religious impression is less visible to the eye, than it is in many parts of Europe. Our immediate forefathers erred, I think, in their anxious proscription of the external signs of faith. When the Spaniard hears the toll of the vesper-bell, be he on the road or by the fireside, in the church or the *paseo*, he reverently joins in the brief aspiration of prayer uttered at once by a million of lips. Can this do evil ? On the contrary, does not the very spectacle itself impress and elevate the soul ? Again. The lofty proportions and the noble architecture of the great cathedral edifices of Europe tend irresistibly to solemnize the mind as you enter them, and to prepare it for the adoration of that Supreme Being, to whose high service they are dedicated. Is it wise to discard or undervalue such influences and impressions ? Surely not. Reason is to be convinced ; but the heart also is to be touched, like the rock of Horeb by the rod of the prophet, if we would make the fountains of purity and faith to gush up from the inmost depths of the soul, and well forth their hidden treasures. True religion is a sentiment or emotion as well as an act of reason. The lawgiver or founder of public institutions, who neglects the means of guiding the conduct through the heart and the feelings, voluntarily throws away the most efficacious of all the implements of good ; and the christian teacher, who, from over-refinement of rationalism, rejects them, leaves them to be employed by others, in the attack or perversion of the faith of the Gospel.

ARTICLE XI.

Modern English Poetry.—Byron, Shelley, Wordsworth.

In the lives and professed principles of several of the illustrious poets, who have made a name in England and the world, since the opening of the present century, we are presented with very much that essentially detracts from the admiration which their genius and their works would, otherwise, command. And while those who speak the language which they so successfully employed, and so richly adorned, appear, for the most part, inclined to forget the faults of intellects whose greatness seems to add something to the dignity of human nature, we confess, that for ourselves, the natural glow of our admiration is dampened, if not entirely smothered, when we see that man in his best estate is yet so earthly and so sensual, so willing to claim kindred with the brute, though he be but a little lower than the angels. When we behold at once the splendor and the filth, "the dirt and the divinity," of such a gifted genius as the author of "*Childe Harold;*"—when we notice the luxurious profligacy of the exquisite Moore; when we hear the philosophic blasphemy of Shelley, and,—alas, that even he should not be an exception—when we consider the reckless life and the one disgusting vice of Coleridge, how are we led involuntarily to adopt the language of a greater than them all,

> " God of our fathers, what is man !
> Nor do I name, of men, the common rout
> That wandering loose about,
> Grow up and perish as the summer fly,
> Heads without name, no more remembered ;
> But such as thou hast solemnly elected,
> With gifts and graces eminently adorned,
> For some great work, thy glory."—*Milton.*

In an age when the world is so far advanced in all that civilizes human nature and refines society, we have seen in England, the heart of Christendom, a constellation of men preëminently adorned and fitted for some great work to the glory of God, who, instead of so consecrating themselves, have allowed their writings to outrage all decency and religion, in a manner more gross and heathenish than would have been tolerable in the dark ages. It is not our purpose now to go into such a review of modern English poetry as shall revive all the clatter and cant which was so rife, and is even yet fluent on the disgusting licentiousness of *Don Juan*, or the blasphemy of *Cain ;* but as Americans, who desire that the literature which is beginning to be formed, in our own dear land, should be free from all that has disgraced our seniors, we cannot but deem it of importance to express our views of the poetry of our language in these times, and to recommend those features of it, which, in our opinion, are alone worthy of imitation.

Not to enter upon a tedious examination of the host of authors who could be introduced to illustrate what we hope to establish, we shall content ourselves with a concise analysis of *three* great masters, under whom most of the others can be arranged in appropriate classes. We have three great contemporary names, which seem a kind of synonymy of the *Progress of Poesy.* In the writings of Lord Byron, we have the wild-fire of the wayward boy, the reckless outburst of the young man's feelings, the instability and error of mind undisciplined. Hence his poetry is chiefly valued by the young, and is too apt to be the first reading of the freshman in society, as it is, in truth, a shining mirror, that reflects the feelings, the passions, and the follies of our early years. In Shelley, we have the advancement of poetry into paths where she is attended by a show of philosophy, and guided by real learning. This poetry recommends itself to maturer mind ; and perhaps we are not too highly complimenting it, when we say that it is of the highest order of merely human song, or *poetry unbaptized.* It is such as we begin to love, when Byron cloys ; and when we are wearied with carving and tinsel, and are willing to turn to the pure sculpture in marble. Had his works been written in the days of Sophocles, they would have ranked with those of the Grecian himself; and Tully would have read them afterwards in his villa, nor dreamed that the Muse could take a higher flight. But the christian reader rests not contented with the soaring that his eye can follow, for unlike the splendid heathen, he knows of worlds beyond Olympus, and of a life that begins, when our mortal years have vanished. Of this glorious elevating influence of our religion the student finds no recognition in the classic pages of Shelley ; and it is then, when fully convinced of this one thing wanting, when sick with disappointment over metres, which lack but virtue to make them perfect, it is then that the mind finds its desideratum in Wordsworth, and contents itself with his spiritual harmonies. This mighty master wins us last, but as he wins us not till we ourselves have entered the most perfect form of our mental education, our love for him is such, as we carry with us through life. When the student throws down the *Cenci*, and has long forgotten the *Corsair*, then may the christian scholar take up the works of Wordsworth, and breathe the pure air of an inspiration, like that which shall be his native air, when unclothed of this earthly clog, and born in heaven.

And so, these poets seem just adapted to the march of mind. Byron catches our boyhood; and if we escape the wretched consequences which his siren numbers are calculated to entail upon us, we yield ourselves to the graceful finger of Shelley, and are led by his upward guidance to fields Elysian of the mind. When passion is sobered, and nature begins to feel the dignity of thought; when the heart's first affections are allayed, and the soul begins to doat on all things lovely; it is then that Shelley comes with a seeming philosophy to seduce the contemplative, and. with his classic finish to enamour the scholar. But if Wordsworth awes us thence, by those mysterious answerings which we find in his every verse, to the yearnings which are naturally felt by him, who can say with the Roman, *omnia fui, et nihil expedit*; then are we liberated and unshackled; then first we feel that we are indeed, at the same time, worshippers of beauty and disciples of true philosophy; and this, because, then first, we begin to appreciate a religion which makes real and enduring all legitimate forms of symmetry and perfection. It is true that Wordsworth is beyond our natural appreciation, very often; but it is so, because he is *above* it; and because he soars, if not with Milton. into the Heaven of heavens, at least, into those regions of pure sunlight, which are far over the vapors and mists of the valley, and into which the eye of the earthling can seldom penetrate.

Of the *poet of passion*, we shall say but little; since, as might be reasoned *à priori*, he is much better known and appreciated than the superior twain, who, in a greater or less degree, may be characterized as *poets of thought*. It has been truly remarked, that Byron's heroes are never *characters*, but only the personifications of *passions*. Of the mass of his poems, it was well said by the great Göthe, that they were only parliamentary speeches in disguise. Those who have read the parliamentary efforts of his lordship know well enough how little there is to commend in the plain prose of thoughts, which, if tagged with rhyme, would have been the thread-bare recitation of every schoolboy. But it is not for us to discuss him, in those manifestations of his own character which he gave us in his Giaour, Lara, or the Bride. We rather follow him to the wanderings which his spirit took in maturer years, when he had become aware of the wrong principles of poetry, which, with all his scorn of *principles of poetry*, he had been following all his life, and when he began to write for immortality, and to dabble in religion, and to assume philosophy. It is in this light, that his character as a poet is too little regarded ; and while the world has been nauseated with reviews and magazine-critiques of his lighter follies, how little do we hear in the way of critical investigation of his tragedies, of the *Mystery of Heaven and Earth*, or even of the more stupendous one of *Cain !* Yet only by these last, can his claim to be called a *great* poet be at all successfully argued. They are certainly the highest efforts of his invention and his only attempts at logic or theology. Perhaps, however, we must except some strophes of Childe Harold, which smatter in metaphysics.

In *Heaven and Earth*, we have a lyric drama, that is sublimer than Æschylus, and which is throughout much in the style of that great dramatist's choral pieces. In this sublime work, while he occasionally allows his numbers to degenerate into irreverence and blasphemy, he generally restrains them, to use his own words, " within the bounds of spiritual politeness." It is, however, by making his blasphemers noble and interesting characters, while the pious are represented not like Abdiel, but tame as " douce Davie Deans," that the poison of his artful irreligion is, perhaps fatally, imparted. But in the " Mystery of Cain," we have from induction to epilogue, one long, inwoven lie, in which the common coin of scoffers since the time of Apuleius has been scraped together, and burnished into a lustre that is still insufficient to set off so much brass for gold. Its chief *personae* are *Abel* and other very religious—*women !* *Cain,* a kind of Lord Byron ; a great philosopher and reasoner, in his own conceit, but in fact a miserable dupe, and a great utterer of sophisms, sounding vastly like sense, but very little like poetry, being, for the most part, the most limping verses in the realm of rhythm : and lastly and chiefly we have *Lucifer*—or the devil himself, introduced to the reader as the friend of man, the great enemy of man's Almighty tyrant, and the particular acquaintance of Cain,—and *the author!* It is amusing to see *Sathanas Agonistes*, treading the abyss of space with his miserable victim, and to hear him holding a very solemn conversation with the first murderer, made up of patches from Voltaire, Bolingbroke, and Thomas Paine.

This drama was very faithfully analysed by the British Reviewers, when England was shocked by its first appearance. Campbell cauterized the versification of his brother bard, in a style truly chirurgical ; while the brilliant Heber—a genius of Byron's order, but dignified by the beauty of holiness—exposed its principles rather to pity, than to chastisement. To them, and to Jeffrey, we commend those who would see a full criticism of the monster ; while for ourselves, we simply take it up, as a point, from which to look back upon the preceding series of the same author, and to confirm our opinion of the whole train, by marking the littleness of this "most lame and impotent conclusion." Yet it is after all, as proportionable a capstone, as could have been placed on the flimsy edifice reared for its support. The great father of lies seems to have designed it as the finishing stroke of the work which he had been accomplishing by means of his pliant tool. Pure reason is impossible in support of an unreasonable cause ; and so, that which enough resembles it to dupe the unwary is the most proper completion which could be given to a structure especially designed to entrap a class of that, by no means, uncommon description.

We cannot but remark this, because we see in the writings of such a poet the work of a greater original than himself ;— who, in his character as the god of this world, is indeed wiser than the children of light. When the great genius, confided by the Creator to some of his favored creatures is, by their own perverse and ungrateful wills, turned from the service of the great author of intellect ; Scripture has informed us, that it becomes the toy or the tool of a far different being. Unconsciously it passes into the service of him whose wages is death ; and the labor it performs is unquestionably instigated by his unseen, but terrible influence. The wonderful control, which the works of Byron have already gained over the immortal destinies of thousands of minds, shows evidently how powerful an engine he must have been deemed by the artful manager whose cause they have subserved.   How cunning was it in a seducing demon to begin by the soft flattery of our fears and feelings, which appears in the restrained licentiousness of Childe Harold.   How well organized was the attack ; and how craftily was it followed up by the small artillery that succeeded !   And when, before society was aware of the sapping which its morals were undergoing, all things were prepared and ready, how consummately did the whole structure fall in with the hollow *diablerie* of " *Don Juan :*" then, how " like an exhalation," did the damning atheism of *Cain* arise from the steaming ruins.   " Is not the hand of *Joab* in all this ?"

They who work for Satan, little know what he is accomplishing, by the apparently trifling tasks which he assigns them. Yet in the end, they have done their share of his work.   The manœuvres and excursions, which they seem making for their own amusement, are all the while the direction of a master mind.   And he, like a skilful general in the management of his serried columns on the field, is very willing that each little captain should be the autocrat of his own platoons, and rejoice in his own epaulettes, and march on totally occupied with the banners and the music which he has arranged to suit himself, if only the great action is all the while going on, and they are in their proper places, unconsciously, but mechanically rolling forward, and sustaining the shock of the battle.   That Lord Byron had actually any design in all he wrote to consummate the baneful end which will assuredly be effected, in the case of any one who yields to its natural tendency, no one, we are satisfied, will pretend to believe.   Such a plan would argue a forethought for which this modern Epimetheus was not distinguished, if there were no other reason for doubting it.   But that he, to whom he abandoned himself, who is at war with God, and who is availing himself of every means to assail his empire, was not using him as a serviceable recruit, is not so apparent.

As an *artist*, Lord Byron was more of a Dryden than a Pope.   He adhered very little to law, except where he was a law unto himself.   This fact, however, detracts nothing from the force of his writings, nor from their power of attracting admiration.   Where he makes his own rules, his style of versification is tolerably pleasing ; but his dramas are the most miserable specimens of English blank verse that exist.   In rhyme, the flow of his verse is better, often luxuriantly sweet, and

sometimes very dignified.   Four verses in a small poem published in his "Hours of Idleness," should have saved his power
of verse-making from the premature lash of the Edinburgh Reviewers; they are worthy of Pope—

> "No marble marks thy couch of lowly sleep,
> But living statues, there, are seen to weep;
> Affliction's semblance bends not o'er thy tomb,
> Affliction's self deplores thine early doom."

But, with all the fame of Childe Harold, it must be allowed
that it contains some horrid mutilations of the Spenserian stanza.
A late number of Blackwood's severely criticises the noble poet
on this point.   It does not even spare his lordship's *English
grammar*, which he ought to have learned at Aberdeen, sufficiently to have kept, forever, from an English classic, such a
bastard line as this

> "And dashest him again to earth;—there let him lay."

Perhaps it is, generally, in the arrangement, rather than in mi-
nutiae, that Lord Byron is happy in the use of Spenser's stanza; and in the arrangement, he certainly often triumphs, beyond art, in the might of original genius.   It is a good rule to
one who instinctively knows its limitations, that the sound should
echo the sense.   But on this rule Byron often practically im-
proves, where he gives a double force to his passages by expressing, in the concealed effect of the rhythm, a thought which
though differing from the signification of the words, still assists
them;—as, for instance, in the following, where, in the simple
narration of a history, he gives us all the *effect* of an arrangement on the battle-field, so that when he concludes with a line
directly descriptive of the battle, we feel as if the whole passage
had been devoted to it.

> "Last noon beheld them full of lusty life;
> Last eve, in beauty's circle, proudly gay;
> The midnight brought the signal sound of strife,
> The morn, the marshalling in arms;—*the day*,
> *Battle's magnificently stern array!*"

Here the first lines while they tell the story *before* the action,
still convey the idea, in connection with the former stanzas, of
a marshalling on the field; and this is carried out until we are
ready for the cannonade—

> "Battle's magnificently stern array."

In which though the words mean only the army in line of battle, the sound has all the thunder of their conflict—the roar of the discharge—the concussion of the atmosphere—the dying away ; and the next line takes up the suppressed effect.   The smoke conceals the combat—

> " The thunder-clouds close o'er it."

But in his dramas, where he attempts to use the verse of England's dictating, all is meagre.   We listen, in vain, for aught of that rhythmical dignity which marks the buskin'd tread of Shakspeare's gorgeous muse, or which often pauses in the measure when "Jonson's solemn sock is on."   The magnificent sonorousness, the "Doric delicacy," the full organ swell, the grand orchestral sublimity of Milton's numbers, seem degraded by comparison with anything that Byron ever wrote.   He seems never to have been a student of the legitimate sublime in *nature ;* even there he was a superficial observer ; and he had totally extinguished in himself any capability, which he may originally have possessed, to appreciate the sublime in morals, at an early period of his history.   We say nothing of the merely intellectual sublime, but of the sublimity of virtue he certainly never conceived.   He could, therefore, very easily represent the pious Abel as a " womanish utterer of weak sentences ;" but he could never command either the thought or the language which Milton has employed to delineate the character of the faithful angel, any more than he was capable of a desire " to vindicate the ways of God, to man."   Where in all his works do we find such a conception, or such a passage as this ;

> " So spake the seraph Abdiel, faithful found !
> Among the faithless, faithful only he ;
> Among the innumerable false, unmoved,
> Unshaken, unseduced, unterrified,
> His loyalty he kept, his love, his zeal."

Here the roll of the numbers, is only equalled by the sublimity of the idea.   Why is it then, that with all his superior charms of verse, Milton is mostly *a name*, not an acquaintance, with the majority of educated youth ?   In our colleges, Byron is devoutly thought *the great English poet*, however they may concede to Milton, the right of possession, to be *called* so.   The mind that has dallied along the flowery walks of his earlier writings, stands thrilled before the fictitious splendor of his

" Cain ;" while the unpretending dignity of Paradise Lost, like a great mountain in the distance, is indeed complimented for its head above the clouds, but is seldom seen, and never visited by the lounger of the garden. Such is human nature ; and the *boy*, who best exemplifies it, will always desert the fireside, where the flute-notes of gentle Cowper are wooing him to the beauty of holiness, or the vaulted sanctuary where the grand organ of Milton is rolling his soul to heaven, if only the fife and drum of gaudier poets be heard in the streets, to lure him to long hours of truant wandering, that surely close in sorrow. Had the great *trio*, whose names we have placed at the head of this article, been given to the world in successive genera- tions, standing each in his own as the great poetic star of his times, no doubt they would be deemed as fair examples of the birth, growth, and perfection of poetry, as we are accustomed to regard Æschylus, Sophocles, and Euripides, in the history of the drama. The painter might delineate them allegorically ; *Byron*, as the serpent, not moving on his belly, but majestically erect, as in Eden, and "more subtle than any beast of the field ;" *Shelley*, like the Rabbinical tempter, " a cherub's face, a reptile all the rest ;" while Wordsworth should stand before us, with none of the dragon left, a true " spiritual being," winged, and ready for flight, but walking the earth awhile, to admire even this poor outskirt of the realms of the all-pervad- ing God. The poetry of Byron is the spirit of the loose Epi- curean, breaking out in wassail-songs over his cups ; the poetry of Shelley, is the breathing of the unchristianized Platonist, standing before the Parthenon at day-break, and absorbed in love and adoration of the beautiful marbles around him ; but Wordsworth's is the high worship of the Christian, rejoicing at morning, at noon-day, and at even, in the beautiful works of God, and ever contemplating the grand in nature, and the sub- limity of virtue, and all that shows anything of the perfection of the original mind.

In passing from Byron to Shelley, we ascend a step in the scale which we are considering. In Shelley, we have unques- tionably a *greater* intellect, and one beautifully cultivated, and expanded by continual philosophical exercise. He seems to have been one with whom deep thought was an instinct ; one of those high minds that never have a boyhood. Before the com- pletion of his fifteenth year, he had written and published two novels, " the Rosicrucian," and " Zasterozzi." At the university, he very soon began to employ the logic which was taught him there in a pedantic endeavor to examine the principles of Christianity. The effect was what might have been anticipated. He published an infidel essay on the Being of a God, which gained him the enmity of his father, and expulsion from his college.

We say this result might have been anticipated, as the natural consequence of the *investigations,* in which he arrogantly engaged. And this, not that we believe true logic will do anything less than more and more illustrate the unshaken truth— nay, the eternal, glorious fixedness—of our holy religion. But still there is something in our faith, so at war with the natural feelings of man, and so at enmity with everything that exalteth itself in the human heart, that the young intellect, just fledged with science, and coming, in its pride, to the examination of things, from which the vulgar are accustomed to shrink with a superstitious awe, is peculiarly ill-adapted to relish the premises on which the Bible bids us reason. The very desire *to investigate* was, in Shelley, incipient infidelity : simply because, it was no desire to discover *truth,* at all hazards, but, on the contrary, an *itching* to rid himself of responsibility, and, if possible, to philosophize truth away. He was dazzled with the world, and desirous of enjoying it, unrestrained. In annihilating the obstacles to such enjoyment, he was radical enough to discover the necessity of disproving the being of God himself : in which, he was certainly more consistent than those, who admitting the existence of a Supreme Being, seek by unsatisfactory excuses to absolve themselves from allegiance to his government. On this account, therefore, we do not praise that " desire to investigate." which many of the great and good are accustomed to commend, because it *sounds* fair, and they have full confidence in truth, as capable of defending itself. If it were, really, what it professes to be, the case would be far different ; but usually it is only a desire to *cavil,* masked under a philosophical outside. Religion so instinctively recommends itself to conscience, that the real lover of truth is little disposed to call it in question : when, therefore, the mind begins to doubt, and to bluster about investigation, we very naturally conclude, that it finds the restraints of religion inconvenient. Of all men, moreover, the young man, is the last, to be encouraged thus to *investigate.* The tyro always loves to come to startling conclusions. This seems to have been the case with Shelley. Hence, they have shown themselves but poorly acquainted with human nature, who have lauded the unhappy man, as one who would " prove all things," and drive truth to its consequences, whatever they might be. Far different was the true state of the case. But alas, poor sophist! let us give him all his due. Shelley was not like Byron, *gross* in his profligacy, or vulgar in his delineations of vice. Their minds were essentially different ; as different as their *styles* ; which, even where they both use the licentious verse of *Pulci*, are as different as the " hells of London," and the groves of Academus. A fair instance of this may be seen, by a comparison of " Beppo," with " The Witch of Atlas," or the translation of Homer's " Hymn of Mercury." Shelley was, always, an intellectual sinner ; but his tendency was downwards, and he waxed worse. The severity of the discipline which drove him from the arms of Alma Mater gained him the sympathy of many false friends, who either censured it as unnecessary, or derided it as bigotry. Again he received the applauses of the ever evil world. Yet apart from religious considerations, he deserved all his punishment and more, on principles of mere social honor. As a sworn subject of a Trinitarian university, and as a subscriber to his belief in scriptural revelation, as well as a professed member of the church of England, and an approver of her thirty-nine articles, he was perjured in his open blasphemy, and richly merited scorn as well as punishment. But there are some crimes, which, in religion the world pardons, while their equivalents, in civil matters, would be punished by the gibbet or the terrible attainder of universal contempt. By virtue of this obliquity of human judgment, away went the atheist boy, praised as a martyr of truth, and dignified with the name of a philosopher. He shortly fell in with the writings of the infidel Godwin, on " Political Justice." Its theory " haunted him like a passion." He became an idolatrous worshipper of a *Themis*, which like the Sculptor, he took not from other men's opinions, but which he chose to originate for himself. It is the difficulty with your *soi-disant* philosopher, that you never can tell exactly what he believes or rejects. He is always arriving at some new conclusion ; and, if cornered in an argument, informs you that he has exploded that part of his creed himself, and now sees the point to which it was only an approximation. No one can tell what Shelley was at this period of his progress, for while he denied a God, he yet absurdly poetized about " some great pervading spirit of intellectual beauty," and at the same time blasphemed and defied the power, which he affected to disbelieve.

And now begins his high poetical career. He published "Queen Mab," in which the most harmonious metres are desecrated to insult the majesty of the great mover of the harmonious spheres, and the dispenser of the bright beams which enlighten them. This work is backed by numerous notes, many original, some from Godwin, and others from the scoffers of France. A more ridiculous farrago than these same *notes*, was never seen. It consists of Jacobinism and *dietetics!* Yes, dietetics; for Shelley was a *Grahamite*; but so far did he improve upon the arguments of the "children of the captivity," that he considered the use of animal food as *only not so bad* as cannibalism. However, his arguments, drawn from the cruelty of destroying life, and directed against a faith that does not forbid it, are so plausible, as, in connection with his poetical views of the subject, to captivate imperceptibly, our sympathies, and through them, perhaps, to influence our judgment.

A poet's life, said Milton, should itself be a true poem. We maintain that it is always *one of his poetical works.* The Task written by another man would not make a Cowper; and what we know of Homer, as the blind and wandering rhapsodist, makes that counterpart to his Iliad and Odyssey, without which the world would have no Mæonides. Milton's life, and Shakspeare's, and Chatterton's, and Byron's, are essential parts of their works, as poets. Their lives, are the canvass, on which their writings seem depicted. Every one feels this; and who does not think of Anacreon, with a sympathy which perfects his notions of the Teian, when he remembers that the poet of love and wine, died, choked by a grape-stone? It is on this account that we continue to speak of the *life* of Shelley, in connection with his writings.

Shelley became an infidel to throw off restraint, but he did not become an abandoned debauchee. The same affectation of philosophy, which led him to enroll himself *Atheist* in an album kept on a Swiss mountain, was happy in preventing him from wallowing with brutes, though it scarcely justified him, in regarding himself, as, in a sense, a divinity.

Having theoretically, annihilated the great lawgiver, he no longer saw any force in law: and this, certainly with greater consistency than characterizes many of his school, who, while they reject the doctrines of any right in the Deity to interfere with the affairs of his own world, still subscribe to the dogma originally penned by an infidel, that "governments derive a just authority *from the consent of the governed !*" Shelley, reasoned otherwise ; and hence he came to regard the divine institution of marriage as unauthoritative, even as a *civil* institution. However, notwithstanding his opinion that it was an "unhallowed tie," he still suffered himself to be bound with it, before his majority ; he married a woman below him in rank, and one every way unfitted for a poet's spouse. But again he perjured himself at the altar ; for shortly after, in a letter to an infidel writer of the day, he enters into an apology for his having submitted to the despotism of priestcraft, and assures his fellow "reformer," that he had only done so, through a willingness to give the poor girl a place in society. In a note to one of his poems he takes occasion also, to ridicule and condemn the cruelty of public opinion in its ostracism of the degraded female. He argues the point with a coolness that sets all decency at defiance, and handles the most delicate subjects with the constrained appearance of ease, which it is common for those to assume, who condemn all modesty, as mawkishness. He affirms that chastity is no virtue, and roundly contends that its loss is no blemish in woman. One would think such *notes* would effectually exclude him from the boudoir not only, but also destroy all the influence of his sophistry ! But his *life* still more forcibly demonstrates the wretchedness of the godless. The vows which, in professed tenderness for the object of his love, he had rashly assumed, were found inconvenient : and as he deemed them no longer binding when the whim was over, he abandoned the mother of his two children, in disgust, and eloped to Switzerland with——whom ? No other than the daughter of the infamous Mary Woolstoncraft, by his old favorite, the infidel Godwin ! What a beautiful tissue was this !.

His passion was now " to reform the world," as he afterward professes in the preface of his master effort. His great *beau ideal* was, that " Love is the sole law which should govern the moral world." On this plausible dogma, he speculates beautifully, but not altogether intelligibly. He evidently means by it something very different from our Saviour's intention in giving almost the same command. He does not refer to that benevolence, that *αγάπη* towards God and man, which Scripture inculcates, and which is only attainable on the principles of the Bible. But he means an imagination of his own—a strange compound of poetry and lust, and desire of ease, pleasure, and a sort of Epicurean *sans souci*, delighting itself in all pleasant things, and disregarding whatever might annoy it.   Still his theory is captivating, because it *sounds* benevolent ; but it ends in the deduction, that the true way to promote human happiness is to allow every one to act his will ; and especially, as to the love between man and woman, it should never be shackled by priestly bands, but should be left to come and go at pleasure. So would the world prosper, he thinks ; and union inseparable with a detested object would be avoided effectually, to the great comfort of our race.   Let us see the practical fruits of such theorizing !   The poor girl, whom he originally swore to love, *committed suicide* in her abandonment ; and he returned to England with Miss Godwin, whom he afterwards married at the solicitation of her father, who seems not particularly to have relished the first illustration of his principles, in his own daughter.   So the farce became a tragedy, admirably adapted to teach mankind, how undesirable is the happiness that would be attained, if the world were only submitted to the tender mercies of *philosophers* and speculators upon Love, as the sole law of the universe.

   But, no more of a history which sets decency at defiance, as well as religion !   Let it go side by side with Byron's, to point a moral, and to teach us Jeremy Taylor's prayer against the dominion of sin and a consuming lust.   We could not but notice it, however, as the most appropriate commentary on his poetry ; for, as such, God seems to have permitted it to exist ; as he did also, for the same great end, the terrible mockery of their philosophy which appeared in the death-beds of Voltaire and Thomas Paine.

   Shelley's principal work, for size and style, is the REVOLT OF ISLAM, originally known as *Laon and Cynthia*.   It is in the verse of Spenser, with some occasional irregularities, and is no less tedious, and more complex than Queen Mab, while it is by no means so ingenious as the "Faery Queen" of his great master.   Still it is instinct with beauty ; and its dedication to his *Mary* is one of the finest short pieces in our language.   We suspect this work is little read even by the poet's warmest partizans, of whom, happily for us, the greater proportion are on the other side of the Atlantic.   It is a dreamy thing in which, as in Spenser's great work, "more is meant than meets the ear." It requires thought and study to be appreciated ; and this is enough to seal the fate of almost any poem, in our newspaper age. *The Revolt of Islam* is, on this account, chiefly known amongst scholars ; which is all the worse for the world, if they happen to be such as will studiously acquire its false principles, to teach them afterwards to the *ignobile vulgus* in forms which the people can more readily appreciate. Shelley was too subtile to allow his poetic talents to be exhausted in trifling. In everything he wrote he endeavored to convey a principle of his own to the minds of his readers. And this " summer-task" itself, however lightly he may choose to speak of it, is, in reality, the crafty offspring of his yearning to *reform the world.* Would that poets, of better principles, had a little more of this wisdom of the serpent, and would always make their songs the servants of virtue and truth ! The Cenci, which is, perhaps, the most popular of his works, is also the least objectionable. But even this is an insidious foe to religion ; and its conception evidently originates in the deepest enmity to the faith of Christendom. It is founded upon a fact in history, connected with the ruin of the powerful Italian family of *the Cenci.* Assuming the base calumny as truth, that the papacy is nothing more than Christianity carried out and exhibited in its proper relievo, the dramatist refers all the cruelties, which his story unfolds, to the Bible and its blessed authors. A recurrence to his own domestic tragedy should have taught him, one would think, that equally accursed results might proceed even from his favorite poetico-philosophical notion of " Love," as the sole religion and law.

In Queen Mab, his early work, which was originally *published* without his connivance, his genius is very fairly exhibited ; while the bitterness of his infidelity taints continually the sweetness of his verse, and shocks, like a tremulous discord in the piano, that constantly recurs, with harsh jarring, in a strain otherwise refined and delicate. Yet his blasphemy is ever glossed with a show of almost Wordsworthian tenderness. He seems to breathe towards his fellows, " perpetual benediction." It is against his God, that he dares to rave. Yet what could be more puerile than an argument against the divine compassion, drawn from the sacrifices instituted to symbolize the stupendous mercy of man's redemption ! The superficial judgment, which is enough, in his intellectual comprehension, to overthrow all the mercy of the plan which the momentary sufferings of a few irrational beings typified, all vanishes into thin air, when we contemplate the substance which they shadowed—the redemption of millions of immortals from the misery to which his idolized *Justice* condemns them. "How much better is a man than a sheep!" The simple eloquence of such a line overthrows all the splendor of the poet's fiction. Yet, alas, the God whom pure angels rejoice to adore is insulted in every verse of Queen Mab, by one who certainly had no excuse for restraining the yearnings of his thirsty soul towards the fountain of sweet waters, of whose living stream he obstinately refused to quaff. The silvery strains of this poem seem born to bless the great Author of all sweet harmonies : the poet's love of the beautiful seems such as would naturally lead him up to converse with him who is all perfect ; and his deep intellectual perceptions seem eminently to mark him for one, who was intended for a high priest of the heavenly muse upon earth. But, in the degradation of an obstinacy which will not remember that this *big* world and these long years are the merest atoms in the universe and in eternity, Shelley stoops from his height of song to curse the spot where Solomon dedicated the temple of God, and where the Son of the Most High died for ingrates like him, in agonies, which he forgets, while he compassionates the beasts that perish ! Christ died in a majesty of suffering, that no rational being is pardonable for not adoring. Rosseau conceded nothing in his confession that "Jesus died like a God !" It was *wrung* from his bitter lips, by the commanding sublimity of the death-scene itself. How is Shelley to be excused then, who, with a soul all alive to the sublime, could close his eyes on the glory of Christ's sacrifice, and turn from the scene of his torture to blaspheme his name, and sing of Prometheus as more to be admired upon Caucasus, than the "lamb dumb before his shearers," on ignominious Calvary.

And withal Queen Mab is opened with such lines as these—

> "How wonderful is death !
> Death, and his brother sleep—
> One, pale as yonder waning moon,
> With lips of lurid blue :
> The other rosy as the morn,
> When, throned on Ocean's wave,
> It blushes o'er the world !"

Here is a fountain-flow of melody worthy of the arch-deceiver himself ; or of him, who in Pandemonium, was so skilful to make the worse appear the better reason. And the rich stream of music rolls on in equal smoothness, delighting the ear, but stupifying the soul that hath not true piety for an antidote, by the noxious vapors it constantly exhales from bitter waters, poisoned by the deadly branches of his deep rooted infidelity.

Still more in his great work, the *Prometheus Unbound*, do we lament the same fatal blemish. This work is a drama, in which all his art, all his classicality, and the whole force of his intellect have been brought into exercise, for the production of a composition, that is after all, more distinguished for its absurdity, than for its greatness in other respects. Poor Shelley! his zeal for reforming the world, destroyed himself. He hints in his preface that much more was in preparation, and might be expected in future developments of his ruling passion. But—"the pride of thy heart hath deceived thee," seemed the lanof God to this *son of the morning.* Like an untimely fruit he fell in his green youth ; and was uprooted as a cumberer of the ground.

The *Prometheus* of Æchylus is the parent, but not the model, of Shelley's. Like its original, however, the modern drama is remarkable for force, sublimity and deep thought. Its plan is essentially different. Adverse to such a degrading catastrophe as the reconciliation of the champion of mankind with man's oppressor, Shelley alters the old story of the Titan's submission to Jove, and of his delivery by the thunderer's permission. With this fine conception he begins his own plot. The first scene represents Prometheus, in his stern endurance of agony, bound to a frozen pinnacle of Caucasus. The daughters of Ocean, Panthea and Ione sit at his feet in constancy of sorrow. The morning is slowly coming up over the shining glaciers. 'Tis silent all ; until amid the sublimity of all that surrounds him, the Titan opens his unyielding lip, and content to suffer what he knows unjust, in the dignity of suffering virtue, he derides his torturer, and taunts him with the misery he makes, in the else, so lovely world. Then comes the calmness of his intellectual superiority to the passion of revenge. His feelings now are but the unruffled hate of principle. He curses no more ; and now is sick at heart that, in the first groans of his torment, he had been weak enough to curse a being already sufficiently miserable in his unenvied tyranny. He calls on the spirits of the mountains and the earth, and the dear Oceanides to repeat his malediction, which he has forgotten, that it may be revoked. They shudder and shrink from such blasphemy of Jove. The phantasm of Jupiter himself is summoned from a shadow world, a limbo of the poet's own. He comes in terrible majesty, and as the apparition approaches, the Ocean daughters speak.

Ione.

"My wings are folded o'er mine ears,
  My wings are crossed o'er mine eyes,
Yet through their silver shade appears,
  And through their lulling plumes, arise
A shape—a throng of sounds !
  May it be, no ill to thee,
Oh thou of many wounds !

Panthea.

The sound is of whirlwind under ground ;
  Earthquake, and fire, and mountains cloven.
The shape is awful like the sound,
  Clothed in dark purple, star-inwoven.
A sceptre of pale gold,
  To stay steps proud, o'er the slow cloud
His veined hand doth hold.
Cruel he looks, but calm, and strong,
Like one who *does*, not *suffers* wrong."

The English language was scarcely ever wrought into such varied harmony. The lyrics that follow are very like passages from Sophocles, particularly the one beginning, " there the voluptuous nightingales." But to proceed with the story. The phantasm repeats the terrible curse ; and Prometheus sublimely revokes it,

"I wish no living thing to suffer pain."

The scenes following are by turns grand, tender, plaintive, and very magnificent. By Jove's order, Mercury comes to beg the Titan's submission and repentance : the furies follow him, like a cloud, steaming up under his feet, and ready to be set on the sufferer, should he still resist. While they are howling for their repast, the victim eyes them without emotion, except that of wonder at their *hideousness*. The suffering adorer of beauty can only think of their wretchedness, not his own : he calmly asks, " *can aught exult in its deformity ?*"

Maia's son is merciful, and endeavors to persuade him to buy his restoration, by surrender. The Titan regards him not.

Mercury reminds him that millions of years must roll on, in torture, and still his torment be only beginning—

Prometheus.

" Perchance no thought can count them, yet they pass !

Mercury.

If thou might'st dwell among the gods, the while
Lapp'd in voluptuous joy—

Pro.

I would not quit
This bleak ravine, these unrepentant pains.

Mer.

Alas, I wonder at, yet pity thee !

Pro.

Pity the self-deluding slaves of heaven !
Not me—within whose mind sits peace serene,
As light in the sun throned.   How vain is talk !
Call up the fiends !"

Qu'il mourut, in Corneille, and the dying Warwick of Shakspeare are not more sublime !

We wish that time and space were afforded us more fully to analyze this noble drama : but we must now speak of its character as a moral work, and of its influence as an English classic.

The *dramatis personae* of " Promotheus Unbound," are all fables, and old mythology.   Hence, the superficial reader, might not, at first, discover its really infidel character.   He would probably regard it with the same *critical* admiration, and *theological* neglect, as we generally accord to the classics of Greece and Rome.   But Shelley's work differs from the writings of the old heathen, in this, that it is written for Christians, and hath a subtle sting in its tail, as deadly as the old dragon's.   More thoughtful readers will see at once, that Shelley's Prometheus is only Lucifer under another name, or perhaps more properly, a personification of the spirit of rebellion against God.   Then it becomes evident that by *Jupiter*, the poet intends the *Almighty*, whether he be known as " Jehovah, Jove, or Lord :" and the whole fable becomes, what Dr. Mason called Pope's Universal Prayer, " *a cursed lie.*"   We are at loss whether to wonder at, or pity Shelley more. The blasphemy is daring beyond all that we could conceive possible in a Christian land ; but the argument is contemptible in the extreme, being founded on the old folly, that he who gave us knowledge at the expense of Paradise, was the benefactor of our race.

But for the seeming irreverence of the allusion, we might observe, that the only analogy in our religion, to the Prometheus of old tradegy, exists in the sufferings of our Saviour himself, when for a time it was allowed for might to triumph over right, and for the beneficent spirit of all good to be made the sport of demons. In the calm stupendous agony of Jesus Christ, is seen a height of the moral sublime, which would have required all the genius of Shelley, and a purer heart, to shadow forth. In him we see the true hero of the fable, yet far greater than even Shelley's conception of his type, in that he did not even *scorn*. Reviled, he reviled not again ; and when the powers of hell gat hold upon him,——more awful than the furies——he suffered alone, unmoving, undisturbed, unruffled by any yearning for revenge——nay with the godlike compassion that triumphed over torture, and broke out through his death-throes, ——" Father, forgive them, they know not what they do."   Oh, here is realized more than the conception of virtue and benevolence, radiant through torment, of which old heathens loved to dream !   Yet Shelley would not choose the original subject of Messiah for his hero, but went back preferring to be a pagan, and to borrow from the fables of idolatry.   Yet he could not but think of Christ, in this connection, and so he refers to him——

> " Remit the anguish of that lighted stare ;
> Close those wan lips ; let that thorn-wounded brow
> Stream not with blood ; it mingles with thy tears !
> Fix, fix those tortured orbs in peace and death,
> So thy sick throes shake not that crucifix,
> So those pale fingers, play not with thy gore."

We may admire Æschylus, who seizing upon the nearest approach which his religion afforded him, to the glorious conception of the subject, so wove it into song, as still to " justify the ways of God to man."   But what are we to think of Shelley, who, with not so much reverence as the heathen's, passed by the Man of Sorrows, and chose to be the varnisher of an old picture, where Angelo would have covered the walls of a temple, with original delineations !

For his own sake, we weep for Shelley : for that of our religion, we but smile at him.   Our faith shines brighter for its puny foes ; and it is a mawkish tear they shed, who grieve that Christianity had not the aid of his talents.   When his church shall have need of such comfort as poetry can bestow, the Lord will anoint for it some man after his own heart.   Of Shelley and Byron, who deserted the captain of their salvation, to war with his enemies, the Christian may speak like the ancient Laconian, "Sparta hath nobler sons than they."   We look upon the poets of whom we have been speaking,—their followers, and *attachés*, the *little* Byrons and the Hunts, and the οἱ πολλοι,—as occupying the same place in the republic of letters, as the Robespierres, the Marats, and the Klootzes, hold, to everlasting infamy, in the pillory of French politics.   The French revolution and the poetry of what Southey branded "the Satanic School," go hand in hand.   Alike, they sicken the souls of christian men, and alike will they be " damned to eternal fame."

Does the good man sigh over such a delineation of the poetry of his own day ; and does he turn his eyes from the blackening picture, for some glimpse of holy light !   Let him look, for the day-star is at hand.   The poetry, which is already beginning to depose the dark, is awakening the dawn.   In the pure light of the morning, the songs of angels will be fitlier heard ; and even now one and another are raising their voices, not like children piping in the market, but like " deep calling unto deep."

We approach the poetry of WORDSWORTH, not to review it, for that would be impossible in the limited space that is left us. But we shall speak of the great characteristics of his writings, and rather introduce them than criticise.   Happily for us, Wordsworth is " becoming the fashion," and poems little known, though written half a century ago, are beginning to win laurels for the gray hairs of the still surviving bard.

Of his chief work, THE EXCURSION, we cannot begin to speak in this article, for we have no room to do it justice.   We must content ourselves with observing the contrast between the mass of his writings and those of the poets of whom we have spoken.   We shall also quote from a few of his minor pieces ; and recommend to those who are strangers to his poetry, some passages, which will easiest serve them, as entrances to his labyrinth of "all sweet sounds and harmonies."

The student, on first examining, cursorily, the volumes of Wordsworth, would be apt to suppose, from their appearance, that he had early drafted his plan, with all the various appendages of his great design, like an architect making an estimate for a palace ; and that, to this plan he had adhered through life, perfecting from time to time its individual parts. He has given us an arrangement of his poetry, by which every line is marshalled to its place, under the heads of poems referring to boyhood, old age, death, immortality, etc. The fancy, the imagination, and the affections, have each their separate stalls ; and into these are driven all his little gems, on the old principle of "everything in its place ;"—the whole suggesting to some minds, no doubt, the idea of an exquisite Mosaic, but to us, conveying no association more dignified, than that of a rack of *pigeon-holes* in a merchant's bureau, each one exquisitely labelled, *bills redeemable, bills payable,* or the like.

It is a fault with literary men, that they will never see a blemish in their idol. It were wiser if they would never choose an idol ; but if, as is natural, they find that they have adopted one, they should be particularly careful not to be found celebrating its deformities. It has been dryly remarked, that all great men have done, in the course of their lives, at least *one* notoriously foolish thing. Let us speak with reverence of the mighty mind, which we are now considering ; but still permit us to inquire, whether this *theory* of Wordsworth, be not that one indefensible thing in him.

The very mention of a theory of poetry hath a most unpoetical sound ; and *à priori,* we feel ready to pronounce the poet of *theory,* no true bard. This seems to have been the effect of Wordsworth's *principles* upon Lord Byron, who detested them at the first blush, and sneered at them, unremittingly, through life. Cowper laughed at Blair, as one who settles what he reads as correct, not by the touch-stone of an original, instinctive taste, but by a calculation of its degree of conformity to certain rules, for certain cases, made and provided. In a perusal of Wordsworth's theorizings, one would suppose that he must write, as Blair read. But this is, by no means, the case. Wordsworth has a mind, as naturally made for philosophy, as for poetry ; and after he has given way to the real influence of inspiration, he cools down to the contemplation of his own work, and of the intellectual operations which produced it, with all the severity of a metaphysical critic. And then he forges out a *theory*, and puts on the shackles, which we are apt to suppose he wore, while at work on the poem. Sometimes, it is true, he seems to have attempted the poetic toil, before he had again thrown off his chains ; and where, in such captivity, he has produced strange manufactures, (all *demonstrably* correct and beautiful *by his own rules*, but, to our natural perceptions, grotesque as the hexagonal trees of Versailles,)—he has certainly *failed*, and of course, has *not* failed to excite the derision of minor critics, of that interesting description who see no joy in the sunlight, because Sol's disc has spots. It is where he has forgotten *theories* and *principles of poetry*, in the innate rush of his glorious perceptions ; and where he has written under the unrestrained impulse of his genius, that this mighty master moves and triumphs.

In his preface to the collected edition of his works, he informs us, that it is his design to leave us, beside the monument of his great effort—THE RECLUSE, of which *the Excursion* is part—the classified total of his minor poems, as a symmetrical counterpart, to his *chef d'œuvre.* The idea of this is very pleasing. It is the natural conception of a mind in love, to sickness, with proportion and propriety. There is a miserable scrap-book effect presented to the eye on opening the volumes of most modern poets, which seems to weaken the character of poetry in our day. How disagreeable is the sight, in many of our finest authors, of *quotations* inserted in the text !—an innovation of a most tasteless nature, at least in serious poetry ! And furthermore, how unpleasant is the introduction of long *mottoes*, and extracts from gazettes, as prefaces to little odes, ballads or sonnets. Even *Notes*, are getting to be nuisances. The old writers got along without them ! Why must modern poets add page after page of dull prose to their volumes, by way of annotation? How would Paradise Lost appear, with half its size additional in notes, such as figure as a bob-tail to Childe Harold ! Yet there are deeper mysteries in the former, than in " my lord Biron." The truth is, POETRY, like EMPIRE, seems getting into the *toes* of their golden-headed type, and is little more, in our time, than iron " mixed with miry clay." Lord Byron has very much of this *crumbiness*, in his minor poems. But in him, perhaps, it is more excusable. The Gothic floridness of his style seems to allow the admission of these thousand little unarranged adornments; and they please us, just as the chapels, nooks, and niches of a great cathedral delight by their variety, and by their very *want* of method. In Shelley we see less of this. There is an Ionic niceness and precision, in the structure of his smallest shrine or trophy. But Wordsworth's Corinthian finish must, to satisfy his design, be so disposed as to exhibit, at a *coup d'œil*, the whole internal construction and harmony of parts. Much better than all, is the unstudied arrangement which Milton's mighty works seem to have fallen into of themselves, with no thought of his own. Of them, we always conceive his immortal epic as reared in a Doric repose of grandeur, upon a height inaccessible, save by the majestic rise, of his lesser productions—his Allegro and Penseroso, his Lycidas, his Comus, his Samson Agonistes.

But Wordsworth, also, gives us a glance at his poetical workshop; and tells us besides, that Cowper and Young made their Task and Night Thoughts, of certain proportions compounded of the Idyl, the Ode, and the Didactic poem. But, while this may be critically *true*, how little would it have pleased us, had they themselves seen fit to introduce those great works to us, with such an announcement! It is, probably, an idea that never entered their heads; and one, which had it been suggested to them, would have been noticed only by a transient smile. Cowper wrote as his genius led him; and his Task exists. It is of no consequence, what kinds of poetry may be detected in it; for it was not compounded like a prescription in Pharmacy. It is unpleasant to see a poet unravelling these things for us, just as it would be disagreeable to see a sculptor, writing the anatomical names of parts of his statue on the marble, or telling us what ligature rounded the fair limb of a Venus, or what muscle nerved the bold arm of the Apollo Belvidere. There are things which we do not like to be told. Such remarks are more agreeable, when they spring up in our own minds, as the fruit of our own investigation. We may go behind the scenes, when buskin'd Garrick has left them; but it is an unendurable irrelevancy, to be bored during the representation, by a pedant at our elbow, who gratuitously informs us that Macbeth's armor is made of paste-board, and that the glare from the witches' cauldron is nothing but the light of burning rosin and sulphur.

Perhaps our illustration is too strong; but it really troubles us, in the perusal of our favorite author, to see on every page a counterpart of the labels of the poor French artist—*voici l'ourse, voilà le renard.*—For all we know the *Idiot Boy* may be " a Poem founded on the affections," but we confess, that in reading such lines as—

> " And now she's at the Pony's tail,
> And now she's at the Pony's head—"

We care very little whether it be akin to Akenside or Mother Goose.   We deem *it*, and *Lines in March*, and the *Pet Lamb*, as only written for the nursery, and published according to the mathematical demonstrations of its propriety, furnished by a *theory*, which is an excrescence, and no part of the poet himself. This, we believe, most of our readers will allow ; though, we doubt not, that should this paper ever meet the eye of the illustrious individual of whom we speak, he would deem far otherwise.   We can fancy him, smiling at our superficial view of the subject, in the serenity of his philosophic abstraction, while we are still assured, that, could he make himself one of those for whom he writes, he would pronounce the same verdict upon a system, in which no one can sympathize with its author.

The true seed of Wordsworth's poetry, the condensation of its plan, seems to be the little fragment, that meets the eye on opening the first leaf of his volume.   Pregnant with thought— all that succeeds it seems born of it.   He has dilated it into glorious compass, and illustrated it with beauties, in untiring variety.   It is a point, from which he has produced a pyramid. It is the expression of an intellectual being, commencing its course for eternity ;—the ejaculation of a man full-grown, but who is still in the sense of our blessed Saviour, " a little child."   Its language is musical, dispassionate and pure, and such as a new-created angel might employ, coming forth in beauty, and looking into worlds unborn.   We envy no one the heart that leaps not up with it, and joins not in its fervent prayer.

> " My heart leaps up when I behold
>   A rainbow in the sky !
> So was it when my life began,
> So is it now I am a man,
> So be it when I shall grow old,
>   Or let me die !
> The child is father of the man,
> And I could wish my days, to be
> Bound each to each by natural piety."

Here is a high-born poet's soul anticipating its career of glory, of fame unfabled, and honor from the fountain of honor above. And here is the love of the dear world, of the beauty of nature, and thence of nature's God—

> " My heart leaps up, etc."

Here, is the poetic unwillingness to loose the hold on fair things of sense, which is apt to slacken with our growing years—

> " So be it when I shall grow old,
> Or let me die !"

And here is a verse which has deservedly become a part of our language—

> " The child is father of the man."

Here is a rising into the sublime on wings of dignified religion—

> " And I could wish, etc."

And could a spirit like this fail to soar towards the heaven, on which his eye was thus early set ! Go, reader, follow him in his flight. Go tread with him the Alps, and gaze with him on clear Como. Or, in his own land, halt with him on the banks of the Wye. Nay, we will give you a glimpse of the picture here. Listen to his reflection ; rejoice in the sweet music of his words ; and confess that to love God and Nature, is to live above the world.

> " Oh, yet a little while
> May I behold in thee, what I was once,
> My dear, dear sister ! and this prayer I make
> Knowing that Nature never did betray
> The heart that loved her.   'Tis her privilege,
> Through all the years of this, our life, to lead
> From joy to joy ; for she can so inform
> The mind that is within us, so impress
> With quietness and beauty, and so feed
> With lofty thoughts, that neither evil tongues,
> Rash judgments, nor the sneers of selfish men,
> Nor greetings, where no kindness is, nor all
> The dreary intercourse of daily life,
> Shall e'er prevail against us, or disturb
> Our cheerful faith, that all which we behold
> Is full of blessings.   Therefore, let the moon
> Shine on thee in thy solitary walk,

And let the misty mountain wind be free
To blow against thee ; and in after years,
When these wild ecstasies shall be matured
Into a sober pleasure ; when thy mind
Shall be a mansion for all lovely forms,
Thy memory be as a dwelling-place
For all sweet sounds and harmonies ; oh then
If solitude, or fear, or pain, or grief,
Should be thy portion, with what healing thoughts
Of tender joy, wilt thou remember me,
And these my exhortations !"

Here we have Cowper, and—we must say—something more.
How is old England blest in her Christian bards ! How in the
pure atmosphere, we are now breathing, we forget that such as
Byron have sung. We stand on Niphates, and all is pure air
and sunlight around us, however the storm may be vapouring
below. We have made the transition through Shelley, from
Byron, for this effect : and now we have reached the top of the
mount, and " methinks it is good to be here." Is religion a
disqualifier for poetry ? Is the world darker, and nature less
lovely, when looked upon by the seraph-eye of the Christian ?
Is there less rapture in the bosom of him who gazes on the
glacier, and the sky above, the lake, the spires, the valley below, and the merry vintagers anear, and all to retain unshaken
our simple creed—

" That all which we behold
Is full of blessings—— ?"

Is there less rapture in such a bosom, than in that of him,
who can leave the glorious scenery of the mountains, and
descend to the mart, and pry into its dark and steaming corners,
to draw out " that dear production of our days—Don Juan ?"
We would rather be Democritus than his opposite : we would
prefer being the *Christian* observer of things earthly, than
either. The natural mind looks on all things *superficially*.
Byron, was all surface. The cultivated mind inquires deeper,
perhaps, but discovers not the nice mechanism of the great
mover. Shelley could look at the misery of the world and
scoff. He might have taken a lesson from Parnell's hermit.
But the christian mind, the true philosopher, can behold the
hand of the first great cause in everything, and smiling say,
" My Father made them all !" He has learned that sublime
degree of confidence, that looks on the blue heaven, and says

with calmness, " shall not the judge of all the earth, do right !"
We cannot but believe, that, in that pure world where all is
harmony, where there is nothing to blunt the nice feelings of
exquisite nature ;—where music is the voice, and poetry the
language ; where the mind is free, ethereal, unclogged—we
cannot but think that there is the perfection of that which the
soul yearns after here,—that great ideal of which the spirit, with
growing wings, delights to dream.   And if this be so, all that is
its opposite is no poetry.   It may be conceit, it may be harmony ; it is not true poetry.   And, consequently, we must
believe that as our little planet rolls on to its long pledged
golden reign, the elements of beauty which it contains, are
destined to arrange themselves in fair and beautiful order, and
to become as clear as crystal.   And now hath this grand
alchemy begun.   Ages on ages of our world had elapsed, and,
save from those who were mouths to the Eternal mind, we
heard no sacred sound.   It is of late only, that the silvery tones
of poetry have begun to breathe religion.   There is our great—
we will not call it *epic*, for it needs not the name.   For Dante's
Commedia, and for Milton's Paradise Lost, we claim a classification by themselves.   They need not be judged by the side
of Homer to be glorious.   But there is our beginning, and the
great star of the constellation, around which the lesser lights of
Cowper, and Thomson, and Watts, and Montgomery, and
Heber are dotting the surrounding darkness.   Amid them,
another luminary of the first magnitude is burning : and though
in his elevation, so far from us groundlings, that his light
has but slowly reached us, we believe that he is surely destined
to become the poet of Christendom, as he is the poet of
Christianity.

We have professed to be merely considering the character of
Wordsworth's poetry, without reviewing his works.   Yet we
cannot allow this opportunity to pass without pointing our
readers to those parts of his writings, where the mind will enter, and feel more speedily at home.   Besides his innumerous
minor poems, he has several collections of sonnets, apparently
disconnected, but in reality continuous works.   Of these, his
ECCLESIASTICAL SKETCHES are in our opinion preëminent.
Except the sonnets of Milton, there are none in the language
to compare with these.   Their harmony not all alone, but their
thought and imagery are generally perfect.   We shall quote
one, by no means the finest ; and that, with the hope that it

will be read, with Wordsworth's own caution,—by a *reader !*
How are the finest passages of our best poets tattered daily, by
the wretched recitations even of educated men. Poetry should
be read aloud, unless by a man of imagination, that the ear
may catch the rhythm. And this sonnet must be read slowly,
sweetly, and contemplatively, or it will never be appreciated.
So read, however, we hear the monks' music ; we feel the
thrill of the monarch ; we float into reflection.

> " A pleasant music floats along the mere
>   From monks in Ely, chanting service high
>   While Caniste, the king, is rowing by.
> " My oarsmen," quoth the mighty king, " draw near,
>   That we the sweet sound of the monks may hear."
>   He listens ; (all past conquests, and all schemes
>   Of future, vanishing, like empty dreams,)
>   Heart-touched, and haply, not without a tear.
>   The royal minstrel ere the choir is still,
>   While his free barge skims the smooth flood along,
>   Gives to that rapture, an accordant rhyme.
>   Oh suffering earth, be thankful ! Sternest clime,
>   And rudest age, are subject to the thrill
>   Of heaven descended piety, and song."

Next to Milton's " *Avenge, oh Lord,*" we should be proud
to adduce this as a specimen of the English sonnet. In the
first line, the sound mirrors the sense ; in the second, we see
the fane on the waterside, and the devotees within. Then
comes the dip of the oar—the royal hand stretched forth to
check it—the ear awake to listen—the far-off chanting—the
effect on the mighty soul ! We feel with him, and the thrill
remains, " as the free barge skims the smooth flood along "—
the oars still suspended, dripping on the soft water, and the vessel itself gliding with its former impulse.

On a Sunday morning, we may open Wordsworth with advantage, when we close our Bibles, to read the *Thanksgiving
Ode.* We may dwell long on its sabbath-morning effect, with
a pleasing delight that sweetly prepares us for worship ; and
lost in revery, our thoughts may wander away—

> " Till hark, the summons ! down the placid lake
>   Floats the soft cadence of the church-tower bells—
> Bright shines the sun, as if his beams might wake
>   The tender insects, sleeping in their cells.
> Bright shines the sun ; and not a breeze to shake

The drops that tip the melting icicles.
Oh, enter now his temple gate !

Inviting words,—perchance already sung,
(As the crowd press devoutly down the aisle,
Of some old minster's venerable pile,)
From voices, into zealous passion stung ;
While the tubed engine feels th' inspiring blast,
And hath begun its clouds of sound, to cast
  Towards the empyreal heaven,
  As if the fretted roof were riven."

But, in fine, we notice the *Ode on Immortality.* It is a glorious development of the lines, with which we set out, and which he has taken for his motto. They might well be the first strophé ; only that this ode is rather the old man looking back on the race, which in the lines we have quoted, he contemplates as before him. The student, who reads this ode for the first time, may understand it, but he will, probably, not appreciate it. One needs to be fully imbued with the spirit of it, before he can love it ; and hence an exception should perhaps be made, in case of a student of high and deeply exercised virtuous genius. He will probably, at once, appreciate it, for he will see in it the traces of kindred ;—a mysterious brotherhood that calls out his inmost soul. Once, truly felt, it will never grow old. Yet to many, who call themselves finished Belles-lettres scholars, the existence of this ode is almost unknown. Others have *read* it ; and others have *looked* at it, but content with calling it Platonism, have abandoned it, with that learned epithet, to be no more a task to their imbecility. We believe, however, that any mind accustomed to look into itself, will, when once it is fully comprehended, truly luxuriate in it ever afterward. How happy then is the noble mind that loves it, with the first sound of its syllables, and that comes to it, in Lord Bacon's way, as if he had thought it all before. To the mass of men it will never be known. Like Gray's Pindarics, it requires some *thought* to be understood ; and who does not know that the mad thousand have no such property ! Coleridge remarked, that its author might well have prefixed to it, the words of Dante—

Canzon ! io credo, che saranno radi
Che tua ragione intendan bene :
Tanto lor sei faticoso, ed alto.

And he has elsewhere adopted Pindar's majestic Greek in its defence : not scrupling, in his heartfelt scorn of Wordsworth's opponents, to apply to them the Theban's indignant epithet of "crows that croak and chatter against the divine bird of Jove."

The ode is a philosophical rhapsody. We are not to attribute its sentiments to the poet, as a *creed*, but only as inquiries, well expressed, as to the dark enigma of our being. Have we lived before ? Did our existence commence but yesterday ? Have we lived in other worlds ? Do we not, by living here, alienate ourselves from a society with things unseen, which we once enjoyed ? These are the misgivings on which the poet dwells. In the sober years of philosophy, he looks back to the years of his first arrival on our earth, and doubts whether he did not then possess a knowledge that has left him. He is *sure*, that, with regard to things eternal, he has lost a delicacy of enjoyment which he once was endowed with. A glory from the grass and the flower, has departed long since. "It is not now as it hath been before." Here the poet begins : and, would that we could quote each mighty strophe, that swells from this natural key-note. But hear a little of the next strophe. He still retains a love for nature—a glow of enthusiastic admiration—but with all, a sense, that his perception of its beauty is diminished.

> "The moon doth, with delight,
> Look round her, when the heavens are bare,
> Waters, on a starry night,
> Are beautiful and fair ;
> The sunshine is a glorious birth,
> But yet I know, where'er I go,
> That there hath passed away, a glory from the earth."

In the third strophe, he pictures the joy of earth and of youth, and of happy animals, in all which, though his hairs are now gray, his heart still mingles. In the *fourth*, he thus addresses them—

> "Ye blessed creatures, I have heard the call
> Ye to each other make : I see
> The heavens laugh with you in your jubilee :
> My heart is at your festival,
> My head hath its coronal,
> The fulness of your bliss, I feel, I feel it all."

Oh, how blessed is this delight, in the happiness of others !

Is it not such as angels feel, when they see God's creatures innocently merry ! But the transition to the *fifth* strophe is wonderful ; and this is more so !

> " Heaven lies about us in our infancy,
> Shades of the prison house begin to close
> Upon the growing boy, etc."

The *eighth* strophe must be particularized, as a remarkable triumph of poetry. An address to a *baby*—but awful as the grave !

> " Thou, whose exterior semblance doth belie
> Thy soul's immensity, etc.——"

Perhaps Milton has sublimer scenes than what follows : he certainly takes us up to heaven : but there is a stupendous moral grandeur in this, and a mystery that sets us, at once, into eternity.

> " —— the eternal deep
> *Haunted forever by the Eternal Mind !*"

Then where was ever a finer stroke of art, than in the transition from this slow, solemn, organ-like passage, to the lively flute notes that follow !

> " Oh, joy that in our embers
> Is something that doth live !"

Passing from this, we thrill along the *ninth* and *tenth* strophes, and rejoice in the

> " faith that looks through death,
> In years that bring the philosophic mind."

The conclusion is worthy of the poem, and its author—

> " The clouds that gather round life's setting sun
> Do take a sober coloring, from an eye
> That hath kept watch o'er man's mortality ;
> Another race hath been, and other palms are won—
> Thanks to the human heart, by which we live,
> Thanks to its tenderness, its joys, its fears,
> To me, the meanest flower that blows can give
> Thoughts that do often lie too deep for tears."

We love to contemplate Wordsworth in the hallowed light of this glorious ode ; and to be thankful that he still remains with us, in green old age, to bless the land of his sojourning. When we consider this truly great and good man's history ; and compare his present condition with the fearful blank, with which we regard the names of the twain who have been associated with him in the present article, we cannot but feel, how true is the word of inspiration, that godliness is profitable, for the world to come, not only, but even for this. Shelly perished poetically, and poets built his funeral pile in the most beautiful part of the world, on the banks of the dark blue sea. Like an old Grecian, he was burned, with incense and wine, and spices : a heathen in his entombment, as he had been in his life. Byron died in tumult, disheartened, and alone, worn out with debauchery and prematurely gray. Both of these were cut down in the prime of life, and ended ere they begun. During their reign, there was no reproach which Wordsworth did not receive from their bitter lips. But he lived along, unreplying, and in dignified silence ; ever comforted by his religion ; and so impressed with the sweet influence of lovely things, that "neither evil tongues, nor slanders, nor the sneers of selfish men," were of any avail to break the peace of his moonlit walk, or the joy of his morning hymn. And they have gone away, despised by all good men ; while Wordsworth lives out all his days, and looks forward to heaven, with no foe on earth, except the wicked. Our little planet is rolling on to her golden age, and to the millennial glory of the Church. In that pure day, who can doubt that Wordsworth shall be still better beloved and appreciated ; while, in the case of the unhappy many, shall be terribly exemplified, the adage, " the name of the wicked shall rot ?"

How grateful must it be to the feelings of the poet now, to read the triumph of principle in his own chequered biography. Unknown and unfriended, and without any meretricious adornment, he appeared on the stage long ago, only to be pilloried there for the amusement of cold-hearted critics. Still, he pursued his steady way, long neglected, and long eclipsed by the false glories that were blazing about him. But the straw has burned out, and the smoke is disappearing, and men of intellect and of soul are turning towards him, in every land, " like the Parsee to the sun." The splendid eulogium lately pronounced on his writings, in the British Parliament, by Sergeant Talfourd, was but the echo of the voice of all who speak the English tongue ; and certainly of that of our own great Empire, from whose distant shores he hears, as from another world, the benediction,

" Serus, in cœlum redeas."

ARTICLE XII.

CRITICAL NOTICES.

1.—*Concordantiae Librorum Veteris Testamenti Sacrorum Hebrai-*
cae atque Chaldaicae secundum literarum ordinem et vocabu-
lorum origines distincte ordinateque dispositae, lexico utrius-
que linguae tum rabbinico tum latino, hoc est, interpretatione
omnium vocabulorum completa locupletatae, atque, fructibus,
quos instituta et nostrâ et patrum memoriâ linguarum orien-
talium investigatio ac collatio praebuit, industrie comparatis
et conditis, accuratissima cum diligentia absolutae, auctore
Julio Fürstio, doctore philosophiae. Lipsiae : sumptt. et
typp. C. Tauchnitii. Sect. I—VI.

This is a work whose appearance cannot fail to be greeted with
the most lively satisfaction as well by Hebrew students in general as
by the grammarian and lexicographer of the sacred language, whose
inquiries it is so admirably calculated to facilitate. The immense
improvements it exhibits both in comprehensiveness of plan and in
beauty and accuracy of execution, are such as to place it far in advance of all preceding works of the kind, to largely augment the
fame of its indefatigable author and enterprising publisher, and in
fine, to rank it as one of the most remarkable literary productions of
the age.
A Hebrew Concordance, i. e. a book exhibiting with some unimportant exceptions all the words found in the Hebrew Bible, together
with the various forms they assume and the connections in which
they occur, has always been and will always continue to be regarded as an immense storehouse of facts which form the basis of many
of the conclusions of the biblical interpreter as well as of the Hebrew
philologist. Such being the case, it may to many appear matter of
surprise that more than two centuries have been suffered to elapse
since the publication of Buxtorf's Hebrew Concordance, (although
from its rarity this has long been difficult of acquisition,) without producing any work of the kind which can be compared to it either for
extent or usefulness. The obstacles which opposed themselves to
the realization of the many plans for a new and improved edition to
which the increasing scarcity of the work and its acknowledged imperfections from time to time gave rise, arose, not from the want of
a conviction of the great benefit to Hebrew literature which would
result from it, but from the enormous amount of labor which its
proper execution would demand even from the most accomplished
oriental scholar, together with the great pecuniary outlay it would
necessarily involve.

If therefore the author and publisher of the present work had merely undertaken to answer these wants by a republication of Buxtorf with some necessary additions and corrections, they would have deserved the encouragement and warmest thanks of every Hebrew scholar. But in truth far more than this has been effected. The enterprising publishing house of Tauchnitz in Leipsic, to whom the literary public is already so highly indebted for correct and beautiful editions of standard works in almost every language to which the typographical art has been applied, have attended to the " getting up" of the work in question in the highest style of art without regard to expense. They have also succeeded in obtaining as its editor the learned and talented Dr. Julius Fürst, who, although but recently become known to the public as an author, by the publication of his Aramaic *Lehrgebäude* and *Perlenschnüre,* has already obtained the reputation of an Orientalist of the very highest order.

In these works, of which in a future number we intend to offer a review, he has proved himself a most able and successful advocate of the *analytico-historical* as opposed to the mere *rational* method of investigation adopted and defended by some writers of the present day. This method, which consists, as its name implies, of combining the evidences afforded by philological analysis with the testimony of tradition, he has employed with great philosophical acumen in tracing out and displaying the degree of relationship between the languages of the Shemitish and Indo-European families which had already been partially demonstrated to exist. His *Lehrgebäude* exhibits in a vast number of instances the success which has attended his investigation in this department of philological inquiry ; and although, as might have been anticipated, he has been severely attacked by the partisans of the rational school, who reject all historical evidence which does not coincide with their own à *priori* deductions, he has forced upon every impartial scholar a conviction of the soundness of his views and of the correctness of the results which their practical application has led him to obtain.

The high expectations to which the novelty and importance of his speculations gave rise among oriental scholars have been fully met by the present publication, which combines in itself a concordance the most comprehensive in its plan and accurate in its execution that has yet appeared, and a lexicon which may be termed perfect as far as relates to the etymological history of the words and the philosophical development of their various shades of signification. The plan of the work is as follows. The words, both Hebrew and Chaldee, are ranged under their respective roots, and preceding the enumeration of the passages in which each one is found is a detailed account of its etymology and meanings in rabbinical Hebrew and in Latin.

These two statements, however, are by no means exact counterparts to each other. In the rabbinical portion the opinions of the most celebrated Jewish doctors and grammarians are stated and discussed, and the meaning of each word settled upon a sound historical basis that will cause to be laid aside as we trust forever many of the far-fetched and unfounded speculations in which modern lexicographers have indulged. The evidence, too, which is thus derived from tradition and from the concurrence of ancient interpreters, is remarkably strengthened by the collateral proof afforded by a most extensive and ingenious comparison of the roots, first with those of the other Shemitish languages, and next with those of the Indo-European stock ; the results of which are as instructive as they are in many cases new and surprising. The frequency of his references to and quotations from the Talmudic writers shows a familiarity with their productions far surpassing even that of the learned Buxtorf, while the purity and elegance of his Hebrew style reminds one of the writings of the Jewish sages of antiquity.

The Latin account of the word which succeeds the Rabbinic is deserving of equal commendation for the beauty and correctness of the style in which it is written. It contains 1, a repetition of the etymologies already given ; 2, a comparison of the equivalent terms in the fragments of the three Greek translations, the Chaldee paraphrases, the Vulgate, and other classical versions ; 3, a complete enumeration of the various Greek expressions employed in the rendering of each word by the Seventy ; and 4, a variety of philological and archaeological observations, frequently of great interest and importance.

It will thus be seen that as a lexicon the work of Buxtorf, which gives but a single meaning to each word, is one which cannot be compared with it for a moment. As a concordance the superiority of the work of Dr. Fürst is hardly less marked. Its principal features in this point of view are as follows :

1. The word to be illustrated is accurately pointed, the place of the accent marked, and its grammatical form stated.

2. The text of the cited passages, here as in Buxtorf left unpointed, has been revised according to the standard edition of the Hebrew Bible by Hahn ; and the places in which various readings occur are pointed out by means of the masoretic signs. In the course of the revision a vast number of errors have been corrected, and we are enabled to state from actual examination that very few indeed have been suffered to remain.

3. The references to book, chapter, and verse, which were given by Buxtorf in Hebrew, are here put for greater convenience in Roman letters and Arabic numerals, while the number of citations has been immensely increased by means of the editor's own researches as well as by the contributions of his friends. Many passages given by Buxtorf, which contain words similar in form to those under

which they are placed but totally different in etymology and signification, are corrected and inserted under their proper heads.

4.   A number of words which Buxtorf had omitted on account of the immense number of times which they occur have found a place in the new Concordance.   All the nouns too, as well as those particles which are derived from verbal roots, are given.   Particles from pronominal roots are excluded from the body of the work, but will be placed in an alphabetical list at the end.

The work as we have stated is arranged on the etymological plan, to the advantages of which those of the alphabetical arrangement are superadded by means of an index at the end containing all the biblical Hebrew and Chaldee words in alphabetical order, with references to the pages of the Concordance on which they are found. There are also several other highly valuable appendages to the work, among which are : An alphabetical list of all the Aramaic, Talmudic, and Rabbinic words explained in the lexicographical division, the number of which is so great as to form an almost complete Aramaic and Rabbinic lexicon in themselves ; a tabular view of the Hebrew roots arranged according to their affinities with those of the other six families of languages of the ancient world ; a collection of the fragments of the old Aramaic Masora, preceded by a history of the same ; and lastly, a chronological table of the sacred writings.   The work is calculated to make ten parts of one hundred and twenty folio pages each, six of which have already reached us. It is truly a herculean undertaking, and we cannot doubt but that in this country as well as in Europe it will meet with the applause and encouragement to which it is so eminently entitled.

2.—*History of the Reign of Ferdinand and Isabella, the Catholic.*
    By William H. Prescott.   In three Volumes.   Fourth Edition.
    Boston : Charles C. Little and James Brown, 1838. pp. 534,
    509, 531.

A brief notice of the first edition of this work will be found in the *Repository* for April last, (Vol. XI. p. 518.)   The *fourth edition* is now before the public, in which several verbal inaccuracies of the *first* are corrected and a variety of new and valuable references and illustrations are supplied.

This large and valuable historical work is such as rarely appears in any language.   It is the fruit of long labor and of learned and accurate research, with advantages which have not been possessed by any previous writer of Spanish history.   The candor and thoroughness with which the author has pursued his investigations and the honesty with which he has submitted his authorities to the inspection of the reader, are worthy of all praise.   One of the first impressions produced by the reading of this book is that the author has thoroughly studied his subject,—that it is trustworthy.

The title of the work does not convey to the reader an adequate idea of its scope and design. The author has accomplished much more than his title promises. It is not the " history of the reign of Ferdinand and Isabella" merely, but of *Spain*, for a considerable time previous to the commencement of that reign, and continued through the regencies of Ferdinand and of Ximenes which succeeded it, to the beginning of the reign of *Charles the Fifth*. The plan of the work is singularly bold and philosophical.

In two introductory chapters of more than ninety pages we have a graphic and very satisfactory view of the political condition of Spain, from the eighth to the fifteenth century. During that long and dreary period, it was broken up into a number of small but independent States, divided in their interests and often in deadly hostility with each other. By the middle of the fifteenth century, these numerous States had become reduced to four ; Castile, Aragon, Navarre, and the Moorish kingdom of Granada. Of the first two of these our author gives a more particular account in his introductory chapters, the history of their constitutions, the characteristics of the people, their religious enthusiasm, the influence of their Minstrelsy, their chivalry, the Cortes, its power, boldness, etc. the nobility, their privileges and wealth, knights, clergy, the poverty of the crown, &c. all which are necessary to enable the reader to understand the origin of subsequent events and the agencies concerned in their production.

We are thus presented with the scattered and heterogeneous materials which were about to be combined to constitute a great nation ; a nation " born to decay," but destined, during the brief career of its glory and its conquests, to exert a more signal influence, on the civilization of Europe and the world, than any other nation of its time.

The marriage of Ferdinand and Isabella first united the crowns of Castile and Aragon. After this, their policy and success in arms soon reduced to subjection the kingdoms of Granada and Navarre, and thus completed the internal national structure of modern Spain. In the meantime Sicily and the Balearic Isles had descended to Ferdinand, with the crown of Aragon, and during the same reign Naples and the whole of lower Italy were added to the Spanish dominions, while the arms of Ximenes acquired for it a new sovereignty in the north of Africa, and the discoveries of Columbus extended the empire of Spain to a world before unknown.

And not only was Spain, at this time, the most interesting nation in the world, but the age of Ferdinand and Isabella's reign was one of the most important points in the world's history. It was an age of revolution and of wonderful expansion of the elements of modern civilization. The properties of the needle had now just begun to be applied to maritime adventure, unfolding new avenues to wealth and knowledge. Gunpowder and fire-arms were beginning to modify the art of war; and printing had just come into use, diffusing intellectual life with a rapidity and to an extent before unknown. It was an age too of *concentration* among the powers of Europe, when the first visible causes began to operate which have resulted in the modern political state of the European nations. The whole European world was in a state of excited action, and the human mind was moving forward with visible and accelerated steps. Learning was about to revive, the impulses were now given which resulted in the glorious Protestant Reformation, and the discovery of the American continent, first opened that broad theatre for the development of the principles of civil and religious freedom, which are so happily illustrated in the Constitution and usages of our own United States, and which are even now exerting a reflex influence so benign and powerful upon the old world.

The history of the reign which embraced the *beginnings* of these great *ends*, is one of more than common interest, not only to the general reader, but to the philosopher, the statesman, the philanthropist and the Christian of every land; while, to Americans, it embraces topics of peculiar attraction.

We deem it unnecessary and out of place to attempt, here, an extended review of this admirable history. Every part of it seems to us so indispensable to the full and correct understanding of the whole, that, to give an adequate exhibition of the merits of the work, we should need to write it over again, and give to our author the credit of original discovery, in regard to most of the important matters of which it is composed. They are such as have never before been presented in the English language. This history is therefore essentially a new one, though the times of which it treats have long since passed away. Robertson's " Charles the Fifth," and the works of Hallam, Roscoe, Milman, Flechier and Sismondi have treated in a popular historical form several topics embracing partial views of Spanish affairs under the administration of Ferdinand and Isabella. Irving, of our own country, in his lives of Columbus and other Spanish voyagers, and also in his chronicle of the Conquest of Granada, has shed a brilliant light upon some of the striking events of that age. But a full history of that reign, its internal policy, its external relations, its important connections with the preceding and subsequent ages of the world, was never attempted by any historian in our language, until it has not only been attempted but *executed* in a most attractive and satisfactory manner by our countryman, Mr. Prescott.

The leading personages in this history, as the title indicates, are the reigning sovereigns of Spain. Associated with them are " the Admiral," Columbus, " the great Captain," Gonsalvo, and Ximenes, whose various characteristics and exploits made him the wonder of his age. Around these several heroes of his narrative, to say nothing of a host of inferiors, our author throws all the life and interest of biography, while the grand events which the history of these individuals draws in its train, introduce the reader, almost unconsciously, to a well arranged and systematic history of Spain in that eventful period of the world.

Next to the discovery of America by Columbus, one of the most interesting topics embraced in this work, especially to the ecclesiastical historian, is the origin and history of the modern Inquisition. Most of the materials of this history, which, until now, have been inaccessible to English readers, have been gathered by our author from the very voluminous documents, in French, recently disclosed by Llorente, a late secretary of that dread tribunal. These are here condensed and the substance of them is presented in a highly attractive form, throwing much new light upon an institution, which must forever remain a blot upon the reign of the beautiful queen. The expulsion of the Jews from Spain, who were the first victims of inquisitorial cruelty, bears still more severely upon the character of one, whose influence in many respects makes us proud to recognize her as the " mother of America." This expulsion, the fall of Granada and the fate of the Jews in Africa, whither they were driven, furnish many scenes of heart-rending interest.

But it is not our intention to enumerate the topics of these attractive volumes. As we have already remarked, a larger portion of the work is new to the English reader, and the materials, rich and various, are arranged in admirable order to produce an ever-growing interest in the reader.

On the whole we are proud to recommend this history, both at home and abroad, as an *American work ;* while we congratulate the author on the rapid sale of the first three editions, and a popularity already acquired, which will ensure him an ample return for his long continued labor and research, under embarrassments of no ordinary character.

3.—*History of the United States from the Discovery of the American Continent. By George Bancroft. Vol. I. Fourth Edition, pp. 469. Vol. II. Third Edition, pp. 468.* Boston : Charles C. Little and James Brown, 1838.

Another *American work ;*—issued by the same publishers, in beautiful style, and worthy to stand by the side of " *Prescott's Ferdinand and Isabella*," as an American and English classic. This work, like the preceding, will compare advantageously with the best standard histories in our language. It is an honor to the country and the age.

We notice these works in the order in which they should be read and pondered ;—for they are worthy of more than a simple reading ; —they deserve to be *studied.* Prescott introduces us to the condition of the world as it *was*, in the incipient stages of modern civilization, and brings us into sympathy with the nation which was honored with the discovery of the new continent. Bancroft takes up the story where Prescott leaves it ; not to narrate the history of the ill-fated Spain, through the glorious reign which succeeded that of the Catholic Sovereigns, to its present humbled and broken condition, but to pursue a branch of modern history, spirit-stirring and buoyant with hope, where, amid many conflicts, it is true, and over numerous and appalling obstacles, the general progress of affairs has been onward, and upward.

We do not intend to intimate by these remarks that " Bancroft's United States" is a continuation of the other work above named. It is a history complete in itself. It covers a portion of the same ground with that of Prescott, and derives its materials, thus far, from the same or similar sources. It will be read, however, with a more lively interest, and its early events be more fully comprehended by readers who are thoroughly acquainted with Spanish affairs, at the time of the discovery of the American continent.

This work is designed to be extended to several volumes. The two volumes named at the head of this notice are already before the public, and the publishers inform us that the third volume is in the press, while the author is diligently pursuing his investigations.

The first volume was published in 1834, and has been sufficiently praised by the Reviewers, as well in Europe as in this country. The second has met with an equally flattering reception, and both have been carefully revised by the author in the editions now before the public.

These volumes are wholly occupied with the Colonial history of this country. The running titles of their several chapters are— " Early voyages—French settlements ;—Spaniards in the U. S. ;— England takes possession of the country,—Colonization of Virginia ; —Slavery, dissolution of the London Company ;—Restrictions on Colonial commerce ;—Colonization of Maryland ;—The Pilgrims;— Extended colonization of New England ;—the united colonies of New England ;—the restoration of the Stuarts ;—Massachusetts and Charles II. ;—Shaftsbury and Locke legislate for Carolina ;—the colonies on the Chesapeake bay ;—New Netherlands ;—the people called Quakers in the U. S. ;—James II. consolidates the Northern colonies ;—the results thus far." Under each of these general heads there is a wonderful variety of incidents of thrilling interest, and many rich trains of thought concerned in placing fully before the reader the leading facts and events of the times. These appear to have been sought out with great care, and are arranged with a due regard to the order of time, as well as to their bearings upon each other, and the whole is presented in a style at once concise, lucid and often highly finished and elegant.

The author possesses the best advantages for original investigation of the early American history, and has already spent years of la-

borious preparation for his work.   Hitherto he has pursued it with
a candor and impartiality which are the crowning excellencies of a
historian, and should his life be spared to complete what he has so
worthily begun, we may hope to possess a standard American history, which future inquirers will find little occasion to correct.

Mr. Bancroft's description of the Pilgrims of New England, in
his first volume, has been so often quoted and so deservedly praised,
that it would be superfluous to refer to it here as a specimen of his
style, whether of language or of thought.   Many other passages of
equal beauty are embraced in these volumes.   His work is studded
with gems of this sort.

4.—*Elements of Psychology : included in a Critical Examination
    of Locke's Essay on the Human Understanding.   With addi-
    tional pieces.   By Victor Cousin, Peer of France, etc.   Trans-
    lated from the French, with an Introduction and Notes, by
    the Rev. C. S. Henry, D. D.   Second Edition, prepared for
    the use of Colleges.*   New York : Gould & Newman, 1838.
    pp. 423.

This work is a translation of ten lectures of M. Cousin, (from the
sixteenth to the twenty-fifth inclusive,) contained in the second
volume of his " History of Philosophy in the Eighteenth Century."
These lectures are pronounced in the Edinburgh Review, (October
1830,) to be " the most important work on Locke since the Nou-
veaux Essais of Leibnitz," and by others, have been lauded as " perhaps the greatest master-piece of philosophical criticism ever exhibited to the public."

Mr. Henry's translation has been before the public since 1834,
and having, as the translator informs us, been " introduced into a
number of our most respectable Universities and Colleges," a judgment has doubtless been formed of its merits by many who have
had more opportunity to study it than ourselves, and whose opinions
will not be affected by any remarks of ours.   Nor is it our design
to depreciate the value of this work as a whole.   It is a splendid
production.   Its classification of the mental faculties is a manifest
improvement upon that of Locke, and, in the chapter on " *Moral
Relations*," our author reasons with triumphant conclusiveness
against the error of Locke, Paley and others, who confound moral
obligation with the influence of rewards and punishments assigned
by law.   Cousin maintains the essential and immutable distinction
between right and wrong, and that, under a wise and good administration, certain actions are required *because* they are right, and
others forbidden *because* they are wrong, independently of the reward promised or punishment threatened to enforce or prevent them.
His chapter also on the " Association of Ideas," his encomium upon
the Third Book of Locke and his observations on *disputes about*

words, are worthy to be imprinted upon the memory of every inquirer after truth. Many other excellencies might be pointed out in these lectures, which commend them as valuable helps in the study of mental philosophy.

His great argument, however, against Locke's theory of knowledge, as we conceive, is strikingly misapplied and erroneous. It is founded in a misapprehension of the meaning which Locke gives to the term *idea*. Cousin speaks of the *objects of ideas*, the conformity of ideas to their *objects*, etc. But this is not the language of Locke, and no such expressions occur in the passages referred to by our author. According to Locke ideas are the *objects* of thoughts, and not the thoughts themselves. Hence to speak of the *object of an idea* is to speak of the *object* of an *object !* This misapprehension has led our author to the startling conclusion, that, according to Locke's theory, we have no knowledge of matter or its qualities, of time or space, of finite minds, of the Infinite Spirit, nor of our own existence ! Such a conclusion, however, adopted by Berkley and Hume, has long since been refuted as erroneous and absurd. And again we wonder at the process of reasoning by which Cousin seems to confound the theory of Locke with that of Condillac and his followers in France, under the common appellation of *sensualism.* Locke derives only a part of our knowledge from sensation ; and uniformly represents *sensation* and *reflection*, as the sources of knowledge.

This work of Cousin, therefore, as it appears to us, on a cursory examination, with all its excellencies, which we admit to be great, is not in all respects unexceptionable. It may be a good book to introduce into our Colleges, and on the whole we are disposed to commend it as such ; but we would have it always in the hands of a professor thoroughly versed in the system of Locke, and who is able to detect the misapprehensions of which we have spoken.

5.—*Religion of the Bible, in Select Discourses. By Thomas H. Skinner.* New York : John S. Taylor, 1839. pp. 323.

This volume, (beautifully executed by the publisher,) is "respectfully presented, by the Author, to the Mercer Street Presbyterian Church," of which he is the pastor. It is in the form of discourses, or essays, the leading topics of which are "Spiritual Religion ;—Spiritual Joy ;—Doing Good, parts first and second ;—Co-operation with God ;—Prayer, parts first and second ;—The Sabbath ;—Restraints on Divine Influence ;—The First Last, and the Last First."

Several of these pieces have been before printed in periodicals and other forms. They are, however, highly worthy to compose a volume, and well adapted to answer the object of their present publication, which is that the respected author may, by this means, "speak more frequently, in their private habitations," to those accustomed to his voice in the house of God. As intellectual productions they are of a high order; systematic in their arrangement of thought, and convincing in argument. In style they are beautiful specimens of pure and elegant English composition, worthy of the pen of the *Professor of Sacred Rhetoric*, and of the zealous, enlightened and persuasive preacher of the gospel. In this respect they exhibit so few faults, that we do not care to name them in this brief notice. In theology they are discriminating, instructive and biblical, indicating clear views, and an abiding impression, on the mind of the author, of that perfect and harmonious system of truth, of which every doctrine of christian theology is a part. In spirit they possess a life and an unction, derived from the closet, not less than from the pulpit; and, though "presented" by the author to the members of his own charge, they are such as other christian pastors may commend, with much promise of usefulness, to their people. As a whole, the book is entirely congruous with the ministerial character, and suited, wherever it may be read, to help the work of the ministry, in elevating the tone of piety, in " the perfecting of the saints," and " the edifying of the body of Christ." We know of but few volumes of discourses, at once so unexceptionable, so attractive, and so well adapted to do good.

6.—*The Catastrophe of the Presbyterian Church, in 1837, including a full View of the Recent Theological Controversies in New England. By Zebulon Crocker, Delegate from the General Association of Connecticut to the General Assembly of 1837.* New Haven: B. & W. Noyes, 1838. pp. 300.

This work has been several months before the public, but we have not, until quite lately, found opportunity to peruse it. It appears to contain a fair account of the principal exciting controversies which have existed, for a few years past, both in the Presbyterian and Congregational churches, by one who has taken pains to inform himself of the facts and events concerning which he writes. The author's mind appears to have been first excited to the importance of preparing this history, by the discussions to which he listened in the General Assembly of 1837, and by the strange and startling positions which were assumed and acted on by the majority of that body, in abrogating the Plan of Union of 1801, exscinding the Synods of Utica, Geneva, Genesee and the Western Reserve, and in passing resolutions discountenancing the operations of the Home Missionary and Education Societies within the bounds of the Presbyterian church. To a Connecticut clergyman these positions and doings may well be conceived to have been astounding, and our author felt that his brethren in New England were deeply concerned to know whereunto were tending their cherished union and coöpe-

ration with the Presbyterian church.   He accordingly set himself to
the preparation of this history of the measures above referred to, in
the accomplishment of which he has found occasion to acquaint his
readers with the origin of the Presbyterian church, the controversies
which have agitated it, from time to time, the differences of theological views, the encroachments on high-church prerogatives, the
" *Act and Testimony*" of 1834, and the memorial which followed
it, the Trials of Mr. Barnes and Dr. Beecher, and in general the
causes which concurred to produce the majority, as it was in the
General Assembly of 1837.

Having accomplished this part of his work, Mr. Crocker, finding
himself in possession of documents to illustrate the contemporaneous
controversies in New England, has embraced an account of these
also in the volume before us ;—the New Haven Controversy ;—
Controversy between Dr. Taylor and Mr. Harvey ;—between Dr.
Taylor and Dr. Tyler :—with Dr. Woods ;—second discussions between Dr. Taylor and Dr. Tyler ;—Discussion on the doctrine of
the Divine Purposes ;—Dr. Spring and Dr. Woods on Native Depravity ;—Measures in Connecticut to suppress New Haven Views ;
—Dr. Tyler's letters to Dr. Witherspoon, etc.

The author has generally exhibited the main positions of the parties in these several controversies, with clearness, together with
their principal arguments, and copious extracts from their writings,
presenting a condensed view of the whole subject.   To which is
added an Appendix, containing an enumeration of publications on
the " New Haven Controversy," and also on the " Unitarian Controversy" in New England.

7.—*American Education : or Strictures on the Nature, Necessity
    and Practicability of a System of National Education, suited
    to the United States. By Rev. Benjamin O. Peers. With
    an Introductory Letter by Francis L. Hawks, D. D. New
    York : John S. Taylor, 1838. pp. 364.*

This is a popular book on a popular subject.   The author has
been for many years engaged in the work of instruction, and brings
to the subject of education, in the language of Dr. Hawks, " the enthusiasm of a mind deeply impressed with its importance."   His
general topics of discussion are " the Political Necessity of religious
Education ;—the essential features of a System of National Education ;—and the Practicability of National Education ;—with an Appeal to the clergy on their obligations to assist in exciting, elevating
and directing public sentiment on the subject of Popular Education."

We have not been able to give this volume the examination which
it deserves, but from the claims of its author to the respect of the
public, and from the strong confidence in the ability of the work expressed by Dr. Hawks in his " Introductory Letter," we do not hesi-

tate to commend it to our readers and especially to those, to whom the author's closing " Appeal " is directed.

8.—*A Manual of Prayer ; designed to assist Christians in learning the subjects and modes of Devotion. With an Introduction by Rev. A. Barnes. Second Edition, enlarged.* Philadelphia : Henry Perkins. Boston : Perkins & Marvin, 1838. pp. 306.

We have perused this little volume with great satisfaction. It is principally designed to furnish an assistant to closet devotion. Its author, we understand, is a layman, who, on making a profession of religion, and feeling the great responsibilities he had thus assumed, experienced much embarrassment, (as most others have in similar circumstances,) in preparing himself for the intelligent and profitable discharge of the social devotions in which he was called on to engage. This preparation he sought in the retirement of the closet, by storing his memory with a vocabulary of his wants, and training his heart to an intelligent and fervent habit of prayer. His experience suggested to him the thought of attempting the preparation of a manual for the use of others. He pursued his object for several years, and has produced a work most happily adapted to the purpose he had in view. The topics of supplication here exhibited are of almost every variety which occur in common life, the language in which they are presented is chaste, scriptural and glowing, and the spirit which pervades them is deep-toned, humble and expansive. They are *christian* and not *sectarian* prayers, and may be safely recommended by pastors of all denominations to the study not only of the lambs of their flocks, but to the attention of all who would improve in the gifts and graces of supplication.

9.—*A Grammatical Analysis of Selections from the Hebrew Scriptures, with an Exercise in Hebrew Composition. By Isaac Nordheimer, Doctor in Philosophy of the University of Munich, Prof. of Arabic, Syriac and other Oriental Languages, and acting Prof. of Hebrew, in the University of the city of New York.* New York : Wiley & Putnam, 1838. pp. 148.

Chrestomathies have, not unfrequently, belied their name. Instead of being easy lessons, they have been among the most difficult compositions which could be selected. The compilers have sought for beautiful pieces, highly rhetorical extracts, rather than those excerpts which would be in the reach of the mere beginner. Some pieces in the Graeca Minora would task the powers of an accomplished scholar. Most of the German reading books which we have seen are open to the same objection. The Arabic Chrestomathies seem to be intended to furnish specimens of the most elegant compositions in the language. They are anything but Chrestomathies. Doubtless De Sacy, Kosegarten and Rödiger would find no stumbling-block in reading them. But alas for the poor tyro! When he opens their pages, he plunges into a black forest. He is at once involved in a labyrinth where there is no clue.

Dr. Nordheimer, we believe, has avoided this sad mistake. Some of his selections are taken from the Hebrew Prophets, but these are found in the latter end of the volume, after ample grammatical analyses and explanatory remarks on a number of chapters in Genesis, several passages from the other books of the Pentateuch, and a few of the easier Psalms. The most difficult points in these prophetical selections are, moreover, elucidated by well-timed observations. Perhaps the student when he reaches these extracts will be able to master all their difficulties. Dr. Nordheimer has very properly confined himself almost exclusively to the clearing up of difficulties of a grammatical nature. The young reader is only bewildered by exegesis. Besides, the study of grammar and of the mere forms, in the hands of an intelligent instructor, can be made to assume much interest. The poetical division of the work is preceded by a succinct statement of the peculiarities which exist in the structure of Hebrew poetry. The advanced reader, who would wish for more ample details, would do well to read De Wette's Introduction to the Psalms, translated by Prof. Torrey of the University of Vermont, and published in the Bibl. Repos. Vol. III. p. 445, First Series. It being universally admitted that the practice of composing in a foreign tongue is one of the surest means of becoming thoroughly imbued with its spirit, Dr. Nordheimer has inserted at the close of his volume an Exercise in Hebrew Composition, with accompanying auxiliary directions.

The volume will add to the well-established reputation of the author, or rather authors, for the Chrestomathy is to be considered as the joint production of Dr. Nordheimer and of Mr. William W. Turner, both having borne an equal share in the plan and execution of it. We believe, that there is but one opinion, among all competent judges, of the Grammar, to which this Chrestomathy is a Supplement, and that opinion is one of high commendation. We shall look with interest for the second volume of the Grammar, which is to embrace a consideration of the Syntax. The whole series will exhibit the author as a very able oriental scholar. We hope for corresponding good fruits in the studies and literary character of the country.

10.—*Democracy in America, by Alexis de Tocqueville, avocat à la Cour Royale de Paris. Translated by Henry Reeve, Esq., with an original Preface and Notes, by John C. Spencer, Counsellor at Law.* New York: George Dearborn & Co. 1838. pp. 464.

This work is written not at all in the spirit which Frenchmen are accused of possessing. There is nothing volatile, fanciful, inconsiderate, from the beginning to the end. If it has errors they do not lie on the surface. They are elaborately reasoned out, or they are skilfully interwoven in the very texture of the work. The volume is one of principles, of abstract reasoning, of solid thinking. The common reader of travels will find nothing in it to his taste. It comprises but few incidents, allusions to passing events, or living characters. The writer takes up our government, and our institutions theoretically, but not in such a sense as to exclude consideration of their practical working. If he refers, however, to an actual event, or to an important political movement, it is merely that he may deduce the principle, or state the reflection, or illustrate some one of his general positions. The book is one of great value, and is, undoubtedly, the most important which has appeared on the United States from the pen of a foreigner. The author shows a more familiar acquaintance with our general and State constitutions, with our political history, with the Federalist, the commentaries of Kent, Story, etc. than most of our own civilians and political writers. M. de Tocqueville is uncommonly fair-minded, unprejudiced, and sharp-sighted. He does not hesitate to say where our principal dangers lie, and where, in his opinion, are the rocks on which we shall split. At the same time, these warnings are given in a very friendly manner, with none of the hauteur of John Bull, with none of that biting censure or hard-wrung praise which our transatlantic cousins are so well pleased to deal out. We hereby thank the author for his profound reflections and his excellent spirit. He has called our attention to the most weighty topics which can engage our attention as citizens of a great republic. If there be any fault in him it consists in an over-refinement of speculation, in endeavors to account for things which do not grow legitimately from our institutions and usages, but which are the result of mere caprice and accident. The author has a passion for philosophising and for generalization. We think that he could have interspersed, without injury to his general plan, more incidents, and a greater number of striking illustrations.

11.—*Handbuch der Christlichen Archäologie, ein neugeordneter und vielfach berichtiger Auszug aus den Denkwürdigkeiten aus der Christlichen Archäologie. Von D. Johann Christian Wilhelm Augusti.* Leipzig: 1836, and 1837, erster band pp. 595, zweyter band pp. 775, dritter band, pp. 759.

This author is one of the oldest professors of theology at the university of Bonn, and author of numerous works.* In the interval between 1817 and 1831, he published, in twelve volumes, a work, entitled, "Denkwürdigkeiten aus der Christlichen Archälogie," (Memoirs on Christian Archaeology). It acquired, notwithstanding

---

* He is not to be confounded with H. E. G. Paulus, the celebrated professor and rationalist leader at Heidelburg, author of many biblical productions.

its size and price, considerable celebrity in Germany and in the northern countries of Europe. The present edition was undertaken in order to effect some improvements and to bring the work into more reasonable limits. An Introduction of considerable length has been added on the object, extent, method and literature of Christian Archaeology. Some matters of comparatively little interest have been thrown out or arranged under other heads and greatly condensed. A very full Index is added at the end of the third volume.

We will now proceed to give some account of the contents. The matters are arranged into fourteen books. Book I. has some general remarks on the ecclesiastical constitution and divine service of the ancient Christians. Book II. is on sacred persons, catechumens, believers, ascetics, coenobites, monks, etc. The sixth chapter gives details respecting the bishop, presbyter, deacon, archdeacon, sub-deacon, and other inferior officers. Book III. contains an account of holy places, churches, altars, cloisters, utensils of churches, etc. Book IV. is on holy times, festivals, anniversaries, the Sabbath, etc. Book V. exhibits the subjects of prayer and psalmody in the church. The fourth chapter has details on psalmody and hymnology in the Latin, Greek and Syrian churches. Book VI. is on the use of the Scriptures in public worship, the particular books which were read, the order in which they were read, lectionaries in various churches, psalters and homilies. Book VII. presents various topics relating to baptism and confirmation. More than 200 pages are devoted to the discussion of these topics. Book VIII. naturally includes the Lord's Supper, the various modes of its observance, the character and admission of communicants, etc. In Book IX. we have the antiquities of penance, confession, and absolution. Book X. contains the views, principles and usages of the church relating to marriage, divorce, etc. Book XI. is on the ordination of priests, with the different ceremonies and rules relating thereto. Book XII. details the last offices which are due to men, extreme unction, burial-service, time, place and manner of interment, etc. Book XIII. discusses extraordinary sacred customs, such as processions, pilgrimages, blessing and anathematizing as practised by priests, etc., lots, ordeals, fasts, etc. Book XIV. is on miscellaneous matters, as liturgies in the eastern and western churches, etc. It will thus be seen that the various topics are handled with much precision and method, in the true German style of division and subdivision. With its full tables of contents, with its numerous references, and large Index, the work will be very convenient for all who are interested in or have occasion to use christian antiquities. So far as we can judge by a perusal of the prefaces, introduction and various controverted topics discussed in the course of the volumes, we have formed a very favorable opinion of the candor, liberality and intelligence of the author. Very recent works on the subject are those of professor Staudenmaier of Giessen on the Spirit of Christianity as exhibited in its sacred seasons, use-ges, and practice ; Siegel's (a clergyman in Leipsic,) Manual of the Antiquities of the Christian Church in alphabetical order ; and the Christian Antiquities of professor Böhmer of Breslau, exhibited theologically and critically.

12.—*Handbuch der historisch-kritischen Einleitung in das Alte Testament. Von H. A. Ch. Hävernick.* Erlangen : erster Theil, erster abtheilung, pp. 312. Zweyter abtheilung, pp. 644. 1837.

This writer has considerable reputation by his work on Daniel. He was, for a brief period, a professor at the new theological school at Geneva, where he published some essays in connection with Steiger. He is now a private teacher in the university of Rostock. In the dedication of the present work to Tholuck, he speaks of his obligations to that pious and distinguished theologian as having been to him a spiritual guide to the truth as it is in Jesus. One cannot but admire the vein of warm-hearted piety which pervades many pages of his works. He prepared the present publication, as he informs us in the preface, with the deep and firm conviction that the object of the Scriptures is to lead man, now sunk in sin and misery, into the way of salvation and peace. After some general preliminary remarks, the author considers the history of the canon, the history of the original languages of the Old Testament, history of the text, history of the translations of the Old Testament, principles of criticism on the text, and special introductions to the Pentateuch, and its various books, and to disputed passages in them, together with some account of the Samaritan Pentateuch, etc. In a late number of the Studien und Kritiken, there is a review of this production of Hävernick, in which considerable fault is found with the author. He is evidently not wanting in critical acuteness, nor in general ability and learning, but he is, not unfrequently, hasty and careless in his statements and conclusions. Much information may be found in the work under notice respecting the most recent investigations on the Pentateuch and the Old Testament generally.

13.—*Memorials of the Right Reverend Father in God, Myles Coverdale, sometime Lord Bishop of Exeter ; who first translated the whole Bible into English ; together with divers matters relating to the promulgation of the Bible, in the reign of Henry the Eighth.* London : Samuel Bagster, 1838. pp. 260.

A re-print of Coverdale's Bible, which was originally published Oct. 4, 1635, was brought out in London on the day of Victoria's coronation. Copies of the first edition are in the possession of the British Museum, the Bodleian library, Public library Cambridge, Sion College, All Soul's College, Lambeth library, Baptist Museum Bristol, of the Duke of Sussex, and the Earl of Jersey. Complete copies are extremely rare. It is yet a controverted point, and, perhaps, is not capable of definite solution, whether Coverdale translated from the original. Mr. Whitaker has attempted to show, that the Hebrew text is by Coverdale, most faithfully and ably translated, and the sense most consonant to the original always adopted. This strong asseveration may well be doubted. Dr. Geddes scruples not to affirm, that this translation is one of more merit, and is more according to the original, (such as Coverdale had it,) than the present authorized version, which is commonly read in the churches. In some annotations to a translation of the New Testament, recently published by Mr. Penn, that gentleman undertakes to prove that hitherto there had been no direct English translation from the Greek, but only through the medium of the Latin, with occasional references to the Greek text ; and in these examples, it will be found, that Coverdale, unlike Wiclif, Tyndale, and the Vulgate, has translated directly from the Greek, and not through the medium of any interpretation whatever. This assertion, so far as Tyndale is concerned, is without foundation. In his Preface to the " Obedience of a Christian Mann," Tyndale writes like one at home in the original languages. " The Greeke tongue agreeth more with the Englysshe than with the Latyne, and the properties of the Hebrue tongue agreeth a thousand tymes more with *y. Englysshe than with the Latyne.*"* It has been the common opinion that Coverdale copied, with some revision, Tyndale's New Testament, and the small portions of the Old which the latter had translated. The compiler of the Life of Coverdale affirms that the contrary will be manifest from an examination of the two versions. This Life is by an anonymous hand. The compiler collects a considerable variety of interesting particulars. The style is, however, not one of a practised writer. There is a very good portrait of Coverdale.

16.—— *China, its present state and prospects, with especial reference to the spread of the Gospel, containing allusions to the antiquity, extent, population, civilization, literature, and religion of the Chinese. By W. H. Medhurst, of the London Missionary Society.* Boston : Crocker & Brewster, 1838. pp. 472.

We received this volume just as the last sheet of the Repository for October was going to press. We have been happy to see that the high opinion which we then expressed of its merits has been unanimously confirmed by the public press. It discusses the prominent topics of interest relating to China in a succinct, candid, and intelligent manner. Just that kind of information is communicated which is fitted to excite an interest in the country and its institutions, and to lead us to search for fuller details. These details may be found in the excellent history of China by Davis, in the journals of the English embassies, and in the Chinese Repository. Mr. Med-

---

* See Dabney's Reprint of Tyndale, p. 25.

hurst's work is of a popular character, but still not deficient in the marks of authenticity and accurate observation. The author is well fitted to tread in the steps and to assume the responsibilities of Morrison and Milne. We hope that there will be, ere long, a sufficient degree of interest awakened in behalf of China both in this country and in Europe, to justify more copious accounts than we have yet had of the structure of the language, of the nature and degree of divergency of the various dialects, of the actual progress made by the Chinese scholars or literati, and of the real value of the writings of Confucius, and of the other more important specimens of the native literature.

We will here subjoin some statements, which we find in a late German periodical, copied from the "Annales de la Propagation de la Foi," touching the Romish missions in China. The missions are divided into three great apostolic *vicariats* and three bishoprics. The vicariats are Chan-Si, Fo-Keen, and Su-Tchuen. The bishoprics have their seats at Peking, Nanking and Macao. The vicariat of Chan-Si embraces four provinces, from three to five bishops, and seventeen native priests. In one district of one of the provinces alone there are 60,000 Christians. The mission in the vicariat of Fo-Keen is in a very flourishing state. In some places public worship is openly celebrated. In one province 30,000 Christians are counted. Two other provinces contain 9,000 Christians. The vicariat of Su-Tchuen has two bishops, nine European priests, thirty native priests and 15,000 Christians. The bishopric of Peking has 40,000 Christians, that of Macao about 40,000. " It needs only one Constantine," thus all the missionary accounts agree, " to bring the 300,000,000 of Chinese into the bosom of the church."

15.—*Friderici Windischmanni, presbyteri, ss. theologiae ac philosophiae doctoris, Vindiciae Petrinae.* Ratisbonae : pp. 135.

This book is written in a very earnest and powerful manner, in opposition to those who doubt or deny the authenticity of the second epistle of Peter. The author has particularly in his eye the work of Meyerhoff. Dr. Hermann Olshausen, whose essay is found in Bibl. Repos. VIII. 88, after a very candid and cautious discussion, decides in favor of the epistle on internal grounds, while the external evidence is, in his opinion, too scanty and feeble to justify much reliance. Windischmann comes to the conclusion, that it was known in the earliest times, that its authenticity was questioned by none, that it differs, indeed, from the first epistle in certain phraseology and sentiments, but that this difference can be well explained by the different nature of the subject discussed, while there are many traces of resemblance, that there are some difficult passages in it, which, notwithstanding, if rightly understood, will particularly confirm the sincerity of the writer, that the description of heretics agrees only with the apostolic times, and that its resemblance to Jude demonstrates its apostolic origin. A large portion of the volume is taken up with an inquiry relating to the time and place when and where both epistles were written. The author concludes that the first epistle was written at Rome (Rome intended by Babylon), and that the second epistle was most probably written in the same place, as Peter in it refers to the epistles of Paul which were written at Rome, and as he speaks of his own death as drawing near, which took place, without much doubt, at the same city. The epistles were addressed, as the writer thinks, particularly to the Jewish Christians, but in an important sense to the Gentile Christians, as Peter refers to the epistles of Paul which were directed to the latter.

16.—*Hoary Head and the Vallies below. By Jacob Abbott.* Boston : Crocker & Brewster, 1838.

The great characteristic excellence of the author is manifest on every page of this little book. We mean the power of most accurate description, a microscopic observation of what passes under his eye, and an exact transference to paper of what he has seen, and in the order in which things appear in nature. Nothing can be more to the life than the description of the mechanic shop with which the first story opens, the conversation between the father and his son, the anxious and complaining solicitude of the mother, and the several incidents relating to sick little Benny. On the question of the general utility of the volume, there will be various opinions, according to the judgment of different persons concerning novel writing. For ourselves we must say, that the great truth intended to be conveyed by the author, namely, that a substance cannot change itself, that the heart of man cannot renovate itself, is very strikingly illustrated. It does not appear merely in didactic statements at the beginning and end of the book, but it is interwoven in the thread of the narratives. We are not hurried away from real life. Real life is described to us. We see what we are, and what we ought to be.

ARTICLE XIII.

Miscellaneous Intelligence.

United States.

A volume of Selections from the German will be published early in the ensuing Spring, translated by Profs. Edwards and Park of Andover. The principal contents will be as follows : 1. The sinless character of Jesus, by

Prof. Ullmann of Heidelberg. II. Specimens of the German Pulpit, by Prof. Tholuck of Halle and others. III. Life of Plato by W. G. Tennemann. IV. Comparison of Platonism with Christianity by Prof. Baur of Tübingen. V. Life of Aristotle by Dr. A. Stahr of Halle. VI. The origin of Sin and Evil, by Prof. Twesten of Berlin. VII. Biblical Articles by Profs. Köster, Tholuck, Umbreit and others. VIII. Miscellaneous articles, by Profs. Neander, Ullmann, and others.

Prof. Emerson of Andover, is preparing for publication a translation of the history of Augustinism and Pelagianism, by G. F. Wiggers, Prof. of Divinity at Rostock, Germany, with notes by the translator. The work will probably soon be put to press.

Prof. Stowe of the Theol. Seminary near Cincinnati, is preparing a translation of Rosenmüller's Commentary (Compend.) on the Psalms, with additional notes of his own; which will be speedily printed.

The above works will be issued from the Press of Gould & Newman, Andover.

Germany.

The controversy occasioned by the publication of Strauss's Life of Jesus continues to rage with unabated fury. Kantists, Hegelians, Rationalists, Semi-rationalists, Supra-rationalists, the disciples of Schleiermacher, and rank infidels have all entered the lists. The firing of Strauss's blunderbuss seems to have been a signal for a general discharge along the whole line. The third edition of the work was published last summer, in two large volumes octavo. He has also published a little work entitled, "Gallerie meiner Gegner," which would still indicate that he holds up with good courage against the storm of missiles which have fallen around him and on him. It is said that the controversy would already fill a respectable library. Among the opposers of Strauss are the names of men no less distinguished than Neander of Berlin, Tholuck of Halle, Harless of Erlangen, Hengstenberg of Berlin, Lange of Duisberg, Müller of Marburg, Paulus of Heidelberg, Sack of Bonn, Ullmann of Heidelberg, Eschenmayer of Tübingen, Baumgarten-Crusius, etc. Archbishop Whately's Historic Doubts respecting Napoleon Bonaparte have been translated and published. Volumes have been put forth in ridicule;—one represented as an appendix critically examining the life of Mohammed from a Schiite tradition, and proving the whole life to be a mythus; another volume, supposed to be written in some future century denying that any such man as Martin Luther ever existed. The controversy shows the extreme, the boundless activity of the German mind, the unsettled state of the religious world, and the eagerness with which multitudes are prepared to rush into open skepticism.

It is sometimes said, that the systems of philosophy in Germany are evanescent, and give place one after another, to an uninterrupted succession of novelties. We observe, however, in one advertisement, a notice of the republication of the works of Kant, Fichte and Hegel. Kant's whole works are in the process of publication under the editorial charge of Rosenkranz, and Schubart. Hegel's complete works are also publishing. Volume X., published last summer, contains his Lectures on Æsthetics. C. L. Michelet has published at Berlin a history of the systems of philosophy in Germany from Kant to Hegel. We are very glad to see a notice of the issuing of the third volume of Ast's Lexicon Platonicum, sive vocum Platonicarum Index. The edition of Plato's works by Ast in nine very convenient volumes, octavo, has long been out. The ninth was published in 1827.—The two Grimms late of Göttingen are preparing a very extensive dictionary of the German language. Jacob Grimm's German grammar is a book of the highest authority. The dictionary will be completed in about six or seven volumes. —The celebrated Lassen is preparing to publish a Sanscrit Manual, and a a manual of Indian Antiquities. The last named was to be in three volumes, the first volume to appear in the course of 1838.—A new edition of Tholuck's sermons on the principal points of christian faith and practice has been published in two volumes.—We collect the following notices of some of the German universities from a late number of the Allgemeine Kirchen Zeitung published at Darmstadt. *Erlangen.* This university contains 184 students, of whom 140 are theologians. *Bonn.* In this university are 689 students, of whom 184 are theologians, 188 attending on the Catholic faculty, and 76 on the Protestant. *Heidelberg.* 468 students, of whom 25 are theologians. *Giessen.* The following was the course of lectures, last summer, in the evangelical theological faculty of this university—Kuinoel on select passages in the historical books of the Old Testament, Credner on Job, on Introduction to the New Testament and on church history, Meier on the epistle to the Corinthians, and on history of doctrines, Palmer on Catachetics and on Symbolic, and Dieffenbach on Dogmatic and Homiletic. *Breslau.* In the evangelical faculty of this university, Schulz lectures on encyclopedia, methodology and on some of Paul's epistles, Knobel on Introduction to the New Testament, the minor Prophets, christian ethics and catachetics, Middledorpf on Introduction to the New Testament, and the Psalms, Böhmer on the *Straussian* controversy or the life of Jesus exhibited in his actual labors, christian antiquities, and church history, Hahn on Dogmatics in connection with ethics and symbolics, and the first part of church history ; Suckow on practical theology. The theological seminary is under the charge of Schulz, Middledorf, Hahn and Böhmer ; the homiletic institute is directed by Hahn and Suckow. *Freiburg.* Hug lectures on the Introduction to the New Testament ; Wetser on Arabic, biblical Hermeneutics, and Hebrew language ; Schleyer on Joel, Amos, Galatians and Ephesians ; Vogel on modern church history ; Staudenmeier on dogmatics, and on the theory of religion and revelation ; Hirscher on christian morals ; and Werk on pastoral theology and liturgies. *Göttingen.* Students in the summer quarter, 1838, were 729, of whom 173 were studying theology.

THE

AMERICAN

BIBLICAL REPOSITORY.

APRIL, 1839.

SECOND SERIES, NO. II.—WHOLE NO. XXXIV.

ARTICLE I.

WHAT IS SIN?

Translation of a passage from Vitringa's OBSERVATIONES SACRAE *in relation to this question, with introductory and other Remarks.*

By M. Stuart, Prof. Sac. Lit. Theol. Sem. Andover.

THERE are times in every Christian country, when accurate definitions of important terms in theology are peculiarly needed. Such a time seems to have already arrived in our own. Disputes have recently arisen among our theologians, and they are so carried on as to assume a grave and somewhat threatening aspect.

There are periods, (there have been such in our country), when pastors and churches can walk together, with the full and quiet persuasion that there is no *essential* difference of sentiment among them, while they are still conscious that differences of opinion in regard to topics not fundamental, or modes of explanation, do actually exist. There have been times, when he that was deemed *weak in the faith*, was still received with cordiality by his brethren, who felt themselves, perhaps, to be more vigorous in their belief; and received, too, in such a way as "did not lead to doubtful disputations." Yet there may be different times, as we are now compelled to believe, which, like some comet portending disaster and filling the public mind with consternation, must pass over us, when every thing appears to be verging to jealousy and disputation. It would seem to matter but little what the actual subject of jealousy and dispute may be, whether a pebble or a crown ; it is enough that such a subject exists.   The smallest trifle will sometimes, in certain states of the public mind, raise up a quarrel as effectually as the most important matter which can be named.   The spirit of the day now and then becomes such as will lead on to a quarrel ; and nothing, it would seem, will appease this spirit, short of the very thing at which it aims, i. e. contention, carried on as vigorously and as far as the nature of the case admits.

The churches of our country, in the North and the South, (I speak now of the evangelical Presbyterian and Congregational churches), have, ever since the settlement of this country, walked together, until recently, on terms of amity and peace. It was once generally thought, and to all practical purposes was fully believed by most Christians, that there were not differences between them of magnitude enough to justify any earnest dispute or active disagreement.   But those happy days, as it now seems, have passed or are passing away ; and what was once regarded, at the most, as being nothing more than a venial error in respect to faith, is now becoming, or has already become, in the eyes of some a dangerous, and of others perhaps even a damnable, heresy.

What can have been the cause of introducing such times as these ?   Is there any development of opinions which are altogether novel, or really heretical, in the North or in the South ? I know of none.   There may be, indeed, now and then a solitary individual who is noisy and assuming, and who throws out paradoxical opinions, more, as I apprehend, to bring himself into notice, than out of any sincere and enlightened regard to religious truth.   Such may be found, here and there, both in the North and in the South.   But this is nothing new.   It has always been so.   Enthusiasts, and ignorant, and self-sufficient, and noisy declaimers of paradoxes, are not peculiar to any age or to any country.

Yet the times have been, among us, when phenomena of this kind did not excite any special commotion.   Our peaceable and quiet pastors and churches looked on the glare of such meteors for a little while, as men are wont to look upon something new and strange ; and then, turning away, went quietly on with their own great business, as usual.   They did not once dream of putting to the account of a whole community, what here and there an enthusiast or an extravagant man either said or did.

They considered him as living and acting in, for, and by himself; not as a federal head of a whole section of country or of a great community.

Who does not spontaneously utter a sigh for the reappearance of this feature of the past, whatever may have been the deficiencies of by-gone days in other respects? Alas! It is difficult now to foresee what may ensue from the present state of feeling, which exists even more extensively, as I apprehend, than most persons appear to be aware of. The time seems to be approaching, when those who profess to be disciples of the same Master, and to love one another as Christian brethren, will not only refuse to support and patronize theological schools in common, but will not unite even in missionary efforts either at home or abroad, or in disseminating the holy Scriptures themselves. Yea, even more; the bonds of brotherhood are not simply to be broken, but active war itself is to be waged, to the extermination, if possible, of one of the parties.

How can the impartial and considerate inquirer account for such an altered state of things? No one cause, that I can name, seems adequate to the effects that have already been produced. Many causes, therefore, would seem to have been combined in the introduction of these threatening appearances;—causes, which it may be the duty of some ecclesiastical historian hereafter to investigate and describe, but which it would be foreign to my design particularly to mention at the present time.

My object in the communication now to be made, is *peace*. "Blessed are the peace-makers," is a sublime and holy sentiment of the gospel—a very expressive portion of the Sermon on the Mount. It is a sentiment worthy of the *Prince of Peace* who uttered it. It should be engraven on the hearts of all his followers.

But although such is my definite object, yet I cannot agree in opinion with those, who think that peace is to be effectually restored and preserved, by quashing all investigation of controverted subjects, or by refraining from the expression of any opinion respecting them. Less still can I agree with such, if such there are, who cry *peace! peace!* to both parties, and talk and write against all public and open discussion, while in their limited and private spheres of action they shew themselves to be devoted partizans, and labour with untiring diligence not only to inculcate their own particular views, but secretly to undermine those of their opponents. I cannot but think this course to be unfortunate, because, where any thing is done on such grounds, it becomes of course a matter of suspicion and jealousy to the public.   Men of an ardent and active temperament, who are usually all energy in regard to any object in which they engage, will hardly obtain credit for being actually silent and inert with respect to the controverted topics of the day, which are deemed to be of high importance.   The reason of this is, their silence is unnatural.   It is therefore construed as a mere *ruse de guerre ;* and for the most part, probably, it is right so to interpret it.

The effects, moreover, of such a suspicion may be easily conjectured.   Jealousy, fear, offence, because there seems to be a want of plainness and frankness and sincerity, are the natural consequences of such a course ; and one need not stop to say, how bitterly such feelings aggravate the animosity of disputants. The more honorable among contending parties are always disgusted with taciturn cunning and wily management, which strives to avoid all open responsibility.   They will sooner bear with a man who is even rash, impetuous, and assuming, while they believe him to be sincere, than with one who says : " Art thou in health, my brother ?" while his dagger is in readiness for a thrust under the fifth rib, so soon as this can be secretly made.

In my apprehension, men appear most magnanimous in times of dispute, who take an open part ; who do not pretend to any indifference as to controverted matters, nor to consider them as unimportant ; but who, notwithstanding their openly professed views and sentiments, have an elevation of feeling and an illumination of mind sufficient to make them kind, and gentle, and forbearing towards those who differ from them.   What magnanimity is there in overlooking that which is wholly a matter of indifference in itself?   None at all.   But if a man can persuade himself to make a separation between things *essential* to religion, and things *unessential ;* between the person and the dress ; between the scaffolding and the building ; and consequently not insist on making heresy out of secondary matters instead of primary ones ; then he may very sincerely think it not by any means an affair of indifference, what kind of costume is worn, (for one kind may surely be more graceful and becoming and comfortable than another), while he still thinks, that it would be rude and even criminal in him, to treat his neighbour with coldness and severity because he did not choose such cos-

tume as he himself prefers.   In short, true magnanimity bears
patiently and meekly with those who differ from us in opinion,
in cases not regarded as altogether unimportant.   But on the
other hand, these causes of difference must not be of an essential or fundamental nature ; for there can be no magnanimity in
refusing to testify against such differences, or to oppose them in
every lawful and proper manner.

Plain and open-hearted frankness is, beyond all doubt, a very
important requisite, in order to heal the breaches which are made
by religious disputation.   The moment that any real ground is
afforded for apprehension that a religious champion is 'crafty
and would catch us with guile,' that moment our confidence,
and in a great measure our respect, are spontaneously with-
drawn.   It is not in human nature to do otherwise than to withdraw it, under such circumstances.   It is, moreover, a just retribution.   But, on the other hand, while every man should be
open and frank, this is no good reason why he should be pug-
nacious, or assuming, or overbearing, or passionate.   There is
some *medium iter*, which good sense and kind feeling and a
proper regard to our own infirmities bid us to choose.   It is certainly very evident, that a man who rears as his only banner
that which is inscribed : *Contend earnestly*, and folds up and
lays aside that which is inscribed : *The servant of the Lord
must not strive, but be gentle unto all men. . . in meekness instructing those that oppose themselves*, will fight, not the good
fight of faith, but the battles of passion and prejudice and dogmatism.   How often is one constrained, who looks with an at-
tentive eye on the contests of party spirit, to ask :   What difference is there between the spirit of combat on the arena of religious controversy, and that on the arena of fashion and honour?
The weapons of the former are not, indeed, the pistol, or the
rifle, or the sword ; but they are not unfrequently the envenomed arrows of deadly tongues and of poisonous breath, which
are designed to smite and to slay with secret wounds, where the
open sight of blood would excite sympathies fatal to the cause
which is thus defended.   There may be gladiators full of the
odium theologicum, who would be duellists in another position
where they sustained another and a different relation to society.

In almost all great disputes, there is, moreover, one party,
if they may be so called, who are perhaps not very numerous
nor prominent, and yet have some distinctive and palpable
characteristics.   I mean those who possess, or profess to enter-

tain, a real apathy as to what is going on, and incline to neither the one side nor the other, just as long as the contest seems to be undetermined. These take to themselves the credit of being peaceable or peace-makers; and they express their wonder how any can interest themselves in *disputes* about matters of religion. Perhaps some of them really possess the indifference which they profess. But in process of time it usually turns out, that they were waiting only to see on whose side victory would declare itself. When the great questions are apparently decided, they some how find themselves to have been all along agreeing with those who are now the majority; and they at last profess to be convinced, that the majority are in the right. All this they make palatable to themselves, and put it to the account of duty, by naming it 'a waiting to see the manifestations of Providence.' But these manifestations, it will be remembered, are always sufficiently plain, whenever either party has attained to a decided, triumphant, and apparently permanent majority.

If now one should ask: What would Luther, Calvin, Zuingle, Jewell, Cranmer, and the whole host of martyrs, have done for the church on such grounds as these? the question would be a very perplexing one to this sort of *peacemakers*. The real truth of the matter after all is, that many such, I think we may truly say, most of such, refrain from forming an opinion on controverted subjects, because it will cost time and hard labour to become so well acquainted with them as to make up an opinion which they would feel able to defend. It saves a great deal of labour, as any one may easily see, not to meddle at all with such matters; and it saves, at least it seems at first view to save, our reputation too, when we can put all this to the account of a peaceable and peace-making disposition of mind, and persuade others that such is the fact.

Much better and more truly Christian is the course of those, who diligently apply themselves to gaining the requisite information concerning all disputed subjects which are matters of interest to the church, and who, when they have acquired so much light as to satisfy their own minds, think and act for themselves, but do it with kindness and charity toward all who may differ from them. "Prove all things; hold fast that which is good." No modern casuistry has been able to improve upon this ancient maxim.

In the course of almost all great disputes, there are times when the voice of reasoning and argument will not be heard.

Should one approach parties contending in mortal combat, while they are actually engaged in contest, could he expect the voice of cool reason and remonstrance to be heard? Can reproof be administered to an inebriate man when under the full influence of the stimulating poison? It is plain that none but empty efforts could be made at such a crisis. Even so with angry disputants on the arena of theology. When they have made up their minds for deeds of violence, can they be dissuaded by the voice of discussion? They have already discussed (in their own view); at any rate, they have already decided; the path of duty appears to them to be open and plain, and it must be trodden, as they judge, let the obstacles be whatever they may.

Yet after a few rounds of contest, and after they have come off beaten, or if not, yet wounded and bleeding, the time at last arrives, while the wounds continue long to annoy and cripple them, when their ears will be open to the questions: Was there sufficient ground for such a contest? Has any thing important been gained by it? Is it probable that any thing important with respect to the real good of the church and the world, can be gained by it? Whenever such a period does arrive, we may hope that fair and sound and friendly discussion will do some good; and it is the duty of those who are able to enter into it, to use their efforts in order to settle controversy, by endeavouring to pour in light upon controverted topics.

No experienced reader of polemic theology can be ignorant of the fact, that a great proportion of the disputes which have existed, or now exist, among sober and enlightened men, in relation to theological subjects, have arisen from defective and erroneous definitions. One believes, for example, in the doctrine of *original sin*; another, who is still a full believer in the total depravity (as rationally defined) of the unregenerate, denies this doctrine. Dispute ensues; it may be fierce, embittered, proscribing controversy. After all, original sin has not, from first to last in the dispute, been fully, fairly, and explicitly defined. Had this been done as it should have been done, the dispute, in all probability, would have never existed.

Each party, in the case now supposed, admits in all important respects the same *facts*, and the same essential *consequences* of them. They differ however about *words*, or rather about *definitions*; and if they proceed to dispute, it must of course be more about *words* than *things*.

Am I correct in this representation? I believe that I am;

and if I can persuade others to think so, (many, I well know, believe it already and do not need to be persuaded), one part of our contentions may be at least diminished, if not entirely done away.

I would fain hope that I may haply obtain an audience among some of my brethren, who have persuaded themselves that they differ from what are called *the New England views of theology* in respect to the nature of sin, when I tell them, that I am going to introduce, on the present occasion, one of their old and familiar acquaintances, in order that he may be heard in respect to the question: *What is sin?* I intend to place before them the thoughts of a man, whose high orthodoxy none will call in question, and who is deservedly viewed, by all candid and discerning judges, as one of the greatest and best men that have adorned the church since the period of the Reformation. That man is the celebrated CAMPEGIUS VITRINGA of Franeker, whose praise is in all the churches, and who has justly won a renown which will endure as long as piety continues to flourish.

The passage which I have selected from him for translation, may be found in his *Observationes Sacrae*, Lib. VI. c. 15. The Essay, of which my translation contains a part, was occasioned by a publication of Peter Poiret, a learned enthusiast, which is entitled *Cogitationes Rationales*, printed near the commencement of the 18th century, in which the author strenuously maintains that sin is merely a *negative* thing, i. e. is not any thing positive and real.

In order to come in a conclusive way to the consideration of the subject, Vitringa occupies nearly the whole of the first part of his Essay in making out the definition of *sin*. This being done, he goes on with an overwhelming argument against his antagonist.

That part of the dispute which is occupied with immediate discussion respecting the positive or negative nature of sin, would be irrelevant at the present time, and quite needless. My object therefore is, to translate only so much of Vitringa's Essay as relates to *definitions* respecting the nature of sin. These are appropriate to the exigencies of our times, and will be listened to, as I would hope, with great respect by all parties. At all events, the thoughts of such a consummate theologian and critic as Vitringa, on such a subject, are well worthy the attention of our religious public.

The reader will see, that before the author gives his own

definition, he passes in brief and rapid review over several of the leading definitions of the times which had preceded. I have deemed it proper to present this part of his Essay, as well as the other, because it helps us to take a more complete view of the whole ground.

VITRINGA ON THE NATURE OF SIN.

Observatt. Sac. Lib. VI. c. 15.

(1) " *Moral good* and *evil* are the opposites of each other. The latter may be regarded as a *habit*, in which case we call it *vitium;* or as an *act*, in which case we name it *peccatum.* Paul, in his epistle to the Romans and sometimes elsewhere, by ἁμαρτία designates *vitium* or *habitual sin*, i. e. vicious habits deserving of condemnation, under the sway of which the unregenerate man performs his actions.

(2) John designates both kinds of sin by the word ἀνομία, i. e. the withdrawing of one's self from the control of law, and consequently from the control of the lawgiver ; which is repugnant to the dictates of right reason.

This word [ἀνομία] is not employed by the classic authors. These commonly make use of παρανομία instead of it.

Habitual sin, in the order of nature and time, precedes sin in the act, which may be scripturally defined παράβασις τοῦ νόμου, or *a violation of the divine law.*

(3) The definition of sin by Augustine, viz., *Concupitum, cogitatum, dictum, factum, adversus divinam legem,* is faulty, because it does not comprise the sin of *neglected* duty, which is commonly named the sin of *omission.*

(4) A learned man [Poiret] has lately said, that sin, generally considered, means *that which is indecorous, incongruous, inconsistent with itself or with its condition.* This seems to me inaccurate. A dependent being who sins, is not *inconsistent* with himself, but acts in a manner repugnant to the law. He who sins is not inconsistent with himself, unless he himself is the rule of action. But creatures are not a rule for themselves ; nor is their condition a rule ; but God, or whatever makes known his will, is the rule. The state of their being is not a rule, unless as determined by a law. Such a sin, therefore, [as M. Poiret describes], can be imagined in no being but a Supreme one, if indeed the condition of such a Being admitted of sin. But this cannot be supposed, without horrible blasphemy.

(5) Another celebrated man [Calvin] has defined sin to be, accurately speaking, *an act which obscures the glory of God.* But all sin is not *act.* Neglect of duty is sin. The obscuring of divine glory is indeed consequent upon sin ; but it does not constitute the nature or essence of sin ; and to this a definition should have peculiar respect.

(6) The celebrated Cocceius defines sin thus : *Something which is deficient in respect to that rectitude in which an intelligent creature was* [first] *formed.* This is less perspicuous than if he had simply said : *Sin is* παρανομία, or παράβασις τοῦ νόμου, i. e. *something committed against the law ;* as we have already defined it. Or the definition of Arminius may be adopted : *A transgression of the divine law, whatever that law may be.* Sins which are committed against those divine laws which are called δόγματα or *ordinances,* would be hardly comprehended within the definition of Cocceius.

(7) The idea of sin involves the conception both of a LAW and of a SUBJECT ; which latter is endowed with properties of such a nature that he can be obligated by law to the doing or omitting of something, and by the promulgation of such a law is actually obligated in this manner. Finally, *it involves also the idea of an* ACT, *commanded or forbidden by the law, either neglected or committed.*

(8) LAW is essential to the idea of sin, because sin is not and cannot be so named, except in reference to a law. "Where there is no law, there is no transgression, Rom. 4: 15."

(9) Grotius defines law to be *the rule of moral actions, obligating to that which is right.* This is a commodious description of a good and just law, which is agreeable to the dictates of right reason. So Tully : "The law is nothing more than right reason, derived from the influence of the gods, requiring what is just and prohibiting what is not."

(10) As we do not here seek after a partial and limited signification of the word, we simply say, that *law is the rule of moral actions ;* or rather, *it is the command or prohibition of a ruler or superior, which regulates the voluntary actions of an inferior who is subject to him ;* (in the language of the Schoolmen, [*Lex*] *modificat liberos actus*).

(11) *Law,* therefore, (as well as *Sin*), involves the idea, (a) OF A RATIONAL SUBJECT, i. e. a free agent, furnished with the faculties necessary for action, who is adequate to determine for himself, deliberately and voluntarily from internal principle, in respect to the doing or not doing of any particular thing.

(12) Consequently, animals destitute of reason; which do not act from design, but from natural impetus and instinct; which have no idea of God, and no consciousness of right and wrong; cannot be obligated by the law to the performance of duty on reasonable principles, and therefore cannot properly be said to *sin* or *to be delinquent.*

(13) But, (*b*) Law implies a *rational subject*, which is inferior to the lawgiver in this respect, viz., that the lawgiver as a ruler or master has the right of command in respect to the actions and deportment of him who is under subjection.

(14) That circumstance, on which the right of command and the reason of obedience are founded, is undoubtedly the dependence of one being on another; and the greater this is, the greater is the right of command and authority over him who is the subject. Entire dependence implies the entire right of authority in him on whom we depend, and obligates the subject to universal and most humble obedience in every action. Such is the authority of God over his creatures; and such the obedience which creatures owe to him, as being entirely dependent on him.

(15) This perfect authority and this entire obedience, from the very fact that they are perfect and entire, exclude all other authority and obedience as just and legitimate, because they are inconsistent with the duty which the creature owes to God, and because the authority of God is not subordinate, and no other authority can be lawful, except such as is in subordination to him. Whatever authority, therefore, parents may have over children, masters over servants, magistrates and rulers over subjects, whatever of duty may be enjoined by the former upon the latter, (and a right to command the former possess, so far as others are subject to them),—all this is derived from divine authority. Πειθαρχεῖν δὲ θεῷ μᾶλλον ἢ ἀνθρώποις, Acts 5: 29. Ὑποτάγητε οὖν πάσῃ ἀνθρωπίνῃ κτίσει διὰ τὸν κύριον, 1 Pet. 2: 13.

(16) But, (*c*) since a rational being cannot be subject as an inferior to another as superior, unless it is of finite perfection, it is plain that law properly regarded, and moreover that sin also, presupposes *a rational subject of finite perfection.* Consummate perfection excludes a law from being prescribed by another, (for it is a law to itself and acknowledges no superior); and therefore it neither admits of sin, nor commits it. If indeed we could conceive of a being absolutely perfect, who should do things inconsistent with the rule of truth and goodness, (which

rule is inherent in the judgment and will of absolute perfection) ; if such a being, I say, could do those things which do not contribute to the glory of its perfections ; then this would be sin, in so much as it would be deserting itself and failing in respect to a proper regard for itself.   But as perfect attributes exclude the idea of self-desertion, so a perfect being must of course be sinless and unimpeachable.   The highest perfection involves the idea of perfect reason ; and this can do nothing contrary to reason, and what is consonant with reason is good and virtuous, it is the opposite of evil and sin.   If now consummate perfection cannot cease to be what it is, then it cannot sin.   But the matter is too clear to need further illustration.

A rational subject then being supposed, who is endowed with the faculty of free agency, and his obligation to a superior being also conceded, the law circumscribes the actions of such a subject.   It *teaches* or *demonstrates* what is to be done or not to be done, (and this is the proper force of the Hebrew word תּוֹרָה, which is derived from הוֹרָה *to teach, to demonstrate,*) ; or it prescribes *in what manner* a thing is to be done or not to be done ; it decides between things to be done and not to be done, and the respective modes of each ; whence the Greek word νόμος [from νέμω].   The object of law, therefore, is twofold ; *actions,* and *modes of actions.*

(18) The law has to do with *actions,* when it either commands or prohibits them, when it orders or forbids this or that to be done ; it concerns *modes of action,* when it merely and solely defines the modes of things to be done or omitted.   For example ; the law which required that the paschal lamb should be eaten, concerned the act itself ;   but the law which required that it should be slain on the evening of the fourteenth day of the month Nisan, and eaten with unleavened bread and bitter herbs, had respect, with regard to these particulars, only to the *manner* in which the passover was to be celebrated.   The apostolic injunction, which forbade women to prophesy with their heads uncovered, had respect only to the *mode* of action ; concerning the act itself nothing particular is prescribed.

(19) The acts of rational beings, and the modes of them, may be modified by law in a two-fold way, either by ordering that they shall be done, or by forbidding that they shall be done. Hence the distinction of law into *precept* and *interdict,* i. e. do or thou shalt do, and thou shalt not do ; which was the most common distinction among the Hebrews.

(20) If such a law is agreeable to the nature and attributes of the ruler who gives it authority, and of the subjects to whom it is prescribed, and also to the mutual relation of the two parties ; *if it does not exceed the ability and strength of the subject ;* and if manifest utility will redound to those who are to obey it, from the observance of it, so that the reason of the law may be clearly seen by all ; then it is named *equitable, just, and good.*

(21) Inasmuch as no one can be obligated by a law to do or omit any thing, unless the pleasure of the lawgiver be made known to him, and expressed in language that is plain and intelligible, it is clear that the notion of *law* and of *sin* supposes or involves the idea, that the pleasure of the lawgiver, as expressed in the law, should be made known to the subject by the clearest indications, or at least publicly promulgated, so that ignorance of the law, without a confession of culpable neglect, cannot possibly be made a pretext for excusing any crime committed against the law.

(22) All these conditions being presupposed, then *sin* may take place ; which is nothing more than a transgression of the law, or something done contrary to law, as we have already described it to be.

(23) Inasmuch as a law either commands or forbids, dilinquency respecting it may be of two kinds ; either by neglecting to do what the law requires, or by doing that which it forbids. Hence the division of sins into those of *omission* and *commission.* The law prohibits theft ; he who steals becomes a delinquent. The law requires us to revere parents and magistrates ; he who neglects to do so, commits sin. To do what the law forbids, to neglect what it commands, is to sin. This seems to be altogether plain and clear.

(24) These considerations are adduced to shew the general nature of sin. They may be easily transferred to offences committed against the divine Being ; the nature of which offences it is our present design to investigate."

After this introductory discussion Vitringa goes on to shew that God is our supreme and rightful Governor ; that we owe him entire obedience ; that his law is holy, just, and good ; and that neglect to do what it requires, or the doing of that which it prohibits, is sin ; and that, considered in this light, all sin is delinquency in respect to the law or a violation of it. This he does for a two-fold purpose; first in order to answer Poiret's book entitled *Cogitationes Rationales,* secondly with an intention to oppose a favorite dogma of many high orthodox theologians of his time respecting the nature of evil. Believing, as these theologians did and rightly did, that *the providence of God extends to all actions and events,* whether good or evil, in order to avoid the conclusion urged upon them by those who doubted or impugned this position, viz., that such a position necessarily involves the belief that God is the author of sin, they defined sin to be merely something *privative,* and not properly an actual thing or a real existence. Hence, as they argued, no *positive* cause was necessary, but merely a deficient or negative cause; and such a cause man himself could be.

In the same way President Edwards endeavours to avoid the imputation cast by some upon such views as he entertained respecting original sin, by the supposition that no positive or efficient cause is necessary. He compares it to the darkness of night, which is not positively occasioned by the influence of the sun, but is a matter of course when the sun once withdraws his light.

Vitringa, in opposition to such views, goes on to shew, that, at all events, sins of *commission* are something positive and real, and cannot be consistently regarded as a mere negation or something simply privative.

It is not to my present purpose to follow him out in his arguments with respect to this topic. They are, as we may easily believe, triumphant and irrefutable. The whole speculation, on the part of those theologians whom he opposes, appears to be nothing more than an illusion, occasioned and sustained by hair-splitting distinctions of terminology, made in entire accordance with the manner of the most subtile efforts of Thomas Aquinas or Duns Scotus.

I cannot refrain, however, from presenting my readers here with one passage from Poiret, whom Vitringa has undertaken in particular to refute. It reminds one so forcibly of many passages with which he meets in the *transcendental* writers of our day, who lay claim to the credit of new discoveries in the art of philosophizing, that he cannot refrain from believing, that after all, "there is nothing new under the sun." I shall not attempt to translate the passage; and this, for the simple but altogether sufficient reason, at least sufficient in respect to me, that I am utterly unable to do so, not understanding what **Mr. Poiret** says nor whereof he affirms.   I give it to the reader therefore in its original and transcendental costume.   It is a summary of his theory in respect to the nature of sin.

Cap. IV. § 14. " Si itaque ego, qui per Deum cogitatio sum spontanea, (at nihil a me), maneam in nihilo, quod est non-determinatio a me, ad me, per me, pro me, sumque mihi ut qui ex me, ad me, et per me nihil sum, volo, opto, eligo, operor, etc., tum non pecco.   Sed si illud NIHIL absit, id est, si ego, res sponte cogitans (qui tamen nihil a me) deficiam a nihilo, a non-determinatione a me, ad me, per me, etc., adsitque aliqua realitatis larva inanis, quâ ego, qui nihil sum, mihi is videar qui a me aliquid sim, sciam, bene optem, velim, operer, tunc eo ipso pecco.   Unde patet, peccatum, non cogitationem spontaneam ejusve positionem actualem esse, sed esse ABSTINENTIAM NIHILI in mente debiti, sive nihili privationem, ipso nihilo longe imperfectiorem et deteriorem ;   etiamsi id vel Dei proxima imitatio interdum esse videatur."

I have my doubts, whether even Coleridge himself, in the most transcendental of all his flights, (which are sometimes counted lofty or sublime by his admirers, as one cannot well avoid believing, because they lose sight of him and think he must of course be soaring aloft),—would have been able, with all his invention and boundless fecundity of words, to go beyond the once admired, but now long-forgotten Peter Poiret.   But all this is by the by ;   let us resume the important topic before us.

I wish to draw the particular attention of the reader to the main positions of Vitringa, in the passage which I have now translated.   These are,

(1) Law is the rule of moral actions.   It is the command of a superior, which regulates the *voluntary* actions of an inferior. See under No. 10 above.

Of course the author means to describe here the *moral* law, i. e. the law of God which regulates our moral actions.   We may speak of the *laws of nature*, i. e. of matter animate and inanimate ; of the laws of our physical being, etc. ; but whenever we employ the term *law* in this way, we merely designate the arrangement or order which the divine being has prescribed to physical nature,—an arrangement which it has no power to transgress, and never does violate.

Let the reader note well here, that Vitringa specificates *voluntary* actions, and those only, as being the proper objects of

moral law. This will be made still clearer, by the next sentiment of his, which I am now going to particularize.

(2) "Law," he says, "involves the idea of a rational subject,
i. e. of a free agent, furnished with the faculties necessary for
action." Nor is this all ; he is more explicit still. This subject or agent must be "adequate to determine for himself, deliberately and voluntarily from internal principles [quod se ex
interno principio deliberaté et έκουσίως . . . possit determinare],
in respect to the doing or not doing of any particular thing."
No. 11 above.

After shewing that the relation of dependence in some sense
must exist between lawgiver and subject, and that both the
matter and manner of actions may be proper subjects of law, he
goes on to say :

(3) A law, in order to be equitable, just, and good, "must
not exceed the ability and strength of the subject." No. 20.

(4) "Inasmuch as no one can be obligated by a law to do
or omit any thing, unless the pleasure of the law-giver be made
known to him, and expressed in language that is plain and intelligible ; it is clear that the notion of *law* and of *sin* supposes
or involves the idea, that the pleasure of the lawgiver, as expressed in the law, *should be made known to the subject by the
clearest indications*, or at least publicly promulgated ; so that
ignorance of the law cannot be pleaded by way of extenuating
guilt." No. 21.

(5) "All these conditions being presupposed, then sin may
take place; which is nothing more than *the transgression of
the law*, or *something done contrary to law*." No. 22.

Putting now these considerations together, we may make out
the following definition of sin, as laid down by Vitringa, viz.,
*The voluntary transgression or violation of a known law of
God, by a rational, free, moral agent.*

I trust that no one will assert this to be an incorrect view of
Vitringa's sentiments, because of what he says respecting *vitium*,
in Nos. 1, 2, of the above extract from his work. His definition of *vitium* is, that it is a *habit* or *habitude* of sinning, by
which he plainly means a *habitual inclination* to sin. This is
clear from the last paragraph under No. 2, in which he says,
that " habitual sin, in the order of nature and time, precedes sin
in the act ;" i. e., if I rightly understand him, the inclination,
in the order of nature and time, precedes the external development by outward actions. Yet this is not all, perhaps, which

he means to say ; for he probably intends to convey the idea, that sinful men possess an inclination to sin which is abiding, constant, or (as we commonly say) *habitual*. It is plain, however, from a comparison of this part of his Essay with what follows, that he did not bestow any considerable time or pains on what he has here said of the distinction between *vitium* and *peccatum*. If the reader will take the trouble to look back and compare Nos. 10, 11, 20, 21, and 22 above, he will see at once that Vitringa means, beyond a doubt, to comprehend within his definition *all* which he calls sin, whether *vitium* or *peccatum*. Indeed the *vitium* which he defines, or rather names, appears to be nothing more nor less than the frequently repeated, i. e. habitual, desire to sin which leads to the commission of what he calls *sinful acts*, and which is itself, (in the sense in which it is here understood by him), forbidden by the law of God.

In a way like to this the apostle James appears to speak, when he says, that " lust, when it has conceived, bringeth forth sin," James 1: 15. It might be a question here, (for such questions have been often raised), whether the lust which conceives and then brings forth sin, is itself a sin. But whatever may be said in order to shew that there must be some ultimate bounds in the genealogical series of sin, beyond which we cannot trace it without running into absurdity or else charging it upon our Maker, yet it is quite plain, at least it is so to my apprehension, that this reasoning will not apply to the lust of which the apostle here speaks. In the context (v. 14) he says : " Every man is tempted when he is drawn away of his own lust, and enticed." I acknowledge, indeed, that some objects which may tempt us, are not in themselves sinful. The tree of knowledge of good and evil, for example, which tempted our first parents, was not sinful. But this was an external object, and not a psychological part or passion of our progenitors. In the case before us, on the contrary, it is our *own* lust that tempts us and entices us ; and this, as the apostle expressly avers, not in such a sense as God tempts men, i. e. tries them or subjects them to trial (see vs. 2, 13), but in an evil sense, viz. entices us to sin. Is it then a forbidden passion *voluntarily indulged*, which the apostle here characterizes under the name of *lust ?* I see no other aspect of the case, which seems to be rational and consistent with scriptural views of the nature of sin. We are not sinners because our nature has a susceptibility of being impressed or excited by objects that may lead us to sin. Adam had evidently such a nature before his fall; the holy Redeemer himself possessed such a nature, else he could not have been "tempted in all points as we are." The point where sinful lust begins, is the point where voluntary encouragement or cherishing of such excitement begins. It is such a lust which " draws away and entices to sin;" and such which the apostle seems plainly to have had in view. And this in itself is sinful; it plainly is, moreover, the parent of actual and outward sins, as they are commonly named.

Vitringa's meaning, then, seems to be of the same general nature as that of James. Although in strictness of speech, as Vitringa has abundantly asserted elsewhere, all sin is an *act* of disobedience or a violation of law, and so lust itself when voluntarily cherished, and therefore sinful, is such a violation, yet in common parlance we speak of a *disposition to sin*, or a *habit of sinning*, or a *habitual inclination to sin*, as something which the mind is prone to separate from the act itself, and to regard as its antecedent. It is in accordance with this common usage of speech, that Vitringa expresses himself in the extract on which I am remarking. But at the same time, if the matter be thoroughly examined according to the whole of his views compared together, nothing will be found plainer or more certain, than that his *vitium* is as really a transgression of the divine law (and of course an *act* of the mind), as his *peccatum* is. And such is evidently the case with the declaration of the apostle James. In both these cases the modes of speech adopted in common parlance are employed, without any special regard to a choice of words which metaphysical nicety or the stricter laws of diction in casuistry would demand.

I may proceed then to remark, that no one, as I trust, will venture to assert that I have not given a fair and legitimate summary of Vitringa's principles and definitions, in what I have said above. And if this be so, the question then arises : Who comes nearest to Vitringa's views, the man who believes that all sin consists in voluntary transgression of known laws by intelligent, rational, free, moral agents ; or he who maintains, that sin may be and is a part of our physiological nature since the fall, and therefore may and does exist antecedent to all thought, knowledge, action, or voluntary exercise of the mind ? This question may be fairly raised ; and it ought to be fairly and candidly answered.

The allegation of *new divinity* ought not to serve, in the present case, as a satisfactory answer to views like those of Vitringa.   He was no new-divinity man, no New England theologian, but an honest, pious, learned, orthodox Dutchman of the next generation after the men of the Synod of Dort itself ; a masterly critic, moreover, a noble linguist, a universal scholar, and a profound theologian.   Here then is Vitringa, with all his orthodoxy and in all his glory, differing as much, in respect to the point before us from what is now called *a man of New England divinity*, as one grape differs from its mate on the same stem.

The reader who is not in unison with the sentiments of Vitringa, may of course regard them as he pleases ; but he will generously concede at least so much as this, viz., that such a view of sin as leads one to define it as being *a voluntary transgression of a known law, by a rational, free, moral agent*, is not *new* divinity, and is not appropriate merely to New England. The time is coming, I trust or at least hope that it is not far distant, when mere expressions of alarm on this subject, and charges of heresy and of forsaking the great *standards* of Protestantism in regard to the nature of sin, will not pass for sound argument.   It surely does not need proof, that such modes of rebuking or of convicting are not kind, brotherly, and rational discussion.   Above all, these methods of urging on the efforts of party, and of kindling into a flame its *odium theologicum*, ought not to have currency with the thinking, sober, candid, and judicious part of our community.   I may be permitted to add here, what I would do in the spirit of meekness and without polemic asperity, that such as have not for themselves fully examined the opinions of the Reformers and their successors, ought especially to refrain from *hereticating* others for a merely supposed difference of opinion.   How easily an error may be committed in this respect, has been strikingly shewn in the learned and excellent exhibition of the sentiments of the Reformation made by the Rev. Mr. Landis, in the Bibl. Repos. Vol. XII., with regard to several points of doctrine concerning which great confidence and much positive assertion have lately been exhibited by some polemic writers of our day.   Every one deeply versed in the theology of the Reformation and of the succeeding age, knows well that the leaders of that day differed as often and as much on some speculative points, which are of inferior practical interest, as theologians do now ; how then

can any one make up his mind to warm contention with Christian
brethren, and even excision of them, on account of matters
which are of such a nature? Bishop Horsley, in a charge to
the clergy of his diocese, told them that 'he did not demand
that they should not oppose Calvinism; but he did insist, that
before they should do so, they should study it sufficiently to
know what it is.' If charges of departure from the doctrines of
the Reformation were made only within the limits of such a
circle as the Bishop here delineates, our churches would be little troubled with the agitation of many questions, which now
occasion great jealousies and much excitement.

On the whole, the entire agreement of Vitringa's views in
respect to the nature of sin, with those that have lately been
stigmatized as new, and subjected to vehement assault, seems
to be too plain to demand, I had almost said to admit of, confirmation. Neither illustration nor confirmation is needed, so
far as the great point of harmony or coincidence is concerned.

For myself I feel constrained to say, that I have no where
found a more brief, plain, intelligible, and almost self-evident
exposition of the subject in question, than this masterly writer
has given us.

But there is a more important question remaining, and which
I would by all means consider as being still entirely open to further discussion, (for we are to call ' no man *master* upon earth');
and this is: *Whether the views of Vitringa are* CORRECT, i. e.
whether they are truly SCRIPTURAL ?

Narrow as the compass of this subject may at first view seem
to be, yet any one who is well acquainted with the state of polemic theology, in times past and at the present day, must know,
as a matter of course, that it would not be difficult to extend
the discussion of it so as to make a volume of no inconsiderable
size; and yet say nothing but what would have a bearing on
some part of the discussions that have already been raised. It
is scarcely necessary for me to tell the reader, that I have no intention of making such a volume. Neither my time nor the
object which I now have in view, would permit me to engage
in such an undertaking. The most that I aim at doing, is to
state in as brief manner as the nature of the case will permit
without exposing myself to be misunderstood, the leading reasons why I prefer and adhere to such a definition of sin as Vitringa has given; while at the same time I do not suppose myself to differ in opinion, so far as material *facts* are concerned,

from those who defend the definitions of sin as given by Turretin and others who in general accord with his views.

I must beg of my readers the liberty, while discussing this question, of pursuing the tenor of my way in such a manner as my thoughts have led me, while revolving the matter in my own mind. Arguments in favour of the opinion which I defend, or objections alleged against it, which appear to be of secondary and inferior importance, I purposely omit. I intend to bring forward only those which have had some sensible influence on my own mind, either in the way of defending or of opposing the sentiments exhibited by Vitringa.

I must also, in justice to myself, say further, that I do not seek to pursue the strict and formal order sometimes maintained in discussions of this nature. I shall first produce some of the leading considerations and texts of Scripture which induce me to entertain the opinion respecting the nature of sin which I endeavour to defend ; and then examine the principal texts of Scripture that are usually relied on in order to establish a different opinion. In doing this, I shall touch here and there on incidental topics which come in my way, and thus make what some of my readers may call *digressions* from my main subject. Into these digressions, however, I shall not fall, unless the topics present themselves to my view not only as disputed ones, but as possessing in themselves no inconsiderable interest. In a word, I intend to canvass the subject more in a familiar way which admits of occasional digression, than in the manner of the more rigid schools ; and I shall do so, because I have thought on the subject in this manner, and it is natural, therefore, for me to suppose that others might not be disinclined to follow the same track. It would not be difficult to throw the whole essay into an order which would answer the stricter demands of rhetoricians or logicians ; but I am not persuaded that the time and pains requisite to do this, would be well bestowed.

A word on one trait more of this discussion, and I have done with prologue. The delicacy of such a discussion at the present time, will be felt and acknowledged by all my readers. I am not the accredited representative, on this occasion, of those whom I suppose to be substantially of the same opinion which I have defended. It is by no concert between us that I have engaged in the present discussion. I have therefore felt it incumbent on me, in order that I might not seem to involve them in any apparent responsibility for what I say, to speak mostly in the first person *singular*, rather than in the first person plural. I am aware of the charge to which I expose myself, in the view of some readers, by so doing. But I had rather incur the hazard of this, than to run the danger of being charged with speaking for others what I am not commissioned by them to say. And besides this, I can truly add, that I have often used the first person singular, when I wished merely to say, that in my own view a thing is thus or so, rather than to make a positive and categorical assertion. If the reader will allow me this privilege, and for such an end, I hope he will not find reason to charge me with egotism of manner, in the sequel of this discussion.

In addressing myself to the work before me, I commence with the leading considerations which have induced me to adopt such a definition of *sin* as Vitringa has given.

(1) The first elements of our moral nature, our consciousness of what is right and what is wrong, our sense of guilt or of innocence, leads us spontaneously to decide, that we are criminal only so far as we voluntarily transgress a known law.

Let it be affirmed a thousand times, and reiterated even with a voice of thunder, that we are guilty of another's sin of which we had no knowledge, which we did in no way aid and abet, or to which we did never even consent, our conscience remains undisturbed and quiet. If we had no sins but such to give us uneasiness, our sleep would be quiet, and our days would pass on bright and unclouded. Or if we are charged with being transgressors of laws of which we had no knowledge, and respecting which it was *impossible* from our state or condition that we should have any knowledge, and consequently it was not our duty in such a state (according to Vitringa's principles) to acquire a knowledge, then our conscience is clear. No burden lies upon it. Metaphysicians may speculate on this subject and make charges of guilt; these may be proclaimed from the pulpit and the press; but conscious innocence still remains undisturbed, and the charges pass by as the idle wind which we regard not.

I make the appeal, now, to every son and daughter of Adam, whether each one has not in his or her own bosom a consciousness such as this? Whether every being made in the image of the living God has not such a principle enstamped on the very elements of his soul, in characters that cannot be effaced or even obscured? Ask all courts of justice and equity, from the highest to the lowest, whether any man can equitably be condemned for that which he not only did not commit, but for that to which he gave no assent, which he did in no way aid or abet, and of which he had no knowledge ; and they will give but one answer.   Ask all legislative bodies, who have any sense of justice, whether they make laws that render guilty those who never voluntarily transgress them ; they respond in the same manner. Indeed, there never has been, there is not, and from the nature of things there never can be, any difference of opinion as to this point of personal guilt and desert.   The disputes, whatever they are, do not turn on this point, but on something diverse from it, and have much more in reality to do with *names* than with *things ;* as I shall endeavor to shew in the sequel.

But if now we are inquired of, whether one man who is innocent, may not *suffer* on account of another's sins, and be greatly injured by them ; yea, not only be injured as to his temporal interests and happiness and comfort, but also as to his spiritual welfare ; we answer, as all men of sober consideration plainly must do, that in this case there can be no more doubt than in the other.   Every day's experience shews us that children suffer on account of their parents' vices ; subjects because of bad rulers ; the peaceful on account of the violent ; the honest by reason of the dishonest ; and, in a word, the world is filled with woes both of a temporal and spiritual nature, which the guilty inflict upon the innocent.   In cases without number misery is suffered, where there was no personal participation in the crime which occasioned it.

I readily admit that this is a point which involves some of the deepest mysteries—some of the most inscrutable principles—of the moral government of God.   Why should it be that the innocent must often suffer on account of others' sins?   Why should the universe be so constituted, that men can do harm, when they are so wicked, to multitudes who do not in any measure participate in their criminality?   These are questions, which, while we admit the facts just stated, we can never, in the present world, fully and satisfactorily answer.   Yet even the most hardy Pelagian would not venture to deny the *matter of fact* as thus alleged ; and whatever there may be in it which is inscrutable, which is either beyond or above our reason, (*contrary* to it we cannot affirm it to be), we are after all obliged, although it may be with reluctance, to admit that the world is, and ever since the fall of our original progenitors has been, filled with the plainest and most indubitable proofs of the fact just stated.

In view of all this, then, why should any one undertake to deny the mischiefs that have ensued, and which the Scriptures, as I believe, do very explicitly declare have ensued, from Adam's fall? He need not, he should not, deny these. And if he does, the same principle would, if he is consistent with himself, lead him to deny that woes spiritual or temporal now come upon the head of those who were not participators in the criminality which occasioned them.

Admitting now all that I have said on this topic, we may still maintain, that sin, properly defined, means *a voluntary transgression of known law*, and that nothing else is properly called sin. Most of those who may seem at first to oppose this view, do not after all, unless I greatly misapprehend them, differ much from it, except in the use of certain *words*. They begin, perhaps, in their reasonings, with this maxim as a self-evident one, viz. that *misery is only and always the consequence of sin*; hence they conclude, that all who suffer must therefore be sinful; and consequently, that infants, because they are *sufferers*, must also be *sinners*. But after all, they do not predicate *actual* sin of infants, and they accede to the definition of sin as given above, so far as what they name *actual* sin is concerned. It is *imputed* sin, then, or (as it is commonly named) *original* sin, which they predicate of infants, and thus make them guilty, in a certain sense, of the sin which Adam committed; while at the same time they would not assign to them any consciousness of personal criminality or actual sin, in respect to his transgression.

Here then, I admit, is a difference seemingly considerable, as to words and modes of explanation between two parties. But I still believe that there is a substantial agreement, after all, as to every important fact in the case. The deleterious and universal consequences of Adam's sin are admitted by both parties; the absolute necessity of renewing and sanctifying grace in all cases is maintained by both; and, in a word, all that is concerned with the actual depravity or real danger of the natural man, is fully admitted. The only difference that is palpable seems to be, that one party in its mode of treating the subject, makes two sorts, or rather two *genera*, of sin, *original* and *actual*, one which is merely putative and another which is actual and personal, in order to account for the guilt and misery of all men; while the other party thinks that nothing is gained by making such a distinction in the way of solving the mystery respecting the mischiefs occasioned by sin, and that no example can be found in the Scriptures of reckoning two sorts, or two *genera*, of sin.   The latter party, therefore, choose to confine themselves to naming that *sin* which is actual and voluntary ; while the other, fully admitting this definition so far as it goes, still extend the use of the appellation in question so as to designate not only the actions but also the *state* or *condition* of all rational beings who are sufferers, of whatever age or in whatever circumstances they may be.

While this state or condition is admitted by both parties to be essentially the same, as to its real attributes, (and this is admitted), why should it be deemed a matter of high importance, and worthy of strenuous dispute, whether the definition of a *word* be more or less extensive, when no change is or can be made thereby in the state of *facts*, or the nature of things ?

But since dispute has arisen, may I be permitted to ask : Is it not a safe and proper way, in such cases, to make the appeal to the Bible, and to follow simply the scriptural usage ?   Who will not here respond in the affirmative ?   Shall we not, then, make the appeal directly to the Bible, and ask, whether the sacred writers do not speak of sin, and treat it, as being *a voluntary transgression of a known law*—and only such ?   This latter circumstance, I am ready to concede, is essential to the object before us.   All are agreed, and there can be no question in the case, that voluntary transgression of a known law is sin ; the Scriptures declare this ; conscience affirms it ; and the only question therefore is : Whether the Bible, like one part of our theologians, goes still further, and names that sin which is merely *putative* or *imputed*, or which is an *original constituent* of the nature with which God has endowed us ?   If so, then the definition of Vitringa must be deemed defective, and instead of his *vitium* and *peccatum*, we ought to have at the outset, *peccatum originale et peccatum actuale ;* and when this distinction was made, the latter might be subdivided, if it should be deemed proper, as the former has already been, in the theology of the schools.

But before we come to the *biblical* investigation now before us, I must be allowed once more distinctly to avow my full belief in the multiplied and mischievous consequences of sin to others, in unnumbered cases where actual personal criminality is not concerned ; and that this is a doctrine widely and often taught in the Scriptures, in a great variety of forms.   But the question, whether a *liability to suffer* by reason of sin which others commit, is to be properly called, or is in the Scriptures called, *sin*, (except in a tropical or a figurative sense), is a question quite diverse from the important facts just stated, and one which can be determined only by fair, accurate, and extensive investigation.

My limits oblige me, however, to be brief; and I can advert only to some leading passages in the Bible. In respect to the tenor of these I would remark,

(2) That the Scriptures seem to me fully and explicitly to declare, that the sacred writers regarded all sin in the same light as that in which Vitringa has placed it. In order to illustrate this, let us ask the question : In what sense are the heathen considered as *sinners* by Paul ? When he is going, in the epistle to the Romans, to shew that all men are sinners, both Gentiles and Jews, (all of course we must suppose him to mean who are capable of being sinners), what does he say, in order to convict the *Gentiles* of sin ? Does he compare their conduct with the demands of the Scriptures ? No, but he makes out another rule of action which they have transgressed. He says : " The wrath of God is revealed from heaven against all ungodliness and unrighteousness of men . . . because what may be known of God is manifest in them [i. e. in the Gentiles, of whom he is here speaking], for God had shewed it unto them." How—where—when ? " The invisible things of him [God] from the creation of the world are clearly seen, being understood *by the things that are made* [and not by revelation in the Scriptures], even his eternal power and Godhead." What follows, then, from the fact that the book of nature had been thus spread out before them ? It follows, that "they are without excuse; because that when they knew God, they glorified him not as God, neither were thankful." The least that can be meant by this last declaration is, that when opportunity was offered to the heathen of knowing and glorifying God, they wilfully refused to embrace it, and so did not glorify him, but were ungrateful. Thus doing, they became sinners, Rom. 1: 20, 21.

Now why need Paul betake himself to such a method of proof as this, in order to shew that the Gentiles were sinners ? Such a method fully exhibits a sense of obligation on his part to shew that the heathen had some knowledge of what was true and right, or at least a fair opportunity to acquire some knowledge of this which they voluntarily and wilfully neglected,—

to shew this, I say, and render it plain, in order to make out
his proof so as to satisfy his readers, that the Gentiles were all
sinners. Why did not Paul choose a shorter and much easier
method of effecting his purpose? Why did he not here declare, that, inasmuch as all men are descended from Adam who
sinned, all men are of course sinners—yea, sinners on this account in a two-fold sense, sinners because of original sin *imputed*, and sinners because of original sin *inherent?* Why should
Paul here hold himself necessitated to make out a charge of actual and voluntary transgression against some plain principles of
right and propriety and truth, in order to bring the Gentiles
under the condemnation of the divine law? According to the
statement of many who advocate original sin imputed and inherent, this last sin is as really and truly worthy of damnation, and
as certainly incurs it, as actual sin. Yet the great apostle
of the Gentiles here begins, continues, and goes on to conclude
his main argument to prove that the Gentiles are sinners, without once adverting to such a principle, or such a position. But
if he had really believed it, in the sense just stated, and had
such views as usually at the present day accompany such a
statement, it passes wonder that he should here overlook and
omit even a hint upon this subject.
    Shall we be told, that he has exhibited, at full length, his
views in respect to this subject, in the fifth chapter of the epistle to the Romans? My answer is, that the exhibition for the
purpose now supposed, comes quite too late. In the first chapter of this epistle Paul concludes his argument to prove that the
Gentiles are all sinners; in the second and third chapters he
maintains and establishes the same charges against the Jews.
In the fourth chapter he removes objections against these charges. In chapter v. he shews what were the blessed fruits of
justification by atoning blood and interceding mercy; and particularly he shows the *wide extent* of the blessings thus procured. It is here, in this connection of thought, and for the purpose of rendering prominent this part of his discourse, that he
introduces the comparison between the mischiefs occasioned by
Adam's fall, and the good occasioned by a Saviour's "obedience unto death." It is not simply or directly to make out the
guilt of Gentile or Jew, that Paul resorts to this; he had already
completed his proof that both were guilty. It was only to shew,
that however multiplied and sore the mischiefs occasioned by
Adam were, a remedy adequate for these, yea, for many more

than these (see v. 16), had been provided by the gospel plan
of salvation.

While Paul then admits, or, as it seems to me, asserts, that
Adam's offence is in some way (he does not say in what one)
concerned as a cause with the sinful character of all men ; while
he declares that " many were *made* sinners by one man's disobedience ;" he not only refrains from saying that this one man's
disobedience was itself the sin of the many, as being imputed
to them, but he declares explicitly that " death passed upon all
men, because that ($\dot{\epsilon}\varphi'$ $\ddot{\omega}$) all have sinned." In the place where
this is asserted (Rom. 5: 12), the necessary implication seems
to be, that the sin of all was, in its essential nature, like the sin
of Adam, i. e. it was a transgression or violation of law. So
the comparison seems plainly to imply : " As by one man sin
entered into the world, and death by sin ; and *so* death passed
upon all men, because that all have sinned," Rom. 5: 12.

How can we reasonably allege, now, that the apostle here
speaks merely of an *imputed* offence, and the mischiefs done to
mankind by reason of this ? Does he not contrast the redemption of Christ here in all its magnitude and glory, with the evils
of sin in *all* their magnitude ? Verse 16th surely establishes the
position that he does. But if he does this, how can it be said,
that he merely contrasts the evils of *imputed* sin (so called)
with the benefits of redemption ? Yet such is the doctrine
taught by the apostle's expressions, if the usual method of making out imputation from this passage is correct. And this consideration is of itself enough, at least so it appears to my mind,
to lead us to suspect the propriety of such an interpretation as
the one just named. Surely Christ did not die merely or principally to atone for *imputed* sin. " The free gift is of *many
offences* unto justification," (v. 16). Those who were " made
sinners by one man's disobedience," committed many—*many*
offences for which atonement was made. And it is these—committed as widely as the human race are spread—these that have
been removed by atoning blood ; and it is this that constitutes
the most prominent glory and benefit of the gospel dispensation.

I cannot admit, therefore, the propriety of an appeal to Rom.
5: 12—19, in order to make out the allegations, that our own
sin is not only what we do in violation of law, but also what
Adam did which is imputed to us, or a part of our nature itself
as given to us by our Maker. Paul does not proceed in this
way, in order to prove that Gentiles or Jews are all sinners.

Nor can it be fairly said, now, in answer to this, that Paul's object was to make out the proposition, that *aggravated* guilt might be justly predicated of all men ; and therefore he undertakes to shew that they are guilty of *actual* sin. For if we adopt such a sentiment, how shall we account for it, (on the ground of those who maintain that there are two kinds of sin), that in his charges he has omitted original sin both imputed and inherent? Surely it would have been a great aggravation of the case in question, had these been added to the bill of impeachment made out by Paul ; I mean that it must plainly have been so, on the ground assumed by those who defend the views which we are examining.

After all that has been said on the meaning of Rom. 5: 12— 19, as establishing the doctrine of original sin imputed and inherent—*sin*, I mean in the scriptural sense of this word—there is yet an entire failure to clear up the mysterious proceeding of Paul as to his form and method of reasoning, in case his creed were as some maintain it to be. Why he did not bring the charge of *original sin* against the Gentiles and Jews in the first part of his epistle, in order to prove that they were all sinners, —a charge which, if correct, must plainly and demonstrably be against *all* men—has not yet been shown. It remains still a *quod demonstrandum* in exegesis and in theology.

Sincerely and undoubtingly do I believe the apostle means to declare, that Adam's first offence has been and is a cause or occasion of all men's becoming sinners. I doubt not he means to proclaim, that human nature has become deteriorated by the fall. But that the sin which he so often mentions in Rom. 5: 12—19 is other than actual sin, i. e. violation of the divine law, I have never yet seen to be proved so as to give satisfaction to my mind. How can the redemption of Christ be limited to a deliverance merely from *original* sin? If mankind are here charged only with original sin imputed or inherent, or with both, then, as the opposite of this, the righteousness of Christ must be considered both as imputed and inherent, in order to carry the antithetic analogy through in a consistent manner. Yet the inherent righteousness of Christ, as transferred to believers, is strenuously denied by nearly all Protestants ; and the *imputed* righteousness of Christ, as belonging to believers was plainly not a doctrine of the early Reformation, but one which sprang up during the subsequent period of theological discussion.

It is then, we may reasonably conclude, a sin different from *imputed* or *inherent* sin, which the apostle puts in contrast with the redemption wrought by Christ. And if so, we are thus far borne out, of course, in our views of sin as an actual violation of the law of God.

I should make an apology for the length of these remarks, were it not that the main passage of Scripture relied on by most to shew that there are two kinds of sin, has been now under consideration. It is impossible to do any justice to such a topic, and to guard against misunderstanding, without going beyond the bounds of a mere skeleton-exhibition.

What has been said may serve to shew, that when Paul undertakes to prove that men are sinners, he resorts to a method of proof which exhibits them as *transgressors* of some rule or law made known to them. What says he, for example, of the Gentiles, to whom no revealed law had been given? He says, that "not having [a revealed] law, they are a law unto themselves; who shew the work of the law [i. e. the work which the law requires] *written in their hearts*," Rom. 2: 14, 15. And what is the consequence? "So many as have sinned without law [revelation], shall perish without it," i. e. they shall be judged and condemned as sinners against the law written on their own hearts.

It would seem, then, as has been already remarked, that in order to justify to the mind of his readers the condemnation of the Gentiles, Paul deemed it necessary to shew, that they had a knowledge of some divine law, even that which was written on their own hearts and consciences, and that they had violated the precepts of this law.

But why, we may here ask, must there be a *law*, and why must men have some knowledge of it, in order that they should be counted *sinners*? The answer may be given by appeal to various passages of Scripture. It is because "by law is the knowledge of sin," Rom. 3: 20; because we "cannot know sin, except by the law," Rom. 7: 7; because "to him that knoweth to do good, and doeth it not, to him it is sin," James 4: 17; because "where there is no law, there is no transgression," Rom. 4: 15. To beings now, which are physiologically incapable of any moral or spiritual knowledge, whose actual condition utterly excludes the supposition of its being communicated or even developed in the soul—to such beings "there is no [moral] law." The God who made them, and made them thus, did not design, that, while they are in such a condition, they should have the knowledge in question.   And if any one should ask how it can be, that they should not sooner come to the knowledge of what is duty, the question involves the same difficulty (and no more), as if one should ask : Why did not God create all men and make them complete moral agents, thousands or millions of years sooner than he has done ?   One thing is very clear in respect to our moral accountability, and this is, that men will never be punished as actual sinners, so long as they cannot commit actual sin. . Be this period sooner or later, heaven will never exact an account of talents not committed to our charge.

There are some things in morals which are too plain to be proved ; and I am almost ready to say, that the question before us appears to be one of those things.   The sacred writers do not express themselves as if they had once thought, that they must needs formally affirm, or establish by a course of reasoning, that *sin is a transgression of law*, and that without a knowledge of law there can be no sin.   They appear to hold as a matter universally conceded, not only that there can be no knowledge of sin without a knowledge of law, but that sin itself cannot exist or be committed without such a knowledge, or (in other words) that "where there is no law there is no transgression."   The case of *wilful* ignorance alone is to be excepted from these remarks.   The consequence of such a state of feeling among inspired authors is, that what we meet with in them respecting the nature of sin, is only what is said *obiter*, i. e. what is now and then thrown in to give intensity to other declarations, by referring the reader to principles already known, established, or rather spontaneously conceded, by every reasonable mind.

Such an assumption of the truth before us the Saviour makes in that solemn declaration of his to the Jews : "If I had not come and spoken to them [the Jews], they had not had sin ; but now they have no cloak for their sin," John 15: 22.   And again : "If I had not done among them the works which none other man did, they had not had sin," John 15: 24 ; i. e. if I had not disclosed my true character to them by the miracles which I have wrought among them, then they would not have contracted their present guilt in rejecting me.   In both of the present cases, the declaration of the Saviour, I readily concede, is not to be regarded as absolute and universal, but as extending to the sin of unbelief and of rejecting him.   But the *principle* sanctioned is altogether the same as that for which Vitringa contends, viz., that sin can be predicated only of cases where there was a knowledge of what was required and of what was forbidden, i. e. of legal precept. In the declarations of Jesus, he takes it for granted that this principle is self-evident. He only declares that the unbelief of the Jews is such that it cannot be excused, because they had enjoyed an opportunity of knowing what the truth is, and had neglected and abused it.

So again, in the Saviour's conversation with the Pharisees, after he had restored sight to the man born blind; Jesus had said : " For judgment I am come into this world, that they which see not might see, and they which see might be made blind" (John ix.), when the Pharisees, who were highly offended, replied : " Are we blind also ?" What is the reply of him who is the light of the world? " Jesus said unto them : If ye were blind, ye should have no sin." Of course, the meaning is not here : ' If ye were physically blind ;' it may be thus expressed : ' If ye were unable to see any moral or spiritual light, then ye would have been guiltless ; but now, your case is very different from this. You yourselves acknowledge that you see ; therefore, your sin remaineth.' " This," said the Saviour on another occasion, in conversation with Nicodemus, " is the condemnation [of unbelievers], that light is come into the world, and men have loved darkness rather than light." It is, not because they could not see any thing of the light, that they are condemned ; it is because that, while they might or did see its glory and excellence, they still preferred the darkness. In John 1: 5 it is said, in our English Version : " The light shineth in the darkness, and the darkness *comprehended* it not, αὐτὸ οὐ κατέλαβε ; this should be rendered, *did not apprehend*, i. e. did not take hold of, embrace, or receive it ; for *did not comprehend it* seems not to be the shade of idea meant to be conveyed here. I take the sentiment to be the same which is exhibited in the passage taken from the conversation of the Saviour with the Jewish ruler.

Need I appeal, finally, to the often repeated and solemn assurance, that " God will render to every man according to his *deeds ?*" Rom. 2: 6. Must it be again repeated, " that the Son of Man will reward every man according to his *works ?*" Matt. 16: 27 ; that " they *who do good* shall come forth to the resurrection of life, while they *who do evil* shall come forth unto the resurrection of damnation ?" John 5: 29. In these, and other cases almost without number, the idea always insisted on is, that *what men have done*, their *actions*, their *transgressions*, the actual *violations* of law whether by commission or omission (for omission always amounts to the doing of something which God has forbidden, under present circumstances, instead of doing one's duty)—in a word, the acts, the voluntary acts of men—are those things for which men are either rewarded or punished. Of course I mean here, not merely such actions as are *external*, but all actual, voluntary, internal desires and affections of the soul, which are contrary to what God has required.

The very names of *sin*, in Hebrew and Greek, are all of an *active* nature. Such a meaning has פֶּשַׁע, עָוֹן, חַטָּאת; such an one has ἁμαρτία, ἐπιθυμία, παράβασις. The very verbs which express the idea of sinning are so essentially active, that they have not even a passive voice ; I mean that there is no *passive* form among them, when they convey the meaning *to sin*.

Add to all this, the great Judge of quick and dead has told us explicitly, as has already been hinted, that the heathen will be judged in the day of retribution, only for such sins as are committed against the light of nature : " As many as have sinned without law, shall perish without law ; and as many as have sinned under the law, shall be judged by the law," Rom. 2: 12. It is scarcely necessary to remark here, after what has been already said, and what indeed lies upon the very face of the whole sentiment, that *law* means *revelation* in this passage. So then, they that have no light of revelation, are not accountable for the privilege or benefit of it, but only for the light of nature. " The Gentiles . . . who have not the law, are a law unto themselves ; . . . these shew the work of the law written in their hearts, their consciences bearing witness, and their thoughts alternately accusing and excusing," Rom. 2: 14, 15.

Thus it appears from the very elements of our nature, from " the law written on our hearts," i. e. our consciences, and from God's holy word, that sin is to be regarded as a violation of known law—a violation committed by a rational, free, moral being. He must be *rational*; for the stones, and trees, and brooks, and rivers, do not and cannot sin. He must be a *free* agent ; for if he is not, then his actions are not his own, and he of course is not accountable for them. Those who have no reason which enables them to choose, or those who are physically compelled to act against their wishes, are not charged by justice, and are not properly chargeable, with *sin*. He must, moreover, be a *moral* agent ; for brutes, and madmen, and *non compotes mentis,* even though they were in some sense free, are not *moral* agents, and therefore they cannot sin.

Apart from theological dispute, it seems to me that there is not an enlightened rational man on the face of the whole earth, who would ever deny these principles. All men spontaneously admit them in legislation, in dispensing justice, in governing, in reasoning—about every thing except theology. A man might as well deny that he has a soul, as to deny that he has one which spontaneously assents to these principles in regard to real criminality.

Such then are some of my leading reasons for believing that Vitringa has rightly defined sin. But whilst I say this, I am fully aware, as I have already intimated above, that all the questions which can be raised, are not decided by these considerations, plain and palpable as they are. It has already been remarked, that those who differ from the views of Vitringa, will still admit his definitions and principles to be correct, so far as they go; i. e. they will admit that these apply, with entire correctness, to all *actual* sin. But they aver at the same time, that the question is not at all decided by this, whether there is or is not such a thing as *original* sin, imputed or inherent, which is not reached by these definitions, and to which none of these principles, however plain and just with respect to *actual* sin, can be properly applied.

On this question views different from those of Vitringa have often been presented, and efforts made to shew, that sin, properly so called, may and does exist antecedent to any actual and voluntary transgression of the divine law. But there is not time nor space enough remaining, to permit us to enter on the discussion of this part of the subject. The prosecution of it must therefore be reserved for a future number.

ARTICLE II.

CAMPBELLISM.

By Rev. R. W. Landis, Jeffersonville, Pa.   [Concluded from p. 130.]

§ II. *Direct Arguments against Campbellism.*

It has already been intimated that Mr. Campbell's views of faith are such as have allowed him to ridicule, in a very indecent manner, the doctrine of the saving influence of the Spirit of God in repentance and regeneration. The faith which he contends for, he says, is " purely historical." " It is one of the monstrous abortions of a purblind theology for any human being to be wishing for spiritual aid to be born again. Transfer such an idea to the first birth, and to what an absurdity are we reduced !" This is a specimen of his ridicule.

According to Campbellism, a belief of the " facts recorded in the gospel," connected with immersion in water, constitutes the real Christian. As we are about to present, in this section, a brief synopsis of direct arguments against the system, we will first, in connection with what has been already advanced, subject the above position to a short examination.

Does the belief of the " naked facts recorded in the gospel," constitute a believer, in the Scripture sense of that term? We fearlessly answer in the negative.

The precise point in debate is illustrated by the following occurrence related by Dr. Jennings, (*Debate*, p. 39). A young, but intelligent female, was urged by a proselyting follower of Mr. Campbell to be immersed; and was told that if she " historically believed the gospel, or the history of our Lord Jesus Christ," that it was all the faith required. She replied, that she could not doubt the reality or sincerity of her historical belief of all that was contained in the Bible;—that she was as conscious of the existence of this belief, as she was of her own existence;—but that she was no less certain, that this belief was different from that faith which is the peculiar characteristic of all the true disciples of Christ, because it did not exert any suitable or lasting influence either upon her heart, or life. The reply was found unanswerable.

It is not our intention to enter into the controversy on the subject of faith, which has of late agitated a portion of the American churches; nor is this necessary, in order to expose the falseness of the Campbellite view.

That a mere naked assent to the truth of the facts mentioned in the gospel, is not that christian *grace* of which we read so much, appears from such passages as the following. Paul (Rom. 15: 13) prays that the Roman Christians might be "filled with joy and peace in believing;" which certainly implies that joy and peace are distinct from a mere naked assent; else why thus pray? To the same purpose Peter says (1 Pet. 1: 8), that "believing, we rejoice with joy unspeakable and full of glory." If this were consequent upon mere naked assent, why speak of it thus as something distinguishing?

But that something more is requisite besides a mere rational assurance, or certainty of the truth of the gospel, to win and overcome the heart of man, is clear from the whole history of the Bible. Can any one suppose that there was one among the people of Israel at Sinai who could have had the least doubt that their law was divine, and that Jehovah had proclaimed it to them? And yet how headlong do they rush into idolatry against its very letter. So in regard to God's constant dealing with that people. And who among the multitudes that followed our Lord could find room to doubt that he came from God, and taught divine truth. Yet how few really *believed* in him, agreeably to the Bible acceptation of that term. And Isa. 53: 1, (applied to Christ by his apostles,) shows that the saving belief of the gospel "report" is connected with the revelation of the "arm of the Lord." Hence we read of those who "believe according to the working of his mighty power," Eph. 1: 19. "No man can say that Jesus is Lord, but by the Holy Ghost," 1 Cor. 12: 3. See also John 6: 63, with verses 35 and 65; also ch. 7: 39 and Isa. vi.

The grievous mistake of these men on this subject arises from supposing that a rational certainty which is sufficient to satisfy the judgment, and silence all its objections; must necessarily be sufficient to overcome the opposite and corrupt inclinations of that heart, which is "enmity against God." But who does not know that a man may have ever so great a degree of the certainty of any thing which is contrary to the inclinations of his wicked heart, and yet that he needs more than the mere evidence of what has made him certain, to determine his will efficaciously against his vicious course. Can a man be more cer-

tain of any thing, than he is that he must die : and yet how few
are even made thereby to think but one moment seriously in
relation to death and its consequences ?   This point is so plain
that we deem further illustration of it useless ; and shall proceed to consider the subject of *regeneration.*

The position on which Campbellism rests,—that *no one can
be discipled, converted, regenerated, until immersed ;* is plain,
comprehensive, and unequivocal.   It is either *entirely universal* in its application to the human race since the commencement of the Gospel dispensation, *or it is necessarily false.*   The
very terms of the proposition, as well as the nature of the system founded upon it, preclude the possibility of any middle
ground ; they do not allow a *single exception ;* for they declare
expressly, that *no one—no person can be regenerated until he is
immersed.*   And in case of any supposed or alleged exception
to the universality of their application, the reply is plain :—the
excepted person is either *not* " converted, discipled, regenerated," or the principle excepted against *is false.*   The terms are
perfectly unequivocal.

The Campbellites must therefore either abandon this fundamental principle of their system ; they must either admit that
persons may be and are saved without being regenerated, or
receiving the remission of sin ; or they must meet the consequences resulting from their principles.   They are, indeed, formidable.   But we leave Mr. Campbell and his followers to
make a choice, while we proceed to point out a few of them.
We shall present them as they occur.

1. Infants who die in infancy, (Campbellite infants likewise),
either are not saved, or they are saved without being *born
again ;* because, as no one can be regenerated until immersed,
and as infants are not immersed, they, of course, are not regenerated.   So that, according to this system, infants dying in infancy are all eternally damned ; or, if not, a vast and innumerable company of the redeemed have not been " scripturally regenerated."

2. Paedobaptists are either lost, or, if saved, saved without
being regenerated—for they do not immerse—and Mr. Campbell declares that " immersion" and " regeneration" are " two
names for the same thing."   Hence Paedobaptists are either
saved without being regenerated, or they perish.   But again :
Mr. Campbell declares regeneration to be essential to salvation ;

and therefore, as Paedobaptists are not immersed, (according to his views,) they are eternally lost.*

But is any Christian seriously prepared to admit that all Paedobaptists who have died are eternally lost? and that all who hereafter die must perish likewise? Is any one prepared to admit that the pious Doddridge, and Henry, and Baxter, and Howe, and President Edwards, and à Kempis, and Fenelon, and Pascal, and Brainerd, and Dwight, and the lovely and apostolic Martyn, with the noble-hearted Heber, and Fisk, and Swartz, and Parsons—is any one prepared to admit that these, with myriads of others as pious and devoted, *are sunk to endless flames,* because they were not immersed? Yet without this admission the fundamental principle of Campbellism cannot be sustained.

Nor is this all. Paedobaptists who are now zealously engaged in promoting the cause of Christ—in conveying the glad tidings of a Saviour's love " to earth's remotest bound"—must, so soon as life terminates, join the " throng of frighted ghosts," *because not immersed.*

Nor let us forget those heroic soldiers of the cross—*the glorious martyrs*—" whom," says Polanus, a contemporary (Syntag. p. 1645), " no promises, no losses, no torments, nor even the direful terrors of the most torturing death that awaited them, could for one moment swerve from their confidence in Christ." The dauntless Huss, and the brilliant Jerome, with Cranmer, and Latimer, and Ridley, and Bland, and Philpot, together with a vast multitude of those valiant sufferers " who were beheaded for the witness of Jesus," or sung praises to the Lamb while the flames were consuming their mangled bodies, all—yes, every soul of them, have taken up their dreary abode amid the unspeakable horrors of the second death—*because they were not immersed.*

---

* Mr. Campbell at first shrunk from this consequence, but consistency drove him on to admit it in his debate with Dr. Jennings (See pp. 172, 173), and his followers now also admit it. One of Mr. Campbell's " best beloved disciples" in his periodical thus meets it: Speaking of Fenelon, and the " hosts of worthy and excellent citizens of every nation and of every age" who have not been immersed, he says: " If therefore we are ourselves honest, we cannot but declare, that in relation to the religion of Jesus, they are unjustified, unsanctified, unpardoned persons." *Author of the Mirror, in Advocate,* Vol. I. p. 215.

The same fate has happened to those devout catechumens of the primitive church, who were dragged to the stake and put to death, before they had received the initiatory rite of baptism. The same too has been the fate of those pagans, who, (as the records of those times declare,) were converted to Christianity upon witnessing the constancy of the martyrs ; and professing their faith under the first impulse of zeal, were barbarously butchered on the spot. But to enlarge on this point were needless.

3. It follows from this system that if a believing penitent is so circumstanced that he cannot be immersed, no matter how ardently he may desire it, he must die without remission of sins ; for immersion is essential to remission ;—he must die without being born again, for no one can be regenerated without being immersed. But if a person dies without forgiveness of sins, or without being regenerated, he of course dies in his sins ; and is of course an enemy to God, and where Christ is he can never come.

These consequences appear so astoundingly absurd, and so unlike the merciful provisions of the gospel, that the Campbellites have done all that men could do to avoid them without abandoning their system. But there is no other alternative. All that they have been able to do, however, has been to produce the following extract from the *Christian Baptist* of Mr. Campbell, Vol. VII. p. 165. "I doubt not," says Mr. Campbell, "but such Paedobaptists as simply mistake the meaning and design of the Christian institution, who, nevertheless, are, as far as they know, obedient disciples of Jesus, will be admitted into the kingdom of glory." But this is not an explanation, it is a contradiction. For how then is regeneration, and forgiveness of sins essential to salvation if Paedobaptists may be saved without either ? And how is this declaration to be reconciled with some others of a different character, (to one of which we have referred,) and made at a later date than the foregoing ? E. g. in his *Extra I. Mill. Har.* p. 30 : "But whether they may enter into the kingdom of future and eternal glory after the resurrection, is a question much like that question long discussed in the schools, viz., Can infants who have been quickened, but who die before they are born, be saved ?" or with the declaration contained in our last marginal note ? Here then, pressed with the difficulties which result from his system, Mr. Campbell endeavors to extricate himself, but only plunges headlong into greater. As old *Gaultier* has it,

" Incidit in Scyllam, cupiens vitare Charybdim."

But even laying aside all this with respect to his contradictions, the relief which the foregoing admission of Mr. Campbell's gives to Paedobaptists, is not worth accepting. To say nothing on the subject of what is necessary to constitute *involuntary* error, it is sufficient to observe that they have no other reason to expect mercy than this very charitable " doubt not." Mr. Campbell has not even pretended to specify a solitary argument, or one passage of Scripture in support of this *pious* supposition. He was too wise to attempt it ; knowing assuredly that any such argument (if a good one) or passage of Scripture, would be of necessity a death-blow to his system.

4. This scheme places the salvation of the human race entirely in the hands of men, and at the mercy of the administrator of the ordinance. For Campbellites do not allow their converts to baptize themselves ; and yet they maintain a person may be " begotten of God, quickened by the Spirit, and impregnated by the word," (*Extra* I.) and yet without immersion will remain " unpardoned, unjustified, unsanctified, unreconciled, unadopted, and lost to all christian life and enjoyment," (see *Ibid.*) Hence the modest and *unassuming protestants*, invest themselves with full as much authority, and the same power over the multitude as his holiness of Rome. They assume the keys of life and death, of hell and heaven ;—and authority " to shut and no man openeth," etc. This sentiment ought to be deeply impressed upon the minds of our countrymen, who have either been led astray by this apostacy, or reside within the sphere of its influence. And it might be worth while also to ask, how this conscientious ministry make out to reconcile it with the moral sense, (to say nothing of the sense of duty consequent upon the sincere adoption of these principles,) to postpone the immersion of applicants for that ordinance, for a number of weeks, or even for a day (as is well known to be a fact of constant occurrence among them,) merely to suit their own convenience ?—and thus endanger the everlasting salvation of their souls. The reader must judge for himself whether this unaccountable conduct arises from the fact that they know their principles to be false ; or that they do not esteem it as a matter of much account to risk the soul's everlasting interest.

5. When any who were originally members of the Baptist church become Campbellites, they are not immersed. The same may be said of apostates from the Campbellite churches,

who have afterwards been reclaimed.   In neither case is immersion repeated. (See *Mill. Har.* Vol. V. p. 187.)   Hence we come to the very edifying conclusions that men may be "*scripturally regenerated*" before they are "converted," and also before they even believe a single word of the Bible.—That a man, no matter how vile he may afterwards become, never can lose the *grace* of this regeneration; it "sticks by him" to that degree, that it never can be lost, and needs not be re-bestowed.

We should here close our remarks upon this ludicrous compound of impiety and folly, were it not that its abettors object to this mode of argumentation.   "No matter what the consequences deducible from it may be," say they, "if the Scriptures do not condemn it, we are satisfied to retain it."   Let us then "to the word and to the testimony," for a moment or two.

6. Nothing can be a more direct contradiction to the principle under discussion than 1 Pet. 1: 2, which, to prevent cavil and needless objection, we present in Mr. Campbell's own version.   "Having been regenerated, not of corruptible seed, but incorruptible, *through the word of the living God*, which remains forever."   Comment here is needless.   See also Jas. 1: 18. John 17: 17, and 2 Cor. 7: 10.

7. Immersion, agreeably to the word of God, is not in all cases necessary to the remission of sin; for Mary, and the sick of the palsy, and the dying malefactor, had their sins remitted without it.   The last of these cases also proves that immersion is not essential to regeneration; for the person then spoken of was regenerated, and saved without it; and none can be saved, agreeably to the Campbellites themselves, without being regenerated. Luke 7: 37—48. Matt. 9: 2. Luke 23: 39—43.

Should they, however, in order to evade this argument, assert that as these instances occurred under the Jewish dispensation, they of course prove nothing with regard to the Christian; I reply, that they lose as much as they gain by this evasion.   For if these occurrences transpired under the Jewish dispensation, it was also under that dispensation that the blessed Redeemer used the words contained in John 3: 5.   And therefore, according to this evasion, that passage has no reference whatever to the christian dispensation.

8. We read of Cornelius "a devout man and one that feared God with all his house," who "prayed always," and "whose prayers and alms had come up for a memorial before God." See Acts x.   So truly eminent was his character for devotion

and piety, that an angel was commissioned from heaven who acquainted him with the fact that his prayers were heard, and his alms-deeds approved in the sight of God. Yet he was not baptized. And of course he was, agreeably to Campbellism, " unpardoned, unsanctified, unadopted, unconverted, unregenerate," etc. etc. Now what can a serious reader of the New Testament think of this ?

9. The Lord " opened Lydia's heart" (Acts 16: 14) before her baptism ; and of course, after her heart was thus opened, by the Lord, she was his " unregenerate enemy." Nathaniel, (John 1 : 43—49) who was " an Israelite *indeed*," which must of course mean something more than one *rationally*, and " in whom there was no guile," was also an " unconverted enemy" to God, agreeably to this system ; because as he had not yet found the Messiah, he had not believed on him intelligently, which is resquisite in adult christian baptism.

10. Simon Magus (Acts 8: 13) is made by this system a convert, a child of grace, and a truly regenerate follower of Christ. " *Simon himself believed also, and was baptised.*" Nothing more is resquisite, besides this, say Mr. Campbell and his followers, to constitute a person a true child of God. And yet so miserably depraved was he still, that he thought to purchase the power of bestowing the Spirit, with money, (v. 18, 19). And this " true convert" on the principles of Campbellism, is thus appropriately addressed by Peter ; " thy money perish with thee—thy heart is not right in the sight of God ;—I perceive that thou art in the gall of bitterness, and in the bond of iniquity," (v. 20—23). Here is a man then, who, though Campbellism makes him a good disciple of Christ, had yet never understood any more of the principles of true religion, than to suppose that the gift of the Spirit could be purchased with money.

11. Zaccheus (Luke 19: 1—10), at the command of Christ, made haste, " and came down (from the tree) and received him joyfully." The evidences which he gave of being truly converted to God, were so perfectly satisfactory, that the Saviour said " this day is *salvation come to this house.*" Yet, as he was not baptized, he was, agreeably to Campbellism, still " unpardoned, unconverted, unregenerate," etc.

12. The case of Paul, (Acts 9: 1—18, and 22 : 16). As we have already remarked upon this passage, we shall merely refer the reader to it, with the single observation, that this system makes Paul an unconverted man after the Lord had said

of him, "Behold he prayeth." We might refer likewise to the case of the eunuch (Acts 8: 26—39), whom though " he believed with all his heart," Campbellism pronounces an " unconverted, unregenerated, unpardoned" man. It would be trifling with the reader's patience to enlarge upon these cases. We will ask attention, however, to a case or two of another kind.

13. Paul declares in 1 Cor. 1: 14—16, " I thank God that I baptized none of you but Crispus and Gaius ;—I baptized also the household of Stephanus : besides, I know not whether I baptized any other." Most persons, taking these verses in connection with the following one, understand Paul to declare that he never himself baptized more persons than he here speaks of. The Campbellites, for obvious reasons, understand him to refer to the Corinthian church alone. And for the sake of the argument we shall grant the assumption.

That Paul was the founder of the Corinthian church all will admit. See Acts 18: 1—17. After his speech at the Athenian Areopagus, he departed thence and came to Corinth, where he remained *a year and six months*, teaching the word of God ; (see **v. 11**) ; and during this time the church was organized and established. Now Mr. Campbell and his followers declare, that " no one can be either a disciple, or convert,—no one could be either discipled or converted, *until he be immersed*." But Paul, the founder of the Corinthian church, did not baptize more than *six* or *eight* of that church. Therefore, as " no one can be a convert until baptized," Paul did not make more than *six* or *eight* converts, during eighteen months' constant preaching, and teaching the Gospel :—that is, Paul, who was " more abundant in labors than all" the other apostles, succeeded in making six or eight converts to the gospel during one year and a half, of unintermitted labor and exertion. If Campbellism be true, this is the sum total of the results of his labors. If it be admitted that he made more than this number, the admission destroys Campbellism at once ; for he must have made them by some other means than baptizing them, which is the only way, according to this system, in which converts can be made.

14. This passage is also subversive of Campbellism in another way. Nothing is more evident than the fact that Paul ardently desired the salvation of mankind ; and he certainly knew that regeneration was essential to salvation. But, say the Campbellites, " no one can be discipled, converted, regenerated—until immersed." If this be a truth, Paul, of course, knew it and believed

it.　Yet we find him *thanking God* that he did not baptize the Corinthians!　That is, *he thanked God that he did not make them converts!*

But again, *why* did Paul thank God that he baptized none, (save a very few) of the Corinthians?　*Simply because he feared that some persons might say he baptized in his own name.* See ver. 15.　Now if one of the sons of Mr. Campbell, (who, we are informed, has several in the ministry,) were on such grounds, to refuse the administration of baptism to applicants, would his father with his present views, consider the excuse a good one?　Would Mr. Campbell himself cease to baptize for such a reason, entertaining the views he does?　No, never! What then is the inference?　Not that Mr. Campbell is more zealous than was the apostle Paul; but that Paul's views on this subject were the very reverse of Mr. Campbell's.　Had Paul regarded baptism as essential to pardon and regeneration, he would have considered all the reports and accusations of baptizing in his own name, as unworthy of the least regard.　What were such things to him, when brought into competition with the salvation of immortal souls? See 1 Cor. 9: 19—22.

15. We think it needless to trouble the reader with more than the following additional argument.　In 1 Cor. 1: 17, Paul says : "Christ sent me *not to baptize,* but to preach the Gospel."　Could he have hazarded so unaccountable a declaration if he believed that no one could be " either discipled or converted" to Christ, without being baptized?　For if this be true, preaching without baptism could do nothing towards saving the soul.—The very *object* of preaching is nullified, if those who believe it do not receive baptism.　Because just so long as they are unbaptized, they are in the very nature of the case, " unconverted, undiscipled, unpardoned, and unregenerated."　But in Acts 26 : 17, 18, Paul himself says that " Christ sent him to the Gentiles, (Corinthians, as well as others,) *to turn them from darkness to light, and from the power of Satan unto God.*"　In other words, *to accomplish their salvation;* for this is unquestionably the meaning of the passage.　But " *Paul was not sent to baptize :*"—that is, according to Mr. Campbell and his followers, he was not sent to " disciple, or make converts" of the Gentiles ; or to procure their " pardon," or " regeneration ;" but to accomplish their salvation without anything of the kind.　This astounding absurdity is true, or the fundamental principles of Cambellism are false.

I am aware that Mr. Campbell pretends to appeal to the testimony of the primitive fathers of the christian church in support of his views on this subject. He claims " *all* the apostolical fathers, *all* the pupils of the apostles, and *all* the ecclesiastical writers *of note*, of the first four centuries." See *Extra* I. Prop. 11. p. 42. And it might be expected, that, in a professed examination of his system, we should pay *some* attention at least, to this appeal. The expectation is reasonable ; and we proceed to answer it by an authority that we have already found of considerable use in this essay ; and which Mr. Campbell and his followers will respect. We refer to Mr. Campbell himself, and to a work written by him antecedent to the full development of his system. When the Campbellites refute the answer to the above objection, which is obviously deducible from the following extracts, we shall hold ourselves in readiness to meet it upon other grounds. " That the ancients *sometimes* (says Mr. C.) used the word regenerate for baptize, I admit ; *but this was far from being common or general.*" " Many of those fathers of whom you have heard, are produced by the Catholics in proof of the doctrine of purgatory, and as evidences of the antiquity of praying to saints and angels—*they were all full of whimsies.* Irenaeus, Justin, Tertullian, Origen, Jerome, Augustine, held and taught wild and extravagant opinions. Some of them taught auricular confession, and the fundamental dogmas of popery." See Campbell's *Debate with M'Calla*, pp. 365— 368. Of course we need add nothing to so high authority.

§ III. *Unitarianism of the Campbellites.*

I employ the term Unitarian, to include both Arian and Socinian ; and as contradistinguishing both from Trinitarian. When I charge this sect with Unitarianism, I do not mean to be understood that every individual is either an avowed Arian or Socinian ; but that the majority are such. Many of them do not appear to know what the sentiments of their leaders are, on this subject, while others " unhesitatingly avow their conviction that not one single truth or fact as taught by Mr. Campbell can be disproved." See e. g. *Mill. Har.* V. p. 173.

Ever since the commencement of his publishing the *Christian Baptist*, Mr. Campbell has been remarkably reserved in the expression of his views respecting the tri-personality in the Godhead ; the distinct personality and deity of the Spirit ; and the underived and independent existence of Jesus Christ. In several of his public disputations, his opponents endeavored in vain to draw from him an expression of his views on these subjects ; till in his encounter with the Rev. Mr. Jamieson of the Methodist Episcopal Church, at Mount Holly, Kentucky, his resources failed. Mr. Jamieson compelled him to acknowledge that " he did not believe Jesus Christ to be the Supreme God." And the author of this Essay has himself heard the doctrine of the trinity ridiculed in the most indecent manner, in a large assembly, by another leading member of the sect.

The Rev. Dr. Jennings, than whom no one could be better acquainted with the character of this sect, and who accepted a challenge of Mr. Campbell, and met him in debate in Nashville, Tenn., employs the following language : " Among this latter class [the Campbellites], I asserted [during the debate with Mr. Campbell], *and still do assert without fear of contradiction*, are found, not only *avowed* Arians, but most of the infidels and semi-infidels or free-thinkers of our country." *Debate*, p. 81.

They fraternize avowed Arians and Socinians, at the same time that they denounce Trinitarians.

The following are specimens of their denunciations. Mr. Campbell addressing Mr. Waterman (*Mill. Har.* V. 156—8) says : " But you only intend a laugh, in your truly Christian spirit, by way of reprisal for ' unchurching you,' or the imputation of a Babylonish parentage to your fraternity. Of this I frankly acknowledge I am worthy of accusation.——I have manifested an ' unchristian' spirit in thinking that the Protestant sects are the ' impure brood' of the mother of harlots. Well, *whose* brood are they ? Or has the Roman Hierarchy any daughters ? And if she have, where shall we find them ? Among Jews, Turks, Pagans, or Christians ?——The grace of the priesthood, which dwelt in the legs and arms of pope Leo X, dwelt in the archbishops of York and Canterbury, and now dwells in J. A. Waterman, and all the regularly ordained ministers of the Methodist *Episcopal* Church."

On p. 147, he utters the following insane sentiment : " There is much strife and division in the christian world ; this I attribute to false teaching. *Crime and infidelity are on an alarming increase*; THIS I CHARGE ON THE PULPIT." After this remark, and thousands of others on the same subject equally indecent, can any one doubt whether Mr. Campbell is to all intents and purposes an infidel under a christian garb ? Upon this subject,

Paine himself, in the whole compass of his *Age of Reason*, has not ventured to employ language more scurrilous.

Once more : " There is not a limb of the Old Mother, be it found where it may, that will not be thrown into the burning fire," p. 157.   See also p. 186, and Dr. Jennings's *Debate*, p. 81, 84, 85.

With equal politeness the author of the *Mirror*, before quoted (and so greatly lauded by Mr. Campbell), remarks : " Well, then, seeing that the spirit of Romanism and Protestantism are the same under similar circumstances,—that they are both ' the hold of every unclean spirit, and the cage of every unclean and hateful bird,' that ' the kings of the earth have committed whoredom with' both,—that they have both trafficked in slaves and the souls of men ;—seeing these things, I turn from the contemplation of these iniquitous scenes, *with the conviction* that I may as soon look for the religion of the church of Christ among the followers of Confutsee, Zeratusht, Juggernaut, Mohammed, or the worshippers of the great goddess of the Ephesians, as hope to find it in the apostate *Isms* of Rome, Augsburg, or Geneva," p. 9.   In chasteness and elegance this extract rivals the most exquisite flowers of the *Age of Reason*, the *Diegesis* of Taylor, or Voltaire's *Philosophical Dictionary*.

Again, on p. 13 : " In this country, about 200,000, within the last ten years, have responded to the call, ' Come out of her, O my people,' " etc.

I have heard this same writer ridicule, in public assemblies, the distinctive doctrines of Trinitarianism, in such language as the following : " The doctrine of the trinity deluged the streets of Constantinople with blood."   " Doctrines which cause such atrocities and abominations, are abominable to the Son of God, they are the language of Ashdod."

But the Campbellites not only denounce Trinitarians,—they openly fraternize avowed Unitarians.

The Unitarian sect of Christyans is well known in this country, and the reader, if not already acquainted with their sentiments on the subject before us, will have an opportunity to become so presently.   In the *Mill. Har.* Vol. III. No. 3, Mr. Campbell with approbation makes the following extract from one of their papers, edited by *Barton W. Stone*, well known as a strenuous Unitarian.

" We are happy to announce to our brethren, and to the world, the *union of Christians in fact*, in our own country.   A few months ago, the reforming Baptists, (known *invidiously* by the name of *Campbellites*,) and the Christians in Georgetown and the neighborhood, *agreed to meet and worship together. We soon found that we were indeed in the same spirit, and on the same foundation,* the New Testament, and wore the same name, Christian. *We saw no reason why we should not be one family.*"

" *To increase and consolidate this Union,* and to convince all of our sincerity, we, the elders and brethren, have separated two elders, John Smith, and John Rogers. The first, known formerly by the name of Reformer [Campbellite], the latter by the name of Christian. *These brethren are to ride together through all the churches, and to be equally supported by the united contributions of the churches of both descriptions.*"

In the same No. of the *Harbinger,* Mr. Campbell expresses his gratification at the receipt of this intelligence. He says: " From numerous letters received from Kentucky, we are pleased to learn that BRETHREN Smith, Stone and Rogers, and others —now go for the Apostolic Institutions."

The Christyans and Campbellites are here declared by both parties to stand upon the same foundation, and to be one people. Ministers are sent out by the societies conjointly, to visit the churches in common, and to preach to them ; to be supported by contributions from each. And this was of course to promulgate the *same doctrines.*

Now as Mr. Campbell and his immediate followers have been so very reserved in communicating their views of those doctrines which are regarded by evangelical Christians as fundamental; and as the Christyans have been more communicative on the subject, it will, of course, not be wronging the Campbellites (as they are "one family"), to take for granted that, to ascertain the sentiments of one sect, will be to ascertain the sentiments of both.

I have before me a number of the standard authors of this last named sect. To quote from all would swell these remarks to an unreasonable length. We will, therefore, confine our quotations principally to one. *Kinkade's Bible Doctrine,* is a text-book of the Christyans. That it may be evident that I do them no injustice by this assertion, I will establish its correctness.

1. Kinkade's *Bible Doctrine* is sold by the ministers of this sect to their people, as containing the views which they entertain of the religion of Christ. Wherever I have travelled

amongst them, I have found this to be the fact.   The same fact has been likewise repeatedly stated in their periodicals.   Among others I instance the "Gospel Luminary" of New York.

2. Mr. William Lane, one of the most popular preachers of this sect, declared during his debate with Mr. M'Calla, that it contained the views of the society to which he belonged ; and *that it contained his views*.

3. In the summer of 1831, I wrote to Mr. Frederick Plummer of Philadelphia, a very popular preacher of this society, requesting him to furnish me with a book, or books, containing a full and accurate expression of the peculiar and distinctive views of the society to which he belonged.   He sent me Kinkade's *Bible Doctrine*, together with a few tracts, one of which he himself had written.

This book, therefore, manifestly contains an acknowledged and approved expression of the views of this society.   Let us then see what views they really entertain respecting some of the fundamental doctrines of Christianity.

I. *The Trinity.*   "The arguments that are advanced at the present day against the Trinity will appear to future generations as the arguments of the prophets against the heathen gods do to us now ; that is, efforts to disprove self-evident falsehoods." "It will appear strange to future generations that professors of religion in the nineteenth century should need long arguments to convince them that three distinct persons are not one being," p. 48.   "Trinitarianism runs me into a dilemma between tritheism and Atheism," p. 40.

II. *The plenary Deity of Christ.*   On p. 41 are the following horrible expressions.   "If Christ is the self-existent God, and at the same time the son of the same God, then he must be the son of himself.   If he is the self-existent God, and if that very self-existent God is the father of our Lord Jesus Christ, then he must be the father of himself.   And if he is the father of that being whose son he is, then he must be his own grandfather."

Again : "The testimony which affirms that the individual person of Jesus Christ, is the uncreated, infinite, independent God ; and at the same time a created, finite, dependent man, only proves itself unworthy of belief," p. 72.   On p. 75 he thus ridicules this sacred subject : "If Christ had been equal with God, in the fullest sense of the word, he would not have denied it ; because it is not likely that the Supreme Being would deny his own power and dignity for fear the Jews would throw stones at him." Will the reader believe it, when I solemnly assure him that the foregoing is far—very far from being the most revolting of his language in relation to this subject? Yet persons who advocate such sentiments, Mr. Campbell denominates " *brethren,*" and extends to them the right hand of fellowship; while with the same breath he denounces all evangelical denominations.

III. *The Holy Spirit.* The following is the caption of Chap. I. Part III. of Kinkade's book: " To prove that the Holy Spirit is not a distinct person from God." On p. 71, he says : " God's Spirit bears the same relation to God, that the spirit of man does to man." " There is not one example in the Scriptures, of prayer, praise, or thanks being offered up to the Holy Spirit ; therefore those that worship it, as a distinct person from the Father, do it without any Scripture authority," p. 186.

IV. *The person of God.* The object of " brethren" of Mr. Campbell, in advancing the following sentiments, is evidently to explode the doctrine of the Trinity. After Socinus, Kinkade says: " Many have thought, and more have believed that his [God's] person fills all immensity.—In my view this very much resembles the doctrine of the ancient heathen, who held that matter is self-existent and that God is the soul of matter." " If this doctrine be true, God must be the origin and container of all the evil in the universe. Hell and the devil, all natural corruption, and moral turpitude, must be incorporated in his person," p. 156. " If his essence fills all immensity, he cannot be an active Being, because there would be no room for him to act in, etc. He cannot even turn round, etc. He cannot have the power of locomotion," etc. p. 157. " It is only from the Bible that we learn the existence of God, and that book ascribes to him nearly all the members of the human body, and represents him to be in the shape of a man.—Ears, hands, and eyes, are parts of an intelligent ruler, and if God has none of these he cannot hear, handle, or see us," etc. p. 160. Mr. Lane, in his debate with Mr. M'Calla, declared expressly, that he adopted these views of the person of God ; and he attempted to support them by reasoning.

V. No doctrine of the Gospel is more precious to the sincere Christian than that " Jesus bore our sins in his own body on the tree." But how do these " brethren" of the Campbellites treat this delightful and soul cheering truth ?   Let us hear.   " Many professors of religion say that Christ bore the wrath of God that was due to sinners, fulfilled the law of God and suffered its penalty in their stead, and so reconciled him to mankind.   But this doctrine is not in the Bible.   There is no text in that book which says, *he made satisfaction to justice for sinners,* or *that he bore the wrath of God that was due to sinners ;* or, *that he fulfilled the law, or suffered its penalty instead of sinners,"* p. 191.   " You see it is impossible that Christ could have suffered the penalty of the law instead of sinners," p. 198.   " There is not one text in the Bible that says Christ fulfilled the law *for us,"* p. 202.   And in attempting to prove that mankind should not ask blessings and mercies for Christ's sake, he says :   " There is no account in the Scripture of any of the prophets or apostles asking any blessings for Christ's sake," p. 217.   On p. 214, he advances the position that man obtains *" salvation by innocence and good works."*   A thousand such extracts might be made from the writings of this sect, but the above will suffice. See also *Clough's Discourses,* passim.

I am aware that Mr. Campbell and his followers will attempt to repel the charge of Unitarianism by producing passages from their writings in which Christ is spoken of as divine, as God, etc.   They equivocate exceedingly on these words.   But evidence derived from such general statements proves nothing ; for the most avowed Unitarians do not hesitate to speak of Christ in precisely the same manner.   Take the following instances.   Thompson, in his *Gospel History,* p. 14, says : " John used the word *God,* when characteristic of the Logos in a subordinate and relative sense."   Dobson, in his *Thoughts on Faith,* p. 70 (though an avowed Unitarian), thus speaks : " All the Gods are commanded to worship him, to whom the title God belongs in a degree immeasurably higher than any or all of them."   But not to multiply instances, we shall conclude with Kinkade ; the author of *Bible Doctrine.*   Though he denies so expressly the doctrine of the Trinity, the personality of the Spirit, the self-existence and atonement of Christ, and the immensity of God, yet hear him : " God is the highest title given to Christ in the Scriptures," p. 99, and 101 also.   On p. 116, he says : Acts 20: 28 only proves that Christ is called God, and that the church belongs to him, *neither of which is denied by any christian preacher."*   Again : *" I conscientiously call him my Lord and my God, and yet I firmly believe that*

he is a created being," p. 118.   " As I have already proved
that the title *God* is frequently given to creatures, it is evident
that he could be *the mighty God,* and yet a subordinate being,
p. 119.   " It is very possible for him to be equal with God in
some things, and at the same time inferior to him in some other
things," p. 107.

These passages may serve to put the unwary on their guard,
and prevent their being entrapped by the equivocal phraseology
of a disguised Unitarian.   We have collected a long catalogue
of positive and direct proofs of the Unitarianism of the Campbellites, but as our Essay has already exceeded its prescribed
limits, and as we must devote a few pages to a review of their
translation of the New Testament, we omit them.

§ IV. *The translation of the New Testament adopted by the
                    Campbellites.*

It was not without reason that our great English moralist
observed : " I do not know any crime so great, that a man could
contrive to commit, as poisoning the sources of eternal truth."*
It is a crime, the extent of whose turpitude, can only be imagined, amid the realities of eternity ; and no instrument, employed by Satan for the destruction of souls, is so ruinous in
its effects.

Ten years ago Mr. Alexander Campbell issued a version of
the New Testament with the following imposing title : " *The
Sacred writings of the apostles and evangelists of Jesus
Christ, commonly styled the New Testament ; translated from
the original Greek, by George Campbell, James Macknight,
and Philip Doddridge, Doctors of the church of Scotland.*"
It has passed through several editions since that time.   The
one referred to in the following review, is " *stereotyped from the
third Edition revised.   Bethany, Brooke Co. Va.   Printed
and published by A. Campbell. 1833.*" Copy right secured.

We shall not attempt to influence the minds of our readers
by declaring the sentiments which this production has led us to
entertain of the character of its author ; but shall merely give a
brief statement of facts in relation to it, that every one who feels
an interest in the subject may judge for himself.

It was not until Mr. Campbell had published several large

* See Boswell's History of Johnson's Tour to the Hebrides, p. 70.

editions of this book that he would consent to correct the false statement in its title page, declaring Dr. Doddridge to be a member of the church of Scotland. That this fact had an important bearing both upon the matter of the translation, and the success of his undertaking, will appear, when it is remembered that after Mr. Campbell had proclaimed Dr. Doddridge to be a *Presbyterian*, he cites him as an important and weighty authority (and one, of course, whose candor had got the better of his presbyterian principles,) to sustain the rendering which his book gives of ἐκκλησία, viz. *congregation*, instead of that given in the common translation. And will the reader credit what is a sober fact ; that Mr. Campbell, even *after* he declares in the book itself, that he had " learned that Dr. Doddridge was not a Presbyterian but a Congregationalist," should issue the book with the same title ? In what estimation can the christian public hold a man, who will, for the sake of promoting the sale of a book, be guilty of such dissimulation ? The effects of it are still felt. I will specify but a single instance. Very lately, in our own immediate vicinity, a clergyman wishing to establish a position which is denied by Presbyterians, appealed to this book of Mr. Campbell's, and gave the authority of " three doctors of the church of Scotland," in favor of it, which was of course, regarded by many as conclusive.* But we shall proceed to examine the work itself.

In order to give a fair and impartial view of the matter, it will be proper first to present the author's own opinion of the book. The following passage is from his *Preface*. " If the mere publication of a version of the inspired writings requires, as we believe it does, the publisher to have no sectarian object in view, we are happy in being able to appeal to our whole course of public addresses, and to all that we have written on religious subjects, to show that we have no such object in view."

The reader has been informed by the title of this book, that Mr. Campbell pledges his veracity and honesty, that it was " translated from the original Greek, by Drs. Campbell, Macknight, and Doddridge." Let him now compare this with the following, from p. 396, of the second edition. " We give no Baptist authorities.—But we rest *the whole authority of this translation on the criticisms of Romanists, Episcopalians, and*

* In a later edition, but not until Mr. Campbell had realized the profits of a very large sale of his book, he has corrected the title page in respect to this point.

Presbyterians;" and he will surely wonder what concern "Romanists and Episcopalians" have in a "translation" made, agreeably to Mr. Campbell's often repeated assertion, by two Presbyterians and a Congregationalist. But hear him again. On p. 448, he says: "From a great many sources and from religious teachers of different denominations, inquiries, suggestions, and criticisms have been received, all directly, or indirectly bearing upon the improvement of the new version. From these, and from our own diligent comparison and examination of all the documents furnished, and within our reach, we have been induced to modernize the style of this version very considerably; *Yet still retaining its original title page!* The reader shall have some specimens of this "modernizing" presently. The single fact is this; *the Version is Mr. Campbell's alone,* (as will fully appear,) and the dishonest artifice of ascribing it to Campbell, Macknight and Doddridge, a crime in no way differing from actual forgery, was resorted to for the purpose of speculating upon the credulity of the public. Hear him again in self-commendation.

"Taking every thing into view, we have no hesitation in saying, that, in the present improved state of the English language, the ideas communicated by the Apostles and Evangelists of Jesus Christ, are *incomparably* better expressed in this, *than in any volume ever presented in our mother tongue.*"

"The whole scope, design, and drift of our labors is to see Christians intelligent, united and happy." "We would only say, that the edification and comfort of a Christian may be greatly promoted by a minute examination of this version, and a diligent comparison of it with the common one." But enough.

As our examination must seriously affect the moral character of this gentleman, we invite attention to another point before we take up the subject directly. It is, that whatever errors, falsehoods, etc., are found in the book, they cannot be attributed to inadvertency, as the following brief extracts will show. In his Prospectus, after saying that he would translate such words as the three Doctors had adopted, he remarks: "But in doing this, *we shall not depart in any instance* from the meaning which they have declared those words to convey." And afterwards, referring to this promise, in his controversy with a "*Friend of Truth,*" he ventures thus to remark: "Now it can be proven in any court of law or equity where the English language is spoken, that *I have not in one instance* departed from this promise." If the reader can compare these solemn asseverations with the passages above quoted and not be shocked by the insincerity which they exhibit, he has more charity than I can pretend to possess. Yet this is scarcely the beginning of what we find to disapprove in regard to this translation.

The following are additional professions of Mr. Campbell in regard to the faithfulness of his labors. " It may so happen that, now and then, once or twice in a hundred years, *an individual* or two may arise, whose literary acquirements, whose genius, independence of mind, honesty, and candor, may fit them to be faithful and competent translators." *See Preface*, p. 8. Now as Mr. Campbell is the translator of this book, and as, on his own showing, these must be the qualifications of translators, he must of course possess them all, and cannot plead exemption from censure as to the merits of his performance, on the score of ignorance.

The reader will bear in mind while he reads the following, that the preface still claims the three doctors as authors of the translation. We quote from the stereotype edition. "The present edition—shows that in the judgment of some at least, the *style* of the whole volume, even of the historical books, was susceptible of some improvement."—"Macknight presented more work for the pen of a reviser than Campbell; and Doddridge, more than either." *Preface*, p. 70.

After professions like the following, what should we not be led to look for on the score of correctness ? " Few readers," says he, " can appreciate the labor and care necessary to the perfecting of an impression of the New Testament.—Aware of all the difficulties in our way, and most solicitous to have the stereotype pocket edition [the one from which we now quote, and to which we shall confine our attention through the remainder of this investigation] of this work as perfect, in its typography, as any in existence, we have been at the labor and expense of preparing two editions at one and the same time ; so that any errata discovered after the sheets of the third edition were worked off, might be corrected in the standing form of the pocket edition. Few, very few errors have been discovered in the third edition ; these are corrected in its errata ; and, of course, do not appear in this." " The sheets of the third edition, after having been repeatedly read by myself and others, were submitted to the examination of Thomas Campbell, sen., and of Francis W. Emmons.—Their classical and biblical attainments have been of much service to us, and to the public, in the completion of this work," pp. 74, 75.

Once more : " This edition being the ultimatum of our critical labors, in comparing, reviewing, and reconsidering our own disquisitions, as well as those of many others, living and dead ; after a full review of the third edition, or Family Testament, while the whole subject was fresh in our recollection, with all the analogies, parallelisms, and peculiarities of the eight authors of the New Testament in full view, exhibits, as we humbly conceive, a correct, and perspicuous translation of the sacred writings of the New Institution, in a style so modernized, and yet so simple, exact, and faithful to the original, as to render it more intelligible than any version in our language." Mr. Campbell is determined not to submit to the inconvenience of waiting, as other authors are compelled to, till the tardy public utter forth their praises of his productions. He has acquired the art of self-praise, and extols himself, and his works still more. He acknowledges obligations to no one in this respect. The following is the conclusion of the paragraph, from which the last quotation is made : " To vindicate and sustain the fidelity of this version to the original now in its most improved form, and its superior accuracy, *we feel ourselves fully competent ;* and therefore do not hesitate in placing it in the stereotype form."

A full year after uttering this language, we find this passage, from under his hand, in the *Millenial Harbinger,* Vol. V. p. 154 : " I am glad to perceive the attention which the New Version is receiving from all denominations ; and if the Lord preserve my life, I hope to be able to defend it *in all capital matters,* against each, and every assault, from any pen or tongue on this continent." And, p. 174 : " Who will undertake to show that the New Version is not to be depended on ?" But we must stop.

We had thought of dwelling upon the translation of particular words, as e. g. ἐκκλησία, which he makes the " three doctors" uniformly render *congregation,* and the word βαπτίζω, which he makes them always render *immerse,* even in passages where *they* are known to regard such renderings absurd, as in 1 Cor. 10: 1. But there are so many things in this translation that require notice, that we are under the necessity of omitting any further remarks on these. For bad as they are, they are nothing in comparison with what is yet to be exhibited.

Incredible as it may appear, Mr. Campbell even while solemnly pronouncing this work to be the translation of Drs. Macknight, Doddridge and Campbell, was mutilating the text, and even leaving out hundreds of passages which they regarded as inspired. The following are a few specimens, in which he has omitted words, phrases, and sometimes whole verses. He omits the following : Matt. 6: 13, " For thine is the kingdom, and the power, and the glory, forever, amen." In 9: 13, he omits the words " to repentance." In 12: 35, the words " of the heart." In 14: 22, " Jesus," and also in v. 25. In 18: 29, " at his feet, and," and in v. 35, " their trespasses." In 20: 6, "idle." 20: 22, "And to be baptized with the baptism that I am baptized with." 26: 9, " ointment." In 27: 35, he omits the following entire passage : " That it might be fulfilled which was spoken by the prophet ; They parted my garments among them, and upon my vesture did they cast lots." In 28: 19, " therefore."

In Mark's Gospel, among other passages he omits the following : 2: 17, " to repentance." 3: 5, " whole as the other." 4: 24, " Unto you that hear, shall more be given." In 6: 11, he leaves out the following : " Verily I say unto you, It shall be more tolerable for Sodom and Gomorrah in the day of judgment, than for that city." 7: 2, " they found fault." In 11: 14, 15, " Jesus" is twice omitted. 12 : 27, " God." 13: 14, " spoken of by Daniel the prophet." 14: 22, " eat."

In Luke's Gospel, the following are omitted : 4: 18, " He hath sent me to heal the broken-hearted." v. 41, " Christ." 9: 56, " For the Son of man is not come to destroy men's lives, but to save." 11: 2, 4, the following words and phrases : " Our —who art in heaven—thy will be done as in heaven so in earth —but deliver us from evil." v. 29, " the prophet." v. 44, " Scribes and Pharisees, hypocrites." 24: 49, " Jerusalem."

In John's Gospel, the following: 1 : 43, " Jesus." 5 : 30, " the Father." 6: 58, " the manna." 8: 20, " Jesus." 8: 59, " going through the midst of them, and so passed by." In Acts 2: 30, he omits, " according to the flesh he would raise up Christ." 8: 37, " And Philip said, If thou believest with all thy heart, thou mayest ; and he answered and said, I believe that Jesus Christ is the Son of God." 10: 6, " He shall tell thee what thou oughtest to do." 10: 21, " which were sent to him from Cornelius." 19 : 10, " Jesus." 23: 9, " Let us not fight against God."

In Romans 1: 16, " of Christ." 11: 6, " But if it be of works, it is no more of grace ; otherwise work is no more work." 13: 9, " Thou shalt not bear false witness." 1 Cor. 6: 20, " and in your spirits which are God's." 7: 39, " by the law." 11: 24, " Take, eat." Galatians 3: 1, " That ye should not obey the truth." Philippians 3: 21, " That it may be fashioned." Colossians 1: 14, " through his blood." 1: 28, " Jesus." 1 Tim. 2: 7, " in Christ." 3 : 3, " not greedy of filthy lucre." 4: 12, " in spirit." Hebrews 10: 9, " O God." 11: 13, " And were persuaded of them." 1 Peter 1: 23, " forever." 1 John 4: 3, " Christ came in the flesh." Rev. 1: 8, " the beginning and the ending." 5: 14, " Him that liveth forever and ever."

In the foregoing omissions, I find that Mr. Campbell has strictly followed in the steps of the Unitarian editors of the *" Improved Version."* He has even been bolder than they ; for in a number of instances, the clauses which they inclosed in brackets, (thereby intimating that there was not sufficient proof of their spuriousness,) he has had the hardihood to *omit altogether.* We cannot trust ourselves to speak the sentiments we entertain of such atrocious treatment of the word of God. No one can be at a loss how to estimate such conduct.

Out of all the foregoing passages, Drs. Campbell, Macknight, and Doddridge have not ommitted a single word or phrase in their version of the New Testament, and yet Mr. Campbell omits them all, *and not less than five or six hundreds of others,* and pledges himself that the version which he offers to the public is made by " Drs. Campbell, Macknight, and Doddridge !"

But this is not the worst of it. He has even left out of *their* version, as he calls it, passages, for the genuineness of which, they strenuously contend. Take a single specimen. In Rev. 1 : 11, (and it will be recollected that Dr. Doddridge was the only one of the three doctors who translated *the Revelation,*) Mr. Campbell omits " I am Alpha and Omega, the first and the last." It is on this clause that Dr. Doddridge has the following note : " I cannot forbear recording it, that *this text has done more than any other in the Bible toward preventing me from giving up to that scheme, which would make our Lord Jesus Christ no more than a deified creature."* Yet does Mr. Campbell make the reader believe that this very text is omitted by Doddridge. The same thing is true in relation to passages contended for by the other translators ; by Macknight, for example, in 1 Cor. 10: 28, etc.

I have myself examined and compared with Griesbach, upwards of three hundred passages from which Mr. Campbell has omitted words, phrases, and texts, nor have I examined by many hundreds, all the passages.   The reader will be satisfied of this when I inform him, that Mr. Campbell in the controversy with a " *Friend of Truth*," was compelled to admit that he has altered the language of Drs. Campbell, Macknight, and Doddridge, in the translation about *three thousand times*.   And the Rev. Mr. Jamieson, before spoken of, states that, upon comparing together the first and second edition of this pretended translation, as far only as Matthew's and Mark's Gospels, he found in this short compass upwards of six hundred alterations in *phraseology*, and *upwards of one hundred in doctrine*.

Now what is the conclusion to which an unsuspecting reader must be led, who confides in the declarations of Mr. Campbell ? One would imagine that no book was ever issued with more scrupulous care bestowed upon it in order to have it correct. And yet I venture to affirm that there has never been a work stereotyped with half the glaring evidences of carelessness, that are to be found in this.   I will specify a few instances.   In his appendix, Mr. Campbell after Griesbach, pronounces the phrase "*And he followeth not with us*" in Mark 9: 38, to be spurious ; and tells us that it is " *rejected* from this improved version ;" and yet by turning to his text we find it still there !   So little has been the care with which he has prepared this work, that he has not even compared his list of " spurious readings" with the text.   He also professes to omit the words " And turning to his disciples he said," from Luke 10: 23, pronouncing them, in like manner, to be spurious ; and telling us in the appendix that he has rejected them from the text : but, upon turning to the text we find them still there !   The word "*you*," in Colos. 1: 10, he after Griesbach pronounces to be *spurious*, and says that he has *rejected* it from his version ; but on turning back, we find it still there !   So shameful has been his negligence while professing to correct the words of eternal life, that he has not only not troubled himself to compare his *spurious readings* with the text itself ; but has made up his appendix by just running over the margin of Greisbach's text and collecting the readings which *he* denominates spurious.   In this way he has pronounced many readings spurious which are still in his text.   He has followed Griesbach so implicitly in this respect, as even to copy his false references ; e. g. in his appendix he tells us, after Griesbach, that the word " Jesus" is left out of John 1: 44, when that word was never in the verse. Thus without even consulting his text he followed Griesbach in numbering his verses. See his Testament on John 9 : 28, also, with appendix. We have not room to specify every instance of this grievous negligence, but the following is too glaring to be passed over. From Phil. 3: 16, he omits the words " Let us walk by the same rule, let us mind the same things ;" and he also declares that he has from the same verse rejected the following clause : " In order that it may ;" when such a clause *was never in the text.* These astounding disclosures, show that, notwithstanding all his professions to the contrary, he has not even been at the pains to give his book even *a cursory perusal,* before issuing it. And remember, reader, we copy all these from the FOURTH EDITION STEREOTYPED ! Such has been the care he has taken, while engaged in expunging from, and adding to, that word which is the savor of life unto life, or of death unto death, to immortal souls ! This is the book of which he says in the preface, " Aware of all the difficulties in our way, and most solicitous to have the stereotype pocket edition of this work as perfect, in its typography, as any in existence, we have been at the labor and expense of preparing two editions at the same time, so that any errata discovered after the sheets of the third edition were worked off, might be corrected in the standing form of the pocket edition," etc. Here, reader, are the naked facts of the case. Such are his professions ; and thus are they proved to lack the slightest shadow of support from the work itself.

As Mr. Campbell professes to rely upon Griesbach as his chief authority for omitting the foregoing words and phrases from his text, (which profession is however most untrue, for he goes further not only than Griesbach, but even than the editors of the Unitarian "*Improved Version*" in rejecting passages ; and he also refuses to admit passages which Griesbach has retained,) it may be desired by some, who have not the means fully to investigate this subject, though most interested in it ; that the christian public should be acquainted with the character of this favorite authority of Mr. Campbell. No one can entertain a higher respect for Griesbach's talents and learning than myself ; yet, notwithstanding a few remarks in his Preface to Vol. II. of his critical edition of the Greek Testament, Unitarians do claim him.

The reader, however, will judge from the following, with what sentiments a serious Christian ought to regard this gentleman's claim to be a follower of Christ. De Wette, a famous professor of neology in the university of Berlin, *maintains that the Pentateuch was composed about the time of the captivity; that the Jewish Ritual was of gradual formation, accessions being made to it by superstition; and that the Book of Chronicles, (which, says he, " Is filled with scraps and inconsistencies,") was foisted into the canon by some of the priesthood who wished to exalt their own order.* His *Beiträge* containing these sentiments, was published a while before the death of Griesbach, and actually came out RECOMMENDED BY HIM. He says, *" If you object to the young literary adventurer* (De Wette) *that he has endeavored to bring Judaism into disrepute, my answer is, that this is no more than Paul himself has labored to do."* This, then, is the man whom Mr. Campbell has professed to follow in his version. Could Paine, or Voltaire, have said more, in so few words, against the Bible?

That he should not be followed implicitly, will appear, if we consider that many of his statements are false; many of his conclusions not supported by their premises. In frequent instances his premises lead to conclusions quite the reverse of his own, while other critics, of as high repute as Griesbach, have published critical editions of the Greek Testament, in which they approximate much nearer the Received Text than he.

1. The celebrated *Nolan,* in his Greek Vulgate, has fully shown that the *criteria* by which Griesbach has made his decisions are fundamentally erroneous.

2. The learned *Wakefield* pronounces Griesbach's testimony respecting a matter of fact, to be " *infamously false."* Griesbach asserted that the reading of Acts 20: 28, in the Ethiopic version was, the " church of *the Lord;*" and it is this to which Wakefield refers. Yet, on the credit of Griesbach, Mr. Campbell (though professing to give the version of Doddridge) reads it in the same manner.

3. Dr. Lawrence, who examined this subject very profoundly, in a tract entitled, " *Remarks on the Systematical Classification of Manuscripts adopted by Griesbach in his edition of the Greek Testament,"* has shown that the general principles of that particular classification employed by Griesbach as the groundwork of all his critical emendations of the *Textus Receptus,* are most incorrect. He illustrates the difference between

---

* See Stuart's Letters to Channing, *sub fine.*

Griesbach's principle of classification, and his own, by an application of both to the disputed text in 1 Tim. 3: 16, *where his own produces a conclusion precisely the reverse of that which had been yielded by Griesbach.* Yet Mr. Campbell without any hesitation omits the word "God" in that passage, on the authority of Griesbach. In the same Essay Dr. Lawrence has likewise shown that Prof. Griesbach's account of facts is frequently *very erroneous.*

4. But Griesbach is far from being the only recent editor of a critical Testament to which the great body of critics attach importance. The celebrated *Matthaei,* styled by Dr. Middleton " *the best Greek scholar that ever edited a Greek Testament,*" published a Critical Testament in twelve volumes, which approaches much nearer the received text than Griesbach, with whom he is at variance. The famous Eichhorn, after giving a high character of this edition of Matthaei, says : " For a long time I have followed *the middle path* between the two parties." The whole system of classifying Mss. which lies at the very foundation of Griesbach's decision, is rejected by Matthaei as entirely worthless. Thus agreeing with Mr. Nolan and Dr. Lawrence.

These animadversions, and numerous others of similar import which might be adduced, show how little reason there is for attributing so much weight to the decisions of Griesbach, as is done by many. If Mr. Campbell's statements respecting his own acquirements in literature, and his qualifications as a translator, are to be relied on, he certainly knew better.

It may be said that many of the passages omitted by Mr. Campbell do not affect the great leading doctrines of Christianity. Be it so; yet the omission of passages which do *not* affect the vitals of Christianity, (when no sufficient reason is offered for their omission,) affords an excuse, and thus prepares the way for leaving out others that do. One of the finest geniuses and most accomplished scholars that America has yet seen, has well observed : " Only unsettle the popular mind as to any one object which it has been accustomed to venerate, and the perversion of it with regard to many others is much facilitated."*

But many of Mr. Campbell's omissions *do* affect the leading doctrines of Christianity. For besides the foregoing long list of passages, he has omitted a great number of others, (not one

---

* Works of Dr. Mason.

of which is omitted by Drs. Campbell, Macknight, and Doddridge,) which go to support the doctrine of the Trinity, the
proper deity of Christ, and the personality and deity of the
Holy Ghost. The following are some of them.

I. *The Trinity.* This doctrine is supported by Colos. 2: 2,
" To the acknowledgement of God, (i. e. the Spirit,) *and* of
the Father, *and* of Christ." Mr. Campbell invalidates this
proof by omitting the words " and of the Father, and of Christ."
He omits also 1 John 5: 7, a passage, of which, with the highest deference to the gentlemen who have abandoned it, I am
bold to say, not only never has been proved spurious, but never
can be, at least on the ground now taken against it. It is granted freely, that in the very few *ancient Greek Mss.* that now
exist, this text has not been found ; and this is granting all that
is demanded, so far as regards the premises. But what then ?
Why—*therefore* the text is spurious ! This conclusion *may* be
legitimate ; but the connection between it and the premises is
not obvious to my mind. In Diocletian's time, how many
thousands of Mss. were sought out and burned ; and in the
great fire at Constantinople alone, A. D. 476, no less than 120,
000 perished in the flames ; and yet from the poor remains that
now exist, this sweeping conclusion must be drawn ! It is unnecessary here to dwell upon the point, but to us the argument
does appear to be utterly irrelevant.

II. *Mr. Campbell omits also the following proofs of the eter-
nal power and Godhead of Christ.*
It is well known that when the New Testament writers apply to Christ, from the Hebrew Scriptures, the name Jehovah,
they always translate it by $K\acute{v}\varrho\iota o\varsigma$, *Lord*, thereby evincing that
Jesus is Jehovah, as in Matt. 3: 3. Proofs of this kind Mr.
Campbell has expunged in abundance : e. g. Mark 9: 24. 2
Cor. 4: 10. 2 Tim. 4: 1. In Matt. 23: 8, in the phrase, "One
is your Master, even Christ," he omits the words " even Christ."
From Phil. 4 : 13, " I can do all things through Christ that
strengtheneth me," he omits " Christ," and has it, " I can do
all things through him who strengthens me." From Colos. 1:
2, he omits the phrase " the Lord Jesus Christ," and thereby
strives to invalidate the evidence that " grace and peace" come
from the Lord Jesus Christ, equally as from God the Father.
In Jude 4, " Denying the only Lord God even our Lord Jesus
Christ." Knowing that the connective $\varkappa\alpha\acute{\iota}$, *and*, must here be
rendered by " even," he omits the word " God" from the text,

and thus renders it : " Denying the only sovereign Lord, even our Lord Jesus Christ."

He leaves out also the word " God" from Acts 20: 28, (*without giving the least notice in his Appendix,*) though Griesbach himself declares that he is not by any means satisfied with fully rejecting it. The passage reads : " Feed the church of God which he hath purchased with his own blood."   From Rev. 1: 11, he omits that whole clause where Christ says of himself: " I am Alpha and Omega, the first and the last."

From 1 Tim. 3: 16, he omits the word " God."   The text reads : " Great is the mystery of godliness, God was manifest in the flesh."   Mr. Campbell makes it read, " who was manifest in the flesh."*   In our common version of the Bible, 1 John 3: 16 is thus rendered : " Hereby perceive we the love of God, because he laid down his life for us."   Mr. Campbell has it " the love of Christ."   The reader can judge for himself of the object of Mr. Campbell in this alteration.

Again, though Mr. Campbell is very willing to follow Griesbach in rejecting proofs of the Deity of Christ ; he has not had the honesty to follow Griesbach where he has inserted new proofs of his Deity.   As, for example, in the following instances : Acts 16 : 7, " They assayed to go into Bithynia, but the *spirit of Jesus* suffered them not."   Eph. 5: 21, " Submitting yourselves one to another, *in the fear of Christ.*"   Colos. 3: 15, " Let the peace of *Christ* rule in *your hearts,*" etc.   These texts being parallel to others in which God is spoken of in precisely the same manner as they speak of Christ, furnish an unanswerable argument in favor of his Deity ; which those Unitarians who follow Griesbach are called upon to meet.   But Mr. Campbell concluded that it was much the easiest way to omit these emendations altogether; though he has followed Griesbach in others, where he thought the Deity of Christ was not so clearly expressed.   As e. g. Rom. 15: 29. 2 Thess. 2: 8, etc.

III. *The Holy Spirit.*   Being sick at heart from witnessing the continued exhibitions of depravity, brought to view by the investigation of this subject, we have omitted many passages which should be dwelt upon in considering the preceding topic ;

---

* I beg leave here tó refer the reader to an admirable article on this passage in *Biblical Repos.* Vol. II. p. 57—80, by Prof. Stuart, of Andover.

and for the same reason, shall give but a few specimens under
the present.   Jude 20, Dr. Doddridge renders, " Praying with
THE Holy Spirit ;" Dr. Macknight, " Praying by THE Holy
Spirit ;" but Mr. Campbell gives the Unitarian rendering,
" Praying by A holy spirit."   And this Mr. Campbell styles,
the translation of Drs. Doddridge, and Macknight !   2 Thes.
2: 13, " Through sanctification of the Spirit ;"   Dr. Doddridge
renders it, " By sanctification of the Spirit ;"   Mr. Campbell,
for obvious reasons, prefers to render it, " Through sanctification
of spirit."   1 Pet. 1: 2, Dr. Doddridge renders, " By sanctification of the Spirit ;" Dr. Macknight, " Through sanctification
of the Spirit ;" but Mr. Campbell has it, " Through a sanctification of the spirit."   Thus does he endeavor to do away with
the personality of the christian Comforter.   Acts 6: 3, " Look
ye out seven men—full of the Holy Ghost and wisdom :"
Mr. Campbell has it, " Full of spirit and wisdom ;" not only
departing from Doddridge's version ; but even going further than
the Unitarian editors of the " Improved Version."   For they
not feeling at liberty to expunge the word " holy," enclosed it
in brackets.   But omitting other instances similar to the above ;
we will name but one more, as a specimen of what Mr. Campbell has done in numerous instances where he feared that it
might appear too glaring to omit the words altogether.   Gal. 4:
6, " The Spirit of his Son :" Drs. Doddridge and Macknight
both give it the same rendering ; and understand the Holy
Spirit to be here referred to.   But Mr. Campbell disposes of the
Holy Spirit, by giving the passage the following expression ;
" The spirit of his Son."   The alteration consists only in the
change of a capital letter for a small one ; but every one knows
that whenever in the New Testament the word *Spirit* is employed to designate the christian Comforter, the first letter is a
capital ; though when used in any other sense it is not so.
    We add but one word in closing this review.   There can be
no doubt that some few errors have crept into the Greek text
of the New Testament.   But then neither Professor Griesbach,
nor any other person, is yet able, from the data which we have,
to point them out with sufficient certainty to justify our rejection
of any portion of Scripture.   And what benefits can possibly
accrue from attempting it ; especially, when it is admitted on all
hands that no doctrine is essentially affected either by the rejection or retaining of all the readings of Mill, Griesbach etc.,
put together.   We object not to the collation and classification

of Mss., but to the dogmatical conclusions attempted to be deduced from such collation. And how absurd is it for those, who maintain that the Greek text is in an unsettled state, to attempt to unsettle popular confidence in the best of all modern translations, by introducing into it the crudities of an unsettled text, at the same time that they admit that all the alterations contended for, do not affect, either pro or con, one solitary article of the christian system.

Conclusion.

In the preceding remarks we have endeavored faithfully to exhibit the system which has been so perseveringly proclaimed as the Gospel of Christ, in several of our Western States and Territories. By keeping its obnoxious features more or less concealed, as occasion required, its advocates have succeeded in distracting and dividing churches, bringing the Gospel into disrepute, and leading a vast number to hope for mercy at the hands of God without experiencing a change of heart. The disastrous consequences that have followed its promulgation, it is impossible even to imagine, much less to estimate, this side the awful tribunal which is forever to determine the destinies of our race. And we cannot conclude this already protracted article, without a short appeal to those who have been led astray from the truth as it is in Jesus, by hearkening to the advocates of this ill digested, and pernicious scheme.

We entreat such persons, not to suffer their minds to be influenced in favor of this system by the consideration that many have embraced it. When the dishonest artifices which are resorted to by these men for making proselytes are taken into consideration; as well as the terms upon which they offer eternal life, to those who are unwilling to embrace the self-denying doctrines of Christ, this fact ought to create no surprise. Moreover, the number of the converts to this system, even allowing it to be as great as its advocates represent, are not to be compared with those who have embraced infidelity. The leading infidels in this country, boast of being supported by 1,000,000 of followers, (a number with which the followers of Mr. Campbell are not to be compared,) and shall we thence conclude that infidelity is truth? Yet it is on this principle, we fear, that many have decided in favor of Campbellism.

But we intreat the followers of this system, calmly to cast

their eyes over the brief sketch of it, comprised in the foregoing pages, and then seriously to ponder the question, whether they are willing to risk the interests of their never-dying souls upon principles so entirely subversive of the word of God? And especially, whether they can safely rely upon the statements of a man who has proved himself capable, not only of selling to the unwary and unsuspecting, a translation of his own manufacture, as the work of three eminent divines, but also of altering and expunging from the word of God itself, contrary to his own most solemn professions? This matter must be decided speedily. Death is at the door, and the soul's eternal interests at stake. We appeal to the conscience of those whom we address, and ask confidently, whether clearer proof can be offered on any subject, than has here been furnished of the radical unsoundness of the entire system of Campbellism? It is proved to be as essential a departure from the religion of Jesus, as Mormonism itself. Our limits forbid our going fully into this part of the subject, or it would be easy to sustain, by innumerable facts, the position that the prevalence of this heresy in any section of the country, is almost invariably followed by the prevalence of infidelity, and a total indifference to all religion. We do not call upon the advocates of these principles, to subscribe to any particular *system* of christian doctrine; but we do entreat them, without any longer tampering with the dreadfully corrupt version of the inspired writings which Mr. Campbell has enticed them to purchase, that they will take the word of God, and examine for themselves the principles which we have here pointed out, and their tendency. Let this be done with fervent prayer, and humble reliance on the Spirit of God, agreeably to his own directions in Proverbs 2: 3—5, and there will be no danger of their continuing in fatal delusion. In matters of this kind, *call no man master*, for to our own Master, even Christ, we must stand or fall.

ARTICLE III.

THE LAW AND THE PROPHETS, FULFILLED IN CHRIST;—AN EXPOSITION OF MATTHEW 5: 17—20.

By Lewis Mayer, D. D. Prof. of Theology in the Theol. Sem. of the German Reformed Church, Mercersburg, Pa.

"Think not that I am come to destroy the law or the prophets : I am not come to destroy, but to fulfil.   For verily I say unto you, Till heaven and earth pass, one jot, or one tittle shall in no wise pass from the law, till all be fulfilled.   Whosoever, therefore, shall break one of these least commandments, and shall teach men so, he shall be called the least in the kingdom of heaven : but whosoever shall do and teach them, the same shall be called great in the kingdom of heaven.   For I say unto you, That except your righteousness shall exceed the righteousness of the Scribes and Pharisees, ye shall in no case enter into the kingdom of heaven."

The terms, "The law and the prophets," or "Moses and the prophets," denote the writings of Moses and the prophets ; as Luke 16: 29, 31, "They have Moses and the prophets ; let them hear them,"—"If they hear not Moses and the prophets, neither will they be persuaded though one rose from the dead." The same terms designate also the religious and moral instructions contained in the writings of Moses and the prophets, and sometimes the moral precepts only.   In Matthew 22: 37—40, Jesus having summed up the practical doctrines of the Old Testament in the two precepts of love toward God and love toward our neighbor, says : "On these two commandments hang all the law and the prophets."   And, in another place, Ch. 7: 12, having laid down as a comprehensive rule of morals, that precept, "Whatsoever ye would that men should do unto you, do ye even the same to them," he remarks : "For this is the law and the prophets."

The passage at the head of this Article seems, at the first view, to be an unqualified declaration of the universal and perpetual obligation of all the commandments contained in the books of Moses and the prophets, even in their minutest parts, and of the incorporation of the whole of Judaism with Christianity.   But this cannot be its meaning.

The apostle Paul taught plainly that the law was abolished

by the christian dispensation. The law was to continue until the seed should come to whom the promise was made.—Before faith came, we were kept under the law, shut up unto the faith which should afterwards be revealed. Wherefore the law was our schoolmaster, to bring us unto Christ.—But after that faith is come, we are no longer under a schoolmaster. Gal. 3: 23—25. Christians are dead unto the law, and as such are freed from it. Rom. 7: 4, 6. Christ has broken down the middle wall of partition between Jews and Gentiles, having abolished in his flesh the cause of the enmity subsisting between them, even the law of commandments consisting in ordinances.—He has blotted out the hand-writing of ordinances that was against us, which was contrary to us, and took it out of the way, nailing it to his cross. Ephes. 2: 14, 15. Col. 2: 14. In accordance with this doctrine Paul zealously resisted the imposition of the law upon the Gentile converts, and exhorted them to stand fast in the liberty with which Christ had made them free. Gal. 5: 1. In consideration of their religious scruples, he permitted the converts from Judaism to continue their observance of the law in the keeping of holidays, abstaining from meats which the law pronounced unclean, or retaining any other parts of its ritual service ; but he pronounced all these things matters of indifference, of no value in themselves, and binding only so far as a weak conscience entertained scruples against the omission of them. Rom. 14: 1—23. 1 Cor. 8: 1—13. At the same time he told the converted Gentiles, " Let no man judge you in meat, or in drink, or in respect of a holy-day, or of the new moon, or of the Sabbath : Which are a shadow of good things to come, but the body is of Christ." Col. 2 : 16, 17. And when the Gentile converts in Galatia had been persuaded by Judaizing teachers to adopt the Mosaic ritual as a necessary means of securing their acceptance with God, he rebuked them sharply, and expressed his condemnation of those who had subverted them in terms of unsparing severity. Gal. 1: 6—9. 3: 1—3. 4: 9—11. 5: 1—12.

It has been asserted that, in this view of the law, Paul differed from Peter and his associates, who were called apostles of the circumcision. I am not aware that any other authority has been alleged for this assertion than the place in Galatians, Ch. 2: 7—14. But that passage certainly affords no just ground for such an opinion. In the part of the same chapter which immediately precedes it, this apostle states that, after he had labored fourteen years in his ministry, he went up to Jerusalem to confer with the apostles who continued there, respecting the doctrine which he had preached. He went up by revelation, and the conference was private, and confined to those who were of reputation, particularly to James, Peter, and John, " lest he should have run in vain, or labored in vain." From this it appears that Paul, who had received his knowledge of the gospel by immediate inspiration, and had never conferred with the other apostles, had by this time begun to entertain a fear that there might be some discrepancy between his teaching and theirs, and was moved by a special revelation to go and confer with the apostles at Jerusalem, in order to put his mind at rest. But in this conference those who seemed to be somewhat, *added nothing to him :* " but on the contrary," says this apostle, " when James, Cephas, and John saw the grace that was given unto me, they gave to me and Barnabas the right hand of fellowship, that we should go unto the heathen, and they unto the circumcision." Paul's difference with Peter was not a difference of doctrine with regard to the Jewish ritual, but a difference of behavior ; and this only in the one instance when certain Jewish Christians, who were zealous for the Mosaic law, had come from Jerusalem to Antioch, where Peter had previously conformed to the practice of the converted Gentiles ; and this difference of behavior Paul represents, not as a fruit of Peter's convictions, but as a consequence of his fears.

That Paul was sustained in his view of the law by the judgment of all the apostles, appears with the fullest evidence from the decision of the council which was held in Jerusalem in relation to this very question. That council was composed of the apostles, with the elders and the brethren of the church in Jerusalem. It was assembled to consider the question which had been raised at Antioch, Whether the converted Gentiles should be required to receive circumcision and to keep the law ? The decision, in which all the apostles concurred, was against the obligation of the law ; and, though it did not satisfy all the zealous Judaizers, and terminate the dispute, it became the law of the church with regard to the admission of converts from the Gentiles, and was observed by all the apostles and their associates. Acts. 15: 1—31. Acts 21: 19—25.

Our Lord himself intimated, on more than one occasion, that the law was soon to be dissolved. He remarked that " the law and the prophets were until John," which seemed, at least, to imply that they then ceased to be what they had been. Luke

16: 16.   He declared that the worship which the law required
to be performed in Jerusalem, should give place to a worship in
the spirit and in truth that would not be confined to any one
place nor to any legal forms. John 4: 22—24.   He predicted
the destruction of the city and the temple in which alone the worship instituted by Moses could be lawfully performed.   Such
declarations were wholly irreconcilable with the idea of the perpetual obligation of the law, and were so understood, at least by
the opposers of the gospel ; for they made them a ground of
prosecutions against Christ, and against his apostles. Acts 6: 11
—14. 21: 27, 28. Mark 14: 57, 58.

It is necessary, therefore, to understand the words of Christ
with some qualification when he says : " Think not that I am
come to destroy the law and the prophets, etc."   To ascertain
his meaning we must distinguish between the form of the law
and its substance.   With respect to the former it is abolished ;
with respect to the latter it is perpetual.

As to its form, the law was adapted to the character and
wants of the people to whom it was given, and of the age in
which they lived.   Its object was to maintain among the descendants of Abraham the knowledge and worship of the one
true God, to preserve them from idolatry, and to prepare them
for the coming of Christ ; and, for this purpose, to keep them
from familiar intercourse with idolaters and the corrupting influence of their example and persuasion.   This was the design of
its priesthood, its tabernacle or temple, its sacrifices, its purifications, its holy-days, its distinction of clean and unclean meats,
and of its entire ritual.   By the operation of this law an Israelite could not eat with an idolater, nor enter his dwelling, without contracting uncleanness which could be removed only by
ablutions, and sacrifices, and the sacred office of the priest.
Familiar intercourse with idolaters was therefore impracticable
when the law was observed ; and this was that wall of partition
between Jews and Gentiles, and the cause of that religious enmity which subsisted between them.

In respect of this form the law was a schoolmaster to bring
the worshippers unto Christ, and was limited to the period which
preceded his coming.   In this respect it was abolished, or rather
superseded, by the new dispensation.   " After that faith is come,
we are no longer under a schoolmaster."—" Christ has broken
down the middle-wall of partition between us, having abolished

in his flesh the enmity, even the law of commandments contained in ordinances."

As to its substance the law of Moses is the law of nature. It contains the eternal and immutable principles of righteousness and goodness, which are of universal and perpetual obligation. It was of the substance of the law that our Lord spoke, when he said : "Thou shalt love the Lord thy God with all thy heart, and with all thy soul, and with all thy mind, and with all thy strength. This is the first and great commandment. The second is like unto it, Thou shalt love thy neighbor as thyself. *On these two commandments hang all the law and the prophets.*" In this respect St. Paul maintained that the law was not weakened by the gospel, but was confirmed by it : " Do we then make void the law through faith ? God forbid : yea, we establish the law." Rom. 3: 31.

Therefore, when Jesus said : " Think not that I am come to destroy the law and the prophets, etc.," he had reference not to the form of the law, but to its substance, to those precepts of virtue and piety which the law contains, and which are in their nature immutable and eternal, and do not depend for their obliging force upon any special legislation or positive commandment. This appears from his subsequent exposition of the law, in which he speaks only of moral precepts, viz. : Thou shalt not kill. Thou shalt not commit adultery. Thou shalt not forswear thyself. Ye have heard that it hath been said to them of old, An eye for an eye, and a tooth for a tooth. Ye have heard that it hath been said to them of old, Thou shalt love thy neighbor and hatet hine enemy.

The prophets were ministers and interpreters of the law. They expounded the law, and showed that the mere ritual service, so far from being the whole of religion, was no religion at all that God would accept, if it was not accompanied with a suitable disposition of mind, and a correct moral deportment. The prophetic testimony to a coming Saviour, which the law contained in obscure types and shadows, was borne by them in fuller and plainer predictions. The prophets are here joined with the law, because their instructions were essentially the same as those of the law, and differed from them only in clearness and fulness. We shall therefore treat the law and the prophets as one subject, and preserve the distinction of form and substance.

With regard to their form, the law and the prophets have

passed away, and have ceased to be what they were. But neither is this passing away a destruction,—it is not a destruction but a change,—and the change is effected, not by violent abrogation, but by fulfilment. The form which God had given to the law and the prophets answered the end which he contemplated; and the end being attained, it terminated there and was lost in it. So far as the Mosaic ritual was typical of a coming salvation, it received its accomplishment in Christ; and so far as the prophets had spoken of a Saviour to come, their predictions were fulfilled in him. The type met its antitype, and the prediction its event. Both now ceased to be what they were before, and their place was occupied by historical facts. With regard, therefore, to the form of the law and the prophets, which has passed away, as well as in respect of their substance, it is true that not a jot nor a tittle has passed from the law until it has been fulfilled.

As to their substance, the doctrine of piety and virtue contained in them, the law and the prophets shall never pass away. Till heaven and earth pass, one jot, or one tittle, shall in no wise pass from the law till all be fulfilled. Heaven and earth were considered the most stable among the works of God, because they remained the same, while all other things were continually undergoing changes, and exhibiting marks of decay. "Till heaven and earth pass"—"Till the heavens be no more"—were forms of expression by which the ancients meant that a thing should never come to pass. So the phrase, "Heaven and earth shall pass away, but such a thing shall not be," conveyed the thought that the one, which yet would never take place, should sooner happen than the other. It is true that Jesus says: "Till all be fulfilled"—ἕως ἂν πάντα γένηται, Till all things come to pass, or are done. But with the duties of morality it is not as with the accomplishment of an end in view, or with the fulfilment of a type or a prophecy, which takes place once for all, and is then done with. The obligations of morality cannot be discharged by a single act, nor by a series of acts. When a moral duty has been performed, we are not done with it; it returns again, and returns perpetually, as often as the same case returns, while we continue to have existence and to possess moral faculties. It could only cease, if God should abrogate it; but before he could do this, he must himself change; and this is impossible. Sooner would the heavens and the earth, even all his works, pass away, than a change take place in him.

Christ, therefore, came not to destroy, dissolve, or abrogate the law and the prophets, but to fulfil : πληροῦν, to make full, to complete, to finish, to perfect, to make effectual,—not to destroy, but to give full effect to them.   This he has done in the following manner.

1. He adopted all the moral precepts of the law and the prophets, and made them the basis of his own instructions. He obeyed them himself, in their minutest points, confirmed them both by his authority and by his example, and caused them to be obeyed by all his disciples.   Never was the law of God honored in our world as Jesus honored it. Never was the intrinsic excellency of its character exhibited, even among the spirits of heaven, as it appeared in him.   The angel obeys, and is without spot or blemish : but the angel obeys in the midst of heavenly bliss, and his obedience still adds to his felicity ; whilst Jesus obeyed in the deepest distress, and every new step in his obedience was another step in pain ; and still he was, like the angel, unspotted and blameless.   As to its intensity, his virtue is without an equal except in the character of God, whose brightest image he is ; all that is great, and all that is lovely, appears in him : yet all this virtue is but the fulfilling of the law, and is therefore only a development of the excellency which is intrinsic in the law itself.   He has thus shewn in his life the dignity and the beauty of the divine law, and has placed it before us in the most favorable light, and the most winning form.

2. He expounded the law, shewing that its precepts apply to the heart, as well as to the outward behavior, and must there regulate the secret thought and the lurking desire, and are there transgressed in secret where no overt act has been committed. The commandment which says, Thou shalt not kill, forbids to be angry without a cause.   The precept which says, Thou shalt not commit adultery, applies to the adultery of the heart, the impure thought that is entertained, the unchaste desire that is cherished, and declares that the crime begins there.   This was a new doctrine at that time, and unlike to that of the Scribes and Pharisees, who made clean the outside of the cup and the platter, but left it within full of extortion and excess. Matt. 23: 25, 26.   But though this doctrine was new, it was that interpretation of the law which alone could make it effectual as a rule of life.   It is vain to attempt the regulation of the outward conduct, if the thoughts and intents of the heart be left at liberty to riot within ; for from the heart are the issues of life ; and as

well may we think to dry up a river by dipping out its waters, while the fountains continue to flow, as to suppress vice by legal enactments that extend only to overt acts, and leave the heart free. Jesus applied the remedy where it was wanted, and laid the axe unto the root of the tree, when he showed where the crime begins, and brought the law to bear upon it in its very inception.

3. He shewed that the essence of the law is love : love to God as the supreme affection, the ruling passion of the soul ; and love toward the neighbor in the same measure in which we love ourselves. Love renders every duty pleasant and easy, and makes the omission of it painful. If there be supreme love to God, it will constrain us to every act of piety and holy reverence ; if we have the same love toward our neighbor which we cherish for ourselves, it will urge us to every act of justice and kindness ; and as the one will effectually restrain us from all irreverence toward the Deity, so the other will prevent us from inflicting injury upon the neighbor. Love is. therefore the fulfilling of the law, and, at the same time, the principle by which the law is made effectual.

4. He furnished new motives to obedience by the clearness and certainty in which he placed the doctrine of a future state of retribution. Jesus Christ has brought life and immortality to light by his gospel. 2 Tim. 1: 10. This important doctrine was but very obscurely intimated in the Old Testament. It constituted no part of the sanctions of the Mosaic law, all of which were only temporal blessings or maledictions. The pious king Hezekiah seems to have known nothing of it, Isaiah 38: 18, 19. Job,* and David, and Solomon spoke very despondingly of the state of the dead. Job 14: 5—12. Ps. 6: 5. 30: 9. 88: 10—12. 115: 17, 18. Eccles. 3: 18—22. 4: 1—3. 9: 2—10. In the time of Christ two parties in the Jewish

---

* The place in Job, ch. 19: 25—27, which is thought to express Job's expectation of a resurrection, has such a meaning only in the translations which have been made since the christian era, and by christian authors, who were acquainted with the doctrine from the New Testament. The Greek version called the Septuagint, which was made by the Jews before the coming of Christ, gives a different meaning to that text. The Hebrew does not easily bear the common translation ; and the meaning which this translation has assigned to it, is moreover at variance with the obvious sense of the passage in ch. 14: 5—12. It is therefore not the true meaning.

church, both in good standing, the Pharisees and the Sadducees, disputed about the doctrine of a hereafter, the former professing to find it in the law and the prophets, and the other denying that it was taught there. It was Jesus that first set this interesting subject in a clear and satisfactory light, and brought it to bear with effect upon the conduct of life. He declared the certainty of another state of being that shall succeed the present one, assured us that it will be a state of rewards and punishments, and that its retributions will be everlasting. He thus connected this world with another, and shewed the relation between them to be as that of a seedtime and a harvest, representing every human act here as a seed which is sown, and which shall spring up and bear its fruit there, whether it be good or evil. A new prospect was thus opened to the mind of man, who was now first enabled to perceive the dignity of his being and the importance of his actions, and a new impulse was given to his moral powers, by the light that was thrown upon his understanding, and the constraining motives that were presented for obedience to the law of God.

5. He imparts ability to the believer to obey the law of God, by the promise of divine assistance in the gracious influences of the Holy Spirit, by the promise of the gratuitous pardon of all his sins, for which the believer himself can make no atonement, and by the prospect which is thus given of the certain and final success of the believer's earnest and faithful exertions to obtain the favor of God and the gift of eternal life. The law could point out his duty, but it could not give him strength to perform it ; it could neither inspire hope, nor kindle love, nor awaken trust in God. But what the law could not do, because it was weakened by the flesh, God has done. He sent his Son in the likeness of the sinful flesh, and as a sacrifice for sin, and condemned sin in his flesh by the awful death which he suffered upon the cross, in order that the righteousness of the law might be fulfilled by us, who are now enabled to walk not after the flesh but after the spirit. Rom. 8: 3, 4. It is the promise of divine assistance in our infirmity, and the assurance of gracious forgiveness under the consciousness of guilt, and the manifestation of the love of God toward us in the death of his Son ; it is this that inspires hope, and love, and confidence in God, and prepares the heart to do his will.

In all these ways has Jesus Christ fulfilled the law ; has made it full, complete, efficient, as a rule of life. For this purpose it was that he came: " He gave himself for us that he might redeem us from all iniquity, and might purify to himself a peculiar people zealous of good works." Titus 2: 14. He came, indeed, to make atonement for us by his death, that we might obtain forgiveness of sins through his blood ; but that atonement itself had for its ulterior object the return of the sinner to God and to his law. " Be ye reconciled to God," was the exhortation which was based upon the fact that God was in Christ reconciling the world to himself, not imputing to them their trespasses. 2 Cor. 5: 18—21. The ultimate design of the coming of Christ was to give full effect to the divine law in us, by removing the obstacles that were in its way, and thereby restoring the harmony that ought to subsist between man and his Creator, and, in restoring it, restoring the fecility to which he was originally appointed.

The design of Christ being thus to fulfil the law in us, he will not permit any one of its precepts to be set aside : " Whosoever, therefore, shall break one of these least commandments, and shall teach men so, he shall be called the least in the kingdom of heaven," etc. *To break* λύειν, *to loosen, to make void ;* the opposite of δέειν, *to bind, to make obligatory ;* as Matt. 16: 19. " Whatsoever thou shalt *bind* on earth, δήσης, shall be *bound* in heaven, δεδεμένον, and whatsoever thou shalt *loose* on earth, λύσης, shall be *loosed* in heaven, λελυμένον. See also ch. 18: 18. John 10: 35.

Jesus has particular reference here to teachers in the church : " Whosoever shall make void one of these least commandments *and shall teach men so*"— " But whosoever *shall do and teach them.*" He evidently alludes to the public teachers of that time, the Scribes and Pharisees, who " sat in Moses' seat." That these did compare the relative importance of the precepts of the law, and distinguish them into greater and lesser, and greatest and least, appears from the question which was put to Jesus by a certain Scribe, saying, " Master, which is the first commandment of all ?" Mark 12: 28. An instance of this distinction is noticed by our Saviour in Matt. 15: 3—6, and Mark 7: 9—12, where he upbraids the Pharisees with making the commandment of God of no effect by their tradition. They appear, from that passage, to have compared the relative value of providing for infirm and necessitous parents, which was a duty included in the fifth commandment, and that of consecrating what the children had to spare, as a gift to the altar, for the benefit of the priesthood, and in obedience to their traditions, to have given the superiority to the latter. The decision was a preposterous one; and there is reason to believe that many others were no better.; but if it had even been just, and the duty of providing for aged and indigent parents were indeed the least of all the duties enjoined by the divine law, still it would be a part of the law which no authority can make void.

Teachers of this description "shall be called the least in the kingdom of heaven." The 'kingdom of heaven' is evidently here the church of Christ on earth; for in the church on earth only, and not in the church in heaven, does the office of teachers subsist. The church is called a kingdom with reference to its constitution, as it has a king and subjects, subordinate officers and a code of laws. It is called the kingdom of heaven, to distinguish it from earthly kingdoms, inasmuch as its origin, its constitution, and its character are from heaven and not of men. Jesus does not mean that these teachers belong to the kingdom of heaven, or that they are recognized as being lawfully in it, when he says: They shall be called the least in the kingdom of heaven; for he presently adds: For I say unto you, that, except your righteousness exceed the righteousness of the Scribes and Pharisees, *ye shall in no case enter into the kingdom of heaven.* The Scribes and Pharisees were guilty of the same sin of making void what they esteemed the least of the commandments of the law; yet they were in high esteem with the people, and the hearers of Christ might suppose that, if they did no worse than the Scribes and Pharisees, they might well be admitted into that kingdom of heaven which Messiah was expected to establish; but Jesus assures them that, if they had not a better righteousness than these had, they should by no means enter into it. The Scribes and Pharisees were not in the kingdom of heaven, but very far from it; and all those who were not better than they, and, consequently, the teachers of whom he speaks, were like them to be exluded. A phrase similar to this one, occurs, 1 Sam. 2: 30, where God says to Samuel, "Them that honor me I will honor; and they that despise me shall be lightly esteemed." In that place, to esteem lightly is related to being despised, just as to honor is related to being honored. To esteem lightly, must therefore mean, To have in no esteem at all; to despise; and the meaning of the phrase is, They that despise me shall be despised, as they that honor me shall be honored. So, in this text, the expression,

They shall be called the least in the kingdom of heaven, can only mean, In the kingdom of heaven they shall be so little esteemed, that they shall not be admitted into it at all.

What our Lord says in this place respecting teachers is true also of private individuals who make void any of the commandments of God. It could not be wrong to teach men so, if it were right that men should live so ; for undoubtedly it is right that men be taught what it is right that they should do in their practice. Whoever, therefore, is not willing to take the whole moral law, expounded as it is by the instructions of Christ, and illustrated by his example, and to make it the rule of his life ; whoever desires to be excused from obeying any one of its precepts, though it should be truly of less importance than others, and even the least of all ; he cannot be recognized by the Saviour as a member of his church. If he be in the church, he is not lawfully in it ; and his connection with it must terminate, when the true disciples of Christ shall be translated into the church in heaven.

"But whosoever shall do and teach them, the same shall be called great in the kingdom of heaven." The teacher of religion must inculcate all the precepts of the divine law ; and what he teaches others, he is expected to practise himself in the conduct of his life. His own example must be a commentary upon his doctrine, from which the hearers may learn the nature and spirit of the duties which he urges upon them ; and the correspondence between his teaching and his practice must convince them of his sincerity, and furnish a proof also that there is a reality in religion, and a power to change the heart for the better. Without such a conformity to the law of God, as we have seen before, he could not be recognized as a member of the kingdom of heaven ; still less could be be preferred in it to the office of teacher ; but if he both obeys all the precepts of the law in his practice, and teaches them to the hearers, he is not only acknowledged as a member of the kingdom, but enjoys also a preeminence among his brethren ; he is great in the kingdom of heaven.

The conclusion to be drawn from the text is, that the moral law, in its whole extent, is obligatory in the church of Christ upon all believers, and forms an essential part of Christianity.

The law is not obligatory as a covenant of works, or a rule of justification before God, but as a rule of life. Justification, that is, the act of God by which the sinner is released from the obligation to suffer the punishment due to his sins, and is reinstated in the favor of God and the hope of eternal life, is entirely gratuitous; it is not of merit but of grace; not by works but by faith in the promise of the gospel : by the works of the law shall no flesh be justified in the sight of God. All that is required here is that the sinner should know himself to be a sinner ; should feel himself to be such ; should so feel himself to be a sinner as to be contrite and broken-hearted ; to feel that his sins are hateful and accursed ; that holiness is lovely and desirable ; and that, despairing of himself, and of every other resource, he should trust in the promise of gratuitous forgiveness which is based upon the death of Christ.

But when the sinner is pardoned, he is at the same time regenerated ; he is made a new creature ; his mind or inner man is freed from the law of sin that is in his members, and is constituted the ruling principle, while his flesh or outer man is subjected, in order that he may thenceforward walk after the spirit and not after the flesh, and that the righteousness of the law may be fulfilled by him. See Rom. vi. vii. and viii.

A rule is necessary to direct the moral action of the regenerated man ; and that rule is the law of God. The necessity of conforming to this law lies in the nature of things. The moral law is the expression of the moral nature of God. To that nature we must be conformed : we must be in harmony with it ; or we must be opposed to it, and at variance with it. To be at peace with God is the source of perpetual felicity. To be at variance with him, is to be at variance with omnipotence, and can eventuate only in our own misery and destruction ; it is to dwell with devouring fire, and with everlasting burnings. If the stubble can contend successfully with the flames, then can we be at variance with the author of our being and yet preserve a happy existence.

Paul says, indeed : "The law is not made for a righteous man, but for the lawless and disobedient, for the ungodly and for sinners, for unholy and for profane, for murderers of fathers and murderers of mothers," etc. 1 Tim. 1: 9, 10. But the apostle does not mean that a righteous man is not obliged to obey the moral law, but that he does not need the law with its sanctions of rewards and punishments to incite him to his duty or to restrain him from vice. He is governed by a higher principle than the hope of reward or the fear of punishment; by the principle of love; that love which is the fulfilling of the law. Rom. 13: 8—10. As a righteous man his life is conformable to the law of God ; for the idea of right or of wrong is only the idea of conformity to the law by which we are bound, or of disconformity to it. The moment a righteous man does wrong, he ceases to be righteous. The moment he is inclined to do wrong, the law takes hold of him and condemns him as a sinner. The moment that his love grows cold and ceases to bear him onward in the path of duty, he needs the law to keep him from unrighteousness, and to convince him of sin.

The same law is given as a rule of conduct to the whole intellectual universe. There can be but one moral law, as there is but one moral nature of God. It is variously modified, as to its form, by the capacity of the intelligent creature ; but its principles are everywhere and always the same. These are contained in the two precepts which our Saviour represents as the sum of the law and the prophets, viz., Thou shalt love the Lord thy God with all thy heart, and with all thy soul, and with all thy mind, and with all thy strength.—Thou shalt love thy neighbor as thyself. No creature can love God more than with all his heart, and soul, and mind, and strength ; and no creature can lawfully love him less. None can love his neighbor more than himself ; but none is permitted to love him less. So the pure spirits of heaven love God. So one angel loves another. This is the cause of the order and the peace of heaven, and the fountain of heaven's bliss.

ARTICLE IV.

BOLDNESS IN THE PREACHER.

By Aaron M. Colton, Theol. Seminary, Andover.

BOLDNESS in the pursuit of *any* object is true philosophy. Consult the page of the historian, the novelist, and the poet. Who have stamped indelibly the impress of their minds on the destiny of nations? Who have wielded most effectively the scourge of war, or swayed over the widest realms the sceptre of empire? Who have been most renowned for hazardous enterprise, in voyage and discovery, in political revolution, in religious reformation? Who—but the Alexanders, the Columbuses, the Hampdens, the Luthers, and the Knoxes? Who—but men bold in the designs they formed, and bold in the execution of their designs? They have all been men linked to their several determinations by an iron band, not to be severed, except by calamity or death. They have all been strangers to fear and timid wariness; undeterred by fatigue, or pleasure, or pain; inaccessible to flattery, or frowns, or ridicule; possessing an instinctive sovereignty of mind, that would assert its way through the world, and, in the face of all obstacles, press its own decisions.

There is *power* in boldness. We bow to a decisive spirit. We do it instinctive homage. The agent may be evil, and then we deplore its mischievous activity. A Caesar's quarrels fill the world with widows and with orphans. We deprecate his doings; but he evinces an energy of mind, from which we cannot withhold our admiration. We are pained that he should have done so much evil. We are tempted to say, it were good for the world had such a man not been born. But the man stands before us, and we look and admire. We begin to philosophize, and are half ashamed of our admiration, and would retire from the sight. But we linger, and turn, and go back to catch one more glance, and our admiration is rife again in spite of our philosophy.

Boldness in a *bad* cause is power; in a *good* cause is *greater* power. Moral goodness has more sublimity than moral evil, and strikes the imagination more strongly. Besides, moral goodness has an attractive grace—a charm of loveliness, which moral evil has not. A *bad* man excites our admiration by evincing lofty resolve. A *good* man reinforces an equal admiration, by enlisting in his favor the best sentiments of the heart. As a sublime moral spectacle, Luther on his way to the Diet of Worms strikes us with greater power than Hannibal scaling the Alps, or Leonidas in the pass of Thermopylæ.

Christianity is unsurpassed as a field for the display of heroic virtue. As an enterprise, never was one so noble in the conception; so arduous in the execution; so momentous in the contemplated results. There is in it a moral grandeur—an intense sublimity, infinitely transcending all the aims of martial heroism.

It is not the recklessness, the impudence, the blunt obstinacy

of the warrior, that is demanded of the Christian ;—but the boldness of firm conviction, full persuasion, conscious honesty of aim,
intense zeal in a good cause—boldness baptized into the christian spirit, and subjected to the christian principle—*christian*
boldness, but *boldness* still, striking, intrepid, effective.

Boldness befits the preacher's office. In determining proprieties of conduct, a distinction is to be made between the *officer* and the *man*. The distinction *is* made, the world over, in
secular affairs. What virtues more noble and useful, can adorn
the *man*, than compassion and forgiveness? But a compassion-
ate and forgiving *judge*, if not a solecism in speech, is an absurdity in morals. The *neighbor*, the *citizen*, may exhibit all the
graces and charities of a kindly nature. His example may be
attractive as "the sweet influences of the Pleiades ;" beautiful as a flower blown in its native bed. But let these very
graces, excellent as they are in their appropriate sphere, be
transferred from the *man* to the *judge*, and the virtue becomes
a vice, and what was beauty, is now a blemish. The sentinel
on duty forsakes his post in the hour of danger. It would, he
says, be arrogance in him to contend against superior skill and
numbers. Is he not a *modest* man ? He is a coward. Modesty
is not to be the crowning excellence of the soldier on the field
of battle. Bravery becomes him there. John Jay, the *citizen*,
is a pattern of all the milder virtues. His is the ornament of a
meek and quiet spirit. But is John Jay, the *ambassador*, characteristically retiring and distrustful of his own opinions ? The
British Cabinet are his superiors in age, experience, wisdom.
Shall he then from modesty submit the Treaty entirely to their
better discretion ? By no means. His *pretensions* to equality
with them, extend not beyond his *office*. In that office he *is*
their equal. His country chose *him*, not *them*, to be its representative. But is he not a man ; and does not modesty become
a frail, erring man ? He is an *ambassador*. He is called to act
as the representative of his country. But is he not fallible ?
His country chose a fallible man, and *knew* they did so. But
might not the choice have fallen on an abler and better man ?
That is his *country's* concern, not *his*. They saw fit to select
him for the trust ; and it becomes him, not in any manner to
apologize for their act, not to impeach, but to vindicate the wisdom of their choice. Apply this distinction to the preacher,
and you sweep away at a breath, every objection to boldness
in his pulpit exhibitions. In all the relations of *private* life, let

him exhibit those graces, which adorn the private life.   In the pulpit, let him be bold.   *God hath seen fit to place him there.* The preacher occupies a place of higher trust, and more momentous responsibility, than any other on earth.   He stands there, not as a mere brother of his congregation, but as the ambassador of Christ.   He is to speak, not his own message, but a message from Christ ; not in his own name, but in the name of Christ.   He is to speak as one having authority.   He speaks in Christ's stead.   Let him speak "boldly as he ought to speak."

Why should not the preacher be bold ?   Shall he be timid through fear of his hearers ?   His call to the ministry, his credentials, his message, are not theirs to give, or take away.   His high aim is not to gratify their tastes, or flatter their vanity, or humor their prejudices ; but to save their souls.   Their opinions are not the rule of his duty, nor their favor the test of his fidelity.   He stands accountable for his stewardship to no human tribunal.   "Who art thou that judgest another man's servant ?   To his own master he standeth or falleth."   "It is a very small thing that I should be judged of you, or of man's judgment ; yea, I judge not mine own self :"—"he that judgeth me is the Lord."   The preacher's crown of life, the prize of his high calling, depends on no human caprice.   It is laid up for him in heaven.

But boldness commends itself to the better judgment of the hearer.   Is the hearer a trifler ?   Timidity will not win him. Boldness may rebuke him.   Is he a man of sense and candor ? Boldness will not offend him.   He will make the distinction between the officer and the brother.   His self-respect, at least, will prompt him to place the preacher upon the basis of his office.   It is assumed, in every step the hearer takes toward the house of God, that the preacher is to address him in the name and by the authority of Christ.   Shall the preacher ascend the pulpit, and there take it upon himself to utter the sentiments of Holy Writ as his own mere *opinions* or *advice ?*   He could not be guilty of greater arrogance.   He could not give his hearers a greater insult.   No !   It is due to *them*, that he demean himself as the servant of Christ ; that he exhibit to them not *advice*, but *authority ;* not *opinions*, but *decisions ;* not the words which man's wisdom teacheth, "but the word of the Lord, which abideth forever."   Boldness in the preacher as the servant of Christ, is modesty in him as a man.

Boldness accords with the character of the christian revelation. Bold, beyond comparison, are the spirit and manner of the Bible—its descriptions of natural objects—its striking delineations of hell, and heaven, and God. Bold are its moral portraitures—its reproofs and rebukes for sin—its denunciations of woe to the guilty—its demands of universal and unconditional repentance—its threatenings, pointing down to the chambers of death—its promises, revealing the gates of life.

The best preachers have been singular for boldness. Such were the Edwardses and the Tennents of our own land. Such were Baxter, and Whitefield, and the Wesleys of Great Britain. Such were Knox, and Luther, and Zuinglius, of an earlier era. Such were " the noble army of martyrs," and " the company of the holy apostles." Such a preacher was Paul. Behold him at Athens. He stands on the summit of Mars Hill. The lofty Acropolis, with its crowning Parthenon, towers behind him. The Ægean, gemmed with green islands, stretches away in the distance before him. The splendid city of Athens, with her temples, and altars, and images, lies at his feet. An immense throng of Athenians have gathered around him. He stands among them, but he stands alone—a barbarian, a *Jew*, a stranger in a city of strangers. He had come from a distant land in fulfilment of a commission from the Saviour of men. He had come to a city, whose laws denounced death to the man who should introduce a foreign deity. He now stands before a most august assembly—a body of men venerable alike for their learning, their experience, and their years ;—before the very tribunal, which had recently condemned the purest and most patriotic of their own philosophers for alleged hostility to their religious rites. He stands to answer for a similar crime. He had preached among them " Jesus and the resurrection "—a doctrine utterly hostile to their civic grandeur, their state policy, their proudest and most cherished superstitions. Will the tribunal, which spared not their own *Socrates*, now spare the *stranger?* The question enters not his mind. He comes forward to this tribunal, not to retract his obnoxious doctrines, but to reassert them ; to bind and rivet them with still greater power upon the judgment and the conscience. He lifts his arm to speak, and it is with the majesty of one on whom rests the Spirit of the living God. He exhibits that last decisive energy of a rational courage, which confides in the Supreme Power—

a courage which makes a man intrepidly dare every thing that can attack him within the whole sphere of mortality—which would make him retain his purpose unshaken, amid the ruins of the world.

ARTICLE V.

THE EFFECTIVE PREACHER—CHARACTERISTICS AND CULTURE.

By Rev. George Shepard, Prof. of Sacred Rhetoric, Theol. Sem. Bangor, Me.

OF Paul and Barnabas it is said, when laboring in Iconium, in a synagogue of the Jews, that they " so spake that a great multitude, both of the Jews and also of the Greeks, believed." They preached effectively. Their style as preachers, as well as their spirit, had much to do with the result. The same remark holds good in respect to all preachers. Much, everywhere, and at all times, depends upon the man, intellectually and prudentially, as well as spiritually. This sentiment is sustained, not only by what we read in the word of God, but also by what we see in his providence,—in his actual withholding or dispensing success. We discover that certain men have been distinguished for success. We are prepared to say, that it was not altogether, because they possessed more piety, or exhibited more truth, than some others, who have been less successful. It was, in part, because they were more skilful in presenting the truth. They drew attention to it ; they produced conviction by it. The Spirit brought many home to God.

Let it here be distinctly and strongly averred, that no fitness or skill in the presentation, will avail to a saving result, unless the Holy Ghost accompanies and gives efficiency to the word. Gabriel may preach, with the eloquence of an angel, through his whole immortality, and without the Spirit, not a conversion would be effected. While we say this, with the utmost strength and sincerity, we repeat the sentiment, that very much depends, in the securing of success, upon the preacher's skill. Indeed, facts on every hand admonish us, to study the art of preaching, with the utmost intentness. Skill, in this work, seems to be almost as important, as if skill were the efficient power.

It is proposed, in this Article, in the first place, to point out some of the characteristics of the truly skilful and effective preacher.

Preparatory to designating some of the prominent elements of the effective preacher, it may be premised, that, by the phrase, is not meant one, who, by mere pleasantness of voice and elegance of style and address, can captivate a luxurious and accomplished auditory ; but one, who can reach and stir the conscience of such an auditory ; who can plant arrows in refined, as well as rustic, hearts ; one, in short, who can convince, agitate, persuade, men in all their states of tenderness and obduracy, roughness and culture.

It is indispensable that the preacher understand, 1. The material he is to work with, namely, truth, in its vast and various relations ; 2. The material he is to work upon, that is, man, in his complex and mysterious attributes.

The effective preacher, then, is a clear and sound theologian. He has a thorough, theoretic knowledge of the whole field of religious doctrine. The properties of the Divine nature, the principles of the Divine administration, the mysterious method of mercy by the cross, the grounds of obligation and duty, lie familiarly in the mind, and are employed as the basis, the fundamental requisite, in all efficient preaching. A minister may, if he chooses, confine himself to the utterance of more prudential considerations,—to the exposition and pressure of the code of a secular morality ; a brief experiment, however, will satisfy him, that his words all go to the winds. He may do more ; he may declaim fervently and move the passions ; he may astonish the people by his soarings upward and outward upon eternity and immensity ; if his sentiments and sentences are the creation of his own fancy, the feelings enkindled by them, and the goodness produced, will pass away like the morning cloud and the early dew. The reason is, he has not used the instrument, which God has put into the hands of his ministers, for the purpose of accomplishing the glorious things, he has ordained. That instrument is truth, the sword which the Spirit employs in all his searching operations. When wielded with sure aim, it will, at first, be painful ; but in the end, it will achieve benignant results. In order to be thus wielded, it must be understood. When rightly understood and appreciated it will be significantly employed. The clear, comprehensive theologian will throw out truth in luminous and heavy masses. His messages will go forth with authority, because they are made up, not of the pretty and sweet things of man's invention ; but of the solid and immense things of God's revealing. He preaches all truth ; even the points the world have called inexplicable, and stumbled against, and quarrelled with. They being in the Bible, he puts them into his sermons ; and though by multitudes they are dreaded, and most hostilely regarded, they sometimes break very hard hearts, and bring down very high looks.

Not only all truth, but truth in its harmony and just proportions, will be presented, when there is this clear view of the whole field ;——not an inordinate prominence and pressing of favorite points ; not a clashing and warring of points ; but every position having its true relative importance, and every single position, coinciding, dwelling in love, with every other position. Nothing can be more fatal to a preacher's influence and success, than through ignorance, or narrow and distorted views of doctrine, to have parts of the same discourse, or different discourses in the same vicinity, standing to each other in a belligerent attitude. One paragraph undoes the impression of another. One sermon nullifies another. The hearer looks on in amazement and confusion, and resolves to put off his reconciliation with God, till the preacher becomes better reconciled with himself.

Again ; In a clear, broad view of truth, its greatness and majesty are seen, and an inspiriting confidence in its efficacy is awakened and sustained. The preacher of this sort, who grasps truth in its amplitude, and sees it in its high authority, has no misgivings from this source, when he stands up in its advocacy ;——no apologies to make in preface of his appeals. He utters his message in freeness and fervor, with the belief that there is an importance, a dignity, a worth attached to it, which the most reckless must respect ; and a power inherent, which the most obdurate must feel. His deep felt confidence in his weapon, his bold relief of doctrine, does often arrest attention, and by the Spirit's aid subdue the heart, when a doubtful and faltering utterance would have been met with the most vacant indifference, if not with positive scorn.

Knowledge is power ; truth is power. The preacher has power, other things being equal, just in proportion to the amount of truth he has compassed and brought under the mastery of his faculties, so that he can use it at pleasure, for conviction, reproof, correction and instruction in righteousness.

Let it here be added, that we speak of truth, not merely as lodged in the head, but lodged and living in the heart. The effective preacher has not simply clear, theoretic knowledge; he has especially a deep, experimental knowledge of the grand system of doctrine. It has all been authenticated in the conflicts and triumphs of his own breast. He speaks what he does know; he testifies what he has seen and felt. He *must* so speak, if he would speak with effect. If he *does* so speak, it will be with effect; even though in other respects, his talents and acquisitions be of a secondary order; for he is prepared to give graphic and vivid pictures, instead of dry, dead abstractions. Indeed, with the scenes of his past history fresh in his mind, he cannot help giving such pictures. Speaking of sin as one who has tasted its bitter fruits and been chained to its detested loathsomeness; of repentance, as one who has bled beneath its anguish, and been blest with its peace; of faith, as one who has been favored with its visions; of love, as one who has kindled and exulted with its flame; of heaven, as one who has foretasted its joys; of hell, as one who has looked into its caverns of wrath and woe, he must speak with an accuracy, a strength, a fulness and descriptiveness of meaning, which gives glowing reality to all he touches, and body and power to all he presents. Such a man does not make a sermon, simply because the hour is coming, when it will be convenient for him to have a sermon; but because his heart is full of something to say; because it is heaving and glowing with indwelling masses of the vivid material. He cannot refrain and be comfortably at rest; for the material accumulates; the mass still enlarges and glows; the fire kindles and burns in his frame; so that he is compelled to pour forth the swelling and struggling contents.

The sermons of the effective preacher are taken especially out of the heart, as all good sermons must be. The effective preacher having a heart of varied and profound experience, every weapon of truth has tried its temper there; and there he goes for his weapons. Truth may be taken from the head, but it must be carried *through the heart*, before it is imbued with the spirit and with power. The preacher who has not felt and lived his materials, but who gleans them from every exterior quarter, and of course takes them on trust, will find them often devoid of interest or efficacy. If he picks up arrows, which others have thrown, they will frequently prove to be blunted arrows. But if he makes his own breast his laboratory, and there casts and shapes, points and burnishes his weapons, he will be far more likely to have those which will do the work intended. Heart answers to heart; heart swallows up the product of heart. It feels what comes from this fountain of feeling. Hence the power of experience; and the necessity, that the preacher who would have power, be a man of experience;—one who has not merely seen the majestic body of truth, but has undergone its transforming spirit. He must unite these two things; theoretic knowledge of the truth, and thorough experience of it. In other words, a clear head, and a warm and active heart. No matter how clear the head, if the heart is only warm; no matter how warm the heart, if the head is only clear.

This leads us to say, that *strong logical acumen*, and *great power of feeling* combined, are requisite, to ensure convincing and effective speaking. These are often found apart, not so often found together. There are many who have one finely developed and vigorous faculty; and if they only had another and contrasted faculty, to be joined, as a true yoke fellow, to the one they have, they would be very strong men. Here is a preacher, who is very warm-hearted. His soul is full of benevolent emotion. But he cannot move five minutes in a consecutive train of thought. There is power; but there is wanting a chain to conduct it from the source to the object. Another is very lucid, very logical; but has no passion, no emotion. He proves his point with sun-light certainty; but the conviction effected is chilly and unproductive. He shows demonstratively, that the sinner should repent; that he has power to comply with the requirement of God. The transgressor is satisfied, that it is so; he sees the truth, bows a full, unhesitating assent, and moves deliberately on to death. Logic alone will make the sinner see that he ought to repent; logic joined with pure and fervid emotion will make him *feel* that he *must* repent. These two together, the reasoning power and the feeling power, will elaborate luminous and burning appeals. You have a preacher who can prove a point and press it,—who can hold up truth convincingly before the mind, or deeply sink it into the hidden recesses of the heart. His passion vivifies his logic; his logic guides and concentrates his passion.

Thus far I have spoken of knowledge doctrinal and experimental,—of the power of reasoning, and the power of feeling, as elements in the truly effective preacher.

In proceeding with our estimate, we may not omit *practical talent.* Perhaps it is better to call it practical *intent,* or the purpose of doing something on the souls of men when we speak, and the skill to do it. It is very important, that there be both the intention and the tact. Indeed, they are indispensable to a truly productive power. There are men, who make admirable sermons; as specimens of reasoning, they are conclusive; in style and structure, they are splendid. On hearing one of these sermons, all admit it was a noble production. But it failed to do the appropriate work of a sermon. It aroused no dormant conscience; it reached and troubled no obdurate heart; because the preacher did not mean to do any such thing. His object was not present, redeeming effect. Such *is* the object of the preacher, whose outline I am trying to give. He is always a man of definite, pointed intention. If he preaches doctrine, it is for its enlightening and sanctifying power, and for the duty which grows out of it. If he preaches duty, it is that he may induce men to do it. His purpose before ignorant men, is to instruct them; before careless men, to awaken them; before skeptical men, to convince them; before the obdurate, to melt them down; in short, to urge if possible, every unsheltered soul to the refuge by God provided. If he has accomplished none of these points, he feels that he has done but little. He cannot be satisfied with the idea, that he is casting seed which will germinate in other centuries. He cannot console himself with the wonders which may spring from his labors, ages after he is dead. His purpose—a purpose his heart has grasped, is, by the grace of God, to accomplish something in the very effort and in every effort.

But the preacher may have an object, and err in the way of reaching it. He may intend to plant the fire of truth in those already inflamed consciences, and yet not know how to do it. The preacher, to be effective, must have the peculiar, and it may be added, rare kind of skill demanded for this thing. He must know the human mind, not merely as learned in books, but as read in the field, the street, the shop, the mart, on the ocean. He must know the common mind, in its variety, its measure of knowledge, its mode of reasoning, its springs of feeling and action; otherwise, he will reason without producing any conviction, and in his most fervid appeals, he will awaken not a particle of emotion. All well enough, it may be, for another order of beings, but not in the least suited to the beings the preacher has before him. The whole elaborate and masterly production goes completely over the heads to be enlightened, and the hearts to be affected. In order to any practical effect on common minds, the preacher must consent to keep down where such minds live and move and have their being. He must consent to think and feel as they do. They are men of this world, on probation for another; and so is he. It is very unfortunate for him to forget that he is a sublunary being, and that he addresses sublunary beings. Some do forget this most egregiously. The moment they begin to move, they rise aloft. They leave the regions of business and real life, and mount up to the domain of balloons; and sometimes we are compelled to infer it is for the same reason,—because they are inflated. When men, living, active, tempted men, are understood and aimed at, the appeal will very likely be a simple, direct, unpretending appeal. The strength will be expended on the object, not wasted in the air. The truths and illustrations employed, will be the very truths and illustrations demanded by the peculiarities of the case. A good aim, the right weapon, an elastic sinew, will ensure an effect. But no matter what the power, or the purpose of the preacher, if he seizes upon an unfitting truth, he will probably accomplish nothing by his effort.

A nice selective talent, then, is of great value to the preacher. Whoever has it, has one of the best elements of power. The kind of preacher we are considering has it. He knows the persons before him; their natures and circumstances; and when thoughts and truths, arguments and appeals, come thronging in his mind, he almost instinctively takes out from the mass, the precise matter which will do the work intended,—the matter which will most surely reach and affect the souls he has to deal with. He is appropriate; every sentence is in its place and worthy of its place. The whole has a meaning for the minds in view. But the preacher, who has not this niceness of discrimination and selection, who puts on his paper or utters from his lips, every thing which comes into his head, loads his discourses with masses of so alien a character, that they cloud its meaning, and cover up its edge. He is clumsy, tedious, oppressive. Whereas if he would only say the things he ought to say, and let the rest alone, he might be attractive, stirring and pungent. "Evil communications corrupt good manners." Bad company is as fatal to the influence of a good idea, as of any thing else. A rich, opportune, robust thought with a dozen abortions cleaving to it, is inevitably impeded in its work.

It cannot move freely and boldly to the commissioned achievement. We say, then, take what is vigorous and fitting, and cast off the rest as an intrusion and embarrassment, incomparably worse than nothing. The right truths, and only these, are wanted.

Power of application is another thing, necessary to make the truly effective preacher. He may be pointed in his intention, select in his matter; but if he is not also actually pointed, urgent, significantly close in his appeal, he will assuredly fail of doing the good he ought to do. Here comes in a certain severity of feeling,—not rudeness, not rash recklessness. He, who is admitted to the most hallowed recesses of the heart, who has to do with its finest and noblest sensibilities, whose hand moves over chords which reach in their vibrations to other worlds and unending ages, should be a man of carefulness and delicacy. In one sense, he should tread lightly, and touch tenderly, where feelings and interests so intimate, sacred, and enduring, are concerned. But if his delicacy is so refined and fastidious, that he shrinks from touching at all; that he forbears to bring the truth in its authority and pungency upon the conscience, he doubtless stands chargeable with a grand deficiency. It is often a morbid delicacy, and he must get rid of it, if he would do his Master's work on the souls of men. He must be willing occasionally to hurt the feelings of people. He must come sharply and roughly across men's hearts, and insert pangs there, which are keen as the probings of the surgeon's knife.

We should all like very well to be excused from this part of our office. But the Lord Jesus will never excuse us. He insists upon having this work done. Until it is done, in some cases, little or nothing is done, in the momentous business of saving souls from death.

We would have go together, this close, searching, truth-applying fidelity, and a wholesome delicacy of feeling. Then, while the preacher delivers his message clearly and strongly; while he goes with it into the heart, and lodges its goading stings in the conscience, he carefully abstains from all wanton and gratuitous severity. While he keeps back nothing either of reproof or alarm, while he uncovers the pit, and gives us visions of its ascending smoke, and audience of its anguished wailings, it is done in the spirit of love; not with a relish, as though he were in his element, when ranging those regions of blackness and terror, and brandishing and hurling the bolts of perdition.   It is done tenderly,—done reluctantly ; but it must be done ; and truth in its most awful, agitating aspect, held up plainly, and urged home faithfully.   It is indispensable to efforts of power and results of redemption.

It has been implied all along, that the effective preacher speaks with a *very considerable plainness.*   It is certain, that if his theology or his rhetoric—his doctrine or his language, have to go through an interpreter, they will get very much diluted on their way to men's hearts.   He should speak not only so that he *may* be understood, but so that he cannot fail to be understood ; indeed, so as to impel his meaning into the minds of his hearers.

It will not answer for him to be always very beautifully and exquisitely finished.   Rounded periods rarely prick.   I speak here of aiming at elegance as an end.   Whoever sits down to make a very beautiful sermon, assuredly will make a useless one.   Occasionally there comes forth such a sermon ; elaborated most deliciously.   Every sentence has a flower ; every line is music ; and every body is charmed.   "He is to them as a very lovely song of one that hath a pleasant voice, and can play well on an instrument ; they hear his words, but they do them not."   This is the character and end of all such preaching, splendid and powerless.

But there is another extreme ; an absolute and arid plainness.   The whole field which the preacher spreads before us, is without bloom, or greenness, or any such thing.   The imagination is exorcised, as if it were an evil spirit, and all its product repudiated, as rank abomination.   Such a man makes a great mistake.   He cannot reach a high point of efficiency.   Certainly, he cannot approach and enter the hearts of men, whilst he refuses to walk in the high way which God has opened to their hearts.   The preacher must *use* the imagination ; he must *address* the imagination.   Men who have swayed and thrilled and melted the popular heart have done so.   Whitefield, Edwards, Payson did so.   There are images which are the best arguments.   There is an elegance, which augments strength ; there is a polish, which touches the temper of the steel.   The sword which hung at Eden's gate had the brightness of fire.   Rhetorically, as well as literally, a blade may be burnished, and still have a terrible keenness of edge.   A discourse may be ornate, and pierce to the dividing asunder of the soul and spirit, the joints and marrow.   The brightness draws the attention; the sharpness cuts the callous heart.

The effective preacher has this chastened elegance,—this polished plainness.   With him ornament is a means used in powerful subservience to the great end of impression.   It is not with labor drawn forth and heaped up; it is rather the spontaneous overflowing of a repressed fountain of beauty within. He writes and speaks as he does, because with the taste and sensibility he has, he could not write or speak differently.   It is not a matter of rule, but of heartfelt, energetic sentiment.   He dares to contravene the written precept, if that contravenes the better law which his own consciousness and good sense have enacted.   He feels that he must move independently, or forfeit the effect which he might otherwise produce.   It is impossible, that he, or any one else, should be a man of power, while he is servilely a follower of other men's rules.   His responsibility to the bar of the rhetorican, should be blotted from mind, by the overpowering conviction of his responsibility to the bar of God. Let him think and write, just as he is compelled to think and write, with an eye on eternal things, with a heart full of truth and love, with inextinguishable purpose, set upon the glory of God, and the redemption of men.   No matter, if thoughts and illustrations break forth, different from any which ever occurred to him before.   No matter, if they occasionally run into forms, different from anything they ever assumed before.   It is all well enough, provided they only lie together, in a vigorous and compact body.   It is better infinitely, than to be forever saying, the same, old, dull things, in the same, old, undeviating way.   Let him yield to the urgencies of the awakened spirit within, when he has such a spirit, and speak freely and boldly, though he speak without a precedent, and it will not be feebly nor in vain. His hearers will not be likely to settle down to their slumbers, while he has them in hand.   They will hardly dare to sleep; for they never will be able to conjecture, what things may be exploded on their organs, before they wake up.

My remarks are not against rules.   Such a course does not become me.   They are only against a servile bondage to other men's rules, or to a particular, arbitrary set of rules.   So used they wither the waking energies of the mind.   They are as chains on the feet, interdicting all strength and freedom of motion.   The preacher cannot manfully do the work of God, with these shackles upon him.   He cannot come up to the expectation of the good on earth, or of the blessed in heaven. He may sit down to write, and if he is thinking about Blair's rules, or any body's else, instead of bringing his mind in arousing contact with the great things of truth and eternity, the product will be something like Blair's sermons, finished, faultless ; but, preached where and how you please, absolutely powerless.

Let me here bring the parts together, that the subject of this discussion may be seen at one view.

The effective preacher is a man of extensive knowledge, not a novice. He has clear and comprehensive views of truth. His mind is filled with its illuminations. He is a man of deep experience ; his heart is pervaded with the spirit and power of truth. He is a man of benevolence ; his soul is filled with intense desires to achieve, by its instrumentality, those grand purposes of love, for which the truth was given. He is a man of logic and of feeling ; he can prove his points and press them. He is a man of simplicity, who aims to be understood ; a man of intention, who means to be felt. He clothes his message in garments of light, imbues it with the energies of emotion, adjusts it to the sensibilities of the heart ; points and pours it into the drowsy chambers of the conscience. He is a man of taste ; he can soar if he pleases ; if he pleases, he can write and speak with a winning beauty and a chastened elegance. He is a man of boldness ; and is not afraid, in distinctness and strength, to utter the whole truth—all doctrine—all duty, whoever may hear, or whoever may forbear. He is a man of independence, his rules are his own, gathered from all proper sources, and incorporated with his habits of thought and feeling. He speaks in his own way, from the impulse of his own spirit and in accordance with his own consciousness and good sense. He speaks not so much for beauty, as for effect. He likes beauty very well, but strength, impression, effect, more. We cannot but approve of his sentiments and course. If he is moving in power, and doing the work of God on the souls of men, we can forgive him, even though in the rush of emotion, he chance to fall upon a figure or a word, at which Quinctilian would frown. If he has strength to lift up and move away mountains of difficulty, and to shiver rocks of obduracy, we will not insist upon his doing the work with absolute smoothness. Let him by all means do the work. The highest exertions of power are sometimes inconsistent with an exact and perfect finish. The sublime and resistless agents of nature are not accustomed to do things very precisely. The lightning does not stop to polish its shafts in its rending, scorching track.

It is not intended by these remarks, to encourage an uncultivated and eccentric power. While we would knock off some encumbering shackles, and concede some liberties to the preacher, in his seasons of excited effort, by all means would we hold him under the dominion of law.

Before closing this Article we subjoin a few remarks upon the cultivation and training of the sort of preacher which has been described. By what process does any one come to be a preacher of his sort?

We say very confidently, that no one becomes a truly effective preacher by accident, or, in these days, by inspiration. He becomes such by diligent labor and prolonged and inflexible intention. It is admitted that some have an original adaptedness to the work, beyond what others have. No one can doubt this who has heard of a Spencer and a Summerfield. But we stoutly deny, that any have become powerful and enduring preachers with no study and no training. Whatever be the gifts, there must be rigid discipline, or there will be ultimate failure. A preacher of sudden and light growth may corruscate and dazzle for a brief season—it is the meteor's brilliancy; it flashes and it is gone.

In all that has been said, it is implied, that the effective preacher, in the best sense, is a solid man;—not a man of sound and show. There are firm and massive materials laid down, deep and strong, at the foundation of his character. It is well, if he has often encountered investigations which have brought into requisition his utmost depth, compass and intensity of thinking. It is to his advantage, if he has grappled with the highest mysteries of mathematics, and threaded the involved mazes of metaphysics; not that he is to demonstrate doctrine by letters and lines; or, in his addresses to men, employ the processes of the schools; but the reach, and vigor, and acuteness he may gain, will impart luminous certainty to his reasonings, and authoritative efficacy to his appeals. We wish it were universally impressed on the mind, that as a preparative to eloquence, in its high and enduring form, there must be a severe and intense intellectual training. Let every young man whose eye is resting on this height of distinction and usefulness, understand, that he will not reach it by the broad, plain, easy road of acquisition, which has been opened in modern times, but by the old fashioned, narrow path, ascending ruggedly, where toil will harden the tendons of the soul, and rocks and roots resist the upward progress. Sinews, which have done such work, when put under the pressure of a fervid spirit, will deal out heavy and effectual blows.

It is hardly necessary to add, after what has been said, that we would insist upon a very thorough and mature preparation for the Theological Seminary. Whoever abbreviates his academical studies, through haste to be in the Seminary and thence into the field, acts very unwisely, and sooner or later will regret what he has done. To come out of the Seminary a finished and strong man, one must enter it with powers and resources sufficient to enable him to avail himself of its advantages. It requires good habits of study previously formed, and the mastery of much language and science, to enable one to encounter successfully the profound and perplexing points of exegesis, and the high mysteries and severe abstractions of theology. The young man who enters with a marked deficiency in this preparatory regimen, will be doomed to go halting through the Seminary, and halting through life. It is not to be expected, that he will go forth into the field a finished and strong man, there to command the respect, and achieve the results of the effective preacher.

Many fail of the desired attainments in their theological course, by their loose and vagrant style of study. They emasculate instead of strengthening their minds. It is indispensable to the right species of improvement and growth in education, that the attention be prominently given to the great subjects of study and investigation which lie in the prescribed course ; the labor, the toil, the intense tasking of the mind should be on these.

The great object of education, theological as well as classical, is discipline ; not first the storing of the mind, but the discipline of it ; not so much the *product* of thinking, as the *power* of thinking. This power can be attained only by close, rigid, continued and connected thinking. Let the mind be held sternly to the subject or pursuit regularly before it. It may come reluctantly ; compel it to come. It may struggle to fly off to more congenial pursuits. Let it be held, during the season of study, to the subject of study, as with " links of iron." One hour thus fixedly employed, is worth more for the great purpose of study, the discipline of the mind, the acquiring of the power of attention, than five hours of loose and intermittent thought.

This fixedness of attention, augmenting the power of attention and of thought, ensures profoundness and accuracy of knowledge. And clearness and accuracy of views are invaluable to the preacher. The attainment of these, should never be lost sight of in his training. A small range of knowledge, where it is thorough, distinct, absolutely and finally mastered, is far better, for all the purposes of knowledge, to the theologian ; than a much wider range, with hesitancy and confusion on every section of his field.

The reading of the theological student and the preacher, we think, should be conducted with special reference to the discipline of the mind and the accuracy of its knowledge. Much progress in these respects may be made by reading, or none at all, according as it is conducted. If it is a restless, unsettled, indiscriminate style of reading, a skimming over of every book, the individual can lay his hand on, it will be but little conducive to those habits which are needed in the work of the ministry. There are those, who, in their course of education are great readers, they read many things, almost everything. The material is laid in, all in a heap ; and it remains without any order or classification. They cloy and oppress their faculties. In the odd but expressive language of Robert Hall, " they pile so many books on their heads, their brains cannot move."

To effect the discipline requisite for the clear and strong preacher, his reading should be limited, select and thorough. It has been well remarked, " that the true student never considers, how *much* he reads, but rather how *little*, and only *what* and *how* he reads." Pliny's advice is to the same effect : " Multum, non multa." A few books of the right sort, are better than more. The great standard works, patiently and firmly put together by the original and massive thinkers of their respective times, authorities and classics in their kind; these are what the student wants, these properly regarded will assuredly *make* him. The right book is the book that will not only feed but stir the mind, the book that will not only convey thought but compel thinking. Such a book is slow reading, if read with any intentness, on account of the thinking it will compel. It is profitable reading, however, for it will make strong by its bracing spirit, rich by its indicated stores, disciplined by its ' iron-linked' logic, excursive by its generous impulses.

From the few good books it is well to select some *one*, the best as near as we can judge, and let that be our ever present and very special friend.   There is an old Latin maxim recovered by the author of the Curiosities of Literature, " Be cautious of the man of one book," for, " whoever has long been intimate with one great author will always be found to be a formidable antagonist."   Demosthenes was a man of one book ; that book was Thucydides, which he read and re-read—copied and recopied, till he obtained a similar closeness and force of thought and diction.   Chatham was a man of one book, and that favorite was the Sermons of Barrow.   A distinguished minister of the American church, who repeatedly read " Edwards on the Will," testifies, " that he is more indebted to that work, than to all other human productions."   The Analogy of Butler, adopted as the favorite, read with numerous and careful repetitions, has been the making of more than one minister.   It is " a work, carefully and closely packed up out of twenty years' hard thinking."   It is absolutely perfect in its kind, resistless in argument, unimprovable in language, altogether unchangeable, indestructible, more solid throughout than the masonry of the pyramids. The reading of such books in the right way, will certainly conduce to very cogent and conclusive thinking and very effective preaching.

In connection with this range and style of reading, there should be the practice of writing, after the same noble and perfected models.   The style and power of writing necessary in the effective preacher can be attained only by the practice of writing ; in every effort raising high the standard and pressing up to the most arduous point of excellence.   Writing as well as reading, especially in the forming period, should be slow, condensed, elaborate.   Some of the first sermons of a young man, may with advantage, receive the thought and labor of weeks, and even of months, instead of days.

There is another practice, which may not be omitted, in the training of the truly able and effective preacher, namely, the practice of extemporaneous speaking.   That the ability to preach without writing in full, is a valuable one in the minister, is generally admitted.   Still we do not believe, that it would, on the whole, be an advantage to have all preaching done without writing.   The most effective orators in the world have been in the habit of writing some portions of their appeals.   It is a fact that many of the most cogent and eloquent discourses, the most intense, pointed, overwhelming paragraphs that have gone forth from human lips, were carefully and fully written.   Demosthenes and Cicero were both very elaborate writers of their spoken matter. The masterly and almost astounding peroration of Brougham's plea in behalf of Queen Caroline, it is said, on the authority of an eloquent English gentleman, was written fifteen several times. It is true, that a sermon, as well as any other sort of address, may be written, and at the same time be warm, simple, direct, attractive and effective to the highest degree. By no means, then, would we have the preacher abandon the pen. If he does so entirely, we do not believe that he can continue to be for a long time, and in the best sense, an effective preacher. But whilst he cultivates the power of writing, he should also cultivate the power of extemporaneous address. Facility and force in this species of address, can be attained only by practice; and the practice should commence early, and be assiduously continued. The mind should be very resolutely made up both to the effort and to the exposure. A little hardihood may be assumed to advantage: "Come what will, I will make the attempt, will persist, will speak and preach extemporaneously. If I fail in some of my efforts, it will not be the worst thing that ever happened." By thus doing the thing resolutely and courageously, the preacher of disciplined powers, will come to utter truth extemporaneously with propriety and effect. He will attain to more influence than he would otherwise have.

The manner also is to be cultivated, the voice, attitude, action, expression. There is great power in these. Whitefield may be adduced as an illustration of the wonderful power of manner. He studied manner till he became a perfect master of it. In most cases, if not all, assiduous cultivation and practice are necessary to secure a significant and forcible manner. Yet most seem to think, that the power of address, if it comes at all, must come without labor—come spontaneously. If God intended that any should be orators, he caused them to be born orators; a perverse and wilful error, persisted in against nearly all the gathered light and remonstrance of past and present examples. All the finished and potent speakers of ancient time became such by an attention to the manner, a toil in practice, which ended only with life; and still we will have it, that we can perform successfully all the high functions of the orator on the most thrilling and momentous themes, with the untutored voice, and the clumsy joints, and the unpractised limbs of nature, corrupted and made worse by that second nature, early habit. It is by this heedless, lazy throwing of this whole great concern, on the drifting tide of chance, that we come so far short in the use of one of the mightiest means of influence and of good of which God has made us capable. It is indispensable that there be in the candidate for the ministry, a zealous study of this thing, an incessant drilling and exposure, if he would arrest attention to, and make effective on the heart, the matter he prepares.

But valuable as these outward accomplishments are, the internal are far more so. Especially must the heart be cultivated ; and let the teacher there be the purifying, enkindling, elevating Spirit of God. Out of a great, warm, illumined heart comes the best eloquence, the most arresting and subduing, the world ever hears.

Prayer, as a means to the attainment in question, should be very prominent. It gives clearness to the understanding and strength and pureness to emotion ; it quickens thought, and vivifies the gathered and otherwise dead material. Sometimes, it lifts the soul to the transfiguring mount, where the enlightened vision reaches to the grand interests and the glorified objects of unseen worlds. Let the preacher be eminently a man of prayer, and grace will be poured into his lips, and he will have the eloquence of the truth and the love and the spirit of God.

ARTICLE VI.

PSYCHO-PHYSIOLOGY, VIEWED IN ITS CONNECTION WITH THE MYSTERIES OF ANIMAL MAGNETISM AND OTHER KINDRED PHENOMENA.

By Samuel Adams, M. D. Prof. of Chemistry, Mineralogy and Geology, Illinois College, Illinois.

THE phenomena of animal magnetism have been regarded with wonder and awe, or with ridicule and disgust, according to the temper of mind, which has been brought to their examination. One has seen in them an important discovery in animal physiology—the dawn of a new science, which challenges the highest admiration of mankind, and whose practical application promises greatly to alleviate, if not entirely to subdue all the diseases incident to humanity. Another has contented himself with classing these phenomena with those of witchcraft and the superstitions of the dark ages, and has regarded them only as fit subjects for satire, and as unworthy a moment's sober investigation. This pretended science has been alternately attacked and defended with uncompromising ridicule and blind enthusiasm. But there is one aspect in which sober philosophy may view the subject without being dazzled with the false splendors, which a bewildered imagination may have thrown around it, and without becoming a mark for the weapons of ridicule and satire.

The sentiment of a Roman poet is applicable to this subject. " Homo sum, et nihil humanum a me alienum puto." The wildest vagaries of the imagination, the most childish follies of ignorance and superstition, are not too trifling to become the subjects of philosophical inquiry. They may not, in our fallen state, be banished from the precincts of sympathizing humanity.

If we cast a backward glance over the history of past ages, we are struck with the frequent appearance of phenomena not very unlike those of animal magnetism,—and which, whether pretended or real, have had an important bearing upon the opinions and practices of mankind. If we explore the murky dens of superstition and trace the path of the whirlwind of fanaticism, we may find a match for each and all of the alleged wonders, which have been brought to light by Mesmer and his numerous disciples.

It is the legitimate office of philosophy to compare these phenomena with each other, to observe their resemblances and differences, to trace them to their true causes, and to inquire how far they may be regarded as springing from a common origin. This we shall attempt, so far as it can be accomplished within the compass of an Article of moderate length.

It requires no very extended comparison of the phenomena in question to enable us to see that they possess much in common. They all exhibit a family resemblance, and lead us to suspect a kindred origin.

In attempting to trace these phenomena to their sources, we are compelled to regard them as originating primarily in the human constitution. The germs of all must have an existence here. Circumstances, it is true, have developed them. But the fact that the weed has from time to time, sprung up and flourished with the wildest luxuriance, demonstrates both the existence of its seeds and the adaptedness of the soil to its production. But when we turn our attention to the human constitution, to discover there the unexplored region, in which it has its growth, the mind involuntarily rests upon the mysterious connection of body and soul—the sympathetic link which unites matter and mind. In other words, psycho-physiology alone can furnish a key to the mysteries of witchcraft, Mesmerism and kindred subjects.

By psycho-physiology we understand that department of the philosophy of the mind, which belongs to the province of physiology, as distinguished from any metaphysical classification or description of the mental powers. Under this head we shall examine briefly the reciprocal relations of the body and the mind. We shall particularly notice the influence of some of the mental states upon the functions of the body ; and shall endeavor to derive from the examination a light, which will enable us to explain the mysteries of animal magnetism and kindred phenomena, which may properly be said to remain, after making the necessary deductions for the deceptions of imposture and the exaggerations of ignorance and credulity.

The execution of our plan will lead us into a brief examination of the physiology of the nervous system. The general truths of this department of science are too well established to require any detailed development in this place. Neither will it be necessary to present the grounds of many of the positions, which we shall assume as already established by the science of physiology. We may take it for granted, that the brain is, *par excellence*, the material instrument of the mind, and that it performs an important office in each of the functions of sensation and voluntary motion.

That our readers may be prepared to appreciate the extensive influence, which the mind exerts over the body, it is proper to state, that the brain, the appropriate organ of the mind, has a direct anatomical and physiological connection with every part of the body. We can hardly bring the point of a needle in contact with any part of the body, without interfering with some nervous twig. This twig, like that of a tree, may be traced to its connection with a larger twig or branch, and this latter to one still larger, and so on till we arrive at the brain. If on the other hand we start at the brain, we may find our way to any part of the body by traversing a cerebral nerve, or the spinal marrow and some one of the spinal nerves.

The office of the nerves is to receive and transmit impressions to and from the brain ; so that an impression made upon the extremity of a nerve may reach the brain, and an impression upon the brain may reach any part of the body through the medium of the nerves.   Here then we are able to discover some of the links of the sympathetic chain, which connects the body and the mind.   An unusual condition of any part of the body, affecting the nerves of that part, propagates a peculiar influence to the brain ;—the state of the brain being thus affected, may modify the operations of the mind.   On the other hand, the acts and emotions of the mind may affect the condition of the brain, and in this way modify the influence, which this organ transmits to the various parts of the body ; thus drawing one or more of these parts into sympathy with the mind.   But this point will be made clearer by a brief examination of sensation and voluntary motion.

In the function of sensation an impression is made upon the extremity of a nerve ; this impression is transmitted along the nerve to the brain, where it is taken cognizance of by the mind. Thus there are three steps in the process of sensation, viz., the change in the extremity of the nerve—the propagation of this effect along the nerve to the brain—the change in the brain, which is appreciated by the mind.   We shall not go into the arguments, which demonstrate the existence of these three steps in sensation.   It is admitted by all physiologists.   We proceed to illustrate this function by one or two examples.

We bring the hand into contact with some body, and we have a sensation corresponding with the tangible properties of the substance touched.   Here an impression is made upon the extremities of the nerves in the ends of the fingers ; this impression passes along the nerves of the hand and arm to the spinal marrow, and thence along the spinal marrow to the brain, where it produces a change which is recognized by the mind.   We direct the eye towards an object ; the light from that object makes an impression upon the retina, which impression passes along the optic nerve to the brain, and thus gives rise to a perception of the object.

Let us next turn our attention to voluntary motion.   Volition as connected with motion is a peculiar act of the mind, which produces an effect upon the nervous system, and through the nervous system upon the muscles ; the muscles contract and produce motion.   This is called voluntary motion.

That part of the function, which belongs to the nervous system is accomplished in three successive steps, which occur in the reverse order of those of sensation. The mind puts forth a volition; this mental act produces an impression upon the brain, which impression is transmitted along the nerves to the muscles, which are thus made to contract, producing motion. Thus we have an impression upon the brain, the transmission of that effect along the nerves and the effect upon the muscles. For example; we will to raise an arm. The volition produces a peculiar change in the state of the brain; this change in the brain propagates an influence along the spinal marrow and nerves to the muscles of the arm, which contract and raise the limb.

This mere glance at the functions of sensation and voluntary motion is sufficient to prepare us to witness without surprise the more unusual phenomena, which result from the union of a spiritual with a corporeal nature. In sensation, an impression is made upon the nervous extremities, and with the swiftness of thought notice of it is carried to the mind through the nerves and brain. In voluntary motion the mind puts forth a volition, and in an instant the mandate is obeyed by muscular contraction. Here, in the first instance, we see a physical effect, at the surface of the body, producing a simultaneous change in the state of the mind; in the second case, an act of the mind produces a physical effect upon the state of the muscles. These phenomena are so common, that they fail to attract our attention and to lead the mind to those trains of reflection, which enable us to reason correctly with regard to the more extraordinary phenomena of our mysterious being. But these simple facts, viewed in the light of sound philosophy, demonstrate the intimate sympathy between the body and the mind. We are prepared to expect, that the varying states of health and disease in the body will give a coloring to all the acts and emotions of the mind—now shedding the radiance of joy and hope on every scene in nature and on every creation of the imagination, and now casting over the present and the future the deep shades of melancholy. When we see a strong mental shock overpowering the physical frame and prostrating the frail body in the dust, we witness but another instance of the effects of that sympathy, which binds together spirit and matter. Who, that has arrived at the meridian of life, has not witnessed, or experienced, the agitation of body, which accompanies that crowd of trembling thoughts and fluttering feelings, that rushes upon the youthful mind, just as the decisive moment is at hand, which must settle the loss or gain of some long-desired object of pursuit ? Who does not know that the powers of the body ebb and flow with the rise and fall of the mental emotions,—as the mind wavers between hope and fear, between the bright anticipations of future good and the gloomy forebodings of evil ? " A merry heart doeth good like medicine ; but a broken spirit drieth the bones."

In the above imperfect view of the physiology of the nervous system, we have spoken of the brain as the instrument of the mind, as a primary organ in the functions of sensations and voluntary motion, in short as the great centre of psycho-physiological sympathy. We are now prepared to enter understandingly upon a more extended discussion of the reciprocal influences of the body and the mind. And in pursuing the subject, we shall endeavor so to arrange and present our conclusions, that they shall be clearly seen to be legitimate deductions from the foregoing propositions.

1. As the brain performs an important office in the functions of sensation and voluntary motion, we should expect, that any change in the state of that organ would be accompanied with a corresponding modification of those functions. Accordingly we observe, that compression of the brain embarrasses or suspends both of these functions. There are other states of the brain which produce exactly the opposite effects. In cerebral inflammation, a feeble light sometimes produces an impression, which is painfully intense, and ordinary sounds are so magnified as to be with difficulty borne. Some diseases of the brain are attended with frantic ravings and exhibitions of almost superhuman muscular strength. A remarkable instance of the effect of cerebral disease in giving increased intensity to the sensations, is recorded by Buffon in his Histoire Naturelle de l' Homme. It was the case of a priest by the name of Blanchet, curé de la Réolle en Guyenne, who passed through a violent fit of insanity, and after his recovery, wrote an account of the feelings which he had experienced. Blanchet thus describes the state of his sensations during the attack. " In this violent malady my senses rose to an excess of delicacy and sensibility, that subjected me alternately to the keenest suffering and the most exquisite pleasure. The light seemed sometimes to dart against my eyes with such splendor and vividness, that l was unable to support its presence. . . . . The sense of hearing also had its accesses and excesses. It was at certain times in such a condition, that the least sound jarred upon the

ear, (l' é branlait)—so delicate and so sensible, that the gentlest undulations of the air became audible sounds. The sound of brass was especially insupportable; the suffering which it caused me was beyond expression. When I heard the ringing of the bell, which was unfortunately too near to me, it seemed to detach itself from the steeple of the church and to rise to the vault of heaven, with which forming one single body and the same instrument, it resounded with a terrific noise, whose shock was so terrible, that I imagined, that all the planets, which are suspended in the immensity of space, were disordered by it, and had fallen upon our earth, making with it one mass of ruins. . . . . The other senses, the taste, the smell, etc., had their vicissitudes of pleasure and pain. I seemed at times to perceive odors and delicious perfumes, whose exquisite savors neither nature nor the art of the chemist could equal. At other times insupportable odors, nauseous and bitter tastes drove me almost to desperation. Even the sense of touch was affected with these extremes of pleasure and pain." There can be no doubt, in this case, that the preternatural state of the senses arose from the same state of the brain, that caused the mental derangement.

We may next notice that class of sensations, which are not preceded or accompanied by any external impression. These are readily accounted for by supposing, that they result from peculiar conditions of the brain. We have seen that a peculiar state of the brain is the last step in the physiology of sensation, and an essential prerequisite to perception. Now if any internal cause should produce the same state of the brain, which results from an external impression, no possible reason can be given why the sensation and perception should not be the same as those resulting from an external impression. Thus an individual would seem to perceive external objects, and he would be unable directly to distinguish these mere states of the brain from those objects.

Dreaming furnishes apt illustrations of this principle. Here the brain passes through the same states, which are produced by converse with the external world, while awake. That dreams often result from the state of the physical system is proved by the fact, that indigestible food, taken late in the evening, frequently causes distressing dreams. Sometimes a narcotic medicine, while it composes to slumber, produces a state of dreamy happiness, with such vivid enjoyment, that the patient on awaking can hardly realize that he has been asleep. In both of these instances the brain is undoubtedly drawn into sympathy with other parts of the body, and thus gives rise to the dreams. In those instances, in which dreams seem to grow out of mental excitement, it is not improbable that the agitation of the mind produces a disturbance of the functions of the brain, and that this disturbed condition of the brain is the proximate cause of the dreaming.

In the delirium of fevers, and often in insanity, the mind mistakes the mere states of the brain for external objects. The case of Nicolai is familiar to most persons of any considerable reading. Esquirol, in the article Démonomanie of the Dictionaire des Sciences Medicales, thus describes the commencement of an attack of insanity. " M————, a woolen spinster, as she was returning from a long walk, became fatigued and lay down upon the ground to rest; in a short time she felt a motion in her head and heard a noise like that of a spinning wheel." In this case the apparent sound of the wheel evidently resulted from the brain's assuming the same state, into which it had before been brought by the real sound. The same author speaks of a young female under his care in the hospital La Salpétrière, who, among other hallucinations, labored under that of the sense of smell. She would frequently request the removal of the cause of some disagreeable odor; at other times she spoke of enjoying the most fragrant perfumes, although in neither case was there any odoriferous body near. It is a circumstance worthy of remark in the account given of this female, that she had lost the sense of smell, so as to be insensible of the presence of natural odors, while the disordered state of her brain was giving her the most vivid perceptions of odors, when none were present to impress the organ of smell. Esquirol also mentions a melancholic patient under his charge, who was subject to a very singular illusion of the sense of hearing. His thoughts were accompanied by their audible expression. A voice seemed to pronounce his thoughts as they flowed along; or as he said " he thought with a loud voice."

In illusions of this kind the sight is the sense, which is most frequently in fault; and its mistakes are sometimes corrected by the more gross and material sense of touch, assisted by the muscular sense, as when an apparent object of sight proves to be an illusion by its want of tangible properties. But when the salutary operations of the will and the judgment become embarrassed by disorders of the brain, when the function of external sensation is suspended, as in sleep, trance, etc., the mind necessarily becomes a prey to the delusion. It receives the mere phantoms of the brain as real existences; it dwells in an ideal world, and sports in the regions of airy nothing, as among the substantial realities of life.

There is one very common instance of an illusion of the sense of touch and of the muscular sense, which we do not recollect to have seen noticed as such by any writer upon the philosophy of the mind. A person on coming to land after a rough sea-voyage frequently continues for some time to feel the motion of the vessel. The earth seems to rock and heave beneath his feet. And here the sight corrects the mistakes of touch and the muscular sense. The illusion would be complete, were not the mistake corrected by the visible presence of surrounding objects. The individual would suppose himself tossed by a raging sea, did not his own eyes convince him of the absence of the vessel, and that he is securely planted upon terra firma. The writer of this article recollects his having been once sea-sick on board a steamboat. In this state of extreme nausea he was exceedingly annoyed by the odor of the oil about the machinery and by the fumes of cigars, which, in his attempts to get a breath of fresh air, he encountered upon the upper deck. After he had left the boat at night and retired to his bed-chamber, he suddenly had a recurrence of the various sensations, which he had experienced while at sea—the motion of the boat, the odor of the oil upon the machinery and of the fumes of tobacco, together with the sea-sickness. Here the sensations were evidently produced by the brain's being made to repeat some of the states, through which it had passed during the day. The same explanation applies to all those cases, in which a person continues to feel the motion of the vessel after landing from a voyage at sea.

Enough has been said upon this point to illustrate the influence, which the states of the brain may have upon the sensations. Disordered muscular contraction in the form of spasms, convulsions, etc., frequently results from disturbed states of the brain. But we need not enlarge on this point.

2. The operations of the mind, depending as they do, upon the instrumentality of the brain, are much affected by the changing states of this organ. We need not adduce any examples to illustrate this position. It is taken for granted in every good treatise on insanity; and upon it is based the whole plan of the medical treatment of that disease.

3. The acts and emotions of the mind may produce an effect upon the condition of the brain ; and as the brain has an extensive sympathy with all parts of the body, the mental state may, through the brain, influence the condition of the external senses and of voluntary motion. We have shown, that the brain may be in such a state, as, not only to influence the sensations, but to give rise to all the phenomena of sensation and perception, without the intervention of any external impression. Now, from what we have said above, it may be inferred, that the mental acts and emotions may produce those states of the brain, from which result the preternatural sensations to which we have alluded.

We shall now proceed to illustrate by a few examples the influence of the mind upon the external sensations. Under this head we may first speak of the voluntary states of the mind, and secondly of those mental states, which are not much under the control of the will. We make this distinction rather as one of convenience, than as possessing much philosophical merit.

Among the voluntary mental states which affect the external senses, we may mention the intense application of the mind to interesting studies. It is a matter of common notoriety, that persons thus engaged in study are unconscious of what takes place around them. They do not hear or feel with the same readiness as when the mind is not intent on any particular subject. We are generally told by metaphysicians that such an individual hears, but from the attention's being directed another way, he forgets having heard. But is not a person's own consciousness the only decisive evidence, which we can have of his hearing or exercising any of the other senses ?——And how can we say that a person hears or feels, when he manifests no sign of it at the time, and has no recollection of it afterwards ? The whole mystery, we apprehend, is explained by supposing that the intense concentration of the mind puts the brain into a state, which renders it unable, for the time, to respond to the external impression, or, which is the same thing, prevents it from acting its part in the physiology of sensation. Some physiologists might explain this fact by saying, that the whole nervous energy is absorbed in the intensity of the mental action, so that there is, for the time being, no power left to carry on the function of sensation ; while some metaphysicians attribute the cause of this phenomenon to the mind, by saying that it has been prevented, by previous engagement, from performing its part in this function. Whether we adopt any one of these hypotheses, or reject them all, the fact that the mental states affect the external senses still remains undisturbed.

In the history of Archimedes we have a remarkable example of the effect of deep study in diminishing or suspending the action of the external senses. We are told, that, being engaged in mathematical investigations, he was entirely unconscious of the noise and tumult attending the capture and sacking of Syracuse, until he was surprised by the armed soldiers breaking into his study ; and perhaps the stroke of the assassin's dagger was the first thing that could break his deep meditation.

It is worthy of remark, that, while these voluntary states of the mind, tend to diminish external sensibility, they are attended with a corresponding increase of mental activity and power. This is remarkably the case with some religious enthusiasts, who, by protracted meditation, become entirely insensible to external impressions, while the creations of the imagination assume all the vividness of real objects ; and the soul seems to expatiate amid the realities of the celestial world.

" The ecclesiastical history of the fourth century," says Montégre, "makes mention of certain monks of Mount Athos, who pretended to have carried meditation and prayer to such a degree of perfection, as to obtain with their bodily eyes a view of God himself, under the appearance of a celestial light. The manner in which they were enabled to arrive at this foretaste of heavenly joys, is thus described. ' Raise thy spirit above the vain things of earth, rest thy beard upon thy breast, turn thine eyes and concentrate the whole power of thought upon the centre of thy belly, and seek within thy body the place of thy heart. At first thou shalt find only thick darkness ; but if thou wilt persevere in this practice night and day, thou shalt find a joy without interruption. When the spirit has found the place of the heart, it then beholds itself robed in light.' "*

Montégre, in the same article, goes on to remark : " In India, where the customs are not subjected to those changes, which among us vary the forms of fashionable folly, there are still found among the fakirs, jouguis and dervishes, with which this beautiful country is infested, a similar species of fanatics, who succeed also in obtaining a sensible communication with the deity by analogous means."

* Dictionaire des Sciences Medicales, Art. Contemplation.

Bernier, a philosophical observer and enlightened physician thus speaks of them. " Among those whom I have just mentioned, there are some who pass for true illuminati and perfect jouguis, or perfectly united to the divinity. They are persons, who have entirely abandoned the world, and who usually retire alone like hermits to very distant groves without ever coming to the towns. If any one carries them food, they receive it, if not it is said that they dispensed with it, and it is believed, that they live upon the favor of God, in perpetual fastings and austerities, and wholly buried in meditation—I say *buried*, because they carry their meditations so far that they pass whole hours in ecstatic raptures, with the function of external sensation entirely suspended, and, (what would be wonderful if it were true,) seeing God himself like a certain white, very vivid and inexplicable light, with a joy and satisfaction not less inexpressible, followed by a contempt for the world and an entire alienation from it. . . . . They prescribe rules for gradually suspending the action of the senses ; they say, for example, that after having fasted for several days upon bread and water, it is necessary at first to stand alone, in a retired place, with the eyes fixed upwards for some time, without the least motion, then to bring them gently down and fix them, both at the same time, upon the end of the nose, and to regard the two sides with equal intensity (a thing sufficiently difficult) and thus retain them bound, as it were, to the end of the nose, until the light appears."*

The life of St. Theresa, written by herself, illustrates the influence of protracted meditation in suspending the powers of the body and quickening those of the mind. " After having discoursed at some length on what she calls the various kinds of orisons and the different degrees, by which man is able to rise in some degree towards the divinity, by the meditations of the mind, or emotions of the heart, she arrives at length to that state, which she designates under the name of *celestial quietude, prayer of union, rapture* and *ecstasy.* ' One experiences,' says she, ' a kind of slumber of the powers of the soul, of the understanding, the memory, and the will, in which, while they are not entirely asleep, they know not the manner in which they operate. The soul experiences a kind of pleasure which re-

---

* Op. cit.

sembles that of a person in the grasp of death, sinking with ecstatic rapture into the bosom of God. The soul knows not what it is doing. . . . . It is in a state of happy *extravagance*, of celestial madness, in which it becomes imbued with true wisdom, and enjoys an inconceivable consolation.' She goes on to speak of the suspension of sight, hearing, touch, voluntary motion, etc. She then remarks: ' As the external powers fail, those of the soul increase in order to enable it to grasp the glories which it enjoys.' She speaks of listening, in this state, to God, to Christ, and the angels, and relates the conversations, which she held with them."*

It is well known to all who are conversant with the history of the human race, that the long continued influence of superstition tends to render prevalent a high degree of nervous excitability. And in the cases to which we have alluded, the constrained attitude of body and mind, the intense effort of the will to prolong that constrained attitude, the high-wrought expectations of celestial glories, which are just ready to burst upon the soul, all tend to bring the nervous system into a state of extreme tension, which could not fail to produce decided modifications of its functions ; and those who are somewhat acquainted with the mysterious nature of these functions, will be prepared to witness the phenomena above described.

Perhaps we may with propriety introduce, under this division of our subject, the case of a certain priest, who, according to the testimony of St. Augustine, was accustomed to suspend at pleasure the action of all the senses, and appeared, like one dead, totally insensible to the tortures which were at those times inflicted upon him. The means, which were used to produce this state in him, were the repetition of cries of grief and distress, and the efforts of his own will. St. Augustine thus speaks of him : "Presbyter fuit quidam, nomine Restitutus in paroecia Calamensis Ecclesiae, qui, quando ei placebat (rogabatur autem ut hoc faceret ab eis qui rem mirabilem coram scire cupiebant) ad imitatas quasi lamentantis cujuslibet hominis voces, ita se auferebat a sensibus, et jacebat simillimus mortuo ; ut non solum vellicantes et pungentes minime sentiret, sed aliquando etiam igne ureretur admoto, sine ullo doloris sensu, nisi postmodum ex vulnere ; non autem obnitendo, sed non sentiendo non movere corpus, eo probabatur, quod tamquam in defuncto nullus invenie-

---

* Dict. des Sci. Med. Art. Extase.

batur anhelitus : hominum tamen voces, si clarius loquerentur, tamquam de longinquo se audire postea referebat.''*

There is another class of mental states which affect the functions of the body, and over which the will has little or no control.   We refer to those powerful emotions of the mind, which spring up spontaneously under the overpowering influence of circumstances.   At one time we see them prostrating all the powers of the body and even producing sudden death, and at another, giving rise to the most alarming convulsive fits.   Again, we see them nerving the frame to achievements of superhuman strength, or rendering it insensible to the most fearful tortures.

All are familiar with the fact, that the sight of blood, or the sudden hearing of painful intelligence, frequently produces syncope or fainting.   The phrase " leaping for joy" is strictly founded in fact, and is expressive of the invigorating and exhilarating influence, which that lively emotion exerts upon the powers of the body.   It is well known, that joy, or any strong mental excitement, will relieve pain.   It may be remarked in reply, that there is no suspension of pain, but merely a diversion of the attention, so that the pain, though it exists, is not perceived. But we are unable to comprehend how it can be known that pain exists, when it is not felt.   We have already sufficiently explained our views on this point.

We often wonder at the fortitude, with which some persons are able to endure the most excruciating tortures.   But we are apt to overlook the influence of strong emotion in rendering the body insensible to pain.   The warrior, in the midst of the excitement of the battle-field, will sometimes receive a severe wound without being conscious of any injury.   Who does not admire the firmness and fortitude of Mutius Scaevola, when in defiance of the rage of Porsenna, and looking his enemy sternly in the face, he held his hand upon the burning coals till it was entirely consumed ?   Yet he was probably rendered nearly insensible to pain by the strong mental excitement under which he was laboring.   The American Indian, who becomes the victim of the tortures of a hostile tribe, endures with comparative composure the most cruel inflictions, which savage ingenuity can invent.   But his patient endurance of torture depends not so much upon his being naturally better able than others to support suffering, as upon the fact, that the struggling emotions of his mind render him nearly insensible to pain.

---

* De Civit. Dei, Lib. XIV. cap. 24.

In all these cases of diminished or suspended external sensibility, the explanation is obvious on the principles, which we have endeavored to explain and illustrate. The brain is so much affected by the intensity of the mental action, that it becomes thereby disqualified for performing its part in the function of sensation.

Another class of phenomena, which are usually treated of under the head of sympathetic imitation, may be referred to, as illustrating the influence of the states of the mind over the body. A person witnessing the natural expression of an emotion of pleasure or pain, feels in some degree the same emotion, accompanied with an inclination to imitate its expression. We see this principle illustrated by the contagiousness of smiling, weeping, yawning, etc. Indeed, there is a propensity to imitate the irregular contortions of the body, which can hardly be considered the natural expression of any emotion of the mind. Nor is it always necessary that these phenomena should be witnessed by an individual, in order that they may be reproduced in himself.

Hecker in his "Tanzwuth" quotes from the (English) "Gentleman's Magazine" of 1787, an account which finely illustrates this principle. In an English factory, one of the girls mischievously introduced a mouse into the bosom of another, who immediately fell into violent convulsions, which continued, almost without cessation, for twenty-four hours. On the following day others were seized with similar convulsions, and by the the fourth day twenty-four were similarly affected. At this time medical aid was resorted to, and this singular disease was speedily removed by the agency of electricity. It is worthy of remark, that five of the individuals who were attacked, had not seen any one affected with the disease, but were seized with the spasms simply from hearing a description of them as they occurred in others.*

We see the influence of sympathetic imitation in the history of the various forms of the dancing mania, which have at different times prevailed under the names of St. John's dance, St. Vitus's dance, Tarantismus, etc.† The same remark applies to the history of the Convulsionaries of St. Medard, and of witchcraft, whenever and wherever it has made its appearance.

---

* Die Tanzwuth, eine Volkskrankheit im Mittelalter, von Dr. J. F. C. Hecker. Berlin, 1832. p. 64.

† See Hecker's Tanzwuth.

Thus far we have endeavored to explain briefly the connection of the body and the mind, and to illustrate by a few examples their reciprocal influence. It may now be interesting to inquire how far the principles, which we have developed, will aid us in understanding the phenomena of animal magnetism.

What then are the agencies concerned in the production of these phenomena? Some have confidently attributed them to the agency of a supposed universally diffused fluid, of such extreme tenuity as to escape the cognizance of the senses, yet endued with such energetic properties as to be capable, when accumulated in the living body, of changing or modifying all its functions, suspending some and giving to others supernatural activity and power; and certain rules are given for directing and concentrating this fluid upon an individual so as to give rise to the phenomena in question. Others have denied the existance of any such fluid or of any real phenomena resulting from this or any other agent. With them the whole is a tissue of imposture and deception.

We shall not stop to examine the merits of either of these hypotheses, but shall proceed to state the views, to which we have been led by a careful examination of facts. In doing this, it will be necessary to describe briefly two leading processes, which have been adopted by the magnetizers in the practice of their art. The processes, which we shall describe, are the one adopted by Mesmer and Deslon in Paris, and that which is in vogue at the present day.

Mesmer commenced his experiments upon animal magnetism in Vienna, his native city, and, after having travelled through Germany and Switzerland practising his new art and propagating his sentiments wherever he went, he at length arrived in Paris, where he set himself up as a great discoverer, and pretended to have under his control a universal remedy, adapted to every case of disease, and destined to supplant every other remedial means. We have the account of his mode of proceeding, in the report of the commissioners appointed by the king to examine into the subject.

In the centre of a spacious room was placed a circular oval vessel (*baquet*), in the bottom of which was placed a layer of bottles filled with magnetized water, and corked and disposed in the form of a radii, so that the mouths of the bottles converged towards the centre of the large vessel. This vessel was then filled with water, also magnetized secundum artem by

Mesmer. Powdered glass and iron filings were sometimes added to the water on account of their supposed agency in concentrating the magnetic fluid. The vessel was covered with a lid perforated with numerous holes, from which proceeded slender iron rods, rendered flexible by means of joints so that they might be bent into any convenient shape.

Thus equipped, Mesmer issued his proposals to the public. From this mysterious tub was to proceed a healing influence, before which the most inveterate diseases must speedily give way. It was even asserted that by the aid of animal magnetism, age would be made to assume the bloom and vigor of youth, and that the human race would soon be restored to ante-diluvian longevity.

Great numbers crowded around the *baquet* of Mesmer. The gloomy hypochondriac there sought relief from his imaginary woes. Nervous females who had tried every other remedy in vain, betook themselves to animal magnetism as their last resort. The worn-out devotee of pleasure sought in this new agent that physical enjoyment which he had ceased to find in the rounds of sensuality. This motley throng were placed in a circle around the magnetic tub with their faces towards it. The iron rods which proceeded from the vessel were brought into contact with the bodies of the patients at the diseased part, if any point could be found, which enjoyed that distinction. A cord connected with a ring in the cover, passed around their bodies, and they were directed to join hands to render the circuit still more complete. Thus situated they waited in fearful expectation for the operation of the mysterious influence supposed to issue from the central vessel. In the meantime, Mesmer splendidly arrayed in lilac satin, waved majestically his iron rod over the expecting multitude. Streams of magnetic fluid were supposed to follow every motion of his magic wand; and his object seemed to be to conduct this agent from the central vessel along the iron rods to the patients seated around.

In this state of things a long time was not required to develop some of the effects of animal magnetism. Some slight spasms and convulsions were first seen in the weaker and more nervous patients. This example was soon followed by others, until all became affected, and a state of things ensued, which by the magnetizers was denominated the crisis. Very different symptoms were manifested by different individuals. Some lay prostrate upon the floor in a state of insensibility, some in convulsions, some were weeping, others laughing, and others leaping about the room with demonstrations of the most extravagant delight.

An improved mode of operation is employed by the magnetizers of the present day. The apparatus of Mesmer is entirely laid aside, and the operator produces the wonderful effects of animal magnetism, by what are called by the French *passes attouchemens*, etc. practised upon a single individual. The person to be operated upon is seated in a chair, is directed to close his eyes, to sit perfectly motionless and to concentrate the whole power of the will and of thought upon the operation. The least motion of the body, or the least intrusion of thoughts foreign to the subject is considered unfavorable to the desired result. Sometimes the patient is instructed with regard to the effects which are expected to be produced, and directed to fix his thoughts immovably upon those effects. The patient being thus seated and thus instructed, the magnetizer takes his place before him, either standing or seated, and embracing the patient's knees between his own. He then commences the operation by placing his hands upon the head of the patient and pressing gently for a few moments, then passing them slowly down over different regions of the body. Sometimes he brings them down over the shoulders and arms and off at the hands, sometimes he passes them down in front of the body and off at the feet, not delaying however to perform some gentle *attouchemens* about the pit of the stomach. These manipulations are practised, for half an hour or more, two or three times every day, until the desired effects are produced or the patient is dismissed as not being susceptible of the magnetic influence. In this process the phenomena produced are attributed to the agency of the magnetic fluid flowing from the hands of the magnetizer into the person operated upon.

It is proper here to remark that this improved mode of operating has been supposed to have given rise to a peculiar phenomenon, we mean magnetic somnambulism. At least, such a phenomenon was never recognized by Mesmer and his immediate followers. It is, however, the principal object of interest with the magnetizers of the present day, on account of the extraordinary powers said to be possessed by persons in that state. We may, in a future number, make this phenomenon the subject of inquiry.

In examining the operations of the magnetizers, it is not difficult to perceive, that everything connected with them is calculated to produce and perpetuate a strong impression upon the mind ; and we apprehend that all the real effects may be accounted for by a reference to the influence of the mind upon the body, on the principles already explained.   Even if these principles do not afford a full explanation of all the phenomena in question, yet nothing, certainly, is gained by attributing them to the agency of a fluid, whose very existence is incapable of any plausible demonstration.

In the operations of Mesmer it is easy to see that his imposing array of apparatus, the solemn pomp and parade in all his proceedings, together with the excited accounts of his mysterious power, which were abroad, were all calculated to seize powerfully upon the imaginations of those operated upon ; and the effects thus produced would be greatly strengthened and prolonged by the power of sympathy.   So that the curious phenomena of animal magnetism in the hands of Mesmer need not be a matter of surprise to any who are at all acquainted with the laws of the human constitution.   It may be supposed however that the experiments of modern magnetizers, performed as they are upon a single person, leave no room for the operation of sympathetic imitation.   But it is clear from what we have already said, that the prevailing reports of the peculiar effects of animal magnetism would strongly predispose all, who are operated upon, to be similarly affected.   It is also easy to perceive, that every circumstance connected with the modern mode of magnetizing is admirably adapted to produce the effects intended.   The motionless posture of the body, the intense and prolonged effort of the will required to keep the thoughts immovably fixed upon one single point, the state of trembling expectancy, in which the mind is held, and the consequent stifled condition of the respiration, all together could not fail to give rise to some unusual sensations.   These sensations being taken as the incipient effects of the magnetic fluid, would tend greatly to increase the impression already made ; and this impression would go on deepening and strengthening till all the faculties of body and mind would be absorbed by the overpowering influence of the imagination.

We have endeavored to unfold briefly some of those principles of our constitution, which grow out of the mysterious union of body and mind, and have attempted to apply these principles to the explanation of the phenomena of animal magnetism.

We might extend this application to witchcraft and other fanaticisms which have at various times prevailed. But this would extend our Article beyond its intended limits. It would be improper for us to close without inquiring how far we are to credit the accounts, which have been given of animal magnetism; lest we should seem to be laboring to explain phenomena, which never had an existence, except in the wild wanderings of a deluded imagination.

Without charging the magnetizers with a greater share of dishonesty than falls to the lot of almost all classes of men, it would be natural to suppose that much deception would be blended with the alleged phenomena of this pretended science. A field which promises so rich a reward to the impostor and deceiver, could not fail to find those disposed to reap its harvest. Certainly it cannot be deemed uncharitable to suppose, that animal magnetism is not free from the charge of imposture, when the very sanctuary of the Lord has been defiled by its unhallowed intrusion.

But even if there were no intended deception in the practices of the magnetizers, it is not difficult to perceive, that the hypotheses which they hold, and the circumstances under which they operate, would naturally lead to deception both with regard to the causes and the nature of the phenomena produced. In order to ensure success in magnetic experiments it is required, that both the magnetizer and magnetizée should be believers in animal magnetism, and that both should *will* the production of the expected effects. It is moreover considered desirable and sometimes indispensable that all the spectators should be believers. M. Georget, himself a magnetizer, tells us that he once saw very dangerous symptoms produced in the magnetizée by the presence of an *incredule*.* The presence of an unbeliever is supposed to produce a counter current in the magnetic fluid or in some way to disturb its regular flow in the desired direction. Where all the witnesses of an experiment are believers, their very credulity may spread a veil of deception over the whole, or prevent them from detecting any fallacy that might exist. If however any one should succeed in discovering any delusion, this very fact would prove his want of faith, which would account for all the failures that might have happened in his presence. Such is the tissue of delusion, in which

* Georget's Physiologie du Système Nerveux.

the magnetizers have enveloped themselves, which effectually shields them from the force of every argument whether drawn from the resources of reason and common sense or from direct experiment. We are aware that all have not carried their speculations to this degree of refinement, yet the above doctrines are held by some of the most enlightened advocates of animal magnetism.

Though there is much deception and fanciful conjecture connected with animal magnetism, yet all its phenomena cannot be considered as visionary and unreal. A knowledge of the principles of our constitution prepares us to believe many of the statements with regard to this subject. But as we have already extended this Article to a sufficient length, we shall reserve for a future number the further discussion of the subject.

ARTICLE VII.

CHRIST PREEXISTENT; — A HOMILETICAL EXPOSITION OF JOHN 1: 1—5.

By Thomas H. Skinner, D. D. Pastor of the Mercer St. Presb. Church, and Prof. Extraordinary of Sac. Rhet., N. Y. Theol. Sem., New York.

" In the beginning was the Word, and the Word was with God, and the Word was God. The same was in the beginning with God. All things were made by him; and without him was not any thing made that was made. In him was life; and the life was the light of men. And the light shineth in darkness; and the darkness comprehendeth it not."

THESE are surprising words. Our familiarity with them, unless it has rendered us unthinking, cannot have diminished our interest in them. There is in these words an abyss of meaning and of power too deep to be ever fathomed by human thought. Francis Junius, of whom, at his death, it was remarked by Scaliger, that the whole world lamented him as its instructor,* was recovered from atheism in a remarkable manner, by

---

* Junius and Joseph Scaliger were Professors at Leyden, at the same time. Scaliger had a strong aversion for Junius in his lifetime,

this passage of Scripture.   Persuaded by his father to read the New Testament, "at first sight," he says, " I fell unexpectedly on that august chapter of St. John, the Evangelist, ' In the beginning was the Word,' etc.   I read part of the chapter, and was so struck with what I read, that I instantly perceived the divinity of the subject, and the authority and majesty of the Scripture, to surpass greatly all human eloquence.   I shuddered in my body ; my mind was confounded ; and I was so strongly affected all that day, that I hardly knew who I myself was : but Thou, Lord my God, didst remember me in thy boundless mercy, and receive a lost sheep into thy flock."

What is the subject of these amazing assertions ?   What is meant by the appellation, THE WORD, by which that subject is expressed ?

In the first place, does it denote a being, or an attribute ; a person, or a quality ?

That a real person was intended, should never, we think, have been questioned.   It is affirmed that this Word was with God, was God,* created all things, was testified unto by John, was made flesh, and dwelt with men, full of grace and truth. There is an irreverent freedom, to suspect nothing worse, in that criticism which ventures to inquire whether the Evangelist meant anything more than an attribute or quality, that is, no real subsistence, by what he denominates the Word in this sublime passage.   He does not more explicitly affirm the personal existence and individuality of Jesus Christ, the subject of his gospel, than the perfect personality of the Word, the subject of his great declarations in this place.

Next, Who was the individual intended by this appellation ? We hesitate not to say that the evidence could not be more per-

---

because the latter took the liberty to contradict him sometimes in matters of chronology, and opposed his having the precedency over all the other professors.   But at the death of Junius, the resentment of Scaliger gave place to the strongest feelings of respect which expressed themselves in an admirable panegyric.

* " On this supposition," namely, that an attribute was intended, "the commencement of the Gospel, would be altogether tautological : ' In the beginning was the wisdom of God, this divine wisdom was with God, and God was this divine wisdom.'   The Evangelist would have had no occasion to establish the identity of the Logos with God, if he had intended to denote by Logos, nothing else than a Divine attribute."—*Tholuck.*

fect than it is, that the self-same person is here spoken of, whom the Evangelist afterwards presents in a human form, and under a human name, as the subject of his narrative. The Word here intended was our Lord Jesus Christ. To argue on this point, implies, in our view, a doubt whether the Evangelist did not mean to practice a deception on his readers.

But why, thirdly, does he give Christ this mysterious appellation? That some reason for this existed, we cannot but think. None of the names given to our Lord, were given arbitrarily. They were all chosen from their being significative of him, in either his nature, or his office. What is there in the present appellation that renders it an appropriate name for our Lord Jesus Christ?

We think with Clarke, that this name should have been left untranslated. The original Logos is, he justly remarks, as proper an appellative of the Saviour of the world, as either of the terms Jesus or Christ. And as it would be improper to say, the Deliverer, the Anointed, instead of Jesus Christ, so it is improper to say, the Word, instead of the Logos.

It should be premised also, that this appellative had been used before the Evangelist wrote, with a deeply significant reference. Philosophers had used it to designate the creative power, to which in opposition to the doctrine of chance, they ascribed the origin of the Universe.* It was in use too among the Jewish teachers, who employed it to discriminate the Deity revealed, from the Deity un-revealed—a distinction which they seem to have derived from certain passages in the Old Testament; assisted, however, as Tholuck thinks, by the ancient oriental theosophy.† This fact accounts for the Evangelist's using

---

* " The Platonists make mention of the Logos in this way :—καθ' ον αει οντα, τα γινομενα εγινετο—by whom eternally existing all things were made."—*Clarke.*

† The passages from the Old Testament cited and commented on by Tholuck are Exod. 33: 14. 20: 23. Is. 63: 9. Mal. 3: 1. Ps. 33: 6. Prov. 8: 23 seq. These passages he shows, we think, contain the distinction; but he supposes it improbable that the Jewish teachers would have discovered it in them, but for their acquaintance with the oriental systems of religion. " In several of these systems, the idea that the highest Being is in himself incomprehensible and unapproachable, is found developed under various modifications. Man is represented as being seized with dizziness, when he attempts to comprehend this idea; and in general there is no transit from this Being to a world of created existences. Consequently it became necessary

the term as if it needed no explanation.* It was a term already in familiar use, and used, unquestionably, to designate a person. Mankind had been taught the doctrine of the Divine unity; they had also received some intimations of the doctrine of the Logos. Their knowledge on the latter subject however was extremely confused. The Evangelist has delivered concerning the Logos sublime and distinct statements, and identified the very person to whom that name appropriately belongs. The true Logos, of whom the Old Testament had given some discoveries and promises, but of whom the philosophers and rabbis had ignorantly discoursed, was, the Evangelist here affirms, Jesus Christ, the Lord and Saviour of the world.†

for God to generate in himself a certain transition-point, to make his fulness comprehensible and communicable; and this he did by producing out of himself from eternity, a Being like unto himself through whom the concealed God was manifested."—The reader will find in *Smith's Scripture Testimony to the Messiah*, Vol. I. pp. 548—569, *third edition*, a collection of the principal passages in the extant writings of Philo, concerning the subject of the Logos. Philo was a Jew of Alexandria, of a sacerdotal family, who is supposed to have been about sixty years old at the death of Christ. His expressions concerning the Logos, have excited great admiration.

* "Since it can be actually proved, that the words ὁ λόγος τοῦ θεοῦ at that time expressed a definite doctrinal conception, and such an one, as is similar to that of John, it is altogether certain that John employed the Word in that determinate doctrinal sense which was prevalent in his time."—*Tholuck.*

† Tholuck rejects the idea, that the Evangelist had allusion to the doctrine of the theosophists on this subject. "Since we find in the first place, that previously in the Old Testament, intimations of this doctrine of the Logos can be pointed out; and secondly, that the apostle Paul teaches the same doctrine of the Logos, Col. 1: 15. 2 Cor. 4: 4. comp. Heb. 1: 3, although he borrowed his mode of teaching neither from the orientals nor from Philo, but from Jewish theologians only; and thirdly, since in Sir. 43: 26 (28), the creative word of God, and in the book of Wisdom 18: 15, the angel which presided over the theocracy of the Old Testament, is called λόγος: it must seem to be most probable, that John did not occupy himself with the dogmas of other religions, but adhered to the Jewish doctrinal theology of his time, which was based on the Old Testament; and that in this way he made known, that the Revealer of God pointed out in the Old Testament—he who directed the administration of the Old Testament theocracy, had actually appeared in Christ. In the Epistles also, 1 John 1: 1, and in the Revelation 19: 13, John calls Christ the Logos,

The propriety of giving Christ this appellation will in some measure appear, by considering that he is, as Philo in speaking on the subject of the Logos, or *Word*, admirably says, THE SAME TO THE SUPREME INTELLECT, THAT SPEECH IS TO THE HUMAN. All who believe in the Scriptures, admit that Christ is in some sense, the REVEALER of God. The Scriptures teach nothing more explicitly than that the Deity, *except as revealed by Christ*, is at this day, and forever will be, hidden out of sight, and out of thought, to the entire universe of men and angels. That God " *could* not make an external revelation of himself in the world, until he had become revealed within himself, that is in the Son" is affirmed (how intelligibly different persons will differently decide,) by the excellent expositor Tholuck ; however this may be, it is the clear teaching of Scripture, that in point of fact, God, by Jesus Christ, has exerted all the power which he ever has exerted, out of himself, and made all the disclosures of himself to creatures which ever have been made.—— That whatever knowledge men have of God and divine things, they have obtained through Christ, he himself affirms : " No one hath seen God at any time ; the only begotten Son who is in the bosom of the Father, he hath declared him." It is related in the Old Testament, that God was seen by Adam, Abraham, Moses, and the prophets ; but they saw him only in the person of Christ ; who also by his Spirit, gave to holy men of old " the lively oracles" of inspired truth. Now as speech is the medium by which knowledge is communicated among ourselves, it is manifestly proper that the source and channel of all true knowledge, should in a revelation given to man, be denominated the Logos ;—a term which signifies speech, or instruction, or the word spoken, or as in our translation, the Word. There is doubtless more of fitness and suitableness in this appellation to the person to whom it is given, than we can understand, but it is sufficiently obvious, that while there is mystery, there is also intelligible and striking propriety, in naming our Lord the Logos.

Having seen that the term in its present use, designates a person, and that this person was Christ, let us proceed to con-

and thereby intimates the important meaning of this appellation." As the Evangelist wrote as he was moved by the Holy Ghost, he was competent to make known, that the Revealer of God pointed out in the Old Testament, had appeared in Christ, without being indebted to either the Jewish theologians of his time, or the eastern theosophists.

sider the announcements concerning him, which follow; remembering that we are attending to utterances indited by omniscience.

The first is, that Christ was in existence at the birth of the creation. The phrase "In the beginning"—the same with which Moses commences the Bible, refers us to the date of the creation, there being nothing to limit or qualify it. The assertion is that the Logos was in the beginning; the question may be asked, in the beginning of what? Of the world as it now is? of the dealings of God with man? of the christian dispensation? And men may give their own answers. The Evangelist is silent. He leaves us with the unqualified affirmation, that the Logos was in the beginning—an affirmation which if taken, in the absolute sense, transfers us to the instant when creation had its origin and time with it, and presents to us Christ, as then in existence.

The assertion here is, unless it should be understood with some restriction of which the Evangelist gives no hint, that Christ was in existence at the creation of the world; that when there were no depths—when there were no fountains abounding with water—before the mountains were settled—before the hills—while as yet God had not made the earth, nor the fields, nor the highest part of the dust of the world—when he prepared the heavens—when he set a compass upon the face of the depth—when he established the clouds above—when he strengthened the fountains of the deep—when he gave to the sea his decree that the waters should not pass his commandment—when he appointed the foundations of the earth*—then existed our Saviour Jesus Christ.

There are those, however, who restrict the words before us, so as to make them mean, in the beginning of the preaching of the gospel. It is not probable that many readers of the Evangelist will adopt this gratuitous exposition. It gives a trivial sense to one of the most remarkable texts of inspiration, and

---

* In this use of Prov. 8: 22—30, to express what we believe to be asserted by the Evangelist as an historical fact, we design not to cite it as a parallel passage. It was, however, understood by the Jews of old, and the christian church from the beginning, of a *person*, the *substantial wisdom* of God; and whatever advances have been made in the science of interpretation, we question the soundness of that criticism which takes it in a different sense. See Waterland's Eight Sermons, pp. 216—218.

thus dooms itself to contempt.* The assertion stands and ever will stand, without limitation or addition.

But taking it thus, what is it, that it requires us to believe concerning Jesus Christ? That he is a Being in the strictest sense eternal!—If he was in existence, when the world and time commenced, he did not himself then come into existence. To make him one of the objects that then came into existence ;—to say that in the beginning he began to be ;—or that among those existences which came forth out of nothing at the command of the Creator, was the Logos, is to contradict the assertion that he was already in existence, when the beginning took place. Well have the ancient Fathers said that " he who was in the beginning comprehended every beginning in himself,"† and that " as to the Being who was from the beginning, no time can be found when he was not."‡ It is therefore the proper import of the words of the Evangelist, that the attribute of eternity, in the most perfect sense, belongs to Christ ; that as the prophet Micah affirms of him, his emanations are from the beginning, from the days of eternity.

We are next informed, that Christ in eternity was the companion of God. This is asserted not once only, but to give it stronger impression it is repeated in the second verse. *The same was in the beginning with God.* Eternal companying with Eternal! An unsearchable mystery, but yet a fact, to which the highest importance is attached in the Scriptures. In the statements of Scripture, concerning both creation and redemption, the proposition that God did not dwell alone in that eternity which anteceded both, that the Logos was with him there, is always implied and is often prominent. We do not give it as the assertion of the Scriptures, though a great commentator has made it, that God could not, except through the Son, have made an external revelation of himself in the world ; but that in point of fact, he has not any otherwise revealed himself in the world, that before creation was entered upon, there was, to speak after the manner of men, a consultation held and an arrangement agreed upon between God and the Logos, and that both creation and redemption were the fruit not of God's agency apart from that of the Logos, but of the concurrence and intercommunion of both ; and further, that but for

---

* Tholuck calls it the *shallow* Socinian explanation.
† Augustine.   ‡ Theophylact.

the part agreed to be fulfilled, and in due time actually fulfilled by the Logos, there never would have been either redemption or creation—is not only a statement, but the leading and fundamental statement of the Bible. That book does not speak concerning the origin and authorship of the universe, as too many do who profess to take it as the standard of their faith. It tells of a creating Deity, but it also tells us of one inhabiting with that Deity the eternity which preceded creation, and equally concerned in accomplishing that glorious work : " The Lord possessed me in the beginning of his way, before his works of old. I was set up from everlasting, from the beginning, or ever the earth was : Then I was by him as one brought up with him ; and I was daily his delight, rejoicing always before him—rejoicing in the habitable part of his earth, and my delights were with the sons of men."* The Bible teaches, that the universe was created *for* Christ, and with reference to a revelation of the divine glory to be made by Christ, through the instrumentality of various redemptive and governmental agencies ; and that redemption itself, except through Christ, was not achievable, without a sacrifice of the divine justice. From which clearly stated premises, the conclusion is, that had there been no Christ, no Logos, in eternity, there had been no world, no creation, no time. We are accustomed in our devout meditations, to trace our salvation to a covenant or agreement entered into, in eternity, between the Father and the Son, and to admit that but for what the Son then consented to do for us, our salvation would have been unaccomplished ; but the Bible leads us to take a wider survey, and to see in the existence and agency of the Logos, the foundation of the existence and perpetuity of all creatures and worlds. The doctrine of a personal Logos, the companion of God in eternity, enters as distinctly into the biblical system of the universe, as the doctrine of a Divine existence ; and the great Lord Bacon has shown himself as sound in the faith, as he was in philosophy, in that memorable confession of his, from which we give the following extract : " That neither angels, man, nor world, would stand, or can stand one moment in God's eye, without his beholding the same IN THE FACE OF A MEDI-

---

* This language is not introduced as proof, but as happily suited to express the sense intended to be conveyed by the author. That it is however applicable to Christ in the strictest sense, was the universal opinion of the ancients (themselves be it remembered *orientals* and therefore) perhaps the best qualified to give the true exposition.

ATOR;——and therefore that before Him with whom all things are present, *the Lamb of God*, was slain before all worlds: but that out of his eternal and infinite goodness and love, purposing to become a creator, and to communicate to his creatures, he ordained in his eternal counsel, that one person of the Godhead should be united to one nature, and to one particular of his creatures; so that in the person of the Mediator the true ladder may be fixed whereby God may descend to his creatures, and his creatures might ascend to God; so that God, by the reconcilement* of the Mediator, turning his countenance toward his creatures, (though not in equal light and degree) made way unto the dispensation of his most holy and sacred will; whereby some of his creatures might stand and keep their state; others might possibly fall and be restored; and others might fall and not be restored to their estate, but yet remain in being though under wrath and corruption: *all with respect to the Mediator*, which is the great mystery and perfect centre of all God's ways with his creatures, and to which all his other works and wonders, do but serve and refer." That doctrine of the Logos, which makes him the companion, in eternity, of the eternal God, was, in the belief of Lord Bacon, as it is in the explicit testimony of Scripture, the foundation-stone of the systems of creation and redemption.

The next of the announcements before us is that Christ, the companion of God in eternity, was also God himself. THE LOGOS WAS GOD. This is not a more explicit assertion of the deity of Christ, than the phrase of which it is the translation. The translation is literally exact. This no criticism questions;

---

* Lord Bacon, on the basis of such scriptures as Job 4: 18. 25: 5. Isa. 24: 23, and of his own exquisite sense of what is fit and seemly, held that the reason or ground of necessity for a Mediator, was the ineffable purity and majesty of God. The writer once questioned if it be consistent with the infinite goodness of the Deity to suppose that he would not converse with innocent and pure creatures except through a mediator. Reflection has convinced him that Lord Bacon is sustained in his belief, by both Scripture and reason. It may be the highest goodness to inspire even unfallen creatures with a sense of infinite majesty and greatness; the want of that sense might be the means of their ruin; and in order to produce it in them, mediation might have been indispensable. God is too good, not to express delight in upright creatures, but it might have been unwise and contrary to goodness, to be regardless of the mode in which his delight should be manifested.

but still there is a criticism which will not take this as a proof-text of the strict deity of Christ. It asserts that he was God, but " if we suppose the word Logos to mean the reason, or wisdom, or power of God, what can that reason, or wisdom, or power be, but God ?"* The evidence however that the word Logos, means not an attribute but a person, is as we have before remarked such, that it requires a degree of opinionativeness not often found, capable of offering it resistance. Recourse therefore has been had to another supposition, namely, that an inferior and subordinate godship is here ascribed to the Logos. He is said to be God, but not the supreme God. If we admit that he was in *some sense* divine, or was God by office, or delegated power and prerogative, we do not reject this testimony concerning him. Here we submit four short remarks. 1. That Christ was a creature in *some sense divine,* or that he was God *by office or prerogative;* and that HE WAS GOD; are not identical propositions. They appear at least to have infinitely different meanings, and wonderful must be the critical ingenuity, that can make them even *seem* convertible. 2. If the incontrovertible meaning of other passages of Scripture would be set aside by taking the words before us in their obvious sense, an attempt to interpret them differently might show respect for the sacred oracles; but there is a great mass of Scripture testimony demanding an adherence to the obvious sense in this place, and not a sentence nor a word to justify a departure from it. There are many Scriptures which assert that Christ was a man, but there is not one which denies his supreme divinity. On the contrary, it might be shown, as it has often been, with the greatest strength of evidence, that this latter point is asserted in Scripture in the most unequivocal manner. 3. The first of these affirmations concerning the Logos, namely, that " he was in the beginning," prepares us to take the present one, in its obvious import. If the Logos was in the beginning, that is, as we have proved the phrase to mean, existed before all created things, and, of course, was distinct from them and uncreated, there should be no hesitation in admitting his deity in the absolute

---

* " A man's word, or thought, is not called *man;* nor would the word, or wisdom of God be called *God,* if a mere attribute, or operation only was intended, and not a real person."—*Waterland.* That a prosopopoeia cannot be here admitted, is further evident from the fact, that it would, as Tholuck has remarked, render the expression tautological : " *The wisdom of God, personified, was God !*"

sense.   After hearing that Christ is an uncreated or eternal being, no surprise should be felt, at being informed that he is the supreme God.   The first of these propositions includes the second.   If anything be peculiar to the great Supreme, it is to have existed from eternity, or to be, without having been created or begun to be.   4.   Since the words refer to Christ as existing in eternity, while as yet there was no world, and no time, to make them declare that he was God by office, is to forget that office implies creatures, over whom it is exercised.   How was he God by office when there were no objects in existence to hold office over?

Zeal for the Divine unity, is the ostensible motive for so explaining this and other Scriptures as to disallow the supreme Deity of our Saviour.   The proposition that there was a Being with God, who was yet himself supreme God, implies, it is alleged, dualism in the divine nature, than which nothing is more contrary to both reason and Scripture.   The implication, we reply, is not included.   God may be one in essence, and more than one in some other respect.   There may be a distinction in the mode of the Divine existence, and yet be perfect unity in the Divine essence.   This is not in itself a contradiction, and if Scripture asserts it, the inspiration of the Bible should be disproved, before it is rejected.   Further; there may be a distinction in the Godhead of *such a kind*, as to admit of more than one impersonation of it, consistently with its numerical unity. That is; the one God may be one in respect of Godhead, and yet more than one in some other respect; and the difference in this other respect may be such as to lay the basis for distinct *personal* attributes and offices.   This is not an inconsistency in itself: No man can show it to be an absurdity: No man can discard it as contrary to reason without making himself wiser than God, provided Scripture has affirmed it.   If now Scripture has affirmed that a person, called the Logos, had union and happiness in eternity with God, and that this person was himself God, supreme and eternal, why, since God may subsist in several persons and yet be one God, should we hesitate to adopt the belief that he does so subsist;—a doctrine, which, while it makes Scripture intelligible and consistent, in the present case, is demanded in explicit terms, by a thousand other texts, and has ever been a fundamental article in the faith of the christian church?—It is not said, that the Logos *as God*, was with God; but that the Logos, as *the Logos*, was with God.   When it can be shewn that the expressions, *the Logos as the Logos,* and *the Logos as God,* mean precisely the same thing, then may dualism in the Divine Essence, be inferred from that interpretation of the phrase, *the Logos was God,* which gives it as a proof-text, of the supreme Deity of Jesus Christ.

We proceed to the fourth of these great testimonies. We are confirmed in the belief, that the Evangelist meant to assert the Divinity of Christ in the former affirmation, by what he now tells us of his agency. He makes him the author of the universe—"All things were made by him; and without him was not any thing made that was made." If he who produced all things from nothing, be not the supreme God, the idea of such a Being has not yet entered into the human mind. This is here said to be the work of Christ in the most emphatic and guarded terms. The universe in general, is first made his workmanship, and then each particular existence composing it, so as to preclude one exception.

It has been said, that the creation here meant, was the new spiritual creation; the state of things in the moral world, as arranged under the New Testament dispensation; and that the assertion of the Evangelist is, that Christ was in all respects, the author of that state and order of things. But not only is this said, without warrant from the context, but it would not have been said, had the preceding testimonies concerning Christ been taken in the only sense, in which, as we have seen, every rule of just interpretation requires them to be taken. It is only those who deny that Christ was, *at* the creation, and therefore *before* it, and supreme God, who take the words before us as referring to the spiritual or moral world. To give them such a reference is taking such liberty with them, as no one would take, who had not some favorite doctrine or interpretation which otherwise must be surrendered. Besides this assertion, so weak in itself, so unsupported, so repudiated by the context, is a virtual denial of what Scripture elsewhere affirms, with the greatest stress. We shall cite a passage to this purport, from Paul's epistle to the Colossians, and subjoin a comment. "For by Him (Christ) were all things created, that are in heaven and that are on earth, visible and invisible, whether they be thrones or dominions, or principalities, or powers, all things were created by him, and for him." "Not one example," remarks Whitby on this place, "can be shown where the creation of all things in heaven and earth, is ever used in a moral sense, or concerning any other than the natural creation. Moreover, in the first place, *all things in earth, and things visible*, must comprise things without life, the inanimate parts of nature, concerning which it is absurd to speak of a moral creation. Secondly, under *things in heaven, invisible, etc.*, must be comprehended the whole celestial hierarchy ; but *good* angels cannot require a spiritual renovation, and Christ came not to convert *fallen* angels, but to destroy their empire." They truly have undertaken a difficult task, who are endeavoring to show that the Scriptures do not make Christ the author of the natural creation. It is the declaration of the Scriptures, that God created all things, but it is also their declaration, that Christ is the creator ; and since they teach that Christ was the supreme God, they are not inconsistent with themselves. They likewise and frequently affirm, *that God created all things, by Christ;* but if while Christ possesses the divine nature, he is in *personality*, distinct from the Father, this expression conveys the sublime and most interesting truth, so clearly taught in other texts, that the Divine person, in whom the creative power directly exerted itself to the production of the universe from nothing, was the same that assumed our nature and dwelt amongst men under the name Jesus Christ. We forbear examining into the grounds of this economy of the creation, or searching for the reasons, why the creative power did not exert itself irrespectively of the personal distinctions in the Godhead, or why the person in which it did exert itself, was the Logos or Christ. Tholuck asserts a necessity in this case. This only would we say on the subject, that if it were only through the mediation of the Logos, that the Deity could converse with created beings, or that such beings, as Lord Bacon says, could stand for a moment in God's eye, it seems meet and reasonable if not morally necessary, that the power which was to give creatures existence, should exist itself in the person of the Mediator.

The fifth of these declarations is, that *in the Logos was life.* We are not to understand by these words, that the Logos was a living in contradistinction to a *lifeless* or *dead* being, in the primary meaning of these epithets. To say this after having affirmed that he was the Creator of all things, were not only unnecessary, but were to sink the lofty strain of the discourse almost beneath contempt. That he was not a *dead being*, by whom the vital universe was made, is an assertion which in the connections before us, no one can seriously think could proceed from the inspired Evangelist. But if *life* here is not to be taken in contradistinction to mere *death*, what is the sense in which we should take it ? It is not difficult to answer this question. There is a life, which is if we may so speak, the life of all life in rational creatures. It is not natural life merely, whether of body or of mind, but the higher life of holiness, or holy joy. Life, in Scripture, often means moral excellence, holiness, benevolence ; and often, also, happiness, the fruit or effect of holiness. These, from their relation to each other, are considered as one, holiness implying happiness as its result, and happiness implying holiness as its cause. We need not therefore in the present instance discriminate : life is holiness ; life is happiness : no account need be taken of the difference. Spiritual life, including both true holiness and true happiness, things dwelling in one another as heat in the sun-beams, is the life which is here said to have been in the Logos. This life, which filled the rational creation, while in its first estate, and we may hope, fills it still with slight exception, had, its fountain in Christ, as the revealing God. All rational creatures awoke into existence in possession of it, which along with existence itself, they derived from Christ. He infused into them the holy vitality which dwelt in himself and filled them with his fulness. That fathomless love which appeared so wondrously in redemption, had been before manifested as perfectly as the nature of things would admit, in the work of creation, when the morning stars sang together and all the sons of God shouted for joy.

This history of our Saviour in his preëxistent state, informs us further that *the life*, that spiritual life of whose nature and fountain we have just spoken,—*was the light of men.*—The sense of this statement cannot be misapprehended. We are in no danger of positive mistake, even if we do not fully and distinctly take the meaning, so as to be able to express it in a perfect definition. Man, when he first awoke from non-existence, found himself in a world furnished magnificently for his use, and gloriously illuminated by those larger and lesser lights, which still pour their splendors from the firmament. Those material beams, however, which gilded the face of nature, and transported the eye with the views of sublimity and beauty which it presented, are not *the light of men.* Nor is this the light of the *understanding*, consisting in ideas or the images of things in the mind and the results of combining and comparing them ;— a light which may or may not be associated with moral depravity, and, if associated with it, is called darkness in Scripture, nay the blackness of darkness. The true light of men is, as Tholuck has happily expressed it, *an ethico-religious knowledge, based on an inward communion with God, and comprehending the theoretical and practical at the same time ;* a knowledge obtained not by mere intellection, but by the blended exercise of the understanding and the heart, when in agreement with the understanding and heart of God ; the knowledge which fills the upright mind, by its inwardly apprehending and loving the divine excellence. This being the end of all material and intellectual light is properly the light of men ; the glory and joy of our rational nature. The source of this light, which shone in man at his creation, purely and perfectly, was in that life in the Logos, of which we have been speaking. It was the communication of that divine life from the Logos to man, that made him the subject of this light. Even as in the new-creation by grace, it is by the soul's partaking again of this same life in Christ, that it acquires the light of the knowledge of the divine glory.* Human teaching may impart the light of external knowledge, the knowledge contained in definitions ; but that sort of knowledge, in which the true light of men consists, is not obtained, until a union takes place between God and the soul ; it is by virtue of that union, that the soul obtains those views of divine things with which it is transported on the day when it is born into the kingdom of God.

This recital concerning Christ in his preëxistent state, closes with these words : " And the light shineth in darkness, and the darkness comprehended it not." No note need be taken of the variation of the tense, since, as it has been justly remarked, nothing is a more distinguishing particularity of the style of this Evangelist, than the confounding of the tenses. The strain of the context manifestly requires, that the past time be understood in both clauses of the sentence. The declaration relates to the Logos in his preëxistent state, and to man as apostate and depraved.

Darkness here means human nature amid the ruins of the fall. Darkness strictly, expresses a state, but the abstract is here taken for the concrete. Man in the darkness of his apostate condition is spoken of, as if he were darkness itself. This mode of speaking concerning depraved man is not peculiar to this writer. Paul declares that Christians before their conversion were

---

* 1 John 4: 7, 8.

darkness : " Ye were sometime darkness, but now are ye light in the Lord." The present testimony then, referring to man as alienated from the divine life, and therefore involved in spiritual darkness, affirms the renewed love of the Logos to him, in these circumstances of guilt and misery. When by transgression he made himself darkness, he who was the light of his soul in innocence, did not forsake him, but continued to shine within him, to the end that he might recover himself by repentance. Through the period before the flood and through all subsequent time, man, a few individuals excepted, was darkness ; but the Logos continued to shine in the world. He shed some rays, even as he now does,* among the most ignorant of mankind, enlightening in some degree every one who came into the world ; but they were shed generally in vain ; the darkness which they penetrated did not comprehend them. The Logos was in the world, but the world knew him not ; he came to his own, but his own received him not. They preferred the creature to the Creator, the finite to the infinite, the visible to the invisible, through the madness of sin. The great mass of all nations made no improvement of the light which shone amongst them and within them, but as Paul teaches, suppressed or perverted it, through their unrighteousness. Even at this day the light is shining in darkness, and the darkness comprehendeth it not. Is the reader acquainted with no individual in whom this Scripture is verified ? Does not his own experience teach him, what the language before us means ? It is true in respect to himself, that the light has been shining in darkness, showing him his immortality, his relations to God, his sin, his danger, his misery, the way of peace, and motives to effort, of infinite power. Is it not also true, that in his case, the darkness has not comprehended the light ; that he has seen as if he had seen not, and perceived as if he had understood not ; that his immortality he has practically disbelieved, his relations to God violated ; his sin he has loved ; his danger disregarded ; his misery not lamented, the way of peace not pursued, motives vast as eternity resisted ?—Where is the man who can seriously reflect on his own moral history, and not know from an interpreter within his own

---

* Some have thought that the constant shining of the Divine light, was intended to be expressed by the use of the present tense, in the first clause ; but we rest not our remark on this criticism, for a reason before given.

breast, what is meant, by the light shining in darkness, and the darkness not comprehending it?

Our reflections on these sublime testimonies concerning CHRIST PREEXISTENT, have deepened our impressions of the truth and importance of the three following statements.

First, That this world's opposition to the christian religion shows it to be a world in rebellion against its own Maker. The author of the christian faith was the author of the universe. The founder of the christian church was he who laid the foundations of the earth and meted out the heavens with a span. The institutions, laws, documents, doctrines of Christianity, rest on the authority of Him who upholds the pillars of creation. To oppose this religion is to lift the hand of treason against the throne of the Almighty. The world have opposed and still do oppose it. "Theophilus of Antioch compared the little christian church in the wide domains of heathenism, to verdant islands in a great raging ocean. Thus too within the pale of Christianity has the congregation of the regenerate always stood in relation to the children of the world." * The testimony of this fact concerning the moral state of mankind, renders a denial of their deep depravity, their "desperate wickedness," the highest possible proof of it.

Secondly, That it is not Christianity, that assigns simple godhead or deity as the cause of the creation. It is coming short of the teaching of Christianity on this subject, only to say, the universe is the workmanship of God. It is rejecting Christianity, in this great article, to exclude Christ's handiwork from the causal influence of the creation. Christianity tells us of a Logos as well as of a Deity, and makes the Deity in the Logos the author of the world's existence. They who assert that God apart from the Logos, or Deity out of Christ, was the maker of the universe, contradict the Scriptures in the most explicit manner. Intimations, that the creative power dwelt in a Divine essence which was pluri-personal, are contained in the narrative of the creation given by Moses,† and throughout the Old Testa-

* Tholuck.

† "After the closest attention that I can give," says Dr. Smith, Scrip. Test. Vol. I. p. 483, "the impression on my mind is favorable to the opinion, that this peculiarity of idiom,—(the use of plural nouns, especially *Elohim* in application to the Divine Being) *originated* in a

ment; but in the New Testament, the subject is set forth in the clearest light, and the express assertion made that the Creator was Deity in the Logos, or God in Christ.

The doctrine that simple Deity was the Creator of the universe, ought never to be published, and if published never received, as a doctrine of Christianity; it may be naturalism, but it is not the gospel. Nay, if it pretend to be Christianity, it is another and a rival gospel, which no true friend of Christ can do otherwise than disavow and condemn.

Thirdly, That the greatest of all wonders is the love of Christ for man. That our maker should for our sakes make himself a man—that he who dwelt in eternity with God,—glorious in all the perfections of the Deity himself, and happy in the complacency of the other Divine persons,—should, to recover us from sin and deserved death, take upon him the form of a servant, and be made in the likeness of sinful flesh; and being found in fashion as a man, should humble himself and become obedient unto death, even the death of the cross—

> " O for this love let rocks and hills
>   Their lasting silence break,
>   And all harmonious human tongues
>   The Saviour's praises speak."

design to *intimate* a plurality in the nature of the one God; and that thus in connection with other circumstances calculated to suggest the same conception, it was intended to excite and prepare the minds of men for the more full declaration of this unsearchable mystery, which should in proper time be granted."—Any exposition of Gen 1: 26, or of the narrative of the creative process given in that chapter, which does not admit this intimation, should, we think, be rejected as unsatisfactory.

ARTICLE VIII.

A BRIEF REPORT OF TRAVELS IN PALESTINE AND THE ADJACENT REGIONS IN 1838; UNDERTAKEN FOR THE ILLUSTRATION OF BIBLICAL GEOGRAPHY, BY THE REV. PROF. E. ROBINSON AND REV. E. SMITH. PREPARED AND READ BEFORE THE GEOGRAPHICAL SOCIETY OF BERLIN, DEC. 8, 1838, AND JAN. 6, 1839.*

By Edward Robinson, D. D. Prof. of Bib. Lit. New York Theol. Sem. New York.

THE journey of which the following is a brief account, had entered into all my plans of life for the last fifteen years. So long ago as 1832, it was the subject of conversation between myself and the Rev. Eli Smith, then on a visit to the United States; and the same general plan of the journey was then marked out, which we have been permitted during the present year to execute. I count it fortunate for myself and for the interests of Biblical science, that I was thus able to secure the company of one, who, by his familiar and accurate knowledge of the Arabic language, by his experience as a traveller in Persia and Armenia, and by his acquaintance with the people of Syria, was so well qualified to remove the difficulties and overcome the obstacles usually attendant upon oriental travel.

---

* [In a letter to the Editor, Prof. Robinson remarks on this Article, that, "having been prepared for a purely scientific Society, there is perhaps less of scriptural reference in it than would otherwise be desirable." It is, however, so rich in its illustrations of scripture scenery, names and history, that no reader of the Bible will fail to peruse it with interest, and the intelligent Christian will readily perceive most of the points of scripture history which it elucidates and supports.

Prof. Robinson was better prepared by previous study, than any other modern traveller in Palestine, for an intelligent investigation of the antiquities of the Holy Land. His authority, therefore, may be deemed conclusive on many points which had been involved in doubt; and we are happy to be the organ of communicating to the American public this rich and interesting outline of his discoveries and observations. It affords us pleasure to add that the author is diligently employed, in Berlin, during the present winter, in preparing a full journal of his travels for the press; and is expected to resume his labors in the New York Theol. Seminary in course of the ensuing summer.—ED.]

I embarked at Trieste Dec. 1, 1837 ; and after spending a fortnight at Athens proceeded to Alexandria and Cairo. The months of January and February 1838, were mostly spent in a voyage up the Nile as far as Thebes. Returning to Cairo in the last days of February, I found Mr. Smith just arrived ; and we now entered on the preparations necessary for our long journey through the desert. We visited mean while the pyramids of Gizeh, the earliest and most vast of all human monuments ; and were ready to set off on our journey on the 12th of March.

I. From Cairo to Mount Sinai and Akabah.

It had been our wish to take a somewhat circuitous route from Cairo to Suez, descending along the eastern branch of the Nile as far as the province Sharkiyeh, and thence along the valley of the ancient canal to the head of the Gulf of Suez. But our time was limited, and we were compelled to take the usual and shortest route, that of Ankebiyeh, the same which Burckhardt travelled in 1816. Our party consisted of three Americans, two Egyptian servants, and five Arabs of the Towara, who have the exclusive right of conducting travellers from Egypt to Mount Sinai. They were the owners of the nine camels we had hired, and were all under the direction of Besharah our guide, one of the men who accompanied Laborde. Just without the city, near the splendid but now neglected tombs of the Kalifs, we halted for a time, to adjust the loads of the camels for the journey, which could not so well be done in the narrow streets of the city. Then we launched forth into the desert ; and traveling onward until darkness overtook us, we pitched our tent for the night in a shallow Wady. This term, in the desert, means a shallow bed, through which the waters of the rainy season are carried off; while in uneven or mountainous regions, it is also applied to the deepest and broadest vallies. It was a new and exciting feeling, to find ourselves thus alone in the midst of the desert, in the true style of oriental travel ; carrying with us our *house*, our provisions, and our supply of water for many days ; and surrounded by camels and the wild sons of the desert, in a region where the eye could find nought to rest upon but dreary desolation. It was a scene which had often taken possession of my youthful imagination ; but which I had not dared to hope would ever be realized.

The desert of Suez is not sandy ; its surface for the most part is a hard gravel, often strewed with pebbles.   Numerous Wadys or water-courses intersect its surface, flowing mostly towards the N. W. to the borders of the Nile or the valley of the ancient canal.   In all these Wadys there are usually to be found scattered tufts of herbs, or shrubs, on which the camels browse as they pass along ; and which serve also as their pasturage, when turned loose at night.   During the present season there had been no rain ; and the whole appearance of the desert and its Wadys, was dry and parched.

Nor did the desert change its character for the better, as we approached Suez.   Hills and mountains, and the long narrow strip of salt water were indeed around and before us ; but not a tree, nor scarcely a shrub, and not one green thing was to be seen in the whole circle of vision.   Nor is a drop of fresh water to be obtained.   All the water with which Suez is supplied for personal use, is brought from three hours' distance across the gulf ; and is so brackish as to be scarcely drinkable.——In the desert we had frequent instances of the *mirage*, presenting the appearance of lakes of water and islands ; and as we began to descend towards Suez, it was difficult to distinguish between these appearances and the distant real waters of the Red Sea.

We reached Suez on the fourth day from Cairo ; pitched our tent on the shore without the walls ; and remained there twenty four hours.   Our attention was naturally directed to the circumstances connected with the passage of the Israelites through the Sea.   We saw the gulf here twice at low water.   Extensive shoals, apparently of coral, stretch out into it for two miles or more below Suez.   These are left bare at the ebb, except a narrow winding channel, by which small vessels come quite up to the town.   A narrow bay runs up for some distance North of Suez.   Anciently the waters of the gulf must have extended much further above the city than at present ; for obviously a large tract has been filled up by sand drifted in from the Northeastern desert.   This tract is still overflowed, when the waters are driven up the gulf by a strong S. E. wind.   Just above Suez, the narrow bay is daily forded at low water.

Our minds were satisfied, in general, that the Israelites must have journeyed from the land of Goshen to the Red Sea, along the valley of the ancient canal, this being the only route on which they could obtain water ; and, also, that they must have passed through the Sea at or near Suez, directly from the great desert plain which extends for ten or twelve miles West and North behind the city. Of course it is impossible to fix the exact point of their passage; but it may not improbably have taken place lower down and near the edge of the present shoals; where even now, at very low tides, the Arabs sometimes wade across. It must be remembered, that the miracle was wrought through the instrumentality of a strong East (or N. E.) wind, which here would act directly to drive out the waters; but would not so act in any other part of the gulf. There are also great difficulties connected with the rapid passage of so great a multitude through the sea at any point where it is wider.

Leaving Suez late the next day, we took our course around the head of the gulf, the better to observe the features of the country. We pitched our tent at night over against Suez, but somewhat lower down, not far from the place where the Israelites probably came out upon the eastern shore. Here, at our evening devotions, and near the spot where it was composed and first sung, we read and felt in its full force, the magnificent triumphal song of Moses : " The Lord hath triumphed gloriously ; the horse and his rider he hath thrown into the sea !" A desert plain extends along the eastern shore of the gulf for nearly fifty miles, bounded on the East by a range of hills or mountains twelve or fifteen miles from the coast. At 3½ hours from the northern end are the brackish fountains of Moses (Ayûn Mûsa) ; and then for eighteen hours or about forty-five miles further, no water is found. This is probably the desert of Shur or Etham, in which the Israelites journied for three days without water. Then occurs the bitter fountain Hawara, corresponding to the ancient Marah ; and two hours further is the Wady Ghŭrŭndel, probably Elim, where are still water and a few palm-trees. From opposite this point a ridge of chalky mountains, Jebel Hŭmmâm, runs along the sea for some distance, and cuts off all passage along the shore. The Israelites must therefore of necessity have passed by the present road inside of these mountains, to the head of Wady Tayibeh, and so down this Wady to the gulf, where they next encamped " by the Red Sea." Thence they would seem to have followed the lower road to Mt. Sinai, through the Wadys Mukatteb and Feirân ; but the stations are mentioned so indefinitely, that no hope remains of their ever being identified.

We took the upper road to Sinai, which leads across a portion of the great sandy tract lying between the high northern

ridge Et-Tih, and the more southern clusters of Sinai.   Et-Tih
is a long level ridge of sandstone, stretching across the whole
peninsula.   Laborde asserts with emphasis that there is only a
single pass through this ridge ; but our Arabs, who had also
been his guides, described to us repeatedly no less than *four*
such passes, three of which are frequented roads to Gaza and
Syria.——We turned aside also to the right a short distance, to
visit the solitary and mysterious monuments of Sûrâbit el-Kha-
dîm.   Travellers have supposed these monuments to be tomb-
stones.   They are evidently of Egyptian origin, being covered
with hieroglyphics indicating a high antiquity ; but they have
nothing of the character of an Egyptian cemetery.

We approached the central granite mountains of Sinai, not by
the more usual and easy route of Wady Shekh, which winds
around and enters from the East ; but following a succession of
Wadys we crossed Wady Shekh and entered the higher granite
formation by a shorter route, directly from the N. N. W. through
a steep, rocky, and difficult pass, between rugged, blackened
cliffs, 800 to 1000 feet high.   Approaching in this direction,
we were surprised and delighted, to find ourselves, after two
hours, crossing the whole length of a fine plain ; from the southern end of which that part of Sinai *now* called Horeb rises per-
pendicularly in dark and frowning majesty.   This plain is over
two miles in length, and nearly two thirds of a mile broad,
sprinkled with tufts of herbs and shrubs, like the Wadys of the
desert.   It is wholly enclosed by dark granite mountains,——
stern, naked, splintered peaks and ridges, from 1000 to 1500
feet high.   On the East of Horeb a deep and very narrow valley runs in like a cleft, as if in continuation of the S. E. corner
of the plain.   In this stands the convent, at the distance of a
mile from the plain ; and the deep verdure of its fruit-trees and
cypresses is seen as the traveller approaches,——an oasis of beauty amid scenes of the sternest desolation.   On the West of Horeb, there runs up a similar valley, parallel to the former.   It is
called El-Leja, and in it stands the deserted convent El-Erbayin,
with a garden of olive and other fruit-trees, not visible from the
plain.

The name *Sinai* is at present applied, generally, to the lofty
ridge running from N. N. W. to S. S. E. between the two narrow vallies just described.   The northern part, or lower summit, is the present Horeb, overlooking the plain.   About 2¼ or
three miles South of this, the ridge rises and ends in a higher

point; this is the present *summit of Sinai*, the Jebel Mûsa of the Arabs; which however is not visible from any part of the plain. West, or rather W. S. W. of the valley El-Leja, is the still higher ridge and summit of Mount St. Catharine.

The plain above mentioned is in all probability the spot, where the congregation of Israel were assembled to receive the law; and the mountain impending over it, the present Horeb, was the scene of the awful phenomena in which the law was given. As to the present summit of Sinai, there is little reason to suppose that it had any connection with the giving of the law; and still less the higher peaks of St. Catharine. I know not when I have felt a thrill of stronger emotion, than when in first crossing the plain, the dark precipices of Horeb rising in solemn grandeur before us, I became aware of the entire adaptedness of the scene to the purposes for which it was chosen by the great Hebrew legislator.

We were kindly received at the convent, after being hoisted to its narrow entrance; and remained there five days, visiting in the interval the summits of Sinai, Horeb, and St. Catharine. As my companion could speak modern Greek with some fluency, we found peculiar favor in the eyes of the good old Superior; to whom the Arabic was almost an unknown tongue. He carried his civility so far, as to accompany us to the top of Sinai and Horeb; but the next day his fervor quailed before the more arduous task of ascending Mount St. Catharine; and he preferred waiting our return at the convent El-Erbayin, where we had lodged.

We left the convent March 29th, on our way to Akabah. We had made our contract at Cairo for camels from that place to Akabah; but we now had in part different men. Our conductor now was Tuweileb, the faithful guide of Rüppell, Linant, and other recent travellers. Our route was again the same as that of Burckhardt in 1816, the usual one to Akabah; descending to the coast of the Eastern Gulf at the fountain Nuweibia, and thence along the shore quite to Akabah. Near this coast, and bearing W. S. W. from the castle of Akabah, is the small island covered with ruins, formerly the citadel of Ailah. It is called by the Towara Arabs, Kureiyeh, which signifies a "town," whether inhabited or in ruins. Out of this Laborde has made *Graia!*

The great valley El-Araba, which we crossed in order to reach the castle, is here about five miles wide; and its general

course is N. N. E.   It is sandy as far as the eye can reach ;
and there is in it no trace of the bed of any stream, not even of
a wintry torrent.   The little water which ever flows in it, appears to enter the gulf at the N. W. corner.   The foundations
and mounds of ancient Ailah (Elath), and the present castle of
Akabah, are on the eastern side, near the shore.

We were well received at the castle by the Aga or governor, to whom we had official letters.   It had been our intention to go from here directly to Wady Mûsa, along the great
valley El-Araba, under the guidance of Hussein, Shekh of the
tribe of Alawîn, who have this territory in possession.   But
learning that he was encamped at some days' distance, and that
we could not hope to set off with him under six or seven days,
we changed our plan, and determined to keep our good Towara guides and take the road across the great Western desert
in the direction of Gaza and Hebron.   We were the more induced to do this, because we everywhere heard a bad character
of the said Shekh Hussein ; and because too this was a route as
yet untrodden by modern travellers.

II. FROM AKABAH TO JERUSALEM.

We left Akabah late in the afternoon of April 5th, and re-
crossing the plain of Wady Araba, began to ascend the western
mountains by the great Hadj route.   We soon encamped for
the night ; and from this point we had *seven* long days' journey
to Hebron.   The ascent afterward is steep and difficult.   The
way is almost literally strewed with the bones of camels, and
skirted by the graves of pilgrims ; all testifying to the difficulty
of the pass.   On arriving at the top of the pass, we soon came
out upon the great plateau of the Western desert ; and found
ourselves higher than the mountain peaks which we had seen
from below, and through which we had just ascended.   Not far
from the top of the pass we left the Hadj route ; and turning off
in a direction about N. N. W. we launched forth again into
"the great and terrible wilderness."

For the first two days, the general character of this desert
was similar to that between Cairo and Suez,—a vast unbounded plain, a hard gravelly soil, irregular ridges of limestone hills
in various directions, the mirage, and especially the Wadys or
water-courses.   All our Arabs gave to this part of the desert
the name Et-Tih, the desert of wandering.   The Wadys are

here frequent ; at first they all ran N. W. into the main water-course of this part of the desert, Wady Jerâfeh ; which, having its head far to the South, runs in a N. E. course to join the valley El Araba nearly opposite to Wady Mûsa. We crossed Wady Jerâfeh about the middle of the second day ; and were struck with the traces of the large volume of water which apparently flows through it in the winter season. On the morning of the third day we reached the water-summit (Wasserscheide) of the desert ; after which all the Wadys run in a westerly direction into the great water-course which drains the more western part of the desert, and flows down to the sea near El Arish.

Almost from the time we entered upon this vast plain, we had before us, as a landmark, a high conical mountain, apparently isolated, along the western base of which we were to pass. It bears the name Araif en-Nâkah ; and a lower ridge extends from it eastward. For nearly three days this mountain of the desert was before us. As we approached it on the third day, the country became rolling and uneven, and the hills more frequent. After passing the mountain, our course turned more towards the N. N. E. and the character of the desert was changed. On our right, to the northward of Jebel Araif, was a mountainous district, composed of irregular limestone ridges, running in various directions, and occupying the whole region quite to Wady Araba, as we had afterwards an opportunity of learning. This mountainous district is penetrated by none of the roads which lead from the vicinity of the Red Sea to Gaza or Jerusalem ; but these roads all fall into the one we were travelling before reaching Jebel Araif, or not far from that mountain. All these circumstances go to show, that our route could be no other than the ancient Roman road from Ailah to Hebron and Jerusalem ; which also, like the present, could not well have been anything more than a caravan route for beasts of burden.

From this mountainous district many broad Wadys flow down towards the West ; and between them are elevated ridges of table land, which the road crosses. We made frequent and minute inquiry after the names of places or stations, which are known to have existed anciently on this Roman road. Of the more southern ones, Rasa and Gypsaria, we could find no trace. Early on the fourth day we crossed a broad Wady called El-Lussân, marking perhaps the site of ancient Lysa ; but we could discover no trace of ruins. In the forenoon of the fifth day, we diverged a little to the left, to visit ruins which had been described to us under the names Aujeh and Abdeh ; and which are doubtless the remains of the ancient Eboda.   They consist of the walls of a large Greek church, and an extensive fortress, both situated upon a long hill or ridge overlooking a broad plain covered with shrubs and tufts of herbs.   Connected with the fortress are cisterns and deep wells, walled up with uncommonly good masonry.   On the S. side of the hill and below, are the ruins of houses ; surrounded by traces of extensive ancient cultivation.

We were now crossing a more sandy portion of the desert ; and in the afternoon of that day, we had our first specimen of the Simûm, or South wind of the desert.   It came over us with violence like the glow of an oven, and filled the air with fine particles of dust and sand so as to obscure the sun, and render it difficult to see objects only a few rods distant.   This continued for about four hours.   We encamped in the Wady Ruheibeh, where we had never heard of ruins.   But on ascending the hill on our left, we discovered the remains of a city not much less than two miles in circuit.   The houses had been mostly built of hewn stone; there were several public buildings and many cisterns.   But the whole is now thrown together in unutterable confusion ; and it would seem as if the city had been suddenly overthrown by some tremendous earthquake.   What ancient city this can have been, I have not yet been able to learn.   The Arabic name suggests the Rehoboth of Scripture, the name of one of Isaac's wells (Gen. 26: 22) ; but the other circumstances do not correspond.

The Wady Ruheibeh opens out towards the North into a fine plain, covered with grass and herbs and bushes ; in crossing which our ears were regaled with the carols of the lark and the song of the nightingale, all indicating our approach to a more fertile region.   Towards noon of the sixth day, we reached Khŭlasah, the sight of ancient Elusa.   It was a city of at least two miles in circuit.   The foundations of buildings are everywhere to be traced ; and several large unshapen piles of stones seem to mark the site of public edifices.   Fragments of columns are occasionally seen ; but no cisterns.   A public well, which is still in use, seems to have supplied the city.

After crossing another elevated plateau, the character of the surface was again changed.   We came upon an open rolling country ; all around were swelling hills, covered in ordinary seasons with grass and rich pasturage, though now arid and parched with drought. We now came to Wady Seba; and on the north side of its water-course we had the gratification of discovering (April 12th) the site of ancient Beersheba, the celebrated border city of Palestine, still bearing in Arabic the name of Bir Seba. Near the water-course are two circular wells of excellent water, more than forty feet deep. They are both surrounded with drinking-troughs of stone for the use of camels and flocks; such as doubtless were used of old for the flocks which then fed on the adjacent hills.——Ascending the low hills north of the wells, we found them strewed with the ruins of former habitations, the foundations of which are distinctly to be traced. These ruins extend over a space half a mile long by a quarter of a mile broad.——Here then is the place, where Abraham and Isaac and Jacob often lived! Here Samuel made his sons judges; and from here Elijah wandered out into the southern desert, and sat down under the Rethem, or shrub of broom, just as our Arabs sat down under it every day and every night! Over these swelling hills the flocks of the patriarch roved by thousands;—we now found only a few camels, asses, and goats.

From Bir Seba to Hebron we travelled 12¼ hours; here equivalent to about thirty miles. The general course was N. E. by E. After an hour and a half we came out upon a wide open plain, covered with grass, but now parched with drought. Fields of wheat and barley were seen all around; and before us were hills, the beginning of the mountains of Judah. At Dhoheriyeh, the first Syrian village, our good Towara left us; and we parted from them not without the kindest feelings and deep regret. For thirty days they had now been our companions and guides, and not the slightest difficulty had occurred between us. The hills and pastures around Dhoheriyeh were covered with mingled flocks of sheep and goats, and herds of neat cattle, horses, asses, and camels, in the true patriarchal style of ancient days.

We took other camels and proceeded to Hebron. Here the "pool" over which David hung up the assassins of Ishbosheth, still remains, and fixes the site of the ancient city. The cave of Macphelah cannot well have been within the city; and therefore the present mosque cannot cover its site. We could not but notice the fertility of the surrounding vallies, full of fields of grain and of vineyards yielding the largest and finest clusters of all Palestine; and likewise the rich pasturage of the hills, over which were scattered numerous flocks and herds.   Yet to a careless observer the country, in general, can only appear sterile ; for the limestone rocks every where come out upon the surface, and are strown over it in large masses to such a degree, that a more stony or rocky region is rarely to be seen.

We took the direct road to Jerusalem.   It is laid with stones in many places, and is doubtless the ancient road, which patriarchs and kings of old have often trod.   But it is only a path for beasts ; no wheels have ever passed there.   We hurried onward, and reached the Holy City at sunset, April 14th, just before the closing of the gates on the evening before Easter Sunday.

III. JERUSALEM.

The feelings of the christian traveller on approaching Jerusalem for the first time, can be better conceived, than described. Mine were strongly excited.   Before us, as we approached, lay Zion, the Mount of Olives, the vales of Hinnom and Jehosaphat, and other objects of the deepest interest.   I beheld them now with my own eyes ; they all seemed familiar to me, as if the realization of a former dream ; and it was almost a painful interruption, when my companion, with the kindest motives, began to point out and name the different objects in view.

Our journey *to* Palestine was now complete ; and our researches and travels *in* Palestine were to begin.   In respect to these we adopted for our future guidance the two following principles, viz. (1) To direct our researches chiefly to those parts of the country which former travellers had never visited ; and (2) To obtain information, as far as possible, not from the legends of monks and other foreigners, but directly from the native Arabs of the land.—We remained for three weeks in Jerusalem, in the house of our missionary friend and countryman, the Rev. Mr. Lanneau ; and afterwards made that city the central point from which to set off on excursions to different parts of the country.   In the mean time we diligently explored every part of the city ; and even here saw or heard of several things, which to us at least were new.

In approaching Jerusalem from Hebron, I was struck with the very rapid descent of the Valley of Hinnom, and the great depth of the Vale of Jehosaphat, into which the former opens. In the city itself, I was prepared, from the descriptions of most travellers, to find the houses miserable, the streets filthy, and the population squalid. But in all these respects I was agreeably disappointed. The houses are better built and the streets cleaner, than those of Alexandria, Smyrna, or Constantinople. The hills and vallies which marked the different quarters of the ancient city, are still distinctly visible. The valley of the Tyropoeum may be traced from its head near the Yaffa gate, to its foot at the pool of Siloam. The hills of Zion, Akra, Bezetha, and Moriah are yet distinct and marked. The latter, on which stood the ancient temple, is now occupied by the mosque of Omar and the extensive court or area around it.

One of the earliest objects of our attention was naturally this area, in reference to its antiquity and connexion with the ancient temple. It is an elevated plateau or terrace, nearly in the form of a parallelogram, supported by and within massive walls built up from the vallies or lower ground on all sides. The southern wall is about sixty feet high. The upper part of these external walls, is obviously of modern origin; but it is also not less easy to perceive, that the lower portions, for the most part, are of an earlier date. These are composed, generally, of very large stones, many of them twenty feet and more in length by five or six feet thick, hewn in a peculiar manner. At the first view of these walls I was led to the conviction that these lower portions had belonged to the ancient temple, and were to be referred back at least to the time of Herod, if not to the days of Nehemiah or Solomon. This conviction was afterwards strengthened, by our discovering, near the S. W. corner, in the western wall, the remains, or rather the foot of an immense arch, springing out from the wall in the direction towards Mt. Zion, across the valley of the Tyropoeum. The traces of this arch are too distinct and definite to be mistaken; and it can only have belonged to the bridge, which, according to Josephus, led from this part of the temple area to the Xystus on Mt. Zion; thus proving incontestably the antiquity of that portion of the wall from which it springs.

We then examined the remarkable tower in the citadel near the Yaffa gate, which even to the unpractised eye bears strong marks of antiquity. Former travellers have already regarded this as the Hippicus of Herod; and we found every reason to assent to this conclusion. So far as we could discover, the lower part of the tower is wholly solid, as described by Josephus; at least there is no known or visible entrance to it, either from above or below.

The present walls of the city were built about 300 years ago; as appears from numerous Arabic inscriptions. Remains of the former wall, which probably existed in the time of the crusades, are still visible on the outside N. W. of the Yaffa gate; also on the North side of the city and in the interior of the N. W. corner. Of the *ancient* wall around Zion, traces may yet be seen for some distance in the scarped rocks below the S. W. brow of Zion. On the high ground North of the N. W. corner of the city, we discovered evident traces of what must have been the *third* or exterior wall described by Josephus in this quarter, erected after the time of Christ. Here must have stood the tower Psephinos; and from this point we were able to trace the foundation of the same ancient wall for a considerable distance further in a N. E. direction.

Of the *second* wall of Josephus, which at the time of the crucifixion was the exterior wall of the city on this side, we could find no remaining traces; unless it be two square ancient towers which we discovered connected with the wall inside the gate of Damascus, one on each side of the gate. These towers are built up of large stones precisely like those mentioned above as belonging to the ancient temple-walls. They have been much injured in building the modern wall of the city; but are evidently ancient, and apparently older than Hippicus. They were, most probably, the guard-houses of an ancient gate upon this spot; and this could well only have belonged to the said second wall. If this hypothesis be correct, it will go far to decide the question as to the site of the church of the Holy Sepulchre; which must then have fallen within this wall, and so within the ancient city. Indeed the church stands upon the very ridge of the hill Akra, which according to Josephus and to every probability, must have formed part of the lower city and been enclosed within the second wall.

Another object of our attention, was the supply of water in and around the city. At the present day Jerusalem is supplied almost wholly with rain-water, preserved in cisterns cut in the solid rock on which the houses stand. Almost every house has one or more cisterns; that in which we resided, had no less than four very large ones. The ancient city was probably supplied in the same manner. With a little attention there can never be any want of water within the walls. The aqueduct which comes from Solomon's pools beyond Bethlehem, brings water only to the mosque of Omar.——Outside of the city, besides the ancient reservoirs, there are wells in various places, some with water and some without. The brook Kidron in the valley of Jehosaphat, flows only when the rain-water descends into it from the adjacent hills. Fountains of running water exist only in this valley ; and of these there are three, viz. (1) The fountain of the Virgin, or of Siloam, just south of the site of the temple ; (2) The pool of Siloam, just within the entrance of the Tyropoeum ; and (3) The well of Nehemiah, or of Job, opposite the entrance of the Vale of Hinnom. This last is a deep well of living water, which in the rainy season overflows ; it is beyond doubt the En Rogel of Scripture. The pool of Siloam is wholly artificial, and receives its waters from the fountain of the Virgin through a subterraneous channel cut through the solid rock. We crawled through this channel and measured it. From this pool the water flows down still a steep descent, and is lost among gardens. The fountain of the Virgin is also evidently an artificial excavation in the rock ; but whence the water is derived, is a mystery. It has a sweetish and slightly brackish taste ; and flows irregularly, or only at irregular intervals. We were witnesses of this irregular flow ; and were told by the women who came for water, that sometimes during summer it ceases to flow for several weeks, when on a sudden the water comes gushing out again in abundance.

Ancient writers have spoken of a fountain of living water as existing under the temple ; though their assertions have in general obtained little credit. Soon after our arrival in Jerusalem, we were told of a similar fountain under the present mosque of Omar ; the waters of which were used to supply a Turkish bath in the vicinity of the mosque. We went to the bath, and found two men drawing water from a deep well. They told us, that the water flows into the well from a passage cut in the rock and leading under the mosque, where is a chamber and a living fountain. In summer, when the water is so low as not to flow out into the well, they go down and bring it out by hand. The taste of the water is precisely similar to that of the fountain in the valley below. We made all our preparations to descend into the well and examine the fountain ; but were hindered at the time ; and were unable afterwards to resume the investigation.——Is perhaps the water of this fountain brought down by a subterraneous channel from some higher point? Is there a connexion between this fountain under the mosque and that in the valley below ; and is the irregular flow of the latter in some way dependent on this circumstance? These questions may, not improbably, at some future time, be answered in the affirmative.

When we arrived at Jerusalem, war was raging between the Druses, and the forces of the Pasha. The city was full of rumors; no one knew where Ibrahim Pasha was; and it was said his troops had been beaten. In this state of things the unquiet spirits of the land began to rouse themselves; several murders and robberies were committed on pilgrims and travelling merchants; and for a time it was doubtful, whether we should be able to travel at all in the country without an armed guard. But soon the certain news arrived, that Ibrahim was at Damascus, and had defeated the Druses. After this, all was again still; and we travelled through the length and breadth of the land without fear or accident,—indeed with the same feeling of security as in England or Germany.

As if we were to have a specimen of all the evils of the oriental world, in a few days after our arrival in the Holy City, the plague broke out,—at first doubtfully, then decidedly, though mildly. Other travellers left the city immediately; and some who were on their way thither, turned back. We continued our investigations without interruption; and a kind Providence preserved us from the danger. On the 19th of May the city was shut up, and none permitted to go out; we had left it two days before, on a long excursion.

Indeed, during the whole journey, although surrounded by war, pestilence, and quarantines, we were enabled to pass through them all without harm or hindrance,—without being detained from these causes even for an hour.

IV. EXCURSION TO THE NORTH EAST AND NORTH OF JERUSALEM, TO MICHMASH, BETHEL, ETC.

Our first excursion from Jerusalem was made on horseback, and occupied two days, the 4th and 5th of May. We were accompanied by friends from the city, and made in all a party of six, besides our attendants. Our road led at first N. E. over the ridge which extends northward from the Mount of Olives; and after crossing several Wadys and hills, we came in about an hour to Anâta, the ancient Anathoth, the birth-place of Jeremiah. It is a miserable village, situated on a high ridge which slopes gradually to the East, with a deep valley on the North.

From this point there is a wide view over the whole eastern slope of the mountainous region ; including also the valley of the Jordan and the northern part of the Dead Sea. The whole tract is made up of deep rugged valleys running eastward, with broad ridges of uneven table land between, often rising into high points. The sides of the vallies are so steep, that in descending into them we were usually obliged to dismount from our horses. The whole district is a mass of limestone rock ; which everywhere juts out above the surface, and imparts to the whole land only the aspect of sterility and desolation. Yet wherever soil is found among the rocks, it is strong and fertile ; fields of grain appeared occasionally ; and fig-trees and olive-trees were scattered everywhere among the hills. Lower down the slope, towards the Jordan-valley, all is desert.— The region now before us was that alluded to in Isa. 10: 28 sq. where the approach of Sennecharib towards Jerusalem is described.

Proceeding from Anathoth northwards, and crossing two deep vallies, we came in eighty minutes to Jeba, the ancient Gibeah of Saul, situated also on high land with a deep valley on the North. West of this, on a conical hill near the Nablous road, is Râm, the ancient Ramah, now a deserted village. Northeast of Jeba, across the very deep valley lies Mŭkhmâs, the ancient Michmash, to which we came in about three quarters of an hour. In the bottom of the valley, directly between Jeba and Mŭkhmâs, are two conical hills, not very high, which are probably the scene of Jonathan's romantic adventure against the Philistines, recorded in 1 Sam. c. xiv.

From Michmash we continued our way northward to Deir Diwân, a large village lying also on the southern brow of a deep valley. In this vicinity must have been the site of ancient Ai. It probably lay a short distance South of the modern village ; where are still the remains of an ancient city, such as portions of wall, reservoirs for water, and sepulchres hewn in the rock. —Proceeding still northward from this village, crossing the valley which seemed deeper and more rugged than any of the rest, and following up a side-valley, we came at last to Tayibeh, a christian village situated on a lofty conical hill, about seventeen miles from Jerusalem. This spot affords a splendid view over the whole eastern slope, the vale of Jordan, the Belka, the Dead Sea, and the eastern mountains. Not far S. E. of Tayibeh is a village on a sharp, chalky, conical hill, still called Rŭmmon ;

probably the same Rock Rimmon to which the Benjamites fled after their defeat and slaughter by the other tribes.

We slept at Tayibeh under our tent ; preferring this to the small and uncomfortable dwellings of the inhabitants, infested as they are with vermin.   The next morning we bent our course nearly S. W. towards the site of ancient Bethel, which now bears in Arabic the name Beit-în.   We reached this spot in two hours from Tayibeh.   It lies just East of the Nablous road, 45 minutes N. E. of Bireh.   Here are ruins of very considerable extent, and among them the foundations of several churches ; lying on the point of a low hill between two shallow Wadys, which unite below and run off S. E. into a deep and rugged valley.   This was evidently a place of note in the early christian ages ; and apparently also in the days of the crusades.   It is now entirely uninhabited ; except that a few Arabs probably from some neighboring village, had pitched their tent here for a time.   In the western valley we spread our carpets and breakfasted on the grass ; within the limits of what was once an immense reservoir.   We obtained here from the Arabs butter of excellent quality, which might have done honor to the days when the flocks of Abraham and Jacob were pastured on these hills.

We passed on to Bireh, which lies on a ridge three hours from Jerusalem ; and thence nearly S. S. W. by Ram-Allah a large Christian village, to Jib, the Gabao of Josephus and the Gibeon of the Scriptures.   This was evidently an ancient stronghold, situated on a sharp rocky ridge rising in the midst of broad vallies or plains, which form an extensive basin, full of cornfields, vineyards, and orchards of olive and fig trees.

Half an hour S. E. of Jib towards Jerusalem, a lofty ridge runs from N. E. to S. W. on the summit of which, in the most conspicuous spot of the whole country, lies Nebi Samwil, a mosque containing the supposed tomb of the prophet Samuel, and usually assumed as marking the site of his birthplace, Ramathaim-Zophim.   The mosque was once a church, built in the form of a Latin cross, and evidently of the time of the crusades.   There are insuperable objections to the hypothesis of its being the birth place of Samuel, arising out of the story of Saul's journey in search of his father's asses, and the mention of Rachel's tomb near Bethlehem in the same connexion.   After long research we were disposed to regard this as the probable site of ancient Mizpeh.——Hence we returned in two hours to

Jerusalem ; crossing the valley of Turpentine (so called by monks and travellers), and ascending a branch Wady which runs down to it from the head of the valley of Jehosaphat, near the tombs of the Judges.

V. From Jerusalem to Carmel, Engeddi, the Jordan, etc.

A visit to Jericho and the Jordan is usually represented as attended with more danger than perhaps any other part of Palestine ; and most travellers therefore take with them a guard furnished by the governor of Jerusalem. But as the soldiers of the government would have been only objects of hatred to the unquiet Arabs whom we might chance to fall in with, we preferred to employ as guards and guides, some of the Arabs who live on the West side of the Dead Sea, who having formerly been themselves robbers, were well known to all the Arabs in the regions we intended to visit. We engaged the Shekh of the Taamra with four of his men ; and had every reason to be satisfied with their fidelity and intelligence.

The excursion on which we were now entering, occupied eight days. We left Jerusalem on the 8th of May, again on horseback, and proceeded by way of Bethlehem, and so along the aqueduct, to Solomon's pools ; and thence to the Frank mountain. This is a steep and lofty hill S. E. of Bethlehem, having the form of a truncated cone, and rising high above all the hills and ridges of the eastern slope. On its top are the remains of ancient fortifications ; and at its base on the North side are traces of an ancient town, probably Herodium built by Herod the Great, who also was buried there. Hence we turned S. W. towards Tekoa ; but pitched our tent for the night near the encampment of our Arabs. Here we had an opportunity of seeing the house-keeping of the desert. The grinding at the mill, the kneading and baking of bread, the care of the dairy, the churning of the milk,—all was carried on by the women in the open tents ; and it was the more interesting to us, as finely illustrating the frequent scriptural allusions to pastoral life.

A short ride brought us next morning, to the elevated site of Tekoa, which still retains its ancient name, and where are the traces of a city of considerable extent. We continued our course southward, inclining somewhat to the West ; and came after a long ride to Beni Naim, a lofty site with some remains of antiquity, about an hour and a half nearly East of Hebron. Passing on still to the South, we came in an hour and a quarter to Ziph, where the ruins are considerable. In about an hour further we reached Kûrmel the ancient Carmel, the scene of David's adventure with Nabal and Abigail. Here seems to have been an important city long after the Christian era. The ruins cover a large extent of ground, and there are remains of several large churches, besides a Roman fortress. About half an hour still further South, is Main, anciently Maon, on a conical hill overlooking the whole district. Hebron bore from here a little West of North ; and in the N. W. we could see the town of Yutta, or Jutta, the probable birthplace of John the Baptist.— Ziph, Carmel, and Maon lie on the East side of an elevated plain surrounded by low mountains, and affording fine tillage and pasturage. We read here the story of David and Nabal ; and were deeply struck with the truth of the Biblical descriptions of manners and customs almost literally and identically the same as they exist at the present day.

From Carmel our course lay directly East, to Ain Jiddi, the ancient Engeddi, on the western shore of the Dead Sea. The way was a continual descent, sometimes by steep passes, and again crossing deep Wadys. As we approached the sea, the region became more desert and desolate than ever. At every moment, we expected to arrive at the shore of the sea and on the level of its waters ; but the way at every step seemed longer and longer. At length, after a ride of seven hours, we came to the brow of the pass of Engeddi. Turning aside to what seemed a small knoll on our right, we found ourselves on the summit of a precipitous cliff overhanging Engeddi and the sea, at least 1500 feet above its waters. The Dead Sea lay before us in its vast deep chasm, shut in on both sides by precipitous mountains ; and, with its low projecting points and flat border towards the South, resembling much a long winding bay, or the estuary of a large river, when the tide is out and the shoals left dry. We descended to the shore by a pass more steep, rugged, and difficult than is to be found among the Alps, and pitched our tent near the fine large fountain which bursts out upon a narrow terrace still 400 feet above the sea. The water of the fountain is beautifully transparent ; but its temperature is 81° of Fahrenheit, or 20° of Reaumur.

The whole descent below the fountain was apparently once

terraced for gardens ; and the ruins of a town are seen on the right. The whole slope is still covered with trees and shrubs of a more southern clime ; among them we found the *ösher*, the fruit of which corresponds best to the ancient descriptions of the apples of Sodom. Nothing is needed but tillage to render this a most prolific spot. The soil is rich, the heat great, and water abundant.——The approach to the sea is here over a bank of pebbles several feet higher than the level of the water, as we saw it. The water of the sea is not entirely transparent ; but objects seen through it, appear as if seen through oil. It is most intensely salt and bitter ; and is exceedingly buoyant. The phenomena around the sea are such as might be expected from the nature of its waters and the character of the region round about, for the most part a naked, dreary desert ; but although we were for several days in its vicinity, we perceived no noisome smell and no pestiferous vapor arising from its waters. Of birds we saw many. Indeed at early dawn, the trees and rocks and air were full of the carols of the lark, the cheerful whistle of the quail, the call of the partridge, and the warbling of innumerable songsters ; while birds of prey were soaring and screaming in front of the cliffs above.

Next morning we were compelled to reascend the pass, in order to proceed northward along the shelving table land above ; the projecting cliffs cutting off all passage below along the water. At night we encamped again on a cliff 1000 feet above the sea, overhanging the fountain Türabeh, which is below on the shore. From this point both ends of the sea were visible. Pigeons were shooting over its surface ; and in the reeds around the brackish fountain below, frogs were merrily croaking. The scene of this evening was most romantic ; the full moon rose in splendor over the eastern mountains, and poured a flood of silvery light into the deep, dark chasm below. Our Arabs were sleeping around us ; only the tall pensive figure of the Shekh was seen, sitting before the door of the tent, his eyes intently fixed upon us as we wrote.——From various data, I judged the length of the sea to be about fifty miles ; its breadth cannot exceed ten or twelve miles.

We continued our course next day, descending again by a difficult pass ; and after travelling for several hours along the shore and over the plain, the soil of which is here in many parts like ashes, we arrived at the lower fords of the Jordan,——a deep turbid stream with a still but strong current. The river is here from 80 to 100 feet broad, winding its way through a cane-brake or jungle, which renders it inaccessible except in spots. It was now the time of wheat harvest in the valley; and we found the river, as of old, overflowing the banks of its ordinary channel; as was the case when the Israelites approached it, Josh. c. iii.   Hence we came in two hours to Jericho, passing on our way the fine fountain Hajleh, the probable site of the ancient Beth Hoglah, on the border between Judah and Benjamin.

Jericho and its environs reminded me strongly of Egypt and its villages.   The plain is rich, and susceptible of easy and abundant irrigation from copious fountains on its western side; it is easy of tillage, and enjoys a climate adapted to produce anything.   Yet it lies almost desert, or overgrown only by a species of thorny tree; and the village is the most wretched and filthy in Palestine.   Only one solitary palm now rears its head in what was once the city of Palmtrees.

From Jericho we took the ancient road to Bethel; proceeding at first N. W. by the fountain of Elisha, and so along the aqueduct at the base of the mountains to the copious fountains of Dûk; and then ascending the mountain by a steep pass. Our way continued up the shelving table-land westward, and along the ravines and precipices connected with a deep valley, to Deir Diwân above mentioned; and so further to Bethel. This is doubtless the road so often travelled by the Jewish prophets and kings.   Along it are found ancient cisterns at intervals, intended for the use of travellers.——From Bethel we returned over Bireh to Jerusalem (May 15th), visiting on our way the site of Ramah, and searching in vain for definite traces of ancient Mizpeh.

VI. Excursion to Gaza, Hebron, and Wady Mousa.

On returning to Jerusalem from our preceding excursion, we found the plague slowly, but constantly increasing; and it was rumored that the city was soon to be shut up.   We therefore remained but a single day, in order to make preparation for our longer journey to Wady Mousa.   This excursion was made only by Mr. Smith and myself with our servants; and lasted twenty-three days.   We set off May 17th on horses and mules; and on May 19th Jerusalem was shut up, and none suffered to go out without first performing a quarantine of seven days.

We had this time no guard, and no attendants save our mule-teers and a guide. We made at first a slight detour, in order to pass by Beit Jâla, a christian village half an hour N. W. of Bethlehem; and then continued S. W. across the mountains to the direct ancient road from Jerusalem to Eleutheropolis and Gaza, through a region as yet unvisited by modern travellers. At a distance on our right was the deep valley of Turpentine, or, as it is here called by the Arabs, Wady Sûrâr, which runs in a S. W. direction until it opens out into the great plain be-tween the mountains and the Mediterranean. On our left was another similar valley, Wady Sûmt. The whole region is full of ruined sites, and ruined villages, some deserted, and some partially inhabited. On our right, beyond Wady Sûrâr, we could see the hill and ruined village Soba, which it has pleased the monks to assume as the ancient Modin, the burial-place of the Maccabees, against the express testimony of Eusebius and Je-rome. We came at night to Beit Nettîf, a large village on a high part of the ridge between the two vallies above mentioned.

The next day was devoted to a visit to Beit Jibrin, the an-cient Betogabris of Greek and Roman writers, of which and its fortress we heard much from the Arabs; and to a search for the site of the ancient Eleutheropolis. From the elevated spot where we lodged, the Shekh of the village pointed out to us several places celebrated as the scenes of Samson's exploits and history, still bearing names in Arabic corresponding to their an-cient Hebrew appellations. Such were Zorah, Timnath, Socho, and others. Four places were also pointed out, respecting which Eusebius and Jerome have specified their distances from Eleu-theropolis, viz., Zorah and Bethshemesh towards Nicopolis, and Jarmuk and Socho on the way to Jerusalem. Following out the specified distances along the ancient road, we came directly upon Beit Jibrin, which lies among hills between the mountains and the plain. Here are the remains of a large Roman fortress of immense strength; which was built up again in the time of the crusades. Around it are the traces of an extensive city.

We had received the impression, that we must look for Eleu-theropolis further West upon the plain; and accordingly turned our course that way to Safîyeh, a conspicuous village lying on an isolated hill. Here however we found no trace of any an-cient site. We then proceeded to Gaza; whence after two days we returned by another route, searching diligently for the sites of ancient Lachish, Gath, and other cities; but finding none except Eglon, on a mound strewed with stones, still called Ajlân. Again arrived at Beit Jibrin, we visited several very singular excavated caverns in the vicinity.——Eusebius and Jerome mention also Jedna and Nazib as being distant from Eleutheropolis, one six, and the other seven miles, on the way to Hebron. These names still exist ; and taking the Hebron route, we found Jedna to be just six miles distant from Beit Jibrin. Nazib lies yet a little further, on another parallel road. This circumstance seems to decide the identity of Beit Jibrin with Eleutheropolis. The former was the ancient name ; the latter was imposed by the Romans, and has been since forgotten. It is also remarkable, that those ancient writers who speak of Eleutheropolis, do not mention Betogabris ; while those who speak of the latter, are silent as to the former.——Rejoicing in this result, we pursued our way to Hebron ; and after a steep and toilsome ascent on a ridge between two deep vallies, we rested for a time at Taffuh, the Beth Tappuah of Judah, and arrived at Hebron in about six hours from Beit Jibrin. Here dismissing our muleteers, we engaged camels for Wady Mousa from the Shekh of the Jehâlin, a Bedawi tribe inhabiting the territory S. E. of Hebron.

We had long before formed the plan to proceed to Wady Mousa by way of the south end of the Dead Sea, and so southwards along Wady Araba, in the hope of being able to decide the pending question, whether the Jordan could ever have flowed through this valley to the Gulf of Akabah. Here too we had hoped again to have been the first ; but were anticipated by the French Count Berthou, who preceded us by three or four weeks, and whom we had seen at Jerusalem after his return. — After being detained two days at Hebron, we set off May 26th ; and passing by Carmel and Maon, and then across a rolling desert in a S. E. direction, we came towards the close of the second day's journey to the brow of the steep descent leading down to the Dead Sea. This descent is in all not less than 1500 feet ; but here and far to the South it is divided into two offsets of nearly equal height. Between these lies a terrace nearly three hours broad, the surface of which is covered with low ridges and conical hills of soft, chalky limestone, verging into marl. At the foot of the second descent is a small deserted Turkish fort, in the narrow Wady Zuweirah, (not Zoar,) which leads out to the sea in about half an hour. . We reached the shore not far from the North end of Usdum, a low, long mountain ridge, running here from N. N. W. to S. S. E. and giving the same direction to the shore of the sea. This ridge, Usdum, is in general not far from 150 feet high, and continues in this direction for two hours to the extremity of the sea, where it tends to the S. S. W. for an hour more, and then terminates. The striking peculiarity of this mountain is, that the whole body of it is *a mass of rock salt ;* covered over indeed with layers of soft limestone and marl, or the like ; through which the salt often breaks out, and appears on the sides in precipices, forty to fifty feet high, and several hundred feet long. Often also it is broken off in both large and small pieces, which are strewed like stones along the shore or fallen down as debris.

The South end of the sea is very shallow ; and the shore continues quite flat for some distance further South ; so that there are traces of its being overflowed by the sea for two or three miles South of the water-line, as we saw it. The western side of this southern valley or Ghor, is wholly naked of vegetation ; but on the eastern side, where streams come down from the eastern mountains, there is a luxuriant vegetation and some tillage. We continued on the western side, along the base of Usdum ; crossing several purling rills of transparent water flowing from the mountain towards the sea, but salt as the saltest brine. Before us, as we advanced southwards, appeared a line of cliffs, fifty to one hundred and fifty feet in height, stretching across the whole broad valley, and apparently barring all further progress. We approached the western end of these cliffs in two and a half hours from the South end of the sea. They proved to be of marl ; and run off from this point in a general course S. S. E. across the valley. All along their base are fountains of brackish water oozing out and forming a tract of marshy land towards the North. Our route now lay along the base of the cliffs ; and after resting for a time at a fine, gushing fountain, we came in two hours to the mouth of Wady Jib, a deep valley coming down from the South through the cliffs ; and showing the latter to be only an offset between the lower plain which we had just crossed, and the higher level of the same great valley further South. The name El Ghor is applied to the valley between the Dead Sea and this offset ; further South the whole of the broad valley takes the name El Araba, quite to Akabah. These apparent cliffs I take to be the Akrabbim of Scripture. The Wady Jib begins far to the South of Mount Hor, beyond Wady Ghüründel, and flows down in a winding course through the midst of El Araba, draining off all its waters northwards to the Dead Sea. Where we entered Wady Jib at its northern end, it is half a mile broad, with precipitous banks of chalky earth or marl, 100 to 150 feet high, and exhibiting traces of an immense volume of water flowing northwards. It may be recollected, that the waters of Wady Jeråfeh in the western desert, which drains the S. E. part of that desert far to the southward of Akabah, also flow northwards into El Araba, and so of course through Wady Jib. Hence, instead of the Jordan flowing southwards to the Gulf of Akabah, we find the waters of the desert further South than Akabah flowing northwards into the Dead Sea. The very nature of the country shows, without measurement, that the surface of the Dead Sea must be lower than that of the Red Sea or the Mediterranean.

We continued our course up the Wady Jib for several hours; its banks becoming gradually lower, and at length permitting us to emerge from it. We were now not far from the eastern mountains, nearly opposite the broad Wady Ghuweir; while before us was Mount Hor, rising like a cone irregularly truncated. We turned into these mountains at some distance North of Mt. Hor, in order to approach Wady Mousa from the East, through its celebrated ancient entrance. A long and steep ascent, the pass of Nemella, brought us out upon the plateaus of the porphyry formation; above which are still the hills of sandstone among which Petra was situated. The entrance to this ancient city, through the long narrow chasm or cleft in the sandstone rock, is truly magnificent; and not less splendid and surprisingly beautiful, is the view of the Khŭzna or temple hewn in the opposite rock, as the traveller emerges from the western extremity of the passage. Then follow long ranges of tombs hewn in the rocky sides of the valley, with ornamental façades in a style of striking, though florid architecture. What we sought in Wady Mousa, was more the general impression of the whole; since the details have been correctly given by the pencil of Laborde. We examined particularly, whether any of these excavations were perhaps intended as dwellings for the living; but could see no marks of such design,—nothing but habitations of the dead, or temples of the gods. There was indeed no need of their being thus used; for the numerous foundations of dwellings, show that a large city of houses built of stone once stood in the valley.

We had nearly completed our observations, and were preparing soon to set off on our return by way of Mt. Hor, when the old Shekh of Wady Mousa, Abu Zeitûn, who caused so much difficulty to Mr. Bankes and his party in 1817, came down upon us with thirty armed men, demanding a tribute of a thousand piastres for the privilege of visiting his territory. We declined payment, of course; but after long and repeated altercation it came to this result, that unless we paid this full sum, he would not suffer us to visit Mt. Hor. We attempted nevertheless to set off in this direction; our own Shekh leading the forward camel; but the hostile party closed around, and swords were drawn and brandished; which however among these Arabs means nothing more than to make a flourish. As it was in vain for us to use force against so large a party, we decided to set off on our return by the way we came. This took the old man by surprise, and thwarted his plans. Messengers soon followed us, saying we might return for the half; and at last, for nothing. We replied that he had driven us from Wady Mousa, and we should not return; but should report his conduct at Cairo. The old man then came himself, to get our good will, as he said, which was worth more to him than money. We thought it better to keep on our way; and suffered no further interruption. It was probably the fear of the Pasha of Egypt alone, that withheld these miscreants from plundering us outright; and we afterwards received compliments from the Arabs in and around Hebron, for the boldness and address with which we had extricated ourselves from the old Shekh's power.

Descending the pass of Nemella, we struck across El Araba in a W. N. W. direction, travelling for a great part of the night. In the morning we reached Wady Jib, here quite on the western side of El Araba; and stopped for a time at the fountain El-Weibi. Other fountains occur at intervals along the valley at the foot of the western hills, both North and South of El-Weibi. From here a path strikes up the western mountain in the direction of Hebron, which is used by the Southern Arabs. Our guides took a more northern road, leading up a very steep pass called Sûfâh, over a broad surface of shelving rock extending nearly from the bottom to the top, an elevation of 1000 or 1200 feet. This is probably the hill Zephath, afterwards Hormah, where the Israelites attempted to enter Palestine, and where they were attacked by the king Arad; Num. 14: 40 sq. 21: 1 sq. comp. Judg. 1: 17. Some miles N. N. W. of this pass is a conical hill still bearing the name of Tell Arad, probably the site of the ancient town.——All these circumstances lead me to place the site of Kadesh in the great valley below, near the fountain El-Weibi or one of the neighboring springs. Here it would be near the border of Edom, opposite a broad passage leading up through the eastern mountains, and in full sight of Mt. Hor. That the Israelites must have approached Palestine through the Wady Araba, is a necessary conclusion from the mountainous character of the district on the West of this valley, through which no road has ever passed.

Our further way to Hebron led us by the sites of Arara, the Aroer of Judah ; and Melh, where is a fine well and the traces of a town, not improbably the ancient Moladah or Malatha. At Hebron we remained a day and a half; being obliged to send for horses to Jerusalem.

We left Hebron again on the 6th of June, taking now a S. W. course by the large village Dûra, the Adora of Josephus ; and descending the mountain to El Burj, a ruined castle of which we had heard much, but where we found no trace of antiquity. Hence we bent our course northward among the hills ; and passing again through Jedna, rested for a time at Terkumieh, the Tricomias of former ages ; leaving Beit Jibrin on our left. We lodged now a second time at Beit Nettif; and the next morning descending N. N. W. we came to the site of the ancient Bethshemesh in the opening of Wady Sûrâr into the plain. The place is now called Ain Shems, although no fountain exists there ; but the situation corresponds to the Scriptural accounts ; and there are evident traces of a large city.——From this point we turned our course N. W. into the plain, in search of the ancient and long lost Ekron. After travelling in this direction for four hours, we arrived at the large village Akir, an Arabic name corresponding to the Hebrew Ekron. The situation too corresponds with the accounts of Eusebius and Jerome. There are now no remains of antiquity visible ; probably because the ancient houses, like the modern hovels, were built not of stone, but of earth.

From Ekron to Ramleh is two hours. Here we lodged, and the next day proceeded to Jerusalem by the camel-road, which also is the ancient Jewish and Roman way, over Lûd (Lydda), Gimzo, Lower and Upper Bethhoron (now Beit Ur), and Jib or Gibeon. The pass between the two villages of Bethhoron is a steep and rugged ascent of some 1500 feet, up the point of a ridge between deep vallies. It is the ancient road ; and has in several places steps hewn in the rock. The present shorter and less feasible route between Ramleh and Jerusalem, appears not to have been in use in the time of the Romans.—Looking down from Upper Bethhoron, a broad valley is seen in the S. W. issuing from the mountains and hills into the plain ; while on the ridge that skirts its S. W. side, is seen a village called Yâlo, the Arabic form for the Hebrew Ajalon. This then is probably the spot, where Joshua in pursuit of the five kings, having arrived at or near Upper Bethhoron, looked back toward Gibeon and down upon the valley before him, and uttered the command : "Sun, stand thou still on Gibeon ; and Moon, in the valley of Ajalon !"

We found Jerusalem still shut up on account of the plague ; and therefore pitched our tent in the Olive-grove North of the city, before the Damascus gate. Here we were joined by our travelling companion and Mr. Lanneau, who had performed their quarantine of seven days. Our other friends held communication with us from the wall ; and once came out to meet us, under the charge of a *guardiano* or health-officer.

VII. FROM JERUSALEM NORTHWARDS TO NAZARETH, TIBE-RIAS, AND BEIROUT.

If my feelings were strongly excited on first entering the Holy City, they were hardly less so, on leaving it for the last time. As we had formerly approached repeating continually the salutation of the Psalmist : "Peace be within thy walls, and prosperity within thy palaces ;" so now we could not but add : "For our brethren and companions' sakes we will now say, Peace be within thee !" Her palaces indeed are long since levelled to the ground, and the haughty Moslem now treads her glory in the dust ! Yet as we turned to look again from the high ground North of the city, I could not but exclaim : "Beautiful for situation, the joy of the whole earth, is Mount Zion on the sides of the north, the city of the great King !" One long, last look, and then turning away I bade those sacred hills farewell forever !

We left Jerusalem July 13th on mules. At Bireh we diverged from the Nablous road to the left, in order to visit Jifna, the Gophna of Josephus. It lies in a deep valley ; and near it are the ruins of a large Greek church. By a circuitous route we

came to Sinjil for the night.   Next morning we diverged again
to the right of the usual road, in order to examine an ancient
site called by the Arabs Seilûn.   We reached it in an hour from
Sinjil, and found it to correspond entirely to the ancient Shiloh,
which Josephus also writes Siloun ($\Sigma \iota \lambda o \tilde{v} \nu$).   We fell into the
usual road again near Khan Lûbban, and crossed the fine though
narrow plain, on the West side of which is the village Lûbban,
the ancient Lebonah.

The country now began to assume a new aspect.   The
mountains in general are less lofty and less steep ; while the
vallies open out into fertile plains or basins surrounded by hills.
Two hours before reaching Nablous, we entered upon the southern end of such a plain, running off N. N. E. four hours in
length and nearly an hour in breadth.   About the middle of the
western side of this fine plain, are seen the eastern ends of
Gerizim and Ebal, 800 to 1000 feet high ; between which runs
the narrow valley of Nablous in a direction nearly N. W.   The
city of Nablous lies half an hour within the valley, and directly
on the water summit ; the waters of the eastern part of the city
flowing east into the plain, while the fine fountains on the western side send off a pretty brook towards the western sea.   We
visited here the Samaritans ; and one of them accompanied us
to the top of Gerizim, and pointed out their Kebla and other
sacred places.   On this summit are traces of a considerable
town ; and also the remains of a large and strong fortress of
stone.

On the way from Nablous to Samaria, where the road turns
up the hills to the right, there is in the valley an ordinary Arab
aqueduct, which leads the waters of the brook to an overshot
mill.   This Richardson and others have magnified into an ancient
Roman bridge !   At Samaria the large ruined church evidently
is the work of the Knights Templars ; as is testified by the frequent crosses of this order.   Many columns also remain of the
ancient temples ; and a long colonnade extends around the southern base of the hill, for more than half a mile.——We now took
the road to Jenîn, on the border of the great plain of Esdraelon ;
passing on our way the former robber fortress Samûr, now a
heap of ruins.

We crossed the great plain from Jenîn to Nazareth by a route
somewhat East of the usual one ; passing through Zer'in, the
ancient Jezreel, and Sôlam, the ancient Shunem ; which Jerome
also writes *Sulem.*   At a distance on the S. W. edge of the

plain, are seen Ta'annuk and Lejyun, corresponding to the ancient Taanach and Megiddo. The eastern part of the plain of Esdraelon has never yet been correctly laid down in the maps. Two mountain ridges run out into it from the East, commencing near the brow of the Jordan-valley, and extending westward to near the middle of the plain. The southern ridge is Gilboa, the northern is the Little Hermon of Jerome. They divide the eastern half of the plain into three parts; of which the northern and southern decline towards the West, and their waters flow off to the Kishon, while the middle portion, between Gilboa and Hermon, slopes to the East, and its waters descend to the Jordan through a broad valley or plain at Bisan, the ancient Bethshean. Jezreel stood on the southern brow of this central valley; in which are copious fountains. One of these is now called Jalûd, the Tubania of the Crusaders, and doubtless the ancient fountain of Jezreel.

From Nazareth we went to the summit of Mt. Tabor, where we spent an afternoon and night enjoying the wide prospect, and dwelling upon the associations connected with this beautiful mountain. Here the remains of a large fortress are visible, evidently of Saracenic origin. We descended by way of the Mount of Beatitudes (so called) and Hottin to Tiberias. The walls of this city were thrown down by the earthquake of Jan. 1837; and still lie in ruins. A single sail-boat now exists upon the lake; but we tried in vain to hire it for an excursion.——We had intended to proceed directly to Damascus; but learned at Tiberias that the Druses of the Ledja and of Antilebanon were in a state of insurrection, so that all the routes from this quarter to Damascus were unsafe. We proceeded however to the North end of the lake; passing by Mejdel (Magdala), the plain Gennesareth with its round fountain, the ruined Khan-Minya, and the remarkable ruins of Tel Hûm. We encamped near where the Jordan enters the lake; and explored the eastern plain, and the site of the ancient Julias, the northern Bethsaida. We made minute and persevering inquiry throughout the whole country, after the ancient names Capernaum, Bethsaida, and Chorazin; but no trace of them remains among the Arab population. If former travellers have heard them, it must have been from the monks of Nazareth or their dependents.——We now bent our course to Safet, which was destroyed by the earthquake of Jan. 1, 1837, and is still little more than a heap of ruins. Here we waited a day for intelligence; hoping yet to be able to visit

Damascus.   But the account became more threatening ; and we were compelled to turn our faces towards Beirout by the way of Tyre and Sidon.

While at Safet, we went to a point an hour North of the town, whence we could see the Castle of Banias and overlook the whole plain and lake of the Hûleh.   The latter is but one lake, eight or ten miles long by four or five miles broad ; the northern half being a mere tract of marsh covered with tall reeds or flags. Between this lake and that of Tiberias, the Jordan flows in a narrow valley, and forms no intervening lake.——On the way from Safet to Tyre, nearly two hours N. W. of Safet, we saw the crater of an extinct volcano ; which was probably the central point or *Ableiter* of the great earthquake of the preceding year, by which Safet and the adjacent villages were destroyed. ——We reached Beirout June 26, 1838 ; and thence returned to Western Europe by Alexandria, Smyrna, Constantinople, and so across the Black Sea and up the Danube to Vienna.

ARTICLE IX.

THE ANTE-COLUMBIAN HISTORY OF AMERICA.

By Henry R. Schoolcraft, Esq. Detroit, Michigan.

Antiquitates Americanae, sive Scriptores Septentrionales Rerum Ante-Columbianarum in America. — *Samling af de i Nordens Oldskrifter indeholdte Efterretninger om de Gamle Nordboers Opdagelsesreiser til America fra det* 10de *Aarhundrede.* — *Edidit Societas Regia Antiquariorum Septentrionalium.*   Hafniae, 1837. 4to. pp. 479.

INTRODUCTORY NOTE, BY THE EDITOR.

[A very brief notice of this learned and interesting work appeared in the Repository for April 1838.   Since that time we have not found it convenient to take up the subject of its important disclosures, until Mr. Schoolcraft has consented to favor us with the present Article.   The work, however, has been in the country some eighteen months, and several notices of it have appeared ; but it has excited less interest than the importance and attractive character of its topics, as well as the learning and evidence with which they are presented, would lead us to expect. The light of authentic history is here shed upon what otherwise must have remained, to a great extent, the " fabulous age" of our country.

That our readers may possess, in as brief a form as possible, an intelligible description of the volume referred to, we insert as an introduction to the Article of Mr. Schoolcraft, the following Prospectus, issued by the Royal Society of Northern Antiquaries, accompanying its publication.]

" Alexander von Humboldt, who of all modern travellers has thrown the greatest light on the physical circumstances, first discovery, and earliest history of America, has admitted that the Scandinavian Northmen were the true original discoverers of the New World; a fact which several later writers of eminence have nevertheless either flatly denied, or called in question. The above mentioned great inquirer has however remarked that the information which the public as yet possesses of that remarkable epoch in the middle ages is extremely scanty, and he has expressed a wish that the Northern Literati would collect and publish all the accounts relating to that subject. The Royal Society of Northern Antiquaries considers it a matter of duty to comply with this wish, embracing a threefold purpose : that of illustrating ancient geography and history ; that of perpetuating the memory of our forefathers, and lastly that of everlastingly securing to them that honorable station in the history of the World, of Science, of Navigation, and of Commerce, to which they are justly entitled. This has appeared to the Society to be so much the more necessary, since the latest researches have rendered it in a high degree probable, that the knowledge of the previous Scandinavian discovery of America, preserved in Iceland, and communicated to Columbus when he visited that island in 1447, operated as one, and doubtless as one of the most powerful of the causes which inspired the mind of that great man (whose glory cannot in any degree be impaired by the prior achievement) with that admirable zeal, which bidding defiance to every difficulty enabled him to effect the new discovery of the New World under circumstances that necessarily led to its immediate, uninterrupted, and constantly increasing colonization and occupation by the energetic and intelligent races of Europe. For this his memory will be imperishable among the nations of the earth. Yet still we Northmen ought not to forget his meritorious predecessors, our own forefathers, who in their way had difficulties to contend with not less formidable, since without knowledge of the properties of the magnet, without aid of compass, charts, or mathematical science properly so called, they dared to navigate the great Ocean, and thus by degrees discovered and partly colonized Iceland in the ninth century, Greenland in the tenth, and subsequently several of the Islands and Coasts of America during the latter part of the tenth and beginning of the eleventh century.

" It is the last of these epochs—very remarkable in the history of the world, yet not sufficiently known—that forms the subject of the work now announced. No separate work has hitherto been devoted to this subject, if we except the Vinlandia of Torfaeus, published in 1705, and now extremely scarce. That work, however, does not contain any collection of the original statements on which the investigation must be based, and such accounts as it does communicate are but few and incomplete. This collection therefore now makes its appearance for the first time as complete as possible, compiled from the numerous and valuable MSS. now extant, and accompanied by a Danish and also *a complete Latin translation;* and by prefatory remarks, archaeological and geographical disquisitions, and other critical apparatus also in Latin. Of its contents we can here merely give a brief sketch, mentioning only the principal sections. Among these may be named, first the historical accounts of Erik the Red, and the Greenlanders, extracted—and now for the first time accurately published—from the celebrated Codex Flateyensis, particularly concerning Biarne Heriulfson's and Leif Ericson's first discovery of the American Islands and Coasts, and the several voyages thither, performed by Leif's brothers and sister. Next the Saga of Thorfinn Thordson surnamed Karlsefne, descended from Irish, Scottish, Norwegian, Swedish and Danish Ancestors, chiefly taken from two ancient MSS. never before edited, and in fact not previously known to the Literati, the one of which is supposed to be partly a genuine autograph of the celebrated Hauk Erlendson, Lawman of Iceland, well known as a compiler of one of the Recensions of the Landnama-book. This very remarkable Saga contains detailed accounts of Thorfinn Karlsefne's and his company's three years voyages and residence in America, whereby an entirely new light is diffused over this subject hitherto so little known. The only knowledge that Torfaeus had of this Saga, which he imagined to be lost, was derived from some corrupted extracts of it contained in the collection of materials for the history of ancient Greenland left by the Iceland Farmer Biörn Johnson of Skardso. It is now for the first time submitted to the literary world in a complete form. The work here announced moreover contains everything else that the Society has been able to collect and discover relating to that knowledge of the New World which our forefathers obtained from the early discoveries and researches of the Northmen. Among these we may mention, 1. Adam of Bremen's accounts of Vineland (in America) written in the eleventh century, being in fact communicated to him by the Danish King Sweyn Estrithson, and compiled from authentic accounts furnished to him by Danes, and now for the first time published from the excellent Codex in the

Imperial Library at Vienna, of which a Facsimile has been transmitted to the Society by the Chief of the Library, Count Dietrichstein. 2. Are. Frode's account of Vineland, written in the same or in the following century ; and also 3, of the eminent Icelandic chief Are Marson, one of his own ancestors, who in the year 983 was driven to a part of America situate near Vineland, then called Hvitramannaland or Great Ireland, whose inhabitants (of Irish origin) prevented him from returning, but at the same time treated him with great respect. 4. Other ancient accounts respecting the Icelandic hero Biörn Asbrandson, in his day one of the Iomsburg Warriours under Palnatoke, and fighting along with them in the battle of Fyrisval in Sweden ; he also in the year 999 repaired to one of the coasts of America, where he was detained in the same manner, but resided there as chief over the natives for about 30 years. 5. Account of an Icelandic mariner, Gudleif Gudlaugson, who was driven to the same coast in the year 1027, and who was rescued from death or captivity by his above mentioned countryman. 6. Extracts from the Annals of Iceland of the middle ages, in so far as they relate to America, particularly Bishop Eric's voyage to Vineland in 1121 ; the discovery of new countries by the Icelanders in the Western Ocean in 1285 ; an expedition from Norway and Iceland in the year 1288—90 ; and also a trading voyage from the ancient colony in Greenland to Markland in America in 1347, as recorded by contemporaries. 7. Ancient accounts of the most northern districts of Greenland and America, chiefly visited by the Northmen for the purpose of hunting and fishing ; among these a very remarkable account (from a letter of a Greenland clergyman) of a Voyage of Discovery undertaken by some clergymen from the Bishopric of Gardar in Greenland, in the year 1266, being —as is corroborated by an astronomical observation—through Lancaster Sound and Barrow's Strait to regions which in our days have for the first time been made correctly known through the zealous exertions of Sir William Parry, Sir John Ross, and Capt. James Clark Ross, and other British navigators. 8. Extracts from the ancient geographical works of the Icelanders, to which is added an outline taken in the thirteenth century representing the earth in four inhabited quarters. 9. An ancient Faroish Qväji wherein Vineland is named, and allusion is made to its connection with Ireland.

" To which are added, I. A description accompanied by delineations and occasionally by perspective views of several *Monuments,* chiefly *Inscriptions, from the middle ages,* found partly in Greenland and partly in the States of Massachusetts and Rhode-Island in North America, on the one hand confirming the accounts in the Sagas, and on the other illustrated by them. II. Detailed *Geographical Inquiries* lately undertaken at the instance of the Society, whereby the sites of the regions and places named in the Sagas are explored, and are pointed out under the names by which they are now commonly known, viz. Newfoundland, Bay of St. Lawrence, Nova Scotia, and especially the States of Massachusetts and Rhode-Island, and even districts more to the South, probably situate in Virginia, North Carolina, and in Florida, which is supposed to be the most southerly land mentioned in the most authentic Saga-accounts, although sundry of the Northern Geographers of the middle ages would seem to intimate their knowledge of the easterly direction taken by the continent of South America. They are chiefly based on the accounts in the ancient MSS. and on the explanations of the *astronomical, nautical* and *geographical statements* contained in the same, which besides receive the most complete confirmation from accounts transmitted by distinguished American scholars, with whom the Society have entered into correspondence, and who, after several journies undertaken for that object in Massachusetts and Rhode-Island, have communicated accurate illustrations respecting the nature of the countries, their climate, animals, productions, etc. and have furnished the Society with descriptions and also with delineations of the ancient Monuments found there. III. *A Chronological Conspectus*, arranging under their proper dates the several voyages to America and the most important events which occurred in that quarter of the world. IV. *An Index of Persons*, in which the names of those persons (of both sexes) who took part in the American Voyages are printed in a different type. V. *A Geographical Index*, in which the same method is followed in regard to names of places mentioned in America. VI. *An Index Rerum*, containing among other things the names of the various productions of the American countries. VII. *Genealogical Tables*, showing the lineage of the most eminent of the Northern discoverers of America, continued down to our days, whereby it is demonstrated that many persons now living in Iceland, Norway, and Denmark, as also the celebrated sculptor Thorwaldsen in Rome, do actually descend from them, that is from men, who 800 years ago were the chiefs of the American natives, or who were at that remote period born in America.

"The work consists of sixty-five sheets large Quarto, and is accompanied by eighteen *large engravings*, viz. eight Facsimiles, some of which represent entire pages of the best of the MSS. employed on the present occasion, in order to give a clear and complete idea of their nature ; by dint of much pains the artist has succeeded in representing them with great accuracy, both as regards the outlines of the letters, which were often much faded away and difficult to discern, and also the color of the different parchments. Further four Maps, viz. 1. One of *Ancient Iceland*, being the first ever made, representing its republican division about the year 1000, constructed by the Icelandic geographer Biörn Gunnlaugson with the aid of Finn Magnusen and other Icelandic scholars. 2. *A Map of the district of Julianehaab in Greenland,* probably comprising the Eystribygd, as it was called, (also important in a geographical point of view,) constructed for the Society by Capt. William A. Graah R. N. from observations and measurements made by him in the country itself, and from such other authorities as were available. On this map are noted the numerous sites (rudera) of churches and houses of the ancient colonists, as far as these are known. 3. *A General Chart* of the Northern Icy Ocean, and of the *Coasts of the Atlantic* for the purpose of exhibiting a view of the voyages of discovery. Here is delineated the Eastern part of North-America, together with such names of countries, capes, firths, islands, and places, from Lancaster-Sound to Florida, as were adopted by the ancient Northmen. 4. *A Map of Vineland,* also with the ancient Northern appellations. Finally, six Engravings being delineations, and partly prospects of the Greenland and American monuments from the middle ages treated of in the work ; several of these are very remarkable, and, for the most part, hitherto quite unknown, such as Inscriptions on Rocks in Massachusetts and Rhode-Island, which from the disquisitions contained in the work, would seem to have been partly intended to indicate the *Landnam,* or the occupation of the country, effected by the ancient Northmen.

" For the convenience of those who prefer reading English to Latin, there is given *in English* a historical view of the Voyages of Discovery, accompanied by the geographical disquisitions, on which account the maps thereunto referring have also *English names.* Moreover the several communications received from the North American Members of the Society's Committee on the Ante-Columbian History of America are also inserted *in English.*"

THE reception which this volume has met with, in America, is decidedly favorable. So far as the principal facts are concerned, we have heard but one opinion. All who have examined it, concur in their testimony respecting the value of the historical materials it embraces, the research and literary labor bestowed on them, and the care with which the leading conclusions are drawn. It is not only evident that America was visited before the era of Columbus, as has been often asserted, but it seems placed beyond doubt that the Northmen made repeated voyages into the northern Atlantic, early in the 10th century, and visited and wintered at various points on the New England coast. A comparison of the ancient and existing maps, and a careful application to this coast of the geographical terms found in the ancient Norwegian and Icelandic Mss. demonstrate, so far as such a problem can be solved, that those hardy navigators visited the entire shores of Massachusetts and Rhode Island, *hutted* themselves for the winter at several points, and brought over cattle, and other means of colonization. It is also quite evident that the discovery and settlement of the country had been purposed and materially planned, and that it was carried on, for a time, with a zeal worthy of all success.

There is as much geographical and general information, embraced in the brief journals of these early sea voyages, as could be looked for, or as was common to the age. In saying this, we may as well express the opinion long entertained, of the ancient journalists of voyages to America, even down to the middle of the sixteenth century, that they were most particularly deficient in every pre-requisite for their office. The business of keeping the journal, or writing the account of an expedition appears to have been left to him, of the party, who was fit for nothing else, in the conceptions of the era. Fighting, discovery, and wild adventure, and not literature, were the characteristics of those ages. It is not surprising, therefore, that we find this department so poorly supplied.

Enough is preserved, by the Scandinavian adventurers, to show that they were more familiar with the arts of navigation and nautical astronomy, than with the science of noting human speech, or describing men and manners. The coast scenery and productions are more minutely noticed. Bays, islands, channels, streams, rocks and straits, were familiar to this race of men, for they dwelt in a part of the globe, unsurpassed for its display of these features. And the language of Scandinavia appears to have been well provided with terms for such objects, and with principles of ready and graphic combination to express their varied appearances. It seems to us, that this facility in the Icelandic tongue, has proved one of the best means, in adjusting the geography, if it has not furnished the key to those early, and century-forgotten voyages.

In allusion to the productions and natural features of the country, the pine tree, the grape vine, and the long sandy beaches, strike us as the most characteristic traits of the New England coast in a state of nature. And it must be borne in mind, that this coast, in its forest state, produced the beach grape, the best of all the wild species, which has now disappeared, or is only to be found, if we are rightly informed, at a

few places.   What is said of "precious" woods, requires to be
received with every allowance for haste and inexactitude of observation.   Similar statements are found in the journals of voyagers to other parts of North America, where there never grew
a mahogany tree.

We think the climate of New England not too favorably
represented.   There have been years, it is true, when owing to
heavy falls of snow and long continued severity, cattle would
scarcely sustain themselves.   But even in these seasons, there
would be less injury done them, while the country was covered
with forests, which would shelter them from the severe north-
east winds.   And so long as the country was a wilderness, it
may be supposed there were numerous fields of grass and native
herbage, near the influx of rivers and along the open bays.   In
ordinary seasons, cattle would winter in New England at this
time, if they could range where there was natural herbage.
We have known cattle to winter themselves, as far north as
latitude 46°, on mere browse.

We have less reason to be satisfied with the accuracy of the
descriptions, given by the north-men, of the natives, who were
encountered on the New England coast.   We doubt whether
the Esquimau race, ["Skroellings"] ever inhabited it.   These
tribes have their affinities with the Greenlanders, and the course
of their migration appears, at all times, to have been directed
through the Arctic circle and along the Arctic ocean completely
across this part of the American continent.   It is certain that
on the landing of the Pilgrims, just 600 years after the death of
Thorwald Ericson, in Massachusetts bay, the Algic * race possessed the entire coast.   They were found not only at Ply-
mouth, near the very burial place of Ericson, but north as high
as the Penobscot, and the French discovered branches of the
same generic stock on the southern shore of the gulf of St.
Lawrence.   Verozani and the Cabots and Hudson found them
south, along the Atlantic, as far as they sailed.   It does not
seem probable to us, that the Esquimaux could have been found,
without these characteristics of the race, his bone fish-spear,
and his seal-skin canoe.   The natives encountered by Ericson,
evinced a degree of bravery hardly compatible with our notions
of the Esquimaux.   A few days of fair sailing would bring the
Scandinavian adventurer from the slaty coasts of Helluland,

---

* This term is a derivative from the words Alleghany and Atlantic.

where the *Skroellings* abode, to the Rhode Island waters, and it does not seem strange that observers who had mistaken the curled maple for mahogany, should not think one race of Indians different from another, when both possessed copper colored faces, had long black hair, and wore a sort of *mantelet* of skins. It is not said they were of small stature, nor that they ate raw fish—the two leading traits in the Esquimaux.

So far as authentic history extends, the Esquimaux tribes have been found north of the latitude of 60°, inhabiting the whole range of islands, gulfs and bays, from the coast of Greenland in longitude 20° to Behring's straits in Asia, in longitude 167°. They have seldom been found more than one hundred miles south of the Arctic sea. The eastern Esquimaux extended down the coast of Labrador to the straits of Bellisle, and were found dispersed, in some instances, as far as north latitude 50°.

The few specimens of the native language introduced from the voyages, rather entangle, than help the inquiry. "Vethilldi," and " Uväege," the names of the father and mother of the captured boys, are certainly not of the Algic vocabulary. The same may be said of "Avalldamon" and "Valdidida," the chiefs of their band. Should it be found that the Icelanders or Norwegians substitute the letter V for B, and L for N in pronouncing foreign languages, analogy might sustain them as Algic derivatives. There is no rule in Rafn's Grammar of the Icelandic,* now before us to settle this point. V is generally dropped before o, u, y, and r, but often retained by the ancient writers. But the question is, if these words are not Algic, are they Esquimaux? By referring to Mr. Gallatin's vocabulary of this language [Vide Archaeologia Americana, Vol. II.] it will be seen that the letter V does not occur.

We are aware, however, from the grammatical examples in the "Mithridates," that the sound is found among the Esquimaux of Kotzebue's Sound, and analogy would lead us to look for it, among the other tribes of this well-marked race of men. Granting all that could be asked on this head, however, it must be recollected that these boys were not captured in Narragansett or Massachusetts bay, but as is stated in general terms, on the voyage home.

Montaup, the true Indian name of Mount Hope, appears to us

---

* Marsh's Translation.

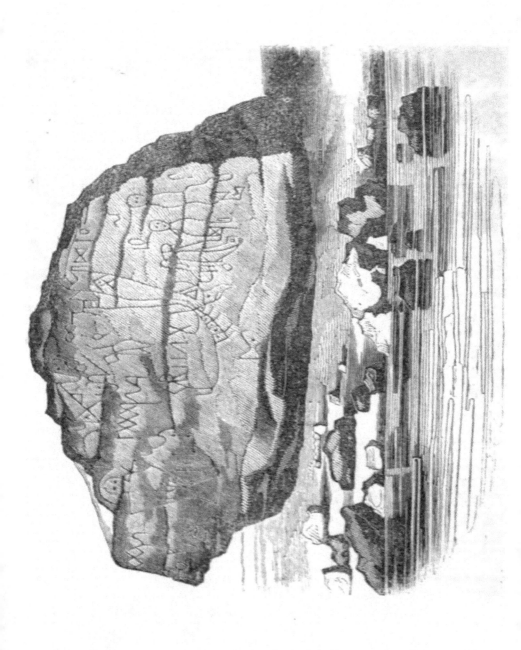

to be rather a derivative from the name of one of the gods of the Algic mythology, than an adoption, by the natives, of the Icelandic noun "Hop." Besides, is it reconcilable with our experience of the dogged attachment of the Indians to their own terms, to suppose they had thus adopted a foreign name, and that too, from an enemy, whom they had fought and driven from their coast?

We have examined cursorily, the several prints of the hieroglyphics on the so called "inscription rock" of Assonet.* We

* [This rock lies on the shore of "Assonet Neck," so called, on the east side of Taunton River, in Massachusetts, and is more commonly known as the "Dighton Writing Rock." Of the inscriptions upon this rock drawings have been taken at different periods, several of which have been published in the Transactions of Scientific Societies in this country; one of the most recent of which is here given, copied from the Am. Antiquitates. Nine of these drawings, together with a picture of the rock itself, are contained in the volume here referred to.

That our readers may the better appreciate the force of Mr. Schoolcraft's remarks on this topic, we give below the translation of a letter from Mr. Magnusen, Vice President of the Royal Society at Copenhagen; (Antiquitates Americanae, p. 378—382.) This letter recognizes the opinion of the editor of the work, Prof. Rafn, and exhibits a brief synopsis of the reasons which have led the learned Society to a conclusion in regard to these inscriptions, which, we think, a more extended examination of the subject may induce them to change. It is as follows.—Ed.]

"Your opinion concerning the inscription and the figures on the Assonet Rock I do not hesitate to approve. That they are in very deed Icelandic, and may be attributed to Thorfinn Karlsefn, I think is beyond all doubt. This, at first view, is demonstrated, as well by the Icelandic letter,  woven in at the left hand of the spectator of the picture, appearing like the prow of a ship, as by the principal images cut in the rock. There are also many criteria, which may prove this even to those who are unacquainted with the inscriptions on stones in Iceland, which, being unpublished, are to the present day nearly unknown to the literary world. These I will endeavor briefly to explain and illustrate.

I. The characters: ΓXXXI
ɳ ᛉ These demand no long explanation. They are, without doubt, numerals; but their united value, or signification, is especially remarkable, since this express number exactly corresponds with the number of men, who, according to the

consider the first three representations of no historical value, unless it be to denote how the preconceived theories of men may lead them to distort facts, even where the data, if properly

history of Thorfinn Karlsefn, made their way, with him, to this region of North America, or rather to this station.   In the 7th chapter of that celebrated history it is related, that the number of men who participated in his expedition was CXL ; but a little after, in chapter 8th, it is stated that nine (IX) of them were lost in that bay denominated by the Icelanders (or Scandinavians) Straumfjoerd, they having sailed northward, by the advice of Thorhall, a hunter, searching for Vineland in that quarter of the world.   Thorfinn himself, with all the rest of his associates, proceeding towards the south or west, came to a place called Hóp, (Hópe i Hope,) where, in fact, his train, as appears from these premises, were CXXXI persons, which number agrees, to a mark, with the inscription at Assonet.   Thus the ancient history or biography of Thorfinn Karlsefn and this celebrated monument in North America, in turn, most accurately, and in a wonderful manner, confirm each other.

Under the numeral characters commonly expressing CXXXI, two letters are seen.   The first, ᚾ , Latino-Gothic, as is known to all, expresses the Latin N ; but the second, ᛦ, is Runic, the common M, for which this character is found inserted in many writings of the middle age, otherwise Latin, both by the Scandinavians and the Anglo-Saxons.   But thus inserted, this character always signifies the word *maðr* (*man, homo, vir,*) or its plural *menn, meðr,* (*men*). Thus I conjecture that these two letters indicate, by way of abbreviation, the two entire words, n(*orroenir*) m(*enn,*) which, added to the number CXXXI, may signify so many (European) *north-men*. The figure, moreover, which we take for a ship, without masts, sails or rigging, standing among these reputed letters, should be noticed. Thus, hieroglyphically, or figuratively, as we conjecture, this fact may be indicated, viz. that those men, borne by ship, came to that land ; but afterwards they despoiled the ship of masts, rigging and sails, that they might desert it, and acquire for themselves permanent little dwellings on the land.   Thus this entire sentence is made out, viz. CXXXI n(*orroenir*) (*ship's*) m(*enn*) i. e. *northern,* (European, or originating from Norway and Iceland,) *sailors.*

II.   Other characters follow, separated from these lines, but, nevertheless, to be regarded as a continuation of them, few indeed, but of grave import, expressed in Latino-Gothic letters—these, for example,

M

◇R.   The first of these very brief lines presents to us something to be abbreviated, similar, in some way, to complex Runics, which, indeed, at first view appears to be made up of two letters, but, on a recorded, would not militate against such theories. All the other representations of these antique and curious devices, from Sewall's in 1768, and Winthrop's in 1788, to that of the Rhode

more thorough examination, it is perceived to embrace three, which make the word, *N A M*, (*nám*). This being appropriate to the ancient language of the Scandinavians and also to that of the Icelanders of the present day, easily takes the same significations; and another word, more common, but compounded, *land-nám*, takes the following,—the occupation of a region or territory, the country thus occupied, or the ground reduced to the possession of the first discoverers or settlers. The word remains to the present time, in Danish, *Nam*, which, according to the great Lexicon of that language, edited by the Royal Scientific Society of Hafnia, is thus defined,—the occupation of anything for the possession and use of the same.—The other word, *O R*, is nothing other than a most ancient and sufficiently well known form of the old language of the Scandinavians, signifying the same as *vor* in modern Icelandic and Danish, which better agrees with the Anglo-Saxon *ure*, and the English *our*. Both words together, *nam or*, exhibit this brief but very forcible signification,—*territory by us occupied, or our colonies.*

III. In the highest part of the configuration, above this inscription, is seen a figure, sufficiently artificial, representing, in our opinion, a great shield, furnished (pede singulari) very similar to a fish's tail, which was called by the ancient Scandinavians, as by the Icelanders, at the present day, *spor ðr*, hence the common denomination of the foot of a shield, *skjaldarsporðr*, the (fish) tail of a shield. This shield, together with the adjoining and inverted head-piece, being the ancient form common among Europeans, I take for signs of the peaceable occupation of that land.

IV. This occupation, or cultivation, of the soil or colony, is furthermore indicated by a very rude figure, cut in the rock beneath the line of numerals, if indeed it represents, as we conjecture it does, a *heifer*, lying down or resting. A day's walk of a heifer, or the full space she travelled over in one (summer) day, in the first settlement of Iceland, used, sometimes, to designate the length and breadth of the soil to be occupied. (See e. g. Landnamae, Lib. 4. Cap. 10.) In the same manner the Phoenician Cadmus, occupying a part of Greece, was led to build his own little dwelling on the spot where a cow, wearied with her long ranging, and nearly overcome, laid herself down to rest.

V. This whole configuration, I think, represents to the beholder this scene,—the ship of Thorfinn Karlsefn, previously destined to Vineland, brought to this shore, the wind being remarkable, as appears by the suspended mast,—his wife Gudrida, sitting on the shore, holds in her hand a key, belonging to their house, built, as appears, some time previous. Before her stands their son, *Snorr*, then three years

Island Historical Society in 1830, are conceived to be more or less important. It is only to be regretted that the care and precision bestowed upon the latter, could not have been applied, in getting an accurate impression, a century earlier.

The event recorded is manifestly one of importance in Indian history. We consider the characters hieroglyphics of the Algic stamp. They are not Runic characters, as we may confidently affirm, with this antique alphabet before us. Some of the principal resemblances to Runes, which appear in the latest copy of this inscription, are wholly unnoticed, in this shape, in the previous drawings. The letters R, I, N reversed, and X appear first on Kendall's drawing in 1807, when the country had been settled and cultivated, and the inscription gazed at, and talked of, in the vicinity, for more than a hundred years. And we think it would be hazarding little to suppose that some idle boy, or more idle man, had superadded these English, or Ro-

---

old, having been born in America. The accompanying men, CXXXI, (or one less,) had then taken possession of Vineland, and thus declared (*n á m o r*) their proper possession to be acquired. One of the ships belonging to them, by which they had been borne thither, being bereft of its sails, for that purpose, is represented as made fast to the shore. The hen-cock, by his crowing, announces domestic quiet or peace, the shield is at rest, and the head-piece, or helmet, is also laid aside. Then, suddenly, war is indicated as near at hand. Thorfinn, the leader of the colonists, is at peace in his dwelling, but, with his shield hastily seized, he endeavors to arm himself against the aggressions of the Skroellings, (or Esquimaux,) who violently attacked the Scandinavians, equipped with clubs, or branches of trees, bow and arrows, and, moreover, with a military machine, (unknown to us,) which, in the history of Thorfinn, is called *ballista*, from which, besides darts and large stones, affixed (as appears) to ropes or cables, shot forth immense balls,—which fact that celebrated history expressly testifies.

VI. Various lineaments, which mark the ropes and other instruments and points of a ship, as also delineations of other figures, in this inscription upon the rock, are composed, as I think, of Ruric cryptographics, or characters, (or enigmas,) such as were in use anciently in Iceland, and even at the present day are found inscribed on rocks, in various mountain caverns, e. g. in the cave which is called Paradisiaca, (Paradisar-hellir). Since, however, the many delineations of the diversified sculpture here presented do not agree with each other, in their representation of these lineaments, we here, especially, hesitate to attempt, at once, their explanation.

FINN MAGNUSEN."

man characters, in sport. These alphabetical marks certainly spell nothing in the ordinary *Runic*, either backward or forward. The mode of explanation adopted by Mr. Magnusen, [p. 878—382] appears to be far-fetched, in some respects cabalistic, and throughout overstrained; and after all, nine tenths of the whole inscription is unintelligible, and is left unexplained. We admire his learning and ingenuity, but rise from the perusal unconvinced.

Take, for example, the characters interpreted as the Latino-Gothic n and the Runic Ψ. They are not found in juxtaposition—they are not identical on the different impressions, but strikingly at variance, and the mass of intervening hieroglyphics is passed over as merely curious, or anomalous. To us it appears, that the character of an ancient inscription should be judged of by its predominant portions, and not its occasional resemblances; and it is the force of this consideration, that leads us to pronounce the inscription Algic and not Runic.

By the term Algic we comprehend that generic race of men, who, (say) in 1600, were found scattered, in various independent bands, along the Atlantic border, between the Floridian peninsula and the gulf of St. Lawrence. We exclude the Muscogee and Cherokee stocks, but excepting these, on the south, this race lined the whole United States border of the Atlantic, and extended westward to the lakes, etc. We, of course, merge in this term, the Powhetannic tribes, the Senapees, Mohegans, Natics and other New England sub-tribes, and the Algonquins of the French. Attention to their history and traditions, and to their languages, and what we must consider their *monumental remains,* indicate that these tribes migrated from south-west to north-east, along this border. The point to which our attention is here called, is, whether the Algics had reached and occupied the present geographical area of New England, previous to the discovery of the country by the Scandinavians, in 1008. Thorwald Ericson, and those who preceded and followed him, called the tribes whom they found at the *most southerly* points of their discovery, Skröellings—a term primarily indicating dwarfs, and applied often ironically, by the northmen. The term has come down to our times as the cognomen of Greenland and Iceland for the Esquimaux. And it is a

---

* Burial places, crania, spear and arrow heads, earth-pots, etc.

question of historical interest, whether the Esquimaux dwelt in the area of New England between the tenth and eleventh centuries ?   The English colonists in 1608, found the whole country occupied by different tribes of the Algics.   The traditions of these tribes made no mention of their having conquered the Esquimaux, or of their having driven north any previous occupants.   They appeared to have possessed the country for ages, and we have never heard that they claimed it as conquest from any other people.

We have already alluded to the inexactitude of observation in the discoverers both of the *ante* and *post* Columbian eras. We think it probable, in the case before us, that the Scandinavian mariners, coming last from the coast of the Greenland or Esquimaux Indians, were not very particular in remarking on the differences between tribes, where there was a general resemblance in the externals of dress, etc.   The Algics of New England were a tall and straight-limbed people, whereas the Skroellings were of a dwarfish appearance.   Yet it is nowhere remarked, so far as we have examined the Copenhagen publications, that the New England Skroellings, so called, were of short stature. On the contrary they appeared to be a quick limbed, active race, who fought with remarkable bravery, were expert in the use of the arrow, and when they found the north-men took to their vessel, hoisted a large heavy ball on a pole,* and let it fall in the midst of their assailants.   All this better accords with our notions of the Algic, than the Esquimaux race.

There is perhaps nothing more characteristic of the mental peculiarities of the Algic race, than their mythology and the system of hieroglyphics, by which they appear, at all times, to have perpetuated events and names.   Whenever a chief or warrior died, they cut or painted on a cedar post or other substance, the symbol of his name, and so many characters as were considered necessary to indicate his principal feats.   Sometimes symbols and characters of this kind were cut or marked on trees.   Sometimes on the bark of the betula papyracea (white birch), which is of an enduring quality.   And, occasionally on rocks, or loose bowlder stones.   It was very common to set up water worn bowlders of a particular figure, in spots supposed to be the residence of spirits, and to decorate them, in various ways.   Sacrifices of

---

* It is probable they sewed up a large stone in a raw skin, for the purpose of sinking the vessel in which their invaders took refuge.

tobacco, etc. were offered at these rude shrines. This is still the custom of the more westerly and northerly of these bands. Figures cut into stone, were certainly very rare. With extensive means of observation, among the remote existing tribes, we can point to but few such instances and nothing of the extensive character of the figures on the Assonet rock. We have, however, witnessed, and have now in our possession, drawings of a far more extensive series of these hieroglyphics taken chiefly from wood and bark. It is from a comparison of these with the Royal Society's plates, that we have expressed the opinion of their identity in point of general character. We think the character of the hieroglyphics a more certain means of satisfactory comparison of tribes than the substance upon which they were impressed or cut. It appears from the letter of Mr. Webb (p. 356) that the Assonet rock is a species of fine-grained grauwacke—a rock so much inferior in hardness to most of the silicious stones, that there could have been but little difficulty in making the impressions with sharp pieces of hornstone or common quartz, such as arrow-heads were chipped with. From the testimony of Dr. Stiles, in 1789, (p. 359) it seems that similar hieroglyphics were found on the Housatonic—a region to which there is no probability that these earlier discoverers penetrated. It is stated, in the same connection, that engraved figures of animals, etc. on a rock, of fifteen or twenty feet surface had been visited by a Mr. Frothingham, at Venango, on the Alleghany river in 1789, which seems to indicate that the Indians had the means of accomplishing this species of inscription.

We throw out these suggestions in a spirit of liberal inquiry, and not with the slightest view of underrating the valuable historical researches of the northern literati. They have shown us the mode of operating, and the high duties an enlightened people owe to the history of the land they live in. As yet but little attention has been devoted, in America, to the subject of Indian antiquities. We have not yet acquired the elements to work with. Their languages—the most curious chapter in the history of tongues, are yet without grammars or lexicons, and lie in a great measure in the rubbish of their prefixed and suffixed verbiage. No attempt has been made to record and explain their prominent system of hieroglyphics. There has been no systematic examination of the crania exhumed from their mounds, with a view of classifying the races. We deem most of the speculations, respecting the mounds themselves, to be but little creditable to American philosophy. Some writers have thought it wonderful that a few thousand cubit feet of soft earth and loam should have been piled up by our Indians over their dead! We have not even an illustrated work, giving accurate descriptions of their utensils, arms and fabrics, ancient and modern. We look in vain for their collected oral traditions and fictitious creations. We do not understand their mythology, and consequently are in the dark as to the true sources of their hopes and fears. In fine, we have but an imperfect knowledge of all that relates to their leading mental and moral peculiarities and characteristics. Enough has been said, and written about the mere external man—his looks and dress—his mode of living and his means of locomotion. But if we may be allowed the term, we know next to nothing of the philosophy of the Indian mind.

But we must not divert the purpose of our present notice into a new channel, albeit, we feel that the topic is one, so far as relates to their hieroglyphics, inseparable from the subject. It is impossible, that we should understandingly, or even willingly, admit the literary evidence brought forward at Copenhagen on this head, without first examining the hieroglyphics of our own tribes. Nor do we suppose from present impressions, that such an examination will militate against the general facts of these early discoveries of the country. The prominent points of doubt is with us, whether either the Indians or the Scandinavians ever recorded any facts connected with these discoveries on the banks of the Cohannet, and whether the country, at that remote era, was inhabited by the Esquimaux or the Algic race. Other topics of deep interest are connected with these. The whole subject is one of the highest literary interest, and one to which, we think, the research and acumen of the country, both individual and associated, is strongly invited. We have merely introduced the topic, and may again advert to it.

POSTSCRIPT.

Since the foregoing Article was prepared, the writer has received the following Note from Mr. Gallatin, respecting the use of the letters V and L in the Eskimau language.

"DEAR SIR,—The letter L occurs in every Eskiman dialect of which I have any knowledge. Thus, heaven or sky is : Greenland, *Killak* ; Hudson's Bay, *Keiluk* ; Kadik Island, *Keliok* ; Kotzebue's Sound, *Keilyak* ; Asiatic Tshuktchi, *Kuilak*.

" I am not so certain about the V, which I find used only by Egede or Crantz (not distinguished from each other in my collections) for the Greenland dialect. In their conjugations I find " We (plural and dual) wash them,"

verb	*pron.*		*verb*	*pron.*

ermikp-auvut and ermikp-auvut.
plural.   dual.

In the Mithridates, the same letter V, is repeatedly used in examples of the Greenland and Labrador dialects, principally (as it appears to me) but not exclusively, in the pronominal terminations

food	ours	debtors	ourś	a prophet—art thou ?

piksau-tivnik,—akeetsor-tivut,—profetiv-vit?

" By comparing these, with the pronouns of the other Eskimau dialects, I suspect that *OO* or *W* are, in these, used instead of V. But the difference may arise from that, [the difference] in the mother tongue, or in the delicacy of the ear, of those who have supplied us with either verbal and pronominal forms, or vocabularies.

Respectfully Yours,
ALBERT GALLATIN.

New York, Feb. 22, 1839."

ARTICLE X.

The Drama of Ancient Greece. A brief View of its History, Structure, Representation, and Moral Tendency.

By Rev. John Proudfit, late Professor of the Latin Language and Literature, University of the City of New York.

Poetry was the earliest form in which thought was embodied. In the infancy of the species as of the individual, the imagination predominated and clothed all the productions of the mind in those glowing images and that musical rhythm which constitute, at once, the essence and the form of poetry. History, philosophy, and even religion did not reject the dress with which the imagination invested them. The moral precepts of Pythagoras, the natural history of Empedocles were *preserved* in the form of poetry, and, among the Hebrews, the most sublime truths of religion, as well as the principal events of their national history, were preserved in the incomparable lyrics of

Moses and of David.   The three principal classes of poetic diction, in which originated all the different species of poetry, are the epic, the lyric, and the dramatic—of which, the epic has been termed the poetry of narrative, the lyric, the poetry of song, and the dramatic, the poetry of action.   " Each of these classes of poetry in its most complete form, became appropriated, among the Greeks, to particular tribes.   The epic was formed and cultivated among the Ionics, the lyric, among the Dorics and Æolics, and lastly, the dramatic among the Attics.   Hence, it arose, that each of these classes, in language, metre and adaptation to music and song, united the characters, and, more or less of the dialect of the tribe in which it was chiefly cultivated, to the peculiarities of its own nature."

The most ancient of these forms is generally allowed to have been the epic, as narrative is one of the first and simplest efforts of the mind.   In relation to Greek poetry it undoubtedly was the precursor and source of the rest ;—the lyric, having, in Greece, to a great extent, derived its poetical language and forms from the epic, and the dramatic being an amplification of the lyric.   For the basis of the drama was the chorus, which was essentially lyric, and the scenes were superadded, as a means of varying the exhibitions, by Thespis, in the age of Solon.

In a universal history of poetry, however, the drama, might, we are inclined to think, claim the priority.   The book of Job is probably the oldest preserved production of the human mind, and it evidently belongs to this class.   Herder has styled it 'an epic representation of human nature;' but with all deference for so high an authority, we would rather entitle it, a dramatic representation of human nature.   What essential feature of the drama does it not possess ?   From the third chapter it is interlocutory to the conclusion.   The introductory narration forms the prologue, and the concluding, the exode to the whole ;—while the striking correspondence between the " beautiful 'elegies" (or as they might, with equal propriety, be termed, beautiful odes,) which occasionally relieve the dialogue, and the chorus of Greek tragedy, completes the resemblance.   Take, for example, the following, which, had it formed one of the choral odes of a Greek tragedy, would have been applauded as an unrivalled specimen of tragic beauty :

> "Man that is born of a woman, is of few days and full of trouble.
>   He cometh up as a flower, and is cut down,
>   He fleeth also as a shadow and continueth not."

The book of Job, viewed as a drama, contains, it is true, but little action ;—quite as much, however, as the Prometheus Vinctus of Æschylus, during the whole episode of which the sufferer remains bound and motionless, while the visits of the Oceanides, Oceanus, Io and Mercury, form the only vicissitudes of the piece, the whole dialogue of which consists of their respective consolations or reproaches with the replies of Prometheus.   In fact, several of the best Greek tragedies contain but a single incident—and the art and power of those great masters is principally displayed in substituting the vicissitude and progress of thought and passion for that of external incident.

The three varieties of dramatic composition among the ancient Greeks were tragedy, comedy, and satyrs.   Of these the earliest was comedy, though brought to its perfection at a later period than tragedy.   In describing its origin, we shall, at the same time, describe the common origin of all the forms of the drama.   The dramatic art " took its birth in the bosom of tumultuous pleasures and the extravagancies of intoxication.   In the festivals of Bacchus hymns were sung which were the offspring of the true or feigned ecstasies of a poetical delirium. These hymns while they described the fabulous conquests of Bacchus, gradually became imitative—and, in the contests of the Pythian games, the players on the flute who entered into competition, were enjoined by an express law to represent successively the circumstances which preceded, accompanied and followed the victory of Apollo over Typhon."*   In this early stage of the art, Susarion, and shortly after, Thespis appeared ; the former enacting his rude and disconnected comedies on a kind of stage, the latter, making the first attempts at tragic representation on a cart—

> Dicitur et plaustris vexisse poëmata Thespis.

Such was the basis of the drama.   Its first materials were the wild effusions of the intoxicated votaries of Bacchus ;—and as it took its rise in connection with the festivals of Bacchus, it retained this connection throughout the subsequent ages of Grecian history.   In this rude state, it was tolerated only in the country ; being excluded from the city, alike by the taste and the laws ;—to the former of which its rustic coarseness was offensive, while by the latter, its unbounded license was condemned as injurious to the public morals.

---

* Barthelemy.

After a long infancy, this species of the drama presented itself in a new and highly improved form in Sicily. Instead of a succession of scenes, without connection or tendency, the philosopher Epicharmus introduced an action, all the parts of which had a dependence on each other, and conducted his subject, without wandering from it, through a just extent, to a determinate end. Comedy was soon after introduced to the Athenians, and was received by that lively and ingenious, but licentious people, " with the same transports which they would have testified at the news of a victory." Though an exotic, its rapid development soon proved how congenial was the soil to which it had been transplanted, and that Attic genius and taste were alike requisite to execute and appreciate it in its highest perfection. It soon became an object of attention and competition to the poets of Athens, and some of them speedily attained a distinction in it which threw into the shade all previous attempts. Such were, among the more ancient, Magnes, Cratinus, Crates, Pherecrates, Eupolis and Aristophanes ; all of whom flourished in the age of Pericles.

But in its moral character and tendency, comedy never underwent any material improvement. Divested of its grossness, that it might adapt itself to the advanced and polished condition of Athenian society, it was rendered the more dangerous by this refinement. It soon became idolized by a population, equally distinguished by its vivacity and licentiousness ; and, attracting all classes to its representation, its corrupting influence was the more extensive and irresistible. The comic writers of Athens were regarded by all wise and good men as the pests of society. This remark, indeed, is not to be received without limitation. Sometimes, undoubtedly, the lash of satire was inflicted on the vices and follies of the time ; on the insolent pride and vulgar ostentation of those who had suddenly risen to fortune and power. In a community like that of Athens, where all things were under the immediate and unchecked control of the capricious multitude, whose favors were much oftener won by popular arts and concessions than by real merit, yet whose vivacity rendered them willing to bear the keenest rebuke, provided it only excited their mirth while it exposed their follies, the political influence of comedy was doubtless wholesome and necessary. The comedians attacked the powerful demagogues of their day with astonishing intrepidity, and their wit and ridicule were often irresistible, where wisdom and eloquence would have reasoned and thundered in vain. Aristophanes, in his comedy of the knights, attacked and completely overthrew the mob-tyrant Cleon, while in the very height of his power. So universally dreaded was this man, that no actor could be induced to personate him, and no artist to model a mask after his likeness. Aristophanes, however, not to be discouraged, brought forward his piece and personated the formidable demagogue himself. The same part in his comedy entitled, "the Peace," happily exposes the absurd and self-destroying passion of his countrymen for war. Nor is it to be denied that the comic poets of Greece, in common with the most licentious writers in all ages, could appreciate and extol the charms of virtue as an abstract conception. We meet with detached passages, especially, in the choral odes, of exquisite beauty, the moral effect of which is purely good. But occasional effusions of this sort will neither counteract nor atone for the influence of a work, the general character and tendency of which is licentious. And that such was the case with the comic drama of Athens is equally evident from the testimony of contemporaneous writers and from the comedies themselves which have descended to our times. To judge from some of the comedies of Aristophanes (the only originals we possess,) or from the Eunuchus of Terence or the Asinasia of Plautus, (both translated from Greek poets, the first, from Menander, the second, from Demophilus,) we can form but one opinion of the auditory which could be pleased with such disgusting indecencies, or of the poet who could pander to an appetite so abominable.. " Paucas reperiunt poetae comoedias, ubi boni meliores fiant," "Poets have composed few comedies by which good men are made better." Such is the concession of one who had before him the whole range of ancient comedy, and was, therefore, incomparably better fitted to judge of its moral spirit than we can possibly be, and who was, himself, in fact, one of its greatest masters. The same poet, while he invites the audience to applaud the chastity of his comedy of "the Captives" and its freedom from all indecent allusions, holds it up as an exception to the general immorality of comedy.*

Profecto expediet, fabulae huic operam dare ;
Non pertractate facta est, *neque item ut celerae ;*

---

* See the Prologue and Catena to the Captives of Plautus.

Neque spurcidici insunt versus innumerabiles;
Hic neque perjurus leno est, nec meretrix mala;

Spectatores, ad pudicos mores facta haec fabula est.

"It will be
To your advantage to attend this play;
For 'tis not in the common style, nor yet,
Like other plays; here are no ribald lines,
Unfit to be remembered; here you'll find
No infamous abandoned courtezan.

"O no.   This play is founded on chaste manner,
Few of that sort of plays our poets find."—*Thornton.*

The fragments which we possess of ancient comedy convince
us that the concession of Plautus is equally candid and true.
" If we peruse these pieces, we shall be convinced that the
sole object of their authors was to please the multitude; and
that, to obtain this end, they considered all means as indifferent;
and employed, by turns, parody, allegory and satire, abounding
in images and language the most gross and obscene."   They
were, also, a kind of legalized slanderers;—or rather, slanderers beyond the reach and power of the law, being protected by
the enthusiastic attachment of the lower classes in " that fierce
democracy."   The shafts of their ridicule were as often levelled
" at errors as at vices," and the most illustrious reputations
were not unfrequently made their peace-offerings to the malignity of the multitude.   Thus it happened that Socrates, whose
pure and benevolent life could have excited, even in a bad
mind, no other evil passion than that of envy, was held up to
ridicule in " the Clouds" of Aristophanes; and Euripides, was,
through his whole life, and even after his death, an object of
persecution to the same poet.

The laws, and the most intelligent and virtuous citizens strenuously opposed these disorders, but in vain.   Successive de-
crees were passed for the regulation of comedy; one forbidding
personalities; another, interference in public affairs; a third,
entirely prohibiting the acting of comedy.   But these laws were
soon either repealed or disregarded, as all laws must be which
are not sustained by public opinion.   Though the chorus and
the mask were laid aside from the alarm and dissatisfaction of
the wealthier citizens, who refused to contribute the means of
these decorations, and thus, a temporary check was given to

the abuses of the stage; yet comedy went on in its downward course, till in common with all the other arts, it shared the ruin which it had accelerated.

The historic classification of comedy is into the old, the middle and the new comedy; the period of the old extending from the first invention of the art to 386 B. C.; that of the middle to the age of Alexander; all that follows belongs to the era of the new comedy, which terminated with Posidippus, in the year 289 before the christian era.

Of the innumerable works produced by all the writers who figured during the three periods of comedy, and many of whom multiplied their productions with that marvellous fertility which was peculiar to the Greek genius, time has spared, in their original form, only eleven comedies of Aristophanes. Exuberance of wit and humor and comic vigor in all its manifestations, as well as profound knowledge of the heart and of the world, have never been denied to this poet. His comedies also, discover a masterly acquaintance with the constitution of his country, and their representation exerted a powerful influence (as we have seen above) on the political events of his time. The Athenians, on one occasion, voted him an olive crown for the service he had done his country by rectifying abuses in its government. The force and boldness of his satire are highly commended by Horace and Persius, who make it the excuse of their own freedom and severity in remarking on the vices of their age. The grace and sprightliness of his language rendered him a great favorite with Chrysostom. His wit, however, appears to have been under no kind of restraint, either from respect for virtue, dignity of station, or religious reverence. The philosophers, the magistrates, the tragedians were all doomed, alternately, to feel the lash of his powerful satire. Admired passages in the serious poets are presented in his pieces in the most ludicrous parodies. The histories and oracles of the gods, and the gods themselves, are treated with the same freedom. His gross indecency often surpasses even the license of ancient comedy, and the persevering malignity with which he persecuted individuals whom all accounts represent as worthy and virtuous men, throws a dark shade over his character as a man, and his many and brilliant excellencies as a poet.

Menander was the most distinguished name of the new comedy. Plutarch, who drew an elaborate parallel between him and Aristophanes, considers him even superior to the prince of the old comedy. Of his many comedies, four only are preserved in the elegant "refashionments" of Terence. Two of the comedies of Terence are translations of Apollodorus. Some of those of Plautus are from the originals of Diphilus, Philemon, Demophilus, and probably of Epicharmus.

The Satyrs were a species of drama between comedy and tragedy. They took their name from a chorus of satyrs, headed by Silenus, whose antic dances and gestures formed a prominent part of the representation. Their materials were mythological and therefore belonged to tragedy. Their end was comic. Their aim was to excite laughter by the juxtaposition of the solemn and the ludicrous, a contrast which is well known to produce this effect in the highest degree. "The satyric drama was distinguished from tragedy by the kind of personages which it admitted—by the catastrophe which was never calamitous, and by the strokes of pleasantry, bon-mots, and buffooneries which constituted its principal merit. It differed from comedy by the nature of the subject, by the air of dignity which reigned in some of the scenes, and the attention with which it avoided all personalities. It was distinct from both the tragic and comic dramas by certain rhythmi which were peculiar to it, by the simplicity of its fable, and by the limits prescribed to the duration of the action." For it was required to be brief as well as of a varied character, being designed merely for the purpose of entertainment and relaxation, after the more serious and absorbing interest of tragedy. Satyrs appear to have been first written by Pratinas; who unable to compete with Æschylus in tragedy, struck out a new path for himself in the invention of these grotesque and amusing parodies, which at once became so popular that it was usual thereafter, to add a satyric drama to each tragic trilogy.* Æschylus, Sophocles and Euripides were all distinguished composers of satyrs. The Cyclop of Euripides is the only extant specimen of this kind of composition.

, The early history of tragedy, (the noblest and most perfect form of the drama, and doubtless, one of the most magnificent productions of the mind,) was, in all important particulars, the same with that of comedy. Like comedy, it had its origin in the songs and revels of the festivals of Bacchus. These were scenes of rustic festivity and unbounded license. The sponta-

---

* This term was applied to the series of three tragedies which, in the early period of the drama, were brought forward at each representation.

neous effusions which they prompted (probably not unlike those of the improvisatori of Italy,) were gradually fashioned into the Dithyramb and Phallic chorus. These were aided by music, the dance and gesture. They were, at first, narrative—but, by an easy gradation, became imitative of the actions of those whose history they commemorated. Imitation, once introduced, speedily wrought important changes. To vary the perpetual recurrence of odes and recitativos, Thespis (in the sixty-first Olympiad, B. C. 535,) introduced an actor and occasional declamation between the odes. This was the basis and these the materials of tragedy. They were, to a certain extent, combined by Phrynichus, the successor and disciple of Thespis. But he who first wrought the erratic and incoherent Dithyrambic and Phallic odes into the regular chorus, and amplified the meagre scenes of Thespis into the complete and majestic drama was Æschylus. Aristotle affirms that he was the first who brought actors into the scene. He, at least, first made the dialogue the principal part, and is therefore, by nearly universal consent, styled, the father of tragedy. His works are marked by the simplicity and fire which characterize the productions of primitive, unconfined and inventive genius. His great and daring mind delighted to expatiate on the confines of human existence —among the vast and shadowy forms of fable. His favorite dramatis personae are demi-gods and heroes—his favorite themes the gigantic prowess and terrific conflicts of Titans. In strength, sublimity and energy, he stands unsurpassed, perhaps unequalled. Along with these excellencies, he exhibits the usually concomitant faults of occasional extravagance and even bombast, and, " in the arrangement of his pieces, there remains much of ancient simplicity and somewhat even of uncouth rudeness. Yet, in the estimation of the right-minded and judicious, he ranked supreme in tragedy. Even the majestic dignity of Sophocles," and, we might add, the impassioned energy of Euripides " bow, at once, before the gigantic powers of Æschylus."

The next in time, and according to the unanimous opinion of the ancients, the next in merit, was Sophocles. This truly great poet, seems in a good degree, to have blended the excellencies and avoided the defects of his precursor and follower—combining much of the sublimity and intensity of Æschylus with the moral elevation and purity of Euripides. Without descending from the dignity of Æschylus, he imparted a more human interest to the mythi which formed the common subjects of their tragedies.

His vivid apprehensions of moral goodness, did not, however, preserve him from irregularities in his early life, though they led him to lament these irregularities in his latter years, since Plato represents him as exclaiming, "I thank old age for delivering me from the tyranny of my appetites." His characteristics are thus exhibited by a recent anonymous English critic : "His language, though at times marked by harsh metaphor and perplexed construction, is pure and majestic. His management of a subject is admirable. No one understood so well the artful envelopment of the incident, the secret excitation of the feelings, and the gradual heightening of the interest up to the final crisis, when the catastrophe bursts forth in all the force of overwhelming terror or compassion. Such was Sophocles; the most perfect in dramatic arrangement, the most sustained in the even flow of dignified thought, word and tone, among the tragic triumvirate." Mr. Schlegel has bestowed on him the highest, and, to a christian mind, the most attractive encomium : "He is," says he, "of all the Grecian poets, the one whose feelings have most in common with the spirit of our religion."

At the same era with Sophocles, though born about fourteen years later, appeared the third and last distinguished ornament of the tragic drama of Greece, Euripides. His parents, as well as those of Sophocles, bestowed on him a most complete and expensive education. He was the pupil of Anaxagoras in philosophy and of Socrates in morals—and has interwoven the sentiments of both in his admirable productions. He is distinguished for his searching discrimination of the inward workings of thought and passion and his singularly vivid and kindling descriptions of them. His unrivalled pathos for which Aristotle entitles him τραγικώτατος τῶν ποιητῶν, induced Quinctilian in ancient and Fenelon in modern times to recommend him especially to the study of lawyers, and why not for the same reason, to all engaged in the cultivation of eloquence. He is remarkable for his fidelity to nature and human life. This was in fact one point of the ridicule of Aristophanes and was censured even by those critics who thought more of consistency with the rules of the drama than with the incidents of human life. He was thus characterized in contrast with his two compeers in tragedy : "Æschylus described men greater than they can be, Sophocles as they ought to be, Euripides as they are." He was also remarkable for the acuteness and vivacity of his dialogue and in fine, for nothing more than the elevated moral tone of his tragedies. This he probably caught from the discourses and the society of Socrates, that name, which both in wisdom and goodness, stands at the head of "all Greek, all Roman fame." Socrates was not only his instructor but his intimate friend, and never attended dramatic representation but when the tragedies of Euripides were exhibited. The intimacy and esteem of such a man outweighs in favor of his mind and heart all the jeers of contemporary comedians and the censures of mere critics. To render the stage a school of virtue was the avowed purpose of this great poet, and the moral and philosophical reflections with which his compositions are replete caused him to be ranked among the sages of Greece, and procured him the merited title of the philosopher and moralist of the stage. In fact, his studious and sometimes it must be owned, unseasonable introduction of such sentiments was regarded by the ancients as one of the defects of his tragedies. But though this feature might render them less perfect as dramatic compositions, it certainly renders them more attractive to the moralist and the Christian ; to those who study *the antique* not principally to gratify their taste or improve their intellect, but to observe the developments of conscience, the revelations of the inward law—to learn, at once, the powers and the wants of heathenism. To such minds the works of Euripides will appear among the richest and most valuable remains of antiquity—and it is perhaps this very circumstance, which has attracted to him more of the attention and admiration of the moderns than to either of his great, perhaps greater competitors. We may add that his tragedies were a favorite study of Milton.

Time has been as unsparing in the destruction of the tragic as of the comic remains of Greece. Of three alone of her many tragedians, have we any complete works remaining, and these bearing a small proportion to the great fertility of those authors. "They are," says Mr. Schlegel, "those which the Alexandrine critics included in their selection of authors, which was to serve for a basis to the study of the older Grecian literature, not as though these were the only valuable ones, but because in them the different styles of tragic art might be recognized." We possess entire only seven tragedies of Æschylus, seven of Sophocles, and nineteen of Euripides. Of these however, many were considered by the ancients the best works of their respective authors.

Having thus given a brief outline of the history, we next turn our attention to the structure of the Greek drama.

It was originally, as we have already mentioned, a string of unconnected choruses. Thespis introduced scenes and the declamation of an actor. Æschylus further developed and perfected these scenes, and added a second actor. Sophocles introduced a third ; and thus, what was, at first, only an accessory, became the principal part, the body of the drama. Aristotle, the great master of dramatic criticism, has given two divisions of the drama ;—the one, with reference to its quantity, the other, to its quality. Those parts which are necessary to its completeness as to quantity are four—the prologue, the episode, the exode and the chorus. The parode and stasimon are subdivisions of the chorus—the former being the first speech of the whole chorus, the latter, including all those choral odes that are without anapaests and trochees. The commoi (or general lamentations of the chorus and actors together,) are found only in *some* tragedies. The prologue is all that part which precedes the first entrance of the chorus. (This term has therefore entirely changed its meaning, in its application to the Roman and modern drama.) The episode all that which intervenes between the first and the last appearance of the chorus. The exode that which has no choral ode after it. The chorus consisted of the lyric interludes introduced between the scenes.

The prologue was the exposition of the subject by one of the persons of the drama. Its business was to give the spectator so much information relative to the incidents of the piece as would enable him to follow the action with intelligence and interest. The episode was the entire development and progress of the plot. The exode, its consummation and result. The subject of the choral interludes was general reflections, philosophical and moral on the progress of the action—an expression of the hopes and fears awakened by the incidents—sometimes, lamentations on the calamities incident to humanity—sometimes, supplications to the Deity for assistance to the dramatic personage whose cause the chorus espoused ; though, in fact, a spirit of disinterestedness and *non-committal* is, in general, one of its most striking characteristics.

The chorus, in its wild, abrupt and impassioned character, and in the boundless variety of its metres, may be regarded as the relic and representative of the original dithyramb. Here, the sprightly and versatile genius of the Greeks delighted to luxuriate through all the possible forms of verse—and the flexibility and "many-sidedness" of their language were peculiarly favorable to the propensity. In fact, all subsequent imitations of the chorus have been comparatively tame and exhibiting a remote and artificial connection with the action—until it has, at last, entirely disappeared from the drama. This may, in part, have proceeded from the conviction that it impairs the probability of the action and its close resemblance to actual life, but the true cause probably lies deeper. Genius loses its juvenile vigor and boldness with the progress of society. It no longer wheels the same bold and airy flights when its wing has been clipped by criticism. As the world grows older, fancy becomes tamed and depressed, in the same proportion as the judgment and the reasoning powers are invigorated and matured. To this cause we are inclined to ascribe it, that the chorus has altogether vanished from the modern drama, and that it has thus become reduced to simple interlocution.

Mr. Schlegel has philosophized on the intellectual character of the chorus in the following characteristic manner. "We must conceive it as the personification of the thought inspired by the represented action—as the embodiment into the action of the sympathy of the poet, considered as the spokesman of collective humanity. . . . The chorus is, in a word, the idealized spectator. It mitigates the impression of a deeply agitating or deeply touching representation, while it reverberates to the actual spectator, a lyrical and musical expression of his own emotions, and bears him aloft into the region of contemplation."

Horace has given a less ambitious but more intelligible account of the province of the chorus in the following lines :

Actoris partes chorus officiumque virile
Defendat; neu quid medios intercinat actus,
Quod non proposito conducat et haereat apté.
Ille bonis faveatque et consilietur amicé.
Et regat iratos, et amet peccare timentes ;
Ille dapes laudet mensae brevis, ille salubrem
Justitiam, legesque, et apertis otia portis ;
Ille tegat commissa, Deosque precetur et oret,
Ut redeat miseris, abeat fortuna superbis.

Those parts of tragedy which constitute its peculiar character or *quality*, are divided by Aristotle as follows—the fable (i. e. the action, the plot, the contexture of incidents) ; the manners, by which is meant the *disposition* of the speaker, his aversions or propensities. The sentiments comprehend *all that is said*—opinions, arguments, general reflections, etc. The diction is the expression of these sentiments by words. The music and decorations were the external accompaniments and embellishments of the exhibition.

The representation of Greek tragedy was managed on a scale of the greatest magnificence. All the arts, which in the most flourishing period of the drama were in their highest perfection, combined to shed attraction and splendor over that which was, not only a favorite national amusement, but an affair of state and a solemnity of religion. The government erected the theatre, educated the chorusses, awarded the crown (by judges appointed for the purpose,) to the successful competitor, furnished the dresses and scenic embellishments, and, in short, defrayed the whole expenses of the exhibition, the magnificence of which was far beyond any private resources.* The theatre at Athens was a noble structure of stone, erected in the age of Æschylus, the previous edifice of wood having fallen beneath the weight of the crowds assembled at a representation. It contained seats for an audience of thirty thousand persons, range above range, and the whole was surmounted by a lofty portico, adorned with statues. Of its interior arrangements and decorations, our limits will not, of course, permit us to speak minutely. All the resources of art and wealth appear to have been lavished to produce the usual theatrical illusions. The vast Σκηνή or stage, presented the appearance of a sea, a forest, a city or a desert, as the occasion required. As the intercourse between heaven and earth is very frequent in the mythological dramas of Greece, the stage-machinery comprehended a great number of aerial contrivances. There was the Θεολογεῖον, which presented the deities in converse aloft, while the platform which supported them was surrounded and concealed by clouds,—the Μηχανή, which, by means of a sort of crane, was employed suddenly to dart out a god or hero before the spectators and as suddenly to withdraw him when his part was performed,—the Αιώραι, a set of ropes which enabled him to walk in the air, apparently unsupported,—the Γέρανος, which caught persons from the stage and bore them aloft to the clouds,—the Βροντεῖ-

---

* Plutarch states that the Athenians had expended more on the representation of their tragedies than on their foreign wars, either of defence or protection.

ον, a contrivance to imitate the rumbling of thunder,*—the Κε-
ραυνοσκοπεῖον, whence artificial lightnings were darted along the
scenic clouds.

Everything in the actual presentation of the pieces was in a
style of extravagance and exaggeration which must have rendered the most consummate art necessary to produce an illusion.
It is evident, however, from the effect, that that illusion was
perfect. It was, of course, aided by the very circumstance
which rendered it necessary, the vast dimensions of the theatre,
which removed a portion of the spectators to a distance of three
hundred feet from the stage. The person of the actor was
raised to heroic stature by the cothurnus, and amplified to heroic
dimensions by the Κόλπωμα or stuffing, which enveloped his
limbs. The masks, which were an invariable appendage of the
representation, were formed and painted with exquisite skill,
and are said to have expressed, with astonishing accuracy, the
peculiarities of age, sex and rank. The voice of the actor was
not only brought to the highest pitch of strength and clearness
by perpetual exercise and a rigid diet, but was further aided by
a mouth-piece inserted in the mask and by brazen vessels fitted
in the intervals (or, as Vitruvius affirms,) under the seats of the
theatre. The chorus was sung, throughout, with instrumental
accompaniment. The scenes appear to have been partly sung
and partly declaimed. The singing was accompanied by the
flute, the declamation by the lyre ; this accompaniment was
doubtless of a very simple character, designed, principally, to
direct and sustain the voice of the actor.

The histrionic profession was amply rewarded and held in
high honor at Athens, and was not attended with degradation in
any respect. On the contrary, distinguished actors were sometimes sent as ambassadors to foreign states. The professional
actors appear, however, to have been regarded as a licentious
and dissipated class by the philosophers and moralists of the age.

The moral tendency of the Greek drama opens to us a vast
field of thought. That its moral influence was extensive and
powerful beyond that of any other mental production of the age,
cannot be doubted, when we reflect that Athens, its favorite seat,
was the intellectual centre of the world—that the festivals, at
which dramatic pieces were presented, were attended by a concourse of foreigners of the highest rank and character, from all

---

* This was effected by dropping stones from a great height into a
vast brazen vessel, rolling them along plates of copper, etc.

the civilized nations—that the drama was often attended by an auditory of thirty thousand, and was impressed on this vast mass of mind by a representation of unparalleled vividness and magnificence.

A single incident related by Plutarch may give us some idea of the extent to which the great dramatists of Greece were known and their influence felt, even during their own age. We quote his own words, which occur near the end of the life of Nicias, after his description of the disastrous defeat and capture of the Athenian army in Sicily :

"Some of the prisoners owed their preservation to Euripides. Of all the Grecians, his was the muse with whom the Sicilians were most in love. From every stranger that landed in their island, they gleaned every small specimen or portion of his works and communicated it with pleasure to each other. It is said that, on this occasion, a number of Athenians, upon their return home, went to Euripides, and thanked him in the most respectful manner for their obligations to his pen ; some having been enfranchised for teaching their masters what they remembered of his poems, and others having got refreshments when they were wandering about after the battle, for singing a few of his verses. Nor is this to be wondered at, since they tell us that when a ship from Caunus, which happened to be pursued by pirates, was going to take shelter in one of their ports, the Sicilians at first refused to admit her ; upon asking the crew whether they knew any verses of Euripides, and being answered in the affirmative, they received both them and their vessel."

Such was the power of a living Athenian dramatist over the rude mariners and common people of Sicily ! Plutarch also relates in his life of Lysander, that when that general with the confederate Greeks, had taken and was about to sack the city of Athens, a few verses of a chorus of Euripides, sung by a minstrel, so affected himself and his associates, that they determined to spare it. Such facts as these suggest that we may easily underrate the influence of literary works before the discovery of the art of printing. Though they were not *multiplied* by the prodigious fecundity of the press, they were *diffused* by the living voice and preserved in the living memory, and their influence on this very account, was probably deeper and more pervading.

Of the moral character and tendency of Greek comedy, enough was said in the course of our sketch of the history of that branch of the drama.   Our present remarks will therefore have reference principally to tragedy.

How evident, from the most superficial view, that its whole power was concentrated upon those already too active and inflammatory elements of our being—the passions !   Here, in fact, lies the secret of its tremendous danger, its invariable perversion.   Good men have thought that the stage *might be made* a school of virtue ; though no one has gone so far as to assert that it is, or ever has been so.   But we venture to assert, that from the very nature of the case, and for the above mentioned reason, *the acted drama never can become so.*   Accompanied by those associations which have ever clustered around it, it gives a dangerous preponderance to sense and passion ;—divest it of these, and you strip it of its attractions.   The mask, the dance, the song, farces, and pantomimes have formed the *cortége* of the tragic muse—and what was the end of all this apparatus of exciting decoration, but to dazzle the senses and inflame the passions ?

If we examine all the tragedies which have been written from the age of Æschylus to the present time, we cannot avoid the conclusion that their object is not instruction, not reformation, but *effect.*   For this purpose, the subjects of ancient tragedy were selected from those who had occupied an almost super-human elevation, whose downfall therefore, would afford the most terrible catastrophe.

> Τῶν γὰρ μεγάλων ἀξιοπενθεῖς
> Φῆμαι μᾶλλον κατέχουσιν.—*Eurip. Hippol.* 1455.

> Τὰ δ' ὑπερβάλλοντ'
> Μείζους δ' ἄτας ὅταν ὀργισθῇ
> Δαίμων, οἴκοις ἀπέδωκεν.—*Id. Med.* 127—130.

So established was this principle that Aristotle lays it down as an example, which has the force of a rule that " the subjects of the best tragedies are confined to a few families,—to Alcmaeon, Orestes, Œdipus, Meleager, Thyestes, Telephus, and others of the like rank."   Jeremy Taylor has somewhere in his moral works, assigned as the reason of this, that the ordinary lot of mortals was not liable to those terrible vicissitudes which are necessary to form the catastrophes of tragedy.   It was sometimes objected, even by ancient critics, that if tragedy would serve the purpose of instruction, its scenes must be laid, occasionally at least, in the ordinary walks of life, and must exhibit the sufferings, duties and temptations, which are incident to the condition of the majority of mankind.　But to this it was replied that these were wanting in the interest and power, necessary to tragedy—that they did not appeal, with sufficient force, to those emotions of terror and pity, the excitation of which is its object.　It is plain, therefore, that the aim of tragedy is to astonish, to agitate, not to instruct or reform the spectators.

Another proof of this is drawn from the *characters* in which tragedy delights.　It is not the firm, consistent, well balanced man of virtue; but those whose passions are stung to madness by suffering or remorse.　It is the aspiring, baffled, tortured and crushed Prometheus,—the maniac Orestes,—the ferocious and vindictive Medea, burning with a demon's passions and wielding a demon's powers of mischief and revenge.

> Λέαιναν, οὐ γυναῖκα, τῆς Τυρσηνίδος
> Σκύλλης ἔχουσαν ἀγριωτέραν φύσιν.

Let it not be supposed that we would measure all the productions of the human mind by the standard of their direct utility.　That wondrous faculty which sheds such a sunlike brightness and beauty over all the objects of intellection, making them not only visible but refulgent, and bathing them in hues as fancied and beautiful as those of a summer's evening—this wondrous faculty is the gift and inspiration of God, all whose creatures are good and all their spontaneous and unperverted developments lawful and beautiful.　The works of the Creator himself are characterized by splendor and vastness, no less than utility.　But all this splendor and vastness have an ultimate relation to utility; and to require as much of the inventions and works of the human mind is only to demand that its glorious endowments of intelligence and imagination be not given up to waste and prostitution.

The actual moral influence of the ancient drama may, however, be estimated with precision and certainty from the accounts we possess of its immediate effects on the population of Athens, where the art flourished in its highest perfection,—and from the statements and opinions of the wisest and best of the ancients themselves, on the subject.　History has preserved both of these in a sufficient degree, to afford us ample satisfaction;—and both tend to confirm us in the belief that its influence was, to the last degree, pernicious.　We have seen that the theatre at Athens would contain thirty thousand spectators, and was often attended by that number.   The citizens, in the most flourishing period, did not exceed twenty-one or twenty-two thousand.*   As every citizen of Athens was entitled by a law introduced by Pericles, to free admission to the theatre and to an obolus besides, for the purchase of refreshments, we may fairly infer that the whole body of citizens was included in the theatrical assemblies.   While the exhibitions continued, they are said to have diffused a delirious excitement throughout the city.   The inhabitants neglected all business, denied themselves sleep, and spent whole days at the theatre, without ever being satiated by the variety of exhibitions.   There were many circumstances, however, which tended to check the disorders arising from these powerful excitements.   The first and principal check was the unfrequency of dramatic exhibitions.   They were only permitted during the three annual festivals of Bacchus.   The principal dramatic contests were, in fact, confined to the greater Dionysia, the principal anniversary of Bacchus. They were, also, under the direct inspection and control of the government.   They formed, in fact, a part of the administration of state.   The government not only bore the entire expense, as we have seen above, but, by officers appointed expressly for the purpose, superintended every part of the preparation and exhibition.   Females were not permitted to appear on the stage ; they were, in all cases, personated by actors of the other sex.   The whole number of actors in each tragedy was limited to three ; and the few who were professional actors were not looked upon as a degraded class ; they were admitted to the most honorable offices of the state.   Nay, the great tragedians themselves, Æschylus, Sophocles and Euripides thought it no degradation to act a part in their own tragedies.

Yet, with all these restrictions, the stage was from the earliest times, an object of alarm and disapprobation to good men. Solon earnestly opposed the innovations of Thespis, as tending not only to improve and elevate the drama, but to increase its fascinations.   " If," said the sage, " we applaud falsehood in our public exhibitions, we shall soon find it in our contracts and agreements."†   The disapprobation of Socrates was expressed

---

* These however bore a very small proportion to the entire population, including natives who were not citizens, foreigners, and above all slaves, who, through almost all Greece, bore an infinite disproportion to the citizens.

† Plutarch's Solon.

by absenting himself from the theatre, except when the moral dramas of his friend Euripides were represented.* We find that the same views of the stage were entertained by reflecting Romans. Tacitus ascribes the virtue of the German women to the absence of theatrical excitements : Ergo, septa pudicitia agunt, nullis spectaculorum illecebris corruptae ;† "They are characterized by inviolable chastity, being uncorrupted by the seductive influence of public spectacles." Seneca is still more pointed and emphatic in his reprobation of these amusements : Nihil, vero, est tam damnosum bonis moribus, quam in ullo spectaculo desidere. Tunc, enim, per voluptatem, facilius vitia surrepunt. Quid me existimas dicere ? Avarior redeo, ambitiosior, luxuriosior ; "Nothing is so pernicious to good morals as to be present at any of these spectacles. Vice easily finds its way into the heart, through the pleasurable emotions which they excite. From such scenes I depart more avaricious, more ambitious, more luxurious than before."‡

Were such the undisputed effects of theatrical exhibitions on the ancient Greeks, and such the sentiments with which they were regarded by the best and wisest who had an opportunity of observing their influence ? The lesson taught by this fact is a very distinct and impressive one ;—and it is the more so, when we reflect on the wide difference between the Greek theatre and that of modern times. There, these entertainments were only permitted during a few days of the year ; they were arranged and superintended by the magistrates ; the actors did not form a large and distinct and, we may add, degraded class ;

---

* Plato quoted by Rousseau : Lettre à d' Alembert sur son article Genève. This treatise contains some admirable views on the subject of the theatre, and exposes with great eloquence, its pernicious influence : "Des spectacles et des moeurs! Voila qui formeroit vraiment un spectacle à voir; d'autant plus, que ce seroit la première fois ! etc.

† De Mor. Ger. c. 19.

‡ Sen. Ep. 7.—To these testimonies may be added one from an enlightened and patriotic American citizen, one whose eloquent writings, contributed not a little to the revolution which gave birth to our liberties : "As a citizen and friend to the morals and happiness of society, I should strive hard against the admission and much more the establishment of a theatre in any state of which I was a member. . . . I am satisfied that the stage is the nursery of vice, and disseminates the seeds of it far and wide with an amazing and baneful success."— *Memoirs of Josiah Quincy, jun., Diary.*

above all, females were, in no case, permitted to appear on the stage, and, at the representation of comedy, do not appear even to have been present at the theatre. Yet even when thus restricted and qualified, this amusement was condemned and avoided by good men. What are we, then, to think of its tendency in our own times, when these checks are removed,—when these compensating circumstances no longer exist,—when it is given up to the license of daily exhibition, dependent on popular patronage, and, of course, graduated to popular taste? The result is, as might have been anticipated. The stage has become, not only the school, but we might even say, the empire of vice. Vice presides over its decorations and animates too often its most admired performances ; and no man, who has a just value of moral purity, and a just fear of the power of temptation, will venture himself, (much less expose the tender and unguarded heart of youth,) in a region so thoroughly imbued with all the influences most hostile to virtue.

The merits of the drama, however, as a subject of solitary study, present quite a different question. And while we maintain that *scenic representation* has, in all ages, been an engine of moral evil, and will never be otherwise, we yet feel that there is no hazard, but on the contrary, great advantage from directing the attention of youth to the study of the ancient drama. Each branch is attended with its peculiar advantages.

Ancient comedy is a picture of ancient life ;—the only picture, of its kind, which we now possess. History presents only an outline of its form ;—epic and lyric poetry a selection of its more beautiful and commanding features. But comedy presents it as it lived and moved. After the lapse of ages and of centuries, it stands an imperishable transcript of the intrigues, the passions, the follies, and, in some instances, of the purer and nobler qualities of those who have long since vanished from the earth. It is, therefore, nearly the only means we now possess of attaining a minute and familiar knowledge of the domestic and social habits of the ancients. And those who love to study human nature in all attitudes and under all circumstances will not be disposed to undervalue this quality. In fact, it must be impossible to appreciate or even understand the works of the ancients, much less to form a just estimate of their moral condition, without this kind of knowledge.

As a means of attaining a thorough mastery of ancient languages, the study of comedy will be found no less important.

The genius of every language is to be sought in its colloquial idioms. Without a familiarity with these, its graver and more elaborate authors can never be read with facility and pleasure. The colloquial idioms of a *dead language* are principally preserved in its comedy. For this plain reason, no course of classic instruction can be considered as complete which does not include portions, at least, of the comic writers. We hazard little in affirming that no student ever found himself at home either in Latin or Greek, without an acquaintance with them.

This study has also, all the sanction which can be derived from the authority of the highest names in classic learning and education. Melancthon exacted from the instructors of youth "a conscientious diligence"[*] in the exposition of certain characters of Terence. Luther did not disapprove even the *exhibition* of the comedies of Terence in schools, (though we confess ourselves far from prepared to go the same length,) and thought that many benefits might be derived from the study of comedy.[†] Jerome was in the habit of finding relief and exhilaration from severer studies and exercises in the comedies of Plautus,[‡] and Chrysostom is said to have kept under his pillow a copy of Aristophanes.

We would not, however, place ancient comedy, either Greek or Latin, in the hands of youth without first rigidly subjecting it to the process of selection and expurgation. We know of only a single comedy in which even the latter would be unnecessary, —the Captives of Plautus.

Tragedy may be read with still less danger and still higher and more important advantages. The old tragedy of Greece is a lofty and stately thing. It is the vehicle of their early history, their philosophy[§] and morality,—it is the development of their intellectual, and to a certain extent, of their social and domestic system. The tragedies of Æschylus, Sophocles, and Euripides, though written by pagans, and, of course, containing much that is defective and erroneous, yet have by no means, in themselves

---

[*] Superstitiosam diligentiam.

[†] Memoires de Luther par Michelet, B. IV. ch. 4.

[‡] Post noctium crebras vigilias, post lacrymas, Plautus sumebatur in manus.

[§] "Aristotle has followed in philosophy, the threads of thought spun from the heads of the tragic poets."—*Brumoy, Theatre des Grecs, Int.*

considered, an immoral tendency. Their authors were enlightened, philanthropic and public-spirited men, far above the vile ambition of corrupting the morals of their countrymen. The moral sentiments, the views of a retributive providence, which they have wrought into their dramas, are often surprisingly high and pure, and betoken an early period, before the minds of men were so extensively pervaded by the multiplying errors and deepening darkness of paganism.* It was not in themselves that these works were considered dangerous by the ancient moralists.† It was when *acted*, when surrounded by the fascinations and excitements of scenic exhibition. The same moralists have made ample use of these works in the philosophy of the human mind. And the great apostle of the Gentiles has repeatedly pointed his own moral reflections by apt quotations from the dramatists of Greece. In connection with an instance of this kind, Calvin thus observes : " We learn from hence that they are superstitious who are scrupulous of obtaining knowledge from profane authors. For since all truth is from God, if anything has been well and forcibly expressed, even by bad men, it ought not to be rejected, because it originally proceeded from God. And since all things are his, why is it not right to apply to his glory, whatever, from any source, is capable of such an application ?"

But it is not enough to say that this study is not unfavorable to morality—it may and ought to be made subservient to it ;—and it cannot fail to be thus subservient, if these works are examined in connection with such inquiries as these :—" What evidence do I here discern of moral perceptions—of distinctions of right and wrong ?—What traces of that law which is written on the human heart ?—What coincidences, either of truth or morality, with the inspired volume ?—What intimations of a belief in the immortality of the soul ?—What views of retributions, present or future ?" Studied on such principles as these, the ancient drama will be found invested with a high moral interest and richly fraught with moral instruction and impression.

To all, then, who wish to become Greek scholars,—who

---

* Antiquitas—quae, quo propius aberat ab ortu et divina progenie, hoc melius ea fortasse, quae erant vera, cernebat.—*Cic. Tusc. Disp. I.* 12.

† The laws of Athens provided that the tragedies of Æschylus, Sophocles and Euripides should be *read* in public every year.—*Greek Theatre*, p. 106. Cambridge, 1830.

wish to imbue their minds with the spirit of the antique, and to
penetrate the intellectual and moral system of that extraordinary
people, the ancient Greeks ; we would say,—study profoundly
the noble remains of their great tragedians ;—but do it in the
spirit of an enlightened and firm eclecticism, knowing how to
" refuse the evil and to choose the good."   And, into what department of literature, ancient or modern, can we safely venture
without the exercise of this discrimination ?

ARTICLE XI.

THE PRESBYTERIAN CONTROVERSY :—ITS OCCASIONS AND PRESENT STATE.*

By Erastus C. Benedict, Counsellor at Law, New-York.

THE controversy in the Presbyterian church, in the United
States, is one of the most remarkable series of events which the
history of religion in our times will present.   Its effect upon
that church, aside from its general disorganizing and schismatic

---

* [As the readers of the Repository are of different denominations,
and, to some extent perhaps, of different views in regard to the subject of this Article, it has occurred to us that some may regret to see
it introduced upon our pages.   But the principles involved in the
controversy now pending in the Presbyterian church are too important, and its consequences are already too widely and painfully felt,
in their bearings upon other denominations and upon the great religious enterprises of the day, to be regarded with indifference by any.
Nor can it be desirable to confine the history of a controversy, so
widely extended, to publications which circulate only among the
parties primarily interested in its results.   In its probable and permanent effects upon the cause of religious liberty and of christian benevolence in our country, generally, it is a topic of universal interest.
To meet the expressed wishes of many, therefore, we have thought
it proper to solicit the present Article from an able writer, whose opportunities of a thorough acquaintance with the subject, as well as
his freedom from any personal interest in the results of the controversy, are such as to inspire confidence in the fairness and candor of
his views.   The Article presents a compendious and consecutive his-

tendency, is to be deeply deplored by its friends. Its members, in some instances, are looking to other communions as a refuge from that injustice, which they attribute to the operation of the Presbyterian system, but which in truth could not exist, except in the widest departure from the plain principles of that system, and in open violations of the constitution of that church, as organized in this country. Independency and Congregationalism are beginning to be regarded by some, as promising, at least for a time, in their feebler power to oppress, that security which the more cautiously devised and stronger built safeguards of the Presbyterian system have failed to afford. Thus a controversy, professedly kept up to save Presbyterianism from the inroads of Congregationalism, has probably done more to bring the former into disrepute and to extend the latter, within the usual bounds of the Presbyterian church, than all the arguments of all the writers on the subject could ever have done, if the judicatories of the church had been true to the principles of their American constitution. The controversy has apparently passed its crisis and, although many readers are but too painfully familiar with its details, still it cannot be amiss to devote a few pages to a sketch of both the ostensible and the concealed causes of the difficulty, the strange history of their action, and the present position of the parties. In thus taking a view, however brief, of the whole subject, it will be necessary to go back to the first organization of the church in this country, and glance at its elementary principles, at the hazard of being trite and uninteresting. The necessity will be a sufficient apology.

As in politics, so in ecclesiastical matters, our character was forming from the time of the first settlements. All along;

---

tory of the controversy, which, as to facts and their relations, may be relied on, and will be of permanent value to such as may wish to trace to their consequences the principles which have been urged on either side. It is, at the same time, an able defence of the constitutional principles and privileges of the Presbyterian church, as they are understood by the writer, and by those, generally, who have opposed the late divisive acts of a party claiming to be the General Assembly of that church. However much, therefore, some may dissent from these principles, we trust that all will regard it, in spirit, and in general interest and importance, as altogether worthy of the space which it here occupies, in a work whose pages are pledged to be open, on all suitable occasions, " to the free discussion of questions of morals ;" it being understood that these discussions shall be conducted with courtesy and candor.—ED.

through one hundred and fifty years, the seeds were sown, which shot up into strength and beauty sixty years ago, when was adopted the now obvious principle of universal toleration —equal rights and equal protection to all,—which laid the foundation of a system of institutions, unlike anything which had before existed. The great experiment, then entered upon, of separating entirely the church from the state, and, with a noble confidence, trusting religion to those proper supports which her Almighty Protector will never fail to provide, has well justified the prophetic hopes of the men of those days.

To the prevalence of popular and republican systems of church government is to be attributed much of the success of that experiment, in the church and in the state. The Congregational and the Presbyterian forms had included, from the beginning, almost all the sects that existed in this country, and they have always been the fast friends and steady supporters of religious and civil liberty. Indeed the principles of liberty and equality are the very principles of these organizations. Both are alike opposed to the despotism of popery and the aristocracy of prelacy. It was this, their republican nature, that led king James to say that "a Scottish presbytery as well agrees with monarchy as God and the devil;"* and that, in the freest monarchy the world has ever seen, condemns them to a sickly and constrained existence. Congregationalism is, in its nature, democratic, trying, judging, governing, by actual assemblies of the people. In the modified form, however, in which it is generally administered in this country, it acknowledges the right of appeal to counsels mutually chosen, and, in some cases, ex-parte-counsels are allowed. Presbyterianism is a republican system, a representative government, relying upon the wisdom and goodness of men chosen by the people for judges and councillors, and, by its carefully provided checks, and its liberal right of appeals, acknowledges, while it guards against, the passions, the prejudices—the imperfections—of the best men. These two systems of government, alike purely ecclesiastical and not sacerdotal, and alike founded upon the principle of perfect equality of right in the members of the church, were widely in

---

* "The *lords* and the rest stood amazed at his majesty's wise discourse; archbishop Whitgift said, undoubtedly his majesty spake by the special assistance of God's spirit. Dr. Bancroft, bishop of London, upon his knee, protested his heart melted with joy."—*Barlow.*

operation in this country. The Congregationalists of various sects occupied almost the whole of New England, and were sparsely scattered through the other States, at the time of the revolution. The Presbyterians — English, Scotch, French, Swiss, Dutch and German, abounded more in the Southern and Middle States. The Presbyterian church proper consisted of four hundred and nineteen churches, scattered through the land. It is worthy of remark that so little did the difference between the Presbyterian and Congregational forms show itself, and so free was the fellowship between the two sects, that, in common parlance, both were called Presbyterians, and they are still called so to a great extent.

From the peace to 1789 the universal mind, in this country, was busy with modelling and organizing our various governments, to adapt them to the new state of things, and it was to be expected that the same spirit would reach the churches. Accordingly the government of the Presbyterian church was reconstructed, and a system of polity adopted better fitted to the change in the institutions of the country. In 1784—5 the subject was agitated. In 1786, the larger presbyteries were divided, and in 1788 the only synod was divided into four.

In that age of written constitutions—the practical application of the idea of a social compact—that church first digested, arranged and codified the rights of its people, the principles of its government, and the forms of its ministrations. Its constitution was formed with a solemnity, and clothed with an authority, superior to the fluctuating changes of opinion, giving to all, in an acceptable form, the creative patent of " the powers that be." It may be observed, that in a new country, of mixed population, without precedents,—looking to no common source of opinion, a written constitution would present advantages not attainable in any other mode. And it is not the least striking evidence of the wisdom of those days, that there was not adopted any old system of government on any known form of social compact, in church or state. A mixed population might be strongly united in favor of a new system of their own making, while any old one would not fail to arouse old prejudices and kindle anew heart-burnings and strifes. Therefore, as in the state, they examined all forms of free government and compiled a system all their own; so in the Presbyterian church, they examined all protestant forms of polity, and compiled a system, presbyterian in its principles, but unlike the constitution of any other church.

It bore the striking family likeness, so obvious in all the American constitutions, in their leading features, while, in detail, no two can be said to be alike.　It was but an individual of another variety having the same general characteristics.　It could not be otherwise, for, like them, it was the work of the chosen representatives of men whose hearts had never fainted, and whose hands had never been weary, in the discouragements and toils of the struggle for independence.

Thus a wisely constituted system of church polity should always partake of the general nature and form of the political institutions under which it is to operate, especially in popular governments, lest one of antagonizing principles, in times of exaltation, should triumph over the other.　" Thus it was, that, under the eye, and with the approbation or permission of the apostles, different modes of church government prevailed in different countries.　The ecclesiastical constitution which might well accord with the national sentiments and civil usages of the Christians of Syria or Persia, or the provinces of Hellenic Asia, might be altogether repugnant to the feelings of the churches of Greece proper, of Italy, Gaul, or northern Africa.　That sort of superstitious, servile and despotic inflexibility, which is characteristic of the arrogant churchman of later ages, assuredly was not the temper of the first promulgators of the gospel.　St. Paul, especially, had learned that high wisdom which is at once immovable in principle and compliant in circumstantials.　He carried about no iron model of ecclesiastical government, from country to country."*　" The liquid and convertible terms" in which the polity of the first churches is dimly and uncertainly shadowed forth in the New Testament, not by inculcation but by diversified example, only authorizes the belief that, by the agency of bishops, elders, and deacons, the churches are to be taught and governed by that system of combinations and rules which is best fitted to existing circumstances ;—bishops, ordained by the laying on of the hands of the presbyters, equal in power and rights, administering the sacraments and instructing the people, in a particular church ;—elders, chosen by the people, the equal coadjutors of the bishops in government and discipline ;—deacons, chosen by the people, to receive and distribute the alms and take care of the poor of a particular church. These are regarded by Presbyterians, as the scriptural elements of ecclesiastical organization, and their combination into various-

---

* Spiritual Despotism.

ly constituted judicial and supervisory bodies with prescribed rights and duties, in the constitution of the presbyterian church, deserves a moment's attention in connection with this subject.

The bishop and elders of a particular church, chosen by that church, constitute the first judicatory, called the church session, which is clothed with the right of admitting new members and is charged with the duty of maintaining the spiritual government of that particular church, subject to an appeal to the presbytery.

The Presbytery is a judicatory formed of all the bishops, and one elder from each church, (chosen by the session,) in a district embracing several churches. This judicatory has the original jurisdiction of licensing, ordaining and judging ministers, and of receiving new churches, and is charged with the duty of visiting the churches, deciding appeals from the sessions and reviewing their proceedings, subject, however, to appeals to the synod. All proceedings effecting the rights or standing of church members must originate in the session, and those affecting clergymen must originate in the presbytery.

The Synod is the next superior judicatory and consists of all the bishops, and an elder from each church, in a district embracing at least three presbyteries. It is charged with the duty of erecting, uniting and dividing presbyteries, and of reviewing their decisions and proceedings, subject to an appeal to the General Assembly, which is the ultimate judicatory of the church. It is made up of bishops and elders in equal numbers, delegated by the presbyteries in their corporate capacity. To this body belongs the power of erecting synods, reviewing their decisions and proceedings, deciding controversies of doctrine and discipline, and of reproving, warning and bearing testimony against error in doctrine or immorality in practice, in any church, presbytery or synod. No one can read the constitution without seeing that its framers were well aware of the truth—so firmly settled by the history of the past—that the tendency of power, in church as well as in state, is to abuse. "It grows by what it feeds on," and nothing can secure right and justice but established, known and wise rules of proceeding and the right of appeal. Thus the principles of discipline and the rules of proceeding, devised with singular wisdom, are carefully incorporated into the constitution, protecting the accused against the spirit of party, the blindness of prejudice and the madness of fanaticism. He is first to be heard before his neighbors, if a layman, in his own church session; if a clergyman, in his own presbytery. Thence, by appeal, the matter may be carried to the presbytery, the synod, and the General Assembly, bodies increasing in numbers, and more and more remote from the prejudices of the controversy, till it reaches a tribunal selected from all parts of the country, bringing to its decision the freedom and impartiality of strangers.

This system, as will readily be seen, is admirably adapted to extension over a large territory, without losing its unity and connection. In this it differs widely from pure Congregationalism, which spends its force in a single congregation no larger than can meet in one place and transact business. This deficiency, however, has been in a measure supplied in the Congregational systems of New England, which approach, more or less, in different States, to the Presbyterian form. Especially in the State of Connecticut has the connection and subordination of ecclesiastical representative assemblies given to the Congregational church a form resembling that of the Presbyterian church. The first settlers of New England—the pilgrims—in some prominent points of their church organizations, were Presbyterians. It is not worth while here to inquire how so many of their descendants have come to adopt a more Congregational form. It seems, however, that their organization, in the several States, into conferences, conventions, consociations, etc. formed of clerical and lay delegates, may well be considered as evidence of a fondness for a representative system, capable of extension, and may, in part account for the readiness with which they and the Presbyterians have always united with each other. The Presbyterian constitution adopted in 1788, abounds in the great principles of freedom of opinion and of conscience, of republican simplicity, of order, and of democratic equality of rights and of powers, and the cognate principles of toleration and liberal charity. These, too, were the cherished principles of the New England Congregationalists. This liberal spirit of the two sects enabled the Independents and Congregationalists, in Presbyterian regions, to come under that constitution, and the Presbyterian church was rapidly extended. The General Assembly did not fail to act on the liberal principles it had adopted, and, under the constitutional "power to correspond with foreign churches," joined hands of brotherhood, from time to time, with the other organized sects, by an interchange of delegates, on plans of union. In 1792, with the General Association of Connecticut ; in 1798, with the Reformed Dutch and Associate Reformed churches ; in 1801 with the General Association of Connecticut, for the new settlements ; in 1802, with the Northern Associated Presbytery ; in 1803, with the Convention of Vermont ; in 1808, with the Middle Association ; in 1810, with the Association of New Hampshire ; in 1811, with the Association of Massachusetts ; in 1819, another was proposed with the Associate Reformed church, which like the first, was not accepted by them, and in 1821 and 1822, the union with that sect was made complete, by the General Assembly, receiving the whole sect into the bosom of the Presbyterian church, and all the members of its General Synod, then in session, into full membership of the then sitting General Assembly. By these various plans of union the delegates were allowed to act and vote as members of the Assembly ; and they were adopted by the respective assemblies, in most if not all of the cases, with entire unanimity ; and, having been, most of them, the work of two, and some of three General Assemblies, they can be no less than the result of a characteristic liberal policy of the church.

The "Plan of Union for the new settlements," formed in 1801, has acquired an importance which entitles it to more notice. It has been used as a means of dividing the Presbyterian church. In 1801 the frontiers of our rapidly extending settlements, were found to embrace emigrants from Connecticut and other New England States, and from the Presbyterian portions of the country, pioneers in religion, as they were in civilization. The settlements were small and scattered, and received only the occasional ministrations of the gospel and its ordinances from the missionaries that a feeble charity sent to preach in the wilderness. These missionaries were of the two sects. As the faithful were multiplied, it became desirable that pastors should be settled, that there might be, at least here and there, fixed lights for the guidance of the people. Neither sect, however, in most cases, could do anything alone. Their united strength could yield but a scanty support to one self-denying minister of religion, and thus, if neither would yield the point of sectarian preference, the fires could not be kindled on their altars. The subject was represented to the General Assembly of the Presbyterian church and the General Association of Connecticut, then being on the most intimate terms of correspondence. These two bodies, to remove the evil above referred to, and to facilitate the spread of the gospel by promoting union and harmony, adopted four joint recommendations, to the ministers, missionaries and people of the new settlements.

1. The promotion, by all proper means, of mutual forbearance and accommodation.

2.—3. In case minister and people should be of different sects, the preserving, by each party, of its ecclesiastical connection and form of government and discipline, and that difficulties between ministers and people should be arranged by a sort of arbitration or council, half of each sect, unless they could agree to submit to the forms of the sect to which the minister belonged.

4. In case of a mixed settlement, they recommended that different views of church government should be no obstacle to their uniting in one church, and settling a pastor—administering the internal discipline by a standing committee of the communicants, with a right of appeal to the presbytery, or to the church, as the accused might be of one sect or the other, the standing committee having the right to be represented in the presbytery when cases of discipline went up on appeal.

This was the " PLAN OF UNION."* It did not provide for the admission of any one into the church or the ministry in violation or neglect of the rules or usages of the sect with which he was united. It recommended no one to give up his own sect, nor to enter that of the other. It only provided substantially that, the pastoral relation might exist between a minister and people of the two sects, without either being guilty of violations of church order. Thus, under the operation of this plan, the Presbyterian minister of a Congregational church and the elder from a Presbyterian church met in the presbytery, and, from the same churches, the Congregational minister and the lay delegate met in the association, and the representation, in both bodies, was complete. As the parties became habituated to the operation of this union, their attachment to the strictness of their sectarian forms must have been weakened in some measure, and, with a broader charity and a kinder toleration, the conviction must have been strengthened that mere form was of little moment, and the parties mutually tended toward each other. The Presbyterians invited their Congregational brethren to sit with them, as corresponding members. They all met together.

---

* The Plan of Union will be found at length in the last July number of the Repository, page 230.

The difference was almost forgotten. Semi-presbyterian and semi-congregational, in their primary assemblies, from necessity, at their feeble beginning, a few of them continued so from choice, when the new settlement had become a city, and the wilderness populous villages. Thus, while in reality the churches without elders were a separate sect, so far as polity was concerned, they did, in some, consider themselves as attached to the Presbyterian church, and entitled to be represented in its higher judicatories. This plainly was not authorized by the terms of the Plan of Union; still nothing was more natural, under the example of the General Assembly, in admitting delegates from Congregational bodies to its full membership, than that the presbyteries should do as much, and that, without much question from any quarter, it should come to be considered a matter of right. And so it was considered, and Congregational ministers and committee men, (quasi-elders,) were allowed to sit in the presbyteries. They had, however, in these cases, no Congregational connections, and were considered as parts of the Presbyterian church. For thirty-six years the undisputed operation of that plan multiplied and increased the churches and the means of religious instruction. It was really a plan of united missionary enterprise,—the first fruits of a liberal spirit, manifesting itself in the concerted action of two great sects;—the same spirit which, a little later, brought so many, of so many sects, together, on the great platform of united action in voluntary association, interchanging the hands of cordial fellowship, and laboring for united success in a common cause. Of these none came foward with a readier zeal, or labored with a more willing industry, than the Presbyterians, urged on by the often repeated recommendations of the General Assemblies. It is refreshing to look back and see all those great men, whose talents and piety have given so much honor to that church, rallying upon the principles which should always characterize American Presbyterians. It would give pleasure to illuminate the page with their names, but we could not do so without calling up some whose subsequent shrinking into narrowness, and falling away into sectarianism, would be such blots upon the lustrous record that it would be painful to look upon.

In the matter of doctrine too, the framers of the constitution were no less considerate. They did not require, as a condition of church membership, the formal adoption of an extended creed or detailed specification of all theological and metaphysical. truth. They well knew that the vast majority of private Christians are unable to form a belief on many of those subjects, upon which the sincerest piety has not secured agreement in divines of the clearest minds, the soundest learning and the deepest study. Besides, "free thoughts,"—liberal investigation,—the right to differ in opinion,—is the foundation of protestantism. Thus, while the constitution declares that "there are truths and forms about which good men may differ," and on which they should exercise mutual forbearance, it sufficiently provides for soundness in the faith by adopting "a system" of theological truth, which candidates for licensure and ordination —bishops, elders, and deacons—are required to receive and adopt, " as containing the *system* of doctrine taught in the Holy Scriptures." It is to be adopted as " *a system*," not as a formula of words, from which there could be no departure ; else illustration and argument, explanation and enforcement of doctrine would be denied to the ministers of religion, and "forms" of preaching, as well as forms of prayer, should have been provided. " Requiring implicit faith and absolute and blind obedience, is to destroy liberty of conscience and reason also," is the emphatic language of our confession of faith.

I have thus, at greater length than I intended, endeavored to sketch such an outline of the organization and principles of the Presbyterian church in this country, and its relations to the Congregational churches, as seemed to be necessary to a full understanding of the pending unfortunate controversy. It was under such an organization, administered on such principles, that this church grew from the one hundred and seventy-seven ministers of 1788 to more than twelve times that number, while the population of the country increased fourfold. It was a great and harmonious sect, and, by the silent operation of principles, it interchanged with our political institutions a mutual and indirect support ten times more efficient than could have arisen from a legal union of church and state, which American Presbyterians have always believed to be as surely destructive of genuine piety as of political and religious liberty.

I said it was a harmonious sect. It would have remained so, if its own principles had not been departed from ;—but where has not discord been, within the last few years ? All human opinions and conduct seem to have been marked by a singular agitation. Religion, morals, politics, learning, have all felt it, and have been disturbed by its malign influence. It has seemed to spring from a zeal of wonderful intensity, pursuing its object with a small and exclusive intellectual vision,—a microscopic eye, which has no field of view, which cannot span a system or appreciate the force of mutually operating causes. Instances will occur to every mind in which a single principle or practice has been on one side attacked, as though it were the last citadel of all the powers of evil, and on the other side defended, as though it really supported the whole "pillared firmament" of truth.   A striking feature of this spirit has been pride and conceited sufficiency,—a practical guardianship of one's neighbor, and of all the interests of earth and heaven,— which says to others, " stand thou there, I am holier than thou. We are the people, and wisdom shall die with us." In short, it is a total disobedience, in practice, of the apostolic command, that we study to be quiet, and do our own business.   The Presbyterian church did not escape this besom of destruction. Individuals began to agitate there, also, and soon gathered a party which took up, in quick succession, the creed, the order, —the infallibility of the church, as the " one idea" with which to work reform.   *The creed*—all its words must be learned and carried by vote, as the essence of truth.   " And they said unto him, say now Shibboleth, and he said Sibboleth.   Then they took him and slew him."   *Order*—a departure, no matter on what expediency, from the forms or usages of the church, must not, in any, the least matter, be tolerated.   *Infallibility*—the church, in her organized and corporate capacity, is, by the appointment of God, the censor of the books, the supervisor of the conduct, the conductor of the education, the collector and distributor of the alms of all mankind.   In the matter of doctrine came doubts and suspicions and jealousies, spending their force, at first, in cold looks and unbrotherly passing by on the other side.   It was whispered in certain places that Mr. —— is unsound,—he has said so and so.   Dr. —— thinks thus and thus.   His principles certainly tend to this or that error.   The hint, the shrug, the solemn shake of the head, the significant regret poisoned the minds of the church and of the presbytery. The pastoral relation was broken up.   Discord began to manifest itself in presbytery and synod, and open charges of heresy, at length, took the place of the *ambiguas voces* of infant calumny.   Men in great favor among the churches were pointed at with solemnity as exercising a dangerous influence, by their words and their writings.   They were accused and convicted of heresies, which they strenuously and honestly insisted they had never believed, and, though the General Assembly restored the victims of local injustice, the peace of the church was destroyed, and disunion and schism began to be openly avowed as desirable.   An acknowledged large majority remained, however, firmly friendly to the peaceful administration of the liberal constitution of the church ; and the agitating party, though they had gained some strength by their exclusive claims of doctrinal purity, were defeated.   They then addressed themselves to the love of the constitution and order of the church, with the same modest practical demand, that all should bow to their interpretations.   The same waking up of excitement, which had been resorted to in the matter of doctrine, told with still more effect on this point.   They seized upon the assumption, that many of the churches in western New York, Ohio and Michigan, were formed on the plan of union,—were without ruling elders, and were Congregational or semi-congregational, in their government.   The cry was raised, "the Congregationalists are trying to overthrow the constitution, and to substitute their own system in its place !"   Every one knew that New England was Congregational, and the western part of our country was filled with citizens and clergymen of New England origin or descent.   This gave a sort of foundation for the cry.   "Look," said they, "at our opponents ! were they not born Congregationalists ?   They are, of course, attached to the form of its government still.—We are the only true Presbyterians.   Look at the men whom we could not overthrow.—They are New England men !—Look, who defended,—New England men !—Look at the majorities in the Assembly,—New England men—Congregationalists !   Look at the West.   Many churches there have no elders, no regular Presbyterian organization.   And the graduates of the schools and seminaries of New England are now flocking thither to take charge of them !   Our Zion is in danger ; and when it is too late, the friends of good order—born Presbyterians,—will be but a handful ;—we shall be driven from the church, or humbled and degraded in it !"   Allegations so absurd and unsupported by proof were seldom noticed or denied by those against whom they were made, and that was made "confirmation strong, as proof from Holy Writ," of their truth.   A portion of the church was fearfully excited and honestly alarmed ;—but even yet the friends of union and peace were a majority.   The General Assembly and the constitution

were still bonds of union.——Then came a new rally, on the
grounds both of doctrine and of order ; and Congregationalism,
and Pelagianism, and Perfectionism, and Taylorism, were rung,
in discord and in unison, without specific charges, till there
could be no peace. A foreign mission board was proposed to
be appointed by the General Assembly. This was opposed by
the friends of united and concentrated effort, as unnecessary,
while the American Board located at Boston was so well performing that duty. This was another fact, to show the progress of Congregationalism ! And the American Home Missionary Society, which had done more to extend the Presbyterian church permanently, than all other organizations, was,
without proof, charged with possessing the power and the purpose to subvert its constitution, simply because its happy plan
of calling out and aiding effort had given it an almost miraculous growth and extension, and many, perhaps most, of those
who had been its beneficiaries, voted against the disunionists ;
and its secretary had never ceased to contend for the integrity
of the church.

Hereupon, suddenly, the American Home Missionary Society, the American Board of Commissioners for Foreign Missions, the American Education Society, (and later, the American Tract Society, and the American Sunday School Union,
etc.) during their whole previous existence, the favorites of the
Presbyterian church, were discovered to be, not the church in
her organized and social capacity, but mere voluntary societies,
and wholly unauthorized to spread the gospel.

There are many who cannot see why errors in administration are not to be charged upon a *general principle* of organization. They confound an *object* with the *abuse* of it. They
see no way to separate adventitious and remediable evil from
inherent and necessary good. To such, an attack upon some
of the oldest, largest and most useful of these societies came
with all the favor which the practical adoption of one's preconceived notions usually finds in the human mind. The disunionists thus acquired much additional strength, in their onset
upon voluntary societies. They did not stop to see that the
evils which were really to be lamented in some voluntary societies were not to be found in all, and had no manner of connection with the voluntariness of the principle of association,
but would all be quite as likely to exist, and many of them with
much greater aggravation, under what is called ecclesiastical

organization. The voluntary principle is the only one that can ever succeed in this country till the principles of our institutions and the modes of thinking of our people shall be changed. It will be long before we shall learn that benevolence, liberality, generosity, almsgiving, are anything but voluntary exercises. They can be the exercises of "the cheerful giver" alone, and can in no manner, fall within the jurisdiction of ecclesiastical courts. They cannot be compelled nor imposed, by a majority, upon a minority. The point, however, was made one of strict religious right. It was said "the world is to be evangelized through the instrumentality of the church—a spiritual society for a spiritual work."—"The word of God knows of but one public association of men for scriptural purposes. That association is the church of the living God."—"All that for which the church was organized was to perpetuate and propagate the truth."—"There should be no missionary society," (no society of any sort,) "but the church," which is "sufficient for every good work and purpose of reform." It cannot be amiss to devote a paragraph or two to these notions.

The word of God was given and is preserved to reveal the truth and to perpetuate it among men. The ministry of the word was established, and has been kept up, to propagate the truth. The church, with its outward organization, was established for the mutual encouragement and care of those whom the Bible and the preacher, under the favor of God, have brought within her sacred enclosures,—those who, having found the truth, still find, in their erring natures, too many temptations to depart from it. The church, in its social capacity, is but the garrison to keep what the soldiers of the cross have conquered. It is not a close corporation, chartered under the great seal of heaven, to enjoy a monopoly in the work of spreading the gospel. The business of sending abroad the word of God and the authorized ministers of religion, to those who have them not, is the individual, personal duty of all who have the means; and it is in no sense the duty of the church, as an organized body. The idea that one man, or any number of men, having the ability, may not, of right, send abroad and support the ministers of religion, is an absurdity which implies a denial of the divine commission of such ministers, received at their ordination. The way it came to prevail is an instance of common false logic, and shows clearly how the most important errors may become firmly established by confounding the literal and figurative use of words.

In a great and laudable zeal to urge on the reformation and conversion of the world, and especially to appeal strongly to professing Christians, all parties, of all sects, instead of speaking of the duty of professing Christians, spoke of the duty of the church, by a common figure of speech, as when we speak of the religious duties of American citizens, we say the *American people* should support the institutions of religion. No one would for a moment suppose that we intended to speak of the American people, in their organized and corporate capacity, and to contend that the government of the United States is alone competent and bound to support the gospel. Yet it is in this way that the duty of private Christians has been transferred to the organized government of the whole church, and, by another similar step, the right to perform the clearest duty is denied both to private Christians and associations. So that "*mother church,*" in the worst style of old Romanism, is to relieve individuals from all duty on this subject, but that of pouring their money into her treasury, at the bidding of her courts, to be used, applied and disposed of, as well as collected, under the requirements of ecclesiastical supremacy. This is not the place to point out, in detail, the practical results of such principles. The dominion of a corrupted priesthood, the bigotry and blindness of a trembling people, the chaining of the pestilent freedom of the press and of opinion, the decking of the church with meretricious ornaments, and, finally, her prostitution to the embraces of the state, are but a few of the consequences, which naturally and necessarily flow from the doctrine, that the church, in her organized and social capacity, is the exclusive agent of heaven for accomplishing all good ends on earth. The history of the Romish church, during all but the earlier centuries of her existence, is but the practical application of that doctrine. Her errors, her corruptions and her crimes were the legitimate offspring of that principle in full operation.

Its reproduction in our day, and in our country, is one of the most singular instances of delusion, which the history of human opinion has furnished. Without one fact, or a single precept in the Bible, from which such a principle can, by any fair interpretation, be deduced, it is wonderful that it has become an article of religion with any of those who maintain that " every addition to the word of God is a corruption." At war with all the political, social and religious principles which are the foundation of our institutions, it is strange that such a principle should have started into quicker life in the midst of us. With the practical application of it, in the case of the Romish church, blazing before them, it is passing strange that its most zealous supporters should be found among those protestants who profess the most fearful apprehensions of the extension of the principles and practices of that aged hierarchy. Utterly and obviously impracticable, in all its senses, in this country, as this principle has been shown to be, in a previous No. of this Journal ;* we marvel that the cause of religious benevolence should be denied the right of all other support. Indeed, as one of its cherished advocates seems to have clearly seen, it lays the axe at the root of all such benevolent action ;—ecclesiastical boards, as well as other associations and individual efforts, are swept away, in one common ruin, by the cardinal doctrine of the creed: " The church contains, in her essential constitution, the elements of incorruption to restore the parts that are corrupt, and the ministry of the word, the officers of discipline and provision for the poor, the Sabbath and the sacraments, are, in all places and cases, sufficient for every good work and purpose of reform."†

" *The Church*" consists of all those who are called to be saints, and it has no corporate, social, organized capacity, or outward oneness of form, in which to act, as an agent, to perform the work of its members. It is broken up into many independent corporate portions, each organized by human wisdom, in its own way, for the purpose of mutual encouragement and discipline. The Presbyterian portion of the church is organized by bishops, elders and deacons, combined in sessions, presbyteries, synods, and general assemblies. Bishops, elders and deacons are its organs. For the Presbyterian church, in her organized and corporate capacity, to enter upon the subject of missions, it would seem that the churches must raise the money, under the order of the bishops and elders, and pay it over to the deacons as almoners,—who would thus be the managers of the church missions. If the church, the Presbyterian church, must be charged, in her church organization, with the education of youth, the schools, it would seem, must be taught by the bishops, ruled by the elders, and fed and clothed by the deacons ;—there must be complaints to the sessions for short com-

---

* Bib. Repos. First Series, Vol. XII. p. 257 seq., Article by Dr. Woods.

† Sermon by Rev. F. S. Mines,—" The Church the Pillar and Ground of the Truth," p. 7.

mons, and appeals, through all the courts, for the correction of errors in scholastic discipline.   Thus the difficulties of science and art, the great departments of education, instead of being left to the voluntary associations, the seminaries of learning, must be under the control of church judicatories !   The absurdity of thus unchurching the church, and making it anything but what it is, cannot be better shown than in this matter of education, nor can the idea of calling an ecclesiastical board, the church in her organized form, be more thoroughly shamed, than by stating, what every body knows, that the Baptists, the Episcopalians, the Congregationalists, the Methodists, the Presbyterians, with church organizations widely unlike, carry on benevolent operations on plans essentially the same.   The business is done by societies, boards, associations, composed of chosen men, and formed and supported by those, and those only, who approve of the object and of that mode of promoting it.   Boards constituted on the principle of elective affinity, the great principle of action of all gregarious animals, *similis simili gaudet.*   On no other principle can men be made to act with efficiency, till their nature be changed.   " Nature is to be subdued only by obeying her laws," said Bacon, and, if he had said nothing else, he would deserve a fresher immortality than the wise men of Greece.   Plainly, all benevolent action is, and must be, voluntary, and, is it not apparent, that the old Romish notion of controlling these matters by ecclesiastical power has been seized upon as a plausible excuse for a more rigid sectarianism ? Does it spring from a love of the church, or of a sect ? from a wish to spread the gospel alone, or to spread Presbyterianism, or Episcopalianism, or some other *ism ?*   Its tendency is to prostrate the glorious flag of the Captain of salvation, which waves its folds of light in the purer skies and steadier breezes of the upper heaven, the guide of associated millions, and to substitute for it, in the cross currents and baffling winds of earth, the fluttering little banners of the captains of fifties, the jealous squads of sectarian troops.   It objects to sending, to the benighted continents and islands of the sea, the gospel, unless it be " under a condition," connected with the strifes, the jealousies, the heartburnings, the quarrels, the beggarly elements of sectarian discord.*

---

* " Our various sectarian missionary societies are now wrestling with omnipotence on this point."—*Spiritual Despotism.*

It was easy to see that the adoption, by the General Assembly, of this principle of church organization would strike a fatal blow at the American Home Missionary Society, the American Board of Commissioners for Foreign Missions, and the American Education Society, and would impair the influence of those members of the Presbyterian church who hold those societies in their "heart's core." It would place in the hands of a party in the church boards of their own formation, composed of their own men, with offices and agencies in their gift, the most efficient means of increasing influence and power. In 1835 and 1836 the great question was debated in the General Assembly, and the attempt to create a board of foreign missions, under the control of that body, was vigorously urged. The majority of the assembly of 1836, however, believed that the great voluntary associations, so successfully in operation, and so strong in the public favor, were better fitted, than mere church judicatories, to manage the great works of christian benevolence. Thus was again defeated that great party which, as the friends of union think they have had too much reason to believe,

> " Had sowen all about
> The seedes of evil words, and factious deedes,
> Which when to ripeness due they growen are,
> Bring forth an infinite increase, that breedes
> Tumultuous trouble and contentious jarre."*

This party, as early as 1834, began to manifest its systematized designs, by secret circulars and party conventions, inviting and digesting a regular organization. It then boldly established *voluntary associations*, for the avowed purpose of compelling and controlling the church in her organized and corporate capacity! These conventions have usually met a few days before the General Assembly, to secure unanimity and concert in "the party," in the Assembly. After the Assembly of 1836, in which the party had been so signally defeated in more than one of its most united onsets, a convention was called to meet a day or two before the Assembly of 1837. It met. Much excitement prevailed among its members, and measures were concerted for a grand catastrophe. In due time the General Assembly was organized; and it was evident that the efforts of the disunionists had produced but too much effect.

---

* Spenser.

They had secured a majority* in the house, submission to the control of bodies, skilled in the management of a popular assembly, and familiar with the means of alarming, arousing and goading on those over whose sympathies they had the mastery. It was soon evident that party measures, of the strongest character, were to be adopted without mitigation, and that schism and disunion were to be thoroughly carried out, without delay, and in such a manner that the party could not be put in a minority, by the strong conservative sense of the church, which they feared would manifest itself in the next Assembly. The first use of their present power was to perpetuate it, and to secure the control over every man's standing in the church. They seemed desirous of driving the minority to immediate secession. A list of heresies was drawn up, apparently with a view to personal accusations, but the proceeding by accusation was liable to the great objection, that it gave the accused a trial, and an opportunity to prove his innocence, and the right of appeal, all which would take time, and might end in an acquittal. In the words of the Assembly "to have done it by personal process would have been impossible, and, if possible, tedious, agitating and troublesome." It was accordingly abandoned.

They then determined upon excision, by means of the plan of union. It was said "where is the local habitation of the liberal party? The region in which the plan of union has operated. Deduct the ministers of that region, from that party, and the residue may almost be counted on the fingers." It was supposed that important consequences would follow the abrogation of that plan, and it was abrogated. This was done on the alleged ground that the plan was a violation of the constitution of the Presbyterian church, and of that of the General Association of Connecticut, and was a plan for introducing into the Presbyterian church, all the Congregationalists in the new settlements, without their adopting our system. Yet the plan of union was neither a law, a contract, nor a constitutional rule. Nor did it bring any one into the Presbyterian church. It was, as has been said, a mere joint recommendation of the two bodies, that, by mutual forbearance and accommodation, Christians of the two sects should endeavor to enjoy together what they could not procure separately, the stated ministrations of

---

* This was effected by their extraordinary exertions and by the failure of several of the friends of union to attend, whose presence would have thrown the majority on the other side.

the gospel ; each party preserving its own ecclesiastical connection. It plainly did not provide that either sect should become incorporated with the other. It made no provision that the united mass should belong to either sect. In times of party excitement, however, the plainest truths are overlooked, and the plan of union, wisely enough abrogated, was abrogated for reasons destitute of foundation. We may presume that those reasons were given mainly because it was intended, as a last resort, to make important measures depend upon them. Those measures, however, were not to be adopted till other means had been tried.

It was therefore proposed to cite, to the bar of the Assembly, certain judicatories, and, by a palpable perversion of the constitution, deny the right of representation, in the next Assembly, to all those judicatories, till all the citations were disposed of. This, if submitted to, would not fail to answer their purpose, temporarily ; but the measure was carried by a majority of only five, in an Assembly of two hundred and fifty, and could not be relied on. It was therefore, allowed to sleep.

It was proposed, as a next resort, that the church should be divided on the spot. It is not to be wondered at, that the friends of union, from the course things had taken, were induced to listen to a proposition which promised peace to the church, and protection from oppression to themselves. There seemed to be no course left but voluntary or violent division, and they consented to negotiate for the former. They soon found, however, that no terms would be proposed or listened to, which could be called equal, or which contemplated consulting the constituency of the General Assembly. The best terms offered were, substantially, that the minority might voluntarily leave the church, if they did not choose to be cut off, by the assumed power of the majority. The negotiation of course failed.

A threat, said to have been made by a prominent member of the committee, was then acted upon without delay, and resolutions were introduced, and urged through the house, cutting off from the church, without hearing or trial, or notice, by a summary edict, the synods of the Western Reserve, Utica, Geneva and Genesee, embracing about five hundred ministers and sixty thousand communicants, entitled to about sixty (more than one fifth of the whole number,) representatives in the General Assembly.

These acts of expulsion were made to depend upon a false principle, and a "false fact,"—a false principle—the unconstitutionality and absolute nullity of the plan of union, and the "false fact,"—the formation of those synods, and their attachment to the General Assembly, by virtue of that plan. This, although asserted and acted on, as a fact, was, in every sense, destitute of truth. The plan did not make any provision, as to synods; and all those synods had been actually formed, by the General Assembly itself, in the constitutional manner, without any reference to the plan of union. They were not attached to the Presbyterian church, by the General Assembly, but were formed, as all the other synods have been, by the mere subdivision of synods as old as the constitution, and they had been several times, every year, acknowledged, and published to the world, by the General Assembly, as courts of the church. In that character alone, (as synods,) had the Assembly any right to meddle with them. They accordingly acted upon the synods, and not the presbyteries, or individuals, that they might seem to have the shelter of the constitutional grant of jurisdiction. It has never been pretended that the Assembly can act originally upon individuals. If, however, individuals were not cut off, then they remained in the church and were pastors, and church-members, and presbyteries still, and, of course, entitled to be represented in the General Assembly. But thus interpreted, no power would be gained by the exscinding acts, for it is the presbyteries, and not the synods, that send representatives to the Assembly. It was therefore determined to give to the resolutions an individual application, as well as an application to synods, presbyteries, sessions and churches, although only synods were named. It was, in effect, declared that all in those regions,—men, women and children, clergy and laity,—were excluded from the church. As a first act, on this construction, they excluded from the Assembly the sitting representatives from the presbyteries in the same regions, and put the clerks of the Assembly under a pledge, not to receive or enroll the commissions of delegates from the presbyteries, in any future General Assemblies. If these proceedings had been legal, or had been submitted to, the end was answered. The majority had perpetuated their power. But such proceedings, under the circumstances, could have no validity. They violated the plainest general principles of Presbyterian government, and the express provisions of the constitution, by disposing of individual rights, without the intervention of the primary courts, and, at the same time, destroying the right of appeal. The grand view of the proceedings, however, was the violation of one of those eternal principles of natural justice, which are superior to all positive enactments. That no one should be deprived of his right, or be punished, without an opportunity of being heard in his own defence, is a principle stamped by the hand of God upon the common understanding of mankind. It has been incorporated in all the codes of all nations, and, in the constitution of the Presbyterian church, it regulates all judicial proceedings. This principle was trodden under foot at every step of these proceedings. There was no pretence of a hearing, or even of notice. The synods and their whole constituency, ministers and church-members, were swept away by the same unforeseen decree, confounding the innocent with the guilty, and condemning all unheard. Wonderful proceedings, indeed! for they were the work of a chosen deliberative Assembly!—for they were the work of a religious Assembly, an ecclesiastical court!—for they were the work of ordained bishops and elders of a christian church!—for the sufferers were their brethren! and the cause of Christ, dearer than all!

The attempt to justify the proceeding, from its form of expression, was too lame and puerile to succeed with the weakest. "It charges no offence, it proposes no trial, it threatens no sentence. It purports merely to declare a fact, and assigns a reason for the declaration." "We simply declare that they are not constitutionally a part of our church." But if the proceeding did not affect the individuals, then it was useless and nugatory. If it did affect them, they clearly were entitled to be heard. Again, "The attempt to excite prejudice against the measure, as a high-handed and oppressive act of power, is uncandid and unfair. Is it an act of oppression for a court to declare that an Englishman is not an American, or that an alien is not a citizen?" Surely it is as much an act of oppression to decide a question of citizenship as it is any other question, against a man, without giving him an opportunity to be heard in his defence. It is certainly a new idea, that a party is not entitled to a hearing, provided the matter in question be simply whether he have any rights at all! The Assembly, after thus cutting away the minority, created a Foreign Mission Board, and after denouncing the American Home Missionary Society, and the American Education Society and their branches, closed its eventful existence. The question now presented itself to those who had been the friends of union, what was to be done? No one doubted that these great measures had been taken, as means to an end,—as only "beating up and levelling down the way" to personal and individual oppressions, from which no prominent man of the minority, now reduced to a powerless handful, would be safe. It was plain too that, unless something was done, the constitution of the Presbyterian church would be a dead letter, and that form of church government be made a hissing and a by-word, among the churches of a free people. Firmly attached to the constitution, they determined to make an effort to vindicate it, and to restore its healthy action, and its original beauty and purity. It was plain to them, that such proceedings, in violation of all the rights of Presbyterians, could have no force or effect to exclude from the church, or to dissolve or extinguish its constitutional judicatories. They did not, however, trust solely to their own, perhaps biassed, opinion, but took the counsel of some of the ablest men and soundest jurists in the country, whose feelings had in no manner been enlisted in the matter. Their clear opinion was, that the proceedings of the Assembly were utterly null, and as though they had not been, and that the constituency of the General Assembly was undiminished. The obvious course, then, was for all the presbyteries to send up their representatives to the next General Assembly, to take their seats, as though nothing had happened, if permitted to do so ; if not, then to take such steps as should secure their rights, and enable them to have the measures tested by the tribunals of the country. They determined firmly and moderately to ask for their rights, and, if denied them, then "to appeal unto Caesar."

It is of the most obvious truth, that, if all the presbyteries were entitled to be represented,—(and they were so, if they were not cut off by those acts of the Assembly,) the representatives must meet on terms of entire equality. No one could have the right to say, "my commission is better than yours, and I shut you out." The commissioners from Philadelphia could as well exclude those from Baltimore, as those from Rochester. Any attempt thus to shut out, in the first instance, a large number of representatives from the organization of the Assembly would vitiate the entire action of those who might remain, and make them a mere convention of certain delegates, destitute of all authority. It was however well understood that the course indicated by the previous Assembly was to be persisted in, and its organs, the clerks, were to make up a partial list, omitting the excluded delegates, which list was to be the sole guide in culling and organizing the Assembly, and was to be defended to the last.   In these circumstances, revolutionary measures would have been justified, as a redress of grievances, and an intelligent community, would not have failed to see the necessity and the righteousness of any proceedings suited to meet the emergency.   The course, however, was a plain one, without resort to revolution.   The commonest principles of the organization of representative bodies gave them a constitutional remedy.

Accordingly, at the appointed time for the meeting of the Assembly, the representatives of all the presbyteries gave their attendance.   Those from the exscinded bodies and the whole body of the friends of union announced to the world, as the constitutional principle, by which they intended to be governed, that no General Assembly could be regularly organized, which should exclude any part of the delegates from their equal rights. They offered their commissions, in the usual form, to the clerks, to be entered on the roll of the members.   They were rejected on the authority of the previous Assembly.   They all, however, resorted to the place of meeting of the Assembly, and took their seats as members; and at the first opportunity, as soon as the preliminary exercises of the Assembly were over, on the ground of the refusal of the clerks to enroll all the members, a motion was made to the moderator, that the clerk be instructed to make up the roll according to immemorial usage, and established practice. The moderator declared the motion to be out of order, because the completing of the roll—the very matter to which the motion applied—was the business in order!   An appeal was, of course, taken from such a decision.   Every body knows that an appeal from a decision of a question of order is always in order when the decision is made; but the moderator declared the appeal to be out of order, and refused to put it to the house; and the mover sat down.   The clerk read his report upon the roll, and the moderator announced, that if any names were to be added, that was the time to move for their addition.   Immediately another motion was made, that the names of the gentlemen, whose commissions had been rejected by the clerk, be added.   The moderator, instead of putting the motion to the house, decided it, on his own responsibility, and declared that they could not be added.   The motion was repeated, and he decided it to be out of order.   An appeal was taken, and he refused to put that also, declaring it to be out of order. A motion was then made by another commissioner, to have his name added, which the moderator disposed of in the same summary manner, showing clearly, that he was willing to pervert what he supposed to be the power of his office to the purposes of a mere party. By the constitution, he was moderator only " till another be chosen," and was, of course, removable at pleasure. A motion was accordingly put to the Assembly, by one of the members, that another person be appointed moderator, which was carried. The party of the moderator, with few exceptions, not voting. In the same manner the pledged clerks were removed, and others appointed in their place, who made out the roll, according to established usage, inserting the names of all the commissioners who had been excluded by the previous clerks, and the Assembly immediately adjourned to another place. The old moderator and clerks, however, declined to consider themselves removed, and, with their party, remained behind, after the Assembly had adjourned, claimed to be the only true General Assembly, and went on and performed the usual functions of that body, as did also the General Assembly. The great difference in the principles of their organization was that the General Assembly embraced, and enrolled, and regularly called, all the members from all the presbyteries, while the party that remained behind, and went on with the old moderator and clerks, excluded, to the end, those who had been excluded by the clerks, in obedience to the command of the previous Assembly. The result was that two bodies were in session, claiming to be the General Assembly of the Presbyterian church.

Among other duties to be performed by the General Assembly, is that of appointing " trustees of the General Assembly," the corporation having charge of the property of the Assembly. Appointments were made by both bodies, and two sets of trustees claim their seats at that board. It is to settle that question that the suit now pending, in the courts of Pennsylvania, is brought, and it depends upon the question, which body was the true General Assembly? This depends upon the validity of the exscinding resolutions. The result of a trial upon the merits must show whether, as the friends of union contend, the church is still one and undivided, or whether the General Assembly of 1837 have really riven it in twain.

Much effort has been made to excite prejudices against the friends of union, because of their having resorted to the courts of law in this ecclesiastical matter. The effort, however, cannot but fail, and ultimately react upon those who have made it. There is too much common sense and common honesty, too much confidence in the tribunals, and too much respect for those, who, in a proper spirit, and for proper ends, resort to them, to look with an evil eye upon an attempt to obtain justice in the usual manner; especially when the wrong consists in a total exclusion from those church judicatories, which, hitherto, had been open to relieve from ecclesiastical oppressions. The glorious law of religious liberty and protection, which puts its heavenly shield over all of us, in this country, and is one of the noblest characteristics of our institutions, had been in vain adopted, if it had not sprung from the sacred character of religious rights, and the universal sentiment that an invasion of them is an attack upon the common interest, which it is every man's business to resist. The confession of faith of the Presbyterian church speaks in no doubtful terms on this subject: "It is the duty of civil magistrates to protect the person and good name of all their people, in such an effectual manner that no person be suffered, either upon pretence of *religion* or infidelity, to offer any indignity, violence, abuse or injury to any other person whatsoever." Who is willing to sit quietly down under oppression? Who likes it the better because it comes in the holy garb of religion? They know little of the common sense of justice in our country, who suppose that 60,000 persons, of both sexes, and of all ages and conditions, would patiently receive a decree of dishonor, and deprivation of their religious rights, an *ex post facto* edict, passed without notice, without accuser, without accusation, without citation, without proof, or pretence of trial, without naming an individual or specifying an offence. It would be slavery indeed where such things could be done, and the injured be, at the same instant, deprived of their rights and of the privilege of resorting to either religious or civil courts for redress.

Time alone can determine what will be the result of the pending suit. It must have a very important influence on the prospects of the parties. The only hope should be that the constitution of the church shall be vindicated, whatever consequences may result to the parties interested. If that is not to prevail, why was it made? why is it retained? If it cannot protect the church, let it be abolished, and let every one do what is right in his own eyes. It is worse than idle to have a false and pretended security, more unsubstantial than the paper upon which it is written. If it is to be violated at the pleasure of few or many, with impunity, the sooner the Presbyterian church is broken up, as a separate sect, the better. It is not only the right, but the duty of all who fear God and regard man, to seek other communions, where freedom and right are respected as well for their own sakes as for the good of society. But such is not to be the necessity. The right, sooner or later, will prevail. *Dabit Deus his quoque finem.* Time and reflection will work wonders, in keeping together parts which have seemed so repulsive, or in bringing them together, if, perchance, it should be decided that the General Assembly had power thus forcibly to sunder the church. No one can look back upon the controversy in a spirit of rational candor, without seeing and feeling how paltry and inadequate were all the causes that led the Assembly of 1837 to work this evil and unnatural division.

Candid minds, on all hands, now admit that there was not, and is not now, any important difference in doctrine between the two parties—they do not differ more than the members of each party differ with each other. There is here and there, in every sect, an individual errorist, or heretic, and of course, in the Presbyterian church. But the line of this excision was not the line of any difference in doctrine. Nor was the question of church order anything in truth. Who can believe that the existence of a few churches without elders, scattered through the new settlements, could, in sober reason, have been made the cause of cutting off, "with one fell swoop," hundreds and hundreds of churches, which were Presbyterian, "after the straitest sect of our religion?" This too, when an indefinite number of churches without elders were retained, and when, too, this very exscinding party, in their letters missive to their missionaries, expressly assert that the existence of an eldership, in a Presbyterian church, may depend upon circumstances. "The only departure," say they, "from the usages of the church, which we can consider as likely, in some cases, to be necessary, is that which relates to the appointment of ruling elders. In the infancy of the church, at some of the missionary stations, it may not always be practicable to obtain suitable candidates for this office among the converts from paganism;" and the apostolic age is properly referred to for authority! When party spirit does not color the medium, how clear the light of reason and revelation shines into the heart of intelligent Christians! Men are beginning to look at this subject, in its true light. All will do so "when consideration, like an angel, comes, and whips the offending Adam out of them." Even those who have been leaders must begin to look back upon their labors with something of the feeling of a conqueror, who has "found quarrel in a straw," when he looks upon "the weltering fields of the tombless dead." The time must come, and that ere long, when many heated minds will be cool, when many blind eyes will be opened, when many who have been driven, will consent to be driven no longer, and many who have been led will consult their self-respect, and think and act for themselves;—and then the strong conservative sense of the Presbyterian church will be again in the ascendant, and her courts will have peace,—and union,—and strength.

ARTICLE XIII.

CRITICAL NOTICES.

1.—*Commentar über das Buch Koheleth, von Augustus Knobel (Commentary on the Book of Ecclesiastes, by Aug. Knobel, Extraord. Prof. of Theology at Breslau).* Leipsig: 1836. 8vo. pp. 372.

In this work it is the design of Professor Knobel to present us with " a new and complete representation of the views of Ecclesiastes concerning the government of the world and the life of man, according to their organic development and their internal connections." In his endeavors to accomplish this aim he seeks " first to thoroughly investigate and settle the meaning of the words and phrases conveying ideas peculiar to Ecclesiastes, and thence by a strict adherence to the connection and to the once ascertained mode of its reasoning, to explain it in harmony with itself."

By pursuing this plan we are furnished with a comprehensive and valuable commentary on a book which has always presented great difficulties to the interpreter and has occasioned the writing of many works for its elucidation. Of these the present is one of the best, if not indeed *the* best that has yet appeared, as will be seen from the following account of its contents. It begins with an historico-critical introduction in the best style of modern German scholarship, affording a masterly exhibition of the character and tendency of the

book under consideration in all its bearings. This introduction is
divided into ten sections and treats in succession of the following
topics : " the title according to its meaning and grammatical form,
the clearing up of contradictions, the design, character, diction, author, age, and finally the views and fortunes of the book." The
opinions previously held on all these points are constantly cited and
weighed, especially in the articles on the character and diction of
the book, points which have been subjected to a most rigid and thorough scrutiny.

The Book of Ecclesiastes is divided by our author into sixteen
sections, extending to the eighth verse of the twelfth chapter, the
remaining verses of this chapter being regarded as an addition of
later date. Each section is preceded by an argument exhibiting its
internal connection ; then follows the translation of the portion which
it comprises, succeeded by an exposition of the meaning of each
verse and of the relation which it bears to those which precede and
follow it. After the manner adopted by Rosenmüller in his Scholia,
but in a much better order of arrangement, are given the views of
other interpreters on the most difficult passages. Our author does
not however follow the ancient Jewish expositions to the same extent ; but, agreeably to the results of his preliminary investigations,
which prove the book to have been composed at least after the return from the captivity (an opinion maintained previously by De
Wette), he enters into an elaborate comparison of the *usus loquendi*
with that of the later Aramaic and occasionally of the Talmudic dialect. In no instance, however, do we see him actuated by a mere
thirst after novelty in his illustrations ; on the contrary he almost invariably selects with a sound and cautious judgment those which are
the most striking and the most apposite, accompanying each sentence
by the parallel passages which present themselves in other writers,
particularly the classic authors, as Horace, Juvenal, etc.

2.—*Chronologia Judicum et primorum regum Hebraeorum. Dis-
sertatio inauguralis. Scripsit Levi Herzfeld.* Berlin, 1836.
8vo. pp. 72.

The great difficulty experienced in settling the chronology of the
book of Judges is owing to the fact that when the several periods recorded in it are summed up, we obtain a greater number of years
(viz. 500) for the government by judges alone than according to 1
Kings 6: 1, elapsed from the time of the nation's leaving Egypt until the building of the temple under Solomon, which is there stated
to have been only 480 years ; not to mention that both the apostle
Paul and Josephus give entirely different estimates of this period.
As, however, the shorter space of time indicated by the book of
Kings is held to be the most correct, it has been usual in endeavor-

ing to harmonize the two accounts, to reduce the number of years as given in the book of Judges, by the obvious method of considering several of the judges whose histories are related in succession to have been contemporary rulers, since in many instances they governed only single tribes. This method was adopted by Jahn in his Introduction, and afterwards by Leo in his History of the Jewish State.

Quitting this expedient however, Mr. Herzfeld adopts another course to prove the correctness of the book of Kings. He makes a distinction between *total* and *partial* conquests of the country by hostile nations. Accordingly such statements as " the land had rest fourscore years," " the land served twenty years" he considers as applicable to contemporary epochs; because while a partial servitude extended over one section of the country, the remaining portion might either have been reduced to subjection by a different invasion, or might have remained in a state of perfect repose. The author regards the conquests effected by the Moabites and Hazorites recorded Judges ch. iii. and iv., as instances of such partial and contemporary servitudes; and by this means he reduces the number of years that elapsed between the Aramaic and the Midianitish conquests (see ch. vi.) from 234 to 117.

The author indeed is not unacquainted with the hypothesis of contemporary judges; but as a whole he rejects it on the insufficient ground, that it is improbable that an inexperienced individual should have been preferred to a judge already known and esteemed for the services he had rendered, or that foreign foes should have' been able to obtain possession of a part of the country under one judge while at the same time another was found capable of protecting himself against invasion. But was the people's choice the only mode of obtaining the supreme power ? and does not the author himself make the assumption that while one part of the country remained in safety, another was in a state of war or subjugation ? In fact we find that Mr. Herzfeld is in one instance compelled to resort to the hypothesis which in general he discards ; this he does by making Eli and Samson contemporary judges, assuming that only the chief judges were always single, and that hence subordinate ones might have existed at the same time, as for instance, those whose powers were restricted to the pronouncing of decisions, among whom was Eli.

As regards the theory of partial servitudes adopted by the author, there is in general nothing to be said against its possibility. Still we demand more specific information as to what foreign nations subdued only single tribes, which our author undertakes to decide by ascertaining whether each invasion was made by one hostile tribe or by several; we desire moreover to know more precisely how far each individual subjugation extended, which when not expressly stated is here deduced from the tribes who took part in the defence. Both of these points, which are thus left extremely doubtful, are rendered still more so by the arbitrary manner in which the author's hypothesis is applied; yet notwithstanding its palpable defects, the work exhibits proofs of a profound study of the subject, accompanied by an independent mode of investigation which on the whole entitles it to a high degree of consideration among the attempts which have been made to establish the chronology of the sacred Scriptures.

3.—*The Missionary Convention at Jerusalem; or an Exhibition of the Claims of the World to the Gospel. By Rev. David Abeel, Missionary to China.* New York: John S. Taylor, 1838. pp. 244.

We have read this volume with great satisfaction. The author imagines that, at the expiration of eighteen hundred years from the ascension of the Saviour, a grand Assembly is convened at Jerusalem to discuss the claims of the various nations of the world to the gospel. Jews, Mohammedans, Pagans, Christians, of every sect, have each their respective delegates at the meeting. They are all, however, supposed to be converted men, and sincerely to desire the conversion of the world.

They first listen to the reading of those portions of Scripture which clearly express the divine purpose respecting the universal triumph of Christianity, and the means by which this triumph is to be achieved. Then follows an animated discussion of the condition and claims of the world, in which the numerous and diversified members of the assembly are represented as making in succession, characteristic speeches and arguments in favor of their own particular countries, nations, tribes and denominations. These exhibit in striking variety of aspects, and yet in general resemblance, the selfish and narrow views of most Christians of every country, each pleading for his own, and undervaluing the importance of all others. In the progress of the discussion, which is continued through six days, the current objections to the missionary enterprise are ingeniously urged and triumphantly refuted, and many important principles are ably defended.

The book is divided into thirty-eight chapters, short, of course, each containing the substance of one or more speeches in the great debate. The result of the whole is to impress the reader with a sense of the importance and the dignity of the Foreign missionary enterprise. The work is unexceptionable in its language and leading positions and is pervaded with the excellent spirit of the author, who, we need not add, is extensively known as one of the most useful of American missionaries to foreign lands, as well by his labors abroad, as by his earnest and successful appeals to the churches at home.—We cordially commend this effort of his imagination, with the results which it presents of his experience, as a missionary, to our readers.

4.—*A Guide to the Principles and Practice of the Congregational Churches of New England, with a brief History of the Denomination. By John Mitchell, Pastor of the Edwards Church, Northampton.* Northampton : J. H. Butler, 1838. pp. 300.

This is a small volume, in rather large type, easily read, and what is much more to its praise, very easily understood. The views here presented are so well digested and so deeply fraught with good practical common sense, that we think the work cannot fail of being acceptable and useful to the denomination of whose polity and history it treats. Nor need its usefulness be restricted to that portion of Christians, since much which it contains is equally applicable to the pastors and the people of other denominations, and is well fitted to remedy some of the prominent evils among the churches at the present day. We should be glad to give a more extended notice of the work, but have space at present for only the following brief notice of the subjects which are discussed respectively in the eleven chapters of which the book consists. ' The origin and history of the Congregational churches—Principles of the Congregational system —Church covenant and watch—Church discipline—Church meetings and church business—Relations of pastor and people—Deacons —Relations of church and society ; parish affairs—Relations and intercourse of churches with one another—Deportment towards other denominations—Doctrines and measures.'

In his next edition, Mr. Mitchell will, of course, correct some pretty serious typographical errors, that are found in this.

5.—*Incidents of Travel in Greece, Turkey, Russia and Poland. By the Author of " Incidents of Travel in Egypt, Arabia Petrea and the Holy Land ;" with a Map and Engravings. In two volumes. Fifth Edition.* New York : Harper & Brothers, 1838. pp. 268, 275.

We find it difficult to keep up with the age in reading books of travels ; and as Mr. Stephens needed not our commendation to aid his popularity as a writer of " Incidents," we delayed to peruse his Greece, Turkey, etc., until quite lately. It has less of scriptural association in it than the travels in Egypt and the Holy Land, and is less interesting to the biblical student. But in animated and beautiful description it surpasses his first effort. His pictures of men and manners are often to the life, and the reader can hardly divest himself of the impression that he is a boon companion of the jovial traveller. It cannot be said, as of the readers of John Foster, that they who travel with him must work their passage. We are borne onward without labor and the thousand annoyances, which, in the East, constitute so large a portion of the traveller's history, are made occasions of ever varying amusement. A vein of humorous satire runs through every line in which American peculiarities and notions are introduced, and truly American in his feelings, he joins the laugh excited by our Yankeeisms.

His remarks on the present state and condition of the people of those countries, their causes and the agencies most likely to produce reform are often truly philosophical and valuable.

We are sorry to add that in too many of our author's descriptions there is a lack of that delicacy and chasteness which belong to true refinement. A popular work which will probably contribute to many an evening's entertainment, at the family fire-side, should be unexceptionable in this respect. No vulgar allusions should stain its pages, however graced with the drapery of humor. Mr. Stephens also indulges too frequently in a sort of reckless trifling with serious subjects. Death is treated with a levity, in some instances, which is very reprehensible. Here humor is misplaced. It were better to omit entirely the description of a scene of melancholy association, than to treat it with unbecoming mirth. We would not advocate that sickly sentimentality in which some travellers have indulged, yet there is a train of thought, a style of moralizing, which is appropriate to serious subjects, imparting a healthy tone to the mind and exerting a beneficial influence on the heart. With these occasional exceptions these volumes are worthy of the popularity which they have attained.

6.— *The Claims of Japan and Malaysia upon Christendom, exhibited in Notes of Voyages made in 1837, from Canton, in the ship Morrison and brig Himmaleh, under direction of the owners. In two volumes.* New York : E. French, 1839. pp. 216, 295.

These volumes are " got up" in good style and present matters of weighty concernment to the christian philanthropist, the American merchant and to the citizens and government of the United States. The vessels named in the title of the work, it appears, are owned by the house of Alyphant & Co. of New York, and being employed in promoting their mercantile enterprises in China and neighboring countries, have been freely and generously used to aid the American Board of Commissioners for Foreign Missions and other benevolent societies in prosecuting their philanthropic labors in those immense regions of darkness and spiritual death. The first volume contains " Notes of the Voyage of the Morrison from Canton to Japan," by C. W. King of New York, a partner in the above firm. It is written with much strength and intelligence, and gives a better view of the history of the Japanese Islands, than is accessible to the

American reader in any other work. This history is contained in an Introduction of some seventy pages, followed by the " Voyage" in which he was accompanied by Mr. Gutzlaff and Dr. Parker an American missionary. The events of this expedition, (though wholly unsuccessful,) were of a highly interesting character. They were not allowed to enter the ports of Japan, but were obliged to return to China, and even to take with them the seven shipwrecked Japanese whom it was one object of the voyage to return to their homes. This treatment was exceedingly barbarous, and on the ground of it Mr. King makes a spirit-stirring appeal to the government of the United States. This appeal is urged with much ability and force, and is accompanied with suggestions which we think highly worthy the attention of the American congress.

The second volume is entitled " Notes, made during the Voyage of the Himmaleh in the Malayan Archipelago. By G. T. Lay, an agent of the British and Foreign Bible Society for Eastern Asia." It is a continuous narrative, written in an easy style, and containing much miscellaneous and valuable information. The volumes are accompanied with well executed maps of the regions described.

7.—Aids to Preaching and Hearing. By Thomas H. Skinner. New York : John S. Taylor, 1839. pp. 305.

Another book from Dr. Skinner so soon after the publication of his " Religion of the Bible," (noticed in the last No. of the Repository,) may be regarded by some as indicating too great haste in its preparation. It is not, however, a sudden and unpremeditated effort of the author, but a choice selection from the results both of his investigations and his experience for many years. It is not a book of skeletons or abstracts of sermons, such as have sometimes been very injudiciously furnished as " *aids to preaching*," nor is it a mass of direct and common-place precepts on the subject of *hearing*, but a thorough and popular discussion of several topics which the author regards as important to be understood by hearers as well as preachers. Hence the book is designed not for preachers only, but for the public. The leading topics discussed are—Mental Discipline,—Studies of a Preacher,—Power in Speaking,—Doctrinal Preaching,—Preaching on Ability, — How to repent, — and Preaching Christ. Most of these discussions we have read, and regard them as among the very best productions of the author. That on " preaching on ability," which is continued through two chapters, is especially clear, discriminating and convincing. It exposes, we think, and refutes, with great ability and entire success the peculiar views of Coleridge on the two topics of Ability and Atonement, which appear not to have been clearly apprehended by most of the admirers of that learned and alluring writer. On the whole, we judge there are few preachers, or hearers who may not be profited by the reading and the study of this book. Its substantial merits, independent of the popularity of the author, will secure for it, we trust, a wide field of usefulness.

8.—*An Elementary Treatise on Astronomy, designed as a Text Book for Colleges and the Higher Academies, with Rules and Tables for the practical Astronomer. By William A. Norton, late Prof. of Nat. Phil. and Astron. University of the city of New York.* New York: Wiley and Putnam, 1839. pp. 485.

We have hitherto possessed no American work embracing the subjects of the above volume in a form adapted to the capacities and wants of the pupils in our colleges. Not that there has been a dearth of books on this branch of science in modern times. There have been books enough of the kind, but none, with which we are acquainted, so well adapted to fulfil the purposes for which this work is especially designed. The works of Herschel, Biot, Laplace, Delambre, Gummere, Francoeur, Bailey, and others are highly valuable, but most of them are defective for practical purposes. In such as have tables for practical astronomy, the calculations in the tables are either not brought down to the present time, or they are deficient in minuteness, so that it would be unsafe to trust to the results obtained from them in the latter case, and there is needless labor left for the practical astronomer in the former. Professor Norton has made his calculations for the tables sufficiently minute for all the purposes of practical astronomy, and so far as we have compared them, they are more correct than most of those now in use, and are brought down to the year 1840.

The plates and diagrams, which are sufficiently numerous for illustration are prepared in good style, and the body of the work, which is intended as a text-book for students, is divided into four parts—1. The determination of the places of the heavenly bodies and their motions. 2. The phenomena resulting from these motions, the appearances, dimensions and physical constitution of the heavenly bodies, etc. 3. The theory of universal gravitation, the great law, by which the motions of the heavenly bodies are regulated, and on which they depend. 4. Astronomical problems, tables, etc.

As an entire work, we think this treatise has been well digested and judiciously arranged. Unity of design and simplicity of style are its characteristics. We are sorry to add that a long list of *errata* disfigures the book, but these we find on examination do not refer to the tables, and may easily be corrected with the pen.

9.—*Demonstration of the Truth of the Christian Religion. By
Alexander Keith, D. D. Author of the " The Evidence of
Prophecy," etc. From the second Edinburgh Edition. New
York: Harper and Brothers, 1839. pp. 336.*

It is impossible to give a full view of what we regard as the peculiar merits and defects of this work in the brief space we can allot
to it in the present notice. Its plan as a whole is original and striking. It does not profess to give a general view of all the evidences
of Revelation, but leaving the more common topics of proof, as already sufficiently established, it takes up in succession the evidence
of the inspiration of the Jewish prophets, derived from the manifest
fulfilment of their predictions,—Hume's arguments against miracles,
which it represents as foretold and confuted in Scripture, and which
our author appropriates as direct proof of prophetic inspiration,—
Antiquity and authenticity of the Old Testament Scriptures, proved
by universal tradition, existing facts, etc.—Objections drawn from
geology refuted, etc.—Connection between the Old and New Testa-
ments,—The origin and progress of Christianity, according to the
testimony of heathen writers,—The genuineness of the New Testament Scriptures, proved by numerous quotations by christian writers,
testimony of facts, recorded in Scripture, and by the arguments of
Celsus, Porphyry, and Julian, appropriated, etc. etc. Under each of
these heads Dr. Keith has collected a considerable amount of learning and information from various sources, and with great ingenuity
has endeavored to press the arguments of infidels of every class into
the service of Christianity. In this, however, we cannot regard him
as having been entirely successful, nor can we vouch for the correctness of some of the geological and astronomical theories which
he seems to take for granted. Yet the book is intensely interesting
and contains enough of learning, of authentic history, of established
facts of antiquity, geology, etc., illustrated by numerous plates and
drawings, to enchain the attention of the reader; and no candid mind,
we may venture to affirm, will turn from the perusal of this work
without feeling itself to have been both instructed and confirmed in
the faith of the Bible.

10.—*Thirteen Historical Discourses, on the completion of Two Hundred Years, from the beginning of the First Church in New
Haven, with an appendix. By Leonard Bacon, Pastor of
the First Church. New Haven: Durrie & Peck. New York:
Gould, Newman & Saxton, 1839. pp. 400.*

We take an early opportunity to introduce to our readers this interesting and valuable volume, reserving for a future No. a more
extended notice of its contents and of certain topics suggested by its
perusal. Though it possesses a high local interest for those who re-

side within the limits of the old New Haven Colony, it is also a most valuable addition to the other memorials of the early history of New-England. The field which the author has occupied was in some important respects an ungathered field, and he has labored in it, with an industrious and enthusiastic ardor, and from it has collected many novel and interesting historical facts. The facts themselves, the graphic manner in which they are recounted, the wisely chosen details by which other times are made to live again before the eye of the reader, the many just reflections upon the important lessons taught us by the past, together with the clear and pointed style which enlivens every page, will recommend the work to all who are interested in the honor of New England, and who reverence the memory of her Fathers.

Among the many volumes, which have been issued to do honor to the early settlers of this portion of the Union, we know of none that in all respects, resembles this. Perhaps there is none which is, for some purposes, and with regard to some points, as valuable. Certainly there is none which presents a greater variety in the sources of its interest to the reader. The two volumes by Prof. Kingsley and Mr. Bacon, both occasioned by the celebration of the 25th of April, 1838, as the two hundredth anniversary of the settlement of New Haven, are in the highest degree honorable to their authors. We shall be disappointed if we do not hear from both of them again, in the field of historic inquiry and illustration.

11.—*Second Annual Report of the Board of Education of Massachusetts, together with the Second Annual Report of the Secretary of the Board.* 1839, pp. 79.

These Reports, though immediately interesting to the people of Massachusetts, are not without great value to the whole country. The Report of Mr. Mann discusses, in an able and philosophical manner, matters which are of universal importance. The Report of the committee drawn up, we presume, by Governor Everett, details at some length the doings of the committee during the past year, particularly in relation to School Libraries and Normal Schools. It is determined to establish two of these schools, one at Lexington in the county of Middlesex, the other at Barre in the county of Worcester. Another will probably be established in Western Massachusetts, and a fourth in one of the Southern counties.

12.— *Territory of Oregon.—Report of Hon. Caleb Cushing.*

The river Columbia was discovered on the 7th of May, 1792, by Capt. Robert Gray, of the ship Columbia, of Boston. Subsequently, Capt. John Kendrick, of the brig Washington, a companion of Capt. Gray, purchased on account of his owners, from the native chiefs on the north-west coast of America, a large tract of land, embracing four degrees of latitude. The deed or deeds for the same were given for a valuable, and satisfactory consideration. In 1811, John Jocob Astor of New York established a factory on the Columbia river. In 1812, the establishment was broken up, and fraudulently sold to the North West Company by one of Mr. Astor's agents, and taken possession of by the British. But the United States claim that *the sale* to the North West Company does not affect the national jurisdiction, which continues of right in the United States. The various historical facts and argumentative considerations pertaining to this interesting subject are exhibited by Mr. Cushing with great clearness and force, in a pamphlet of fifty pages.

13.—*An Address delivered before the Mercantile Library Association, Boston, September* 13, 1838, *by Edward Everett, and a Poem by James T. Fields.* pp. 58.

Non tangit quod non ornat, may be applied to all which Governor Everett does. His resources of fact and happy illustration seem to be absolutely inexhaustible. No matter what be the subject or the occasion, every thing is fresh, pertinent, eloquent. The poem of Mr. Fields is no unworthy accompaniment. The lines are flowing and graceful, and the wit is sparkling.

14.—*Poems by George Lunt,* New York : Gould and Newman. 1839, pp. 160.

This little volume contains true poetry. While no piece falls below mediocrity, there are several compositions which, in sentiment, imagery and versification are of very high order. We have been much gratified with the tone of moral purity which pervades the whole volume.

15.— *Travels in South-Eastern Asia, embracing Hindustan, Malaya, Siam, and China, with notices of numerous Missionary stations, and a full account of the Burman Empire ; with Dissertations, Tables, etc. By Howard Malcom. In two volumes.* Boston : Gould, Kendall & Lincoln, 1839. pp. 273, 321.

These volumes are beautifully executed, accompanied with maps and numerous illustrations in neat and tasteful engravings ; but they have come to hand too late to allow us time to peruse them. We shall examine them hereafter and give a more extended notice in the next No. of the Repository. In the mean time we have no doubt the interest felt in the subjects and the character of the author will secure for them a wide circulation.

16.—*Additional Notices of New Publications.*

The following books have been received, some of which will be further noticed hereafter.

Notes Explanatory and Practical on the First Epistle of Paul to the Corinthians. By Albert Barnes. Second edition. New York : William Robinson; Boston : Crocker & Brewster, 1838. pp. 357. The reputation of these "Notes" is evinced by the rapid sale of the first edition. From an occasional reading and the known ability of the author we have no doubt of their practical value.

Notes, Critical and Practical, on the Book of Genesis ; designed as a general help to Biblical Reading and Instruction. By George Bush. In two volumes. Vol. 1. second edition. New York : E. French, 1839. pp. 364. This book has also obtained a deserved reputation. We shall hope hereafter to examine it more thoroughly than has yet been in our power to do.

Lectures upon the History of St. Paul, delivered during Lent, at the Church of the Holy Trinity, Upper Chelsea. By the Rev. Henry Blunt, A. M. First American, from the seventh London Edition. Philadelphia : Hooker & Claxton, 1839. pp. 382. Mr. Blunt is a sensible writer, and this is doubtless a good book.

Union ; or the divided Church made One. By the Rev. John Harris, author of "Mammon," "The Great Teacher," etc. etc. Revised American edition. Boston : Gould, Kendall & Lincoln, 1838. pp. 301. Mr. Harris's works are always read with interest.

The Crook in the Lot ; or a display of the Sovereignty and Wisdom of God in the afflictions of men. By Rev. Thomas Boston. Philadelphia : W. S. Martien. New York : Robert Carter, 1839. pp. 162. An old book, republished ;—a good specimen of the quaint and homely style of the author's age, pious and comforting to the afflicted, whose taste is not revolted by its oddities.

Rambles in Europe ; or a Tour through France, Italy, Switzerland, Great Britain and Ireland, in 1836. By Fanny W. Hall. In two volumes. New York : E. French, 1839. pp. 228, 246. These volumes are written by a young lady, in an easy and pleasant style, and will not suffer in comparison with most books of travels by transient visitors to Europe.

Wales, and other Poems. By Maria James ; with an Introduction by A. Potter, D. D. New York : John S. Taylor, 1839. pp. 170.

The Women of England : Their Social Duties and Domestic Habits. By Mrs. Ellis, (late Sarah Stickney,) author of "The Poetry of Life," "Pictures of Private Life," etc. New York : D. Appleton & Co. 1839. pp. 275. This book is doubtless in the very first class of its kind. The reputation of the writer is established for beauty of style, good sense, and purity and elevation of sentiment.

A Discourse delivered before the Connecticut Alpha of the Φ. B. K. at New Haven, August 14, 1838. By Heman Humphrey, S. T. D., President of Amherst College. New Haven : L. K. Young, 1839.

The Choice of a profession : An Address before the Society of Inquiry in Amherst College, August 1838. By Albert Barnes. Amherst : J. S. & C. Adams.

Annual Circular of Marietta College, with the Inaugural Address of the President, delivered July 25, 1838. Cincinnati, 1839.

The Harmony of the Christian Faith and Christian Character, and the Culture and Discipline of the Mind. By John Abercrombie, M. D. F. R. S. E. New York : Harper & Brothers, 1839. pp. 146.

Dr. Bell's Lessons on the Human Frame. Designed for Schools and Families. Illustrated with upwards of fifty engravings. Philadelphia: Henry Perkins, 1839. pp. 158.

An Inaugural Address, delivered at Marshall College, Mercersburg, Pa. September 1838. By Albert Smith, Professor of Languages in that Institution. Chambersburg, 1838. This is a sensible discourse, in which the author maintains with learning and ability, that education separated from religion furnishes no security to morality and freedom.

ARTICLE XIII.

LITERARY AND MISCELLANEOUS INTELLIGENCE.

United States.

Postscript.—Presbyterian Controversy:—The Law-suit decided.

[We have delayed the present No. of the Repository a few days for the purpose of obtaining the decision of the court in the great cause referred to, (page 497,) as " pending in the courts of Pennsylvania." We insert it, as furnished by Mr. Benedict, who was present at the trial, and, (though necessarily out of place,) as a supplement to his Article closing on page 500. The principles laid down by Judge Rogers are the same which the author has so ably defended in his Article referred to, and with him and the friends of constitutional liberty at large, we gladly unite in expressions of profound gratitude to God that justice in this case has been honored, and a result so propitious obtained. May wisdom be granted from above to guide the successful Assembly in the discharge of their now confirmed and increased responsibilities.—ED.]

The cause came on to be tried at the Philadelphia *nisi prius* before the Hon. Judge Rogers of the Supreme Court of Pennsylvania, on the 4th March inst. The court and jury were addressed by the following counsel : —On the part of the friends of union by Josiah Randall, Esq. and William R. Meredith, Esq. of Philadelphia, and George Wood, Esq. of New York. On the other side by F. W. Hubbell, Esq. and Joseph R. Ingersoll, Esq. of Philadelphia, and the Hon. William C. Preston of South Carolina.

It need not be said that the merits of the cause were fully and ably discussed, when it is known that ten days (in the aggregate) were devoted to the addresses to the jury by counsel of such distinguished ability. The charge of the learned Judge was given to the jury on the 26th day of March. It was in writing, and occupied an hour and a quarter. It was characterized by great simplicity, force and beauty. The breathless anxiety of an assembly crowded almost to suffocation showed the intense interest which was felt in the opinion of the court, while the friends of constitutional Presbyterianism were gratified with hearing the great principles for which they have been contending, clearly and ably vindicated. The following conclusions of the learned Judge were distinctly and emphatically laid down, with other subordinate points, as the law of the case.

First—That such a suit was the appropriate and best mode of determining the matters in controversy.

Second—That the Plan of Union was constitutional, and, at the time, expedient under the early policy of the church ; and that the General Assembly and the General Association were competent to make it, and to rescind it.

Third—That if it were void, the existence of the four synods could not be destroyed by its abrogation, because from the nature of the Plan they could not have been attached to the church by virtue of that Plan, and the fact was undisputed that they were created like all the other synods, by the General Assembly and in the same manner.

Fourth—That the acts exscinding those synods and all their constituent parts, without notice or trial, were contrary to the eternal principles of justice, to the law of the land and to the constitution of the Presbyterian Church, and were null and void, and that of course the commissioners from their presbyteries were entitled to their seats in the General Assembly of 1838.

Fifth—That the clerks and moderator in excluding these commissioners and preventing their cases from coming before the house, if it was the result of concert with a party to carry out those exscinding acts, was grossly erroneous, and called for the notice of the house, and the house was competent to remove them by appointing others.

Sixth—That those who are present and have an opportunity to vote and decline to vote, no matter for what reason, are bound by the majority of those who do vote.

Having stated to them (without intimating an opinion) the questions of fact upon which they were to pass, he adjured them in the solemn language of their oath, "as they should answer to God at the great day," that with unprejudiced minds they should decide according to the evidence. The jury having been out about an hour returned with a verdict for the plaintiffs.

Thus has closed this most remarkable trial! Its result is matter not for selfish triumph, but for devout gratitude to the Great Disposer of events, that thus another beacon-light has been kindled on the highway of time, to light up the onward path of the friends of religious liberty ! Let the victims of ecclesiastical oppression in their " night time of sorrow and care" look to its " pillar of fire," thank God and take courage !

March 27, 1839.

Robinson & Franklin, New York, and Crocker and Brewster, Boston, have in the press and will soon publish, *Notes, critical, explanatory and practical on the Book of the Prophet Isaiah ; with a New Translation. In two Volumes, 8vo. By Albert Barnes.* A few sheets only of these volumes have been furnished us by the publishers, from which we have derived favorable impressions of the thoroughness and general excellence of the work. The author is already too well known, as an annotator on other portions of Scripture, to require our commendation, and we need only add that his forth-coming Notes on Isaiah have been in preparation for a series of years past, and, in his own language, are " the production of many a laborious, but many a pleasant hour." Our readers may expect a more extended notice of these volumes hereafter.

Hooker & Claxton, Philadelphia, are about publishing Winer's large Greek Grammar of the New Testament, translated by Professors J. H. Agnew and O. G. Ebbeke of Philadelphia. In the German it is a volume of about 600 pages 8vo. and is spoken of in the highest terms by those who are qualified to judge. The translators are also making arrangements to offer to the public Winer's Greek Lexicon of the New Testament, which they prefer to either Wahl or Bretschneider.

Henry Perkins, Philadelphia, has in the press the first American edition of Greenfield's Polymicrian Testament, on which he is sparing no pains to secure typographical accuracy.

Harper & Brothers, New York, have in press Indian Tales and Legends, in two volumes. By Henry Rowe Schoolcraft, being the first of a series of volumes in preparation by the same author, denominated " Algic Researhes, comprising inquiries respecting the mental characteristics of the North American Indians." From the character of the author and his familiar acquaintance with these subjects, as superintendant of Indian affairs on our North-western frontier for many years past, the public may expect some interesting and instructive developments in these volumes.

Perkins & Marvin, Boston, will publish, in the coming month, a Memoir of Mrs. Sarah L. Smith, wife of the Rev. Eli Smith, missionary in Syria.

C. C. Little & James Brown, Boston, have in press " the complete works of the Right Hon. Edmund Burke in 9 vols. 8vo, also the poetical works of Edmund Spencer, with notes, etc., in 5 vols. 8vo. and 12mo.

We are happy to learn that George Alexander Otis Esq. of Boston, the translator of Botta's History of the American Revolution, has translated, at the suggestion of John Quincy Adams, the Tusculan Questions of Cicero. We have every reason to suppose that this noble production of the orator has been rendered into English by Mr. Otis with accuracy and elegance.

Scotland.

It affords us much pleasure to announce that the Edinburgh Biblical Cabinet, (noticed in the Repository Vols. V. 485, and IX. 319,) is still continued by its enterprising projector and publisher, Mr. Thomas Clark. The series has reached the twenty-third volume. It consists of translations, mostly from the German, of commentaries and other treatises designed to explain and illustrate the Scriptures. We earnestly commend the work to our readers. It may be procured for about one dollar a volume. We shall revert to it again at an early day.

INDEX TO VOLUME I.

ADVERTISEMENT.

American Biblical Repository,

SECOND SERIES.

Price Five Dollars per annum, in advance.

PROPOSITION TO SUBSCRIBERS.

To obviate all objections on account of the expense of the Repository to distant subscribers, and to place it within the reach of intelligent individuals and families of limited means, in all parts of the country, the proprietors submit the following proposition, viz. :

To each subscriber wishing to receive the work by mail, and who will forward *five dollars in advance, postage paid*, the numbers will be promptly sent, *postage paid by the proprietors*. And at whatever time during the year five dollars shall be received from a subscriber, the subsequent numbers for the year shall be sent, postage paid as above.

This offer, if accepted, will save to each subscriber, receiving the work by mail, during the year, at a distance less than 100 miles, *one dollar* or more, and at a distance of more than 100 miles, nearly *two dollars.*

So large an allowance cannot long be continued, unless it shall result in a corresponding increase of subscribers. The proposition is made for the current year, however, with the confident expectation that its liberality will be appreciated, that many who might otherwise feel unable to possess the work, will embrace these peculiarly favorable terms, and that thus an amount of patronage will be received which will enable the proprietors to sustain the enormous tax imposed upon the transmission of periodicals, by our existing post-office laws, and to continue to furnish the Repository to its most distant readers, as cheap as to city subscribers.

N. B. Letters concerning the Repository, the names of subscribers, etc. may be addressed to Mr. JOSIAH ADAMS, General Agent, corner of Fulton and Nassau streets, New York, or to the EDITOR, at the same place.

ERRATA.

Page 436 7th line from top, for *materially* read *maturely.*
" 448 2d " " for *cubit* read *cubic.*
" " 24th " " for *points* read *point.*

CPSIA information can be obtained
at www.ICGtesting.com
Printed in the USA
BVHW081438260819
556817BV00017B/2297/P